Real Estate Development Workbook and Manual

Howard A. Zuckerman

George D. Blevins

PRENTICE HALL
Paramus, New Jersey 07652

Library of Congress Cataloging-in-Publication Data

Zuckerman, Howard A.
    Real estate development workbook and manual / by Howard A.
Zuckerman and George D. Blevins.
        p.   cm.
    Includes index.
    ISBN 0-13-763491-9
    1. Real estate development.   I. Blevins, George D.   II. Title.
HD1390.Z83   1991   91-21946
333.73′15—dc20   CIP

Printed in the United States of America

10

This publication is designed to provide accurate and authoritative information in regard to the subject matter covered. It is sold with the understanding that the publisher is not engaged in rendering legal, accounting, or other professional service. If legal advice or other expert assistance is required, the services of a competent professional person should be sought.
—*From the Declaration of Principles jointly adopted by a Committee of the American Bar Association and a Committee of Publishers and Associations*

ISBN 0-13-763491-9

90000

9 780137 634910

ATTENTION: CORPORATIONS AND SCHOOLS

Prentice Hall books are available at quantity discounts with bulk purchase for educational, business, or sales promotional use. For information, please write to: Prentice Hall Career & Personal Development Special Sales, 240 Frisch Court, Paramus, New Jersey 07652. Please supply: title of book, ISBN number, quantity, how the book will be used, date needed.

PRENTICE HALL

On the World Wide Web at http://www.phdirect.com

Howard A. Zuckerman

for my wife and partner, Amy, and my three children
Lindsey, Carley, and Adam

for my parents and sister

to the memory of Dr. James Graaskamp
may his legacy continue with the
thousands of students he taught

George D. Blevins

for Jeanne, Joy, and Juli, my wife and children

and

my father and mother, George and Doris Blevins

Howard A. Zuckerman
Acknowledgments

This book entailed a long process of sifting through old files and notebooks to try to detail in a manner which will guide the reader through the real estate development process. Many long hours were spent on our trusty word processors to complete this publication.

I would like to give special thanks to my wife and kids, who have had to live with my coming home late at night and then sneaking away so the book could be finished.

I would also like to thank the many other individuals who have given their counsel, information, and encouragement. In addition, special thanks should be given in the memory of Dr. Jim Graaskamp, Professor of Real Estate at the University of Wisconsin, who taught me many years ago the basic concepts of real estate and the value of "sticktoitiveness."

Additionally, I would like to thank: Milton (Gimp) Fromson and Danny Rocker, D.D.S. for giving me the opportunity to start in the real estate field in 1973; Richard Katz for showing me the fundamentals of real estate number crunching; Michael Feiner for informing me about the University of Wisconsin Real Estate Program; Mike Komppa and Steve Leaffer for spending hours on the telephone discussing "deal philosophy"; Joseph Harman for backing me on my first development deal; and Wayne Pratter for giving me the opportunity to joint venture with his service corporation.

Finally, the following individuals are also to be thanked for their time and help in preparing this manuscript:

William H. Howell, President, William Howell & Associates, Atlanta, Georgia
Chuck O'Brien, Pieper, O'Brien, Herr Architects, Partner, Atlanta, Georgia
Harold Cunniliff and Mike Kilgallon, Partners, Pacific Group, Atlanta, Georgia
Dale Henson, President, Dale Henson & Associates, Atlanta, Georgia
Norm Cohen, President, Habersham Homes, Atlanta, Georgia
Mark Johnson, President, RESystems, Atlanta, Georgia
Mike Verner, Partner, Verner & Perling, Atlanta, Georgia
Leo Dolan, Vice President, DIHC, Atlanta, Georgia

George D. Blevins
Acknowledgments

The opportunity to complete a work of this magnitude is a rare privilege and I am grateful to God not only for that opportunity but for the abilities which He has given me to use in my contributions to it.

In addition, I would like to thank Howard Zuckerman for allowing me to coauthor this publication. His faith and confidence in me is appreciated. I have enjoyed the association, and learned much from it.

I would like to acknowledge and express my appreciation to Blaine Kelley, Robert Lutz, Donald Brooks, and Donald Rutland of The Landmarks Group, a multi-disciplined real estate development company in Atlanta, Georgia. Without their kindness in providing me with opportunities within the real estate development business, my contributions to this publication would not have been possible.

Finally, the following people must be thanked for all that they have contributed to this publication:

Ray Hoover, Partner, Thompson, Ventulett, Stainback, and Associates, Inc., Atlanta, Georgia

Joe Ann Lee, Vice President of Marketing, Northside Realty Associates Inc., Atlanta, Georgia

Brian Bowron, Director of Property Management, The Landmarks Group, Atlanta, Georgia

William Pinto, Vice President, The Hardin Group, Atlanta, Georgia

Gordon Davis, Mike Cenker, Cecil Copeland, Davis International, Atlanta, Georgia

Robert Hughes, Partner, Ashley and Associates, Atlanta, Georgia

Richard Stonis, President, Associated Space Design, Atlanta, Georgia

Bill Stevens, Partner, Long, Aldridge and Norman, Attorneys, Atlanta, Georgia

Greg Logan, Partner, Robert Charles Lesser & Company, Atlanta, Georgia

Surber and Barber, Architects, Atlanta, Georgia

The Authors

HOWARD A. ZUCKERMAN

Howard A. Zuckerman is President of The Seville Companies, a real estate acquisition and development firm in Atlanta, Georgia. Since 1976, Mr. Zuckerman has been active in the acquisition, development, financing, and equity placement of income producing properties valued at over $100,000,000.

His experience covers a wide range of real estate, including syndication of new and existing residential and commercial properties; the development, construction, management, leasing, and resale of residential and commercial properties; and brokerage of residential and commercial properties throughout the sun belt. These activities have involved single-family homes, apartments, offices, shopping centers, and mini-warehouses.

The author's scholastic background includes an undergraduate degree in Marketing at Ohio State University and a Masters of Science in Real Estate Urban Land Economics and Appraisal at the University of Wisconsin.

Mr. Zuckerman's other business affiliations, past and present, include memberships in local and regional real estate trade groups, including the Real Estate Securities and Syndication Institute (RESSI), the National Association of Realtors (NAR), the National Association of Home Builders, the National Mini-Storage Institute, and the Urban Land Institute (ULI).

He has been the subject of numerous articles in regional and national trade and business publications and has been included in "Who's Who in Real Estate" and "Who's Who in Finance and Industry." He is also the author of *Real Estate Investment & Acquisition Workbook* (Prentice Hall, 1989) and *Real Estate Wealthbuilding, How to Really Make Money in Real Estate* (Dearborn Financial Publishing, 1991).

GEORGE D. BLEVINS

George D. Blevins' 12 years of real estate development experience have equipped him to communicate effectively within all the disciplines of the real estate business.

As a Vice President with The Landmarks Group, a multidisciplined real estate development company, his responsibilities included tenant development, predevelopment, design and construction, and development management. He provided leadership for The Development of Concourse and Promenade, major mixed-use projects in Atlanta.

Mr. Blevins, as a graduate of North Carolina State University, received his architectural registration while working with Thompson, Ventulett, Stainback and Associates, Architects, Inc.

He has been successful in the development of systems for management, resolution of company-wide organizational issues, setting the pace for quality developments, and preparing winning proposals for 4,000,000 square feet of real estate development with a value exceeding $900,000,000.

Mr. Blevins' experience includes commercial office, hotel, retail, historic and residential developments. In addition, he has served on the Board of Directors for the Atlanta Midtown Business Association. Mr. Blevins founded the Blevins Company in 1989, a Real Estate Development Advisory created to provide services to developer's of real estate investments. The use of the Blevins Company's services allow development firms to function more efficiently by streamlining their staff and overhead, yet to maintain the experience necessary for success. Recent accomplishments include the development of a real estate asset management program with Van Landingham Associates for the Georgia Power Company and Development Management for Henderson's Wharf, a Residential, Historic Inn and Marina mixed-use development in Baltimore, Maryland, for Boston Bay Capital, Inc.

Contents

How This Workbook Will Help You Develop Successful and Profitable Real Estate xix

Foreword xxi

Chapter 1
Fundamentals of Real Estate Development 1

Real Estate Development 1
The Key—Marketing and Marketing Research 2
Decision Making: Choose a Target and Set a Goal 3
Create Your Investment Strategy 4
Successful Developments 4
Market Constraints 8
Market Timing: Four Cycles That Affect Development 9
Weighing the Risks 10
Managing the Risks 12
Reaping the Rewards 13
Public and Private Interface in Development 16
Types of Developers 18

Chapter 2
Planning a Strategy with Development and Financial Criteria 20

Market Research Identifies the Need 20
Decision Making—Selecting a Target 23
A Need for a Site Or a Site for a Need? 32
Identify Development Criteria 36
Identify Unique Challenges to Be Encountered 36
Conduct a Feasibility Study 38
What to Include in a Feasibility Study 39
Identify Financial Criteria 51
Choose the Appropriate Ownership Vehicle 53
Flexibility During the Process 55

Chapter 3
Selecting the Site: Location, Analysis, and Purchase 56

Establishing Land Development and Selection Criteria 58
Finding Available Land 64
Land Development Trends 67
Site Research 68
Initial Site Visits 73
Site Evaluation 74
Community Politics and Issues 76
Land Cost Evaluation Process 78
Helpful Hints (Do's and Don'ts) 80
Possible Strategies for Use 81
The Greater Fool Theory 82
Land Acquisition Forms 82

Chapter 4
Contracting and Financing the Land Acquisition 89

Land Purchase Techniques 90
Items to Consider When Making an Offer 92
Determining the Land Offer 95
Structuring the Financing for the Land Acquisition 98
Other Creative Land Purchasing Techniques 99
Legal Documents Required to Purchase Land 100

Chapter 5
Responding to the Governmental Regulatory Process 115

How Governmental Regulations Affect Development Management 121
Decision-Making Considerations in Site Acquisitions 122
No Construction Without a Permit 134
Regulations in Project Finance and Accounting 139
The Sale and Leasing of Real Estate 141
Safety and Protection of Building Occupants 141
Working with Government Officials 143

Chapter 6
**The Predevelopment Process: Developing Cost Estimates,
Schedules, and Financing 145**

Creating the Program 146
Selecting the Team 153
Linear Responsibility Matrix 160
Values in the Selection of Consultants 163
Requesting Proposals and Predevelopment Budgeting 163

Managing the Budget: The Developer's "Seed Money" 164
Scheduling Work Tasks 168
Managing the Process 173
Responsibilities of the Players 177
Coordination of Meetings: Making It Happen 188
Value Engineering: An Ongoing Challenge 189
Project Management 194
The Developer's "Go" or "No Go" Decision 197
Preparing to Close the Financing 200
Retaining Information: The Developer's File System 201
Postclosing Memorandum: A Complete Record of the Development 213
Team Selection Forms 222

Chapter 7
Preparing for Construction by Careful Design 232

Programming for Success 233
Creating Construction Documents 233
The Design Team Members 255
Miscellaneous Design Criteria 256
From Proposals to Contracts 268
Tenant Development Design 271
Checklist for Reviewing Plans and Specifications 276
Design Forms 288

Chapter 8
Crunching the Numbers to Determine Financial Feasibility 290

How to Prepare a Development Proforma 291
Cash Flows and Preparing the Operating Proforma 301
Five-to-Ten Year Operating Forecasts 306
Process of Refinement 308
Approaches to Financial Feasibility 308
Backdoor Approach to Feasibility 312
Sensitivity Analysis: "What if" Scenarios 312
Value and the Real Estate Development 315
Projecting Taxable Income 319
Lender Ratios and Other Measurement Tools 325
Financial Rules of Thumb 326
Using Computers to Assist the Developer 331
How to Make the Development Value Judgment 332
Case Study: Sutton Place Apartments 332
Additional Case Studies 350
Financial Forms 350

Chapter 9
Financing for the Real Estate Development 353

Maximizing Financial Returns 355
Financing for the Development Phase 357
Funding the Permanent Loan 381
How to Prepare a Loan Package 392
How the Appraisal Process Works 396
Negotiating the Terms and Conditions of the Loan 401
Closing the Loan 408
Permanent Lender's Closing Checklist 408
Refinancing the Property 411
Financing Forms 411

Chapter 10
Raising the Equity 413

How to Find Sources of Equity 414
Determination of the Required Equity 414
Finding Equity and the Offering 415
Preparing the Investor Package 416
Professional Raising of Equity 424
How to Select Potential Investors 424
Checking of References 425
Structuring the Equity Transaction 426
Partnerships 427
Checklist for Establishing a Limited Partnership 428
How to Terminate a Partnership 432
Responsibilities of Partners 432
Fees Paid to Developer for Services Rendered 433
Profit and Tax Losses: Structuring the Benefits 435

Chapter 11
The Construction Process 437

The Role of the General Contractor 438
Selecting the General Contractor 440
Construction Strategies 445
Controlling Costs 447
Agreements to Construct 450
Insurance and Risk Containment 453
Construction Management Process 457
Cost Monitoring 460
The Art of Construction Scheduling 463

Quality Assurance—Quality Control 466
Proposals for Quality Assurance—Quality Control Programs 468
Construction Phase Insights 470
Construction Phase Forms 474

Chapter 12
The Marketing Process: Selling the Product 489

Preparing the Market Study 490
Marketing Professionals—Choosing the Team 494
Marketing Strategies—Creating the Business Plan 498
Leasing and Sales Criteria 503
Legal Agreements 505
Marketing Files 507
Financing and Concessions 509
Media Placement 509
Reporting Procedures 511
Visual Aids and Collateral Materials 511
Sales or Leasing Offices 518
The Model Suite 520
Description Packages 520
Preparation of Marketing Budgets 522
Marketing Campaigns: Matching Product with Prospect 526
Finding the Users 526
Preselling the Market 529
The Presentation—Or the Sale 530
Closing the Sale—Leasing and Sales Agreements 531
The Leasing Agreement 532
Marketing Forms 538

Chapter 13
Maximizing the Returns Through Property Management 544

Who Will Manage the Property? 545
The Management Agreement 549
Management Company Responsibilities 551
Property Management Policies and Procedures 555
Service Contracts 556
Preparing the Operating Budgets 557
Real Estate Taxes 567
Insurance Coverage 568
The Accounting System 570
Inventory and Supplies 578
Tenant Leases 579

The Owner's Association 580
Property Management Forms 580

Chapter 14
Sale of the Development (The Developer's Final Reward) 583

Reasons for Selling 583
Sale Pricing—Terms and Conditions 584
Sale Transactions 585
Preparing Successful Sale Packages 587
Ten Steps of a Profitable Sale 589
Sale Forms 597

Chapter 15
Responding to Changing Cycles of the Real Estate Industry 598

Causes of the Real Estate Decline of the 1980s 600
Analysis of the Situation or the Diagnosis of Potential Problem Areas 603
Prescriptions and Solutions for Problem Areas 606
Project Development Prescriptions 606
Development Business Prescriptions 621
Prescriptions for Personal Life 639
The 1990s and Economic Factors about Which the Developer Should
Be Aware 642

Chapter 16
Project Economics for Various Product Types 645

Product Type No. 1: Retail 646
Product Type No. 2: Industrial Building (Build to Suit) 653
Product Type No. 3: Corporate Summit Office Building 673
Product Type No. 4: Residential Subdivision—Land Development 685

Appendix
Real Estate Development Procedural Diagram 693

Glossary 694

Index 725

COMPLETE DEVELOPMENT FIGURES, FORMS, TABLES, AND DOCUMENTS

FIGURES

1–1   The Components of a Successful Development 5
1–2   Real Estate Development Market's Cycles 9
1–3   Risk-Yield Curve 12
1–4   Risks versus Rewards Decision Making 14
1–5   Basic Real Estate Development Relationships 17
2–1   Developing a Strategy 22
2–2   Evolution of Real Estate Market Information (1970–2000) 23
2–3   Analysis Process: The Search for a Site for a Use 34
2–4   Analysis Process: In Search of a Use for a Site 35
3–1   Components of a Demographic Study 59
3–2   Land Development Trend 68
3–3   Aerial Photograph Provides Information Concerning Shape, Form, and Proportion 69
3–4   Aerial Photograph Provides Information Concerning Patterns and Trends 70
5–1   Federal Departments 117
5–2   State Departments 118
5–3   County Departments 119
5–4   City Departments 120
5–5   The Re-Zoning Process 131
6–1   Team Relationships Diagram 151
6–2   Linear Responsibility Matrix 161
6–3   Professional Work Order System 167
6–4   Predevelopment Budget Form 169
6–5   Predevelopment Schedule 170
6–6   Work Order Request 171
6–7   Invoicing Instructions 172
6–8   Summary Schedule 174
6–9   Summary Design and Construction Schedule 175
6–10   Detailed Design Schedule 176
6–11   Boundary and Topographical Survey 180
7–1   The Design Process 235
7–2   Master Site Plan 238
7–3   Site Plan 239

7–4   Alternative Sketches 244
7–5   Schematic Design Drawing 249
7–6   Rendering 250
7–7   Design Development Drawing 251
7–8   Working Drawing 253
7–9   Commercial Measurements 258
7–10   Landscape Architecture Presentation Drawings 265
7–11   Landscape Architecture Working Drawings 266
7–12   Tenant Space Planning 273
8–1   Capital Costs 300
8–2   Cash Flow Calculations 305
8–3   Refinement Process 309
8–4   Feasibility: Frontdoor Approach 310
8–5   Financial Feasibility: Backdoor Approach 313
8–6   Sensitivity Analysis 314
8–7   Appraisals 316
8–8   Depreciation Tables 321
9–1   Construction Loan 360
9–2   Sources of Financing 382
9–3   Self-Amortizing Loans 385
9–4   Lender Ratios 403
10–1   Limited Partnership Organizational Chart 433
11–1   Construction Methods 446
11–2   Contractor Organizational Chart 460
11–3   Detailed Foundation and Superstructure Schedule 464
11–4   Detailed Construction Schedule 465
11–5   Near Term Schedules 467
12–1   Marketing Presentation (Master Plan) 513
12–2   Marketing Presentation (Floor Plan) 514
12–3   Marketing Presentation (Interior Design Detail) 515
12–4   Marketing Presentation (Building Sections) 516
12–5   Marketing Presentation (Architectural Model) 517
13–1   Property Management Staff Diagram 546
13–2   Operating Expenses 561
13–3   Chart of Accounts 572
13–4   Profit and Loss Statement (Variable Budget) 573
13–5   Balance Sheet 575
13–6   Trial Balance 575
13–7   General Ledger 576
13–8   Cash Deposits 577
14–1   Sale Process 589
14–2   Calculation of Sale Proceeds 595

FORMS

3–1   Land Checklist Form 82
3–2   Land Rating Form 88
6–1   Team Player Checklist Form 223
6–2   Code Synopsis Form 225
6–3   Construction Cost Analysis Form 226
6–4   Tenant Allowances Form 227
6–5   Architect Selection Form 228
6–6   Contractor Selection Form 229
6–7   Cost Control Report Form 230
6–8   Cost Control Report Form 231
7–1   Square Footage Calculation Form 289
8–1   Development Proforma Form 351
8–2   Operating Proforma Form 352
9–1   Lender Checklist Form 412
11–1   Schedule Summary Form 475
11–2   Commitment Dates Form 476
11–3   Unresolved Issues Form 477
11–4   Summary Costs Form 478
11–5   Design Costs Form 479
11–6   Construction Costs Form 480
11–7   Exposure Items Form 481
11–8   Risk Identification-Damage Containment Form 482
11–9   Application and Certification for Payment Form 484
11–10 Draw Request Letter Form 485
11–11 Change Order Request Form 486
11–12 Project Cost Report Form 487
11–13 Lien Release Form 488
12–1   Residential Data Form 539
12–2   Commercial Data Form 540
12–3   Lease Checklist Form 541
12–4   Commercial Lease Summary Form 542
12–5   Leasing Status Report Form 543
13–1   Budget Forecast Form 581
13–2   Residential Lease Summary Form 582
14–1   Sale Prospect Form 597

TABLES

11–1   Evaluation System 444
12–1   Sample Market Study Summary 495
12–2   Case Study 504

DOCUMENTS

4–1   Sample Letter of Intent 101
4–2   Land Purchase and Sales Agreement 104
9–1   Loan Commitment 363
12–1   Sample Tenant Work Letter 506

DIAGRAM

Matrix, following page 693

How This Workbook Will Help You Develop Successful and Profitable Real Estate

This workbook provides information which is needed to prepare for successful real estate development. It offers a comprehensive guide for the planning and implementing of the development process. It includes necessary tools such as ready-to-use forms, checklists, sample agreements, examples of systems, diagrams, and case studies along with narrative concerning various issues.

Whether you are a first-time developer or a seasoned professional, you will find this a handy reference leading you step-by-step through the major phases in the development process, including:

- How to find the right parcel of land for the development
- How to structure and negotiate the land purchase
- How to prepare market studies and analyze the market
- How to handle the zoning process
- How to design the product for the proper market
- How to prepare and analyze the development costs and operating proforma
- How to obtain construction and permanent financing
- How to raise the necessary equity that is required
- How to administrate and coordinate the development process
- How to handle the accounting process
- How to contract and oversee the construction process
- How to bring the product to the market
- How to manage the property during lease-up and after completion
- When and how to dispose of the property

In addition, checklists and financial tables have been provided for ready use; there is also an extensive glossary of most commonly used terms within the real estate and development industry.

The sample forms and outlines included in this workbook can be used "as is" or modified to suit your individual needs. They are designed to help you quickly recall and analyze the necessary information concerning your development.

There are no guarantees in the real estate development business. Many challenges exist which the developer must overcome. Your opportunity for success will increase proportionally to your preparation. Through this Development Workbook, you will be prepared to make intelligent planning decisions—decisions that will play a crucial role in reaching your personal financial goals.

REAL ESTATE DEVELOPMENT PROCEDURAL MATRIX DIAGRAM

Before you begin reading, it is suggested that you refer to the Appendix for the Real Estate Development Procedural Matrix Diagram. This diagram is designed to not only give a comprehensive overview of the development process, but can also be used as a guide or index in referencing various issues in the overall study of this book.

Foreword

First of all, it is a distinct pleasure and honor to have the opportunity to write the foreword for this new book. To all of us who have had the opportunity to play a role as either the developer or simply to be involved in any aspect of the real estate development process, its publication is a great break-through.

Too often, limited experience fails to provide us with the tools and foresight to understand real life situations. In this publication, the authors have successfully provided a developer's perspective into real life from a practical and meaningful application. Unlike theory, we must have guidelines and strategy which can be used in each situation for that particular project at a given time. This book's reference points constantly remind us to examine the variables along the way. It is hoped that this publication will be a great source of insight for the developer or the potential developer.

Additionally, I am pleased that the book has shown great respect for completing your homework by planning a strategy prior to beginning in this industry. We are reminded to carefully examine the market and when we find that the "lights are green," continue to proceed with caution. As many have learned, discipline is critical and oftentimes perseverance is the only difference between success and failure.

The role of the developer in risk taking throughout the process is respected. Too often, little is mentioned about risk taking even though it is such a critical component in the development formula. Knowing about risk taking is not enough. The risk must be measured and found acceptable to the developer by considering the constraints of the financing and the work tasks necessary for the project to reach its profit and return objectives.

Finally, this workbook is long overdue and should have been available to the savings and loan institutions which have departed. Their lack of discipline and failure to understand the process contributed to their demise. I am delighted that the authors have taken the time to create such a meaningful and practical tool which can help the developer achieve the desired success.

With wishes for a great success . . . .

> Michael A. Feiner
> Feiner Enterprises, Denver, Colorado

## Chapter 1

Fundamentals of
Real Estate Development

REAL ESTATE DEVELOPMENT

The experience of developing real estate is extremely exciting. It is a game with very high stakes and one where fortunes are made or lost. It is a game for the entrepreneur and one which will test skills of prediction and decision making. It is a game where amateurs create a tremendous amount of confusion and a game where professionals make significant blunders. It is a business where one can create monuments to their immortality and a business which shapes our environment and communities.

Real estate development is the process of responding to a real estate need in our society by creating and financing a product which satisfies that need. It is a process which involves leadership, market research, marketing, public relations, design and construction, financing and accounting, and property management. It is a business like others, where one has to adhere to the ethical and moral laws of our society through codes and ordinances. It is a business where products created can generate regular ongoing cash flows for the developer and investors over long periods of time. It is a business which works with the physical features and forms of our environment and can be created in land, water, or air. It is a business which responds to the changes of technology, socio-economics, demographics, architecture, laws, entertainment and recreation, manufacturing, and industry by reflecting those changes in planning, process, and form. It is a business which deals with the past in historic preservation and reaches to the future in master planning. Somewhat like the renaissance people in history, the developer's hand is in a little bit of everything involved in the community.

This chapter has been written to give a picture of the real estate development process and the type of person who is involved in this process. As you move through the concepts presented, we will set a cornerstone of marketing research, encourage you to choose an objective, provide you with the key questions to ask in developing your investment strategy, give you a bird's-eye view of the components of a successful development, focus on market constraints, timing, and cycles, picture the risks and rewards, and discuss developing in general. It is our hope that you will clearly see that one must always have a strategy, be aware of its associated risks, use resources wisely, and serve the customer—to be able to reap the rewards—in accomplishments and increased net worth.

THE KEY—MARKETING AND MARKET RESEARCH

Once, I was asked, "If you were given $20,000,000, as a real estate developer to do with as you pleased, what would you do?" After careful thought and in an ideal world, I responded that I would spend the first $1,000,000 on market research so that I know the markets better than my competition. Then, I would spend another $1,000,000 on assembling the very best development and marketing team. Then, I would use the remaining $18,000,000 as equity to pursue that which I learned from my marketing research to develop as many properties possible.

Whereas one would find it very hard to find an investor who would go along with this plan, the example does make a very good point. Too often, many developments have begun without marketing research other than abbreviated generic market studies, the enthusiastic feelings of the entrepreneur developer, and the naivety of the investor. The cornerstone of one's efforts in development must be marketing and market research. Only in this way can we know how to sell to the ultimate user and know when and what these users need. It is possible for some developments to create a need in themselves, but this is not often the case. When developers fail to use market research adequately, they will generally make one or more of the following mistakes.

- They will miss the market opportunity that exists.
- They will make mistakes in positioning the property relative to the competition.
- They will have inadequate market evaluation.
- They will not have priced the product strategically.
- They will over- or underestimate market demand.

While *market research* is what planning and developing must be based, marketing is the process of finding the customers which will in their rent payments or purchases fuel the development. In the previous example the investment in the creation of an outstanding marketing team was paramount after generating the needed market research. Without the mature marketing team, the public will not be informed properly about the development's offering and when interested prospects are identified, the sales presentation may be poor. Consequently, few customers will be convinced that your product is better than the competition. In addition, the aspect of marketing, which is essential for repeat business is property management. Fuel for the development as stated is provided by rent payments, and renewals of leases or repeat business will continue to provide that income necessary to produce cash flow and cover debt services.

DECISION MAKING: CHOOSE A TARGET AND SET A GOAL

Typically, the market will dictate the development side of this decision. If the market is overbuilt and the financing costs are too expensive, the feasibility of developing is poor. The developer might then choose to either buy an existing property and create "added value" by renovating that property or converting that property to a new use. An alternative may be to buy a piece of land and wait until market conditions dictate the development of his chosen product type. Since this book is about the development process, the following paragraphs will briefly discuss the three land options of the developer.

Buying a Parcel of Land to Hold for Your Future Development

In this option, the developer finds a piece of land that, based on market trends, has future potential profit possibilities. It is necessary to remember when making the purchase, that there must be sufficient funds to carry this land until market conditions change. This purchase could be through an option to close at a future date, an all cash purchase, or a purchase that is either financed by the seller or a lending institution.

Flipping the Land

Another option available to the developer is that of flipping the land to someone else in the future. It is hoped that this action results in a profit. Flipping the land is a term used to describe the process of buying a parcel of land at one price, making minimal improvements or upgrading the zoning, and selling to a new buyer. The new purchaser of this land might be a land speculator or another developer. Many times a profit taken can be a wise decision. Often, land is flipped without even taking possession. Some contracts are sold for a profit prior to closing.

Creating the Development Master Plan and Then Selling

This process entails the developer securing the property either through an option or by outright purchase, then creating the master plan for the property, and then rather than complete the development himself, he will sell off the property and the master plan to another developer who will complete the development process.

CREATE YOUR INVESTMENT STRATEGY

Once the decision is made to jump into the development arena, the developer must decide on what type of personal risks are necessary for potential rewards. Questions to be asked are:

- Am I in this business for the short or long term?
- Do I need immediate cash flow or am I patient for the return?
- How much cash can I afford to invest in any one development?
- Do I need development and marketing partners?
- Do I need financial partners to bear the financial risks?
- Do I have all the necessary expertise to pull off a successful development?
- Do I have the drive and ambition to complete what I set out to do?
- Do I want to build to hold or sell at completion?
- Am I willing to live in a stressful environment?
- Do I have the management and marketing expertise to lease-up and manage the property after completion?

SUCCESSFUL DEVELOPMENTS

There are many factors that play into that which makes a successful real estate development. All of these factors interact with the other and will be affected by the marketplace's demands (see Figure 1–1). Brief descriptions of these interacting factors are given below.

Location

All successful real estate developments have "Location, Location, Location." Location is relative to each product type. What is a good location for one user will differ with the next user. Residential housing does not want to be close to a freeway

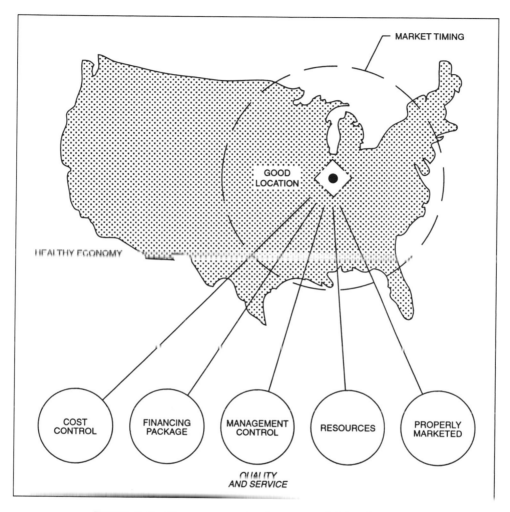

MARKET TIMING

GOOD
LOCATION

HEALTHY ECONOMY

COST
CONTROL

FINANCING
PACKAGE

MANAGEMENT
CONTROL

RESOURCES

PROPERLY
MARKETED

QUALITY
AND SERVICE

Figure 1-1   The components of a successful development.

or railroad, but an industrial warehouse might require both features. A good location will provide amenities and services such as shopping, dining, transportation access, housing, and governmental services as closely as possible.

Planning

Successful real estate developments do not occur without proper comprehensive planning. The initial concept until the final sale should be thought out well in advance. Very few businesses succeed by crisis management. There will be times during crisis that decisions will have to be made to "make the deal," or stay on schedule. These decisions will ultimately be the best decisions, because of proper planning. It always helps to have preplanned your options. The best developments occur because of anticipation rather than reaction.

Market Timing: The Window of Opportunity

Market timing is crucial. Many a well-thought out project has failed due to poor timing. Factors such as unexpected inflation, a rise in interest rates, competition startups, and utility moratoriums all affect the final outcome of the development. It is also extremely difficult to second guess what the buying psychology of the consumer will be at any given point in time. Market research will help in this area as much as possible. Additionally, many developments go through an extended time period from concept to final completion. Many large projects can go through more than one market cycle and take years in predevelopment. When the correct window is open, the developer must be able to seize the opportunity and make a move.

Financial Staying Power

Due to the fact that many projects take longer than expected to absorb their product, the developer must have the financial resources to bridge slumps in the marketplace. Many a developer has lost a project due to downturns in the market. Part of the development equation is deciding whether or not you have extra cash reserves to weather potential storms.

Control of Construction Costs and Schedules

Without careful monitoring, construction costs have a nasty habit of creeping over budget. Many construction projects go over their planned budgets due to unanticipated costs, such as unforeseen soil and rock conditions, materials cost increases, and poor estimating of construction costs. Each component of the construction cost should be analyzed and reanalyzed over and over again prior to starting construction. During the construction process, the total team should be challenged to continually find ways to minimize costs, while still maintaining quality.

In addition to cost control, time control is essential. Knowing that lease-up schedules affect cash flow, and construction schedules affect interest charges, the project must be constructed within the allotted time or one will face severe penalties in capital cost projections. See Chapters 6 and 11 for more information concerning scheduling.

Properly Marketed and Targeted

All successful developments have marketing programs that target and aggressively pursue the customer. Very few developers succeed by waiting for the market to come to them. After proper market research, identifying the market, and creating a product to satisfy the needs of that market, marketing plans must be developed which define objectives, describe the personnel necessary to reach those objectives and budgets. Then with the enthusiasm of a "salesperson" that plan must be executed.

A Well-Conceived Financing Package

A good financing package can add to the profitability of the development. The lower the cost to service the debt, the more profit for the developer's pocket. The structure of the financing will play a primary role in the evaluation of risk, and how one should react should the project fail to perform as projected.

Management Control

As in all successful businesses, the developer must have total control over the development. Not only must all the management systems be in place, but they must be fine-tuned and monitored regularly. Every system can be improved but the saying, "Keep It Simple Stupid" (KISS) should always be followed. Oftentimes the bureaucracy of a large lethargic organization will negatively affect the success and profitability of a development as well as the developer.

A Healthy Economy

Starting developments during an "unhealthy economy" can be suicide. If the buying mentality of the customer is in a holding pattern, obviously your product will not sell as well as before.

The Art of Compromising

One must realize that in the process of real estate development, compromises will always be made. One may have to build a little less to be within the budget, one may have to build a little more to respond effectively to the competition, or one may have to build differently to follow governmental ordinances. In the process, do not be discouraged, because ultimately, your development will likely improve because of these adjustments.

Quality and Service

To win over the competition, the successful development must excel in quality and service. The customer usually desires the most quality and service for his investment. The competitive edge, profits, and success will always belong to those who set the pace in quality and service.

Good Old-Fashion Luck

Even after all of the above, for ultimate success, the developer needs a little luck. With all the pieces that it takes to assemble any type of real estate development, "Murphy's Law" can occur. Murphy said that if something can go wrong it will. Since we are not absolute, the unexpected can occur, but with proper planning, your successes will outdistance your failures.

MARKET CONSTRAINTS

Many constraints can hinder the success of any development. Since these factors constantly change, developers must develop a "sixth sense" for reading the markets.

Customer Mentality

Since the consumer is the ultimate user of the developed product, knowing their thought processes is essential. One of the main criteria for making decisions is money. When the economy is healthy and unemployment low, the customer will spend, but when the economy is uncertain, the customer will conserve in large purchasing decisions.

Mortgage Rates

When mortgage rates increase, it is more difficult to borrow for the development. Not only will the cost to borrow be more expensive, but also the lender will loan less to the developer, causing the developer to have to generate more equity for the project.

Governmental Regulatory Policies

Many times changes in the zoning ordinances will discourage a proposed development. A reduction in the zoning classification or approved density could alter the future profitability of the development and prohibit it altogether. If already begun, future planning may have to be altered.

Market versus Investor Demand

A critical lesson to learn from the development boom of the mid 1980s is that development demand should be responsive to the demand of the consumer, and not the investor. During this time period, great sums of equity and debt funds were available to the developer. Many developers lost sight of true market demand and only saw "green" in potential fees. Much of the glut of property in the late 1980s is product which should never have been developed. With this easy money, many first-time developers built a product that was both ill-conceived in design as well as in marketability. Developers should learn from the mistakes of others and study past market trends to enhance effectiveness.

MARKET TIMING: FOUR CYCLES THAT AFFECT DEVELOPMENT

As mentioned above, timing is critically important in the development of property. The general rule, "buy low, sell high," applies to real estate as it does to any type of investment. The following four cycles are predicated on a market with "classic" conditions and economic ebb and flow (Figure 1–2). They assume that the economic base of the area is sufficiently stable to enable it to recover from hard times, and that there is a continual need for additional residential and commercial properties. These cycles will vary in duration and severity depending on many outside and intangible forces. Markets may have sub-markets which behave differently during the same period; the north side of the city could be booming, while at the same time, the south side is stagnant. Nevertheless, the ability to recognize these cycles can give the developer the added edge in making investment decisions.

Down Cycle (DC)

The down cycle is when the market is overbuilt and vacancies start to rise. This market is a buyer's marketplace. Rent concessions are commonplace and properties are in foreclosure due to the financial pressures of carrying empty buildings. This period of the market is when the developer needs intensive marketing efforts, financial strength, and "staying power" until the market changes. Very little if any new construction occurs during this period. Most lenders discontinue their lending

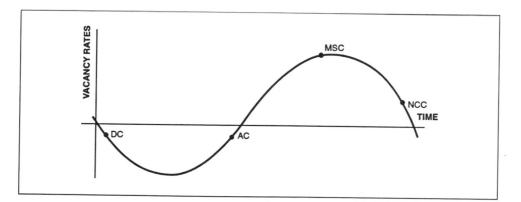

Figure 1–2   Real estate development market's cycles.

operations until there is an upturn. Sales prices will be discounted and the developer will be forced to accept lower sales prices.

Absorption Cycle (AC)

Due to the lack of new construction resulting from the down cycle, the market forces of supply and demand begin to take effect. The market will now pass through the absorption cycle of the overbuilt inventory of space. As the excess inventory is absorbed, the rental rates begin to climb and rental concessions decrease. New development activity will begin to occur due to the increase of new demand and the shortage of supply.

New Construction Cycle (NCC)

The new construction cycle, following the absorption cycle, will see new demand in the market, with the supply of available space decreasing. Developers will be aggressive to build product to satisfy this demand. Rental rates will increase, as well as sales prices for the property. During a recovery cycle, the rate of inflation and construction costs will increase. In order for the developer to realize his desired profit margins, these increased costs must be passed along in the form of higher rents or sales prices.

Market Saturation Cycle (MSC)

The fourth and final cycle begins once the market has peaked and begins its slide downward. Occupancy levels begin to decrease, rent concessions begin to reappear, and development activity will slow to a halt. The market has now gone full cycle.

The prime time to develop property is either during the last stages of the absorption cycle or during the new construction cycle.

WEIGHING THE RISKS

In all of life there is risk and associated with that risk is reward; the greater the risk, the greater the reward. The following is a list of the risks associated in any real estate development. A prudent investor will take the time to consider each prior to beginning a new venture.

Financial Risk

As in all types of business investments, there is a possibility that part or all of the invested equity may be lost. The possibility also exists that the developer may have to fund "out of pocket" for negative cash flows, due to changes in market conditions. The developer may even have to sell at a loss, or even lose the property through foreclosure. In the worst possible scenario, the developer may have personal liability for the loss incurred to the lender. This potential risk is substantial and should be evaluated carefully. A list of reasons for development losses and a clearer definition of financial risk is given below:

- Poor assumptions in proforma
- Construction cost overruns
- Extended lease-up, sell-out, or construction schedules
- Lower than anticipated rents or sales prices
- Increase in interest rates
- High vacancy, low absorption rates in market
- Poor acceptance of the product by the market
- Inaccurate operating costs

Opportunity Risk

There is also risk associated with losing the profit you would have received if you had invested your funds elsewhere. In the above example, the developer could have lost some or all of his invested capital. The loss of these funds could mean that he has also lost the opportunity of investing in another development, hopefully a profitable one.

Inflationary Risk

The added factor of inflation in the economy can further erode the developer's return on invested capital. Assuming that the developer finally gets a profit, this profit may be worth less than on day one, due to inflation.

Physical Destruction Risk

The physical asset of the development could be totally destroyed through a natural disaster such as a flood, fire, or earthquake. Although insurance can replace the building improvements, the physical destruction could severely affect surrounding market conditions and hinder replacement of the existing tenants or the availability of new tenants.

Liquidity Risk

Since real estate is not a liquid investment, as are stocks and bonds, the developer may have to hold the development for a longer period than originally intended.

This lack of liquidity may hinder the developer from having the cash funds available to begin another development or make another investment.

Health, Family and Ego Risk

Three risk factors often overlooked by the real estate developer are those of physical health and well-being, stress in one's family life, and the damage to pride and ego. Oftentimes, unfortunately, many of these factors ride on the success or failure of a development. The stress of a financially unprofitable venture can not only wipe out one's projected profits, but also their life savings. This financial burden can create great strain on one's life. It is a sad commentary when not only one's business fails, but their family also, because of failure to evaluate and be aware of these risks and to manage them effectively.

MANAGING THE RISKS

Whereas real estate developers cannot totally eliminate the risks, they can minimize them as much as possible. Only in this way can the probability of success be at its greatest. The following will describe ways in which the risks heretofore discussed can be managed effectively. A risk-yield curve is shown in Figure 1–3.

Doing Your Research

Market research into the product type and market area is critical to success. The more research completed prior to the development process, the better the chances for reducing risk.

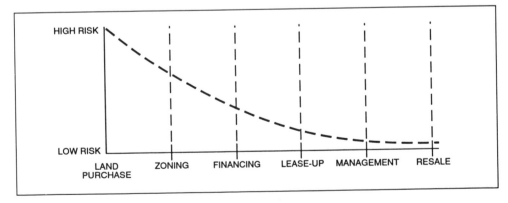

Figure 1-3 Risk-yield curve.

Land Purchase Contingencies

To protect the developer against financial losses during the land acquisition stage, various contingencies should be added to the contract. More information concerning the subject can be found in Chapter 4.

Diversifying Your Development Activities

The saying, "Don't put all of your eggs in one basket," applies here. Diversify your development activity into other product types as well as other geographic market areas.

Shift Rental Risk to the User

Negotiate leases in which the user pays for increases in operating costs and rents to protect against inflation.

Limiting Financial Liability of Ownership

The developer should try to negotiate nonrecourse financing for any loans on the property. Another method of limiting liability is through financial partners who will help carry the financial liabilities.

Ownership Investment Vehicle and Legal Liability

The type of ownership vehicle selected should be chosen to protect the developer from personal liability. This will protect the developer from litigation from tenants, vendors and consultants, contractors, and the public. Additionally, assuming the developer is required to personally endorse a mortgage loan, a corporate investment vehicle should be used to shield the developer's personal assets.

REAPING THE REWARDS

If now you have used your vision and entrepreneur skills to research, plan, design, finance, construct, and lease or sell your development, obviously you as the developer should be compensated for your efforts and compensated well for the risks taken. This is where this business is exciting because of the many vehicles for profit that exist. The following will illustrate the many ways a real estate developer can profit for a job well done. Figure 1–4 briefly outlines the varying risks and rewards that may occur and be evaluated during the decision-making process.

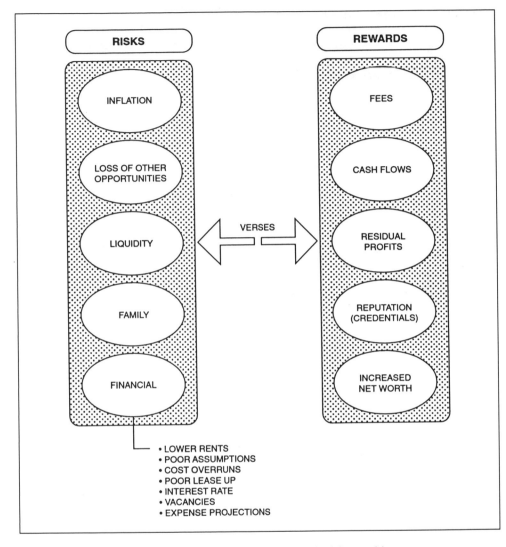

Figure 1–4   Risks versus rewards decision making.

Generating Up-Front Fees

Most developers generate some type of development fees during the construction and rent-up phases. These fees are used to pay overhead costs and place profit into the developer's pocket. Examples are given below.

Development Fee

This is a fee paid to the developer for services. It is used to offset overhead and is paid through the development process. It is usually based on a percentage of the costs, dollars per buildable square feet, or dollars per unit.

General Contracting Fee

If the developer builds the project himself, this fee is based on a percentage of the costs to build the property.

Construction Management Fee

If the developer contracts with a general contractor to oversee the construction management, this fee can be based on a monthly retainer fee, a percentage of the construction costs, or a set fee.

Marketing or Leasing Fee

If the developer markets the project, this fee is based on either a flat rate per square foot or unit or a percentage of the rents generated.

Property Management Fee

The developer who manages the project is entitled to a management fee. This fee is usually based on a percentage of the collected revenues.

Cash Flows

After all the revenues (rents and expenses) are collected and the operating expenses and debt services are paid, the cash flow remaining is distributed to the developer and any partners per joint venture agreements. Obviously, as expenses are controlled, debt is paid, and rents escalate, these cash flows increase, giving the investors a greater return over time.

Using Available Tax Shelter

Depending on whether the developer is considered active or passive in the management of the development, there are various types of losses to offset other incomes. As in all tax shelters, this is deferred tax and will be considered gain at the time of sale. At the time of a sale, regardless of an active or passive management, the developer can use all losses to offset gain on this sale to the degree of the losses and the law.

Creating Net Worth—The Residual

If the property is developed and performs according to the developer's financial proforma, there should be a spread between the property's market value and the cost of the development less any equity that the developer was required to invest. This spread is the potential residual for the developer. If over the holding period this spread increases due to increases in the net operating income or inflation, then the developer is creating and enhancing his net worth.

Accomplishment in One's Work—The Ultimate Credential

Once again, if the property performs financially as planned and is a service to the tenants and the community, the developer can take great pride in his work. Although this does not put any extra money directly into his pocket, it is an intangible benefit that can be derived. In addition, each project successfully developed becomes a credential that will help in the development of future work, thereby creating the opportunity for repeat business.

PUBLIC AND PRIVATE INTERFACE IN DEVELOPMENT

For real estate development to occur, there are three basic groups which must strategically interact and mutually support each other. Their relationship and response to the other is paramount to the development opportunity and successful relationships within the community. They relate by having an identity which then sends signals of need or availability, which when satisfied, create a vibrant healthy community. Figure 1–5 is a diagram illustrating these relationships and interactions.

Space Consumer (User) Group

The space consumer groups are the ultimate users of the property, whether they be renters or purchasers. This group makes decisions based on location, sense of satisfaction, security, and cost. Each requirement is made in conjunction with the others and unless cost is no object, decisions made through a series of trade-offs and compromises. This group receives the net benefits of the development in space and environment provided and pays rents to the space producer group for the space. They receive benefits from the public infrastructure group that pays taxes for the services provided.

Space Producer Group

The space producer group are those who, as a team, assemble the final product that the space users need. They include the developer and other professionals with

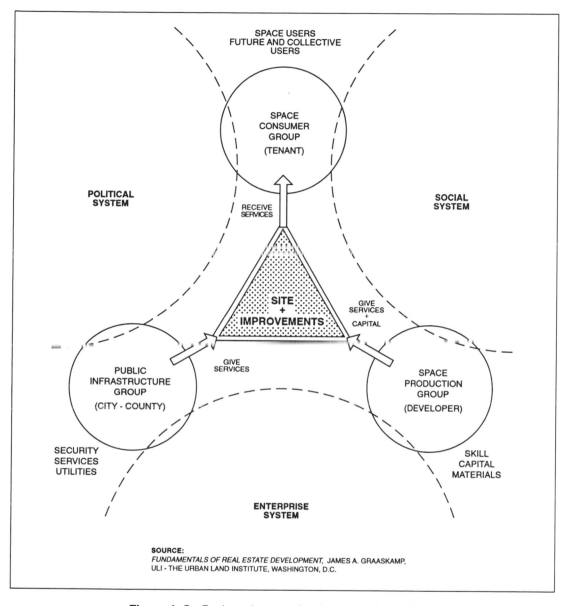

Figure 1–5 Basic real estate development relationships.

abilities in the architectural, engineering, construction, financing, marketing, and property management disciplines. They provide capital and services to the development and receive capital gain potential in cash flows, fees, and residuals in the future.

Public Infrastructure Group

The public infrastructure group includes those that provide all of the off-site systems. This infrastructure includes the networks of local streets, utilities, public services (police and fire departments), schools, and other governmental agencies. This group provides services to the space user group as well as the development. They are compensated for these services through taxes and user fees.

TYPES OF DEVELOPERS

Once you have made the decision to work in a particular market segment and to develop your product, other decisions must be made to further define your objectives as the developer. There are many different types of developments and by the same token there are many different types of developers. The following are a few ways in which real estate developers function.

Land Developers

Land developers develop parcels of land by rezoning and constructing needed infrastructure. Then they market various parcels of land to other developers or end users.

Speculative Developers —Building to Own

Speculative developers will develop a project with only a commitment from a few or even no tenants. This type of developer is developing to own and is looking for the annual cash flow income stream, as well as the long-term equity increase and appreciation of the property. Since the speculative developer will own the property longer, the property is usually designed for low operational and maintenance costs.

Merchant Builders

A merchant builder develops a property for immediate resale either prior to the start of construction, during the construction phase, or immediately after construction. In negotiating the sale of the property, the developer can take a lower sales price and sell the completed property without any tenants or he can get a higher sales price by guaranteeing the new purchaser a totally leased property.

This developer may design less quality into the finished product, knowing that his association with the product may be short.

Fee Developers

Fee developers are developers who will contract with an owner to develop a property for a fee. These individuals are experienced in all phases of development, and essentially averse to risk. They may also lease and manage the property for additional fees.

Renovators and Converters

If market conditions or the right opportunity presents itself, the developer may choose to purchase an existing property and improve its value through creativity and hard work. Although not starting from the "ground up" in creating this product, the developer is still developing, using the conventional process, described herein.

Chapter **2**

Planning a Strategy
with Development
and Financial Criteria

MARKET RESEARCH IDENTIFIES THE NEED

The most important ingredient used for planning development strategy is market research. Only when we know the market and its demands will we be able to have the basics for an effective plan. Without market research, we will be developing projects intuitively and have a very risky venture on our hands. There is a verse in the Bible, in the book of Proverbs, which states that success comes from wise counsel, considering the costs, and careful planning. King Solomon used this wisdom before building his temple and passed this advice on to us. Take the time to gather the market data and spend the time to analyze it before beginning your venture and your probability of success will increase.

Consider the following example. A developer in a large metropolitan area decided to develop a golf-oriented residential project. He followed the normal processes of hiring an architect with extensive experience and planned what seemed to be an exciting project. His public relations firm made sure that the advertisements were in every major publication and newspaper and of course the ground-breaking and grand-opening ceremonies were like no other. Now after 18 months of operation and millions of dollars spent on the project, the project is in financial difficulty. They cannot sell memberships to the club and last year, only six lots were sold. Memberships to the golf club have to be given away as concessions to lot purchasers. Interestingly enough, this is in a market where typical golf course communities sell 45 to 65 lots per year and without the golf club memberships. So, what happened? The error which the developer made was to plan this project as if it was just another golf course in the community. It was his belief that the surrounding residential development's only requirement should be one-half acre lots similar to other developments in the area. In addition, the developer thought that the price for these lots was simply a function of the cost of the land, development costs, and financing. Further analysis revealed that not only was this course difficult to play, but the amenities in this context were overdeveloped. This overdeveloping placed additional cost burdens on the project's economics. It was also observed that the surrounding residential golf communities were thriving with similar sized lots, easier courses, in a more attractive and efficient setting, and for the same price. Essentially, in the planning of this development, the developer did not know his market well and did not approach the development of the golf course as the development of a business rather than as an amenity. He did not understand the minimum basic requirements of his market to position his development properly relative to the competition. The problems which are being faced at this point could have been avoided through market research and a thorough understanding that all of the parts of the development fit together as a whole and the way that they work together many times sets your development apart from others. This superiority to competition may be amenities offered, views to the surroundings, the architecture, access to parking, aesthetics, environments, landscaping and all for the same price. It is a challenge, but one that is achievable.

To plan a strategy for development, it is essential to know your market and that your market evaluation consider the supply by price and type, demand by price and type, the profile of your competition, and competitive standards. Then with this information, the strategy for development should be to position the project relative to the competition, giving the customer choices which position your development in a leading position now and in the future. Any development should be positioned relative to the competition, because in the final analysis, they are nothing more than a business. The market research factors to consider when developing a strategy are shown in Figure 2–1.

Over the past 20 years, the focus of market research has been evolving from just a quick accumulation of information to a sophisticated science of interpreting this data and how it relates to the total market. Figure 2–2 outlines the evolution of the process.

In this chapter, we will discuss various choices for the developer to make in a business venture, criteria for decision making, unique challenges to be faced, feasibility studies, financing issues, and ownership of property. In the process of completing your development strategy, all of these should be addressed and, if carefully

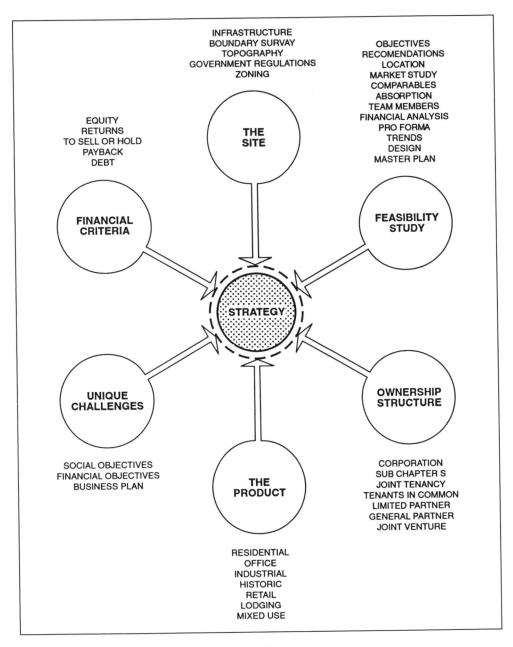

INFRASTRUCTURE
BOUNDARY SURVAY
TOPOGRAPHY
GOVERNMENT REGULATIONS
ZONING

OBJECTIVES
RECOMENDATIONS
LOCATION
MARKET STUDY
COMPARABLES
ABSORPTION
TEAM MEMBERS
FINANCIAL ANALYSIS
PRO FORMA
TRENDS
DESIGN
MASTER PLAN

EQUITY
RETURNS
TO SELL OR HOLD
PAYBACK
DEBT

THE SITE

FINANCIAL CRITERIA

FEASIBILITY STUDY

STRATEGY

UNIQUE CHALLENGES

OWNERSHIP STRUCTURE

THE PRODUCT

SOCIAL OBJECTIVES
FINANCIAL OBJECTIVES
BUSINESS PLAN

CORPORATION
SUB CHAPTER S
JOINT TENANCY
TENANTS IN COMMON
LIMITED PARTNER
GENERAL PARTNER
JOINT VENTURE

RESIDENTIAL
OFFICE
INDUSTRIAL
HISTORIC
RETAIL
LODGING
MIXED USE

Figure 2–1   Developing a strategy.

	1970–1976 (The Age Of Innocence)	1977–1985 (Tax-Driven Deals)	1986–1989 (Return to Economics)	1900s (Proactive Decision Making)
Geographic Coverage	Metropolitan area	Metropolitan area Downtown/suburban	Metropolitan area Downtown/suburban Multiple submarkets	Building-by-building data Flexibility to design competitive market
Typical Usuage	Background	Background Due diligence	Background Due diligence Project-specific Assumptions	Comprehensive real estate information management system Acquisition Asset management Disposition
Qualitative Description	Anecedotal "broad brush" Non-data-intensive	Reporting without interpretation Limited data	Moderate iunterpretation Limited data	Highly interpretive and analytical Data-intensive
Delivery System	Consulting reports	Consulting reports Publications Newsletters	Consulting reports Publications Newsletters Limited databases	Automated databases Real estate expert systems
Forecasting Techniques	Chamber of Commerce "Area outlook"	Extrapolation of recent past	Increasing reliance on economic and demographic indicators	Reliable predictive models integrated with economic and real estate databases

Reprinted with permission from The REIS Reports, Inc., New York, N.Y.

Figure 2–2   Evolution of real estate market information (1970–2000).

considered relative to what the market will be, play a role in your development's success.

DECISION MAKING—SELECTING A TARGET

The developer's level of experience will determine the choices available. The beginning developer is advised to tackle a simple project first to develop elementary expertise—then equipped with this experience, become involved in larger projects. Obviously, the larger developer will generally be involved with the larger projects not only because of the size of their staffs, but for the substantial rewards which can be earned. The following is a master listing of types of developments and their variations.

Residential

Residential properties provide dwelling space for individual tenants. Rental and for-sale properties are available as follows:

Rental Properties Housing Types

Rental properties are those residential properties that are rented to tenants on a weekly, monthly, or annual basis to generate revenue.

Single-Family Homes: Individual houses to be rented to a tenant are single-family homes.

Duplex, Triplex, Quadraplex: Two, three, or four units, which may be attached, and rented to tenants comprise this group.

Mobile Homes: These prefabricated homes are purchased or rented to tenants, either in a single or double width.

Mobile Lot Rentals: An investor can also receive rental income from lots on which mobile homes or recreational vehicles are placed.

Multi-Family Apartments: Properties with five or more rental units. Multi-family housing can be designed in the following styles:

Garden Style: One- to three-level apartment buildings

Townhouse: Properties that contain multi-level units attached in rows

Mid-Rise: Three to six stories, with elevators

High-Rise: Over six stories, with elevators

Weekly Rental Apartments—Single Room Occupancies (SRO):   These properties cater to residential users who lease by the week or month.

For-Sale Housing Types

Homes developed or purchased by an investor for immediate resale. For-sale housing is sold to the purchaser who will live in the housing or rent the housing to another individual.

Single-Family: Single-family housing is designed to accommodate housing for only one family. The following are types of housing styles.

Cluster Housing: High density housing, either attached or detached housing, may be called cluster housing.

Zero Lot Line: High density housing on very small lots, usually 60 to 80 front feet per lot is termed zero lot line.

Condominium: Ownership of an individual residential unit in a multi-unit building. The owner gets a divided ownership interest in the building and an undivided interest in the common areas, including the lobby, hallways, stairways, exterior sitework.

Townhome: Ownership of an individual residential unit in which all the units are attached. The owner gets fee ownership of the unit and the land directly underneath the structure.

Cooperative: A type of ownership whereby the owners of a building are stockholders in a corporation that owns the real estate. Each shareholder then gets a proprietary lease to his or her unit.

Planned Unit Development (PUD): A planned unit development is a master plan for a large tract of land. It usually contains various types of residential or commercial development.

Resort: Investing in vacation property to rent or to sell. This includes single-family and condominium ownership as well as:

> **Time Share:** A form of ownership in which the property is owned by several parties. Each owner has the ownership rights to the property for a specific time period.

Conversions: Of multi-family projects from rental to for-sale. Conversion can be either changed to condominium or cooperative ownership.

Rehabilitation: Renovating residential property or upgrading it to meet current demands are types of rehabilitation.

Senior Citizen: Housing designed for a senior citizen market is available in the following:

> **Retirement Housing:** Housing that is either rented or sold to the retirement market. This includes pure rental communities, nursing home facilities or congregate care facilities, a combination of both.

> **Personal Care Housing:** Housing provided for residents for protective care and watchful oversight, but do not have an illness, injury, or disability needing chronic or convalescent care, including medical and nursing services.

> **Nursing Facilities:** Buildings used to care for older adults in need of continuous medical care are considered nursing facilities.

Market Segments

Each type of residential property will need to be designed and marketed to a different market. The following are various types of markets:

Rental Housing

> **Low Income:** This is basic housing for low-income tenants. Units range from one to four bedrooms. The rent can be subsidized by the government or the developer's mortgage might be subsidized by a governmental low interest rate loan. Amenities usually include a pool, playground, and laundry facilities.

> **Moderate Income:** This market will pay for more features and amenities than are available to the low-income market but not the high prices of the upscale market.

> **Upscale:** This market demands quality in the unit features, amenities and they are willing to pay for it. Units range from efficiencies to three bedrooms. The units include upgraded appliances, flooring, wallcovering, oversized rooms, ceiling molding, upgraded lighting, and upgraded

cabinetry. Amenities include clubhouse with party room and exercise facilities, tennis, pool, laundry facilities, maid service, doorman and concierge, and additional building security systems.

All Adult: All-adult housing is designed for either singles or childless couples. Amenities include pool, tennis, clubhouse with party room and exercise facilities, and laundry. Unit sizes range from one to two bedrooms.

Family: Family housing is designed with larger bedrooms and unit sizes from two to four bedrooms. Amenities include pool, playground, laundry facilities, tennis, and clubhouse with child-related activities.

Senior Citizen: Senior citizen housing is designed to meet the needs of the aged and physically handicapped. Unit features include special security and emergency buzzers, and handicapped bathroom and kitchen facilities. Amenities include individual and group activities. Unit sizes range from efficiencies to two bedroom units.

Student: Student housing is located either on a college campus or just adjacent to the campus. Units range from one to three bedrooms. Many bedrooms are oversized to accommodate more than one student. Unit features are basic. The amenities include laundry facilities, transportation to and from campus, pool and tennis.

Military: Military housing is located adjacent to military bases. It is designed as low-cost basic rental housing. Units range from one to three bedrooms. Amenities include laundry facilities, pool, and playground for the children.

Corporate Suites: Corporate suites are designed for the business user who wants to rent on a weekly or monthly basis. Unit sizes are small efficiencies to one bedrooms with small kitchenettes. The units are fully furnished, including kitchen and bathroom accessories. Maid service is also available.

Weekly or Short-Term Housing: Weekly or short-term housing caters to the blue-collar market. Units are efficiencies with kitchenettes. Amenities include a pool and public telephones (single residence occupants).

For-Sale Housing

Entry Level: The entry-level housing market is usually young individuals or young married couples moving from their parents' house or an apartment. The price range of this housing is the lowest level of the market. Unit sizes range from two to four bedrooms. Unit features include dishwasher, washer and dryer connections, and patio area.

Move-Up Level: This market has graduated from the entry-level housing market and because of increased purchasing power or family size needs a larger and more expensive home. Unit features include upgraded flooring, cabinets, appliances, wallcoverings, larger room sizes, basements, and covered parking.

Luxury Level: This is the top of the line level. These units feature upgraded flooring, wallcovering, cabinets, appliances, custom molding and lighting fixtures. Units range from three to five bedrooms. Amenities include pool, tennis, or membership to the community association.

Move-Down Level: This market is moving down to a smaller home due to a reduction in family size. They still require the same unit features and amenities as they have had in the past. Unit sizes range from one to two bedrooms with a den.

Historic Renovation

Historic properties, even in their dilapidated conditions, often provide the richest of character for our communities. Many times they are renovated for residential, office, or retail use even though their original use was industrial or warehouse. Often, their high ceilings, rich detailing, and large windows provide unique character. In addition, tax laws provide incentives for development by allowing the use of income tax credits to offset income dollar for dollar. The qualifying properties must be certified for the National Historic Register. Some developers focus only on these properties and some investors use them as investments to shelter income. To have one's building certified for the Historic Register is a very detailed and lengthy process both nationally and locally. The potential developer is cautioned to research this matter carefully prior to beginning a development with this type of product. Additional information is contained in Chapter 5.

Commercial

Commercial properties provide space for businesses. Essentially, space is provided for the conducting and management of business, storing and selling of goods, or the temporary lodging of the business person. The following will list the major categories and a brief description of each.

Retail

Convenience Center (Strip Center): A small retail center, usually one-half to four acres having between 5000 and 40,000 square feet. Typical tenants are a convenience market, dry cleaners, laundry, and liquor store.

Neighborhood Center: A shopping center with a supermarket or drugstore as anchor tenants. Typically located on five to ten acres, having between 50,000 and 100,000 square feet of rental space.

Community Center: A medium-size center, with about 50 stores. Typically located on 15 to 20 acres and having between 150,000 to 200,000 square feet of rental space. Typical tenants will include a variety of soft-goods and hard-goods retailers.

Regional Center: A large center, usually enclosed, with at least two department stores and from 400,000 to 1,000,000 square feet of rental space, located on 80 to 100 acres.

Hyper-Center: A large regional enclosed center, with 750,000 to 2,000,000 square feet of retail space, located on 50 to 150 acres. They usually have between two to five department stores and 100 to 200 stores.

Theme Center: A retail center designed around a common theme.

    Off-Price Center: A retail center that caters to tenants that offer merchandise at discount prices.

    Factory Outlet Center: A retail center that caters to manufacturers who sell their goods directly to the public.

    Fashion Oriented Center: A retail center that deals in high-priced, high-fashion merchandise.

    Car Care Center: A retail center that caters to tenants who deal in the automobile aftermarket business.

The following listing briefly describes the types of tenants that can be found in the above referenced retail centers.

Local Tenant: The local tenant is a business that may have more than one location. Space sizes range from 1000 square feet to 10,000 square feet for a restaurant. Leases for local tenants range from three to five years, with options to renew.

Regional Tenant: Regional tenants are either company owned or franchised operations. Multiple locations are located in the city or region. Sizes range from 1000 square feet to 20,000. Leases for regional tenants range from five to ten years with options to renew.

National Tenant: National tenants are similar to regional except they are located nationwide.

Anchor Tenant: The anchor tenant is the tenant which draws the most business to the retail center. They can be a grocery store, drugstore, or department store. Sizes range from 10,000 square feet in a neighborhood center to 250,000 square feet and up in a super regional mall. Leases for anchor tenants range from 10 to 30 years.

Kiosk Tenant: Kiosk tenants are small specialized tenants that rent space in the common areas. Sizes range from small pushcarts to 100 square feet. Leases for these tenants are short term.

The rule of thumb for a retail center is roughly 10,000 square feet of building area and 30,000 square feet of parking area for each 40,000 square feet (approximately 1 acre) of site area.

Neighborhood Center   5 to 7 acres
Community Center   10 to 30 acres
Regional Center   35 to 80 acres
Super Regional Center   80 to 125 acres

Office

Office buildings are rented to non-retail commercial users. These buildings are designed as garden, mid-rise or high-rise structures. In low to mid-rise office buildings, assuming a 100,000 square footage building, the land required will be approximately 7 acres. In high-rise office buildings, the total square footage of the tower will equal the square footage of the parking deck. They feature space for most any kind of business. They are as follows:

Office Building: Generally an assortment of office buildings ranging in height of one to 20 stories depending on zoning ordinances and density requirements. They are exclusively used for office space and usually feature lush landscaping and a park-like atmosphere. Office space users are those which sell a product, or sell and administrate a service to the public but do not need a retail location. They are classified as Class A, Class B, and Class C, with Class A being the very best quality. The following types of tenants might occupy office space.

Local Tenant: Local tenants are community oriented. Space requirements range from 500 square feet to over 100,000 square feet. Leases range from three to ten years with options.

Regional Tenant: Regional tenants have national headquarters and locations in different regions. Space requirements range from 500 square feet to over 100,000 square feet. Leases range from three to ten years with options.

National Tenant: National tenants have national headquarters and locations all over the nation. Many of these tenants are in the Fortune 500 largest companies. Space requirements range from 500 square feet to over 100,000 square feet. Leases range from three to ten years with options.

Anchor Tenant: The anchor tenant of an office building is the largest tenant. Most new buildings constructed today require an anchor tenant before the lender will fund construction. They typically take 25 to 50 percent of the total space with expansion options. Their leases are long term with options and possibly ownership of the building.

Executive Suite Tenant: Executive suite tenants are businesses set up by outside companies or the developer that cater toward the small space user. Offices are either furnished or unfurnished. Amenities include secretarial services and support facilities. Leases range from daily to yearly, and as these tenants grow in size, they become potential tenants for the building.

Medical: Buildings that cater to medical users are usually located near hospitals and provide space for doctors of all types with special utilities as required for additional plumbing and electrical.

Business Parks: A group of office building type structures that generally provide for office space near entrances and parking, often with warehouse type storage space and truck docks. Business park properties cater to similar type users as office buildings, except these users require some warehouse and loading facilities.

Industrial

Buildings that provide rental space to users of bulk storage feature very small office space. Industrial buildings are designed for users which require a small percentage of office space (10 to 20 percent) with the balance in large spanned warehouses with loading facilities. Industrial properties are broken down into the following:

Office-Warehouse: Light industrial users typically warehouse products or manufacturer and non-smokestack type product. The tenant can be either local, regional or national. Space requirements range from 1000 square feet to over 100,000 square feet.

    Service: Ceiling height 0–16 feet, drive-in loading, and 31 to 100 percent office.

    Distribution: Ceiling height 16.1 to 23 feet, drive-in and dock-high loading, and 11 to 30 percent office.

    Warehouse: Ceiling height 24 feet, drive-in and dock-high loading, and 0 to 10 percent office.

Bulk-Distribution: Large storage space for central receiving for distribution. Direct railroad access is not absolutely necessary.

Manufacturing Facilities: Heavy industrial users typically require extra facilities for rail shipping or increased utility availability. The tenant can be either local, regional or national. Space requirements range from 1000 square feet to over 1,000,000 square feet. Normally developed in the same way as a corporate use in build to suit.

Mini Warehouse Properties: Mini warehouse properties cater to users of small storage spaces. Unit sizes range from a 5′ × 5′ to 20′ × 30′ storage area. Leases range from monthly to yearly. Security and 24-hour availability are required. Some mini warehouses have heated and air-conditioned areas for those tenants who require this option. They are buildings designed for approximately 25 to 600 square feet. They cater to the following type of users.

    Residential Tenant: Residential users typically live within three miles from the property and have no room at home to store all of their possessions. Unit sizes that cater to this market range from 5′ × 5′ to 10′ × 15′.

Commercial Tenant: Commercial users typically have their business located within three to five miles from the property. Some smaller businesses even run their operations out of these storage spaces. Unit sizes range from 10' × 15' to 20' × 30'.

Incubator Space: Buildings designed for newly started, smaller business. The typical space use is 800 square feet to 1200 square feet.

Lodging

Properties that lease living space to individuals per day can have price ranges from budget to luxury. They can be marketed to the transient, resort, vacation, convention, or business person user. They are as follows:

Motel: A leased space providing a bedroom and bath with parking immediately adjacent. This type of property is usually a two-story walk-up building with few amenities.

Hotel: A property that features the same elements as a motel but with amenities such as restaurants, shops, exercise rooms and pools, meeting and ballroom areas, and bars and lounges. These properties can be garden style, mid-rise or high-rise in design.

Suites: A lodging property that offers a living area and a bedroom area. These can be in a high- or mid-rise design or as cluster housing.

Lodging property users come in many shapes and sizes. Some lodging properties cater to a specific market while others will cater to many markets. Most lodging properties include some type of food facilities.

Economy and Budget: The economy or budget class is designed for the user who just wants a basic safe and comfortable room for sleeping at a reasonable price.

Business: The business class is designed to meet the needs of the business traveler. Amenities include meeting rooms, secretarial services, and travel services.

Vacation and Resort: Vacation or resort properties include the amenities that are required by the vacationers or are in close proximity to these facilities.

Convention: Convention properties include the amenities required by this market: meeting facilities, travel services, and multiple food facilities.

Extended Stay: This market is now serviced by the "all suite" concept of lodging. This market requires more than just a sleeping area. All suites include a separate living area.

Mixed-Use Developments

Developments that combine two or more of the previously discussed uses are mixed-use ones. Multi-use projects can either be low-rise suburban projects or high density high-rise urban projects. Mixed-use projects were created to satisfy a convenience and marketing demand using valuable property for its highest and best use. To have lodging convenient to the office user's visitors provides an advantage in marketing the space to potential tenants. In addition, the synergy created with the various uses of retail, lodging, dining, and office provides vitality for the development. Some mixed uses have become mega-structures in which the space captured between the structures becomes an entirely different use altogether. Oftentimes the value created by the combination of these uses is superior to a development which has solely one use. They are normally advertised as total environments in which the inhabitants can find satisfaction for all of their needs, be they residential, lodging, shopping, business, dining, or recreation.

Other Types of Commercial Properties

Condominium: Commercial properties that are either converted or developed to be sold to the users. These can be either retail, office, or industrial properties.

Recycling: Upgrading a property for the purpose of changing its present use—that is, converting an old industrial building to a retail or office property, or for historic renovation.

Single Purpose Buildings: Properties designed for a specific purpose, for example a theater or a bowling alley. Other single purpose buildings include

Restaurants and fast-food convenience outlets

Athletic and sporting clubs

Day care and education

Prison facilities

A NEED FOR A SITE OR A SITE FOR A NEED?

The question of which comes first, the product or the land, depends on the developer's assets, experience, and business plan. In order to develop a parcel of land for its "highest and best use," the developer will determine the most appropriate product type for that site through market research. If the developer has specific expertise in a particular product type alone, he will then conduct a search to find the best possible site for that product. With a diversified product type either method can be chosen.

Deciding on the Correct Product Type to Meet Market Demand

Assuming that the developer desires to develop a certain product, such as multifamily housing or an office building, he must first study the market. By completing a market study, the developer will know which segment of the market is in demand. This market study will reveal the rental rates, features, amenities, and occupancy history of adjacent similar properties. Using this information, the developer will be able to pinpoint the product's needs and program the development for success.

Reviewing the Economic Growth Potential of an Area

The potential market area should be in a positive growth mode. If the development is adding inventory to the existing market area, the market area should be able to absorb the new space in a relatively short time period. The direction of the growth should also be studied to ensure that the proposed development is strategically located to take advantage of new growth. Timing is critical because oftentimes, a developer has suffered financially while waiting for growth to catch up.

Reviewing the Absorption Trends

The market area should demonstrate a history of annual absorption. Developing in an area with high vacancy percentage will add inventory to an overbuilt situation and will negatively affect your proforma projections. Finding market niches is one way to overcome this challenge.

Reviewing the Target Market

The market study should carefully review the market segments that are in demand. As mentioned in the preceding paragraph, even in an overbuilt market, specialized niches may exist. In the apartment market, that niche may be a property which caters toward families with children. Office markets might target users of less than 2000 square feet which desire garden style buildings.

Reviewing the Rental and Sales History

A careful analysis of the past and current rental rates and sales costs will reveal the strength of demand for the product. If prices are stabilized, it demonstrates that market demand is not increasing. Consequently, when price discounts appear, it reveals an oversupply. If prices are escalating rapidly, it reveals that there is a good demand for the product.

How to Find the Best Piece of Land to Develop Your Product Type

If the decision is made to develop a certain type of product type, a search should be made for the best parcel of land available in the marketplace which will suit that product. This process should consider four different factors (Figure 2–3):

- Profile attributes
- Preliminary screening of alternatives with use profile criteria

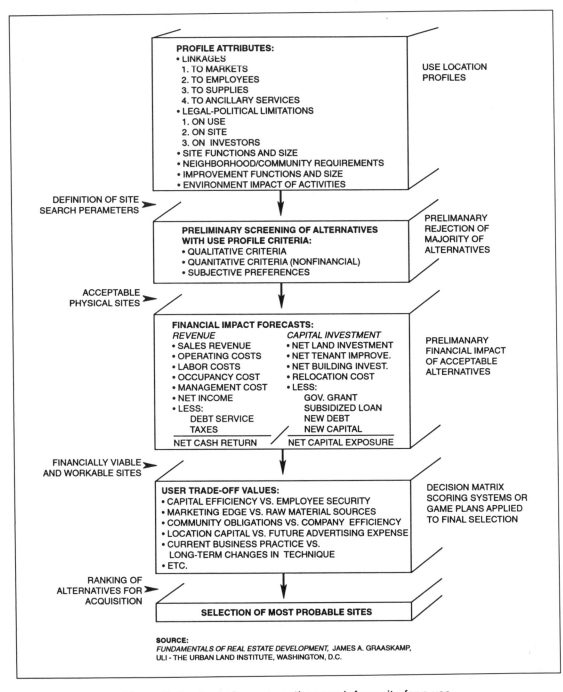

PROFILE ATTRIBUTES:
• LINKAGES
  1. TO MARKETS
  2. TO EMPLOYEES
  3. TO SUPPLIES
  4. TO ANCILLARY SERVICES
• LEGAL-POLITICAL LIMITATIONS
  1. ON USE
  2. ON SITE
  3. ON INVESTORS
• SITE FUNCTIONS AND SIZE
• NEIGHBORHOOD/COMMUNITY REQUIREMENTS
• IMPROVEMENT FUNCTIONS AND SIZE
• ENVIRONMENT IMPACT OF ACTIVITIES

USE LOCATION
PROFILES

DEFINITION OF SITE
SEARCH PERAMETERS ➤

PRELIMANARY
REJECTION OF
MAJORITY OF
ALTERNATIVES

**PRELIMINARY SCREENING OF ALTERNATIVES
WITH USE PROFILE CRITERIA:**
• QUALITATIVE CRITERIA
• QUANITATIVE CRITERIA (NONFINANCIAL)
• SUBJECTIVE PREFERENCES

ACCEPTABLE
PHYSICAL SITES ➤

FINANCIAL IMPACT FORECASTS:

REVENUE	*CAPITAL INVESTMENT*
• SALES REVENUE	• NET LAND INVESTMENT
• OPERATING COSTS	• NET TENANT IMPROVE.
• LABOR COSTS	• NET BUILDING INVEST.
• OCCUPANCY COST	• RELOCATION COST
• MANAGEMENT COST	• LESS:
• NET INCOME	GOV. GRANT
• LESS:	SUBSIDIZED LOAN
DEBT SERVICE	NEW DEBT
TAXES	NEW CAPITAL
NET CASH RETURN	NET CAPITAL EXPOSURE

PRELIMANARY
FINANCIAL IMPACT
OF ACCEPTABLE
ALTERNATIVES

FINANCIALLY VIABLE ➤
AND WORKABLE SITES

USER TRADE-OFF VALUES:
• CAPITAL EFFICIENCY VS. EMPLOYEE SECURITY
• MARKETING EDGE VS. RAW MATERIAL SOURCES
• COMMUNITY OBLIGATIONS VS. COMPANY EFFICIENCY
• LOCATION CAPITAL VS. FUTURE ADVERTISING EXPENSE
• CURRENT BUSINESS PRACTICE VS.
  LONG-TERM CHANGES IN TECHNIQUE
• ETC.

DECISION MATRIX
SCORING SYSTEMS OR
GAME PLANS APPLIED
TO FINAL SELECTION

RANKING OF
ALTERNATIVES FOR ➤
ACQUISITION

SELECTION OF MOST PROBABLE SITES

SOURCE:
FUNDAMENTALS OF REAL ESTATE DEVELOPMENT, JAMES A. GRAASKAMP,
ULI - THE URBAN LAND INSTITUTE, WASHINGTON, D.C.

Figure 2–3 Analysis process: the search for a site for a use.

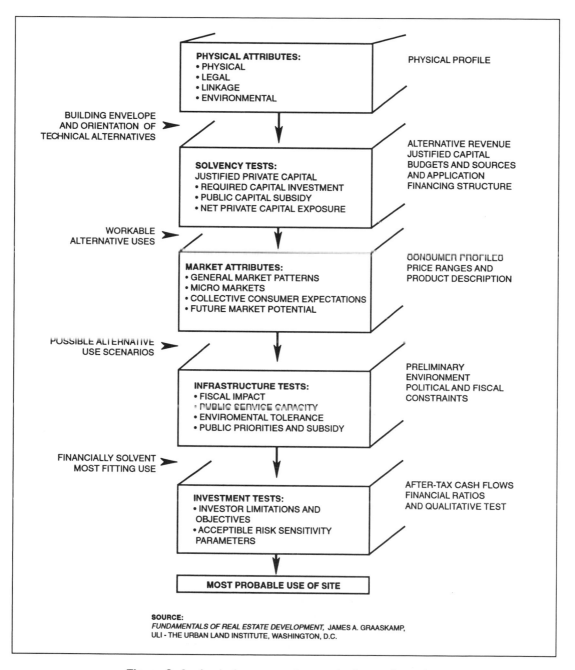

PHYSICAL ATTRIBUTES:
• PHYSICAL
• LEGAL
• LINKAGE
• ENVIRONMENTAL

PHYSICAL PROFILE

BUILDING ENVELOPE
AND ORIENTATION OF
TECHNICAL ALTERNATIVES

ALTERNATIVE REVENUE
JUSTIFIED CAPITAL
BUDGETS AND SOURCES
AND APPLICATION
FINANCING STRUCTURE

SOLVENCY TESTS:
JUSTIFIED PRIVATE CAPITAL
• REQUIRED CAPITAL INVESTMENT
• PUBLIC CAPITAL SUBSIDY
• NET PRIVATE CAPITAL EXPOSURE

WORKABLE
ALTERNATIVE USES

MARKET ATTRIBUTES:
• GENERAL MARKET PATTERNS
• MICRO MARKETS
• COLLECTIVE CONSUMER EXPECTATIONS
• FUTURE MARKET POTENTIAL

CONSUMER PROFILES
PRICE RANGES AND
PRODUCT DESCRIPTION

POSSIBLE ALTERNATIVE
USE SCENARIOS

INFRASTRUCTURE TESTS:
• FISCAL IMPACT
• PUBLIC SERVICE CAPACITY
• ENVIROMENTAL TOLERANCE
• PUBLIC PRIORITIES AND SUBSIDY

PRELIMINARY
ENVIRONMENT
POLITICAL AND FISCAL
CONSTRAINTS

FINANCIALLY SOLVENT
MOST FITTING USE

INVESTMENT TESTS:
• INVESTOR LIMITATIONS AND
OBJECTIVES
• ACCEPTABLE RISK SENSITIVITY
PARAMETERS

AFTER-TAX CASH FLOWS
FINANCIAL RATIOS
AND QUALITATIVE TEST

MOST PROBABLE USE OF SITE

SOURCE:
FUNDAMENTALS OF REAL ESTATE DEVELOPMENT, JAMES A. GRAASKAMP,
ULI - THE URBAN LAND INSTITUTE, WASHINGTON, D.C.

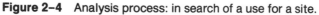

Figure 2-4   Analysis process: in search of a use for a site.

- Financial impact forecasts
- User trade-off values

IDENTIFY DEVELOPMENT CRITERIA

After the developer has selected the type of property to develop and its location, the following decisions regarding development criteria must be made.

Development Size

The size of the development will be based on the developer's financial strength, the amount of potential equity available, or the borrowing potential with other lenders or investors. This along with market demand will determine the size and magnitude of the development.

Potential Tenants

The quality of the development, its character, and amenities will be guided by the desired tenant profile. The quality of the development is usually described as Class A, Class B, or Class C, with Class A being the highest quality with higher tenant profiles.

Construction Type

The type of construction used for the development will be a function of the type of desired product, the site location, the budget, and the market demand.

Quality of the Development

The quality of the development will be a function of the market. If the developer is going after a high end market, then he will have to put more visible quality into the product, through types and details of materials, features and amenities.

IDENTIFY UNIQUE CHALLENGES TO BE ENCOUNTERED

Prior to any decision making concerning the what and where of the development, the developer must first determine his objectives, including both his short and long term goals. These objectives can be divided into social and financial objectives. In addition, he must consider any unique challenges which he may encounter because of his selected objective. Each product type in its development has its own set of unique requirements for operations and financial success. In programing the development, each of these requirements must be considered. For instance, managing office buildings is quite different from managing a hotel, requiring a staff with special training and expertise. Managing the one-story office building in comparison to a 50-story office building tower is quite different and requires personnel with varying sophistication.

Social Objectives

Social objectives are those goals that pertain to the community in general. If the developer has a mind-set of taking from but not contributing to the community, our environments will suffer and our communities will be undesirable for living. In the long run, this may contribute to the destruction of what was a strong market. Consequently, even the developer's proforma will suffer. The developer must always contribute to the community. These social objectives might include bringing affordable housing into the marketplace or designing a project that blends into the social and historical setting of the community. This could also include sensitivity to surrounding neighborhoods, traffic patterns, and replacing many of the trees which were destroyed. It might also include using material and designs that are sympathetic to local customs. Signage and graphics can also be constructed tastefully. Before beginning the development, the unique challenges associated with a particular location should be considered carefully.

Financial Objectives

Since almost all business decisions are made financially, the developer must determine how much profit is worth the risk of the development. The financial goals may be on short- or long-term basis. This decision is typically based on the current financial position of the developer. With a current cash flow and a good net worth, long-term profit might be considered. Conversely, if the developer is in need of cash, he may want to take a quick profit and move onto the next development.

In addition, if a particular development will have a long predevelopment period due to difficult zoning, environmental, or community issues, it is best to consider the challenges encountered when one's "seed money" is tied up due to attorney and consultants' services. Controlling the land with large amounts of earnest money will also reduce available "seed money." If lender's are not to finance speculative ventures, then less speculative ventures should be considered. The developer must pause once an objective has been selected and consider "what" to avoid spending his resources only to arrive at a dead end.

CONDUCT A FEASIBILITY STUDY

To further define the specifics of the development criteria, the developer should be prepared to spend both time and money to prepare a feasibility study. An outline for such a study is found later in this chapter. Studies which may be included in the presentation of the feasibility study are as follows.

Strategy Review

This study analyzes the objectives, tactics, and decision criteria of the developer.

Market Study

The market study reviews both the micro and macro issues within certain qualified market areas. Above all, this study should identify the price and quantity of your niche market, target your efforts, determine price and market depth, and stick to reality avoiding the real estate romance. See Chapter 12 for more definitive detail on market studies and their impact.

Consumer Marketing Study

This study reviews and analyzes the needs and desires of the consumer.

Legal Study

The legal study reviews the legal constraints of development in the market. It reviews the zoning and political issues of the community and determines the possibility of change.

Design Study

This study includes the engineering, land planning, and architectural studies. In addition, any unique local ordinances should be considered. Along with preliminary design, a code synopsis should be requested to reveal any issues that may affect marketing. Master planning is critical to determine if the desired product at a defined density will in fact fit physically on the site. Preliminary sketches can be used to illustrate the function abilities of the site.

Environmental Impact Study (EIS)

This study reviews and analyzes the impact of the development on the environment. It includes information relative to the traffic system, tax base, county services, environmental concerns, and other public policies.

Financial Study

This study reviews the actual economics of the development. It reviews the development and the operations costs of the property. Various rates of returns are analyzed. Sensitivity analysis considers both the upside and the downside of the development. Early projections must be reviewed to influence early decision making prior to approving additional expenditures.

WHAT TO INCLUDE IN A FEASIBILITY STUDY

As the feasibility study is completed during the due-diligence phase to assist the developer in decision making, this study should be completed by an expert in the area of intended use. In order for the study to be unbiased, the analyst should review the information supplied by the developer and make final recommendations based solely on market conditions. The following is a general outline for this feasibility study. This is a comprehensive outline, giving the developer the opportunity to fashion his own outline in response to his product's specific needs.

Feasibility Study Outline

    I.   Cover letter (scope of work)

    II.   Table of contents

    III.   Scope limiting conditions

    IV.   Developer's objective and constraints

          A. Financial

             1. Leverage, liquidity

             2. Yield

             3. Risk

          B. Nonfinancial objectives

          C. Resources, capabilities, constraints

          D. Development strategy

    V.   Conclusions and recommendations

          A. Conclusions

          B. Recommendations

             1. Type of property to develop

                a. Commercial

                   (1) Building information

                      (a) Total square footage (gross/net)

                      (b) Square footage per floor (gross/net)

    (c) Number of floors

    (d) Design of building

    (e) Type construction

    (f) Desired zoning

  (2) Parking requirements

  (3) Projected rental/sales rates

    (a) Projected rental/sales concessions

    (b) Lease term

  (4) Tenant interior finish allowances

  (5) Real estate commission policy

  (6) Property amenities

  (7) Projected target market

  (8) Projected absorption period

    (a) Phasing of property

  (9) Projected marketing game plan

  (10) Potential lender sources

    (a) Residential

 b. Residential

  (1) Building information

    (a) Total number of units

    (b) Unit mix

    (c) Unit type

    (d) Design of building

    (e) Type construction

    (f) Desired zoning

  (2) Parking requirements

  (3) Projected rental/sales rates

    (a) Projected rental/sales concessions

    (b) Lease term

  (4) Unit features

    (a) Options

  (5) Real estate commission policy

  (6) Property amenities

  (7) Projected target market

  (8) Projected absorption period

    (a) Phasing of property

  (9) Projected marketing game plan

  (10) Projected lender sources

VI.   Property description
     A. Identification of the property
     B. Legal description
     C. Neighborhood boundaries
     D. Current zoning
     E. Property plat
     F. Topography
     G. Maps
         1. State
         2. City
         3. County
         4. Neighborhood
VII.   Overview of the city
     A. Demographics (census tract)
         1. Past
         2. Present
         3. Projected
            a. Population
            b. Age
            c. Income
            d. Sex
     B. Employment trends
         1. Largest employers in the area
            a. Number of employees
         2. Unemployment statistics
     C. Purchasing power
         1. Past
         2. Present
         3. Projected
            a. Per person
            b. Per household
VIII. Building permits (number, dollar, volume)
     A. Past
     B. Present
     C. Projected
         1. Residential
            a. Single-family
            b. Condominium/townhome

            c. Mobile home

            d. Multi-family

        2. Commercial

            a. Retail

            b. Office

            c. Industrial

            d. Lodging

IX.   Supply versus demand

    A. Past

    B. Present

    C. Projected

        1. Residential

            a. Single-family

            b. Condominium/townhome

            c. Mobile home

            d. Multi-family

               (1) Total number of units

               (2) Total number of properties

               (3) Occupancy

               (4) Absorption

        2. Commercial

            a. Retail

            b. Office

            c. Industrial

            d. Lodging

               (1) Total square footage

                   (a) Class A

                   (b) Class B

                   (c) Class C

                   (d) Class D

               (2) Total number of properties

               (3) Occupancy

               (4) Absorption

X.   Overview of subject area

    A. Demographics (census tract)

        1. Population

        2. Age

    3. Income

    4. Sex

   B. Neighborhood analysis

   C. Proximity to

    1. Residential

    2. Commercial

     a. Retail

     b. Office

     c. Industrial

     d. Lodging

   D. Transportation

   E. Religious institutions

   F. Educational institutions

   G. Municipal services

   H. Recreation

 XI. Legal, political, and environmental constraints

   A. Legal feasibility

   B. Political feasibility

   C. Environmental feasibility

 XII. Comparables

   A. Residential (rental properties)

    1. Type of property

     a. Single-family

     b. Duplex-quadraplex

     c. Multi-family

      (1) Garden

      (2) Townhouse

      (3) Mid-rise

      (4) High-rise

     d. Mobile home

      (1) Mobile home lot rental

    2. Name of property

    3. Location

    4. Year built

    5. Ownership

    6. Management company

    7. Marketing company

8. Acreage
9. Density (units/acre)
10. Building information
    a. Exterior construction
    b. Roof
    c. Utility system
    d. Number of floors
11. Unit mix (number of units)
12. Square footage (gross/net)
13. Parking
14. Unit features
15. Amenities
16. Quality of property
17. Condition of property
18. Resident profile
    a. Age
    b. Sex
    c. Marital status
    d. Length of tenancy
    e. Income
    f. Employment
19. Absorption history
20. Occupancy history
21. Rental rate
    a. Rent concessions
    b. Furnished rates
    c. Parking
    d. Who pays utilities?
22. Rent per square foot (gross/net)
23. Lease term
24. Security deposit
    a. Fees
25. Pet policy
26. Real estate commissions
27. Site plan
28. Floor plans
29. Pictures
30. Brochure

31. Location map
32. Copy of
    a. Lease
    b. Application
B. Residential (for-sale)
    1. Type of property
        a. Single-family
        b. Condominium
        c. Cooperative
        d. Townhome
        e. Mobile home
        f. Lot sales
    2. Name of property
    3. Location
    4. Year built
    5. Developer
    6. Marketing company
    7. Acreage
    8. Density (units/acre)
    9. Building information
        a. Exterior construction
        b. Roof
        c. Utility system
        d. Number of floors
    10. Unit mix (number of units)
    11. Square footage (gross/net)
    12. Parking
    13. Unit features
    14. Amenities
    15. Quality of property
    16. Condition of property
    17. Resident profile
        a. Age
        b. Sex
        c. Marital status
        d. Income
        e. Employment
    18. Absorption history

19. Sales price
    a. Options
20. Sales price per square foot
21. Association fees
    a. Breakdown
22. Earnest money deposit
23. Financing terms
    a. Lender
    b. Interest rate
    c. Amortization period
    d. Term
    e. Buydown
    f. Closing costs
24. Real estate commissions
25. Site plan
26. Floor plan
27. Pictures
28. Brochure
29. Location map
30. Copy of
    a. Sales contract
    b. Condominium/cooperative documents
    c. By-laws
C. Commercial (rental properties)
    1. Type of property
       a. Retail
          (1) Strip center
          (2) Neighborhood center
          (3) Community center
          (4) Regional center
          (5) Super regional center
          (6) Theme center
       b. Office
          (1) Business park
       c. Industrial
          (1) Light industrial
          (2) Heavy industrial
          (3) Mini warehouse

   2. Name of property
   3. Location
   4. Year built
   5. Ownership
   6. Management company
   7. Leasing agent
   8. Acreage
   9. Density
  10. Building information
      a. Exterior construction
      b. Roof
      c. Utility system
      d. Number of floors
      e. Number of buildings
      f. Ceiling height
      g. Bay depth
      h. Dock loading
  11. Total square footage (gross/net)
      a. Square footage per floor
      b. Square footage per building
  12. Parking
  13. Tenant finish allowance
  14. Amenities
  15. Quality of property
  16. Condition of property
  17. Tenant profile
      a. Type business
      b. Length of tenancy
  18. Rental rate (per square foot—gross/net)
      a. Rent concessions
      b. Who pays utilities?
      c. Common area maintenance
      d. Lease options
      e. Escalation
      f. Participation leases
  19. Lease term
  20. Security deposits
  21. Roster of tenants

22. Real estate commissions
23. Absorption history
24. Occupancy history
25. Site plan
26. Floor plan
27. Picture
28. Brochure
29. Location map
30. Copy of lease

D. Commercial (for-sale)
  1. Type of property
     a. Retail
     b. Office
     c. Industrial
  2. Name of property
  3. Location
  4. Year built
  5. Ownership/developer
  6. Management company
  7. Leasing company
  8. Acreage
  9. Density
  10. Building information
      a. Exterior construction
      b. Roof
      c. Utility system
      d. Number of floors
      e. Number of buildings
      f. Ceiling height
      g. Bay depth
      h. Dock loading
  11. Total square footage (gross/net)
      a. Square footage per floor
      b. Square footage per building
  12. Parking
  13. Tenant finish allowance
  14. Amenities

15. Quality of property
16. Condition of property
17. Buyer profile
18. Sales price (per square foot—gross/net)
    a. Sales price concessions
    b. Owners association fees
19. Earnest money deposit
20. Financing
    a. Lender
    b. Interest rate
    c. Amortization period
    d. Term
    e. Buydown
    f. Closing costs
21. Roster of buyers
22. Real estate commissions
23. Sales absorption history
24. Site plan
25. Floor plan
26. Picture
27. Brochure
28. Location map
29. Copy of
    a. Sales contract
    b. Condominium documents
    c. By-laws
E. Lodging
    1. Type of property
       a. Motel
       b. Hotel
       c. Suites
    2. Name of property
    3. Year built
    4. Ownership
    5. Management company
    6. Acreage
    7. Density

8. Building information
   a. Exterior construction
   b. Roof
   c. Utility system
   d. Number of floors
9. Unit mix (number of units)
10. Square footage (gross/net)
11. Parking
12. Unit features
    a. Furniture
13. Amenities
14. Quality of property
15. Condition of property
16. Tenant profile
17. Occupancy history
18. Rental rates
    a. Weekday
    b. Weekend
    c. Special discounts
19. Site plan
20. Floor plans
21. Brochure
22. Location map

XIII. Property comparison analysis
   A. Price (rental or sales) per square foot
   B. Features
   C. Amenities
   D. Financing
   E. Correlation of data in relation to subject

XIV. Surveys
   A. Sample

XV. Projected absorption schedules
   A. Unit type
   B. Square footage or number of units per month

XVI. Financial analysis
   A. Cash flow analysis
   B. Ten-year forecasts

C. Back up schedules
D. Sensitivity analysis
E. Financial ratios

XVII. Marketing strategy
A. Models
B. Sales/rental office
C. Theme
D. Sales/rental strategy
E. Public relations
F. Advertising
G. Promotions

XVIII. Development team
A. Developer
B. Design planning
C. Marketing
D. Management
E. Financing
F. Exhibits
1. Resumes
2. Company brochures
3. Key personnel resumes

XIX. Qualifications of the analyst
A. Firm
B. Principals
C. Analyst

IDENTIFY FINANCIAL CRITERIA

In addition to the development criteria previously discussed, the developer must also identify the financial criteria of the venture. Both must be considered and carefully reviewed for appropriate strategic and tactical planning. The following will list various aspects of this financial criteria which must be considered.

The Amount of Equity Required

The financial study will determine how much equity is required by the development. The equity is the difference between the total development costs and the loan amount that is available.

Development to Sell or to Hold

The developer must determine if he will sell the development prior to the start of the construction, during construction, after completion, or if he will hold the property after completion and provide property management. Knowing these factors is important in that the strategy of the investment will determine the structuring of the proforma and its budgets. If a particular market demands a level of quality, then the budget must be responsive to this demand and carefully managed to protect projected profits. If one can save on construction costs and still obtain the same residual at sale, then this strategy should be followed. Typically, if the developer sells the property before or just after completion, he will not spend money on some construction items as if he would if he were to own and manage the property for a long term. Having to manage the project long term will often result in emphasis on management and maintenance items which can increase construction expenditures but reduce long-term operational costs.

What Type of Financial Return Will Be Required?

Since profit is the primary motive for business ventures, the developer must determine what return will be worth the risk of completing and managing the development. The developer's risk is a function of the following:

- Money invested
- Potential money that could be lost should the development fail
- Present value of the future rewards of the development
- Payback period of the development
- Percentage return on invested money
- Intangible opportunity cost of time

In addition, product types vary in their risk. Much of this risk is determined by the user base of the product. A Class A office building may have less risk than a Class C office building, because the developer may have a greater probability of collecting rents from some tenants in Class A space, due to the strength of their credit ratings. Generally, single-tenant buildings, such as restaurants, face greater risks than multi-tenant offices or industrial warehouse buildings. Losing one tenant can affect all cash flow in the single-tenant building, while losing one of many tenants can only affect some of the cash flow.

Payback Period

Most investors want to receive their equity return as soon as possible. The payback period is determined by the number of months or years necessary to return the equity principal.

Rates of Returns

Establishing a minimum rate of return on investment is an essential business decision which the developer must make prior to proceeding with the development. This rate of return will be a function of the risk associated with the development and the rates available for other types of investments.

CHOOSE THE APPROPRIATE OWNERSHIP VEHICLE

There are many types of ownership vehicles from which the developer can choose. These are legal entities which are devised relative to the developer's long-term attitude toward risk and methods of conducting business. The best way to choose a vehicle is to discuss your needs with your attorney and accountant. Each developer has a unique set of criteria used for decision making which will drive this decision. By carefully considering the various options, the developer can provide self-protection in the future should the deal go sour or if he is sued for other reasons. The main issues to be considered are potential liabilities, tax consequences, control and the degree of liquidity desired. The following will briefly discuss the various types of ownership vehicles currently available.

Sole Ownership

Sole ownership is the simplest and most basic vehicle. The developer is investing by himself in his own name. You have no partners and you are responsible for all decisions.

Tenants in Common

As tenants in common, each owner receives his or her own income or loss directly without regard for the others. Each owner has his own tax election. There can be any number of investors. In this case, if one of the parties dies, that share in the property reverts to the estate. This vehicle is good only for passive investors or those investors who desire an inactive role in the daily management of the property. These properties should not be management intensive.

Joint Tenancy with Right of Survivorship

In joint tenancy with right of survivorship, if a partner dies, the ownership passes to the other partners. This type of ownership vehicle should be used only when family members are partners, due to the fact that ownership passes to the surviving partner upon death. If your partner is not a family member, this vehicle works only when there is "key man" insurance used to buy out the deceased partner's family.

Corporation

A corporation is an entity that is chartered by a state or federal government and is considered to be legally separate from the person who owns it. Nevertheless it can own property, borrow money, or enter into other legal agreements much in the same way that individuals can. Corporations are attractive vehicles for several reasons. For example, owners can only lose what they have invested, thus limiting their liability. Ownership can easily be transferred through the sale of stock, and a corporation can survive beyond the owner's lifetime. By using a corporation, the investor can limit liability, but personally loses the pass through of the tax benefits.

Subchapter S Corporation

This is an offshoot of the corporation. Under this method of ownership, the investor can get the best of both worlds. There are the benefits of limited corporate liability as well as limited pass through of tax benefits. The Subchapter S corporation may have no more than ten individual shareholders. Each shareholder's personal tax return will include the pro-rata share of capital gains, ordinary income, and tax preference items.

Limited Partnership

Limited partnerships can be structured for the passive investor. In this vehicle, the passive investor can pool resources with other investors to acquire larger properties not available individually. By using this method, the investor will play a passive role and the general partner will control the management activities. The investor will then only be liable for his investment. This type of investment vehicle limits control and liquidity because daily decisions are made by others. Resale can only take place with a majority vote of all partners involved.

General Partnership

In a general partnership, two or more investors can acquire ownership in property. In this case, all the partners are liable, but have an equal vote (if they have equal ownership) in the management decisions.

Master Limited Partnership

In a master limited partnership a group of limited partnerships are combined. Shares in the master limited partnership may be sold. If shares are publicly traded they give the investor liquidity in his investment.

Joint Venture

Joint ventures are used in lieu of a general partnership and are limited to owner-ship of a defined property or properties. In some joint ventures, one party is the working partner who contributes knowledge and labor, while the other partner supplies the equity and financing.

Real Estate Investment Trusts (REIT)

Real estate investment trusts (REIT) are vehicles that are regaining the popularity they enjoyed in the early 1970s. In this vehicle, the investor purchases stock in a company that is either purchasing properties or making mortgages on properties. The investor is passive, and all management decisions are made by the executives in the REIT. The investor is liable only for his or her investment but does not get the benefits of any of the tax losses. An advantage of this type of investment is that the investor has liquidity—that is, he can resell his investment. This does not necessarily mean that he or she will make a profit.

Equity REIT

The equity REIT invests in the ownership of property. It purchases property by either paying all cash, assuming the existing debt, or placing new debt on the property.

FLEXIBILITY DURING THE PROCESS

Now we have developed a framework of decision-making criteria that provides us with the foundation for all future decisions. We know what the market needs, its unique challenges, our financial objectives and the basic structure of the deal which will be acceptable to our development team. One issue that must be remembered in all development is flexibility. Normally, all that we started out to do will change. For example, with a new piece of information, we may decide that another ownership vehicle would be better. As we work within a community, we might find that one piece of information which was previously overlooked sending the venture into another direction. In addition, we may find other opportunities which have a greater return and ease of financing. We may develop relationships with partners which have their own set of objectives. A new tenant who wants to lease 75 percent of our building may bring a whole new program and property management require-ments which will change our design. All in all, the development is in a constant status of flux being responsive to the needs of the marketplace before and after completion. Be flexible! Have a definite direction, but be willing to change to take advantage of the opportunities that you may discover.

## Chapter 3

Selecting the Site:
Location, Analysis,
and Purchase

In the selection of the site, as stated before, market research is the key to the creation of a successful development. Market research will provide the developer the essential criteria for the proper selection of the site. Usually it will include personal observations or market studies of regional or local areas which give an understanding about trends of development as well as trends in demographics. The trends in development will inform the developer about the successes or failures of like kinds of development and the demographics will describe growth patterns from which a development's program criteria evolve.

Trends may result from the need for more or fewer employees within the community due to an industrial or manufacturing plant's relocation. In other instances, an area may change its employment base from agriculture to high-tech industry. A similar shift could result in changes in the demographics within the community which then become catalysts for development trends. In another instance, the industry itself may generate new neighborhood concentrations. These concentrations of residential development would then become catalysts for other developments that provide services for the neighborhoods such as recreation, retail, office, or dining. In one instance, the developer may choose to develop because of a growth trend, whereas in the other instance, the choice to develop may be due to the needs created by demographic change. The location of a regional retail mall generally responds to community growth trends on a regional level and is immediately followed by additional developments of residential, other retail, hotel, and office development along with other ancillary services occurring on adjacent sites. By carefully keeping abreast of the shifts and changes within the community, region, and nation, the developer will begin to observe patterns. These patterns of change provide indications of opportunities. In other instances, these changing patterns may indicate that opportunities no longer exist. A timely response by the developer in either direction will help to maintain a profitable business, by positioning developments for success. Failure to respond to this market input will generally result in missed opportunities or projects completed for which there are no customers.

In the final analysis, the demographics of the region and its changes due to other phenomenon will be the indicators to observe when choosing the general area for your site selection. The following paragraphs will provide insights into demographics studies for site selection, as well as illustrate how the potential developer can collect and analyze the data required for the proper site selection.

Market Studies Overview

To fully understand market choice, the developer should obtain market data provided by local chambers of commerce, as well as studies provided by regional or national market research firms. This information provides property name, location, rental rates, and occupancy levels of product types within the chosen area. The following companies provide studies on a regional and national level:

> REIS Report (office, industrial, retail, residential)
> REIS Report, Inc.
> 250 W. 57th Street
> Suite 1710
> New York, NY 10107
> (212) 247-4433

If retail is the developer's product choice, then the following publications are provided to list all retail locations, their sizes, marketing agents, and tenants.

> *Directory of Major Malls*
> MJJTM Publications Corp.
> P.O. Box 1708
> Spring Valley, NY 10977
> (914) 426-0040

Shopping Center Directory
National Research Bureau
310 S. Michigan Ave.
Suite 1150
Chicago, IL 60604
(312) 663-5580

Demographic Criteria of the Site

The developer must decide initially which data should be measured for development, the area to be measured, as well as current and future forecasts. Oftentimes the information is based on a 1-, 3-, and 5-mile radii. For instance, retail developments measure income population counts and income levels as well as the household formations. The following types of data are provided in demographic studies.

- Population counts
- Household formations
- Population by race
- Estimated income levels
- Population percentage by age
- Population percentage by sex
- Owner occupied housing
- Housing costs (rental/sales)
- Marital status of the population
- Travel time to work
- Occupation of the population
- Education levels of the population
- Sales by retail category
- Number of vehicles per family

Figure 3–1 is a sample of how this demographic information is supplied.

ESTABLISHING LAND DEVELOPMENT AND SELECTION CRITERIA

Once the decision has been made to develop in a particular area and to develop a product based on trends and demographics, the developer must select the very best site for the best price suitable for product type. The first step in this process will be the development of site selection criteria. This criteria will include the following considerations.

DEMOGRAPHICS

PEELER RD. AND N. PEACHTREE RD.
DUNWOODY, GA

SITE 263451
COORD. 33:56.10 84:17.70
5 MILE RADIUS

19__ ESTIMATE

AGE/ INCOME	15-24 YEARS	25-34 YEARS	35-44 YEARS	45-54 YEARS	55-59 YEARS	60-64 YEARS	65+ YEARS
HOUSEHOLDS	3674	16320	17483	14199	5716	5143	7006
	5.28%	23.47%	25.14%	20.42%	8.22%	7.40%	10.07%
$75K +	85	1605	4773	5533	2045	1291	610
$50-75K	248	3693	4959	3870	1340	1101	746
$35-50K	747	4198	3410	1974	950	986	1048
$25-35K	812	2976	1780	1191	500	690	1046
$15-25K	904	2477	1518	956	387	599	1358
$7.5-15K	475	869	607	399	263	262	1105
<$7.5K	100	600	106	276	231	214	1003

	19__ CENSUS	19__ ESTIMATE	19__ PROJECTION
POPULATION	121333	166057	191762
HOUSEHOLDS	44743	69586	86242
POPULATION BY RACE	121333	166057	191762
WHITE (NON-HISP)	94.27%	93.37%	92.81%
BLACK (NON-HISP)	2.62%	3.13%	3.41%
HISPANIC	1.66%	1.85%	2.00%
OTHER (NON-HISP)	1.45%	1.65%	1.78%
AVERAGE INCOME	$29,186	$55,511	$70,354
MEDIAN INCOME	$25,755	$49,238	$63,238
POPULATION BY SEX	121333	166057	191762
MALE	48.67%	49.07%	49.01%
FEMALE	51.33%	50.93%	50.99%

HOUSING UNITS	COUNT	%	OCCUPIED UNITS	COUNT	%
TOTAL	44743	100.00	BY OWNER	33288	80.00
OCCUPIED	41610	93.00	BY RENTER	8322	20.00
VACANT	3133	7.00			

HOUSING VALUES	COUNT	%	MONTHLY RENT	COUNT	%
<$20K	2996	9.00	<$100	0	0.00
$20-39.9K	3995	12.00	$100-149	0	0.00
$40-49.9K	5357	16.00	$150-199	664	8.00
$50-79.9K	6658	20.00	$200-249	1240	15.00
$80-99.9K	5992	18.00	$250-299	1824	22.00
$100-149.9K	4660	14.00	$300-399	3120	37.00
$150-199.9K	2663	8.00	$400-499	1050	13.00
$200K +	1007	3.00	$500 +	424	5.00
MEDIAN VALUE	$62,564				

Figure 3-1 Components of a demographic study.

Location of the Land

The search should be focused on a specific geographical area within the community. The location should demonstrate indicators of growth potential, high occupancies, and a demand for the product type.

Zoning Classification

The land should have the required zoning or have the probability of being rezoned. If the land must be rezoned, the developer must decide if the long-term rewards are worth the lengthy process of rezoning relative to costs and timing. Often this process takes months, even years to complete, depending on the trends of the community.

Parcel Size

The parcel size required is determined by the needs of a particular type of development and the density of that development along with its requirements for parking and open space. It should be noted that this will vary from community to community. Sometimes, the site size is a function of the zoning classification. For example, if the market study reveals that there is a demand for 300 apartment units, and based on the current or potential zoning classifications, the developer must decide how much area will be necessary to build 300 units, along with its associated parking and green space. One parcel of land may be 20 acres, but zoned for 15 units per acre, while another parcel of land is 15 acres and zoned for 20 units per acre. In addition, some parcels contain non-buildable land, such as flood plains, or land with restricted uses. Another concern will be the conditions or covenants which are placed on the land. In addition, buffers and easements can greatly reduce the site's buildable area. A wise decision to make when considering a site is to hire a consultant to produce a master plan for testing layout and to confirm the site's feasibility for your particular development. In summary, the following must be considered in determining the size required for your intended use:

- Parking requirements by zoning
- Typical floor plan of the intended use
- Required green space
- Density allowed by zoning
- Special conditions or easements imposed on the site vertically or horizontally
- Developments' required amenities
- Traffic access

Current or Past Uses of the Site

The site should be reviewed for any past uses that might prohibit the developer's intended use or greatly add to the cost of the development. Environmental assessment studies should be performed to determine the presence of toxic waste.

Surrounding Land Uses

Adjacent land use should be reviewed and studied relative to compatibility with your intended use. Incompatibility in appearance or the presence of noise can greatly affect the marketability of your product. One should not only study that which exists but seek to determine if there are any future plans that will negatively affect the development. The following are some items for consideration:

- Overhead power lines
- Cemetery
- Landfill
- Adult entertainment establishments
- Railroads, freeways, or expressways
- Airport glide paths
- Parking decks or roof tops
- Sewer and water plants
- Manufacturing plants
- Quality of surrounding developments

Price of the Land

Depending on the situation, land is priced by the parcel, acre, or the foot. The developer should analyze the land cost per its intended use. One piece of land may have an acceptable price for a use, but be too expensive for another use. The density and projected cash flows of the development will have substantial impact on the land's price. For example, if 10 acres of land is to be developed as apartments with a density of 10 units per acre, and the economics reveal that you can afford to pay between $6000 to $8000 per buildable unit for the land, consider the following comparison:

$$10 \text{ acres @ } 12 \text{ units/acre} = 120 \text{ units}$$
$$120 \text{ units} \times (\$6000 \text{ to } \$8000/\text{unit}) = \$720,000-\$960,000$$
$$\$720,000-\$960,000 \text{ land cost}/10 \text{ acres} = \$72,000-\$96,000/\text{acres}$$

Therefore you can afford to pay $72,000 to $96,000 per acre.

In comparison, the developer is planning an office building of 150,000 gross square feet. The economics reveal that of the total cost, the developer can pay only $10.00 per square foot of gross buildable area for the land and the site will require the same 10 acres of the apartment complex.

$$150,000 \text{ square feet} \times \$10 \text{ per square foot} = \$1,500,000$$
$$\$1,500,000 \text{ land cost}/10 \text{ acres} = \$150,000 \text{ per acre}$$

Therefore for the office building land, the developer can pay $150,000 per acre.

Characteristics of the Site

One can attempt to develop anything on any site if they have the time and are willing to pay the development costs. Prior to purchase, the physical characteristics of the site should be reviewed and tested through master planning with your architect or land planner. Some site features lend themselves to certain types of developments. For instance, residential tends to be more successful on sites with rolling terrains and dense landscapes, whereas office buildings seem to function more efficiently on level, above-street terrain.

The Shape of the Property

The configuration of the property can influence the shape and size of the floor plan of the building and its associated parking layout. The architect or land planner's master plan will illustrate building layout viability. The site's area as well as its configuration must work appropriately and satisfy the needs of the development.

Visibility and Access to the Consumer

The customer must not only be aware of product, but must also have ease of access to the product. This is extremely important for some types of developments. Some retail developments rely heavily on sight lines from surrounding streets. Some office developments market well not only because of their proximity to freeways but their profile on the skyline. To outdistance the competition, the developer's site must be equal to or better than others within the marketplace. Educated tenants with a host of choices will often make their final decisions based on visibility and ease of access.

Traffic Patterns

A study of street patterns may reveal ease of access to the site, but without further analysis, the developer may overlook other key factors. If at certain times of the day, the streets are overloaded with traffic in grid lock, resulting in hindered ease of access, marketing of the development will suffer. Prior to the purchase of the site, review the situation, including your intended master plan with a traffic planning engineer to understand the complete traffic situation. In this review, the following issues should be considered.

Ingress and Egress from the Site

Determine what possibilities exist for ingress and egress. In addition, what size should the entrances be relative to traffic movement and the interface with off-site traffic? If the property is on a corner, will entrances on both streets be required?

Speed of the Traffic

Study the speed of the traffic passing the site. A site where traffic is moving at 50 miles per hour will make it difficult for ingress and egress. Similarly, traffic that is backed up past the development's entrance will do the same.

Side of the Street

In retail developments, the developer should know if the property is located on the coming to work side or the going home side of the street. Depending on the type of retailer, this can have a tremendous effect on sales.

Traffic Counts

Retail users depend on customers buying their product and need exposure to as many cars passing the site as possible.

Curb and Median Cuts

Due to the size of the development more than one curb cut may be needed. If the existing or proposed median cuts do not match up with the entrances or exits for the development, it impedes access to the development.

Availability of Utilities

Since no property can be developed without utilities, the site should have availability of the following services per the proposed developments required capacities.

- Gas
- Electricity
- Water
- Sewer
- Telephone
- Cable TV (residential only)

Ideally, these utilities should be adjacent to the site. If not, the developer must consider the cost to bring them to the property and include these costs in the project economics either as part of land or construction costs. Sometimes access to the site will require easements through others' property. The utilities availability will be determined by community future planning for infrastructure, the utility company's ability to provide these services, and when they can be provided.

Availability of Support Services

Some support services that can positively affect the development are:

- Employment centers
- Residential neighborhoods

- Freeway systems
- Retail centers
- Education systems
- Cultural centers
- Hospitals and other medical facilities
- Fire and police departments
- Railroad/boat shipping
- Recreational facilities
- Hotels

FINDING AVAILABLE LAND

The following ideas will aid the developer in his search for the "perfect site."

Land Broker

Some real estate brokers specialize in different types of land transactions. The developer must identify those brokers who market the type of desired land. The developer should interview several brokers to determine their market knowledge and commission requirements. Brokers are usually paid a fee in the 10 percent range for land sales, and this fee should only be paid at a closing. A reliable broker will recognize and identify even those opportunities not in the open market. If the ideal site is found, make an offer, even if it is not on the market.

Local and National Newspapers

Most local and national newspapers have a classified or a business section that lists properties for sale. If you cannot find that for which you are looking, place an ad in the same publication describing the type of site you need. Many "gems" are found this way.

Trade Magazines

Throughout the real estate industry there are local, regional, and national trade publications on various segments of the markets. These publications carry advertisements from sellers, buyers, and brokers. Depending on how active you are, you may want to compile a list of these sellers or even subscribe to these publications.

- *National Real Estate Investor*
- *Shopping Center World*
- *Southeast Real Estate News*
- *Southwest Real Estate News*

- *National Mall Monitor*
- *Multi-Housing News*
- *Professional Builder*
- *Commercial Times*

Local Banking Community

A local banker may have knowledge of potential sellers. Frequently, local bankers have a portfolio of "real estate owned" (REO) properties that have been acquired through foreclosure. Since banker's are not in the real estate business, they would rather sell to a new capable buyer. Oftentimes, the terms will be to the developer's benefit, because of a lower price and financing. Purchasing property in this manner is also a way to avoid paying brokerage fees thereby improving your economics.

Local Federal Housing Administration (FHA) Office

Once a number of properties have been acquired through foreclosures, the FHA is required to dispose of them through public auction. Contact your local FHA office for more information.

Auction Companies

Become familiar with local auction companies. Watch for announcements in the newspapers or other trade publications or have your name added to their mailing list. These companies specialize in selling unwanted property, and not all of the properties are distressed. Many times people sell through auction companies to expedite the process.

Foreclosure Reports

The investor should check for any pending foreclosures in the local or legal newspapers. In addition, there may be periodic foreclosure auctions in the area. Properties under foreclosure can usually be purchased for below-market prices.

Title Companies

Many times a local title company will have knowledge of properties not yet on the market. Build relationships with the people of these organizations to increase your knowledge of these possibilities.

Attorneys and Accountants

In many instances, local attorneys and accountants will have clients who are considering selling their property.

Architects and Engineers

Since architects and engineers provide services for many different developers or land owners, they can be an excellent source of leads.

Estate Sales

Check on estate sales. Property can be purchased at bargain prices. Often heirs do not realize the value of the property and need a quick sale to pay estate taxes.

Property Management Companies

Property management companies will be knowledgeable about adjacent properties. If you purchase the property because of their lead, they may have a shot at management or even a fee for the referral.

Letters to Property Owners and Real Estate Brokers

The developer can also develop a form letter that lists his or her purchasing criteria and mail these letters regularly to local property owners and real estate brokers.

Visual Inspection of an Area

Another method for finding opportunities is to just drive through an area and identify potential purchases. After you have compiled a list of these properties, visit the local tax department and research the tax records for the ownership of these properties. Contact these owners and ascertain their interest in selling the property. Stay in contact with these owners, because they might not be interested in selling today, but they might sell tomorrow. People have different reasons for selling. Their circumstances of life are in constant change. They may be transferred, lose their jobs, become divorced, have a death in the family, retire, or undergo changes in their financial situation.

Other Developers

Other developers, whether competitors or not, may have knowledge of available parcels through their research or may even be interested in selling some of their surplus land.

Real Estate Property Tax Services

Real estate property tax services represent property owners in property tax matters. Often these companies are aware of who must sell their property.

County Planning and Zoning Department

Since the local county planning and zoning department keep track of all the land in the area, they generally have an idea of available property.

Local Industrial Development Agencies

The local industrial development agency may be able to provide the developer with potential site locations as well as companies that need to expand or relocate.

Summary

Even after you have established a solid network, there is no guarantee that deals will materialize. Do not become frustrated. The objective is to expose yourself to as many potential opportunities as possible. You may have to review 100 possibilities to find five worth pursuing. Use the "Babe Ruth Theory." For a time Babe Ruth held the record for the most home runs while also being the strike-out king. Remember that to hit the home runs you must be persistent and take a lot of swings.

LAND DEVELOPMENT TRENDS

Land matures through three phases of life: dormant phase, growth phase, and maturity phase. The phase which the land is in at a particular time determines its use and value. Land values are very difficult to measure annually. Land can remain dormant for long periods of time with a stabilized value only to have its value rise dramatically and quickly when it reaches its development period. The following will discuss each phase; Figure 3–2 illustrates the effect.

Dormant Phase

During the dormant phase the land value stays relatively low and purchase is highly speculative with great risk. Acquisition in this phase will take patience and staying power. It is recommended purchases be made with cash.

Growth Phase

During the growth phase, real estate speculation begins and increases creating demand for the land. As the pace quickens, speculation brings higher values.

Maturity Phase

During the maturity phase, the land value tends to rise to its highest value based on potential uses and then stabilize. During this maturity period, land buyers tend to be users and not speculators.

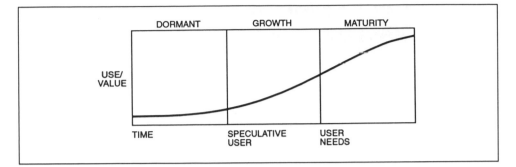

Figure 3–2   Land development trend.

SITE RESEARCH

After finding suitable sites for your type of development, additional research will be necessary to make a final decision. Some insightful "tools of the trade" to help in this decision-making process are given below.

County Plat Books

Every county has books that contain the plats of every parcel located in their jurisdiction. These books show parcels of land by district, land lot, and parcel.

County Tax Books

Once a parcel of land has been identified, the developer should find the parcel's owner in the county tax records. With the district, land lot, and parcel number, the owner of record can be found. The ownership may appear under a corporate name, post office box number, or an owner's agent. Consequently, the developer will have to locate the person who controls the property.

Aerial Photography

One way to review an area is to obtain an aerial photograph. Most larger cities have more than one land aerial photography service which re-photographs at least once a year. These aerials can be enlarged to present a more detailed view of the subject property. Aerials are available in 90 degree or oblique views. The 90 degree view will be shot from directly above and be two-dimensional, while the oblique view will be shot from anywhere from 45 to 85 degrees and give a view from the air but giving a more three-dimensional effect. Photography in winter will give a better view of the land because of the absence of tree foliage. Figures 3–3 and 3–4 provide two examples of types of aerial photographs. The first gives

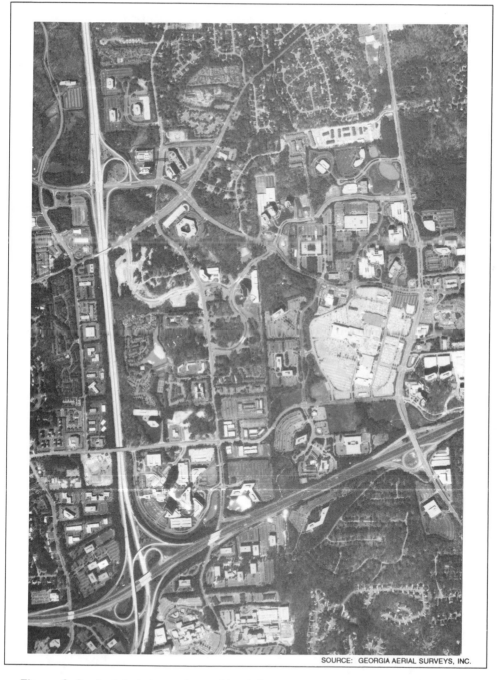

SOURCE: GEORGIA AERIAL SURVEYS, INC.

Figure 3–3 Aerial photograph provides information concerning shape, form, and proportion.

SOURCE: GEORGIA AERIAL SURVEYS, INC.

Figure 3–4   Aerial photograph provides information concerning patterns and trends.

information concerning shape, form, and proportion, while the second provides information concerning patterns and trends.

County Planning and Zoning Departments

A visit to the local planning and zoning department is imperative. Call and set an appointment to discuss the local communities' planning and zoning concepts. Ask them to give you some insight into the zoning and planning problems encountered on sites in your area. This meeting will not only be informative, but be an opportunity to begin a relationship with those individuals whose recommendations can make or break your transaction. Be sure to obtain copies of the following items:

- Land use maps
- Zoning ordinance, including any amendments
- Building code, including any amendments
- Street maps
- Information on utilities
- List of permit and building fees

Yellow Pages

Most of your competition is listed and after spending some time tracking their locations, you will not only know who they are, but where they are.

Local Real Estate Guides

Most cities today have publications that contain lists and advertising for apartments, retail centers, and office buildings. Use of these guides will help you to gain additional information concerning your site and its surroundings.

Local Chamber of Commerce

The Chamber of Commerce can supply economic and general demographic data. Their purpose is to positively influence the growth of commerce within the community. They will not only know who may assist you in your endeavor, but provide additional information about various sites which are available. They will understand the trends of the community, giving you further insights for marketing your product.

Utility Companies

The local utility companies will supply information on availability of utilities within an area. Seek to learn about the complete process of interface with these companies. Reviews of your plans, schedules of installation, future planning,

construction and operational costs, impact and utilities fees are all valuable information for planning. Sometimes, larger utility companies can supply the developer with additional market research.

Local Newspaper

The local newspaper's historic files can provide the developer with recent articles
on the real estate market. Additionally, since most real estate owners or their
tenants advertise, the newspaper may have a market research department.

Department of Transportation (DOT)

The communities Traffic Planning Bureau or State Department of Transportation
can assist in broadening your knowledge of the road systems. They will supply
information concerning existing or proposed road planning. These departments
will control access to your site by their approvals of curb and median cuts. They
have the right to make your building permits subject to their conditions. For instance, they may know of a street widening, which will require a larger right of way
and reduce the amount of buildable area on your site. In addition, they will control
directional flow of traffic and signalization. Because most utility lines are located
above or below the streets, these departments will also be concerned about capacities available and future construction which would affect planning.

Geodetic Maps and Surveys

The Federal Government has developed a complete set of topographical data for
the nation. Most large cities have offices where these are available. These surveys
will give overall information about an area relative to flood plains and soil conditions. If the developer finds that an area is in the flood plain or the soil is
unsuitable for building, then no further research saves time and money.

Demographic Information Companies

The U. S. Census Bureau or national demographic information companies have
the most current information available. After identifying the closest street intersections or a census track number, they will supply you with extensive information. The following are a few demographic information companies.

Donnelly Marketing
70 Seaview Avenue
P.O. Box 10250
Stanford, CN 06904
(203) 353-7214

Equifax Marketing Decision Systems
539 Encinitas Blvd.
Encinitas, CA 92024
(800) 877-5560

National Planning Data Corporation
P.O. Box 610
Ithica, NY 14851
(607) 273-8208

CACI
9302 Lee Highway, 3rd Floor
Fairfax, VA 22031
(800) 292-2224

INITIAL SITE VISITS

After identifying a number of sites, the developer should make initial visits to the site to simply get a sense of the "lay of the land." An experienced developer will be able to envision the "idea" based on knowledge of the product type. Subsequent visits should be used to introduce the site to other professionals such as geo-technical engineers, land planners, architects, and surveyors, who will provide services in the analysis of your site. Some features will be obvious and will be the seed beds for future design, while others are subterranean and will not be known until further study. Three ways to visit the site are walking, visual sighting, and flying.

Walking the Site

The first stage of the land analysis is just plain walking the site. Proper clothing such as boots and blue jeans is preferred. On this visit, look for potential problems such as rock formations and drainage. In addition, there may be evidence of waste disposal or utility easements. Amenities may also be observed. A grove of trees, a lake or stream, or a particularly good vista if used properly can become valuable marketing assets in the future.

Sighting the Site

Knowing about the surrounding conditions adjacent to the site will also prove helpful. Simply sitting in your automobile and observing traffic and the other developments in the area will give the developer a sense of the surroundings. Knowing that traffic peaks at different times of the day, be sure that you pick the time most critical to your product type.

Flying the Site

During the morning and evening traffic peak hours, the developer should fly over the site to observe traffic and community growth patterns as well as other features not readily seen on foot. Having obtained the aerial photography similar to that illustrated in Figures 3–3 and 3–4 before flying the site will allow the developer to focus on areas of interest.

SITE EVALUATION

A visit to the site and a study of plat plans will only reveal a portion of the conditions and features of the site. More extensive research must be conducted prior to completing acquisition. This research and analysis should include the following.

Poor Soil Conditions

Because of the uncertainty of subterranean site conditions, contractor's contracts and cost estimates will contain qualifications relative to site construction costs. If these costs are underestimated, the economics of the development will be severely affected. Poor soil conditions must be discovered early for proper planning. The evidence of weak soil conditions may influence a developer's decision to find another site, because the type of soil along with the location of rock determines foundation design.

Rock

Rock exists on all sites. Its location and type must be known. In addition, the developer, through consultants, must know what effect rock will have on a particular building type. The geo-technical engineer will not only provide information on soil conditions and water locations, but also through borings, the location and type of rock. If the rock is near the surface and an underground parking or subterranean basement is required, then its removal with grading or blasting must be considered. In addition, perk tests giving information about water absorption into the soil can be obtained.

Underground Water

Water tables exist underground at some locations. Flood plains have water on the surface, thus creating wetlands. Knowing the exact location of the water is critical for foundation and underground construction. Foundation construction costs will increase and special waterproofing methods may have to be used to counter-act the presence of water.

Surface Water

All water to and from the site must be controlled, not only to prevent damage to your property but to prevent damage to adjacent properties. If the clearing of your site creates additional runoff from your site and into surrounding streams, reten-tion and detention ponds must be used. These can become features used for marketing or structures built above or below the ground to collect the water and control its feeding into the surrounding streams or storm sewers. These can be expensive and must be included in initial economic projections for site costs.

Mines

The presence of underground mines if not detected prior to purchase could prove to be disastrous. If they exist, the cost for filling them with proper soil must be considered.

Land Restrictions and Covenants

By completing the title search, land restrictions, covenants, and easements which run with the land will be known. These restrictions may totally prevent the devel-oper from developing the project. Title searches will research ownership as far back as 100 years if the property has been held by one family for many generations.

Boundary and Topographical Surveys

Before developing a master plan, it is essential that an accurate boundary and topographical survey be obtained. The boundary survey will give the metes and bounds of the property and illustrate its relationship to surrounding properties. In addition, it will give accurate area takeoffs, legal descriptions, and precise dis-tances and directions of the boundary lines. The topographical survey will give elevations, contours intervals, key site features, including building locations, and underground utilities. To minimize site costs, the secret is to balance cut and fill. The topographical survey must be completed to sitework cost estimates.

Environmental Assessment Studies

Before financing the purchase of the land, a lender will require an environmental assessment study to determine the presence of toxic chemicals above or below the soil. Research will be conducted by a consultant into the uses of this and surrounding sites historically. Soils will then be tested to determine if the soils have absorbed harmful chemicals. If this due diligence has not been performed, the developer may be liable at some future date. Other environmental impact studies may be requested depending on the location of the site and any special adjacent features. Environmental assessment studies can answer questions relative to the chemical content of the soil as discussed above, traffic conditions, water runoff, and quality of water issues. The information researched in these studies is as follows:

- Investigation of the site for possible contamination
- Review of the public records (local officials, state officials, federal regulatory agencies)
- Review of the past ownership that may have used or stored hazardous materials on the site or on adjacent sites
- Site reconnaissance (inspection of the property in question and adjacent property)
- Assessment of the existing and potential environmental conditions
- A report of the findings and recommendations
- Investigation of the extent and nature of the on-site contamination
- Sample collections of the surface soil, subsurface soil, surface water, groundwater, and any building materials
- A toxicological risk assessment to determine any potential threat to human health or the environment
- An evaluation of the regulatory compliance

COMMUNITY POLITICS AND ISSUES

In addition to the physical issues of site analysis heretofore discussed, other concerns affect the decision to develop. These concerns stem from the local community's political and special interest groups.

Environmental and Conservation Groups

Quality of life seems to be the main issue of concern for these groups. They serve to be a balancing factor preventing development, simply for the sake of profit, from removing too many trees, or negatively effecting the other eco-systems of our communities. The challenge occurs when there are differing opinions as to the effect that a development will have on the environment. Prior to the purchase of the site, find out if your site is located in the "hot bed" of one of these issues. Then, consider if you are willing to encounter these groups, pay the legal costs, and endure the negative publicity. For the total community interest, it is recommended that the developer sets the pace in cooperatively working with these groups.

National Soil and Water Conservation

The Department of Natural Resources has developed specific guidelines for obtaining permits for land disturbing activities. If the local city or counties decide to not adopt such ordinances, the Environmental Protection Division (EPD) of the Department of Natural Resources will have permit and enforcement responsibilities. Their concerns will be clearing, dredging, grading, excavating, transporting, and filling land changes relative to sediments into state water. The developer must illustrate how to control erosion and sedimentation during and after construction. Some states like Florida require Development of Regional Impact Studies (DRI) for specific size developments and require comprehensive plans for controlling water quality protecting fish and wildlife. Approval for developments requiring these studies will be extremely expensive and will require a great deal of time in working with local, state, and federal departments.

Neighborhood Opposition

Zoning plans for communities have been instituted to control the growth of communities. Without a careful mixing of land uses, residential owners find themselves living adjacent to large manufacturing facilities resulting in a devaluation of property values. Obviously, if a planned development will increase the tax base of a community, one can see why local governments will grant a favorable rezoning. The problem occurs when the proposed site is located adjacent to a neighborhood which views this change as unfavorable. Generally, local residents will organize to stop your development or delay its timing. There are ways to respond to the neighborhood needs through buffers, traffic planning, and building heights, but they are all compromises. Be prepared to spend great amounts of time presenting your ideas, and looking for ways to convince them that you have their interests in mind. In addition, your economics and marketing plans must take into consideration these compromises.

Utility and Building Moratoriums

Unless the community has wisely planned for growth in the future, expansion may outstrip the capacity of services. When this occurs, building permits are conditional upon the availability of utilities. When considering the selection of a site, find out about the availability of utilities now and into the future. Find out if a fee can be paid to reserve the capacity which your project will need. You will be presented with quite a dilemma if you are carrying land costs, and ready to develop, but a moratorium has been placed on needed utility services.

Historic Preservation Groups

If the selected site has an existing building which is located on the National Historic Register or if that building holds great sentimental value to the community, and your development plans for its demolition, be prepared for a long delay. Since all demolition and building permits are issued by local government, these groups can march, create negative publicity, and appeal to the mayor to change your plans. Since the use of historic structures can provide tax incentives, consider using the structure for your intended use, or finding a way to compromise with these groups to avoid the fight.

Archeological Sites

Even after all the due diligence possible has been completed, there is still another challenge for the developer, one that can delay a project indefinitely. One generation's trash can become another generation's history and we live in a society which is always interested in that which was not heretofore known. This is why a previous societies' trashpile can become another's archeological dig. If all permitting has been approved and sitework has begun, only to find some significant archeological artifacts, be prepared to have construction stop, while hundreds of professors and students clamor over your site collecting pieces of history.

LAND COST EVALUATION PROCESS

Without relating the asking price of the site to the overall economics of the developer's chosen product, there is no way of knowing if the price is right. The price may be comparable to other comparables in the area and still not be right for your project. On the other hand, the price may be right just as a piece of dirt, but still be overpriced relative to infrastructure improvements required for service. Since land cost is a function of the improvement to the real estate, only a careful analysis of the total development costs will reveal if the price is justified. The following will provide benchmarks for the "real costs" of land.

Price per Acre

Land is typically priced by the acre. The developer should review cost relative to gross and net buildable area. Gross buildable area is land area which is totally available and the net area is land which is available after deducting non-buildable land area due to flood plains, lakes, ponds, or other natural features. For example, if a 10-acre parcel of land is priced at $1,000,000, but it has 2 acres in the flood plain, the gross and net prices per acre are as follows:

$$\frac{\$1,000,000}{10 \text{ acres (gross)}} = \$100,000 \text{ (gross)}$$

$$\frac{\$1,000,000}{8 \text{ acres (net)}} = \$125,000 \text{ (net)}$$

Price per Square Foot of Land

The price per square foot of land is the price per acre divided by 43,560 square feet or square feet per acre. For example, if 1.4 acres cost $121,968, then the cost per square foot is $2.00.

$$43,560 \text{ sq.ft.} \times 1.4 \text{ acres} = 60,984 \text{ sq.ft.}$$

$$\frac{\$121,968}{60,984 \text{ sq.ft.}} = \$2.00 \text{ per square foot}$$

Price per Unit

The price per unit measurement is the cost of the land divided by the buildable number of units. If the land for an apartment property is priced at $800,000 and 100 units can be built, then the cost per unit is $8000 per unit.

$$\frac{\$800,000}{100 \text{ units}} = \$8000 \text{ per unit}$$

Price per Buildable Footage

The price per buildable square footage (gross or net) is the cost of the land divided by the total gross or net square footage to be built. For example, 100,000 gross square feet (85,000 net square feet) is to be built on a 10-acre parcel of land that costs $1,000,000. The price per buildable footage is $10.00 (gross) and $11.76 (net).

$$\frac{\$1,000,000}{100,000 \text{ sq.ft.}} = \$10.00 \text{ per gross sq.ft.}$$

$$\frac{\$1,000,000}{85,000 \text{ sq.ft.}} = \$11.76 \text{ per net sq.ft.}$$

Price per Front Foot

Many times, property which is zoned for commercial use is priced by the front foot. For example, a one-acre parcel with 200 foot of frontage might be priced at $500,000 or $2500 per front foot.

$$\frac{\$500,000}{200 \text{ ft.}} = \$2500 \text{ per front foot}$$

Land Costs as a Percentage of Total Development Costs

The percentage of total development costs is that cost of the land divided by the total cost of the development. For example, if the land cost $500,000 and the total development costs including the land were $4,000,000, then the percentage of the land is 12.5 percent.

$$\frac{\$500,000}{\$4,000,000} = 12.5\%$$

Land Cost Adjustments

The asking price for the land does not represent the total cost of the land acquisition. The following items can greatly increase the ultimate cost of the purchase:

- Excessive cut or fill dirt
- Rock removal
- Flood plain, underground water, wetlands
- Removal of toxic waste, including asbestos
- Building demolition and removal
- Cemeteries
- Buying and moving utility easements
- Cost of retaining walls
- Buying access easements
- Absence of utilities
- Neighborhood acceptance compromises
- Zoning fees
- Legal fees
- Environmental impact studies
- Impact fees
- Renovation of historic features
- Required water retention and detention
- Pool soil conditions

HELPFUL HINTS (DO'S AND DON'TS)

The following are some helpful insights to remember when contracting for the purchase of your selected site.

To Do (Do's)

- Buy in proven growth areas.
- Buy in areas where utilities are available.
- Buy land with high visibility.
- Buy in areas with high residential and commercial occupancy rates.
- Buy in areas that have increasing rental rates.
- Contract for land with as many qualifiers as possible.
- Always complete due-diligence efforts prior to closing including completing project economics.
- Buy land based on your market research and not just your feelings.

To Not Do (Don'ts)

- Don't buy land to hold unless you can fund interest carry costs for an extended period of time.
- Don't buy land on the down cycle.
- Don't buy inappropriately zoned land or land that will be difficult to rezone unless you are willing to pay the price of time and money.
- Don't buy more land than is needed for the development unless you are prepared to subdivide and speculate.
- Don't construct infrastructure prematurely.
- Don't spend excessive predevelopment costs unless property is under contract (under control).
- Don't place large amounts of earnest money down until you have had a chance to perform due diligence.
- Don't contract for purchase without a real estate attorney's counsel.

POSSIBLE STRATEGIES FOR USE

The developer must have a reason for purchasing land which will ultimately result in profits. As discussed in Chapter 2, the purchase must be based on an investment strategy. To achieve your objectives, the following strategies can be used.

Land Banking

Land is sometimes purchased during its dormant phase and a long time before its growth phase. If land can be purchased at lower prices now and at bargain prices, the developer will control a key site and position his future development to take advantage of escalating land values which will occur with future development. If the developer believes that market trends will ultimately bring a return on the investment, then the risk of carrying the land for a long period of time is worthwhile. If he purchased the land for a much lower price than his competition, he will have a marketing advantage. The cost of carrying this land is not only built into the price of the land, but calculated into the price asked for the land. Land banking carries high risk and should be accomplished with a patient joint venture partner, who has patient money.

The developer can also structure a transaction for purchase of the land at a predetermined value in the future. Even though the land may have a higher price, the developer will be in control of the prime site when it is needed.

Land Subdividing

Purchasing more land than needed is a good strategy if there is demand for market sites. The developer who has a strategy for subdividing, developing the product, and marketing the remainder of the land, can not only reduce the original principle, and increase the value of the land being held, but also realize a profit. Selling off select parcels of land can help carry a larger tract of land. When subdividing, the developer should review and evaluate the potential and future value of the remaining parcels. Access to the remaining parcels and available infrastructure are primary considerations for its marketing.

THE GREATER FOOL THEORY

The Greater Fool Theory states that there is always someone who will pay more for something than yourself. Land values should be based on development strategy and projected returns. Do not allow competitive pressure to force you into paying more than your project economics reveal that the property is worth. Profit is made going into a deal. Overpriced land will make the venture carry more risk, prevent you from gaining the returns projected, and reduce your individual profitability.

LAND ACQUISITION FORMS

Land Checklist Form (3-1)

These forms assist the developer in reviewing the various land parcels.

- Property data
- Physical data
- Neighborhood characteristics
- Accessibility

LAND CHECKLIST FORM

PREPARED BY _____

DATE PREPARED __/__/__

PROPERTY DATA

PROPERTY ADDRESS _____   LEGAL DESCRIPTION: LANDLOT ___ DISTRICT ___ SECTION ___ BLOCK # ___
_____   BOOK # ___ PAGE # ___ TAX I.D. # ___

PROPERTY OWNER _____ BROKER _____   TAX ASSESSMENT: YEAR _____ ASSESSMENT $_____
ADDRESS _____ ADDRESS _____   MILLAGE RATE (YEAR)_____ _____
_____   _____   MILLAGE RATE (YEAR)_____ _____

TEL. NO. (___)_____   TEL. NO. (___)_____

LAND SIZE: AREA (ACRES) _____ FRONTAGE (FT.) _____ LEFT (FT.) _____ RIGHT (FT.) _____ REAR (FT.) _____ UNUSABLE AREA _____

PHYSICAL IMPROVEMENTS: NONE ___ YES (DESCRIBE) _____
RENTAL INCOME (PER MONTH) $_____ EXPENSES (PER MONTH) $_____

CURRENT ZONING CLASSIFICATION _____ POTENTIAL ZONING _____

CURRENT DEBT: LENDER _____ LOAN BALANCE $_____ TERM (YRS) _____ MATURITY DATE __/__/__
PREPAYMENT PENALTY _____ ASSUMABLE: YES ___ NO ___ FEE $_____

DESIRE TO SELL: FIRM NO ___ MAYBE ___ YES ___ VERY ANXIOUS ___
TYPE SALE: OPTION ___ ALL CASH ___ TERMS ___ GROUND LEASE ___ JOINT VENTURE ___
SALES PRICE: $_____ PER ACRE $_____ PER FRONTAGE $_____

PHYSICAL DATA

ALTITUDE OF LAND (FT. ABOVE SEA LEVEL): FRONT _____ CENTER _____ REAR _____
TOPOGRAPHY (%): LEVEL ___% ROLLING ___% SLOPING ___% STEEP ___%
VEGATATION: NONE ___ YES ___ TREES ___%
TYPE TREES: PINE ___ HARDWOOD ___ OTHER _____
SOILS CONDITION: SANDY ___ CLAY ___ ROCKY ___ ADOBE ___ CALICHE, HARD ___ CALICHE, SOFT ___ SULFATE ___ GRAVEL ___ CEMENTED GRAVEL ___
ALKALI ___ SALT ___ CONGLOMERATE ___ OTHER _____
ROCK: OUTCROPPING _____ ADJACENT PROPERTY _____

SOILS TEST: BORING (# SAMPLES) _____ SEISMIC _____ PREPARED BY _____ DATE __/__/__
RESULTS _____
ARE ADDITIONAL TEST REQUIRED: YES ___ NO ___ ARE SOILS TEST FROM ADJACENT PROPERTY AVAILABLE: YES ___ NO ___

MAPS AVAILABLE: TOPOGRAPHY (DATE) __/__/__ SURVEY (DATE) __/__/__ AERIALS (DATE) __/__/__ PLAT (DATE __/__/__

ARE BOUNDARIES STAKED: YES ___ NO ___

NEIGHBORHOOD CHARACTERISTICS

HEAVY TRAFFIC: NO ___ YES ___ HEAVY AIR TRAFFIC: NO ___ YES ___ RAILROAD TRACKS: NO ___ YES ___ DUMP AREA: NO ___ YES ___
HIGH WATER TABLE: NO ___ YES ___ POWER LINES: NO ___ YES ___ FLOOD PLAIN: NO ___ YES ___ CHEMICAL ODORS: NO ___ YES ___
WATER VIEW: NO ___ YES ___

ACCESSIBILITY

DOES LAND HAVE ROAD FRONTAGE: NO ___ YES (FT.) _____
FRONTAGE ROAD: DIRT ___ PAVED ___ PRIVATE ___ COUNTRY ROAD ___ CITY ROAD ___ STATE ROAD ___ # LANES _____
TRAFFIC COUNT (DATE __/__/__): NORTH _____ SOUTH _____ EAST _____ WEST _____

UTILITIES TO SITE

	AVAILABLE	DISTANCE TO SITE (FT.)	COMPANY NAME	TELEPHONE NO.	CONTACT	DEPOSIT FEE
ELECTRICITY	YES ___ NO ___	_____FT.	_____	(___)_____	_____	$_____
GAS	YES ___ NO ___	_____FT.	_____	(___)_____	_____	$_____
WATER	YES ___ NO ___	_____FT.	_____	(___)_____	_____	$_____
SEWER	YES ___ NO ___	_____FT.	_____	(___)_____	_____	$_____
TELEPHONE	YES ___ NO ___	_____FT.	_____	(___)_____	_____	$_____
CABLE TV	YES ___ NO ___	_____FT.	_____	(___)_____	_____	$_____

SIZE LINES (INCHES): GAS _____ WATER _____ SEWER _____
UNDERGROUND UTILITIES: ELECTRIC ___ TELEPHONE ___ CABLE TV ___

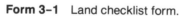

Form 3-1 Land checklist form.

LAND CHECKLIST FORM

GOVERNMENTAL REQUIREMENTS

LOCATIONAL JURISDICTION _____

LOCAL SERVICES: POLICE _____ FIRE _____ TRASH _____

INSURANCE RATING _____

DEVELOPMENT ATTITUDE: LOCAL AUTHORITIES: FOR _____ AGAINST _____ CITIZENS: FOR _____ AGAINST _____

COMMENTS FROM (NAME, DATE, TEL. NO.)

PLANNING DEPT: _____

_____

_____

BUILDING DEPT. _____

_____

_____

ZONING DEPT. _____

_____

_____

IS UNIFORM BUILDING CODE USED: NO ____ YES ____

ARE BONDS REQUIRED: NO ____ YES ____

IS THERE A LOCAL ARCHITECTURAL COMMITTEE: NO ____ YES ____

DESGIN CRITERIA (FT.): FRONT SETBACK _____ REAR SETBACK _____ SIDE SETBACKS _____ HEIGHT: FEET _____ STORIES _____

FEES: ZONING $_____ DEVELOPMENT $_____ ROAD BOND $_____ BUILDING $_____ OTHER $_____

HOW OFTEN ARE ZONING MEETINGS HELD: _____ IS THERE A WAITING PERIOD IF TURNED DOWN: NO ____ YES ____ HOW LONG (TIME) _____

IS THERE ANY THREAT OF COMDEMNATION FOR SUBJECT PROPERTY: NO ____ YES ____ IF SO, WHEN PLANNED _____ HOW MUCH LAND (ACRE) _____

IS THERE A MASTER ZONING PLAN FOR THE AREA: NO ____ YES ____

IF REQUIRED, IS THERE POTENTIAL OPPOSITION TO A REZONING: NO ____ YES ____ BY WHOM _____

IS THE SUBJECT LAND IS A SPECIAL ZONED AREA: NATIONAL FOREST _____ WILDLIFE PRESERVE _____ FIRE HAZARD AREA _____ EARTHQUAKE ZONE _____

HISTORICAL SITE _____ 100 YEAR FLOOD PLAIN _____ HAZARDOUS DUMP SITE _____ ARCHEOLOGICAL SITE _____ OTHER _____

POTENTIAL LAND USE

RESIDENTIAL (PER ACRE/TOTAL UNITS): SINGLE-FAMILY ____/_____ MULTI-FAMILY ____/_____

COMMERCIAL (PER ACRE/TOTAL SQ.FT.): RETAIL ____/_____ OFFICE ____/_____ INDUSTRIAL ____/_____ LODGING ____/_____

MARKET ANALYSIS

COMPARABLE VACANT TRACTS OF LAND IN THE AREA:

MAP #	ADDRESS	MILES TO SUBJECT	GROSS ACRES	NET ACRES	ASKING PRICE	TERMS	CURRENT ZONING	POTENTIAL ZONING	DATE LISTED
_____	_____	_____	_____	_____	$_____	_____	_____	_____	_/_/_
_____	_____	_____	_____	_____	$_____	_____	_____	_____	_/_/_
_____	_____	_____	_____	_____	$_____	_____	_____	_____	_/_/_
_____	_____	_____	_____	_____	$_____	_____	_____	_____	_/_/_
_____	_____	_____	_____	_____	$_____	_____	_____	_____	_/_/_
_____	_____	_____	_____	_____	$_____				

COMPARABLE SOLD TRACTS OF LAND IN THE AREA:

MAP #	ADDRESS	MILES TO SUBJECT	GROSS ACRES	NET ACRES	ASKING PRICE	TERMS	CURRENT ZONING	POTENTIAL ZONING	DATE LISTED
_____	_____	_____	_____	_____	$_____	_____	_____	_____	_/_/_
_____	_____	_____	_____	_____	$_____	_____	_____	_____	_/_/_
_____	_____	_____	_____	_____	$_____	_____	_____	_____	_/_/_
_____	_____	_____	_____	_____	$_____	_____	_____	_____	_/_/_
_____	_____	_____	_____	_____	$_____	_____	_____	_____	_/_/_
_____	_____	_____	_____	_____	$_____				

Form 3-1 Land checklist form. (*Cont'd*)

LAND CHECKLIST FORM

MARKET INFORMATION

RESIDENTIAL:	SLOW	MODERATE	HEAVY	AVE. RATES		OCCUPANCY
SINGLE–FAMILY	____	____	____	$____	PER HOME	____%
MULTI–FAMILY	____	____	____	$____	PER MONTH	____%
COMMERCIAL:						
RETAIL	____	____	____	$____	PER SQ.FT.	____%
OFFICE	____	____	____	$____	PER SQ.FT.	____%
INDUSTRIAL	____	____	____	$____	PER SQ.FT.	____%
LODGING	____	____	____	$____	PER NIGHT	____%

MARKET ANALYSIS

DISTANCE TO (MILES):		NAME	MAJOR EMPLOYERS	# EMPLOYEES	DISTANCE TO SUBJECT
FREEWAY ENTRANCE	____	_____	_____	____	____
NEIGHBORHOOD SHOPPING CENT	____	_____	_____	____	____
REGIONAL SHOPPING CENTER	____	_____	_____	____	____
HOSPITAL	____	_____	_____	____	____
MEDICAL OFFICES	____	_____	_____	____	____
PUBLIC TRANSPORTATION	____	_____	_____	____	____
ELEMENTARY SCHOOL	____	_____	_____	____	____
MIDDLE HIGH SCHOOL	____	_____	_____	____	____
HIGH SCHOOL	____	_____	_____	____	____
PRIVATE SCHOOL	____	_____	_____	____	____
COLLEGE/UNIVERSITY	____	_____			
TRADE SCHOOL	____	_____			
MILITARY INSTALLATION	____	_____	UNEMPLOYMENT RATE: ____% YEAR ____		
OFFICE CENTERS	____	_____	TREND: UP ___ DOWN ___ STABLE ___		
LIBRARY	____	_____			
CITY HALL	____	_____			
AIRPORT	____	_____			
RECREATIONAL FACILITIES	____	_____			

DEMOGRAPHICS

PREPARED BY _____

DATE __/__/__

	1 MILE	3 MILE	5 MILE
POPULATION:	____	____	____
WHITE	____%	____%	____%
OTHER	____%	____%	____%
AVERAGE AGE (YRS)	____		
AVERAGE INCOME ($)	$____	$____	$____
MEDIAN INCOME	$____	$____	$____
HOUSEHOLD SIZE	____	____	____
# VEHICLES/FAMILY	____	____	
OWNER OCCUPIED	____%	____%	____%
RENTER OCCUPIED	____%	____%	____%

SITE REVIEWED

FHA

DATE __/__/__

REVIEWER'S NAME _____

TEL. NO. (___)_____

COMMENTS _____
_____
_____

VA

DATE __/__/__

REVIEWER'S NAME

TEL. NO. (___)_____

COMMENTS _____
_____
_____

HIGHEST AND BEST USE OF PROPERTY

	# UNITS	SQ.FT.	DENSITY	
RESIDENTIAL:				TIME OF DEVELOPMENT (YEARS) ____
SINGLE–FAMILY	____		____ PER ACRE	POTENTIAL YEARLY LAND APPRECIATION ____%
MULTI–FAMILY	____		____ PER ACRE	
COMMERCIAL:				POTENTIAL FUTURE ASSEMBLAGE: NO ___ YES ___
RETAIL		____	____ PER SQ.FT.	
OFFICE		____	____ PER SQ.FT.	
INDUSTRIAL		____	____ PER SQ.FT.	
LODGING		____	____ PER SQ.FT.	

Form 3–1 Land checklist form. (*Cont'd*)

LAND CHECKLIST FORM

COMMENTS (NAME, DATE, TEL. NO.)

BROKERS _____
_____
_____
_____

BANKERS _____
_____
_____
_____

TITLE COMPANY _____
_____
_____
_____

TAX ASSESSOR _____
_____
_____
_____

BUILDERS _____
_____
_____
_____

MERCHANTS _____
_____
_____
_____

CONTRACTORS _____
_____
_____
_____

MORTGAGE BROKERS _____
_____
_____
_____

ENGINEERS _____
_____
_____
_____

ARCHITECTS _____
_____
_____
_____

DEVELOPMENT MGR. _____
_____
_____

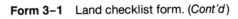

Form 3-1 Land checklist form. (*Cont'd*)

- Utilities to site
- Government requirements
- Potential land use
- Market information
- Demographics
- Highest and best use
- Comments

Land Rating Form (3–2)

This form should be used to rate various parcels of land.

LAND RATING FORM

FORM 3-2

PREPARED BY _____

DATE PREPARED ___/___/___

EXCELLENT	5
VERY GOOD	4
GOOD	3
AVERAGE	2
POOR	1

DESCRIPTION	PROP. #1	PROP. #2	PROP. #3	PROP. #4	PROP. #5	PROP. #6	PROP. #7	PROP. #8	PROP. #9	PROP. #10
LOCATION										
ZONING										
PRICE & TERMS										
DEMOGRAPHICS										
PHYSICAL SITE										
SHAPE										
VISABILITY										
TRAFFIC PATTERNS:										
INGRESS/EGRESS										
SPEED OF TRAFFIC										
SIDE OF STREET										
CURB CUTS										
MEDIAN CUTS										
TRAFFIC COUNT										
AVAILABILITY OF UTILITIES:										
ELECTRICITY										
GAS										
WATER										
SEWER										
TELEPHONE										
CABLE TV										
AVAILABILITY OF SUPPORT FACILITIES:										
EMPLOYMENT CENTERS										
HOUSING										
FREEWAY SYSTEM										
SHOPPING										
SCHOOLS										
CULTURAL CENTERS										
FIRE & POLICE DEPARTMENTS										
RAILROAD/BOAT SHIPPING										
RECREATIONAL										
_____										
_____										
_____										
_____										
_____										
TOTAL										

	ADDRESS	LANDLOT/DIST/PARCEL	PRICE/ACRE	BROKER	TEL. NO.
PROPERTY #1	_____	___/___/___	$_____	_____	(__)_____
PROPERTY #2	_____	___/___/___	$_____	_____	(__)_____
PROPERTY #3	_____	___/___/___	$_____	_____	(__)_____
PROPERTY #4	_____	___/___/___	$_____	_____	(__)_____
PROPERTY #5	_____	___/___/___	$_____	_____	(__)_____
PROPERTY #6	_____	___/___/___	$_____	_____	(__)_____
PROPERTY #7	_____	___/___/___	$_____	_____	(__)_____
PROPERTY #8	_____	___/___/___	$_____	_____	(__)_____
PROPERTY #9	_____	___/___/___	$_____	_____	(__)_____
PROPERTY #10	_____	___/___/___	$_____	_____	(__)_____

Form 3-2   Land rating form.

## Chapter 4

Contracting and Financing
the Land Acquisition

After selecting a site that satisfies the needs of market research, project economics, and master planning, the developer must gain control of the property. Control of the property may be through a purchase or some type of ground lease transaction. It can also be through a joint venture where the basis in the land is used as a portion of the equity and the original owner becomes a joint venture partner in the total development because of his or her contribution.

Sometimes, the developer will find that the desired land is owned by an unwilling seller. Gaining control of this land may be most challenging. The developer must not only present a market sensitive offer, but also must motivate the seller to sell. The joint venture is one of these motivators to sell. Others which have been used include parks, buildings, and streets which carry family names as well as a total development which carries a name which gives the original owner an intangible ownership. Another idea is a life estate which gives the buyer ownership, while the seller retains possession until death. "Like-kind" exchanges are another way for the developer to gain control. Essentially, like-kind exchanges are trades. If the developer finds that the seller desires another piece of property, he can purchase that property and make it a simple step for the seller to realize his dreams. An example of this occurred in Atlanta, Georgia, in a $30 million plus transaction. A large corporation desired a key corner piece of property from an unwilling seller, who just happened to have occupied the property for 20 to 30 years. This seller did not want to have the problems of developing another corporate headquarters as well as pay the tax on the gain realized by the sale. Therefore the developer for the large corporation found another key corner site within the city which another developer wanted to develop. A building to meet the seller's criteria was designed and built. Then, that building along with the land was exchanged for the original corner site desired by the corporation. The seller received his price in the new land and building, and paid no taxes, and the large corporation gained control of the desired corner piece of property, by paying for another piece of property along with its real estate improvements.

Gaining control of the property is more than simply making an offer and presenting a contract. If there is stiff competition for a particular piece of property, the developer may desire to gain control quickly prior to being assured that the property will totally satisfy the potential development needs. One low-risk method, with a carefully worded contract, is to make an offer with a 60- to 120-day "free-look" period or a due-diligence period for very little earnest money. While maintaining control, the developer has the time necessary to research zoning, master planning, financing, environmental, and geo-technical issues.

Purchasing the land is one of the simplest aspects of the development process, but it is one of the most important, because this decision sets the foundation for the total development. The land is the only real estate involved, while everything else is nothing but improvements to that real estate. To make an error in this aspect of the transaction will cost the developer a steep price throughout the total development. That price can be paid in the following ways:

- The price can be too high and the economics for the remainder of the development could price the project out of the marketplace.
- The zoning may not allow for sufficient density of development to realize projected returns.
- The master plan did not consider that 30 percent of the site was flood plain and therefore the overall price paid for the land was too high.
- An environmental aspect of the land was overlooked, and after a significant investment of "seed money" was invested, financing could not be obtained.
- Building setbacks were not considered, which reduced the amount of buildable land to such a degree that the building would not fit on the site.
- Utilities such as sewer and water were not available to the site, making development impossible.

LAND PURCHASE TECHNIQUES

To close on the purchase of the land, it is essential for the developer to have completed research in detail prior to consummating the offer. To enter negotiations without understanding the market, comparable land prices, the mood of the seller, the seller's needs, and the preliminary economics for the development will weaken the developer's ability to negotiate and close effectively. The following steps must be followed for adequate preparation.

Step 1: Research the Property, Developing Knowledge of Its Use

Prior to negotiating a deal, the developer should establish an offering price range based on market comparables and project economics. The developer should know property and the market. A thorough knowledge of the mortgage market will also help in negotiations. Sometimes a property should be refinanced. Knowing the lender's terms can expedite the negotiations.

Step 2: Verify All the Facts

A smart developer will doublecheck all information. Remember, "garbage in, garbage out."

Step 3: Research the Seller: Learn His or Her Needs

As much as possible, the developer should know the strengths and weaknesses of the selling party. A careful background check of the seller is advised. The seller may have hidden motives for selling. In addition, the seller may have financial problems, thus giving you a stronger bargaining position. Learn the "hot buttons" and what turns on and what turns off the seller. How you relate to a seller can eventually determine the strength of the deal which you negotiate. Sometimes, on very large transactions, private investigators can be helpful in learning more about persons and companies.

Step 4: Have Alternate Plans

The developer who is well prepared, will have Plan A, Plan B, Plan C, and, if necessary, Plan D. Since every transaction and every seller are different, the developer should be prepared to react to the seller's counteroffers. The developer's counteroffers should be based on a "sensitivity analysis" performed, providing a broad range of knowledge about the flexibility of the deal. In other words, the developer should know enough about the implications of various decisions to create a "win-win" situation.

Step 5: Have Patience

If you have not developed patience, now is the right time to start. In the process of acquiring land, you may be negotiating with a non-business person, a property owner who does not wish to sell, or one who is not ready to sell. For the right price and at the right time, everything sells. The developer must present precisely the right combination of terms which will give the property owner incentive to negotiate and sell.

Regardless of the type of transaction and the negotiations for that transaction, the most important issues which must be considered are the amount of the offer and the terms of that offer. By now, with all of the preliminary data gathered, the developer should be able to negotiate a safe price for the land. The following paragraphs will discuss items to remember, determining the final offer, possible financing arrangements, and the documents needed to finalize the transaction.

ITEMS TO CONSIDER WHEN MAKING AN OFFER

The following listing will provide insight into the comprehensive offer which the developer must negotiate to gain control of the selected site.

Purchase Price: The price paid by the developer for the land.

Cash Downpayment: The amount of cash the developer will pay at closing should the land owner provide financing.

Seller Financing Terms: The amount of financing the land owner will provide to the developer.

Closing Date: The date set for the closing.

Earnest Money: The amount of money required at the signing of the contract to demonstrate the buyer's sincerity. Carefully determine when the earnest money will be "at risk."

Inspection Period: The time period which the developer will have to perform due diligence for review and inspection of the property. The developer should exercise care in estimating the time needed. This inspection period should expire in a predetermined number of days after receiving all information requested from the land owner or after contingencies have been waived.

Closing Costs: These are the expenses paid by the buyer or seller at closing. Each party's responsibility should be clearly defined. The following are different types of closing costs.

1. *Title insurance:* The premium due for the insurance to protect the buyer against any title defects.
2. *Transfer tax:* The tax due for transferring the deed from one owner to another. It is based on the sales price and a rate established by law.
3. *Mortgage registration tax:* The tax due the state for the registration of the mortgage.
4. *Recording costs:* The fee charged by the local municipality for recording mortgage and deed documents.

5. *Survey:* The cost of the property survey which verifies the legal description.

6. *Legal:* Attorney's fees which are usually paid by both the buyer and seller.

Closing Extension: The option to extend the closing date should the developer not be able to close on time. It pays to be prepared for the unexpected.

1. *Additional monies:* An additional amount of earnest money when the closing time is extended. They can either be additional proceeds paid for the property or can be included in the sales price.

2. *Notice to seller:* The time required by the contract for notification that the developer will exercise the extension option.

Closing Prorations: These are the expenses of the property which will be prorated between the seller and the developer as of the day of closing. It should be agreed by both parties that late revenue or expenses which are not collected as of the closing date will be reconciled within 30 days after the closing.

1. *Revenue:* Any revenue from the land should be prorated as of the date of closing.

2. *Real estate taxes:* The real estate tax due as of the date of closing.

3. *Operating expenses:* If there are any operating costs for the property, they should be prorated as of the date of closing.

Brokerage Commission: If a broker was involved in the sale of the property, he should be named and the amount of his commission disclosed. If either the buyer or seller is a licensed real estate agent, it should also be disclosed in the contract.

Seller Warranties: These are the representations and warranties which the developer may require from the seller.

1. *Power to sell:* The seller is the authorized party to execute the sales agreement.

2. *Conveyance:* That the sale of the property does not violate any governmental regulation.

3. *Utilities:* That the required utilities are available to the property.

4. *Soil conditions:* That the property was never used as a cemetery, landfill or as a repository for toxic waste.

5. *Liabilities:* That all liabilities which encumber the property are disclosed.

6. *Condemnation proceedings:* That there are no current or proposed condemnation proceedings pending.

7. *Material defects:* That there are no defects which will adversely affect the property.

8. *Road widening:* That there are no known current or proposed road widenings which will reduce the area being purchased.

9. *Utility moratoriums:* There are no known current or proposed utility moratoriums which will adversely affect the property.

10. *Current leases or service contracts:* That there are no outstanding leases.

Deal Contingencies: Detailed issues which are critical for the consummation of the transaction and if not verified as believed at the signing of the contract will cause the contract to be terminated unless waived.

1. *Land survey:* Verification of a certain amount of buildable acreage.

2. *Zoning/variance:* Required rezoning or variances for the developer's intended use.

3. *Market studies:* Substantiation of market supply and demand relative to the owner's intended use.

4. *Financing:* Substantiation that financing for the land and the development can be obtained.

5. *Project feasibility:* Time necessary for the developer to verify the project economics and proforma work.

6. *Utilities:* Availability of or the costs necessary to provide needed services for the development.

7. *Appraisal:* Verification that the asking price is close to market prices for other similar property.

8. *Site development costs:* Because of the presence of some unusual features, and the liability usually associated with sitework costs, estimates should be obtained and included in project economics.

9. *Soil and environmental tests:* Conduct studies to verify presence of rock or soil strength or the presence of other hazardous material.

10. *Land spin-off:* Preselling a portion of the land prior to closing may be necessary for the project economics to work.

11. *Real estate taxes:* The current real estate taxes may be higher than other comparable properties, or a new assessment may increase the taxes. Depending on the value of the property, the amount of this tax could adversely affect the economics and an appeal may be necessary.

12. *Raising the equity:* Since the transaction will most likely require equity, the purchaser may require time to raise the equity.

Transaction "Outs": When to Consider Terminating the Contract: In formulating the deal, the developer should insure that should certain events not occur prior to the closing, the deal can be terminated. The developer is justified in making such requests, because should certain of these events occur, the property may no longer be worth the purchase price. The following are items to consider for termination.

1. *Lien free:* If the seller does not clear up all liens on the property prior to closing, the transaction will be in default.
2. *Clear title:* The contract should state that at the closing the developer will receive land with a clear title. If someone clouds the title prior to closing, the purchaser should have the right to terminate.
3. *Transfer of the existing financing:* The deal might have been contingent on assuming an existing mortgage debt. If the underlying lender does not approve this assumption, then the purchaser may terminate.
4. *Condemnation or right of eminent domain:* If the local or state government decides, prior to closing, to condemn and take all or part of the property, the purchaser should have a right to terminate.

Right of Contract Assignment Clauses Help Developers Avoid Losses: Since each developer should try to negotiate into a deal as well as a way out of a deal, the developer should have a *right of assignment* clause in the contract. This clause will give the developer the right to assign the contract to a new entity, prior to the closing, or to assign the contract to another party. If the developer has substantial resources at risk and it appears that he will be unable to close, he might be able to sell his contract to another party to reduce his losses or even to make a profit. Many sellers are reluctant to give this right because they want to know the buyer. If unable to negotiate an unlimited right of assignment, the developer should negotiate for this right with a "not to be unreasonably withheld" clause.

DETERMINING THE LAND OFFER

Prior to making an offer, the developer should determine the land's values. This real cost of property relative to the development was discussed in Chapter 3. Value is generally related to density and every parcel of land is not valued the same. A one acre tract of land in the central business district zoned for a high-rise office building may be $1,000,000, while a one-acre tract of farm land could be valued at only $2000. An appraiser can be used to substantiate the value prior to making the offer.

Comparable Properties Land Appraisal

One method of valuing the land acquisition is by requesting an appraisal. The appraiser will review comparable properties recently sold in the marketplace. The following is a list of information normally used in an appraisal.

- Address of property
- Grantor/grantee
- Date of sale
- Sales price
- Size (acreage)
- Zoning classification
- Utilities to site

After this information is obtained, the appraiser will make adjustments (pluses or minuses) in the sales price relative to comparables based on the time of the sale, financing terms, or added costs due to unusual site conditions. Once these adjustments are made, the appraiser will study and compare this information to arrive at the market value.

An example of this process and its calculations are presented as follows:

The subject property is located at 3186 Bayard Rd. It is 10.0 acres. The proposed date of sale is January of 1990. Property appreciation is 6 percent per year. The property is zoned RM-10 (residential multi-family, 10 units per acre).

Summary of Comparable Land Sales

Sale No.	Location	Grantor/ Grantee	Sale Date	Sales Price	Size/ Acre	Zoning	Util
1	12 W. Main	Jeff Felman/ Jeff Yankow	6/XX	$500,000 All cash	8.5	RM-10	All
2	18 1st St.	Mike Bloom/ Dale Markowitz	7/XX	$660,000 All cash	10.4	RM-10	All
3	28 S. 2nd	Peter Rowe/ Steve Leaffer	4/XX	$740,000 All cash	10.5	RM-10	All
4	2 Pate St.	Rbt. Krill/ Billy Levine	9/XX	$320,000 All cash	4.7	RM-10	All

Land Sale Adjustments

Sale No.	Time	Financing	Site	Location	Adjusted Price	Adjusted Price/Acre
1	+ $17,500	+$0	+$10,000	+$ 0	$527,500	$62,058
2	+$16,500	+$0	−$ 5,000	+$10,000	$665,000	$63,942
3	+$29,600	+$0	+$ 0	+$ 0	$769,600	$73,295
4	+$ 4,800	+$0	+$ 0	−$ 5,000	$319,800	$68,043

In correlating this information, the appraiser finds that the adjusted comparables range from $62,058 to $73,295. Since the third sale is very similar in all features, the appraiser values the land at $75,000 per acre or $750,000.

The Backdoor Approach to Land Value

The second method of land appraisal is the "backdoor" approach. This approach estimates the price for a parcel of land from a reverse direction. Assume we are using the 10-acre parcel previously used. The developer plans to purchase a 10-acre tract of land and desires to build 120 apartment units. The market study reveals that there is a demand for 40 one-bedroom, one-bathroom units (600 square feet) which can rent for $500 per month and 80 two-bedroom, two-bath units (900 square feet) which can rent for $600 per month. The vacancy factor is 5 percent. The miscellaneous income is based on $25 per unit per year. Operating expenses are $2200 per unit. The value is based on a 9.5 percent capitalization rate. The building costs are $35 per square foot. The soft costs are $789,806 less $217,600 in rental income. The developer is putting in $500,000 in equity and is looking for a potential equity value in the development of 125 percent of this investment or $625,000.

Unit Information

40 1 BR, 1 BA units @ 600 square feet =	24,000 sq.ft.
80 2 BR, 2 BA units @ 900 square feet =	72,000 sq.ft.
Total	96,000 sq.ft.

Operating Statement

40 1 BR, 1 BA units @ $500 per month =	$ 20,000
80 2 BR, 2 BA units @ $600 per month =	$ 48,000
Total	$ 68,000
	× 12 Mo.
Gross potential income	$816,000
Less vacancy @ 5%	($ 40,800)
+Miscellaneous income @ $25 per unit	$ 2,850
=Effective gross income	$778,050
−Operating expenses @ $2,200 per unit	($264,000)
=Net operating income	$514,050

Value

Based on 9.5% capitalization rate	$5,411,053
−Construction costs @ $35 per foot	($3,360,000)
−Soft costs (including interest and negative cash flow)	($ 789,806)
+Projected rental income	($ 217,600)
=Remaining balance	$1,478,847
−Required profit (equity × 125%)	($ 625,000)
=Land value	$ 853,847

In reviewing these two approaches to value, the appraiser reports that the land is worth $75,000 per acre or $750,000 but he can afford to pay up to $853,847 or $85,385 per acre for the 10-acre tract of land.

STRUCTURING THE FINANCING FOR THE LAND ACQUISITION

There are many ways to acquire property and each has its own idiosyncrasies. The following will describe structures for these transactions.

All Cash

The owner is paid all cash at closing. This method may include arranging financing with the seller for a portion of the sales price and paying the difference in cash.

Seller Financing

This method requires that the seller take back part of the sales price in a mortgage and will include the following terms defined.

Mortgage Amount: The principal amount which the seller will finance.

Interest Rate: The interest rate which the seller will charge for financing the loan.

Mortgage Amortization Period: The time period over which the loan will be amortized.

Maturity Period: The time period after which the loan will become due.

Mortgage Payment: The monthly or annual debt service payment.

Due-on-Sale Clause: This clause states that the seller financing is due upon the resale of the property.

Right-of-Transfer Clause: A clause which states that the developer can transfer the mortgage to another party.

Transfer Costs: The amount of money which the seller will charge to allow the mortgage to be transferred.

Escrow Clause: A clause which states that real estate taxes and the insurance will be escrowed as part of the mortgage document.

Prepayment Clause: This clause states whether prepayment penalty is allowed or not. If allowed, it further describes any penalties for prepayment.

Release Clause: This clause defines how parcels of land will be released (if applicable) to the transaction.

Mortgage Recourse: Personal guarantees by the developer are described within this clause.

OTHER CREATIVE LAND PURCHASING TECHNIQUES

Joint Venture

Rather than bringing in additional equity partners, the developer may wish to structure the land purchase as a joint venture with the seller. The transaction can be structured in two ways.

- The land owner has a subordinated mortgage (to the construction loan and then the permanent loan) which bears interest and receives a percentage of the cash flows and future residuals at sale.
- The land owner places his or her land into the development as the required equity for a negotiated price and then shares in the cash flow and future sale profits. The developer can offer the seller a preferred return on cash flows until the equity investment is retired.

Options

An option is the future right to purchase at a predetermined date in the future. The developer may not need all of the land at closing and not desire to carry this extra land due to the high carrying costs. By using an option, the developer can structure the transaction so that only the current needs are purchased and then options all or part of the remaining land at predetermined values at closing dates in the future. For the option, the land owner is paid earnest money either up front or at a specified date in the future.

Ground Lease

One option for gaining control of the land is through a ground lease. Some owners do not sell because of emotional reasons. The land may have been in the family for many generations. Some do not want to sell for financial reasons like having to pay taxes on the gain at sale. The ground lease offers the property owner a way to obtain yearly income while maintaining ownership of the property. Additionally, the ground lease offers a way to escalate rent each year keeping pace with inflation and the comparable land values.

From the developer's position, since land is not depreciable, it does not make any difference relative to taxes. In addition, the land rental can be deducted as an operating expense. Since the land represents between 10 to 20 percent of the total development costs, overall up-front development costs will be reduced.

When structuring the group lease payments, the developer should make sure that the future escalations do not place burdens on the operations of the property. The terms of the ground lease must be carefully reviewed relative to structuring of financing. At a minimum, the lender will require that the ground lease extend at least 25 percent longer than the normal loan amortization period. The developer should also be aware that when this ground lease expires, the property will revert back to the original land owner. For this reason, the developer should negotiate for a 99-year lease. If this lease is negotiated for a shorter period, the developer should at least negotiate an extension. While not legally owning the land, the lease agreement should give the developer all the rights of ownership, while under his or her control.

Ground Lease with an Option to Purchase

Under this method, because the owner wishes to delay the sale of the property until the future, the developer can take a ground lease with the right to purchase the property at some future date. The future price can be based on an updated appraisal or a predetermined value.

Land Contract

Under the terms of a contract, the developer will take possession of the property, even though the seller retains the title. Upon a specified loan paydown the seller will release the title to the purchaser.

LEGAL DOCUMENTS REQUIRED TO PURCHASE LAND

As a word of caution, when submitting letters of intent or land purchase and sales agreements, use an attorney regardless of your experience level. Their knowledge about changes in real estate law will be invaluable during negotiations because they can advise you of ways to minimize your risk. Their experience in many different real estate transactions will give you a broader base of knowledge with which to negotiate. Improper wording of documents can bring severe judgments in future litigation. Sample documents such as the letter of intent and the sales purchase agreement are provided within this publication. The letter of intent can be found in Document 4–1, while the purchase agreement can be found in Appendix K.

Letter of Intent

The first step in negotiating the purchase is to send the seller a letter of intent. This letter should be as thorough as possible and include all of the terms of the transaction. At the end of the letter, the seller can acknowledge agreement to the terms and conditions by signature. This letter should also state a required time period for the response from the seller.

Since this is the initial offer to the seller, it is likely that renegotiations will occur. Using this form and the attached exhibits will save both time and money. After the letter of intent is signed by both parties, transmit a copy to the attorney for drafting of the purchase agreement.

DOCUMENT 4–1   Sample letter of intent.

July 18, 19_____

Mr. Ken Myers
4233 Hindsale Road
Atlanta, Georgia 30062

RE: 10 Acres located at _____
      Atlanta, Georgia

Dear Mr. Myers:

Based upon the information which was provided by you, the following terms and conditions are described below the terms and conditions under which I will acquire the above referenced property.

1.	Purchase price	$800,000.00
2.	Cash downpayment	$250,000.00
3.	Purchase money mortgage	
	A. Loan amount	$550,000
	B. Interest rate	Ten percent per annum
	C. Maturity period	Ten years
	D. Amortization period	Interest only
	E. Mortgage payment:	$4,583.33 per month
	F. Due-on-sale clause	None
	G. Right-of-transfer	Allowed, seller cannot unreasonably withhold approval
	H. Transfer costs	None
	I. Escrows	None
	J. Prepayment penalties	None
	K. Land release	None
	L. Mortgage recourse	None
4.	Closing date	January 15, 19_____
5.	Earnest money	$25,000.00 paid into escrow with Chicago Title Co. All interest will accrue to the Purchaser. Earnest money will go "at risk" at the end of the inspection period.
6.	Inspection period	Thirty days from the later of the execution of the purchase agreement or the delivery to the purchaser of all of the items in Exhibit A.

(Cont'd)

DOCUMENT 4–1   Sample letter of intent. *(Cont'd)*

7. Closing costs
   A. Title insurance premium   Paid by purchaser
   B. Transfer tax   Paid by seller
   C. Intangible tax   Paid by purchaser
   D. Recording costs   Paid by purchaser
   E. Survey   Paid by seller
   F. Legal fees   Each party pays own
8. Closing extension   Thirty days
   A. Additional earnest money $10,000.00 applied toward the purchase price
   B. Notice to seller   Seven days prior to original closing date
9. Closing prorations   All revenue and expenses are to be prorated as of the day of closing. Any late receipts or expenses will be prorated within 45 days after the closing.
10. Brokerage commission   Seller shall be responsible for and shall pay at its sole cost all brokerage fees and/or real estate commissions of any kind due to any third party who has dealt with the Seller. Purchaser will warrant that it has dealt with no other persons in negotiating this sale.
11. Seller warranties   Seller will warrant to the best of his or her "knowledge" that
                                 1. The land was never used for a land fill, toxic waste dump, or cemetery
                                 2. All utilities are available to the property
                                 3. There is no condemnation proceedings against the property
                                 4. The property is currently zoned RM-1

It is my intention to purchase the above-referenced property under the terms and conditions stated above. If these are acceptable, please acknowledge at the bottom of this page and return this agreement within five (5) business days to

DOCUMENT 4-1 Sample letter of intent. *(Cont'd)*

the undersigned. Upon receipt of the executed letter, I shall instruct my attorneys to draft a purchase agreement.

Sincerely,

General Properties, Inc.

Ed Davidson
President

ED/rke

Enc.

Accepted and agreed upon this _____ day of _____, 19_____

BY: _____

Exhibit A (Required Items)

1. Utility Letters:
   a. Gas
   b. Electricity
   c. Water
   d. Sewer
   e. Cable television
   f. Telephone
2. Legal Description
3. Property Survey
4. Last two years' property tax bills
5. Copy of zoning letter

Land Purchase and Sales Agreement

After a letter of intent has been negotiated and signed, the developer's attorney will prepare the purchase agreement. This document will include all of the business terms and conditions to which the developer and the seller have agreed, but will present them in the proper legal language defining the rights and obligations of each party. Once the first draft is completed and reviewed, both parties will then refine the language to be acceptable to each party's attorney. When all issues are satisfied, each party will sign the document. If there are any future disputes in the transaction between the two parties, this document is used to define their obligations and to make judgments. Document 4–2 is a sample land purchase and sale agreement.

DOCUMENT 4–2   Land purchase and sales agreement.

STATE OF _____

_____ COUNTY

    THIS AGREEMENT is made and entered into this _____ day of _____, 19_____ by and among _____ (hereinafter referred to as "Purchaser"), _____ (hereinafter referred to as "Seller"), and _____ (hereinafter referred to as "Broker").

WITNESSETH:

    THAT FOR AND IN CONSIDERATION of the mutual promises and covenants contained herein and the earnest monies paid and to be paid hereunder, the Seller, Seller's successors and assigns, covenant and agree to sell, transfer and convey to the Purchaser and its successors and assigns, who hereby covenant and agree to purchase and accept, that real property located in the County of _____ and the State of _____, more particularly described on the attached Exhibit A (hereinafter referred to as the "Property"). Said sale and conveyance shall be made under the following express terms and provisions hereof:

    1. **Purchase Price and Payment Terms:** The Purchase Price shall be _____ ($_____) and NO/100 DOLLARS. The Property is to contain _____ acres. _____ ($_____) and NO/100 DOLLARS shall be paid at Closing. _____ _____ ($_____) AND NO/100 DOLLARS shall be paid _____ days after the _____ County zoning approval. The Seller shall take back a _____ ($_____) and NO/100 DOLLAR Purchase Money Mortgage for a period of _____ (_____) months from the date of the Zoning Approval. This mortgage will be paid at _____ percent (_____%) per annum on the outstanding balance. This mortgage will be paid on a _____ basis, starting _____ months after the payment of the _____ DOLLARS. This Mortgage will be due in full payment at the _____th month or upon the placement of a Construction Loan on the property. Said Purchase Price shall be due and payable in full cash or Federal funds check, at the option of Purchaser, at closing, and shall be adjusted for any prorations provided herein.

DOCUMENT 4-2 Land purchase and sales agreement. *(Cont'd)*

2. **Closing Costs and Prorations:** At the closing of said sale, all real estate taxes payable on the Property in 19_____ will be prorated as of the date of Closing. If the actual amount of said taxes is not known on the date of the Closing, the same shall be prorated on the basis of the amount of said taxes payable in 19_____ and shall be adjusted between the parties when the actual amount of said taxes payable in 19_____ is known to Purchaser and Seller. The cost of _____ property transfer tax, property recording fees, and Seller's attorney's fees will be paid by Seller, and Purchaser's attorney's fees, mortgage tax, loan recording costs, survey, title examination and title insurance fees, rezoning costs, topography and soils engineering will be paid by the Purchaser.

3. **Marketable Title:** Subject to the remaining provisions hereof, Seller warrants that it shall convey good and marketable fee simple title of the Property to Purchaser by a General Warranty Deed, subject only to the permitted encumbrances listed upon Exhibit B, attached hereto and hereby made a part hereof. Marketable title shall mean title which is insurable without further exception by a national title insurance company, such as Lawyers Title Insurance Corporation, Ticor Title Insurance Company of California, or Chicago Title Insurance Company at its standard rates and at Purchaser's selection.

4. **Title Examination:** Seller represents that Seller holds good and marketable fee simple title to the Property. Seller further warrants that Seller shall take no actions to change or vary the status of title from this date and until the conveyance is made to Purchaser, except for such changes as are necessary to satisfy and title objections, as set forth below. Purchaser shall, on or prior to the termination of the Inspection Period described in Paragraph 6A hereof, in good faith have the title to the Property examined and shall furnish the Seller with a written statement of any objections to Seller's title, including any which may result from documents listed upon Exhibit B hereto. Seller shall, within _____ (_____) business days after receipt of said objections, clear and cure the same if required by this Agreement. The Seller shall take all reasonable steps to so cure and satisfy any such defects at Seller's expense. In the event any defects or objections such as Deeds to Secure Debt, taxes, assessments, etc., can be cleared by the payment of specific sums of monies, Seller shall clear all such defects or objections so that title can be conveyed free and clear of the same. In the event Purchaser's examination reveals any exceptions or objections which the Seller cannot clear by reasonable effort and which are due to no fault on Seller's part, then at Purchaser's option, Purchaser may: (i) terminate the Agreement and receive a full and complete refund of all Earnest Money (as hereinafter defined) paid; or (ii) waive such objections and close the purchase. In the event the Purchaser is not satisfied with the condition of said title after payment to clear any such monetary defects and Seller is not able to further clear said title to

(Cont'd)

the satisfaction of Purchaser, at Purchaser's option the Earnest Money shall be refunded to the Purchaser, this Agreement shall be terminated, and neither party shall be further bound hereby. Purchaser shall have no claim for damages due to Seller's failure to deliver title satisfactory to Purchaser.

5. **Survey of Acreage and Engineering Studies:** Purchaser shall, within _____ (_____) days from the date hereof, obtain an accurate survey of the Property, showing the acreage on the Property to the nearest one-hundredth (1/100th) of an acre, and acquire any engineering studies desired by Purchaser. Said survey and studies shall be prepared by a surveyor and by an engineer both licensed in the State of _____, and copies shall be provided to the Seller within said _____ (_____) day period. Such survey shall show access, the location of all easements, driveways, streets, ditches, rights-of-way, indicating whether paved or unpaved, fences, power lines, and encroachments, if any, a flood plain certification certifying that the Property is not within a 100-year flood plain or any area that has been designated a flood prone or flood hazard area, and shall be addressed to reserves the right to make written objections to title based upon such survey within _____ (_____) days after receipt of said survey by Purchaser. Any such objections to title shall be deemed to be rendered under and governed by the terms of Paragraph 4 hereof. Purchaser shall have the right to go on the Property for purposes of running all desired engineering tests, soil tests, surveys, and other such examinations. Purchaser shall not cause waste to the Property, except as may be necessary in making said engineering studies. Purchaser shall pay all costs of these studies, and Purchaser shall indemnify and hold the Seller harmless from and against any costs or damages incurred by Seller through the exercise by Purchaser of such rights and privileges. This provision shall survive any termination of this Agreement.

6. **Earnest Money and Satisfaction of Contingencies:** The Purchaser has paid to the Seller earnest money (the "Earnest Money") in the amount of _____ ($_____) AND NO/100 DOLLARS to be held in an interest-bearing account by Purchaser's title insurance company. Seller acknowledges receipt of Purchaser's check in said amount. Said Earnest Money held by Purchaser's title insurance company and used in the manner hereinafter provided for.

    A. In addition to any other rights Purchaser may have under this Agreement, Purchaser shall have a period (the "Inspection Period") of _____ (_____) days from the later date of when this Agreement is executed by all parties hereto or the date in which the Purchaser has received any requested items in Exhibit E has in which to inspect the Property and to make all required surveys, verification of current and future zoning, engineering studies, soil tests, and zoning

DOCUMENT 4–2   Land purchase and sales agreement. *(Cont'd)*

studies relating to the Property that Purchaser deems appropriate. Purchaser shall have the right to terminate this Agreement within said _____ (_____) day Inspection Period if Purchaser determines, at its sole discretion, that the Property is not suitable for Purchaser's intended use. Written notice of termination shall be given by Purchaser to Seller in the manner set forth in the notice provision hereof. In the event of such termination, the Earnest Money, together with all interest earned thereon, shall be refunded to Purchaser and this Agreement shall be of no further force and effect. The Purchaser's failure either to terminate this Agreement within this _____ (_____) day Inspection Period shall constitute Purchaser's acceptance of the Property.

B. This transaction is contingent on the Purchaser obtaining zoning approval by the _____ County Plan and Review Board to develop a project in the _____ zoning classification. Purchaser agrees to apply by _____, 19_____ for the _____, 19_____ zoning hearing.

C. This agreement is contingent on the Purchaser being able to obtain _____ residential lots or _____ buildable square footage of commercial space.

D. This agreement is contingent on the Purchaser being able to obtain _____ curb cuts from the Department of Transportation and the local governmental authority.

E. This agreement is contingent on the Purchaser being able to obtain an acquisition and development loan for the intended use.

7. **Termination of Agreement:** In the event Purchaser does not elect to terminate this Agreement during the Inspection Period, the Earnest Money and all interest earned thereon shall then be held, applied, and disbursed in the following manner:

A. In the event the sale is consummated, the Earnest Money, together with all interest earned thereon, shall be applied against, and as a part of the Purchase Price.

B. In the event the Purchaser shall materially default in the performance of any of its obligations hereunder, the entire Earnest Money deposited hereunder shall be retained by the Seller as consideration for the execution of this Agreement and as full liquidated damages arising out of Purchaser's failure to consummate this sale, actual damages to the Seller in the event of Purchaser's breach being difficult or impossible to measure. In such event, this Agreement shall be of no further force and effect

(Cont'd)

and none of the parties hereto shall be bound hereby. In the event of Purchaser's breach, neither party shall have any remedy against the other except as specifically set forth in this paragraph.

C. In the event Seller materially defaults in any of its obligations hereunder Purchaser shall receive a refund of all the Earnest Money and any interest earned thereon and shall be entitled to pursue such right to institute proceedings in any court of competent jurisdiction to enforce the performance by Seller of the terms hereof.

8. **Broker's Commission:** If, and only if, this sale actually closes, the Seller covenants and agrees to pay to Brokers a sales commission equal to _____ (_____%) of the Sales Price. Said commission shall be due and payable in full in cash at the time of the closing. In the event the zoning is not approved for any reason whatsoever, even if due to the fault to any party hereto, no commission shall be payable. Purchaser and Seller shall each indemnify the other against and shall hold such other party harmless from any and all claims, damages, costs or expenses of or for any real estate brokerage fees, finder's fees, or any other fees or commissions of any kind or nature other than the sales commission to Brokers set forth above and shall pay all such fees or commissions by third parties with whom such party has dealt, including reasonable attorney's fees.

9. **Closing:**

A. If Seller and Purchaser have kept and performed their obligations hereunder and all contingencies have been fulfilled, then the closing of this sale shall be held on or before _____, 19_____. The Closing shall be held in _____, _____, at a time and place designated by Purchaser and during normal business hours.

B. Seller agrees to extend said closing by _____ (_____) days for an additional _____ NO/100 DOLLARS (\$_____) in Earnest Money.

C. At Closing, Seller shall execute, where necessary, and deliver to Purchaser the following.

     1. A General Warranty Deed in recordable form, conveying the Property to Purchaser free and clear of all liens, charges and encumbrances, with the exception of those encumbrances listed upon Exhibit B attached hereto and hereby made a part hereof.

     2. An affidavit indicating that, as of the Date of Closing, there are no outstanding or unsatisfied judgments, tax liens, suits, or bankruptcies against or involving the Property or Seller; that there are no unpaid assessments affecting the Property; that there has been no skill, labor, or material furnished to the Property of any kind; and

DOCUMENT 4–2 Land purchase and sales agreement. *(Cont'd)*

that withholding is required under the Internal Revenue Code. Without such affidavit, Purchaser shall withhold as required.

3. Such documentation as may be reasonably required by Purchaser's title insurance company to evidence that the above-described instruments have been duly and validly authorized, executed and delivered by Seller and its duly authorized representatives, and that said instruments are sufficient to vest title to the Property in Purchaser.

4. All other documents affecting title to and possession of the Property and necessary to transfer the same of Purchaser, free and clear of all liens, charges, and encumbrances not hereinbefore specifically excepted.

10. **Representations and Warranties by Seller:** Seller represents and warrants to Purchaser that:

A. Seller has all requisite power and authority to execute this Purchase Agreement, the closing documents, and all other documents required to be delivered by Seller.

B. The conveyance of Property pursuant hereto will not violate any private restriction or agreement to which Seller is a party of any applicable statute, ordinance, governmental restriction or regulation.

C. To the best of Seller's knowledge, the Property has never been utilized as a cemetery, landfill, or repository for toxic waste substances.

D. All utilities, including but not limited to electricity, gas, cable TV, public water, public sewer, and telephone service are available to the boundary lines of the Property.

E. There are no liabilities which encumber the Property, except as set forth on Exhibit B; and there are no obligations, direct or contingent, and no leases, contracts or other commitments relating to the Property.

F. There is no administrative agency action, litigation, condemnation proceeding or proceeding of any kind pending against the Seller which relates to or affects the Property.

G. Seller knows of no material defects relating to the Property of which it has not advised Purchaser.

H. To the best of the Seller's knowledge there is no proposed widening of the roads adjacent to the property.

I. To the best of the Seller's knowledge there is no planned water or sewer moratorium planned within the next _____ months after the planned closing of this transaction.

(Cont'd)

J. If there are any current leases or service contracts on the Property, the Seller acknowledges that they can be canceled within a _____ day cancellation period with no termination penalty.

K. On the date of Closing, Seller will have complied with all of its obligations hereunder, unless such compliance has been waived in writing by Purchaser, and all warranties made hereunder shall be true and correct on said date.

Seller hereby agrees that truthfulness of each of said representations and warranties and of all other representations and warranties herein made is a condition precedent to the performance by Purchaser of its obligations hereunder. Seller shall reaffirm the truthfulness of all of the foregoing on the date of Closing. Upon the material breach of any of these representations and warranties, or upon the material breach by Seller of any other representation, warranty, condition, or provision hereof, Purchaser may, prior to the date of Closing, declare this Agreement null and void and all Earnest Money and interest earned thereon shall be returned to Purchaser, or Purchaser may elect to close the sale.

11. **Eminent Domain and Damage:** If, prior to Closing, any judicial, administrative, or other condemnation proceedings are instituted in which a taking is proposed which exceeds $_____ in value including any consequential damages to the Property, or the Property is materially damaged, Purchaser shall have the option of declaring this Purchase Agreement to be null and void. Within five (5) days of receipt by it of notice of the institution of any judicial, administrative, or other condemnation proceedings involving the Property or of any damages thereto, Seller shall give written notice thereof to Purchaser. Upon receipt by Seller of written notice of an election by Purchaser to treat this Agreement as null and void which notice must be given by Purchaser to Seller within ten (10) days after Purchaser has received the written notice from Seller of any such condemnation proceedings or damage, all Earnest Money and any interest earned thereon shall be returned to Purchaser. If purchaser elects to proceed and to consummate the purchase despite the damage or the institution of condemnation proceedings or damage all Earnest Money and any interest earned thereon shall be returned to Purchaser. If Purchaser elects to proceed and to consummate the purchase despite the damage or the institution of condemnation proceedings, or if it appears that the value of the proposed taking or the damage, including any consequential damages to the Property, shall total $5000 or less, there shall be no reduction in or abatement of the purchase price, and Seller shall assign to the Purchaser all of the Seller's right, title, and interest in and to any award, settlement, or insurance proceed made or to be made.

12. **General Provisions:** This Agreement constitutes the sole and entire agreement between the parties with respect to the Property. No representation,

promise, or inducement not included herein shall be binding upon either party hereto. No failure of either party hereto to exercise any power given hereunder, or to insist upon strict compliance with any obligation specified herein and no custom or practice at variance with their terms hereof, shall constitute a waiver of either party's right to demand strict compliance with the terms hereof. In the closing of this sale, all parties shall provide proper evidence of their authority to make this conveyance of all evidence required of compliance with all applicable state and federal laws. Such evidence must be reasonably acceptable to the other party and to any title insurance company insuring title to the Property.

13. **Notice:** Any notices required to be given to the respective parties shall be addressed as follows:

TO PURCHASER: _____
_____
_____
_____
_____

TO PURCHASER'S _____
ATTORNEY: _____
_____
_____

TO SELLER: _____
_____
_____
_____
_____

TO SELLER'S _____
ATTORNEY: _____
_____
_____
_____

TO BROKERS: _____
_____
_____
_____
_____

Any notice required to be given, or furnished, under this Agreement, to Seller, Purchaser, or Broker shall be deemed to be so given: (i) when hand

(Cont'd)

delivered, or (ii) when addressed as set forth above to the party intended to receive the same and said notice is either delivered to such address, or three (3) days after the same is deposited into the United States mail as first class, certified mail, return receipt requested, postage paid, whether or not the same is received by such party. Either party may change the address to which any such notice is to be delivered or mailed by furnishing written notice of such change shall be effective, unless and until it is received by such other party.

14. **Failure to Close:** In the event that Purchaser, for any reason, fails to close this transaction, Purchaser shall give to Seller copies of all tests, surveys, studies, engineering reports, etc., that Purchaser has obtained regarding the Property.

15. **Execution Date:** Seller shall have _____ (_____) days from the date of execution by Purchaser to accept/execute this Agreement.

16. **Assignment of Contract:** Purchaser may freely assign its rights, duties, and obligations under this Agreement without the consent of Seller. Seller shall not assign its rights, duties or obligations hereunder without the proper written consent of Purchaser.

17. **Controlling Law:** This Agreement has been made and entered into under the laws of the State of _____, and said laws shall control the interpretation thereof, except for any local law which shall govern the interpretation and enforcement of any mortgage on the Property.

18. **Time of the Essence:** Time is of the essence of this Agreement.

19. **Survival:** All of the terms, covenants, conditions, representations, warranties, and agreements of this Purchase Agreement shall survive and continue in full force and effect and shall be enforceable after the Closing.

20. **Captions:** The paragraph headings or captions appearing in this Purchase Agreement are for convenience only, and are not a part of this Agreement, and are not to be considered an interpretation of this Agreement.

21. **Entire Agreement; Modification:** This Agreement constitutes the entire and complete agreement between the parties hereto and supersedes any prior oral or written agreement between the parties with respect to the Property. It is expressly agreed that there are no verbal understandings or agreements which in any way change the terms, covenants, and conditions herein set forth, and that no modifications of this Agreement shall be effective, unless made in writing and duly executed by the parties hereto, provided, however, a waiver of any condition or obligation need be executed by the party whose benefit the condition or obligation was imposed and further provided that a copy of such unilaterally executed waiver shall be promptly delivered to the other party hereto in accordance with the notice provisions of this Agreement.

DOCUMENT 4–2 Land purchase and sales agreement. *(Cont'd)*

22. **Special Stipulations:** Any Special Stipulations that are attached to this Purchase Agreement as Exhibit E shall take priority over any other language in this Purchase Agreement.

23. **Effective Date:** The effective date of this Agreement shall be the date of the last party to sign and initial this Agreement, which effective date shall be inserted in the introductory paragraph hereof.

IN WITNESS WHEREOF, the parties hereto have caused this instrument to be executed as of the date on which the last party to sign has executed this Agreement.

SELLER

DATE OF EXECUTION: _____

By: _____

WITNESS: _____

Title: _____

NOTARIZED: _____

PURCHASER

DATE OF EXECUTION: _____

By: _____

WITNESS: _____

Title: _____

NOTARIZED: _____

BROKER

DATE OF EXECUTION: _____

By: _____

WITNESS: _____

Title: _____

NOTARIZED: _____

SCHEDULE OF EXHIBITS

A. Legal description
B. Permitted encumbrances
C. Plat
D. Copy of leases (if applicable)

(Cont'd)

DOCUMENT 4–2   Land purchase and sales agreement. *(Cont'd)*

E. Special stipulations

    1. Seller will furnish to the Purchaser a copy of the last two (2) years tax bills for the Property.

    2. Seller will furnish to the Purchaser all copies of the current leases and lease applications of the current tenants.

    3. Seller will provide Purchaser (within _____ days of the execution of this document) copies of all mortgage documents that will be assumed by the Purchaser. Seller will also provide Purchaser (within _____ days of the execution of this document) a letter of approval by the mortgagee for this loan assumption and transfer.

    4. If rezoning is required the Seller agrees to assist Purchaser in obtaining said zoning.

## Chapter 5

Responding to the Governmental Regulatory Process

The real estate developer's challenge is to create a successful development within a highly regulated environment. This is known as the entitlement to-use process. Governmental regulations control and restrict, provide criteria for decision making, and often create a tremendous amount of additional work and analysis for the developer. In addition, these regulations, in their complexity, result in expense of time and resources for compliance. Therefore, it is essential that the developer understand procedures for responding to these regulations and include this knowledge within the decision-making framework. The developer must balance aesthetic and economic desires with social and private interests while positioning development for maximum marketing effectiveness. He or she must become a master of responding to the growth needs of society while also responding to that society's demands for a certain "quality of life."

Because of the tremendous growth experienced to date, we have become more and more concerned about the quality of our social existence. This has occurred because we have seen firsthand the results of uncontrolled growth within our communities. Pollutants have been poured into our streams while lakes and landscapes in their natural beauty have been destroyed. Community infrastructure of roadways and utilities have suffered to the detriment of residents, because of lack of planning.

It is human nature to be free to make our own decisions and to govern our own life. Unfortunately, when we attempt to make these decisions often with greed incentives and a lack of caring for others, we find that we have damaged portions of our environment or even caused the death of some. Truly, "The love of money has become the root of all evil."

Consequently, federal, state, and local governments have taken action through legislation to tightly control the activities of brokers, builders and developers. At first the regulations were very simple, but with larger populations, and over time, they have become more complex. To make this process even more complicated, we have differing laws, codes, or ordinances on local, state, and national levels. Not only do we have to be aware of various codes, but we have to even understand jurisdictions relative to particular issues. The issue becomes further complicated because we have the right to press for changes of laws to which we are opposed, through legislation and variance. The regulatory process is in a constant state of flux and makes the game of real estate development very interesting.

Areas of Concern

By and large, across the country, the real estate developer will have to be concerned with the following areas.

- Conformity to local and state land use plans
- Adequacy of water supplies and drainage
- Avoiding erosion
- Avoiding air and water pollution
- Avoiding traffic congestion
- Impact of development on education and other governmental agencies
- Conservation of energy
- Preservation of scenic areas
- Preservation of historic sites
- Preservation of natural resources
- Business decisions and tax implications
- Leasing, sale, and management of investment properties

Governmental Agencies

The diagrams in Figures 5-1, 5-2, 5-3, and 5-4, illustrate in organizational form the various federal, state, county, and city departments that regulate the developer's actions and decision per laws and ordinances.

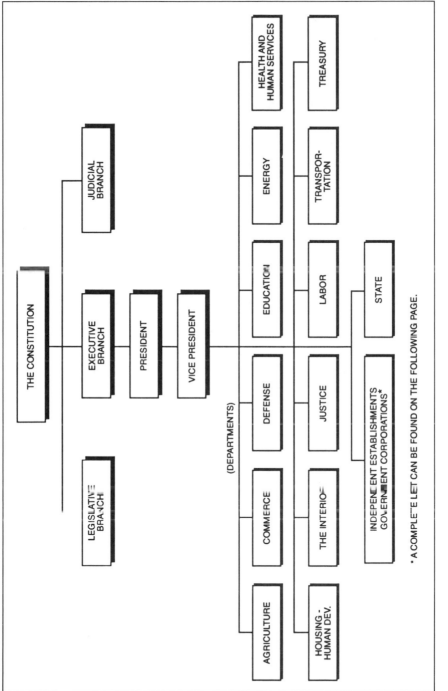

* A COMPLETE LIST CAN BE FOUND ON THE FOLLOWING PAGE.

Figure 5–1 Federal departments.

117

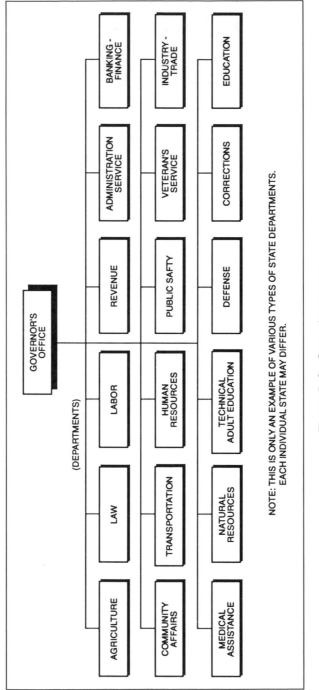

Figure 5-2 State departments.

GOVERNOR'S OFFICE

(DEPARTMENTS)

AGRICULTURE · LAW · LABOR · REVENUE · ADMINISTRATION SERVICE · BANKING-FINANCE

COMMUNITY AFFAIRS · TRANSPORTATION · HUMAN RESOURCES · PUBLIC SAFTY · VETERAN'S SERVICE · INDUSTRY-TRADE

MEDICAL ASSISTANCE · NATURAL RESOURCES · TECHNICAL ADULT EDUCATION · DEFENSE · CORRECTIONS · EDUCATION

NOTE: THIS IS ONLY AN EXAMPLE OF VARIOUS TYPES OF STATE DEPARTMENTS. EACH INDIVIDUAL STATE MAY DIFFER.

118

Figure 5-3 County departments.

NOTE: THIS IS ONLY AN EXAMPLE OF COUNTY GOVERNMENT.
EACH INDIVIDUAL COUNTY MAY DIFFER

PLANNING COMISSION

COUNTY COMMISSION

COUNTY MANAGER

POLICE

PLANNING ECONOMIC DEVELOPMENT

ZONING ADMINISTRATION

(DEPARTMENTS)

PUBLIC WORKS

INSPECTION AND PERMITS

HEALTH

FIRE

ROADS

WATER

SEWER

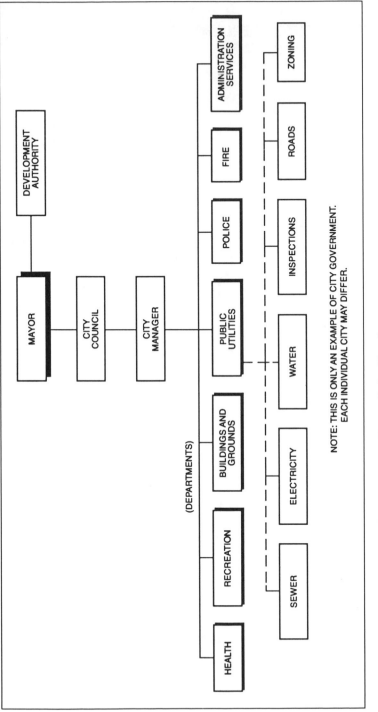

NOTE: THIS IS ONLY AN EXAMPLE OF CITY GOVERNMENT. EACH INDIVIDUAL CITY MAY DIFFER.

Figure 5-4 City departments.

HOW GOVERNMENTAL REGULATIONS AFFECT DEVELOPMENT MANAGEMENT

The following will give a bird's-eye view of how governmental regulations affect development management, financing, construction, leasing, and property management. As the developer orchestrates the various disciplines within the process, each will encounter its own set of unique challenges.

Development Management

During the site acquisition, the "deal making" side of the business must be aware of zoning, land planning, environment, and traffic issues, all of which can directly affect the value and function of a particular site. In addition, all legal documentation must be created to represent the law.

Design and Construction

All construction documentation and contracts must be completed in compliance with local building codes. Without strict compliance, there will be no issue of building permits. Permits are withheld until construction documentation reflects code compliance. In addition, occupancy is withheld until construction complies with these codes.

Project Finance and Accounting

Project economics must respond to real estate taxes and depreciation of the property over time, and to take advantage of historic tax credits, certain certifications must be completed. Accounting procedures must be set up as per direction from the Internal Revenue Service.

Leasing, Marketing, and Brokerage

Depending on the location, state Real Estate Commissions will not only license brokers and salespersons to sell real estate as a business, but also set standards of conduct for the sale of that real estate. Failure to comply can result in legal action and loss of both business and brokerage licenses.

Property Management and Operations

Once a project is complete, the property manager must on a continuing basis comply with building operations codes. Failure to pass ongoing inspections of fire protection systems, means of egress, elevatoring, and clean air can result in fines and even condemnation. Other environmental concerns which will be addressed will be use of chemicals, employee protection, health concerns in eating establishments and air quality.

DECISION-MAKING CONSIDERATIONS
IN SITE ACQUISITIONS

Prior to the site acquisition, the developer must consider all of the governmental regulations of the local community relative to the selected site. During the due diligence/predevelopment period, costs due to governmental regulations are considered. Without a careful analysis, the following may occur.

- The developer may end up owning land that can never be zoned for its intended use.
- The project economics may be based on square footage of land which is unbuildable.
- The demolition of buildings on the site may be prevented because of their historic significance.
- Building height may be restricted because of conditions previously placed on the site.
- Project economics may be based on a density of buildable square footage per acre on the site which is greater than that allowed.

To prevent the aforementioned dilemmas, the developer and consultants must consider all of the possibilities that could occur due to governmental regulations, eliminate the nonapplicable ones, and focus on those that require response. The following primary issues must be considered and in the following paragraphs, they will be addressed.

- Local zoning and land use policies
- Air traffic
- Historic buildings and sites
- Hazardous waste
- Wetlands
- Flood plains
- Erosion and sediment control
- Stream banks protection
- Air pollution regulations
- Waterways
- Storm water management

Local Zoning and Land Use Policies

Each local city or municipality has established rules and regulations regarding how land will be used. These have been established for economic as well as social issues. Land uses are described as zones. By designating zones for particular uses, the communities can encourage or discourage development and protect land values. Since these rules and regulations guide the developer in planning and vary from place to place, the developer must understand the rules of the game and the workings of the political system.

What Is Zoning?

Zoning is the act of a governing authority that specifies the uses for which property may be used. Each local municipality usually has a department that establishes, reviews, and approves all zoning changes.

In 1922 the U.S. Department of Commerce developed the first of two major pieces of zoning legislation. The Standard State Zoning Enabling Act gave the local governments the control to legislate the height, area, size, location, and use of buildings into zones or districts. In 1928, the Standard City Planning Enabling Act outlined a master plan for these governments which would be planned and reviewed by a local planning commission. Most current zoning rules and regulations are based on these two pieces of legislation.

Our communities are always in a constant state of change. Due to the success of commercial areas, they grow and infringe on residential areas and often displace residents who prefer to live elsewhere. The developer who is a part of this process, oftentimes, is involved in rezoning. Rezoning is possible because communities benefit from changes which benefit the tax base, which is in turn used for services to that community. Since the rezoning process can be very political and at times emotional for the surrounding land owners, the developer should be adequately prepared to accomplish all objectives—in other words, be knowledgeable about the following:

- Attitudes of adjacent land owners and the likely opposition
- Commissioners or politicians and their attitudes toward growth and change and how to positively influence their decisions to vote favorably
- The strength of his team in the community (when unfamiliar with a community, it is best to hire attorneys, architects, land planners, and civil or traffic engineers from that community)
- Reputation for quality developments which are sensitive to neighbors

Most zoning ordinances include zoning conditions for the following types of developments:

- Residential
    One family (various types)
    Two family
    Multi-family
    Mobile home park
    Townhouse
- Agricultural

- Commercial
  - Neighborhood business
  - Central business
  - Commercial limited
  - Commercial redevelopment
- Institutional
  - Medical
  - Educational
  - Industrial park
- Industrial
  - Light industrial
  - Heavy industrial

Land Use Plans

As part of the system to protect the health, welfare, and safety of the public, the local governmental agencies regulate land use and development through a combination of:

- Zoning ordinances
- Planning and subdivision requirements
- Master planning
- Site plan reviewing
- Fire protection requirements
- Utility standards
- Architectural design standards
- Regulated environmental ordinances, such as noise, clean air, and billboard regulations

Local Moratoriums

Many areas will use building or utility moratoriums to help slow down the growth. These moratoriums serve as a "no growth" policy for the area possibly because an abundance of new growth results in an overburdening of the transportation networks, the school, and utility systems. The developer should know about all current and proposed moratoriums.

The following methods are used by local municipalities to control growth.

- Disallowing certain types of zoning
- Restricting building lot sizes
- Restricting buildable square footage
- Requiring land dedications
- Extended zoning process
- Restrictive covenants
- Costly permit fees

- Utility moratoriums
- Zoning rollbacks
- Building permit ceilings
- Large impact fees

Building and Development Fees (Impact Fees)

Each area will have its own fee schedule for building. The developer should contact the local building departments for these costs and should also check to see if there are any planned increases. These fees are assessed to the developer for funding ongoing maintenance and improvement of infrastructure.

How the Developer Should Approach Zoning

If the developer is planning an acquisition of land, it is necessary to first contact the local zoning department to verify its current zoning status. If the land requires rezoning or a variance for the planned use, the developer should obtain the current zoning ordinances, and learn the application process.

Role of the Zoning Attorney

The developer who lacks in-depth knowledge and strong political relationships within an area should acquire the services of a local attorney specializing in the real estate zoning process. This attorney should have a reputation for expertise and effectiveness in the rezoning process.

Preparing the Zoning Application

The zoning application will ask the developer to describe the proposed development. It will include questions on:

- Current owner
- Land area to be rezoned
- Zoning classification requested
- Building density, total number of square feet of improvements to be built per acre
- Total number of parking spaces
- Amenities included in the development
- Description of the exterior design
- Unit mix (if residential)
- Projected sales price (if residential)
- Projected automobile trips per day generated by the development
- Landscaping buffers planned
- Effect on the local school systems (if residential)
- How the development will blend into the surrounding neighborhood

- Exhibits
    Copy of the current deed
    Current legal description
    Current survey
    Copy of paid tax receipt
- Development plan to include:
    Master land plan or site plan
    Floor plans
    Elevations
    Renderings
    Traffic impact study
    Hydrology study

Questions That Will Be Asked of the Developer

The following is a list of questions that the developer should be able to address during the rezoning process.

- What is the present flow of traffic in the area? Will this rezoning impact that flow? Will additional curb cuts be hazardous to the traffic flow?
- How will rezoning affect the local support systems?
- Will the additional lighting of the development cause any inconvenience for the adjacent property owners?
- How will the future trash removal from the development be handled?
- What buffers will be used with the adjacent property owners?
- How will the construction traffic be handled?
- How will drainage be handled during and after construction?
- Will the rezoning of this property affect the adjacent property owner's land values?
- Can the subject property be utilized profitably at its current zoning?
- An impact analysis may be required to answer the following:
    Suitable use?
    Any adverse affect on adjacent property?
    Does current zoning have reasonable economic use?
    Excessive impact on traffic, utilities, schools?
    Conforms with comprehensive development plan?
    Other conditions affecting use or development?

Zoning Variances

Various restrictions apply within zoning classifications, such as the required setbacks, buffers, square footage, and height requirements. Under certain circumstances, these restrictions may be waived and a variance granted. Typically, these variances are granted in cases where adherence to the restrictions would be extremely difficult and would cause hardship for the developer, but not adversely affect the public. Usually, the process to apply for a variance is similar to applying for rezoning.

Administrative Approval

Before asking for a variance, the developer should ascertain whether or not a complete rezoning process is necessary, or if the planning department can make the decision administratively.

Density

The ultimate value of the land is in proportion to its density. Density is the magnitude of development which is allowed to occur on the land. It is usually expressed in units per acre, square feet per acre, or the minimum size of lots allowed for residential developments.

Asking for Revisions to Building Density Allowances

Since the developer will be paying a substantial price for the land, a certain density of buildable area may be required for the economics to work. Typically, each zoning classification will outline the currently allowed buildable area. If the density required is greater than the density allowed, the developer will need a variance. To obtain this density variance, the developer must prove that a financial hardship will exist under the current density and that the newly requested density will not overburden the area's infrastructure. There should be more than one game plan. The developer should know the minimum density required, and since the zoning process is one of negotiations and compromise, always ask for more density than is needed. As the negotiations proceed, he can then compromise at a level acceptable for his economics. Any less density than that which is required for the successful planning of the project should result in termination of the land purchase contract. It should be noted that all contracts where specific zoning requirements are needed should be contingent on achieving acceptable rezoning.

Placing the Rezoning Signs on the Property

After the rezoning or variance application fee is paid and processed, the zoning department will give the developer a sign to place on the property. This sign will be notice to the public of the time and place of the impending rezoning hearing.

Notice to the Neighbors

Within days of the submission of the rezoning application, the zoning department will notify in writing the surrounding property owners of the rezoning hearing.

Meeting with the Local Planning and Development Agencies

After meeting with the local zoning department, the developer or a representative should contact the local planning and development departments. This department will be familiar with the property, its zoning classification, and potential uses. This department's recommendations will play a major role in the acceptance of rezoning requests.

Negotiating with the City Officials

In many cases, the developer may need to negotiate with the city to help speed along the zoning process. This negotiating may include a request by the city officials for the developer to assist in the cost of road construction or even to donate land for public use. Conversely, in order to make the development financially attractive, the developer might need to request a forbearance or reduction of real estate taxes for a period of years.

Neighborhood Planning Areas: Learning to Compromise

After the visit to the local planning and development agencies, the developer should contact the adjacent properties' owners or the head of the homeowner's association. These individuals or groups will be directly affected by the new development and will desire input into the planning process. Consequently, it is a good idea for the developer or a representative to develop positive relationships with these groups seeking to reassure them of cooperation in response to their needs. This process will be the most emotional of any phase of the development. Typically, the more expensive the neighborhood the more vocal and active they will become in this process. Many times these groups will hire an attorney to represent them. Be prepared for an interesting experience.

Many meetings will be required with the homeowners' group to negotiate the final deal. It is very important that the developer be able to come to terms with this group, so that at the rezoning hearing, the voice of the public supports his request.

The following is a list of items the developer may be asked to negotiate with the neighborhood groups:

- Architectural style
- Exterior building materials
- Signage and graphics
- Lighting
- Buffers and setbacks and height
- Number of curb cuts
- Landscaping
- Density of development
    Residential (units per acre)
    Commercial (square footage per acre)

- Parking
- Trash removal (time of day)
- Location and size of retention area
- Recreational area restrictions
- Potential cross easements for adjacent property owners
- Development and construction schedules
- Clean up during construction
- Road repairs and improvements
- Neighborhood improvements

City/County Zoning Boards

In many municipalities, an elected group of individuals preside on the zoning board or the county commission. Since they are elected officials, they are "politically oriented" and must be convinced that the development benefits the area and their constituents. Each member of this group should be visited prior to the hearing. At the meeting they should be presented with the developer's credentials and the proposal for the development plan. They will normally ask many questions about the development and its benefits to the area. The developer should be aware of any objections prior to the meeting and be prepared to provide a presentation which will persuade them to vote favorably. If unable to overcome all of their objections, the developer must ensure that he at least has the necessary number of votes for approval.

Zoning Hearing

At the zoning hearing, the developer should use the following aids to present the proposal to the zoning board and the community in his presentation:

- Area maps
- Project renderings
- Master or site plans
- Floor plans
- Elevations
- Market studies
- Area demographics
- Traffic studies
- Hydrology studies
- Environmental impact studies

After the developer's presentation, the zoning board will ask questions and then request input from the audience. Usually, anyone speaking for or against the proposal will have a short period (under five minutes) to state their opinion.

Afterward, the zoning board will take their vote. Sometimes this vote is made in public while at other times it is in private, depending upon the sensitivity of the issue.

Zoning Appeal Process

If rezoning or variance request is turned down, the developer should make an appeal. Many municipalities have requirements that the rezoning cannot occur again until a specified time period has elapsed. If the developer concludes that he is not being treated fairly, he should file suit against the municipality and request that his case be taken to the state court system. If the developer follows this route, it will be an expensive, long, and drawn out process.

Playing the Local Political Game

The developer should maintain an active political contact base. This could include contributing to the right policy makers election campaigns or assisting in raising of their campaign funds.

Being a Concerned Citizen as Well as a Businessman

Since the developer can reap financial rewards with a successful project, he should make every effort to contribute to the commercial success of the community. This can be accomplished through participation in public service groups or local funding events. The developer is in a position of public leadership with responsibility to contribute to the community which made success possible.

A Word of Caution

Always review the local zoning board's agenda prior to making your presentation. If, per chance, your presentation will follow a highly contested issue, which is turned down, it is likely that the tone of the whole meeting will be negative—preventing you from successfully obtaining rezoning. It would be a better decision to wait till a more favorable time to present your case to provide better chance of approval. A summary of the rezoning process is shown in Figure 5–5.

Air Traffic

When the Federal Aviation Administration's (FAA) procedures are overlooked within the development process, the implications can be very costly in terms of redesign and delay in schedule. There is nothing worse than to have spent predevelopment budgets in preparation for construction only to learn that your project is in an undesirable location relative to FAA requirements. This can happen when the developer focuses only on the land and not the air above.

When the selected site is in proximity to any airport or there is evidence of fly-over by aircraft, it is best to have a meeting with local FAA officials to ascertain any existing regulations. Often, unique challenges will be encountered when the selected site is on a hill near an airport or a high-rise structure is planned.

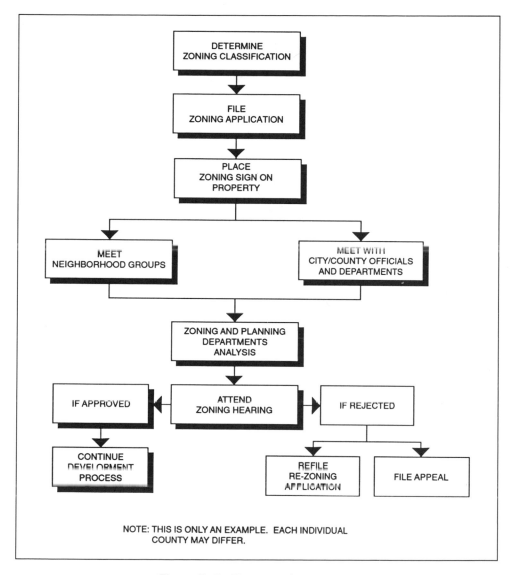

Figure 5–5 The re-zoning process.

The FAA's concern is twofold: one is the glide path of the aircraft, and the second is radar's location and the direction of its beam. Sometimes the building design will have to be reconfigured, while at other times its location may have to be moved. The glide paths are set at specific elevations, while the radar issue is much more complex.

The FAA requires that a form entitled, Notice of Proposed Construction, be completed and submitted along with a site plan, location map, land lot data and topographical drawings. It should be noted that this process for review can take as long as eight weeks.

Historic Buildings and Sites

If the selected site has buildings which qualify for placement on the National Historic Register, the developer will have to comply with a governmental certification process. If the selected site contains a building which is already on the National Historic Register the developer will be prevented from demolition or renovation without approval from the State's Historic Trust. These historic trusts are greatly influenced by local preservation groups and the Department of the Interior's National Park Service and the demolition of one of these buildings is usually prohibited.

If the developer wants a building located on the site to be placed on the National Historic Register, he will have to work closely with the State's Historic Trust in submitting an application. Reasons for having a building placed on the National Register are twofold: One is to protect the structure from demolition, while the other is to take advantage of the investment tax credits derived from the costs of the developer's renovation per the 1986 Tax Reform Act. The process of certification for the use of tax credits involves three steps.

> **Step One:** An evaluation of its significance including a detailed description of the building's history and outstanding architectural features.
>
> **Step Two:** Description of the rehabilitation which is proposed, giving a detailed explanation of the renovation including how the exterior materials will be finished. Detailed descriptions must be provided along with photographs, specification, and construction documentation. This should be approved prior to construction. If the building is on the Historic Register, it must be approved prior to receiving any local building permit.
>
> **Step Three:** Final certification of the rehabilitation, which is final approval by local and national agencies that the project has been completed as agreed. This will normally require explanations about items in question, final inspections, and photographs.

Hazardous Waste

To protect the public against past storage of hazardous chemicals and other waste products, the U. S. Environmental Protection Agency (EPA) has developed procedures for inspection, identification, and removal of these wastes. Generally, they will be addressed in Environmental Assessment Studies, along with recommendations for removal.

Wetlands

Wetlands are described as frequently saturated soil areas which support vegetation adaptable to wetland type environments. These wetlands and their modification or destruction are regulated by the Federal Government. The provisions of the Clean Water Act (Section 404) concerning wetlands and waters of the United States describes activities permitted and the permitting process. Permits are approved by the U. S. Army Corps of Engineers, and reviewed by EPA and the Fish and Wildlife Department. The EPA has veto power regardless of the Corps' of Engineers approval. In addition, the disturbance of wetlands must be reviewed by all state, county, and local agencies prior to approval. Jurisdictions are carefully described relative to the characteristics of waterways and the developer will usually hire a biologist to assist in the process along with a host of other consultants.

Flood Plains

Building within and the control of flood plains is usually administered on the local Government level with strict adherence to rules established by the Federal Emergency Management Agency (FEMA), a division of Housing and Urban Development (HUD) Department of the Federal Government. If building adjacent to flood plains, the developer will not be able to obtain flood insurance without strict adherence to these regulations. Generally, the Development/Engineering Departments will use subdivision ordinances or development regulations to administer these requirements.

Erosion and Sediment Control

When land changes or land disturbing activities result in soil erosion from water or wind and the movements of sediment into state water or onto land within the state caused by the following, local and national environmental agencies will become involved in the planning and construction permitting process

- Clearing
- Dredging
- Grading
- Excavating
- Transporting
- Filling

When local city and county governments fail to adopt ordinances enforcing provisions of the federal law, then the Environmental Protection Division (EPD) of the Department of Natural Resources will have permitting and enforcement responsibilities. In addition, some states have Erosion and Sediment Control Acts which are administered by local soil and water conservation districts.

Stream Banks Protection

State laws have been created to provide natural buffers along these waterways. Local units of government will administer and review all development that affects these areas.

Air Pollution Regulations

Certain areas of the United States require that real estate developments demonstrate compliance with the Air Quality Control Act.

Waterways

Whenever development or construction must cross waterways or a walkway or traffic way is required, regulations developed by FEMA must be followed. The Corps of Engineers is responsible for review and approval.

Storm Water Management

If a development is located adjacent to waterways and/or coastal areas, retention of water is required for runoff of water from the development's site. This runoff is stored and allowed to soak into the soil. Away from these areas, detention is required. Detention only impedes the free flow of this runoff and controls the velocity and amounts that feed into surrounding streams.

NO CONSTRUCTION WITHOUT A PERMIT

Local governmental departments have developed a network of approvals to insure that your construction plans and specifications have been carefully reviewed prior to issuing any type of building permit. Usually, during the design and construction of the project, three permits are required: land disturbance permit, building permit, and certificate of occupancy.

Land Disturbance Permit

Once the site plan has been approved for zoning and land use, and before dirt can be moved on the site, the developer must have a land disturbance permit. To obtain a land disturbance permit, the following are usually provided and approved.

- Site plans
- Grading, drainage, and hydrology plans and specifications
- Sewer plans and sections

- Site plans illustrating other utilities
- Erosion control drawings
- Landscape and tree protection drawings
- Other plans as necessary for illustration of flood plains

Building Permit

Complete plans and specifications must be provided along with the appropriate permit fee before final review of these plans for permitting begins. It is advisable to have as many preliminary reviews as necessary for specific interpretations of the code so that revisions to these drawings when submitted will be minor. The permit set should be kept on site during construction to be reviewed by inspectors from the building departments. After construction is completed, they should be filed for future reference.

Certificate of Occupancy or Occupancy Permit

Before the building can be used for its intended use, the local building department must approve a certificate of occupancy. The certificate certifies that the construction has been substantially completed and complies with all building codes as intended. The contractor is responsible during the construction process to have the building inspected at various times by these officials per their instructions.

Cooperation During the Permitting Process

The most important point to remember during the permitting process is that the officials reviewing your plans have the right by law to interpret local codes. This means that developing a relationship of cooperation and interest in the public welfare will go a long way toward a successful permitting process.

Use Your Design Consultants

Choosing consultants with a wealth of experience in working with local building departments will make the process smooth and successful. The experts have in-depth knowledge about the "hot points" and usually know key officials on a first-name basis. In addition, they have probably developed trust through repeated contacts within the building departments.

Programming Using Code Synopsis Review

During the programming of the project, the developer can become familiar with the key code issues that affect the design and construction of the project if he will require his consultant to prepare a code synopsis prior to beginning architectural and engineering design. That synopsis should consider the following:

- Area limitations
- Building type allowances for exiting (square foot/person)
- Construction types
- Dead-end distances
- Exit requirements
- Exit units
- Fire protection systems
- Floor, wall, column, and beam fire resistance ratings
- Handicapped requirements
- Height limitations
- Minimum travel distance to exits
- Required hardware
- Required opening protection
- Separation requirements
- Smoke ventilation and detection requirements
- Structural loading requirements
- Unusual electrical requirements
- Unusual mechanical requirements
- Unusual plumbing requirements
- Use groups

Safety During Construction

Generally, there are four governmental regulatory issues which the contractor must consider during construction. These are:

Workers Compensation Insurance: Check local and state laws to determine the limits of coverage required to provide protection for construction workers.

Licensing: Some states have extensive testing requirements for securing a business license for construction.

Environmental Protection Agency: Since hazardous materials are used in the construction of projects, the EPA requires that certain procedures be used in their storage and use.

Occupational Health and Safety Administration (OSHA): Regulations: The following issues are addressed in these regulations and must be monitored c 'he construction site.

- Abrasive grinding
- Accident record keeping and reporting requirements
- Air tools
- Band saws
- Belt sanding machines
- Chains
- Circular saws, portable
- Compressed air usage
- Compressed gas cylinders
- Concrete, concrete forms, and shoring
- Cranes and derricks
- Disposal chutes
- Drinking water
- Excavating and trenching
- Explosives and blasting
- Eye and face protection
- Fire protection
- Flagman
- Flammable and combustible liquids
- Floor openings, open sides, and hatchways
- Gases, vapors, fumes, ducts, and mists
- General duty clauses
- General electrical requirements
- General requirements
- Grounding of electrical
- Hand tools
- Head protection
- Hearing protection
- Heating devices, temporary
- Hoists for materials and personnel
- Hooks
- Housekeeping
- Illumination
- Jointers
- Ladders
- Lasers
- Liquefied petroleum gas

- Mechanical power transmission
- Medical services and first aid
- Motor vehicles and mechanized equipment
- Noise
- Personal protective equipment
- Powder-activated tools
- Power transmission and distribution
- Radial saws
- Radiation and ionizing
- Railings
- Respiratory protection
- Rollover protective structures
- Safety nets
- Swing or sliding cut-off saws
- Scaffolds, general
- Scaffolds, mobile
- Scaffolds, swinging
- Table saws
- Tubular welded frame scaffolds
- Stairs
- Steel erection
- Storage
- Tire cages
- Toeboards (floor and wall openings and stairways)
- Toilets
- Wall openings
- Washing facilities
- Welding, cutting, and heating
- Wire ropes, chains, ropes
- Woodworking machinery

Compliance with Codes During Construction

To secure a building permit and to pass all inspections during construction, the architects and engineers must produce drawings while the subcontractor's must build the systems in compliance with local and national codes. The following are a sampling of the types of codes most often used.

Building Codes Most Often Used

National codes:

- Southern Standard Building Code (Southeast, with some exceptions)
- Uniform Building Code (West, with some Midwest)
- Basic Building Code (Northeast, with some Midwest)

Local codes:

- Life Safety Code, NFPA 101
- Appropriate Mechanical Engineering Code
- NFPA 90–A, NFPA 96–Mechanical Reference
- Appropriate Plumbing Code
- National Electric Code
- Appropriate Gas Code
- Appropriate Energy Code
- ANSI (American National Standard's Institute) A–117.1, Handicap Code
- ANSI A–17.1, Elevator Code
- Appropriate Fire Protection Code

REGULATIONS IN PROJECT FINANCE AND ACCOUNTING

When ready to begin to formulate project economics and to seek financing, the developer must consider the regulations issued by the Internal Revenue Service (IRS), which have long-range affects on any decision making. The section provides a "broad brush" review of the major issues addressed in project finance and accounting.

Our tax laws are constantly changing as the systems of our society change. Since the beginning of Income Tax law in 1913, there have been revisions to that law in 1939, 1948, 1954, 1963, 1971, 1976, 1978, 1980, 1981, 1982, 1984, 1985, 1986, 1987, 1988, and in 1989. Obviously, they will continue changing and the developer is not guaranteed that the validity of decisions today will be as valid in the future.

Tax laws originate in the House of Representatives, then once approved by the Senate, they are sent to the President for signature. The IRS is a department of the U. S. Treasury Department. The IRS is responsible to interpret tax laws, issue regulations, collect taxes, perform audits, initiate legal action, and design the forms for reporting.

Not only are income tax laws created to fund the services provided by the government for the general public, but they have also been created to encourage and provide incentives for purchases which fuel the economy. For instance, allowing the taxpayer to deduct interest and property taxes from income reduces income tax payment and encourages the taxpayer to purchase a home. In addition, allowing the developer-owner of real estate to deduct losses from expenses and depreciation from gross income reduces tax payments and increases cash flow giving further incentive to develop more.

The regulations of the IRS have serious implications. The following is a listing of various issues that must be considered.

- Deduction of passive losses from active and passive income
- Choice of either cash or accrual tax accounting methods
- Types of taxpayers (ownership structure types) that can be used in the tax accounting methods
- Accounting periods
- Calculation of the basis on a piece of purchased property
- Cost recovery and depreciation tax shelters allowed including the types of property that qualify for these deductions
- Classification of assets and the treatment of losses and gains in each situation
- Taxable entities
- Exchange transactions
- Investment tax credits for expenses in the rehabilitation of older commercial and industrial properties whether certified historic structures or not
- Income tax credits for the development of qualified low-income housing projects
- Deductibility of interest in project financing and the handling of prepaid interest and loan points
- Capitalization of construction period paid interest
- Rules relative to the deductibility of losses per the developer's risk taken
- Installment sales transactions
- Disposition of real estate interests

This is only a sampling of the issues affecting the real estate development's investment strategy, long-range planning, project economics, project finance, and accounting. Volumes and volumes are written on these issues each time the tax laws are revised. We have only intended to paint a small picture of the magnitude of government regulations that will directly affect the economics of the real estate development venture. It is our recommendation that prior to consummating project finance, land transactions, or setting up your accounting procedures, counsel from a tax attorney, a certified public accountant (CPA), or a financial planner be used.

THE SALE AND LEASING OF REAL ESTATE

The developer who will serve also as broker in the sale or leasing of real estate may have to be licensed to practice in the state where the development is located. If a local broker is commissioned to serve as leasing agent, the developer should be aware of the laws regulating these practices. Some states have licensing laws developed by State Real Estate Commissions. These have been developed to protect the public against unscrupulous practices. To conduct business as a licensed broker or salesperson and receive a fee for that service requires extensive education and experience to qualify. In addition, the Real Estate Commission regulates the broker and salesperson's activities so that they are legal and ethical. The Real Estate Commission's rules and regulations cover the following:

- Practices of the broker
- Operations of the brokerage office
- Disclosures of information and relationships
- Judgment in case of violations
- Organization of the Real Estate Commission
- Earnest money and escrow funds
- Relationships between salespersons and brokers
- Responsibility
- Advertising procedures
- Training of salespersons and brokers
- Real estate contracts
- Enforcement of Civil Rights Act of 1968—the broker cannot refuse to sell or rent or make unavailable or deny a dwelling to a person with regards to race, color, religion, sex, or national origin
- Laws of agency
- Taxation
- Rules of conduct

The developer should research the matter completely prior to leasing or marketing product in a particular state. Some have licensing laws while others do not. In addition, in selecting marketing personnel, make this an important consideration.

SAFETY AND PROTECTION OF BUILDING OCCUPANTS

Once the project is complete and turned over to property management, a new phase of responsibility to governmental regulations begins. In many ways it is similar to the others, but in this case it is ongoing for the life of the project. The following are those issues which must be addressed.

Environmental Issues

Air Quality

Since the mechanical equipment was designed, balanced, and inspected to perform as per specifications, it must be checked periodically and cleaned to ensure that there is no leakage of chemicals within the systems. Since most buildings have no operable windows, the equipment must provide adequate fresh air and the proper number of air changes.

Asbestos

EPA requires that when there is any substantial renovation, asbestos material must be removed and handled per their specifications.

Underground Tanks

Recent regulations require the reporting of fuel tanks for emergency generators and a complete report on their status.

Ozone Layer

It seems that there is concern about the effect which chiller refrigerants have on the ozone layer's destruction. Regulations are forthcoming from the EPA specifying new chemicals to be used.

Chemicals for Cleaning and Landscaping

The U. S. Department of Agriculture requires licensing for the use of chemicals in a commercial setting. Annual inspections are conducted to review use and storage. In addition, material safety data sheets are required to be kept on every chemical used.

Employee Safety

OSHA

The Department of Labor has established regulations to protect workers on the job. Refer back to the "No Construction Without a Permit" section of this chapter for specific areas covered by these regulations.

Worker's Compensation Insurance

Some states require this type of insurance to provide funds for job-related injuries and accidents.

Automobile Insurance

Some states require auto insurance with minimum coverage for employees who operate company vehicles.

Tenant Development Construction

During the planning and construction of tenant space, all of the same codes and ordinances which were required for the original construction of the building apply. In addition, no tenant construction can occur which alters the original life safety systems that were approved for the occupancy permit. Normally, building permits are required for tenant construction along with required inspections.

Ongoing Inspections

The following types of inspections will occur per the local or state building inspections department.

- Fire extinguisher testing (possibly once a year)
- Fire alarm inspection (possibly twice a year)
- Walk through of building ingress and egress systems to ensure that fire stairs have not become storage areas and existing hardware functions as approved
- Checking of handicapped systems, including access and parking to ensure that their presence is maintained
- Elevator inspections to check the operation of the equipment, the status of the hoistways, cleanliness, and electrical systems

WORKING WITH GOVERNMENT OFFICIALS

In working with governmental officials, there are a few key suggestions the developer should bear in mind.

- Spend time getting to know the components of the approval process so that your strategy for gaining approvals can be set with understanding.
- Develop relationships with the various departments and their personnel for long-term communications and approvals which may be necessary in the future.
- Be persistent. Often the circuitous route which one has to take makes little sense at the time, but it is the established method. You are in the development business, not governmental transformation. There is more profit in development than fighting city hall. Sometimes the secret to getting approval expeditiously is nothing more than persistence.
- Pay attention to the direction which you are given and if at all possible, comply with it. Don't take an adversarial position.
- Walk things through approval processes rather than allowing the governmental officials to route your paperwork. Your interest will be better served and the attention to your request will be immediate.

- Set your schedule for completion of the project providing ample time for approvals. They will take time. It is better to accept it and work within these time frames.

The responsible real estate developer must be able to balance his or her quest for profit with a sensitivity to the quality of life required by the community. He must know the law and work within it to protect the public and his reputation. He must be able to compromise between the private needs of individuals and the needs of society as a whole. In addition, the developer must be able to recognize and preserve, in every way possible, the delicate balance of nature which exists in any setting.

## Chapter 6

The Predevelopment Process: Developing Cost Estimates, Schedules, and Financing

The most important objective for the developer during the predevelopment process is to minimize assumptions and to project the most accurate cost estimates and schedules. The quality of work accomplished during this period of the process will minimize risk to the developer and set in motion the forces needed for a quality project. The quality and comprehensiveness of this planning will be directly proportional to the development's success. This chapter will consider programming, selection of the team, budget control, scheduling, managing the process, preparation of economics, closing, and construction starts.

Predevelopment

The predevelopment phase is that period after the site and the product type have been selected. It is that work effort expended after the selected site is under contract and due-diligence efforts are underway to determine the feasibility of the project with respect to further design, cost estimates, development of project economics, financing, further market studies, and schedules. It is that period of time in the project when "seed money" in addition to the earnest money required to control the site is used, fully realizing that it is at risk, if in the final analysis, the developer decides to pass on the opportunity. It is the first major risk the developer must assume in the total development process. It is laying of the foundations for the future development. Therefore, the developer must focus as never before on all of the factors that can affect the success of the development. It is that time when the developer must gather all the facts, look in to a crystal ball of reasoning and intuition, and make a "go" or "no go" decision.

CREATING THE PROGRAM

Because most developers are entrepreneurs and because they spend their efforts in deal making, minimal time is spent in programming the project prior to beginning the predevelopment process. Often, time and money are wasted finding direction. Having a clearly defined program is essential because it is the track on which all of the predevelopment activity relates. The developer should decide precisely what is best for the site and the market and place these thoughts on paper in a program. These decisions compiled into a formal presentation will give all of the team members an opportunity to understand the objectives and provide accurate proposals for costs and schedules. Placing these thoughts on paper provides an opportunity for logic to be tested and the best solutions be found.

The program is a series of statements which respond to all of the components of the project giving detailed direction, which will ultimately accomplish stated objectives. The uniqueness of the program will be found in the special way a particular development company operates, the development type, market conditions, and whether or not the development company provides services in all of the real estate development disciplines. This chapter will go into detail concerning suggested components of this program.

As the key leader in this process and program, the developer's leadership will be most effective. If the developer has a well-informed team, clearly knowing the who, what, when, where, and why of the deal, it will be easier for them to give the developer a project within the budget, built and leased on time. In addition, they will have a sense of ownership which will result in the highest quality work.

During predevelopment the developer may be working with two types of teams.

1. The first team will be that team within the office. The larger developers have teams of development managers, construction managers, leasing executives, property managers, and project finance managers.
2. The team outside of the office is comprised of consultants such as architects, contractors, engineers, surveyors, brokers, appraisers, and so on.

Regardless of the composition of the developer's team, including the total team's input in the programming process, the program will provide the very best direction for all of the disciplines because each will have assisted in the formulation of direction early in the process.

The following is a listing of items to be included in the program. Some will be addressed in greater detail elsewhere in this chapter.

Introduction

The introduction sets forth the overall intent of the project and the very basic work efforts to be expended. It will create a vision of what the development can be.

Objectives

Those tasks to be accomplished during the predevelopment and development process should be specifically stated as objectives.

Master Planning

From the developer's vision, knowledge of the market, and from having walked the site, the master planning section should set direction for how various elements of the master plan are envisioned to fit together. This section can include previous master plans, aerial photography, location maps, existing boundary and topographical drawings, site analysis studies, and any other specifics about the site.

Building Description

An experienced hotel or office building developer will have great knowledge from marketing, construction, and property management staff as to what works and what does not work. This knowledge will have been developed over time. The inexperienced developer will have to use consultants to develop direction relative to function, operations, and finishes for the proposed project. The following is a list of descriptive data which, often times, depending on whether the project is developed for an anchor tenant or a corporate user, an architectural and interiors program will be developed for use. This section of the overall development program is an appropriate place for its insertion.

- Height limitations
- Entrance expressions
- Exterior form
- Vistas desired
- Exterior plazas
- Bay depth
- Interior atriums or exterior spaces articulation

- Security systems
- Fire protection
- Exterior and interior lighting
- Total square footage
- Desired floors and ceiling heights
- Ceiling systems
- Handicapped provisions
- Mechanical systems and any desired characteristics
- Special communications provisions
- Elevator lobbies and elevators
- Energy optimization
- Special features relative to the competition
- Core configurations, corridor length, and descriptions
- Tenant sizes, unit sizes, unit mixes, or room mixes depending on the particular building type
- Floor sizes or number of units or rooms per floor
- Art, graphics, and signage systems
- Materials and colors desired
- Postal service
- Specialized furniture, fixtures, and equipment provisions
- Expansion
- Basements and service areas
- Telecommunications
- Individual programs for specialized use
- Landscape conceptualization relative to overall intent of the project

Zoning

Since the site has been selected and the zoning determined to be acceptable or just requiring minor variances, this section should include applicable zoning ordinances complete with amendments, conditions, and covenants. Any applicable drawings for clearer explanations should be included.

Traffic

To accomplish rezoning, traffic studies were probably completed. Copies of such studies will be essential for the planners to use during the master planning phase. This is important in the planning of major projects where substantial work must be completed on and off the site.

Existing Data

Oftentimes in the process of purchasing a site, a previous developer may have conducted studies which did not prove feasible. Any existing data which the developer thinks will provide insight for the team should be included in this section.

Energy Use Optimization

The energy consultant can develop options which can be considered for energy conservation to lower operational expenses. If these options result in additional costs without payback over a reasonable time (5 to 10 years) that should be omitted.

Philosophy

Any special issues that should be kept in mind during the development or vital project—relative to the developer's objectives and beliefs, mission, and value systems—should be included.

Interior Design

This section will specifically set out the responsibilities of the interior designer for the development of the proposal. If previous programming has been completed to date, then that program should be included here. The following issues will be addressed.

- Conceptual building and space utilization studies
- Public spaces
- Design intent details for predevelopment cost estimates
- Presentation board's descriptions
- Development of tenant standards (for office buildings and multi-family housing projects)
- Graphics, art, and signage
- Furniture, fixtures, and equipment (F,F, & E)

Marketing

A synopsis of the marketing strategy for this particular product type will give the team insight into the methods to use in the sale of the product. In addition, the preliminary marketing research summaries and conclusions should be included. The program should include descriptions of the competition's offerings so that the total team can creatively provide amenities and features which surpass the competition and make the sale more effective. This section will also lay down guidelines for the development of a preliminary marketing plan.

Scheduling

To properly develop proposals and agendas for the completion of the total project, the developer must have a preliminary schedule which considers all activities on a "broad brush" basis to understand cash flow needs over time, see critical path activities, and have a comprehensive understanding of the total process. This pre-development schedule will be an effective tool for the management of the process.

Team and Team Relationships Diagram

This section of the program will list all members selected, their addresses, phone numbers, and representatives. If some members are not selected to date, then their generic titles can be used to indicate the total composition of the team. Because it is essential that each member knows responsibilities, a team diagram can be included to describe those relationships. With this knowledge, each team member can copy all those affected with various information, thus promoting better communications and interaction (see Figure 6–1 and Form 6–1).

Presentations

Included in the predevelopment process should not only be scope or design development drawings for pricing, but also marketing oriented visual aids for presentations used in financing and marketing proposals. These are the colored plans, elevations, diagrams, and renderings which the design consultants must complete. Any special needs for the developer's project should be clearly defined so that their completion costs are included in the consultant's proposals. Sometimes, models are required.

Area Calculations

In different areas of the country, square footage calculations are measured differently. To avoid wasted time, set direction for how you wish for these calculations to be measured. Building Owners and Managers Association (BOMA) standards are used for office buildings. Depending on the product type, each will have different requirements. The calculation of square footage should be consistent for the whole team for the most accurate formulation of capital costs and project economics.

Pricing and Cost Estimates

Two efforts should be considered: (1) the documents which the architectural and engineering teams prepare explain the design and (2) the presentation of the

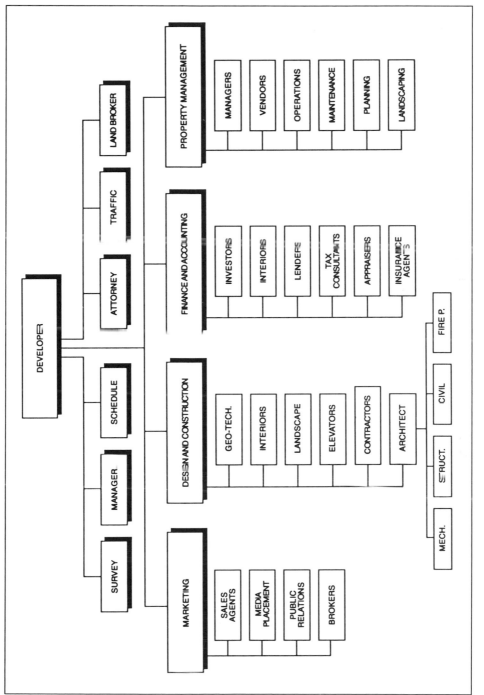

Figure 6–1   Team relationships diagram.

151

contractor's cost estimates. Give clear direction concerning the formats required for this information. The following examples can be used.

Architectural and Engineering

- Floor plans required at a designated scale
- Sections at a designated scale
- Elevations at a designated scale
- Wall sections at a designated scale
- Code analysis of life safety and fire protection requirements
- Schematic designs for all programmed features
- Outline specifications
- Completed area calculations sheets
- Foundation recommendations
- Typical structural bay design
- Civil engineering site drawings
- Mechanical floor distribution and systems comparisons and specifications
- Electrical floor distributions, vertical feeders, and specifications

Landscape Architecture

- Schematic illustrations of intent and a budget

Interior Design

- Schematic drawings and budgets for F,F, & E items, art work, and special finishes specifications

Graphics Designer

- Budget for interior and exterior signage

Contractor

- Cost estimates should be submitted per the following illustration at the end of this section with detailed backup sheets. All alternatives and allowances should be listed on separate sheets and should be comprehensive enough to provide the developer with the building described in the program (see Form 6–3).

Tenant Allowances

Since the contractor will price tenant allowances on a unit-by-unit basis and their description is included in the architect's outline specifications, the developer must develop a list of offerings for the tenant. The tenant allowance must be formulated directly from marketing research into the competition's offerings (see Form 6–4).

Technical Data

All geo-technical and environmental assessment studies will be included in this section. Usually, the developer is responsible for providing zoning data, boundary and topographical surveys, environmental assessment studies, and geo-technical information. If the developer desires to shed this risk, the architect or contractor can be made responsible.

Code Synopsis

The code synopsis will give the consultant direction in the completion of the code analysis for the developer (see Form 6–2).

SELECTING THE TEAM

Due to the many work efforts required in the development process, the developer must be able to effectively manage a team of professionals in his quest for a successful venture. In smaller projects, the developer may play the role of more than one function. The larger, more complex developments will require many professionals at great expense. This team of professionals will assist in analysis of the development potential of the land, running the financial analysis to review the potential risks and rewards, raising the equity and financing, designing the product, constructing the product, marketing the product to the user, and managing the development during ownership.

The care used in the selection of these team members will play a major role in the ultimate success of the project. Selections should be based on experience, track record, fees, relationships, unique needs of the developments, politics, service, and product type. Each member is like the link in a chain. If one link is weak, the whole chain is weak. If that particular link is critical to the project's success, the developer will experience failure. The developer is a generalist in need of many specialists.

The following is a comprehensive list of team members from which the developer can select. From this list, the developer can decide on team composition. Each development is different, so it is impossible to create the perfect team. The developer will have to make that judgment. Later in the chapter, we will explore how to actually make the final selection of a particular team member.

The Development Team

Developers

Those who transform raw land and concepts into the product offerings are developers. They are the overall team leader. They are entrepreneurs, master planners, visionaries, and financial risk takers.

Land Brokers

These brokers locate land and assist in negotiations for its purchase by the developer.

Project/Development Manager

In larger development firms, the development manager is the overall manager of the project.

Construction Managers

They oversee the design and construction progress and report progress and status to the developer and the lender. Construction managers can be within the developer's company or with an outside consultant.

Schedule Consultant

The developer will hire a schedule consultant to assist in coordinating the scheduling of the development and construction phases.

Tenant Development Coordinator

The individual who oversees the planning and construction of tenant improvements is the tenant development coordinator.

Design Team

Architect

Project architects design the product, produce construction documents, and provide construction administration.

Land Planner

These team members master plan the site for development. They can also be architects.

Interior Designer

The individuals who design the public areas, marketing models, sales and leasing offices, including their finishes, and specifications for the furniture, fixtures, and equipment are interior designers.

Space Planner

These team members who provide layouts for the interior space of tenants.

Landscape Architect

The interior and exterior landscape plans including planting, land contours, fountains, exterior spaces, lakes, garden, art, and irrigation are developed by the landscape architect.

Graphics Designer

The directional and informational signage for the project is handled by the graphics designer.

Engineering

Civil Engineer

Following direction from the architect or land planner, civil engineers design sitework relative to public utilities interface for connections into storm and sanitary sewer, water mains, etc., hydrology requirements, environmental concerns, roadway design and drainage, and earthwork and erosion control. In addition, they will interface with local, state, and federal authorities relative in obtaining land disturbance permits.

Surveyor

The registered surveyor will provide boundary and topographical surveys including legal description, title searches, descriptions of easements and certification.

Structural Engineer

Structural engineers evaluate geo-technical studies and provide structural design for sub-grade and elevated structures.

Mechanical Engineer

The design of the environmental control systems that provide heating and air conditioning is the job of mechanical engineers. They also provide extensive studies relative to energy use optimization.

Plumbing Engineer

Interior building sanitary, storm sewers, water and gas systems are designed by plumbing engineers.

Electrical Engineer

Electrical engineers design the service, transmission, transformation, and distribution systems needed for power to the building. They specify lighting fixtures for exterior and interior lighting, as well as electrical panels for power distribution to elevatoring, fire annunciation, and smoke detection systems. They also provide extensive studies relative to energy use optimization.

Fire Protection Engineer

Sprinkler designs and connections to the fire annunciation system are handled by fire protection engineers.

Geo-Technical Engineer

A geo-technical engineer is hired to identify the soil types and location of subterranean rock or water. They provide information concerning possible foundation types, percolation, and strength of soil.

Environmental Engineer

Specialized testing relative to the presence of hazardous materials and chemicals on the site is done by an environmental engineer.

Parking Consultant

Maximum use of the site for parking facilities or parking deck is designed by the parking consultant.

Traffic Engineer

The traffic engineer provides roadway systems analysis to study and make recommendation for traffic flow improvement. By studying the growth of an area, they can provide future planning to avoid grid lock. Their studies will reveal the waiting time at intersections and traffic counts by sites. In addition, they can provide insight into how access from your site should interface with surrounding roadway systems.

Specialty Consultants

For specific areas in the development project, a specialized consultant will be hired to join the team. Several types of specialists are listed here.

Lighting consultant: designs lighting systems to respond to unique lighting requirements

Kitchen consultant: designs the layout of food service facilities for their most optimum and efficient use

Curtain wall consultant: designs and provides insight into the challenges associated with major curtain wall installations on high-rise buildings

Acoustical engineer: provides studies and recommendations relative to the control of sound transmission and reverberation

Restaurant consultant: provides total programs for menus and food service procedures

Roofing consultant: provides analysis of roofing problems and recommendations for roof types in unique situations

Concrete consultant: depending on the uniqueness of the situation and the use of special concrete finishes, they provide specification and procedural ideas to ensure quality control

Elevator consultant: designs elevatoring systems to provide the most efficient cost effective systems for people movers

Fountain engineer: specializes in the design and specification of controls for water

Construction

General Contractor (GC)

The generalist, overall coordinator, and expediter who identifies the work, contracts, schedules, and manages the construction is the general contractor, who in turn, hires the subcontractor for the individual disciplines.

Subcontractor

The subcontractor generally works for the contractor in the following disciplines: sitework, concrete, drywall, masonry, curtain wall, painting, elevators, mechanical, plumbing, electrical, and so on.

Job Superintendent

The individual who runs the construction project for the general contractor is the job superintendent.

Tenant Construction Contractor

Individuals who coordinate the completion of the tenant's construction improvements are tenant construction contractors.

Materials Supplier

Materials supplier refers to those companies that supply the various construction materials required for construction.

Testing Service

Developers contract with a testing service to check curtain wall and roofing systems to ensure that the design will function as planned.

Quality Assurance/Quality Control

To assure that the project is being constructed per specifications, a testing firm to measure the quality of welding, concrete, soil compaction, and so on, can be hired to inspect and report those aspects of construction which have the greatest liability at failure.

Debt and Equity Financing

Mortgage Broker/Banker

The individual who finds and helps negotiate the terms and conditions for the construction and permanent financing is the mortgage broker/banker.

Mortgage Lender

The provider of the land acquisition, construction, or the permanent loan funds for the development is referred to as the mortgage lender.

Equity Money Raiser

This individual will help coordinate the raising of any equity required.

Financial Consultant (Investment Banker)

Consultants provide insight and financing packages for submission to local and international lenders concerning innovative financing concepts.

Inspecting Architect

Selected by the lending institution and contracted for services with the developer, the inspecting architect is responsible for visiting the site and verifying the status of the work for the lender.

Insurance

Agent

This individual finds and negotiates the best insurance available for the builder's risk and permanent insurance coverage after completion.

Carrier

Those companies which provide insurance coverage for the various needs of the developer and the project are called carriers.

Tax Consultant

This individual reviews the potential real estate and personal property tax liability that is projected for the development, as well as seeking to reduce the assessed property taxes after completion if they are higher than market comparables.

Appraiser

This individual appraises the property for both the construction and the permanent loans. In addition, he or she evaluates property values and provides recommendations at sale.

Marketing

Market Analyst

A market analyst studies and prepares the market studies for the area and gives analysis of competition. This study assists in determining the "highest and best use" of the property and development and provides underwriting for the proposed concept. In addition, vacancy and absorption trends provide direction for the developer in projecting cash flows for project economics.

Brokers and Leasing Agents

These agents identify potential tenants or buyers and negotiate the terms of the lease or contract either independently or for the developer.

Advertising Agencies

Developers often contract with advertising agencies to develop programs and visual aids to be used in providing advertising to the public.

Public Relations Agencies

Working closely with advertising agencies, public relations firms develop and send messages of image to the public for the project or the developer.

Marketing Manager

A marketing manager generally works for the developer in the overall marketing of the project.

Property Management

Property Manager

This individual manages the project during and after lease-up and often handles lease renewals.

Maintenance and Operations Managers

This individual or individuals manage or maintain the physical plant of the property and respond to tenant or occupant requests.

Service Vendors

Service vendors are those companies responsible for providing services such as elevator repair and maintenance, landscaping, janitorial, security, window cleaning, major equipment preventive maintenance, water treatment, irrigation, supplies, and equipment rental.

Asset Manager

This individual oversees the property management company when the developer contracts with other management companies for marketing and property management.

Attorney

The counsel provides insight into all real estate matters in negotiations, and agreement, financing, zoning, securities, litigation, and taxes. Since many are specialists, the developer may have many different individuals within one company or different companies providing the required service.

Accountant

Individuals or a company is hired to provide accounting and records of the cash flow of revenue and expenditures. Large developers have their own accounting departments responsible for all accounting procedures.

LINEAR RESPONSIBILITY MATRIX

The linear responsibility matrix (see Figure 6–2) defines each of the development work tasks and indicates the individuals responsible for those tasks. This matrix can be used to develop the list of services required for your development as discussed previously and assist in the formulation of the total development team and budget projections.

How to Select the Team Members

Based on the size of the developer's in-house staff and experience level in the product type to be developed, the developer should list the potential work tasks required for the project. From this list, the team composition can be determined. The team will vary in size depending on the type of property to be developed. Some team members will come from his staff, while the remainder will be from outside professionals. The process used to assemble the team should be as follows:

1. Determine a list of services required.
2. Make a list of potential professionals.
3. Ask for proposals from the professionals.
4. Interview the principals and their staff: It is important to evaluate the consultant's staff in that they will be your daily contacts and will accomplish the work.
5. Check references and financial strength of company if important (i.e., contractors).
6. Develop a short list.
7. Conduct additional interviews to develop list of intangibles.
8. Make a decision and negotiate contracts prior to final selection. (Ensure that each has or can carry adequate errors and omissions insurance.)

LINEAR RESPONSIBILITY MATRIX

PROPERTY _____

TASK DESCRIPTION	DEVELOPMENT	FINANCING	APPRAISER	CONSTRACTOR	CONST. MGR.	ARCHITECT	ENGINEERS	CONSULTANTS	MANAGEMENT	MARKETING	LEGAL	ACCOUNTING
DETERMINE DEVELOPMENT CONCEPT	X											
SITE SELECTION ACTIVITY:												
FIND LAND PARCEL	X											
OBTAIN ATTORNEY	X											
IF ZONING IS REQUIRED:	X											
MEET WITH COUNTY OFFICIALS	X										X	
MEET WITH NEIGHBORHOOD GROUPS	X										X	
MEET WITH PLANNING BOARD	X										X	
CONTRACT FOR THE PROPERTY	X										X	
ADVANCE EARNEST MONEY	X										X	
COMPLETE TITLE SEARCH												
PUT UP EARNEST MONEY DEPOSIT	X										X	
SELECT LIST OF POTENTIAL TEAM PLAYERS	X											
INTERVIEW AND SELECT POTENTIAL TEAM PLAYERS	X											
COMPLETE SURVEY							X					
COMPLETE TOPOGRAPHIC SURVEY							X					
COMPLETE SOILS TEST							X					
ORDER/REVIEW PROJECT STUDIES:	X											
ENVIRONMENTAL STUDIES								X				
GEO-TECHNICAL STUDY								X				
WETLAND STUDY								X				
TRAFFIC STUDY								X				
PRELINIMARY CONSTRUCTION COSTS				X	X							
MARKET STUDY	X								X	X		
REVIEW DOT REQUIREMENTS					X		X					
DETERMINE PROCEED/QUIT DECISION	X											
PRE-DEVELOPMENT ACTIVITY:												
PRELIMINARY SITE SCHEMATICS					X							
DRAFT PRELIM. DEVELOPMENT & OPERATING PRO-FORMAS	X											
PUT TOGETHER LENDER PACKAGE		X										
OBTAIN PRELIMINARY LENDER FINANCING INTEREST		X										
PUT TOGETHER INVESTOR PACKAGE		X										
OBTAIN/REVIEW APPRAISAL		X	X									
DETERMINE LENDER/OBTAIN LOAN COMMITMENT		X										
PUT UP LENDER COMMITMENT FEE	X											
IF PRE-SALE/LEASING REQUIRED:												
PREPARE LEGAL DOCUMENTS FOR SALE/LEASE						X	X					
DRAFT MARKETING STRATEGY						X						
PREPARE MARKETING BROCHURES						X						
PREPARE MARKETING BUDGET						X						
OBTAIN MAJOR TENANT INTEREST						X						
SIGN PRE-LEASES/SALES	X					X						
COMPLETE WORKING DRAWINGS & SPECIFICATIONS					X							
PRICE OUT/REVIEW CONSTRUCTION COSTS			X									
COMPLETE VALUE ENGINEERING	X		X	X	X	X						
MAKE FINAL GENERAL CONTRACTOR SELECTION	X			X								
FINALIZE DEVELOPMENT & OPERATING PRO-FORMAS	X											
MAKE "GO" OR "NO GO" DECISION	X	X	X	X	X	X	X	X				
IF "NO" REQUEST EARNEST MONEY DEPOSIT	X											

Figure 6–2 Linear responsibility matrix.

LINEAR RESPONSIBILITY MATRIX

PROPERTY _____   Page 2 of 2

TASK DESCRIPTION	DEVELOPMENT	FINANCING	APPRAISER	CONSTRACTOR	CONST. MGR.	ARCHITECT	ENGINEERS	CONSULTANTS	MANAGEMENT	MARKETING	LEGAL	ACCOUNTING
PRE-CLOSING ACTIVITY:	X											
SET UP OWNERSHIP ENTITY	X											
ORDER TAX I.D. NUMBER	X											
SET UP BANK ACCOUNTS	X											
REVIEW ALL LOAN DOCUMENTS	X	X									X	
CLOSE PROPERTY/LOAN	X										X	
SET UP DEVELOPMENT FILES	X											
POST LOAN CLOSING ACTIVITY:												
CONSTRUCTION ACTIVITIES:												
OBTAIN ALL BUILDING/DEVELOPMENT PERMITS				X								
OBTAIN ALL BUILDER RISK POLICIES				X								
OBTAIN COMPLETION BOND				X								
COMMENCE CONSTRUCTON				X								
REVIEW CONSTRUCTION SCHEDULE				X	X							
REVIEW CHANGE ORDERS				X	X							
REVIEW LIEN WAIVERS				X	X							
REVIEW CONSTRUCTION DRAW REQUESTS				X	X							
OBTAIN G. C. COMPLETION CERTIFICATE				X								
OBTAIN CERTIFICATE OF OCCUPANCY				X								
COMPLETE PUNCH LIST	X			X	X							
REVIEW G.C. OPERATING MANUAL	X				X							
COMPLETE ALL WARRANTY WORK				X								
MANAGEMENT ACTIVITY:												
ESTABLISH ACCOUNTING CONTROLS									X			
ESTABLISH MANAGEMENT POLICIES									X			
ESTABLISH MAINTENANCE POLICIES									X			
PREPARE YEARLY OPERATING BUDGETS									X			
PREPARE YEARLY CAPITAL EXPENDITURE BUDGETS									X			
PREPARE YEARLY TAX RETURNS												X
MARKETING ACTIVITY:												
IMPLEMENT MARKETING PLAN									X	X		
OBTAIN/REVIEW & SIGN LEASES	X								X			
TENANT BUILD-OUT ACTIVITY:												
DESIGN/REVIEW TENANT SPACE				X								
COST OUT T.I.				X								
BUILD-OUT SPACE				X								
PUNCH-LIST				X								
OBTAIN CERTIFICATE OF OCCUPANCY				X								
MOVE-IN TENANT									X			
COLLECT TENANT CHARGES									X			
RESALE ACTIVITY:												
DETERMINE ASKING PRICE	X									X		
DETERMINE IF BROKER USED	X											
INTERVIEW & SELECT BROKER	X											
PREPARE LIST OF POTENTIAL PURCHASERS	X									X		
COLLECT PURCHASE OFFERS	X									X		
NEGOITATE OFFERS	X									X		
REVIEW TAX RAMIFICATIONS	X											X
CONTRACT FOR PROPERTY	X										X	
CLOSE PROPERTY	X										X	
IF REQUIRED COLLECT MORTGAGE PAYMENTS	X											

Figure 6–2   Linear responsibility matrix. (*Cont'd*)

Architect and Contractor Selection

Since the developer's greatest liability in hard costs lies in the quality of architectural/engineering design, and the quality of construction, the selection of these team members should be exercised with great care. In addition, on very large projects, the use of a well-known world class architect or contractor can be used for good advertising and public relations. Forms 6–5A and 6–5B can be used for evaluating these professionals so the very best selection can occur.

VALUES IN THE SELECTION OF CONSULTANTS

In hiring employees and commissioning work, the developer normally makes his selections based on the consultants' credentials, slickness of the brochure, magnitude of work accomplished to date, referrals, and size of staff only to find that the service, creativity, and overall relationship during the project is difficult and disappointing. The relationship is then terminated and the developer must go through the process of developing another team, which can be very time consuming. One of the reasons for this dilemma is neglecting to focus on the value system of the potential employee or consultant. The values of a person or a company are those inner characteristics which drive the individual to accomplish at a particular quality level. It is easy to sell someone with a slick presentation, but how do they perform in day-to-day challenges? This is written as a challenge to the developer to search this matter out carefully and develop a process for understanding this intangible in the selection of a team. Form 6–1 contains a segment that can be used to evaluate the values which individual team members in their disciplines must possess to perform a successful service.

REQUESTING PROPOSALS AND PREDEVELOPMENT BUDGETING

In formulating the budget for predevelopment costs, after the team members have been selected, a proposal should be requested based on the program. Each consultant should prepare a proposal broken into the following parts.

- The scope of responsibilities should be broken into the various services to be performed. Since the planning efforts could be terminated prior to completion, each professional should list each service by phase.

  Predevelopment services

  Construction documentation services

  Construction administration services

- The schedule of time necessary to perform the service should be determined. Since the developer will be on a tight schedule, each professional must be committed to perform in a specified time. Sometimes penalties can be defined for a failure to perform.
- Another part of the agreement is the fee and payment schedule. The fee schedule can be negotiated as a fixed fee, an hourly rate, or a percentage of the costs. It is advisable to have the consultant quote a fee with a guaranteed maximum cost for the service, but billing only actual costs until the ceiling has been reached. This allows the developer to terminate the service at any time and pay only for work accomplished to date.
- It is as important for the consultant to define what his or her service is as well as what it is not. Be sure to review all of quoted billings. For instance, what are reimbursable costs in addition to fees and what are not? Computer services and expensive architectural models and renderings, and multiple copies of reports and construction documents cannot be overlooked. If the consultant is from out of town, expect extensive travel and communications costs.

Proposed Contracts

After you have received the proposal, request that the consultant or contractor send you a copy of a standard contract with any special stipulations which this project may require. A cursory understanding of the consultant's perspective of the working relationship before the performance of any service should be understood. If it is unsatisfactory, then another consultant can be chosen. A careful review of these contracts by your attorney will reveal many issues that should be resolved.

Predevelopment Budget

Now with a list of the work required during predevelopment and proposals from the individual team members, the developer can formulate a predevelopment budget and as can be seen in Figure 6–5, develop schedules for cash flow analysis and predevelopment management. The predevelopment budget format in Figure 6–4 will provide a basis for developing this budget and approving expenditures for each phase of the work. This budget format is very simple and can be expanded or reduced. If one of the items listed is not used, simply leave blank. If others are needed from your team listing, delete some and add others.

MANAGING THE BUDGET: THE DEVELOPER'S "SEED MONEY"

After the completion of the predevelopment budget, the developer must identify sources for these funds. He may have already used some of his own resources such as earnest money for the land contract, so the balance of the predevelopment budget must be funded before beginning these work efforts. These funds will be at risk so the developer must manage them carefully. This "seed money" as it is called, comes from the developer's funds, joint venture partners, or from lines of credit. If in the final analysis, the venture is a "no go" then these resources will be lost forever. This section will list potential expenditures for this seed money at various points along the development process.

Phase 1: Site Selection Seed Money

Phase 1 is the period from land contracting until the time that feasibility studies and legal review are completed.

Land Acquisition

- Earnest or option money
- Legal fees for the contract
- Title fees
- Survey
- Topographic survey
- Soils tests
- Rezoning
- Aerial photography

Project Studies

- Feasibility studies
- Market studies
- Environmental impact study
- Traffic study
- Development scheduling
- Contracting strategies

Phase 2: Predevelopment Seed Money

Phase 2 is the period from the end of the completion of the feasibility studies and legal review until financing has been secured.

Design Fees

- Lender's package (architectural/engineering and cost estimations)

Marketing Expenses

- Preliminary brochure
- Marketing costs to obtain an anchor tenant

Financing Expenses

- Costs of financing package

Phase 3: Preconstruction or Preclosing Seed Money

Phase 3 is the time period from the "go ahead" decision or securing financing up until the closing of the construction loan.

Construction Expenses

- Advances to the general contractor to mobilize and order long lead time materials
- Permits and other fees
- Demolition
- Sitework

Design Expenses

- Preparation of construction documents

Marketing Expenses

- Final brochures and marketing material
- Design of marketing office and model rooms
- Advances to marketing personnel
- Promotional expenses

Financing Expenses

- Commitment fees

Phase 4: During Construction Seed Money and Equity Advances

Phase 4 begins once the construction loan is closed and the construction is started. Depending on the timing of construction loan draws, the developer may advance funds from out of pocket for short periods of time until reimbursement by lender. Equity advances will be funded if the development is over budget and the construction loan for those expenses is expended.

Predevelopment Budget Management

To manage these seed monies effectively, a system must be developed for the manager to use, to expedite approvals, initiate work efforts, control expenditures, approve invoices, and accurately report expenditures. The system which will be described can be used by the manager throughout the total development process, and if managed effectively, will result in a great savings of time. The following paragraph and diagrams will describe what we call the Predevelopment Work Order System.

Predevelopment Work Order System

This system was developed to control the work efforts and expenditures during the development process. After agonizing hours of telephone conversations seeking to reconcile invoices, the system was developed whereby a manager

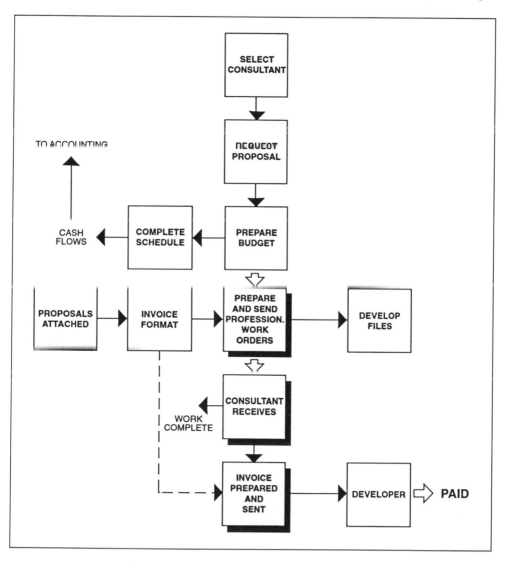

Figure 6-3 Professional work order system.

PREDEVELOPMENT BUDGET

PROJECT _____

APPROVED BY _____
DATE ____/____/____

DESCRIPTION	AMOUNT
ARCHITECTURAL DESIGN–ENGINEERING	$_____
LANDSCAPE ARCHITECTURAL DESIGN	$_____
INTERIOR DESIGN	$_____
MASTER PLANNING	$_____
TENANT PLANNING	$_____
CIVIL ENGINEERING	$_____
ENERGY CONSULTANT	$_____
CODE CONSULTANT	$_____
PARKING DECK DESIGN	$_____
BOUNDARY–TOPOGRAPHICAL SURVEY	$_____
SOIL EXPLORATION/GEO-TECHNICAL STUDIES	$_____
TRAFFIC STUDIES	$_____
ELEVATOR CONSULTANT	$_____
LAND OPTION	$_____
ATTORNEY	$_____
GRAPHIC CONSUTLANT	$_____
SCHEDULING CONSULTANT	$_____
CONSTRUCTION MANAGER	$_____
MARKETING VISUAL AIDS AND MODELS	$_____
MARKET STUDIES	$_____
FINANCING PACKAGE	$_____
DEVELOPER REIMBURSIBLES	$_____
CONSULTANT REIMBURSIBLES	$_____
CONTINGENCY	$_____
MISCELLANEOUS	$_____
_____	$_____
_____	$_____
_____	$_____
_____	$_____
_____	$_____
_____	$_____
_____	$_____
TOTAL	$_____

Figure 6-4   Predevelopment budget form.

could understand exactly what expenditures had been authorized, what the consultants understood had been authorized, the percentage of work completed to date, and easy approvals of consultant invoices in minutes. The system is made up of the following:

- An approved predevelopment budget (Figure 6–4)
- A schedule of those activities to be performed per this budget (Figure 6–5)
- The proposals (received from consultants)
- Individual work order requests (Figure 6–6)
- Invoicing procedures including their format (Figure 6–7)
- Folder to contain all work order requests for that project (to be acquired and filed)
- Cash flow projections per month developed from the schedule (bottom of Figure 6–4)

Copies of the complete set of forms for use in this process will follow this section.

Work Order System Procedures

The diagram on page 167 shows the sequential procedures to follow in using the work order system (see Figure 6–3).

SCHEDULING WORK TASKS

The best way to project development costs and to manage the development process is to schedule all the activities to be accomplished by the team. Using scheduling tools will give duration of activities, set milestones for work task completions, and identify critical path sequencing. Only in this way can the developer relate the complex set of work tasks to be completed. Valuable insight into the relationships between zoning, financing, design, marketing, construction, and a host of other activities will be gained. Use of the schedule will allow the developer to manage the team so that vital input is received when critical decisions are necessary.

Schedules will be used for different reasons at different times during the process. Some formats will be the similar, but differing objectives, depending on the composition of the team at that time. Obviously, the initial schedules will be "broad brush" or summary types listing major work tasks with few details. Then as the team grows and the frenzy of activity increases, the schedules become more detailed. In the development process, the development manager, the construction manager, the contractor, and the schedule consultant should have the capability to develop detailed schedules for the process to flow smoothly. Even though we are discussing the predevelopment process, we are going to describe schedules

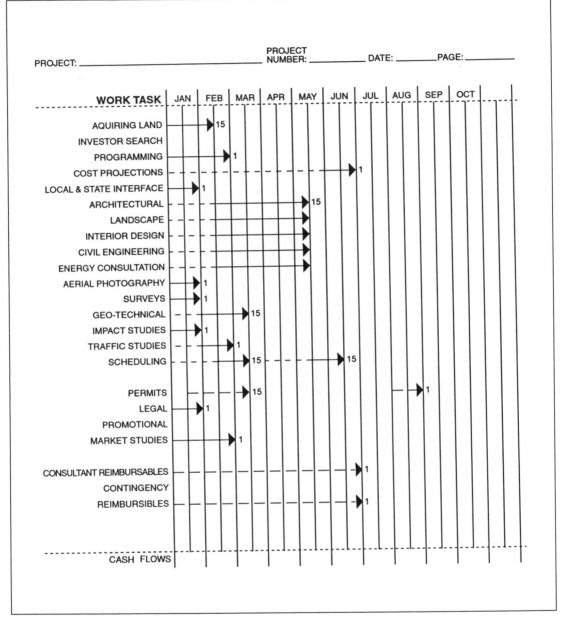

Figure 6–5 Predevelopment schedule.

WORK ORDER REQUEST

PROJECT: AT & T PROMENADE   NO. 3511

PROFESSIONAL WORK ORDER # 24

TO: THOMPSON, VENULETT, STAINBACK & ASSOCIATES
    CNN TOWER
    TWELFTH FLOOR NORTH
    ATLANTA, GEORGIA 30303

WORK DESCRIPTION:
    Predevelopment/Pricing documents for office building & parking deck as per item number I & II
of the September 7, 19XX proposal. Basic services: Architecture plus structural, mechanical,
electrical, plumbing, and fire protection engineering.

COMPLETION DATE: ASAP   COPIES NEEDED: As requested

FEE NOT TO EXCEED $502,000
                  ($81,371) Deleted Civil and Parking Master Plan
                  ----
                  $420,629
                    $1,518 Post Office
                   $37,450 Energy Study
                   $21,400 Pkg. Deck Functional Design
                    $4,708 Elev. Consultant, Phase III
                   $46,945 Revised Scope Doc. (Bldg. 1)
                   $36,035 Demolition Design

                  $568,685

REIMBURSABLES NOT
TO EXCEED: $30,000
                  $15,000 Revised

                  $45,000
                  $15,000 Revised

                  $60,000

REVIEWED AND AUTHORIZED
_____
DATE ___/___/___

Figure 6–6 Work order request.

INVOICING INSTRUCTIONS

Attached is a Work Order Request form which is your written authorization to preform the work described at the authorized cost indicated on the Work Order Request. This authorized cost my not be exceeded without first receiving additional approval from _____.

This Work Order Request form serves not only as your work authorization, but also as our means of tracking design costs. It is imperative that you reference the project number as well as the correct Work Order Number when invoicing. Please submit your invoices in a format which includes the following information for each item included on the invoice to help us expedite the process necessary for your payment.

All reinbursable expenses require backup documentation, Also when invoicing for work performed on an hourly basis with guaranteed maximum fees, hourly recapitulations are required.

PROJECT NAME _____

WORK ORDER # _____

AUTHORIZED FEE AMOUNT	FEE EARNED	LESS PAYMENTS RECEIVED	NET DUE
$_____	$_____	$_____	$_____

Thank you for your cooperation,

Sincerely,

Figure 6–7 Invoicing instructions.

that will come into play after the construction start so that the potential developer can see what is needed ahead of time.

The type of schedules used in this section will be time-scaled precedence diagrams. They are a combination of the bar chart diagram and the critical path method of scheduling. They are time scaled and networked with precedence relationships. Only in this way can the team see which activities are planned to be accomplished simultaneously. These schedules can be produced using computer simulation programs, manually, or with computer aided design (CAD).

The following will describe the varying types of schedules to be used and give examples of their appearance.

Predevelopment Budget Scheduling

This schedule can be found in the previous section on predevelopment budgets. It is simplified and gives the total picture for the development manager, allowing him to budget, select the proper team, and project cash flow (see Figure 6–4).

Summary Schedule

Used in marketing and financing proposals, the summary schedule gives only the key overall tasks to be completed and their durations. In a major project, it would illustrate the various major components to be completed on the master plan—that is, office buildings, sitework, hotels, residential, and athletic clubs (see Figure 6–8).

Summary Design and Construction Schedule

This schedule will focus only on the design and construction and provide more general detail for these work tasks only (see Figure 6–9).

Detailed Design Schedule

Meetings will be held with only the design members of the team to gather detailed information about their needs from other team members. With commitments from these members of the team to produce defined amounts of work within specific periods of time, this schedule is developed to manage the process. Using this schedule, biweekly meetings are held using near term scheduling to manage the process and to provide reports on the progress (see Figure 6–10).

The three previous schedules will occur during the production of construction documents. The detailed foundation superstructure and skin schedule, the detailed construction schedule, and near-term schedules occur at the beginning and during construction. These three are described in detail in Chapter 11.

MANAGING THE PROCESS

Once the predevelopment budget is approved, the team is selected, and the overall work tasks are scheduled, a startup meeting of the total team is recommended before beginning the work. In this meeting, the program can be reviewed, regular coordination meetings set, communications and relationships can be established, and questions answered. The developer may want to break the team down into smaller groups like design and construction, marketing and

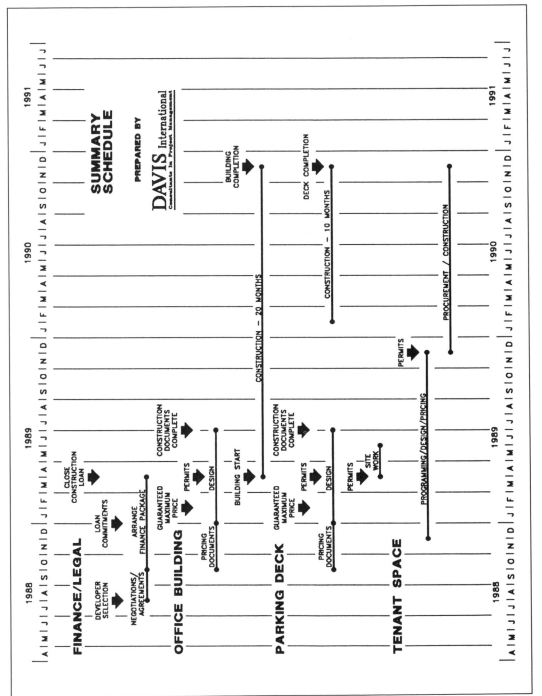

Figure 6-8 Summary schedule.

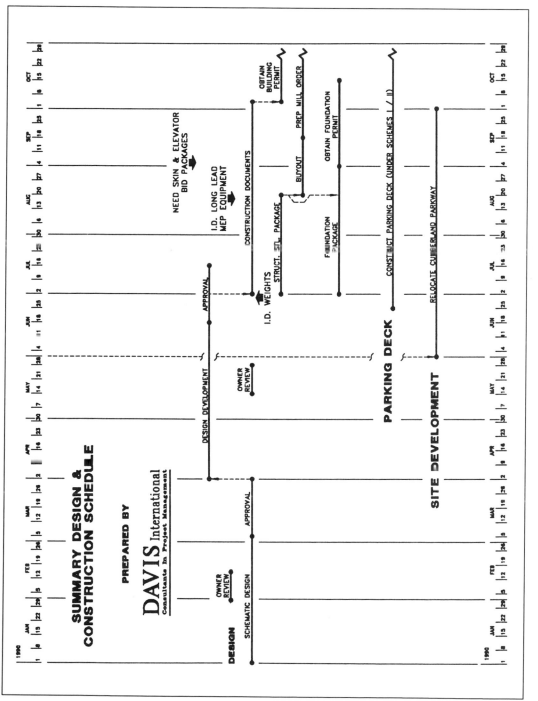

Figure 5-9   Summary design and construction schedule.

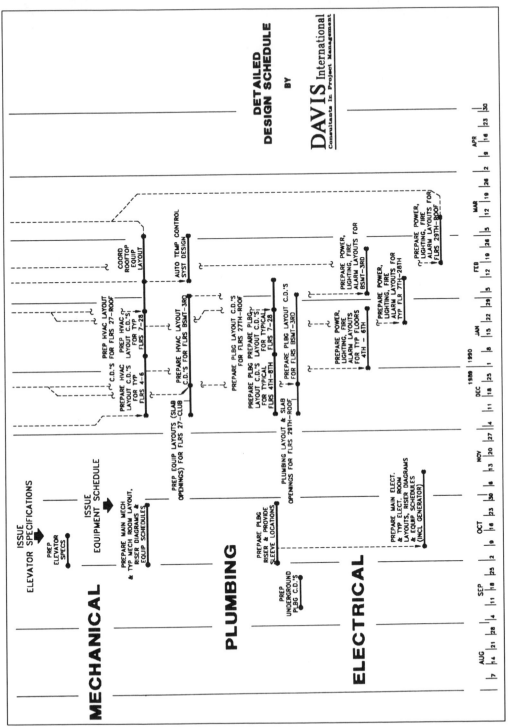

Figure 6–10 Detailed design schedule.

176

property management, or legal and project finance, if appropriate. Very large projects are managed more effectively in this manner.

As the leader, the developer must understand the responsibilities of the team members to fully understand and use them effectively. Once the team is in motion, the developer becomes the expediter and decision maker, and to accomplish this with the fewest problems, he must know his team. The following paragraphs will consider the responsibilities of the team, the coordination of the team, and value engineering.

RESPONSIBILITIES OF THE PLAYERS

The following is a list of the development functions and the team members who will manage these functions. In our communities some of these functions can be handled differently. This is just a typical pattern for generalized information.

Legal Matters

All legal matters are usually managed by an attorney with real estate experience. The developer should contract with an experienced real estate attorney who is an expert in all legal matters pertaining to the development. Some of these are as follows:

Land Purchase Agreement

Initially, the attorney will prepare and help negotiate the land purchase agreement.

Zoning

The properties zoning classification should be verified. The attorney can contact the local zoning department and request a letter be sent on their stationary verifying the classification. If the property has to be rezoned or needs a variance, the attorney can develop a checklist of the steps required by the local zoning authority and then submit an application. A more in-depth analysis of the zoning process was given in Chapter 5.

Title Search

The attorney can initiate the title search to verify the owner of record, as well as reveal defects on the title. Since the developer will not be able to finance property with clouds on the title, the sooner the developer is aware of potential title problems, the more time there will be to correct them. The title search will also show recorded land and deed restrictions.

Survey

Once the survey has been certified by a registered surveyor, the attorney will review it to verify its completeness. The survey should illustrate recorded easements or encroachments.

Existing Leases

If the property involves any current leases, the attorney should review their terms and conditions. If the developer must terminate the existing leases, the attorney can give guidance into legal procedures.

Potential Litigation

Since the development process involves many legal documents, there is always the possibility of litigation between parties. An attorney who is an expert in contract law can help the developer avoid this litigation.

Professional Services Agreement Documentation

The documents for professional contract should be drafted and reviewed by the attorney.

Scheduling

From the beginning to the end of development projects, a scheduling consultant can provide the necessary expertise for managing and illustrating on a schedule the activities of the development. This is addressed in more detail earlier in this chapter. The scheduler can provide the following types of schedules and reports in general; the development manager and contractor can also be responsible for these functions.

Development Scheduling: The development scheduling will detail all of the functions of each of the team members and will show in a visual graphic the time allotted for each.

Design and Construction Scheduling: The design and construction scheduling should be done in conjunction with the various design consultants and the general contractor. These schedules will show the design and construction process from starting the sitework to the end of the warranty periods.

Project Status Reporting: The schedule consultant and contractor can provide monthly status reports for the developer and lender's staff.

Engineering Specialists

Engineering specialists collect data, study that data, or provide recommendations as to existing conditions. In the beginning of land development because of many unknowns, there are many risks. These engineers must be commissioned to uncover problem areas or verify that there are no problems on your selected site, which must be overcome. The way in which the challenges are resolved will help minimize the developer's risks. If the following items are left as unknowns, they can represent significant risk to the development.

Boundary Survey

A registered surveyor should be retained to complete an updated survey of the property. To help the developer visualize the total land involved in his purchase, the civil engineer should place markers and flags along the boundaries of the property. This survey will help to confirm the actual area that will be purchased. Many land purchase contracts will be based on a fixed dollar amount per actual acreage.

Topographic Survey

A registered surveyor will illustrate on drawings through field work the contours or topography of your site. This survey is essential in determining the amount of earthwork that will have to be moved during sitework construction. The topographic survey will show the contours of the land in predetermined intervals, usually from two to ten feet. Earthwork is a costly item in sitework construction costs. Therefore, it is very important to be as accurate as possible when calculating these costs.

- Title, property location, owner's name, engineer certification, and date of survey
- True and magnetic north
- Scale
- Existing easements, rights of ways on or adjacent to the subject property
- Names of the adjacent property owners
- Location of any existing structures on the property, building elevations, wall, curb, step, tree wells, drives, and parking lot locations
- Location and sizes of existing storm and sewer systems
- Outline of any wooded area, locations, types, and sizes of large caliper trees
- Water features: lakes, ponds, or streams
- Utility pole locations
- Rock outcropping locations
- Road elevations at predetermined intervals
- Grid system of elevations at predetermined intervals
- Predetermined contour intervals
- Utilities
- Existing building locations

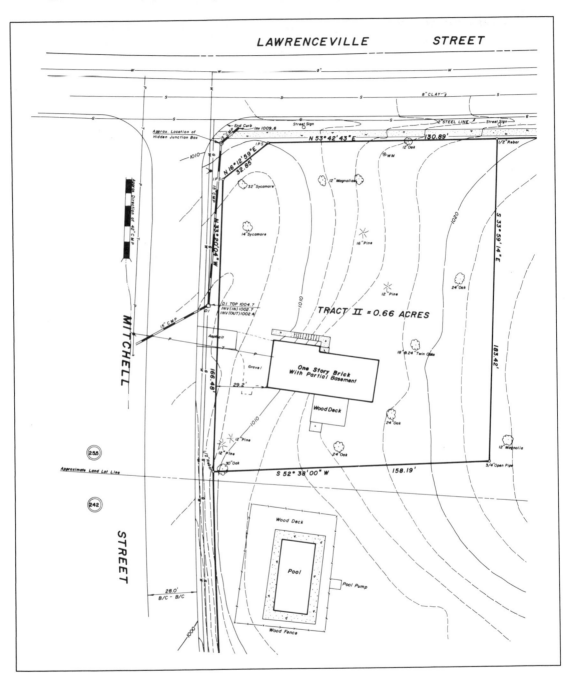

Figure 6-11 Boundary and topographical survey.

- Legal descriptions
- Metes and bounds

Geo-Technical Studies

One of the great unknown development costs is due to unseen soil conditions. Rock formations, underground water, poor soil, or hazardous toxic soil can add to site development costs. If these are discovered, the purchase price should be renegotiated. The following are used to determine the soil conditions: Materials and soils testing engineers or geo-technical engineers will be responsible for this work.

Soil Borings: Borings are taken of the soil and rock at different elevations and these samples of the soil are tested to analyze the soil contents and type of rock formations.

Seismic Tests: Seismic tests are taken using sound waves to verify the depth of rock formations.

Compaction Tests: Compaction tests are used when the dirt has been moved to another area of the property. It verifies the compact strength of the new soil.

Perk Tests: Perk tests are used to measure the absorption of water into the soil.

Sound Control

Often, depending on the use for the property, the local authorities might require a sound control study. This study will show the potential increase of noises to the area. This is typical along freeways, near airports, or for large manufacturing facilities.

Environmental Testing

Environmental testing is used to verify the presence of chemical pollutants in the air or soil.

Traffic

New development attracts more people and more people use more automobiles. Traffic engineers study the movement of traffic in response to growth of communities. In addition, they have expertise in the design of roadways and parking decks. They play major roles in the rezoning of property and the design and analysis of roadway systems.

Utility Services

The engineer should confirm that existing utility services are adequate for the proposed development. If the utility services are not adequate, the engineer must determine whether they can be improved, and at what cost. Since utility letters showing service to the property are required by lenders, the engineer should request that each utility should send written acknowledgment of availability. Civil engineers can supply assistance in these matters.

Storm Water Detention and or Treatment

Civil engineers will work with local and national regulatory agencies in the control and preservation of wetlands and waterways. Local development authorities will require a plan for releasing water from the property. Since the detention of water is a potential user of the land, it directly affects the square footage of developable land. It should be determined exactly how much area will be required to comply with applicable codes and policies, and where on the site the required facilities will be located.

Ground Cover

The landscape architect and civil engineer will provide assistance for these efforts. Certain local tree removal and preservation ordinances can effectively prevent the development of certain sites unless there is compliance with set standards. The costs for these improvements should be determined as early as possible in the planning stages of the development.

Specially Designated Property Uses

The registered surveyor should review the property to see if it is included in any of the following restricted property uses and note these items on the survey:

- National forest
- Wildlife preserve
- Fire hazard area
- Earthquake zone
- Historical site
- Flood plain
- Hazardous dump
- Archeological site

Master Planning, Architectural, and Engineering Design

The architect and his structural, mechanical, electrical, and plumbing engineers are responsible for analysis of the development program in the context of the community, using codes and creativity to create the product which the developer markets.

Schematic Drawings: The architect and engineers produce schematic drawings for developer approval to illustrate the master plan and architectural design.

Design Development Drawings: These drawings are produced by the architect and engineers as the second stage in documents production for designing and pricing the product for development and marketing. Twenty percent into design development drawings is a good definition for the predevelopment documents, lenders package, pricing documents, or scope drawings.

Construction Drawings: The third and final stage in the production of drawings for pricing and construction. The set which will be bid for bid proposals. The set by which the building will be constructed.

Specifications: Produced by the architect and engineers, these specifications give more specific and detailed information not found on the construction drawings. Together with the construction drawings they become the total construction documents set.

Program

The development program is created and managed by the development manager, architect, or interior designer depending on the exact scope and magnitude relative to the project.

Construction Administration

During the construction phase of the project the architect and engineers verify that the building is constructed according to plans and specifications and approve construction draw requests by the contractor relative to percentage of work completed.

Master Planning

During the predevelopment phase, the architect or land planner will meet with the developer to discuss the development concept. The developer will then give the architect the basic property and development information.

- Property location
- Property size (acreage)
- Current zoning
- Type of proposed development
- Copy of the survey and topographic survey

After the review, the architect will contact the local zoning and building department to verify the current zoning and acquire the necessary building codes to which the development must conform. The architect should obtain the following information:

Local Planning Department

- Current zoning use
- Possible zoning classifications

- Building restrictions
  - Units per acre
  - Square feet per acre
  - Height limitations
  - Setback requirements
  - Parking ratios
  - Opening requirements
- Procedure for rezoning and variance
- Rezoning decision in process
- Approval of variances
- Approvals for entrance signage

Local Building Department

- Plan approval process
- Necessary permits and process
- Cost of permits

Local Utility Departments

- Contacts for information
- Current or proposed moratoriums
- Permit process
- Utility hook-up fees
- Easements required
- Construction timing
- Monthly operating charges per square foot
- Services guarantee or allotments

Local Fire Department

- Fire safety requirements
- Interpretation of codes
- Applicable codes

Local Department of Transportation

- Acceleration and deceleration lane requirements
- Is a bond required for this work?
- Specifications for this work?

With this information in hand, the architect can then lay out the preliminary plans and sketches. The preliminary plans and specifications will then be incorporated into the developer's financial package, which will include the following:

- Site plan
- Exterior elevations
- Interior floor plans
- Wall sections
- Rendering
- Outline specifications

This package of preliminary plans will then be given to the general contractor. Based on this information and his past experience, the general contractor should be able to provide the developer with a very accurate cost for the development. If the development will be bid out by more than one general contractor, the developer should ensure that a detailed bid specification sheet requests the detail of the estimates which the developer desires to see in the estimated costs. By using this method, the developer will be able to compare "apples to apples" in the bid process, the developer can be sure that all bidders have included all of the items which are required.

Graphics

Graphics are sometimes designed by the architect, interior designer, or graphics designer, who is responsible for the directional signage of the project and the identifying signage at the buildings and entrances to the site.

Interior Design

The architect or interior designer can perform this service. The responsibility can include programming, selection of finishes, furniture, art work, graphics, fixtures, and equipment.

Construction

The general contractor, fabricators, and subcontractors perform the role during construction.

Contractor Selection

The developer, with recommendations of architect or engineers, is responsible for contractor selection.

Subcontractor Selection

The contractor with approval by developer and recommendation from the architect, engineers, and interior designer is responsible for subcontractor selection.

Construction Cost Estimate

The responsibility of construction cost estimates lies with contractor and subcontractors with review by architects and engineers.

Project Economics, Capital Costs, and Cash Flows

The development manager (developer) along with the staff of financial analysts and accountants are responsible for capital costs and cash flows.

Hard Costs: (design and construction numbers) Developer's design and construction managers with estimates and proposals contractors, architects, engineers, and other consultants produce estimates of hard costs.

Soft Costs: (financing, insurance, revenues and expenses) Soft costs are the responsibility of development manager, marketing manager, property manager, financial analysts and accountants.

Marketing Feasibility

Marketing feasibility refers to data collected by the development and marketing managers using real estate brokers or market analysts. During this period, the marketing staff will review current market conditions. If the developer requires any preleasing or presales, the marketing managers will be seeking commitments from potential space users. This process will take a series of meetings between the prospect, the developer, the design team, and the general contractor. The final outcome of these meetings will hopefully be a signed lease which will be prepared by the developer's attorney.

Advertising and Public Relations

Generally, the advertising and public relations matters are produced by firms who specialize in these disciplines, but approved, managed, and commissioned by the development and marketing managers.

Budgets and Strategic Planning

Created by the directors of marketing services, development and marketing managers create the budgets and strategic planning. Responsibility of developer to monitor for results.

Marketing Centers and Visual Aids

Many team members work with visual aids and marketing centers. They are programmed by marketing managers, designed by architects and interior designers, staffed by agents and brokers, and managed by the developer and marketing managers.

Marketing Agreements

All marketing agreements are negotiated by the developer, the attorney, and the marketing manager.

Tenant Leases and Sales Contracts

Standard forms are developed by the attorney, but negotiated and completed by the developer or marketing manager.

Property Managers and Operations

Managers ensure that the property and equipment function as planned. They provide input into the programming for the proper design of systems. They not only provide tenant interface to satisfy the needs of the customer, but also are responsible for formulating the operating and capital improvements budgets annually. They manage the property to perform under predicted proforma. Their staff supervises equipment maintenance, landscaping, janitorial, lease renewals, capital improvements, renovations, and tenant construction.

> **Service Contracts:** These contracts are provided by the vendors, reviewed by the attorney, and negotiated by the property manager.
>
> **Management Contracts:** Created by the attorney, management contracts are negotiated by the developer and property manager.

Financing

Depending on the size of the development company, the developer, chief financial officer, or the director of project finance will have day-to-day contact with various funding sources. If not, then when a potential development is identified, the developer must find financing for debt or equity. The developer will either obtain the financing required or will contract with a mortgage broker to find it. See Chapter 9 for additional information.

Accounting/Draw Requests/Payment of Billings

Most accounting issues are managed by the developer's staff or contracted out with a CPA (certified public accountant).

Equity

Equity can be from many sources: the developer's own funds, the funds of friends, other lenders, or syndicators.

Debt

Debt is usually acquired by the developer or broker from banks, institutions, or corporations such as insurance companies.

Agreements

All agreements are negotiated using attorneys, developer, and staff of financing and accounting department.

Taxes and the IRS

The accounting department or the CPA handles tax and IRS matters.

Partners and Joint Ventures

Sometimes found by the developer, attorney, or financing staff search for suitable partners.

COORDINATION OF MEETINGS: MAKING IT HAPPEN

In the process of making the development happen, the developer should develop a series of ongoing meetings to ensure that all activities are being coordinated properly by the team and that the development is proceeding as planned. The following listing and descriptions provided are a sampling of the types of meetings that can be used to make management more effective.

Initial Team Member Interviews

At these meetings, the potential consultant presents his or her credentials and the developer completes an evaluation. The initial team member meetings are primarily for major consultants and contractors.

Initial Startup Meetings

When the total team comes together for a review of the program, direction, and for questions and answers prior to starting work, the members help set up overall organizational issues.

Biweekly and In-House Staff Meetings

The total in-house development team, including development, design and construction, marketing, property management, and project finance meet biweekly to review and report on the status of the project. Usually, schedules and cost reports are provided.

Biweekly Scheduling Meetings

The total design and construction team meets to report on status of commitments and to set strategy for future work tasks. This meeting also becomes a forum for requesting information and providing answers to various questions previously asked.

Monthly Joint Venture Meetings

Usually on a monthly or quarterly schedule, members involved in the joint venture meet to report on the total progress of the project and to solicit decisions on joint approvals. Such meetings also serve as a forum for developing future strategies.

Business Planning Meetings

On an annual basis, the total developer's staff should meet to develop strategic and tactical planning for the coming year; this meeting usually occurs in the later months of the year.

Design Review Meetings

Because the physical form of the project represents the tastes of the developer and that which he wishes to provide for the customer, the developer will need ongoing meetings to approve the design decisions. The issues presented and discussed can cover subjects from landscaping to graphics.

Biweekly Marketing Review Meetings

Because the success of marketing determines the success of the initial phases of the project, the developer will desire to keep abreast of the status of prospecting and signed leases. Reports should be provided and sent to the lenders.

Helpful Hints for All Meetings

In the process of being a part of a meeting or providing its leadership, the developer should direct that the following issues be addressed to use time wisely.

- Have a clear objective
- Have a typed agenda
- A set time and place
- A set duration
- Require punctuality
- Counsel team members privately on effectiveness
- Always be prepared
- Minimize the number of meetings
- Minimize interruptions
- Minimize the number of participants (Rule: The length of the meeting will be directly proportional to the number of people present)
- Produce memorandums of the decisions (copy for appropriate team members and file for future reference)
- Make each session a time where decisions are made so that action can be taken as soon as possible.
- Make sure each person is introduced
- If not necessary to meet, then don't

VALUE ENGINEERING: AN ONGOING CHALLENGE

Value engineering is the act of making decisions affecting the costs of a project in such a way that the development not only retains its value, but its value increases over time. The value engineering process is ongoing until the project is complete and the sum of its decisions must strengthen and not weaken your potential for success. Each decision, like changing one item for another, must in the total, give the developer, marketing and property managers a product that will lease effectively and perform efficiently.

Value engineering is a process which begins with the initial production of the project economics and continues through the initiation of capital improvements long after the contractor has departed from the site. Almost every economic decision made by the developer will involve value engineering. The experience of value engineering is like firing a missile from a ship, yet not knowing the missile's final destination. Over time and with each piece of information, the target is clearly defined. Then using radar, and with each new piece of information, and the known target, the missile is guided carefully to the objective. While guiding the value engineering process, the developer must be flexible and resourceful in finding solutions for each new challenge.

Each piece of cost information provided at different times within the process will be directly related to the assumptions which are made in providing that information. The secret of value engineering is to minimize the number of assumptions which exist. When these are eliminated, the guarantee of a project produced within the budget and on time will be in sight.

The process of value engineering is a dynamic process. It involves all the members of the team and their individual desires and goals for the project. The developer as the key decision maker must have his objectives clearly set to move through the myriad of opinions presented. Input must be evaluated in terms of marketing, property management, financing, and risk. Each discipline must realize that the key to a successful venture is satisfying the customer's needs rather than illogically demanding their pet project. The magnitude of the value engineering effort will occur during the predevelopment and construction phases of the project. Herein, we will focus on that period.

Within this chapter we will provide some general discussions concerning value engineering as well as a list of the most obvious issues that the developer should consider when the price of the contractor is too high.

Miscellaneous Ways to Reduce Costs

- Reduce the amount of sitework
    - Balance cut and fill calculations
    - Minimize retaining walls
    - Use natural drainage techniques
    - Reduce the amount of paved surfaces
    - Keep as many natural areas as possible
    - Locate building for shortest distance for utility lines
    - Build using the contours of the land
- Construction of the exterior of the building
    - Check on the safety factor of the structure (are they too high for normal engineering practices)

Consider other alternatives for the exterior facade

Consider other alternative for the roofing material

Use sloped system instead of a builtup roofing system requiring interior drains

Too many detailed surfaces make the construction of other items complicated

Reduce the amount of glass

Insulated glass may not be needed in this situation (believe it or not, there are some areas where insulated glass is not required)

If gutters are not absolutely necessary, eliminate them or devise less expensive ways to control the water

Check if an interior fireplace flue can be used instead of an expensive brick one

Choose alternatives for exterior construction which require less installation time.

- Construction of the interior of the building

Check the flooring materials—can carpet be used instead of wood or slate or whatever you are using

Reduce the height of the ceilings

Use less expensive toilet fixtures

Change the finish on the hardware

Change the type of specified accessories

Consider less expensive alternative to heating and cooling

Stack the plumbing fixtures within the building vertically to minimize distances for plumbing of water and sewer

Use paint instead of wall covering

Re-layout the floor plan to minimize doors and length of walls

Use a different kind of door

Change the window treatment—use blinds instead of curtains

Re-select paint colors for less expensive paint

Use a less sophisticated temperature control system

Reduce the number of electrical outlets

Select equipment not requiring separate circuits for the electrical

Eliminate skylights

Use standard cabinetry instead of custom design

As can be seen, the process of value engineering is unique because of the type of project, the contractor which is being used, the objectives of marketing and property management, and the project economics. There are no absolutes to use every time. The preceding were some directions where ideas for reducing cost can be explored. The next section will give a more expanded discussion concerning the subject.

How to Review Working Drawings and Specifications

When the cost estimate received exceeds the projected budget, the developer will request suggestions from all consultants about how to reduce costs. With the preliminary working drawings and specifications in hand, the development team will analyze each aspect of the design for potential ideas. These ideas will be re-priced and presented for evaluation. Then the total development team will provide input as to the implications of each decision.

Where to Cut Costs While Not Sacrificing Value

Site Work

Changing the elevations to reduce cut or fill, or raising the building to avoid rock excavation cuts costs. Relocating the roads to avoid excavation can also be helpful. In addition, the quality of roadway design can be reduced and drainage systems re-routed to save piping is a viable idea.

Landscaping Design

The landscaping design will be critical to the final outcome of the development, since it adds to the curb appeal which helps sell the final product. Using less planting and smaller planting will often reduce these costs.

Landscape Contractor: The landscape contractor will review the plans and specifications with installation costs and ultimate maintenance costs in mind. Using the landscaper, this criteria and the time of year for the planting, can recommend revisions.

Marketing: Marketing will want as much seasonal color as possible. This will give the property a better appearance.

Management: The management people will review the landscaping plan with an eye toward the maintenance costs. They will want a functional plan that has a good appearance but fits within the forecasted maintenance budget.

Exterior Building

General Contractor: The general contractor will try to reduce the construction budget by suggesting alternative materials that have a similar appearance but cost less. In reviewing the plans it might be noticed by the marketing group that by reorientation of the building a larger number of tenants can gain a better view of the adjacent lake. By making this design change, the general contractor estimates no additional construction costs, while marketing believes that they can obtain an additional $.25 per square foot rent which will increase cash flows and ultimate value.

Management: The exterior design will be analyzed by the management group to identify ideas for reducing future maintenance and replace costs. Management will also review the fire safety plan to reduce insurance costs.

Marketing: Since sizzle sells, the marketing group will want the property to show well. They will probably want to keep all of the "bells and whistles."

Interior Building

Marketing: The design of the interior spaces will be reviewed by marketing to ensure that the floor plans are competitive in their layout options in the market. It might be noticed that by increasing the size of a residential floor plan, the developer can obtain another $600.00 per year in rent because of the addition of a walk-in closet. The cost for this extra 20 square feet might be $20 per square foot or $400. The final analysis shows that for a $400 additional cost, the value of the property can be increased by $4200 ($600 × 7.0 Gross Rent Multiplier).

Management: Management can review the plan relative to efficiency in maintenance and accessibility when making major repairs.

General Contractor: The general contractor will review the plans for structural changes which can be made without altering the layout of the space.

Interior Designer: The interior designer will review the interior floor plans to identify where less expensive finishes can be used.

The Amenity Package

The amenity package will add additional costs to the development costs and the future operating costs, but without these amenities the market might not prefer this development over others.

General Contractor: The general contractor will review the amenity plans with an eye toward cost reduction and ease of installation.

Marketing: Once again, marketing will need the amenities to sell the product.

Helpful Hints for Value Engineering

Use the team members effectively in this process because the "master mind" power of their creativity will find solutions to every problem. That idea which solves a problem, costs less, and is easily maintainable is in the final analysis better than the original. Making value engineering modification like this is a lot like finding a treasure, especially when the overall project is more successful.

The developer must be an effective leader in this process because of the sensitive personalities of the designers and the pressures on the team to perform. Schedule time in the process for value engineering, because it is one of the inevitable natural activities. Don't be surprised when it must occur. Embrace it as a friend.

PROJECT MANAGEMENT PHASES

If the developer does not have in-house construction management staff and the type of project or the size of the development is substantial, he must hire a construction manager to assist in the development process. This individual or company will assist the developer in overseeing the design, construction, and scheduling of the project from concept through the post-completion activities. The following are the four phases of development that the construction project manager will need and the work tasks to be performed.

Predevelopment Phase

- Assembling the development team
- Producing development schedules
- Developing the project team organizational structure using the linear responsibility matrix
- Reviewing and assisting in negotiations of the professional services agreements
- Assisting in selecting and negotiating the fee of the general contractor
    Determining the type of contract to use
    Holdbacks
    Draw requests
    Arbitration versus litigation clauses
    Change order policies
    Scope of responsibilities
- Preparing construction and testing manual (can be prepared by the architect)
    Establishing detailed inspection procedures
    Outlining acceptance/rejection procedures
    Preparing a chart showing all the required tests, when they are needed, the frequency of sampling, the material being tested, who will perform the tests, and who will review the testing results
- Determining rights of way and construction easements
- Reviewing construction insurance policies for proper coverage

- Reviewing construction bond submittals
- Establishing the construction bid process (if applicable)
- Reviewing construction cost breakdowns
- Organizing preconstruction conference meetings
- Drafting project emergency information
- Coordinating notices to proceed
- Monitoring general contractor mobilization

Design Phase

- Development of the project team organizational structure using the linear responsibility matrix
- Production of a design schedule to coordinate all design disciplines and related procurement and developer input
- Design of a cost control model for the control of the estimated construction cost
- Development of a summary construction schedule to be used in establishing the design and procurement sequencing
- Participating in the team member meetings to verify and review the status, identify problems, obtain commitments to problem resolution actions, and develop near-term schedules
- Updating all schedules and cost controls, analyzing trends, and making recommendations
- Verifying procurement status through vendor contacts, including on-site inspections and review of vendor production schedules
- Trouble-shooting on critical problem areas to develop recovery plans and ensure their implementation
- Reviewing specifications
- Assisting in the value engineering
- Coordination of the development of a quality control plan
- Coordination of the development of a quality assurance plan

Construction Phase

- Development of the project team organizational structure using the linear responsibility matrix
- Detailed scope of work documentation with each individual contractor and subcontractor
- Development of startup occupancy activities and sequencing with the developer's staff

- Use of the team scheduling conferences to lead the construction team in the development of a coordinated overall project schedule consistent with previously established design and procurement sequencing and the startup/occupancy requirements of the developer
- Refinement of the construction cost control model to reflect the buyout status of the project
- Update and enlarge the procurement scheduling model and integrate it with the on-site construction schedule
- Coordinate the incorporation of the quality control system into the general contractor's operational procedures
- Coordinate the project team meetings on a regular basis to analyze and verify the status, identify problems, obtain and document problem solution steps, and develop near-term schedules for the next implementation cycle
- Updating all schedules and cost controls, analyzing trends, and making recommendations for action
- Review of the scheduled personnel needs in light of the area's availability, and assistance to the general contractor in developing specific plans for resolving personnel problems
- Management of the design/procurement/construction interfaces as specific potential trouble areas
- Control change order processing to minimize disruption in construction scheduling, while controlling impact of the total cost
- Pay request verifications based on earned-value schedules, stored materials verification, and quantity measurements where appropriate
- Monitoring of quality control system implementation
- Conduct the status review and projection meetings for the developer
- Coordination of the punch-out and warranty phases of the construction phase

Delay Claims Analysis Phase

Since the construction process is complex and for an extended period of time, the possibility of future developer claims against the general contractor can exist. The project construction manager should provide the following:

- Detailed review of available documentation, including schedules and schedule updates, job meetings notes/memos, progress meeting minutes, architect/engineer (A/E) site reports, superintendent daily logs, subcontractor daily logs, job-site photographs, change order requests, executed change orders, and correspondence relating to the delay claim
- Development of an as-planned schedule, reflecting initial schedule of activities and logic, to serve as a baseline for the comparison in the delay analysis

- Development of an as-built schedule, reflecting the actual schedule progress and significant events which transpired "behind the scenes" and resulted delaying impact on scheduled operations
- Analysis of results, by comparison of as-planned and as-built schedules, indicating the periods and causes of delay or acceleration, and review of the implications of the analysis with the claims team
- Preparation of a chronological summary of pertinent correspondence for attorney/client issues
- Preparation of an indexed listing of correspondence pertaining to specific claims issues
- Development of a summary of change order requests/executed change orders, reflecting basis for change order, time extensions requested versus approved, and net increase or decrease in contract amount
- Analysis of actual weather conditions versus yearly norms for job-site location based on the U.S. Weather Service Data
- Analysis of selected personnel utilization on an as-planned versus as-built basis
- Preparation of graphical displays for presentation to claims team for review, to opposition for negotiation of settlement, or for use in litigation proceedings
- Furnishing deposition information, review of plaintiff's depositions, and provision of expert testimony

THE DEVELOPER'S "GO" OR "NO GO" DECISION

Once all the team members have completed their preconstruction assignments, the developer will call a meeting to determine if the development will proceed ahead or terminate. At this meeting, the developer will once again review all of the facts and recommendations provided by the team members. The team members in this meeting will be primarily the in-house staff. The developer will confirm that management approves the building plans and specifications. If preleasing or preselling is required by the construction lender, he will verify with marketing that these commitments are firm. The developer will confirm that the mortgage broker can obtain construction and permanent loan commitments if required, under the terms and conditions most economically sensible.

The developer will ask the attorney if all of the legal documents required to close the deal are approved. The general contractor will state if all systems are "go" for beginning construction. And finally, the developer will once again review the development and operating proforma to verify that the venture makes economic sense.

If the developer does not get positive feedback from the development team, then the choice is to ask everyone to once again review their findings or pass on the deal.

At this point, if the developer does not feel just right about the deal, he should not be pushed into developing the project just because so much time and money is invested. In the long run, he will be dollars ahead of the game, if he "folds his cards" and takes short-term losses. Better to crawl out of a shallow hole than to be stuck in the bottom of a deep pit.

If the developer feels comfortable with the deal concept, but the timing is not right, an alternative would be to purchase the site and hold it until the timing improves. If this is the case, the developer must ensure these are the best terms for the purchase and that he is capable of carrying the land for an extended period of time.

To assist in the "go" or "no go" decision-making process, the developer can request the team develop a project development plan.

Project Development Plan (PDP)

The PDP is a document prepared by the development project manager describing all the various aspects of the development as currently known. Each discipline in the development process is required to provide essential input and to initial as approval on the cover of this document that all within is accurate. The developer—as the final decision maker—will review this document prior to making a final decision. The components of this document are as follows:

I.   General description of the project activity
  A. Name
  B. Description
  C. Concept
  D. Timing
II. Ownership entity
  A. Form
  B. Ownership
III. Land
  A. Location
  B. Size and features
IV. Proposed improvements
  A. Buildings
  B. Parking
  C. Amenities
  D. Plans and specifications
  E. Interior design
  F. Leasing status

V. Project economics
   A. Capital costs
   B. Project income projections
   C. Operating expenses
   D. Standard tenant allowance
   E. Tenant design budget control
   F. Projected value
   G. Projected value to developer
   H. Projected cash flow to developer
   I. Land sale proceeds
   J. Land cost allocation
VI. Development plan
VII. Development marketing strategy
VIII Financing
   A. Interim financing (construction financing)
   B. Permanent financing
   C. Guarantees and risks
IX. Administration
   A. Real estate services
   B. External team members
   C. Internal team members
   D. Fees to the development team
X. Marketing
   A. Target market
   B. Target industries
   C. Presales and preleasing
   D. Average unit or tenant size
   E. Lease-up schedule
   F. Rental rates or sales schedule
   G. Escalation
   H. Lease or sale terms
   I. Renewal or resale terms
   J. Tenant improvement allowance
   K. Concessions
   L. Commissions
   M. Parking
XI. Exhibits as needed

The Decision to Pass on the Venture

Using the previous information, the following are some reasons why the developer may pass on the development.

- Rezoning application was turned down
- Developer cannot line up an anchor tenant
- Current financing costs are too expensive to make the numbers work
- Market is starting to be overbuilt
- Projected design costs are too high
- Land sitework costs are too great
- Zoning which the developer can obtain does not give him the required density to justify the land and the development costs
- Equity requirements of the development are more than the developer can afford

PREPARING TO CLOSE THE FINANCING

Once the decision has been made to go forward, the developer and the team will make plans to close on the land and construction loan as soon as possible. The following are items that the various team members will handle during this phase.

Attorney

Financing Documents

Any documents that relate to the financing of the land or improvements should be carefully reviewed and negotiated. These documents may be the land acquisition loan, the construction loan, or the permanent loan.

Equity Venture Documents

If any partner equity is required by the developer, the attorney will prepare the partnership or joint venture documents.

Marketing Documents

The attorney should prepare the leasing, sales agreements, or any other legal documents which will be required to market the property.

Marketing

Prior to closing the construction loan, the marketing team will complete any of the necessary documents required by the lender. These documents will include:

- Executed leases or sales agreements
- Final working drawings and specifications (initialed by all parties)
- Estoppel certificates signed by the tenants

RETAINING INFORMATION: THE DEVELOPER'S FILING SYSTEM

Now that the land and the construction financing have been closed, the construction, marketing, and the management process will start. The developer and project manager should establish monitoring systems to observe every phase of the development process.

Setting Up the Development Files

An important part of the development process is to keep a well-organized set of files. The following is an outline that could be used.

1.0   Development
   1.1   Internal office correspondence
   1.2   Strategy and programming
   1.3   Project schedules
   1.4   Project development plan (PDP)
   1.5   Project reporting/meetings/correspondence
      1.5.1   Inter-office meetings
      1.5.2   Joint venture meetings/correspondence
      1.5.3   Construction lender meeting/correspondence
      1.5.4   Permanent lender meeting/correspondence
      1.5.5   Major user/correspondence
      1.5.6   Special tenants
      1.5.7   Other
      1.5.8   Management team members
      1.5.9   Civic/community organizations
      1.5.10   Legal correspondence
   1.6   Proposals
   1.7   Development proformas
   1.8   Operating proformas
   1.9   Tenant/owner's association proformas

2.0 Land Acquisition
2.1 Letter of intent
2.2 Legal description
2.3 Utility letters
    2.3.1 Electricity
    2.3.2 Gas
    2.3.3 Water
    2.3.4 Sewer
    2.3.5 Telephone
    2.3.6 Cable TV
2.4 Demographics
2.5 Maps
    2.5.1 State
    2.5.2 City
    2.5.3 County
    2.5.4 Census tract
    2.5.5 Sewer
2.6 Traffic counts
2.7 Zoning manual
    2.7.1 Zoning application
    2.7.2 Correspondence
2.8 Land studies
    2.8.1 Soils testing
    2.8.2 Hydrology study
    2.8.3 Environmental impact studies
    2.8.4 Traffic studies
2.9 Land closing documents
    2.9.1 Survey
    2.9.2 Title policy
    2.9.3 Escrow agreements
    2.9.4 Deeds
        2.9.4.1 Limited warranty
        2.9.4.2 General warranty
        2.9.4.3 Quitclaim
    2.9.5 Easements
    2.9.6 Closing statement
    2.9.7 Transfer tax form

2.9.8   Loan payoff letter

2.9.9   Consent of buyer

2.9.10   Consent of seller

2.9.11   UCC financing letter

2.9.12   Purchase money mortgage

2.9.13   Guarantee

3.0   Design and Engineering

   3.1   Internal office correspondence

   3.2   Government authorities/approvals/correspondence

      3.2.1   Federal

      3.2.2   State

         3.2.2.1   Department of transportation

         3.2.2.2   Fire/life/safety

         3.2.2.3   D & R/DRI/dredge and fill

      3.2.3   County

         3.2.3.1   Permits/building occupancy

         3.2.3.2   Administrative/commissioners

         3.2.3.3   Planning department

         3.2.3.4   Zoning department

         3.2.3.5   Fire/life/safety

         3.2.3.6   Public works/water/sewer

         3.2.3.7   Traffic/roads

      3.2.4   City

         3.2.4.1   Permits/building occupancy

         3.2.4.2   Administrative/commissioners

         3.2.4.3   Planning department

         3.2.4.4   Zoning department

         3.2.4.5   Fire/life/safety

         3.2.4.6   Public works/water/sewer

         3.2.4.7   Traffic/roads

   3.3   Team selection

      3.3.1   Architects

   3.4   Public utilities

      3.4.1   Electricity

      3.4.2   Gas

      3.4.3   Telephone

      3.4.4   Water/sewer

3.5 Project description sheets
3.6 Master planning date
3.7 Area calculations
3.8 Consultants correspondence
    3.8.1   Landscape architect
    3.8.2   Civil engineer
    3.8.3   Structural engineer
    3.8.4   HVAC engineer
    3.8.5   Plumbing engineer
    3.8.6   Electrical engineer
    3.8.7   Interior designer
    3.8.8   Geo-technical and testing
    3.8.9   Schedule consultant
    3.8.10 Associate architect
    3.8.11 Vertical transportation consultant
    3.8.12 Traffic consultant
    3.8.13 Cost estimator
    3.8.14 Sprinkler and fire safety consultant
    3.8.15 Concrete consultant
    3.8.16 Code consultant
    3.8.17 Acoustical consultant
    3.8.18 Food service/laundry consultant
    3.8.19 Lighting consultant
    3.8.20 Graphic/signage consultant
    3.8.21 Art work
    3.8.22 Audio/visual/TV consultant
    3.8.23 Model/rendering/art consultant
    3.8.24 Energy consultant
    3.8.25 Environmental consultant
    3.8.26 Site survey consultant
    3.8.27 Parking consultant
    3.8.28 Furnishings, fixtures and equipment consultant (F,F, & E)
    3.8.29 Tenant design consultant
    3.8.30 Photography/map consultant
    3.8.31 Minority participation consultant
    3.8.32 Retail consultant
    3.8.33 Club consultant
    3.8.34 Wind tunnel consultant

3.9   Project budgeting
3.10   Scheduling
    3.10.1   Predevelopment
    3.10.2   Summary design/construction
    3.10.3   Overall project schedule
    3.10.4   Biweekly scheduling meetings
    3.10.5   Other
3.11   Drawings
    3.11.1   Site
    3.11.2   Elevations
    3.11.3   Floor
    3.11.4   Landscape
3.12   Street addresses
3.13   As-built survey
3.14   Architect completion certification letter
4.0   General Contractor
  4.1   General contractor interface
    4.1.1   Resume
    4.1.2   References
  4.2   Preliminary cost estimates
  4.3   Pricing documents estimates
  4.4   Value engineering
  4.5   Guaranteed maximum costs
    4.5.1   Sitework
    4.5.2   Base building
    4.5.3   Parking dock
    4.5.4   Tenant work
    4.5.5   Off-sitework
  4.6   General correspondence
    4.6.1   General requirements
    4.6.2   Sitework
    4.6.3   Concrete
    4.6.4   Masonry
    4.6.5   Metals
    4.6.6   Carpentry
    4.6.7   Thermal and moisture protection
    4.6.8   Doors, windows and glass
    4.6.9   Finishes

4.6.10   Specialties

4.6.11   Equipment

4.6.12   Furnishings

4.6.13   Special construction

4.6.14   Conveying system

4.6.15   Mechanical

4.6.16   Electrical

4.7   Notice to proceed

4.8   Applications for payment

4.9   Sitework change orders

4.10 Base building change orders

4.11 Parking deck change orders

4.12 Tenant work change orders

4.13 Off-sitework change orders

4.14 Close out

4.15 Disputes

4.16 Miscellaneous

4.16.1   Liens/bonding capacity/notices

4.16.2   Other contractors correspondence

4.16.3   Daily reports

4.16.4   Monthly cost reports

4.17 Quality assurance/quality control (QAQC)

4.17.1   Project summary

4.17.2   Photography/job progress

4.17.3   On-site inspections/misc.

4.17.4   Subsurface investigation reports

4.17.5   Pavement reports

4.17.6   Foundation reports

4.17.7   Steel reports

4.17.8   Concrete reports

4.17.9   Precast concrete reports

4.17.10 Torqueing/weld reports

4.17.11 Other

4.17.12 Field inspection daily reports

4.17.13 Punch lists

4.17.14 Roof inspection reports

4.17.15 Curtain wall inspection reports

4.17.16 Curtain wall wind torque reports

5.0   Agreements
   5.1   Real estate services agreements
      5.1.1   Brokerage agreements
            5.1.1.1 Correspondence
      5.1.2   Legal agreements
            5.1.2.1 Correspondence
      5.1.3   All other agreements
   5.2   Land acquisitions agreements
      5.2.1   Correspondence
   5.3   Ground lease agreements
      5.3.1   Correspondence
   5.4   Joint venture/partnerships agreements
      5.4.1   Correspondence
   5.5   Construction loan agreements
      5.5.1   Correspondence
   5.6   Permanent loan agreements
      5.6.1   Correspondence
   5.7   Major user agreements
      5.7.1   Correspondence
   5.8   Purchase/technical service agreements
      5.8.1   Correspondence
   5.9   Management agreements
      5.9.1   Correspondence
   5.10 Marketing agreements
      5.10.1   Correspondence
   5.11 Agency agreements
      5.11.1   Correspondence
   5.12 Architectural agreements
      5.12.1   Correspondence
   5.13 Construction agreements
      5.13.1   Correspondence
   5.14 Subcontractors agreements
      5.14.1   Correspondence
   5.15 Miscellaneous design consultants agreements
      5.15.1   Correspondence
   5.16 Development agreements
      5.16.1   Correspondence

5.17 Ground lease agreements
    5.17.1   Correspondence
5.18 Condominium documents
    5.18.1   Correspondence
5.19 Lease agreements
    5.19.1   Residential
    5.19.2   Commercial
5.20 Owner's agreements
    5.20.1   Condominium agreements
    5.20.2   By-laws
    5.20.3   Rules and regulations
5.21 Developer warranty agreements
    5.21.1   Correspondence
6.0 Marketing
6.1   Correspondence
6.2   Market analysis/market feasibility studies
6.3   Strategic planning
6.4   Budgets
6.5   Traffic reports
6.6   Competition studies
6.7   Advertising
    6.7.1   Media placement
        6.7.1.1 Newspaper
        6.7.1.2 Magazine
        6.7.1.3 Radio
        6.7.1.4 Television
        6.7.1.5 Billboard
    6.7.2   Advertising proofs
    6.7.3   Advertising copy
6.8   Public relations
    6.8.1   Groundbreaking
    6.8.2   Topping out
    6.8.3   Grand opening
    6.8.4   Media coverage
6.9   Broker lists
6.10 Broker relations
6.11 Direct mail

6.12 Brochures
    6.12.1   Price lists
    6.12.2   Options
    6.12.3   Projections
6.13 Visual aids
    6.13.1   Renderings
    6.13.2   Display boards
    6.13.3   Model
6.14 Signage
6.15 Office
    6.15.1   Design plan
    6.15.2   Furnishings
    6.15.3   Equipment
    6.15.4   Supplies
6.16 Model
    6.16.1   Design plan
    6.16.2   Furnishings
6.17 Leasing reports
    6.17.1   Prospect status reports
    6.17.2   Proposals/leases
    6.17.3   Other
7.0 Financing
  7.1   Correspondence
  7.2   Construction loans
    7.2.1   Lender package
    7.2.2   Lender status reports
    7.2.3   Closing checklists
    7.2.4   Closing documents
    7.2.5   Correspondence
  7.3   Permanent loans
    7.3.1   Lender package
    7.3.2   Lender status reports
    7.3.3   Closing checklists
    7.3.4   Closing documents
    7.3.5   Correspondence
  7.4   Appraisals
  7.5   Title insurance

8.0 Equity Partner
    8.1 Correspondence
9.0 Property Management
    9.1 Tenant correspondence
    9.2 Strategic planning operations/maintenance
    9.3 Operating budgets
    9.4 Budget status reports
    9.5 Security
    9.6 Inventory
        9.6.1 Office
        9.6.2 Maintenance
        9.6.3 Common area
    9.7 Business support centers
    9.8 General consultants data
    9.9 Guarantees
    9.10 Warranties
    9.11 Maintenance manuals
    9.12 Monthly reporting
    9.13 Insurance
        9.13.1 Policies
    9.14 Real estate taxes
    9.15 Service agreements
    9.16 Banking
        9.16.1 Property—checking account
        9.16.2 Property—money market account
    9.17 Tenant files
        9.17.1 Application
        9.17.2 Credit report
        9.17.3 Reservation agreement
        9.17.4 Lease
        9.17.5 Key agreement
        9.17.6 Move-in/move-out form
        9.17.7 Correspondence
        9.17.8 Work orders
        9.17.9 Tenant improvement selection form
        9.17.10 Tenant drawings

9.17.11 Tenant building permit

9.17.12 Tenant certificate of occupancy

10.0 Accounting

    10.1 Correspondence

    10.2 Yearly property tax returns

    10.3 Yearly investor tax returns

    10.4 Business permits

    10.5 Annual partnership registration

11.0 Legal

    11.1 Correspondence

    11.2 Securities

    11.3 Zoning

    11.4 Tenants

12.0 Unit Closing

    12.1 Unit sale

        12.1.1 Reservation agreement

        12.1.2 Purchase and sales agreement

        12.1.3 Selection form

        12.1.4 Closing documents

        12.1.5 Closing statement

        12.1.6 Pest-letter

        12.1.7 Punch out form

        12.1.8 Correspondence

13.0 Sale

    13.1 Sales package

    13.2 Potential purchasers

    13.3 Letters of intent

    13.4 Sale closing documents

    13.5 Disbursement of funds to partners

    13.6 Purchase money mortgage

Construction Reporting

During the construction phase, the developer must know quickly and in detail about delays in construction progress. Since the marketing team will be seeking to move tenants into the building as soon as possible, any construction delays must be coordinated with tenant planning. During the construction phase, the project manager and developer will be using the following tools to review this process.

Daily Construction Logs

The daily construction logs used by the construction superintendent will give great insight into the construction progress. This log will include information about the weather conditions, the progress of each subcontractor, and any potential problems.

Construction Draw Schedules

The construction draw schedules can be compared to the original projected draw schedule. This will show if the project is ahead or behind schedule.

Monthly Construction Progress Reports

These reports can be prepared by the general contractor, the construction manager, and the schedule consultant. They will show the progress of each trade on a building, per unit, or per floor basis. This report will also show how many days ahead or behind schedule the project is.

Schedule Consultant Meetings and Monthly Reports

Since the schedule consultant will be working on near-term schedules, a monthly report will provide detailed problems concerning delays.

Architects and Engineers Inspection Reports

As part of construction administration responsibilities, the architects and engineers on a weekly or biweekly basis will visit the site. During their walk-through, they will observe work not being completed per construction documentation. Copies of these reports are sent to the total team (see Form 6–6).

Quality Assurance Quality Control Engineers

As part of their contracted responsibility during various phases of the work, these engineers will inspect the installation, fabrication, and finishing of construction to verify its performance per specifications. Reports are forwarded to the contractor, architect, and developer.

Closing Out of the Construction Phase

Once the construction is completed the following items should be completed by either the developer or a representative.

- Complete inspection of the property by the engineers, architects, and developer's staff to develop a comprehensive "punch list" of items yet to be completed. A punch list is a list of items that is not complete to the satisfaction of the developer. These items must be completed prior to declaring substantial completion.
- Obtain a completion letter from the general contractor
- Obtain certificates of occupancy from government regulatory agencies

- Release the general contractor's final payment and all holdbacks
- Obtain all lien waivers from the general contractor
- Obtain the construction operational manual containing all warranties and guarantees
- One-year warranty

Management Systems

The management team will prepare monthly financial accounting reports that show all the revenue and expenses incurred during that time period and will compare them to the original or revised operating budgets.

Marketing Reporting

On a weekly basis, the marketing team will prepare marketing reports that show the status of the marketing progress. It will show the traffic to the property during the week, any unusual weather conditions that might have slowed down potential traffic, and the status of the prospects' interest.

Finance and Accounting

On a monthly basis after draw requests and payments to various consultants and contractors, the accounting staff will prepare monthly cost reports providing the following information.

- Original budgets
- Revised budgets
- Actual costs incurred to date
- Unexpended committed costs
- Estimated amount to complete
- Current projected costs
- Variances to the revised budget
- Variance explanations

POSTCLOSING REPORT: A COMPLETE RECORD OF THE DEVELOPMENT

The postclosing development memo is a list of information that can be used to produce a manual for use during the duration of the development. It can be prepared by the developer, project manager and staff. It should include all of the information regarding the development. It will be used in the future as a reference tool. The following is an outline of this memo.

Postclosing Development Memorandum Outline

I. Overview of the deal
- A. Summary of the players (name, address, telephone number, contact)
  1. Land seller
  2. Ownership entity
     a. General partners
     b. Special limited partners
     c. Joint venture partner
  3. Seller's attorney
  4. Purchaser's attorney
  5. Lender
  6. Lender's attorney
  7. Note lender
  8. Note lender's attorney
  9. Note surety company
  10. Note surety attorney
  11. Property management company
  12. Leasing company
  13. Architect
  14. Landscape architect
  15. Engineer
     a. Civil
     b. Structural
     c. Mechanical
     d. Electrical
     e. Plumbing
     f. Surveyor
     g. Soils test
  16. General contractor
     a. Bonding company
  17. Construction manager
  18. Title company
  19. Accountant

        20. Money raiser
        21. Real estate broker
        22. Mortgage banker/broker
        23. Appraiser
        24. Tax consultant
        25. Insurance company
        26. Interior designer

   B. Summary of the investors
        1. Name
        2. Address
        3. Telephone number
        4. Social security number
        5. Number of investment units purchased
        6. Total dollars invested
        7. Sales representative

II. Banking information
   A. Property operating account
        1. Checking account
           a. Bank name, telephone number, contact
           b. Account number
           c. Signatures
           d. Interest earned
        2. Money market account
           a. Bank name, telephone number, contact
           b. Account number
           c. Signatures
           d. Interest earned

   B. Ownership entity operating account
        1. Checking account
           a. Bank name, address, telephone number, contact
           b. Account number
           c. Signatures
           d. Interest earned
        2. Money market account
           a. Bank name, address, telephone number, contact
           b. Account number

         c. Signatures

         d. Interest earned

    C. Security deposit escrow account

       1. Checking account

         a. Bank name, address, telephone number, contact

         b. Account number

         c. Signatures

         d. Interest earned

       2. Money market account

         a. Bank name, address, telephone number, contact

         b. Account number

         c. Signatures

         d. Interest earned

III. Tax identification number

IV. Investor call for funds

    A. Dates due

    B. Amount due

    C. Letters to investors due date

       1. Where to send payments

V. Debt service payment instructions (for each mortgage)

    A. Lender

       1. Address

       2. Telephone number

       3. Contact

    B. Surety

       1. Address

       2. Telephone number

       3. Contact

    C. Account number

    D. Account debt service paid from

    E. Payment responsibility

       1. Address

       2. Telephone number

       3. Contact

    F. Mortgage payment due date—first payment

    G. Mortgage payment due date

    H. Mortgage payment late date

    I. Monthly payment—amount due
        1. Payment increase date
           a. New payment amount
    J. Loan maturity date
    K. Balloon payment amount
    L. Debt service amortization schedule
    M. Lender reporting requirements
        1. Monthly statements
        2. Quarterly statements
        3. Yearly statements
           a. Audit statements
           b. Borrower financials
    N. Escrows
        1. Real estate taxes
        2. Insurance
VI. Real estate tax escrow
    A. Bank
        1. Type of account
           a. Checking
           b. Money market
        2. Address
        3. Telephone number
        4. Contact
    B. Account number
    C. Payment responsibility
    D. Due date
    E. Monthly payment
    F. Interest earned
    G. Tax consultant
        1. Yearly fee
    H. Local tax department
        1. Address
        2. Telephone number
        3. Contact
    I. Tax account number
    J. Most recent tax assessment

K. Most recent millage rate

L. Date tax bill due

VII.   Insurance escrow

    A. Insurance company

       1. Address

       2. Telephone number

       3. Contact

    B. Effective date of coverage

    C. Name of insured

    D. Yearly premium

    E. Is premium paid in advance?

    F. Monthly escrow

       1. Bank

          a. Address

          b. Telephone number

          c. Contact

       2. Due date

       3. Interest earned

    G. Policy coverage (dollar amount)

       1. Liability

       2. Content

       3. Rent loss

       4. Fidelity bond

    H. Renewal date

    I. Copy of policy

VIII.   Reporting requirements (sent by managing partner)

    A. Investors

       1. Quarterly reports

       2. Yearly summary

       3. Tax returns

       4. Call for funds

    B. Lender

       1. Monthly cash flow

       2. Yearly statements

       3. General partner financials

    C. Money raiser

       1. Weekly traffic reports

       2. Monthly cash flow statements

           3. Quarterly reports

           4. Yearly summary

IX.   Reporting requirements (sent by management company)

    A. Weekly traffic reports

    B. Monthly cash flow statements

           1. Monthly variance reports

    C. Monthly profit and loss statements

    D. Quarterly comparable report

    E. Quarterly property report

    F. Yearly property report

    G. Yearly budget

           1. Line item summary

           2. Capital budget summary

X.   Partnership service fees

    A. Paid to

    B. Payment due date

    C. Fee amount

    D. Responsibility to send out

XI.   Deposits

    A. Insurance

    B. Utilities

           1. Gas

           2. Electricity

           3. Water

           4. Sewer

           5. Cable TV

           6. Telephone

           7. Equipment

           8. Furniture

XII.   Service contracts

    A. Landscaping

    B. Janitorial

    C. Laundry

    D. Vending

    E. Tax consulting

    F. Pool

    G. Mechanical

    H. Pest

         I.   Trash
        J.   Window cleaning
       K. Sprinkler system—landscaping
       L. Sprinkler system—building
      M. Elevator
      N. Parking lot sweeping
      O. Sign maintenance
       P. Vehicle maintenance
      Q. Equipment maintenance
      R. Plant maintenance
       S. Security system
       T. Security personnel

XIII. Inventory (item description, location, serial number, dollar value)
      A. Office
      B. Model
      C. Maintenance shop
      D. Pool area
      E. Units
         1. Appliances
         2. Mechanical

XIV. Builder warranties
      A. Copy of warranty
         1. Roof
         2. Plumbing
         3. Mechanical
         4. Electrical
         5. Pool
         6. Paving
         7. Landscaping
         8. Flooring
         9. Elevator
       10. Sprinkler systems—landscaping
       11. Sprinkler systems—building
       12. Equipment
       13. Appliances

XV. Subcontractors (name, address, telephone number, contact)
      A. Mechanical
      B. Electrical

    C. Plumbing
    D. Landscaping
    E. Paving
    F. Drywall
    G. Painting
    H. Wallpaper
    I. Flooring
    J. Cabinets
    K. Pool
    L. Windows
    M. Appliances
    N. Signage
    O. Security system
XVI.   Material identification (manufacturers, model number, color)
    A. Appliances
    B. Cabinets
    C. Flooring
    D. Paint
    E. Wallpaper
    F. Lighting
    G. Landscaping
    H. Signage
    I. Bathroom fixtures
    J. Security system
XVII.   Operating manuals (copies)
    A. Appliances
    B. HVAC
    C. Hot water heater
    D. Pool
    E. Sprinkler—landscaping
    F. Sprinkler—building
    G. Elevator
    H. Security system
XVIII. Seller warranties (copies)
    A. Rent-up guarantee
    B. Negative cash flow
    C. Construction completion

XIX.   Closing statement
    A. Land closing
    B. Mortgage closings
XX.   Reconciliation of purchaser closing costs
    A. Payee
    B. Amount
    C. Check number
    D. Date
    E. Explanation
XXI.   Completion certification letter from lender
XXII.   Lien waiver release at closing
XXIII. Construction penalty computation
XXIV.   Copies of all certificates of occupancy
XXV.   Date tickler file (date, amount, responsibility, comments)
    A. Property information
    B. Investor call for funds
    C. Payments to sellers
    D. Note financing payments
    E. Cash flow distributions
    F. Debt service extension payments
    G. Loan maturities
    H. Seller guarantees
    I. Lender reporting
    J. Partnership reporting
    K. Tax returns
    L. Insurance renewals
    M. Real estate taxes
    N. Fees receivable
    O. Miscellaneous
XXVI.   Copy of investor information package

TEAM SELECTION FORMS

Team Member's Checklist Form (6–1)

This form can be used to qualify the various types of professionals that will make up the development team.

- Real estate broker
- Appraiser
- Architect
- Landscape architect
- Structural engineer
- Mechanical engineer
- Electrical engineer
- Plumbing engineer
- Surveyor
- Consultant
- Management company
- Marketing company
- Mortgage broker
- Attorney
- Accountant
- General contractor
- Construction management
- Interior designer
- Insurance agent
- Tax consultant

TEAM MEMBER'S CHECKLIST FORM

FORM 6–1

TEAM PLAYER

REAL ESTATE BROKER	_____
APPRAISER	_____
ARCHITECT	_____
LANDSCAPE ARCHITECT	_____
STRUCTURAL ENGINEER	_____
MECHANICAL ENGINEER	_____
ELECTRICAL ENGINEER	_____
PLUMBING ENGINEER	_____
SURVEYOR	_____
CONSULTANT	_____
MANAGEMENT COMPANY	_____
MARKETING COMPANY	_____
MORTGAGE BROKER	_____
ATTORNEY–CORPORATE	_____
ATTORNEY–REAL ESTATE	_____
ATTORNEY–TAX	_____
ATTORNEY–SECURITIES	_____
ATTORNEY–PARTNERSHIP	_____
ACCOUNTANT	_____
GENERAL CONTRACTOR	_____
CONSTRUCTION MGR.	_____
INTERIOR DESIGNER	_____
INSURANCE AGENT	_____
TAX CONSULTANT	_____

GENERAL INFORMATON

YEARS IN BUSINESS	_____
NO. PROPERTIES MANAGED	_____
NO. UNITS/SQ.FT. MANAGED	_____
NO. OF EMPLOYEES	_____
YEARLY SALES VOLUME	$_____

SPECIALIZATION

RESIDENTIAL:	
SINGLE–FAMILY	_____
MULTI–FAMILY	_____
COMMERCIAL:	
RETAIL	_____
OFFICE	_____
INDUSTRIAL	_____
LODGING	_____

VALUE EVALUATION MATRIX

	REF #1	REF #2	REF #3
CUSTOMER ORIENTATION	____	____	____
LISTENER	____	____	____
PUNCTUALITY	____	____	____
INITITATIVE	____	____	____
RESOURCEFULNESS	____	____	____
DECISIVENESS	____	____	____
EXCELLENCE	____	____	____
DILIGENCE	____	____	____
COMMITMENT	____	____	____
INTEGRITY	____	____	____
GOAL ORIENTATED	____	____	____
COMMUNICATIONS	____	____	____
LOYALTY	____	____	____
DELEGATION	____	____	____
PRUDENT	____	____	____
LEARNER	____	____	____
POSITIVE ATTITUDE	____	____	____
FLEXIBLE	____	____	____
TEAM PLAYER	____	____	____
TOTAL	____	____	____

KEY: (1) EXCELLENT (2) GOOD (3) AVERAGE (4) POOR

FEE STRUCTURE

HOURLY $_____ BILLED EVERY (MIN.) _____
BILLED: WEEKLY ___ MONTHLY ___

RESIDENTIAL:	
SINGLE–FAMILY	_____%
MULTI–FAMILY	_____%
COMMERCIAL:	
RETAIL	_____%
OFFICE	_____%
INDUSTRIAL	_____%
LODGING	_____%

REFERENCES

BUSINESS:
DATE ___/___/___
BUSINESS NAME _____
CONTACT _____
ADDRESS _____
_____
TEL. NO. (___)_____

BUSINESS:
DATE ___/___/___
BUSINESS NAME _____
CONTACT _____
ADDRESS _____
_____
TEL. NO. (___)_____

BUSINESS:
DATE ___/___/___
BUSINESS NAME _____
CONTACT _____
ADDRESS _____
_____
TEL. NO. (___)_____

Form 6–1 Team player checklist form.

Code Synopsis Form (6-2)

This form is to be used to understand the code compliance issues.

CODE SYNOPSIS FORM

FORM 6-2

PROJECT _____

DATE ___/___/___

ISSUE	CODE	SPECIFIC REQUIREMENT	DISCUSSED LOCALLY	VARIANCE REQUIRED	ACTION
ZONING					
CORP. OF ENGINEER					
REGIONAL IMPACT STUDIES					
ENVIRONMENTAL REGULATIONS					
BUILDING:					
(USE GROUP)					
(CONSTRUCTION TYPE)					
(HEIGHT LIMITS)					
(AREA LIMITS)					
(SQ.FT./PERSON)					
(EXITS)					
(SEPARATION)					
(EXIT UNITS)					
(TRAVEL DISTANCE)					
(DEAD ENDS)					
(HARDWARE)					
FIRE RESISTANCE RATINGS:					
(FLOOR RATING)					
(WALL RATING)					
(COLUMN RATING)					
(BEAM RATING)					
OPENING PROTECTION					
STRUCTURAL LOADING					
FIRE PROTECTION SYSTEMS					
SMOKE VENTILATION					
SMOKE DETECTION					
ELECTRICAL REQUIREMENTS					
MECHANICAL REQUIREMENTS					
PLUMBING REQUIREMENTS					
STRUCTURAL REQUIREMENTS					

Form 6-2 Code synopsis form.

Construction Cost Analysis Form (6–3)

This form is to be used to determine the construction costs from the contractor.

CONSTRUCTION COST ANALYSIS FORM

FORM 6-3

PROJECT _____

DATE ___/___/___

CODE	DESCRIPTION	COST	COST/SF	COMMENTS
0100	GENERAL CONDITIONS	$_____	$_____	_____
0200	SITEWORK	$_____	$_____	_____
0230	FOUNDATIONS/EARTHWORK	$_____	$_____	_____
0235	UTILITIES	$_____	$_____	_____
0300	CONCRETE (CAST-IN-PLACE)	$_____	$_____	_____
0340	CONCRETE (PRE-CAST)	$_____	$_____	_____
0400	MASONRY/STONE/MARBLE	$_____	$_____	_____
0500	METALS (STRUCTURAL/MISC.)	$_____	$_____	_____
0600	CARPENTRY (MILLWORK)	$_____	$_____	_____
0700	ROOFING (WP/INSULATION)	$_____	$_____	_____
0810	DOORS/FRAMES	$_____	$_____	_____
0840	ENTRANCES/WINDOWS/WALLS	$_____	$_____	_____
0920	DRYWALL/PLASTER/STUCCO	$_____	$_____	_____
0930	TILE	$_____	$_____	_____
0950	ACOUSTIC CEILINGS	$_____	$_____	_____
0960	FLOOR COVERING/CARPET	$_____	$_____	_____
0990	PAINTING/WALL COVERING	$_____	$_____	_____
1000	SPECIALTIES	$_____	$_____	_____
1100	EQUIPMENT	$_____	$_____	_____
1200	FURNISHINGS	$_____	$_____	_____
1400	ELEVATORS	$_____	$_____	_____
1540	PLUMBING	$_____	$_____	_____
1550	HVAC	$_____	$_____	_____
1560	ELECTRICAL	$_____	$_____	_____
1600	FIRE PROTECTION	$_____	$_____	_____
___	_____	$_____	$_____	_____
___	_____	$_____	$_____	_____
___	_____	$_____	$_____	_____
S-TOT	BASE BUILDING COSTS	$_____	$_____	_____
0102	TENANT WORK	$_____	$_____	_____
	CONTRACTOR'S FEE	$_____	$_____	_____
S-TOT	BASE + TENANT + FEE	$_____	$_____	_____
	EXTRAORDINARY ITEMS	$_____	$_____	_____
___	_____	$_____	$_____	_____
TOTAL	ALL CONSTRUCTION COSTS	$_____	$_____	_____

Form 6-3 Construction cost analysis form.

Tenant Allowances Form (6–4)

This form is to be used to identify the tenant allowance costs.

TENANT ALLOWANCES FORM

FORM 6–4

PROJECT _____
TENANT NAME _____
SUITE NO. _____
DATE ___/___/___

DESCRIPTION	QTY.	UNIT COST W/ FEE	UNIT COST W/O FEE	TOTAL COST W/ FEE	TOTAL COST W/O FEE
JOB PLANT	_____	$_____	$_____	$_____	$_____
PARTY WALLS	_____	$_____	$_____	$_____	$_____
TENANT WALLS	_____	$_____	$_____	$_____	$_____
ENTRY DOORS	_____	$_____	$_____	$_____	$_____
INTERIOR DOORS	_____	$_____	$_____	$_____	$_____
CARPET OZ.	_____	$_____	$_____	$_____	$_____
BASE BUILDING COLUMNS	_____	$_____	$_____	$_____	$_____
PAINT COLUMS	_____	$_____	$_____	$_____	$_____
PAINT EXTERIOR WALLS	_____	$_____	$_____	$_____	$_____
LABOR CEILING TILE	_____	$_____	$_____	$_____	$_____
PERIMETER ACOUSTIC SOFFIT	_____	$_____	$_____	$_____	$_____
WALL SWITCHES	_____	$_____	$_____	$_____	$_____
DUPLEX WALL OUTLETS	_____	$_____	$_____	$_____	$_____
LIGHT FIXTURES	_____	$_____	$_____	$_____	$_____
DIFFUSERS	_____	$_____	$_____	$_____	$_____
VENETIAN BLINDS	_____	$_____	$_____	$_____	$_____
MULLION CLOSURES	_____	$_____	$_____	$_____	$_____
SPRINKLER HEAD RELOCATION	_____	$_____	$_____	$_____	$_____
SPRINKLER HEAD ADDITIONS	_____	$_____	$_____	$_____	$_____
EXIT SIGNS	_____	$_____	$_____	$_____	$_____
FIRE EXTINGUISHERS	_____	$_____	$_____	$_____	$_____
PUBLIC ADDRESS SPEAKERS	_____	$_____	$_____	$_____	$_____
FIRE DAMPERS	_____	$_____	$_____	$_____	$_____
THERMOSTAT INSTALLATION	_____	$_____	$_____	$_____	$_____
BUILDING PERMITS	_____	$_____	$_____	$_____	$_____
FUTURE CORRIDORS	_____	$_____	$_____	$_____	$_____
TENANT ENTRY ALLOWANCE	_____	$_____	$_____	$_____	$_____
MISCELLANEOUS	_____	$_____	$_____	$_____	$_____
_____	_____	$_____	$_____	$_____	$_____
_____	_____	$_____	$_____	$_____	$_____
_____	_____	$_____	$_____	$_____	$_____
_____	_____	$_____	$_____	$_____	$_____
_____	_____	$_____	$_____	$_____	$_____
_____	_____	$_____	$_____	$_____	$_____
_____	_____	$_____	$_____	$_____	$_____
_____	_____	$_____	$_____	$_____	$_____
_____	_____	$_____	$_____	$_____	$_____
_____	_____	$_____	$_____	$_____	$_____
TOTAL		$_____	$_____	$_____	$_____

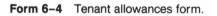

Form 6–4   Tenant allowances form.

227

Architect Selection Form (6–5)

This form is to be used to evaluate the architectural firm options.

ARCHITECT SELECTION FORM

FORM 6–5

PROJECT _____
DATE ___/___/___

ITEMS TO BE EVALUATED	FIRM 1	FIRM 2	FIRM 3	FIRM 4	FIRM 5
SERVICES PROVIDED	_____	_____	_____	_____	_____
FIRM HISTORY	_____	_____	_____	_____	_____
PRIME CONTACT	_____	_____	_____	_____	_____
SIZE OF ORGANIZATION	_____	_____	_____	_____	_____
VOLUME OR WORK (LAST YEAR)	_____	_____	_____	_____	_____
PROJECTED WORKLOAD	_____	_____	_____	_____	_____
PRODUCT EXPERIENCE	_____	_____	_____	_____	_____
LOCAL FAMILIARITY	_____	_____	_____	_____	_____
DESIGN EXPERTISE	_____	_____	_____	_____	_____
FAST TRACT EXPERIENCE?	_____	_____	_____	_____	_____
PERSONAL CHEMISTRY	_____	_____	_____	_____	_____
REFERENCES #1	_____	_____	_____	_____	_____
#2	_____	_____	_____	_____	_____
#3	_____	_____	_____	_____	_____
OFFICE LOCATION	_____	_____	_____	_____	_____
FEE STRUCTURE	_____	_____	_____	_____	_____
LIABILITY INSURANCE	_____	_____	_____	_____	_____
TEAM COMPOSITION	_____	_____	_____	_____	_____
LITIGATION	_____	_____	_____	_____	_____
FIELD ADMINISTRATION	_____	_____	_____	_____	_____
VALUE ENGINEERING	_____	_____	_____	_____	_____
CADD	_____	_____	_____	_____	_____
SUMMARY TOTALS	_____	_____	_____	_____	_____

RANKINGS: (1 = Excellent) (2 = Good) (3 = Fair) (4 = Poor)

Form 6–5 Architect selection form.

Contractor Selection Form (6–6)

This form is to be used to evaluate the construction firm options.

CONTRACTOR SELECTION FORM

FORM 6–6

PROJECT _____
DATE ___/___/___

ITEMS TO BE EVALUATED	FIRM 1	FIRM 2	FIRM 3	FIRM 4	FIRM 5
MANAGEMENT RATING					
LABOR MANAGEMENT STRUCTURE					
SCHEDULING REPUTATION					
EFFECTIVE MINORITY RELATIONS					
EXPERIENCE					
TOTAL ASSETS VS. LIABILITIES					
BONDING CAPACITY					
YEARLY VOLUME OF WORK					
SCHEDULING					
CONTRACT IMPASSES					
PROPOSED SCHEDULE					
REFERENCES					
#1					
#2					
#3					
PROPOSED FEE					
SITE COSTS					
PARKING DECK COSTS					
TENANT ALLOWANCE					
OTHER					
PERSONAL CHEMISTRY					
VALUE ENGINEERING					
LITIGATION					
SUMMARY TOTALS					

RANKINGS: (1 = Excellent) (2 = Good) (3 = Fair) (4 = Poor)

Form 6–6   Contractor selection form.

229

Architect's Inspection Report Form (6–7)

This form is to be used by the inspecting architect or engineer.

ARCHITECT'S INSPECTION REPORT FORM

FORM 6–7

PROJECT _____
PROJECT NO. _____
FIELD REPORT NO. _____
DATE PREPARED ____/____/____
TIME PREPARED _____
PREPARED BY _____

WEATHER CONDITIONS _____
TEMPERATURE _____
PERCENT COMPLETED _____%
SCHEDULE CONFORMANCE _____

WORK IN PROGRESS

_____
_____
_____

OBJECTIONS

_____
_____
_____
_____
_____
_____
_____
_____
_____
_____
_____

UNRESOLVED ITEMS

_____
_____
_____

ITEMS ATTACHED

_____
_____
_____
_____

Form 6–7   Architect's inspection report form.

Cost Control Report Form (6–8)

This form is to be used to keep track of the development's "hard costs."

COST CONTROL REPORT FORM

FORM 6–8

PROJECT _____

DATE ___/___/___

CODE	COST CATEGORY	ORIGINAL BUDGET	REVISED BUDGET	ACTUAL COST TO DATE	UNEXP. COMMITTED COSTS	EST. AMOUNT TO COMPLETE	CURRENT CURRENT PROJ. COST	VARIANCE TO ORIGINAL BUDGET
____	PREDEVELOPMENT	$____	$____	$____	$____	$____	$____	$____
	SUB-TOTAL	$____	$____	$____	$____	$____	$____	$____
____	LAND							
____	ACQUISITION COST	$____	$____	$____	$____	$____	$____	$____
____	IMPACT/UTILITY/TAP	$____	$____	$____	$____	$____	$____	$____
____	SUB-TOTAL	$____	$____	$____	$____	$____	$____	$____
____	DESIGN							
____	ARCHITECT/ENG.	$____	$____	$____	$____	$____	$____	$____
____	LANDSCAPE ARCHITECT	$____	$____	$____	$____	$____	$____	$____
____	TENANT INTERIOR FEES	$____	$____	$____	$____	$____	$____	$____
____	TENANT REIMB.	$____	$____	$____	$____	$____	$____	$____
____	PUBLIC AREA FEES	$____	$____	$____	$____	$____	$____	$____
____	SURVEY/SUBSURFACE	$____	$____	$____	$____	$____	$____	$____
____	SCHEDULE CONSULT.	$____	$____	$____	$____	$____	$____	$____
____	QUALITY CONTROL	$____	$____	$____	$____	$____	$____	$____
____	CONSTRUCTION MGMT	$____	$____	$____	$____	$____	$____	$____
____	MISC. DESIGN	$____	$____	$____	$____	$____	$____	$____
____	REIMBURSIBLES	$____	$____	$____	$____	$____	$____	$____
	SUB-TOTAL	$____	$____	$____	$____	$____	$____	$____
____	CONSTRUCTION							
____	BUILDING SHELL	$____	$____	$____	$____	$____	$____	$____
____	SITEWORK	$____	$____	$____	$____	$____	$____	$____
____	LANDSCAPING	$____	$____	$____	$____	$____	$____	$____
____	PARKING DECK	$____	$____	$____	$____	$____	$____	$____
____	TENANT ALLOWANCES	$____	$____	$____	$____	$____	$____	$____
____	SPECIAL TENANT ALLOW.	$____	$____	$____	$____	$____	$____	$____
____	ALLOWANCES	$____	$____	$____	$____	$____	$____	$____
____	SUB-TOTAL	$____	$____	$____	$____	$____	$____	$____
____	F, F & E							
____	FURNISHINGS	$____	$____	$____	$____	$____	$____	$____
____	SECURITY	$____	$____	$____	$____	$____	$____	$____
____	SUB-TOTAL	$____	$____	$____	$____	$____	$____	$____
____	TOTAL	$____	$____	$____	$____	$____	$____	$____

Form 6–8   Cost control report form.

## Chapter 7

Preparing for Construction by Careful Design

Architects and engineers should never be allowed to create buildings as monuments to themselves, especially in the development business. Each project's development should be in response to a market need in location, form, services, and rental rate structure. Should the developer ignore the market need, the investment will fail for lack of demand. The developer should study the market and become an expert in understanding the competition. The designs should respond to the psychology of the user and be used as key features in closing the sale. Each element of the design should uniquely fit its intended market and this should be apparent.

The developer should value the input of brokers and marketing managers in decisions concerning the function and aesthetics of the project. Their knowledge about the markets can prove invaluable in fashioning a development which can be enthusiastically sold. Regardless of the type of development, the buyer should be able to sense a level of quality, either in the materials used or in the way in which the materials fit together. A wise architect stated that it is not just the cost of the project which denotes quality, but the way in which the pieces fit together. The project must be designed with quality and creativity and built with care. There must be order and energy in site planning, landscaping, building shape, floor plan layout, building materials selection, interior spaces and graphics systems, and that quality must be sensed in its presentation.

During the design phase, the developer is able to define his vision and have it drawn on paper for evaluation. This is an exciting time for the developer who can see the concept mature. The developer must always be looking for the fresh and new ideas that can propel him to the forefront of the industry in advertising and leasing success. This is the time when these ideas begin to become reality.

To realize design and construction success, the developer should select team members who are leaders in their own right. These team members should possess outstanding communication and presentation skills to not only know what the development must be, but also to illustrate that image to the host of other players on the team. The developer must challenge the design team to produce ideas which are not only cost effective, but set the pace in responding to the market with the highest level of creativity.

In Chapter 6, we learned that during the predevelopment process the designers of the team will create and produce concepts and outline details of the project for pricing. This chapter will discuss this design process in detail and the creation of these pricing drawings, as well as the construction documents for the actual building of the project.

PROGRAMMING FOR SUCCESS

It is hoped at this moment in the development process, you as the developer have created the program. This was discussed in detail in Chapter 6. This program may now be used to further develop your design ideas. After initial presentation of the development's concept, additional ideas will become apparent. Using these new ideas, the program should be revised. Just as business planning is essential to the success of any business ventures, so the program is essential for the success of the design. The effectiveness of the program will be determined by its completeness in response to market conditions. Market conditions change and if the developer were to keep track of the evolution of the project, and constantly update the program, it would be quite different at the end from the beginning. The developer who spends the time required to document his desires and objectives will find that the development process will flow smoother.

CREATING CONSTRUCTION DOCUMENTS

In the process of designing the project for the developer, the experienced designer will follow a series of phases in the preparation and execution of design documents for construction. These phases are known as research and planning, master planning, schematic design, design development, construction documentation, bidding and negotiations, and construction administration.

Using these phases in the process, the total development's concepts can be envisioned by the developer, allowing the designers to conceptualize and create concepts for physical form. The following diagram describes the total design process for the production of construction documents and the percentages of the work tasks (Figure 7–1). The remaining portion of this section will describe the expectations and details of the activities occurring during this process.

Research and Planning for the Design Phase

Prior to starting the design process, the designer must gather pertinent data relative to the site, the surrounding environment, the product type and its specialized functions and criteria. In another section of this chapter, a listing of miscellaneous design criteria is given as an example of the type of information which must be gathered during this phase. The following is a checklist the designer can follow in research and planning.

I. List of contacts (name, address, telephone number)
    A. Building inspector
    B. Zoning official
    C. Fire inspector
    D. Electrical inspector
    E. Plumbing inspector
    F. State highway engineer
    G. Health or sanitary engineer
    H. Electric company representative
    I. Gas company representative
    J. Water company representative
    K. Telephone company representative
    L. Cable television representative
    M. Environmental agency representative
II. General site conditions
    A. Indicate the location and type of buildings adjacent to the subject site.
    B. Describe the existing adjacent highways or roads and suitable entrance possibilities. Include frontage on major streets, side streets, and back streets.
    C. Indicate whether there are any highway alterations or additions planned which would affect the site. Indicate right-of-way lines.
    D. Analysis of the site:
        1. Approximate area in square feet (taken from the survey or tax records)

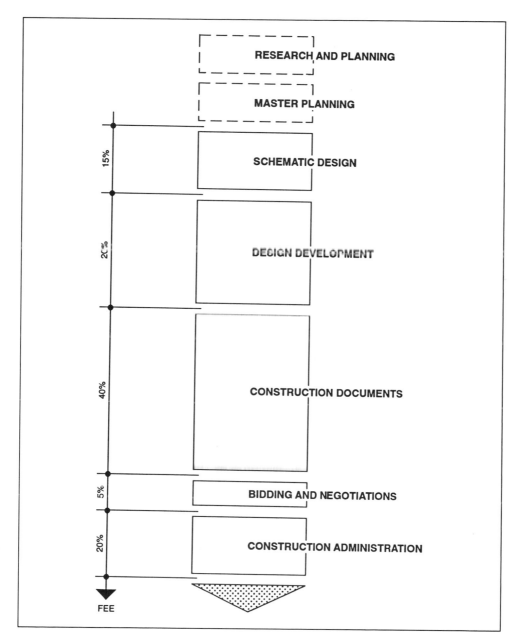

RESEARCH AND PLANNING

MASTER PLANNING

15%

SCHEMATIC DESIGN

20%

DESIGN DEVELOPMENT

40%

CONSTRUCTION DOCUMENTS

5%

BIDDING AND NEGOTIATIONS

20%

CONSTRUCTION ADMINISTRATION

FEE

Figure 7–1 The design process.

      2. Topography

      3. Existing improvements

      4. Wooded areas, trees

      5. Streams, brooks, or ditches (investigate seasonal variations, flood conditions, etc.)

      6. Lakes, ponds, marshlands (investigate seasonal variations, flood conditions, etc.)

      7. Ground water table (investigate seasonal variations, flood conditions, etc.)

      8. Type of surface soil, visible boulders, rock outcroppings

      9. Miscellaneous comments

  E. Suitable pylon sign locations having maximum visibility from the highway

  F. Acquire survey and topographic map

  G. Acquire soil analysis and borings

  H. Acquire aerial photographs of the site and surrounding area

  I. Determine location of water and electricity main lines

  J. Become familiar with any existing buildings to be left remaining, removed, or demolished

  K. Understand setbacks required and exceptions

  L. Understand parking ratio requirements and any exceptions

  M. Understand parking requirements

  N. Understand landscaping requirements for parking lot, buffer strips, and perimeter roads

  O. Indicate any easements of record or other matters affecting a clear title

III. Storm drainage

  A. Research runoff of watershed area

  B. Indicate any existing storm sewers and obtain sizes, locations and connections

  C. Determine where the storm water can be discharged (streams, lake, ditch, adjacent property)

  D. Determine whether roof drainage can be discharged directly into storm sewers or drained onto the site

  E. Determine any possible long-range planning of the city for disposal of the storm water

IV. Sanitary sewage

  A. Indicate existing sanitary sewer lines and tap fees required

  B. Determine whether a separate sewage treatment plant is required for the development

      1. Types of treatment required
      2. Types of treatment used by other similar developments in the particular region
      3. Governmental authorities with jurisdiction
      4. Special requirements to be met in regard to sewage of restaurants, laundries
      5. Where effluent of treated sewage can be discharged—stream, lake, dry wells
    C. Determine possible long-range plans of the city for permanent disposal of sewage; secure positive statement as to the possible assessment district fees involved in connection with these disposal facilities
    D. If sanitary sewer is available, what are the restrictions, impact fees, etc.
  V. Electric lines
    A. Indicate any existing high voltage lines or other electrical equipment on the site
    B. Indicate the proximity of off-site primary lines
    C. Determine the electrical company's participation in the site underground electrical distribution system
  VI. Public transportation authority
    A. Location and movement of existing and proposed public transportation facilities
    B. Public transportation pick-up points
    C. Public shelter facilities
    D. Possibility of having bus routes within development
  VII. Geo-technical data
    A. Determine what borings are needed by structural engineer
    B. Determine soil testing required by civil engineer
    C. Secure a copy of geo-technical testing

Master Planning Phase

Master planning by the architect and land planner is usually needed on larger tracts of land where more than one type of product is to be developed. For example, based on the market demand, a one-hundred acre tract of land may be planned for both multi-family, retail, and single-family residential, as well as areas set aside for lakes or parks. All of these land uses will be master planned and include schematics for roadways and utility infrastructure.

    The process of land planning will include analysis of the site for natural vistas and wooded areas. The topography of the site will influence drainage, the

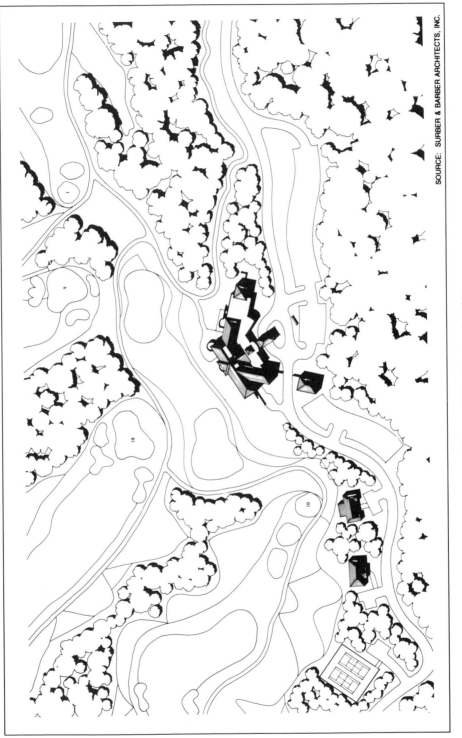

Figure 7–2   Master site plan.

roadway system, and sometimes the location of structures. In addition, soil conditions on the site will influence the location of underground utilities, building locations, and their structural systems. Also, the accessibility and availability of public transportation and utility systems will be studied. An example of a master plan drawing can be found in Figure 7–2.

Site planning is the design of the site for a specific building. This planning will normally occur in the schematic design phase, but is a direct result of master planning. The objective of the site plan is to place the building in the most economical and aesthetically pleasing location on the site. In site planning the following should be carefully considered. Figure 7–3 is a drawing of a site plan drawing.

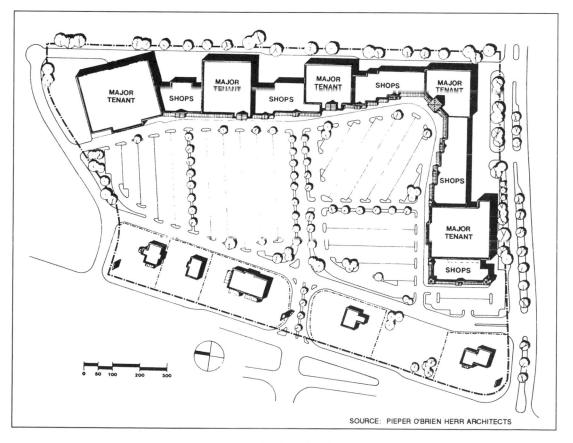

SOURCE: PIEPER O'BRIEN HERR ARCHITECTS

Figure 7–3 Site plan.

Natural Factors

In an analysis of the site, the location of the building should respond to the natural conditions.

- Geology—rock conditions
- Physiography—relief, and topography
- Hydrology—surface and groundwater, wetlands and floodplain
- Soils—uses and classification
- Vegetation—plant ecology
- Wildlife—habitats
- Climate—weather conditions, solar orientation

Boundary and Topographical Survey

These are discussed in detail in Chapter 6. The shape of the land and the changes in elevations will influence the location of all structures.

- Location of any existing structures on the property, building elevations, walls, curbs, tree wells, driveways, and parking lots
- Location and sizes of the storm and sewage systems
- Outline of any wooded area, locations, types, and sizes of large caliper trees
- Hydrographic features: lakes, ponds, streams, creeks
- Utility pole locations
- Rock outcropping locations
- Road elevations at intervals
- Elevations at predetermined intervals
- Contour intervals

Site Grading and Drainage

The slope of the land must be studied and shaped to control water and route it from buildings or roadways. Many times the water runoff can be rerouted on the surface or piped underground.

The shapes of the land can also be fashioned to provide special features for landscaping. Other items to review will include:

- Erosion control
- Land contouring
- Swales and ditches
- Subsurface drainage

Vehicular Circulation

Since most developments include automobiles, the site planners will be required to ensure that vehicles have ease of ingress and egress to and through the property. This is crucial in developments where large vehicles need access to truck docks and entrances for moving the tenants into their spaces. The following are types of vehicular circulation patterns:

Grid System: A system of equally spaced streets that run perpendicular to each other.

Radial System: A radial system directs the traffic flow to a common center.

Linear System: This type of system links the traffic flow between two points.

Curvilinear System: A curvilinear system is designed to follow the topography of the land.

Parking and Parking Decks

Parking layout must not only comply with local codes, but provide ease of access for tenants and visitors. Since many sites are designed on tight or irregular sites, this is often a challenge. Parking is designed in 45, 60, and 90 degree angles. In parking lot design, the tenant should not have to walk up to the car in the evening and lots should be well-lighted and planned with good drainage. The tenant's route to entrances should prevent crossing as few traffic ways as possible.

Angle	Width (ft)	Curb Length (ft)	Length of Space (ft)	Aisle Width (ft)	Total
45°	9 stall	9	19	24	62
60°	9 stall	10.4	21	18	60
90°	9 stall	12.7	19.8	13	52.6

Service Areas

Service areas should be designed to give the various types of vehicles adequate room for maneuvering. Service areas should be located away from the entrances and screened with landscaping.

Street Widths

The following is a listing of various types of width which are used in traffic planning.

Minor streets	9–11 feet per lane
Major streets	10–14 feet per lane
Collector streets	10–18 feet per lane
Parallel parking, on street	8–10 feet per side
Private drives	8–9 feet per lane
Service drives	12–14 feet in width

Residential streets

Collector streets, with emergency parking	36 feet in width
Multi-family, with parking	32 feet in width
Single-family, with parking	26 feet in width
Cul-de-sacs, with parking on one side	20 feet in width

Turning radii

Minor streets	12–15 feet
Major arteries	35–50 feet

Pedestrian Circulation

Circulation to and from the building and its amenities should be planned for ease of access and provide for enjoyable experiences.

Easements

If the property includes any easements, either from adjacent property owners or utilities, the site plan should respond to these appropriately. Underground utility easement sometime prevents construction. These areas can be designed as landscaped or parking areas.

Utilities

The location of these lines must be cost effective and provide for ease of access.

Fences and Walls

Any required fences or walls should be designed for security, maintenance, and be cost effective.

Exterior Lighting

The design and planning of exterior lighting should be designed considering the following:

- Pedestrian
- Vehicles
- Aesthetics

Signage

Signage should be located for clear visibility and designed to complement the architecture of the development. Signage should include:

- Project identification at the entrance
- Address identification of the development and the individual buildings

- Office/model identification
- Traffic, street, and parking identification
- Handicapped parking identification

Schematic Design Phase

After program review, research, and master planning, the designer will provide the developer with evaluations of program and budget requirements. Then, the designer will provide the developer with alternative approaches to the design of the project (see Figure 7–4). Based on an approved direction, the schematic design documents will be produced illustrating scale and the relationships of project components (Figure 7–5). Prior to starting this process, the architect and engineers should do the following regarding the proposed development:

- Refine the budget estimates
- Prepare a detailed design schedule
- Recommend basic materials and construction systems
- Prepare function and circulation flow diagrams
- Prepare conceptual sketches
- Prepare preliminary specifications
- Retain outside consultants (if applicable)
- Conduct environmental studies (if applicable)
- Provide alternative design ideas
- Supervise energy optimization study
- Lead in design team value engineering
- Establish reporting and accounting procedures for his consultants
- Develop the construction bid package format
- Identify the long-lead purchase items
- Be prepared to present the design per developer's request
- Initiate some preliminary governmental regulatory reviews
- Initiate preliminary utility company reviews
- Review project design with insurance companies
- Update the conceptual estimate
- Provide schedule revisions
- Review contractor's budgets
- Build three-dimensional study models
- Prepare presentation boards
- Review other consultants' work for input

SOURCE: SCOGIN ELAM AND BRAY, ARCHITECTS

Figure 7–4 Alternative sketches.

Design Development Phase

Twenty percent into design documentation usually is the stopping point of pricing documents for contractor pricing. The design development phase is a continuation of the schematic design phase and the time when the designer completes more of the initial details of the design. Manufacturers are consulted, drawings are revised, and more of the comprehensive design is completed. More extensive reviews by the local building department occur for better understanding of the use of materials. Pricing efforts are repeated and value engineering continues. Based on approved schematic design documents and any revisions requested by the developer, the designer will complete documents for approval necessary to describe the size and character of the entire project. At the completion of this phase a rendering will be produced similar to Figure 7–6 for marketing purposes. The following are issues to consider during design development.

Building Construction and Safety Requirements

- Evaluate local and state building codes.
- Obtain approval of the local authority for crossing streets or municipal property or other property for utility services to the site.
- Work out cost-sharing arrangements for continuation or oversizing of the municipal services to the site, if applicable.
- Obtain approval of the traffic department for access and curb cuts. Discuss the need for new traffic signals.
- Obtain particular requirements by the building or fire inspector.
- Consider availability of building materials.
- Is seismic design of the structure required?
- Determine the methods of trash removal.
- Obtain FFA approvals.
- Consider environmental impact of pollution issues.

Electrical

- Obtain copies of all rate schedules available and determine whether primary service is economical and available.
- Specify applicable electrical code. Give any other codes or ordinances differing from the National Electrical Code which are applicable.
- Determine the type of service available.
- Is service supplied underground or overhead?
- Are underground conduits required?
- Determine specifications for transformer pads. Indicate whether pad-mounted, fully enclosed transformers are available.

- Determine the types of metering allowable (outdoor, indoor, or individual).
    - Types of wiring to be used
    - Emergency lighting
    - Exit lighting
    - Electric signs
- Determine whether there are reduced rates for heat pumps or electric heating.
- Does the utility company rent fixtures on poles for parking lot lighting.

Water Supply

- Who installs water lines and at what cost? What types of easements must be granted?
- Obtain water pressure, including residual pressure (in pounds per square inch) in mains opposite property. Obtain a flow test. Determine whether there is any variation in the water pressure during the day.
- Obtain a water analysis. Determine the hardness of the water in parts per million, and if hard (more than 100 ppm), whether future treatment by the water company is contemplated—how much reduction and when.
- Obtain the lowest temperature of the tap water in the winter.
- Specify whether the water supply will be obtained from a raw water source, millpond, or open top reservoir.
- Indicate whether the water is objectionable for any use.
- Determine who furnishes the water meters and are there any special metering arrangements required. Indicate whether the meters are preferred inside or outside of the building and if a master meter is required.
- Determine the sizes of the water meters required.
- Ascertain if air-conditioning equipment can function with city water.
- Determine the acceptable water main construction materials.
- Does the water company furnish fire hydrants? At what cost?
- Do the fire hydrants have to be metered?
- Are back flow preventers required? What are the specifications?

Plumbing

- Obtain applicable plumbing codes.
- Determine whether indirect wastes from food-containing units can be spilled into
    - Floor drains
    - Floor sinks
    - Individual hub drains
- Can wastes from sinks and water stations located under the service bars and counters spill into

Floor drains
Floor sinks
Individual hub drains

- Check condition of and location of grease traps and whether they are indoor or outdoor.

Sprinklers

- Is the sprinkler system required and does it have to be metered?
- Does the sprinkler system have to have a separate supply?
- Can the sprinkler system drainage lines be discharged into the rainwater leader?
- Can the sprinkler flow test pipe be discharged into the sanitary system?
- Determine if the water supply and distribution system must be reviewed by insurance underwriters.

Fuels

- Determine the fuel most used for heating similar buildings.
- Determine the fuel most commonly used for cooking in local restaurants (if applicable).
- Indicate whether gas lines on site are installed by the gas company at its cost.
- Determine the type of gas available (natural or artificial).
- Determine the specific gravity and BTU/cu. ft.
- Determine the pressure of the gas oz./sq. ft.
   At the main opposite the property
   At consumption side of the meter
- Indicate whether the pressure is reduced at the main or the meter.
- Determine the local requirements for the location of the gas meters (inside or outside of the building). If a meter access is required, indicate the desired location and the size of the metering for the anticipated gas input.
- Indicate whether the gas meters are furnished by the utility company or by the owner.
- Obtain a copy of the gas rates.
- Obtain a copy of the gas burning regulations.
- Determine any special installation requirements.
- Indicate any limitations on new installation capacity requirements.

Telephone

- Who furnishes the site conduit system?
- Indicate whether the conduit system in the building is to be furnished by the owner or by the utility company.

- Determine whether the telephone company can run cable above the hung ceiling.
- What are the space requirements for the telephone closet?

Construction Documentation

Based on the approved design development documents and any revisions requested by the developer, the designer should prepare, for approval by the developer documents consisting of drawings and specifications in detail for the construction of the project. These documents will become a part of the designer's contract for services. Figure 7–8 illustrates a typical detail in construction document.

Bidding Documents

Bidding documents are the documents which will be presented to the general contractors and subcontractors for their use in preparing bids with cost estimates of the work. These documents include the following:

- Invitation to bid
- Bid instructions
- General information and bid form
- Bid bond information
- Construction documents

Contract Documents

The contract document is the actual form of legal document between the developer and the general contractor. These documents also detail the bond requirements and any other certificates that must be executed.

General Conditions

This section outlines the rights and duties of the developer, the general contractor, the architect, the engineers, or construction manager.

Construction Specifications

The specifications are prepared by the designer or by a professional who coordinates the writing of these specifications for the designer. Construction specifications are divided into 16 major sections. They are as follows:

- Bidding and Contract Requirements

    Division 1   General requirements
    Division 2   Sitework

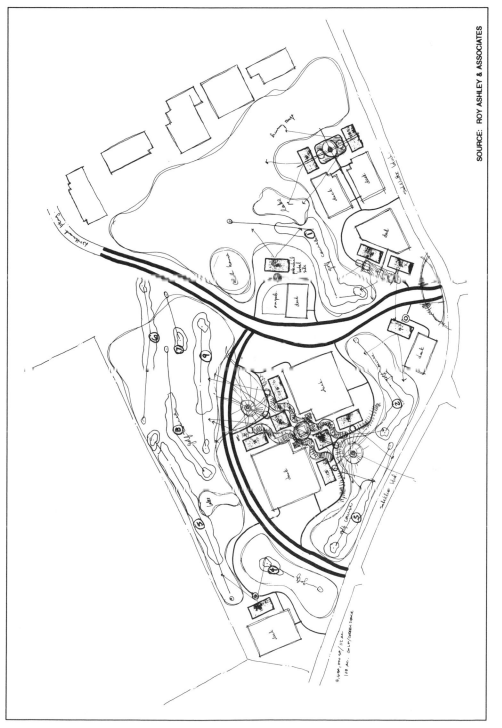

Figure 7-5 Schematic design drawing.

Figure 7-6 Rendering.

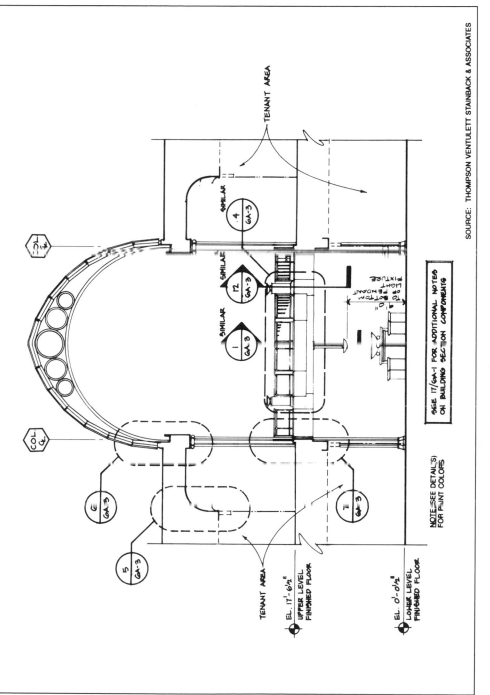

SOURCE: THOMPSON VENTULETT STAINBACK & ASSOCIATES

Figure 7-7 Design development drawing.

251

Division 3	Concrete
Division 4	Masonry
Division 5	Metals
Division 6	Wood and plastics
Division 7	Thermal and moisture protection
Division 8	Doors and windows
Division 9	Finishes
Division 10	Specialties
Division 11	Equipment
Division 12	Furnishings
Division 13	Special construction
Division 14	Conveying systems
Division 15	Mechanical
Division 16	Electrical

Working Drawings

The working drawings are a series of graphic drawings that will be used in the construction process (see Figure 7–8). These drawings illustrate plans, elevations, sections, isometrics, details, schedules, and diagrams for dimensional relationships. The drawings will include the following:

- Architectural drawings
- Structural drawings
- Mechanical drawings
- Plumbing drawings
- Electrical drawings
- Sprinkler drawings
- Civil engineering drawings
- Landscape architecture drawings
- Interior design drawings
- Kitchen equipment drawings
- Graphics and signage drawings

Depending on the size of the development each of these areas can include additional detail drawings. Each sheet of drawings in these sets will include:

- Project title and address
- Owner's name and address
- Names and addresses of design professionals
- Name of individual who completed drawing

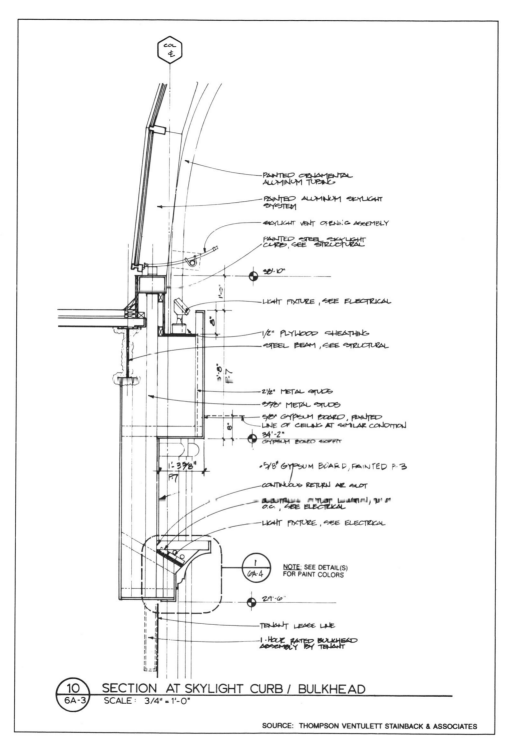

COL
℄

PAINTED ORNAMENTAL
ALUMINUM TUBING

PAINTED ALUMINUM SKYLIGHT
SYSTEM

SKYLIGHT VENT OPENING ASSEMBLY

PAINTED STEEL SKYLIGHT
CURB, SEE STRUCTURAL

38'-10"

LIGHT FIXTURE, SEE ELECTRICAL

1/2" PLYWOOD SHEATHING

STEEL BEAM, SEE STRUCTURAL

2 1/2" METAL STUDS

3 7/8" METAL STUDS

5/8" GYPSUM BOARD, PAINTED
LINE OF CEILING AT SIMILAR CONDITION
34'-2"
GYPSUM BOARD SOFFIT

5/8" GYPSUM BOARD, PAINTED P-3

CONTINUOUS RETURN AIR SLOT

ELECTRICAL OUTLET CHANNEL, 72" 0"
O.C., SEE ELECTRICAL

LIGHT FIXTURE, SEE ELECTRICAL

1
6A-4

NOTE: SEE DETAIL(S)
FOR PAINT COLORS

29'-6"

TENANT LEASE LINE

1-HOUR RATED BULKHEAD
ASSEMBLY BY TENANT

10
6A-3

SECTION AT SKYLIGHT CURB / BULKHEAD

SCALE: 3/4" = 1'-0"

SOURCE: THOMPSON VENTULETT STAINBACK & ASSOCIATES

Figure 7–8 Working drawing.

- Dates
- Dates of any revisions
- Designer's seal and signature (if required by law)

Bidding and Negotiations

The designers can assist the developer in the selection of bidders and the evaluation of the bids. If required, the designer can manage the total process for the developer. Their responsibility can include the issuing of bidding documents and answering any questions.

Construction Administration

This service begins at the developer's issuance of a notice to proceed to the contractor and will terminate when the final payment to the contractor is made or normally 90 days after the date of substantial completion of the work. The designer can provide administration of the contracts for construction during this period. The designer will act in behalf of the interests of the developer. The designer will visit the site at intervals and at appropriate stages in the construction to become familiar with the progress and quality of the work and to determine if the work is proceeding in accordance with construction documents. Field construction administration, written inspection reports, and certificates for payment can be provided as required. Other issues addressed during this period are listed below.

Shop Drawings Submittal

Detailed drawings produced by subcontractors, fabricators, and manufacturers which are submitted to the general contractor for approval during the construction phase. These are checked carefully with construction documents by appropriate designers.

Addenda

The addenda includes any new documents issued during the bidding or negotiation phase.

Contract Modifications

This activity includes modifications (change orders or supplemental instructions) to the scope of the work described in the construction documents.

Punch List

The punch list is produced jointly by the designer, developer, and the contractor as a listing of all work yet to be complete under the construction contract at such time that the contractor designates as substantial completion.

Warranty and Guarantee Manual

This manual produced by the contractor and reviewed by the designers sets forth all documentation of warranties and guarantees.

THE DESIGN TEAM MEMBERS

To accomplish all of the design tasks required for the construction of the development, the developer will need many different designers. The following briefly describes the types from which the developer can choose. It should be noted that the work of many of these is regulated by governmental agencies not mentioned in detail in Chapter 5. In addition, a more detailed description of their responsibilities is included in Chapter 6.

- Land planner
- Architect
- Civil engineer
- Structural engineer
- Mechanical engineer
- Electrical engineer
- Plumbing engineer
- Fire protection engineer
- Landscape architect
- Parking consultant
- Traffic consultant
- Elevator consultant
- Lighting consultant
- Kitchen consultant
- Curtain wall consultant
- Space plan designer
- Interior designer
- Graphics designer
- Fountain designer

Team Relationships and Composition

Often the landscape architect, architect, interior designer, traffic consultant, graphics designer, and land planner work directly for the developer. The civil, mechanical, electrical, plumbing and fire protection engineers, kitchen consultants, and fountain designers normally work directly for the architect even though the developer can mix and match them in any way. For example, sometimes the landscape architect and interior designer work directly for the architect on smaller projects.

As a side note, it is preferable to structure the team for efficiency and the dynamic of creativity. Having a number of designers reporting directly to the developer can be advantageous, though time consuming. This team structure places the designers in a more competitive, yet cooperative position to prove their worth to the team. Otherwise the architect can control all input prior to the developer's presentation.

In addition, never force one consultant to hire another consultant against his wishes. Since the first consultant will have the liability for the other consultant's work, he should have the final approval.

When selecting a consultant for out-of-town projects, there are other considerations. A local consultant may have more knowledge and leverage in final design approvals and be able to get started quicker. On the other hand, out-of-town consultants tend to be more expensive because of travel expenses. In addition, communications are more limited. All of these challenges can be overcome if you have the funds, time, and patience.

MISCELLANEOUS DESIGN CRITERIA

Obviously, during the design process, thousands of judgments and decisions are made. The quality of decisions will be based on the quality of criteria. The criterion is the force which shapes the design and gives basis for its worth. In the section where the various phases of the design process were discussed, insights were given into research in the designer's search for criteria. This section will expand those sections.

Measurement of Space

One of the first tasks to be completed by the development team is a definition of the proposed space measurements. These are the physical sizes of the components. Without specific definitions of space, marketing teams can be selling more or less space than is actually available and the general contractor's estimate will be inaccurate.

Residential Measurements

Residential developments are measured by heated and non-heated area. Heated area includes all the space to be heated, while non-heated areas include the garage, patio or balcony, and possible sections of the basement. Measurements are taken from inside wall to inside wall.

Commercial Measurements

Commercial buildings are quoted by rentable and usable area (see Figure 7–9). The Building Owners and Management Association (BOMA) defines these areas as:

Rentable Area: The rentable area is the tenant's pro rata portion of the entire office floor, excluding any elements that penetrate through the floor to areas below. The total rentable area on a floor is fixed during the life of the building. The rentable area of a floor shall be computed by measuring to the inside finished surface of the dominate portion of the permanent outer building walls, excluding any major vertical penetration of the floor. No deductions will be made for columns and projections within the building. The rentable area ratio of an office shall be calculated by the following formula:

$$\frac{\text{Rentable area}}{\text{Usable area}} = \text{Rentable/usable ratio (R/A)}$$

Usable Area: The usable area measures the actual occupied area of the floor or an office. The amount of usable area can vary in a building as the corridors on each floor expand and contract with the moving of tenants. The usable area of an office is calculated by measuring to the finished surface of the office side of the corridor and the other permanent walls, to the center of the partitions that separate the office from the adjacent usable areas, and to the inside finished surface of the dominant portion of the permanent outer building walls.

General Contractor Measurements

Most general contractors measure space by the total heated and cooled square footage, from the outside wall to outside wall. Prior to approval of plans and specifications, it is advisable to request the general contractor to measure this square footage. The worst thing that can happen to the developer is to have the general contractor give a "ballpark" figure for estimated costs per square foot and then find out that each is using a different method of measurement. In the conclusion of pricing efforts, request that the contractor and designer meet and confirm all area calculations. Most contractor's quote their prices based on gross square footage. Always check on their definition prior to accepting and contracting for their services.

Exterior Design and the Use of Materials

The use of materials will be a function of their availability, their costs, the designer, and developer's preferences, and market response.

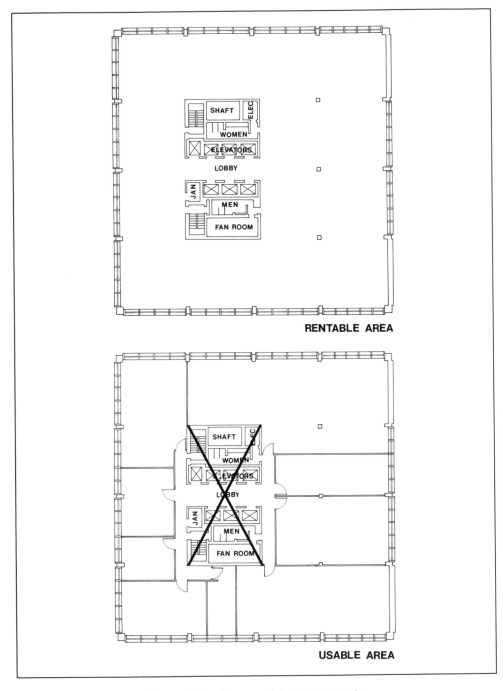

Figure 7–9   Commercial measurements.

Colors

Depending on whether the developer desires the development to stand out or blend with the surroundings will determine the color scheme to be used. Since the exterior skin of the building is quite expensive, the colors used should be colors that withstand the tests of time. It is a marketing disaster to select colors only to find at project completion, the style and desires of the marketplace have changed. On the other hand, those interior finishes that are changed every few years can be exactly what is most up-to-date in the marketplace.

Roof Treatment

The style of roof treatment should be compatible with the overall design style of the development and must fit within the construction budget of the project. Any roof equipment should be designed with a parapet to screen visibility of this equipment. Additionally, future maintenance should be kept in mind when specifying the roof system.

Parking Structures

If individual parking structures are designed with the development, they should be designed to blend in its surroundings and should be located in close proximity to the main building. Landscaping is essential to soften the appearance of these structures.

Visual Design Factors

In the creation of design which demonstrates delight, dynamic, and order, the designer will use various techniques to find the most appropriate design for the development. The following expressions will be used by the designer in presentations.

- Sequence
- Repetition and rhythm
- Balance
- Proportion and scale
- Pattern, texture, and color
- Shape, form, and size

Interior Design Specialty Issues

As the architect/designer produces the design of the site and building, the interior design shapes the interior spaces and gives them character and life. To be able to accomplish these tasks, the following criteria must be used.

Residential Interior Design

The design of the residential unit should be based on market demands. The architect should consult the marketing staff for current trends in the local housing market. Since these trends change quickly, the designer should be aware of new market trends. The following are in a state of constant flux.

Floor Plan: The floor plan should be designed for livability and traffic flow. The designer must design a plan which is within the budget of the consumer and can be built for the general contractor's estimate.

Kitchen: The kitchen is one of the most important rooms in the residential unit. This room should be designed so that it functions well in the preparation of meals. Additionally, in many upscale residential units, this room must have special appeal and become a living area.

Bathrooms: Similar to the kitchen, these rooms will not only have to function well, but may have extra "sizzle."

Storage: Storage is an extremely important feature in residential development. Ample storage must be available in sleeping, kitchen, and bath areas. Additional storage should also be designed into the basement, attic, or garage area.

Room Sizes: Today's consumer desires larger room sizes which function well with latest furniture designs. The room sizes must have adequate square footage as well as a functional shape.

Windows: In today's modern design, windows are more than just a place for a view. Their size and shape add to the character of the space. Their sense of delight add to the project's marketing effort. In themselves, they become design features.

Ceiling Height: The height of the ceiling, 9 feet or vaulted, adds volume and spatial effect to the residential unit.

Molding: The more expensive the residential unit, the more interior molding will be included. This molding not only conceals construction defects, but gives a feeling of elegance and visual interest.

Energy Conservation: Without high cost of utility bills, the home should be designed with all current energy saving systems. The buildings should be oriented to the sun's angles and provided with appropriate insulation.

Handicapped Requirements: Because of the current handicap requirements, the architect should include these features into the design. These requirements will include:

Oversized doors and hallways

Ramps and elevators

Lower cabinets and sinks

Bathroom grab bars

Lower electrical switches
Emergency buttons

Commercial Interior Design

Each product type and each building will have many unique design features. The following are the main design features that should be considered.

Service Cores: Each floor of a commercial building will have an area called the "core" which will contain the elevator shafts, the interior emergency stairways, and the mechanical shafts and rooms. Typically, this core is in the center of the building or in proximity to the entrance or lobby areas. Most services to the tenants spaces run from these cores.

Depending on the space requirements of the tenants, the distance from this core can be important in the marketing efforts. If the building will be marketed to small space users which are under 5000 square feet, the greater the distance from the core to the outside windows, the more difficult it will be for the tenant to have efficiently designed space. Conversely, large space users need greater distances from the core to the exterior windows. The most economically efficient and typical office buildings are designed with approximately 30 to 40 feet from the corridors to the exterior wall.

Lobby Area: The lobby area is located near the main entrance to the building. This area will be designed as a public area and include a building directory. Elevator lobbies will be in proximity and lead to tenant corridors. The corridors should be designed to be efficient, well-lighted, and pleasant.

Elevators: Most buildings over two floors will require passenger elevators. The speed of these elevators will usually depend on the number of floors of service. The number of elevators per building will be a function of the number of floors, the square footage of the floors, the floor type, desired interval of waiting time and the budget. Service elevators are needed for moving furniture, equipment, and mail. Elevator rooms are usually located on the roof along with the cooling tower and other mechanical and electrical rooms.

Janitorial Areas: For larger commercial properties, janitorial rooms are included on each floor. These rooms include slop sinks, drains, and supplies.

Mail Room: Depending on the size of the building, a separate mail room might be required. These rooms are usually located on the main floor or in the basement area of the building. Their layout must be approved by the U. S. Postal Service.

Structural Columns: Each building should be designed with as few columns as possible, because of their effect on tenant layout. The location and size of these columns should be as small as possible. The most economical column layout is one which is close to a square and contains between 900 to 1000 square feet (30 ft. × 30 ft. bays).

Ceiling Height: The height of the ceiling gives the tenant the feeling of spaciousness. Depending on the type of tenant, the ceiling height may have to be increased. It should be noted that the higher the ceiling the greater the costs. A higher ceiling requires an oversized piece of drywall that will have an increased construction cost as well as an increased cost of operating the HVAC (heating, ventilation, and air-conditioning) system. Ceiling grids should be coordinated with the window modules. Grid sizes of 2'-0" increments seem to work best. In industrial developments, ceiling height will be extremely critical to the tenants. This increased ceiling height is used for vertical storage and for movement clearance of equipment lifts.

Window Sizes, Mullions, and Modules: The window sizes, the mullions (the metal strip between the windows), and the modules (imaginary squares that divide the vertical surface of the building) are typically between 3 to 5 feet. The importance in their sizing lies in the planning of tenant offices. A 4-foot wide window will dictate an 8- or 12-foot office whereas 3-foot window sizes allow 9- or close to 10-foot width which are typical and most efficient.

Floor Loads Capacity: The structural capacity of the floors will result directly from the functions of the user. Codes set standards for floor live loading in typical buildings. Dead loading is added for those tenants using heavy machinery, libraries, and computers for their business. Typically, the floor load of the average building will be between 75 to 100 pounds per square foot. Increases in the capacity will add additional construction costs.

Number of Building Corners: The building floor design will dictate the number of corner offices available. Since the more corners designed, the more expensive the construction costs, the availability of more than four corner offices is usually designed in higher priced office buildings for marketing purposes.

Bay Sizes: Retail properties will be marketed by the width and depth of the bays. Smaller tenants will only require a 15- to 20-foot bay width with a 50- to 70-foot bay depth, while larger tenants may combine a multiple bay width and require additional depth.

Space Flexibility: Since most developers cannot predict exact tenant space requirements, the building design should include as much flexibility as possible. Additionally, even if a building is owned today, tomorrow it may want to be sold. The marketability of the building will be directly proportional to the building's flexibility in responding to another owner's needs.

Mechanical and Telephone Rooms: Mechanical rooms should be located on each floor of the building. Inside these rooms various mechanical equipment is located. This area can include the telephone equipment.

Utility Systems: The utility system designed for the building will be based on current installation costs and current uses charges for service.

HVAC Design: The heating, ventilation, and air-conditioning systems, commonly known as the HVAC, should be designed with the comfort of the tenant in mind. This system should take into consideration the number of people in a particular location at different times of the day or night. It is a property management nightmare to have hot tenants in the summer and cold tenants in the winter. Most buildings are designed with HVAC zones. Each floor or portions of the floors can be zones. Additionally, the developer can have the choice of tenant or building management control of the thermostat settings.

Energy Use Conservation: Due to the high cost of energy consumption, all buildings should be designed with energy use optimization ideas. Many new buildings include a computerized system of energy management. The computers are programmed to control HVAC during peak periods.

Plumbing Design: Since various tenants have different plumbing requirements, the building should be designed for flexibility. A wet column is vertical plumbing which is encased inside the cladding of an interior column. These pipes can be used for providing plumbing uses for wet bars, kitchen sinks, showers, and additional bathrooms. These wet columns avoid the expensive runs which would otherwise be necessary without them. Also, the codes control the number of fixtures which must be provided for men and women along with drinking fountains. Retail developments, during initial construction, omit the ground floor concrete slabs until the tenant's design is complete for ease of plumbing installation.

Electrical Design: The electrical design of the building will depend on the type of building and the type of tenant. Certain tenants will require additional electrical servicing capacity for equipment and computers. Most systems are designed for a 3 to 5 watt capacity per square foot.

Floor Ducts: Many buildings today are designed with underground electrical service through the floor system. For large service-oriented tenants with large bullpen areas, flexible service is provided to the employee's desk by floor electrical and telephone outlets. Since there is an absence of walls, this design prevents the use of electrical cords running from the ceiling or along the floor. These systems give the tenant great flexibility.

Security Systems: Security can be provided by a service security desk which not only monitors the building 24 hours a day, but monitors television camera and audio listening stations. Special locking devices can be used for the elevators and the tenant entrances. In addition, lighting is one of the greatest security features.

Life Safety Features: The designer should equip the building with all current life safety features economically feasible. These items will reduce insurance premiums and can be used as marketing features. The following are some examples:

Specially treated fire doors
Manual fire alarms
Emergency power
Elevator recall service
Smoke detectors
Automatic door-release system
Emergency phone service
Emergency exit doors
Remote stairway unlocking
Automatic sprinkler systems
Central control console
Smoke evacuation system
Building standpipe

Loading Facilities: The loading dock needs of tenants should not be overlooked. Many tenants require daily shipments of supplies. The loading dock should be located for ease of access from surrounding roadways. In addition, the dock should be located adjacent to the service elevator. Railroad access is essential for industrial-warehouse facilities and loading docks must be located carefully for vehicular and rail access.

Trash Removal Facilities: Since all tenants generate trash, an organized system of trash removal should be included in the building design. Some options which can be used are trash chutes on each floor, separate service elevators, and trash compactors or dumpsters.

Landscape Architectural Design to Soften and Cover

Depending on the size and scope of the development, either a landscape architect or a landscape contractor will provide the design and selection of plant materials. Landscaping provides great curb appeal for the development and reinforces marketing efforts. The more appealing the property, the greater the occupancy and the higher the rental rates. The landscaping portion of the development budget will dictate the size and quantity of the landscape material. With larger landscaping budgets, more mature plant material can be used and the beauty and completeness of the project will be realized sooner. Even in the scope of total cost, the budget for landscaping is quite small. Exercising care in landscape design can accomplish wonders for mediocre developments and make smashing successes for great developments. Figure 7–10 shows a landscape architecture drawing, while Figure 7–11 shows a landscape architecture working drawing. Landscaping design should consider the following areas.

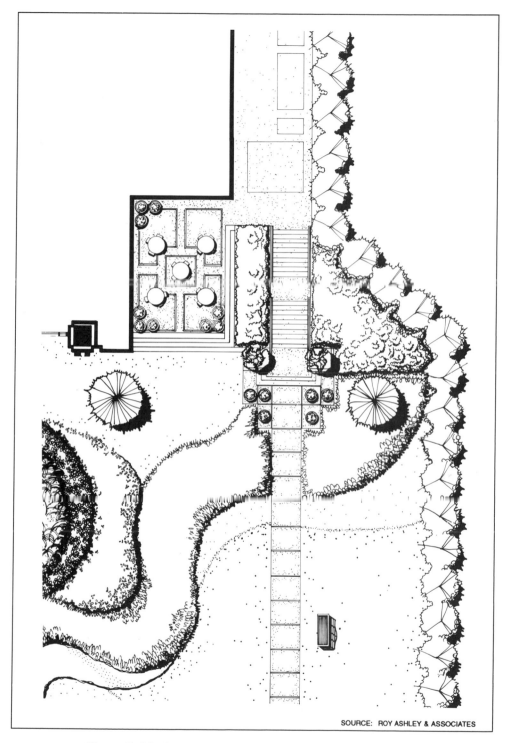

Figure 7–10 Landscape architecture presentation drawings.

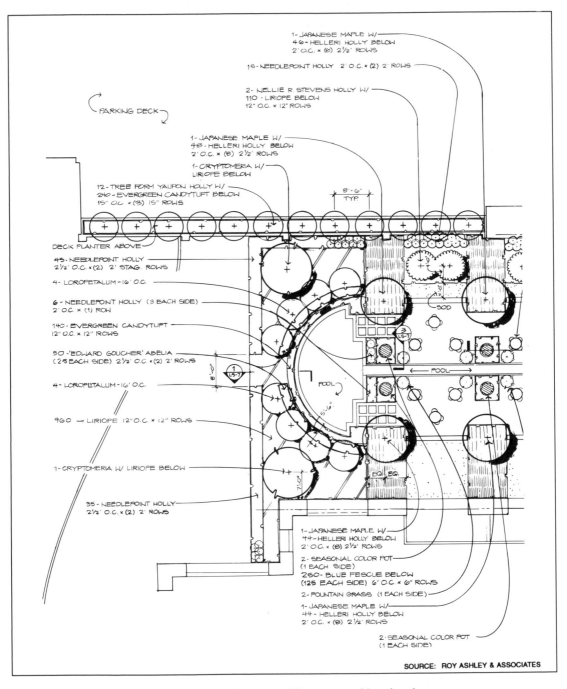

Figure 7–11 Landscape architecture working drawings.

- Property setbacks
- Property entrances
- Interior roadways
- Property buffers
- Amenity areas
- Exterior furniture
- Exterior building common areas
- Interior building common areas
- Water features and water edges
- Walkways
- Interior lobbies and atriums
- Existing features such as lakes, forests, and special ornamental trees

Choosing the Right Plant Material

The process of choosing the correct planting material will depend on the development's landscaping budget, the time of year the plants are installed, the soil conditions, and the weather conditions in that part of the country.

Irrigation

To make sure that the plant material is healthy, the landscape designer should include some method of providing moisture for the plants. This will include either an underground sprinkler irrigation system or a manual watering schedule.

Energy Conservation

Energy conservation should also be reviewed when designing the landscaping plan. Certain types of shade trees can be planted around the building to shield the sun for vertical wall surfaces.

Architectural Details

To add vitality to the development, additional architectural details can be added—for example:

- Paving materials and colors
- Landscaping walls
- Stairways
- Sculpture
- Pools and fountains
- Night lighting
- Pedestrian seating
- Gazebos and trellises

FROM PROPOSALS TO CONTRACTS

The initial step to contracting for services is the proposal. Using proposals and with a minimum of effort, the developer can review the scope of services offered, the fees for those services and the credentials of the consultant. This aspect of contracting was discussed in detail in Chapter 6. Often for minor services, these proposals, with appropriate signatures, can become agreements and no further contracting is needed. As explained in Chapter 6, when multiple consultants are used, a work order system can be used for convenience. Usually, in the early predevelopment phases of the process, these mini-agreements are acceptable, because the liability on the project at this time is minimal due largely to the fact that only drawings or reports have been produced. Now that we are serious about the construction of the project, it is imperative that standards for their production and the liabilities for errors and omissions be discussed. In addition, formal relationships between team members must be addressed. For a smooth working construction project, all of the contracts must be coordinated together as a total with each company recognizing its responsibilities to the other.

In this section, we will discuss those proposals which must be changed into contracts. They are as follows:

- architect's agreement
- interior designer's agreement
- landscape architect's agreement

Negotiating the Professional Services Contracts

Once the consultant has been chosen, the developer should focus on the following issues.

Fee Structure

The fee structure can be based on an hourly rate, a fixed fee, fee per square foot, or a percentage of the total construction costs.

Payment Schedule

The payment schedule will outline when the various fees are due to the design team members. Normally, they will parallel the completion of various phases of the design process.

Hiring of Design Professionals

Depending on what is desired the developer may choose to hire design professionals individually or may decide to have the architect coordinate this effort. If the architect accepts this extra responsibility, he will receive an additional administration fee for these additional services.

Ownership of Drawings

Most architects retain the rights to their designs and drawings. If the developer desires to own these rights, the rights must be negotiated into his contract. The developer usually pays for the service, and not the ownership of the drawings.

Re-Use of Drawings

Many times the developer will re-use the design more than once. The developer and the architect must negotiate a re-use fee for these drawings.

Scope of Work

The term scope of work defines the work to be accomplished for the stated fee.

Schedule of Completion

In order to maintain the developer's schedule, the design professionals must provide the developer with dates of completion for various stages of work. The developer must remember that compliance with the designer's needs for information and approvals will determine this schedule's final outcome.

Outlines for Architectural, Interior Design, and Landscape Architectural Agreements

The following will provide listings of the various issues encountered in the development of these agreements. It is recommended that an attorney be used for negotiations, production, and review.

Architectural Contracts

The basic form for most architectural contracts is the American Institute of Architects (AIA) standard form contract. It should be remembered that the architect usually has contracted with engineers prior to consummating this contract. The developer can request a copy of those documents if required. The items addressed in the architect's agreement are as follows:

Article 1   Architect's services and responsibility
Article 2   Owner's responsibility
Article 3   Construction cost
Article 4   Direct personnel expense
Article 5   Reimbursable expenses
Article 6   Payments to the architect
Article 7   Architect's accounting record
Article 8   Ownership and use of documents
Article 9   Arbitration
Article 10   Termination of agreement

Article 11   Miscellaneous provisions
Article 12   Successors and assigns
Article 13   Extent of agreement
Article 14   Basis of compensation
Article 15   Other conditions of service
Exhibit A   Architect's insurance
Exhibit B   Site plan
Exhibit C   Design baseline
Exhibit D   Phase approval form
Exhibit E   Call back authorization form
Exhibit F   Subordination agreement
Exhibit G   Lien waiver
Exhibit H   Consent of assignment

Interior Designer Contract

The magnitude of this agreement will be determined by the type of project. Hotels, clubs, restaurants, and casinos require extensive programming in design and construction documentation. Space planning is also another work effort which is extensive and complicated. The following is a listing of major issues considered in the interior designer's agreement.

Article 1   Scope of work
Article 2   Scope of service
  Phase 1   Planning
  Phase 2   Concept
  Phase 3   Architectural
  Phase 4   Contract documents, including F, F, & E drawings and specifications
  Phase 5   Bidding and negotiations
  Phase 6   Design implementation
Article 3   Services not included
Article 4   Implementation of interior design
Article 5   Fees
Article 6   Reimbursable expenses
Article 7   Additional services
Article 8   Cancellation and partial services
Article 9   Credit and press release
Article 10   Assignability
Article 11   Phase approval forms

Landscape Architecture Contract

The following are included in this contract and can be expanded to use any of the articles used in the interior designer or architectural contracts if the landscape architect's work efforts merge into these disciplines.

- Information provided by the developer
- Preliminary landscape design
- Final design
- Rendered landscape plan
- Bid and contract documents
- Supervision of construction
- Selection of plant materials
- Warranty reports
- Documents
- Payment
- Termination or abandonment of improvement

TENANT DEVELOPMENT DESIGN

Tenant space planning is addressed at this time because it usually lies outside the standard architectural or engineering contracts. It is an important aspect of commercial construction because in marketing the property, the efficiency of the layout and the costs for construction are crucial pieces of the decision-making process of a prospective tenant. Selecting designers whose services aid the marketing process will prove to be helpful in the developer's overall marketing success. It should be noted that the architect, interior designer, or space planner can provide this service.

The tenant development process begins prior to the completion of the project and continues long into the future after the completion of the project. The developer should have a person or a department which is responsible for the overall design and construction of tenant space. Project management and property management usually manage these efforts.

Anchor Tenant Space Planning

Anchor tenants who have decided to lease prior to the completion of construction documents and the beginning of construction can have a substantial effect on the design, overall appearance, and function of the project. These anchor tenants usually are essential for the financing of the project. In addition, they will exercise powerful influence in the decision-making process. Their space planning contracts will have provisions for design approval. Also, the programming, scheduling, and design can affect the building's overall construction schedule. Figure 7–12 is a diagram showing tenant space planning.

Tenant Development Systems

Because rents from leasing the space is the fuel which runs the development, the developer should establish systems and procedures for the tenant development process to ensure that maximum efficiency in design, cost and schedule control, and responsiveness is maintained. The systems should be carefully formulated and fashioned for the uniqueness and location of the development. The following are items or work tasks which must be considered in the planning of these efforts.

Responsibilities of the Staff

The tenant development personnel will interface with marketing, accounting, and property management throughout the tenant build-out phase. Each should be aware of their responsibilities to the other and the need for smooth communications in winning and satisfying prospective tenants.

Tenant Interface

Tenant development personnel should interface with the prospective tenant from the beginning in conjunction with marketing personnel. Only in this way will the tenant's needs be clearly understood from the moment the lease is signed to the moment the space is occupied.

Space Planner and Tenant Contract

Space planners should be chosen for their creativity and responsiveness. If the space planners who are hired cannot perform up to marketing's expectations, the potential tenant finds another project in which to locate. Prior to signing a contract, schedules and fees for work as well as additional services should be clearly understood. In addition, they must also be sensitive to controlling cost through efficiencies in their design.

Tenant Construction and Their Contracts

Experienced tenant construction contractors will give the best results. Selecting these can be on a unit price bid basis as well as references to their past work. They must be acutely aware of schedule constraints and be able to perform consistently in this manner. Their contracts should be structured so that a guaranteed maximum price is given.

Cost Estimations and Unit Prices

The prospective tenant who is considering your development must know the rent and additional fit-up expenses early in the process. Having standard

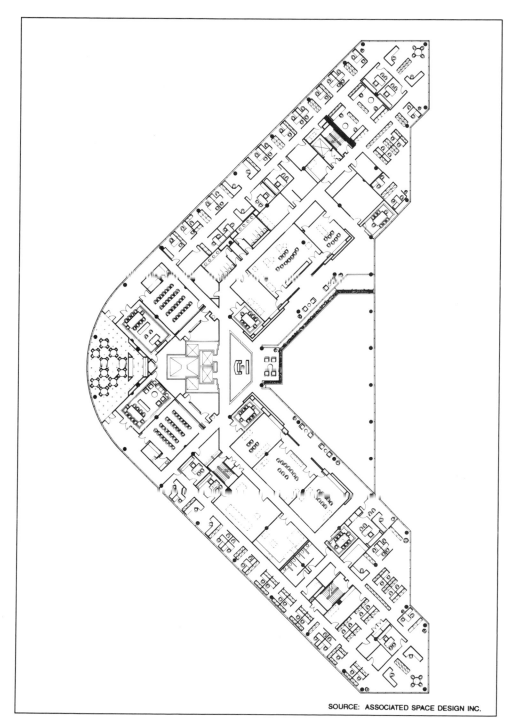

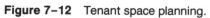

Figure 7–12   Tenant space planning.

tenant allowances which have been priced on a unit basis is quickest way to respond to this need. It is only a matter of knowing the components, measuring the components, multiplying the math, and addition general conditions. Having unit prices sometimes allows the tenant development manager to provide a quick estimate without contractor involvement and the time that it takes for a contractor to respond.

Standard Tenant Allowance

In the pricing of the building and formulation of project economics for the hard costs of the development, costs for standard tenant allowances will be included. This allowance schedule includes all of the items offered by the developer from floor to ceiling. It is from this standard tenant allowance that unit prices are derived.

Mechanical, Electrical, and Plumbing Engineers

The easiest way for the documents required for mechanical, electrical and plumbing to be produced is with the original engineer for the construction. If this engineer is located in another city, then it is better to use a local one. To function effectively, they must understand the systems that are designed and be able to work well with the tenant development manager and the space designers.

Standard Tenant Finishes and Their Presentations

In the formulation of interior design concepts for the public areas of the new development, the interior designer should include standard tenant finishes. These will include carpet options, paint and wall covering options, hardware finishes, graphics for doors, plastic laminate for countertops, ceiling tile, and window treatments. It is better for the public areas interior designer to select these finishes for them to work well with the total building. The visual aids that are created can be used by marketing for tenant presentations.

Production of Base Drawing

Once the construction of the development is under way and construction drawings have been approved, a base drawing should be produced. This drawing is usually created by the architect or the interior designer. It is a drawing of all of the floor plans of the building on which new tenant layouts can be drawn. It does not contain all of the details of the construction document so that only the layout of the new tenants can be seen in relationship to the whole floor plan. Base drawings must be completed for finishes, and electrical, mechanical, and plumbing plans.

Coordination with Governmental Agencies and Building Permits

Obviously, this construction, as any other, must comply with the standard requirements of local government agencies relative to codes and inspections prior to receiving an occupancy permit.

Standard Leases

It is important for the tenant development manager to thoroughly understand the lease so that all construction, costs, and schedules are in compliance with it.

Punch Lists and Acceptance of Premises

Once the construction of the tenant space is complete, the marketing agent, tenant development manager, the new tenant, and the contractor should visit the space to identify any deficiencies. These should be produced in a punch list and after they are corrected, the tenant will sign a document accepting the premises. The tenant can sign an acceptance of the premises which is conditional upon the completion of these items.

Design Approvals

Once the tenant design process is under way, it is critical that all changes to the drawing be approved by marketing, property management, and the new tenant. Each should sign off in terms of cost, schedule, and design.

Finishes and Hardware Selection

It is best to have standards which all tenants must use. Otherwise, control of costs will be difficult and property management will be almost impossible.

Tenant Construction Authorizations

No construction should begin without authorization. The authorization will be activated by the signing of the lease. Only at this time is the tenant liable for the construction costs. Beginning at any other time means that the developer is liable for the costs. This is also true in additional services request which is discussed next.

Additional Services Request

After the tenant space is completed, there are always other items which the tenant may need. These are referred to as additional service requests. When received, they should be priced and, prior to completion, there should be an authorization signed which states that the tenant will pay for the extras.

Invoicing Procedures

Procedures should be devised which require the contractor to invoice on a standard format making it easy to track the actual costs of the development. There should be a linear track from cost estimation to final payment.

Guaranteed Maximum Costs

Using guaranteed maximum costs will minimize the developer's liability for cost overruns and allow him to sign leases with a degree of security.

Scheduling

All members of the tenant development team must be sensitive to schedule because of the penalties in delayed rent payment should they fail to have the tenant's space ready on time. On very large projects, these payments can be very large and their absence can have adverse effects on the development's economic projections.

Change Order Request

All change order requests by the contractor should track the additional services requests which have been previously signed and which are above and beyond the guaranteed maximum costs.

Final Inspection and Certificates of Occupancy

These must be timed to coincide with the tenants' dates of occupancy. For this to occur, it is important to provide a three-to-seven-day safety factor.

Applications for Payment

Use of the standard contractor application for payment is acceptable.

Professional Work Orders

This system was discussed in Chapter 6; it is the same but in a reduced scope.

Progress Reports

The contractor and tenant development manager should make weekly reports to marketing as to the status of the work. If a delay is anticipated, it is better than a late surprise.

Contractor's Affidavit or Release of Liens

As the contractor receives payment for work accomplished, he should always sign a lien release to prevent a subcontractor which he did not pay from adversely affecting the work.

CHECKLIST FOR REVIEWING THE PLANS AND SPECIFICATIONS

The following is a checklist which the developer or representatives can use in reviewing plans and specifications. The success of the overall team's effort will be directly proportional to how everyone assists everyone else in the completion of their work. The developer and managers must approve all of the designer's presentations and the contractor's cost estimates. This checklist will build confidence that all important issues have been considered.

I. Review of preliminary and final working drawings and specifications to evaluate the overall adequacy of
A. Site Planning
    1. Site plan
        a. Citing of improvements
            (1) Relation to topography
            (2) Relation to view
            (3) Relation to sun
        b. Grading plan
        c. Traffic flow
            (1) Vehicle
            (2) Pedestrian
            (3) Emergency vehicles
    2. Soils tests
        a. Soils test
    3. Drainage control
        a. Erosion control
        b. Retention areas
            (1) Design
            (2) Capacity
            (3) Screening
        c. Location of catch basins
    4. Utilities
        a. Location of meters
            (1) Water
            (2) Sewer
            (3) Electric
            (4) Gas
            (5) Telephone
            (6) Cable TV
    5. Retaining walls
        a. Location
        b. Type of materials
    6. Paving
        a. Type of material
    7. Curb and gutter
        a. Type of curb
        b. Condition

  8. Sidewalks
    a. Type of material
    b. Handicap access
  9. Fire hydrants
    a. Location
 10. Dumpster
    a. Location
    b. Design
    c. Screening
    d. Truck access
 11. Parking
    a. Location to buildings
    b. Number of spaces
    c. Handicap parking
      (1) Number of spaces
      (2) Location
    d. Striping
    e. Bumper guards
 12. Fencing
    a. Location
    b. Type of material
    c. Design
 13. Exterior lighting
    a. Review location
    b. Review design
    c. Review size of lights
 14. Mail boxes
    a. Location
    b. Design
 15. Signage
    a. Entrance sign
      (1) Location of signage
      (2) Type of material
      (3) Design
      (4) Lighting
    b. Guest parking
      (1) Location of signage
      (2) Type of material
      (3) Design

      c. Office
         (1) Location of signage
         (2) Type of material
         (3) Design
      d. Model unit
         (1) Location of signage
         (2) Type of material
         (3) Design
      e. Miscellaneous signage
         (1) Location of signage
         (2) Type of signage
         (3) Type of material
         (4) Design
16. Landscaping
      a. Landscaping plan
      b. Plant materials
         (1) Quality of materials
         (2) Sizing of materials
      c. Maintenance schedule
17. Irrigation system
      a. Irrigation design
      b. Watering schedule
B. Exterior of buildings
   1. Building exterior
      a. Materials
      b. Warranty
      c. Durability
      d. Color selection
   2. Roofing
      a. Type of roof
      b. Material selection
      c. Color selection
      d. Flashing
      e. Roof bond
      f. Warranty
   3. Address signage
      a. Material
      b. Location

      c. Design

      d. Color selection

  4. Exterior lighting

      a. Location

          (1) Building

          (2) Unit entrances

          (3) Breezeways

          (4) Handicap

      b. Photo-cells and timers

      c. Design

      d. Material

  5. Air conditioner condensers

      a. Location

      b. Screening of units

      c. Size of units

      d. Warranty

  6. Exterior stairways and walkways

      a. Location

      b. Material

          (1) Steps

          (2) Railings

      c. Handicap access

  7. Doorbells

      a. Location

  8. Unit entrance doors

      a. Type of door

      b. Peephole

  9. Roof access

      a. Location

10. Roof overhang

      a. Design

11. Gutters and downspouts

      a. Location

      b. Design

      c. Splash blocks

      d. Roof diverters

12. Hose bibs
    a. Location
13. Windows
    a. Location
    b. Materials
    c. Design
C. Interior of buildings
    1. Foundation plans
        a. Design
        b. Type of materials
    2. Floor plan
        a. Floor plan for traffic flow
    3. Flooring
        a. Floor system
        b. Type of material
            (1) Residential
                (a) Kitchen
                (b) Bathroom
                (c) Utility area
                (d) Foyer
                (e) Living areas
            (2) Commercial
    4. Wall and ceiling areas
        a. Location
        b. Type of material
            (1) Paint
            (2) Wallpaper
        c. Design
    5. Heating, ventilation, and air conditioning (HVAC)
        a. Design
        b. Capacity
        c. Material
        d. Warranty
    6. Hot water heater
        a. Location
        b. Capacity

     c. Design
     d. Warranty
  7. Kitchen
     a. Design
     b. Appliances
        (1) Type of appliances
        (2) Refrigerator
        (3) Oven
        (4) Dishwasher
        (5) Disposal
        (6) Washer
        (7) Dryer
        (8) Trash compactor
        (9) Microwave
        (10) Inventory
        (11) Color selection
        (12) Warranties
     c. Review cabinets
        (1) Material
        (2) Quality
        (3) Color selection
        (4) Design
        (5) Hardware
     d. Review plumbing
        (1) Materials
        (2) Design
        (3) Sink/hardware
  8. Smoke detectors
     a. Location
     b. Type
        (1) Electric
        (2) Battery
  9. Bathroom
     a. Bathtub
        (1) Material
        (2) Design

    b. Stall shower
      (1) Material
      (2) Design
    c. Cabinets
      (1) Material
      (2) Design
      (3) Color selection
    d. Mirror
      (1) Location
      (2) Size
    e. Medicine cabinets
      (1) Location
      (2) Size
    f. Countertops
      (1) Style
      (2) Color
    g. Sink
      (1) Style
      (2) Color
    h. Commode
      (1) Style
      (2) Color
    i. Hardware
      (1) Style
      (2) Color
    j. Handicap facilities
      (1) Code compliance
10. Insulation and soundproofing
    a. Specifications
      (1) Floors
      (2) Exterior walls
      (3) Ceilings
11. Electrical
    a. Location of electrical outlets
    b. Location of switches
    c. Location of panel boxes
    d. Location of telephone outlets

      e. Lighting fixtures

      f. Electrical capacity

      g. Light sizes

12. Cable TV

      a. Location

13. Window coverings

      a. Material

      b. Design

      c. Color

14. Fireplaces

      a. Location

      b. Design

      c. Type of material

15. Trim work

      a. Location

         (1) Ceiling molding

         (2) Chair rail molding

         (3) Door casing

         (4) Window casing

         (5) Floor molding

16. Mechanical utility system

      a. Heating system

         (1) Electric

         (2) Gas

         (3) Location of supply and return ducts

      b. Water heating system

         (1) Electric

         (2) Gas

      c. Air conditioning system

         (1) Electric

         (2) Gas

      d. Cooking

         (1) Electric

         (2) Gas

      e. Clothes dryer

         (1) Electric

         (2) Gas

17. Plumbing
    a. Water pressure capacity
18. Utility room
    a. Location
    b. Appliances
       (1) Washer
       (2) Dryer
    c. Sink
19. Doors
    a. Location
    b. Material
    c. Color
20. Closets
    a. Location
    b. Shelving
    c. Lighting
    d. Size
21. Parking area
    a. Garage
    b. Carport
    c. Parking deck
       (1) Location
       (2) Design
       (3) Materials
22. Janitor's area (commercial property)
    a. Location
23. Mechanical area (commercial property)
    a. Location
    b. Equipment
24. Elevators
    a. Location
    b. Design
    c. Specifications
25. Commons areas
    a. Location
       (1) Lobby
       (2) Hallways
       (3) Stairways

b. Design

c. Color selection

d. Material

26. Fire protection

a. Location

b. Design

27. Security

a. Location

b. Design

c. Specifications

D. Amenity package

1. Clubhouse

a. Location

b. Design

c. Material

d. Color selection

e. Mechanical

f. Plumbing

g. Electrical

h. Furniture, fixtures, and equipment (F, F, & E)

2. Laundry facilities

a. Location

b. Design

c. Plumbing

d. Mechanical

e. Electrical

f. Color selection

g. Interior finish

h. Equipment

3. Public restrooms

a. Location

b. Design

c. Fixtures

d. Color selection

e. Cabinets

f. Electrical

g. Mechanical systems

      h. Plumbing

      i. Hardware

  4. Office

      a. Location

      b. Design

      c. Color selection

      d. Interior finish materials

      e. Electrical

      f. Mechanical systems

      g. Plumbing

  5. Pool

      a. Location

      b. Design

      c. Specifications

      d. Decking area

         (1) Material

         (2) Size

      e. Inventory

      f. Pool equipment room

      g. Diving board

  6. Tennis court

      a. Location

      b. Design

      c. Lighting

      d. Fencing

      e. Materials

  7. Playground area

      a. Location

      b. Design

      c. Lighting

      d. Inventory

      e. Materials

      f. Fencing

  8. Lake area

      a. Location

      b. Design

II.   Review of the plans to determine:
      Gross/net leasable square footage
      Number and type of units
      Size of each unit
      Number of parking spaces
III. Review and verify the plans and specifications to:
      Make sure they comply with all zoning and building codes
      Obtain the certificate of occupancy
IV.   Prepare an independent cost analysis by trade and by line item to determine if:
      Project can be completed for the dollars indicated
      There are any "front-loaded" costs
      There are any incorrect or underestimated costs
V.   Determine if the project can be completed per schedule
VI.   Review the construction contracts
VII. Draft a report to summarize the findings to include:
      Completeness of the plans and specifications
      Unusual features and/or construction techniques employed
      Cost estimates
      Time schedules
      Recommendations for correcting any deficiencies

DESIGN FORMS

Square Footage Calculation Form (7-1)

The square footage calculation form is to be used to calculate the various types of square footage in a building.

SQUARE FOOTAGE CALCULATION FORM

FORM 7–1

PROJECT _____

DATE ___/___/___

FLOOR	GROSS BLDG. GRA	GROSS INT. GIA	RENT RA	USABLE MIN. UA	USUABLE MAX. UA
SUB TOTAL					
ATTRIUM					
PENTHOUSE					
TOTAL					

EFFICENCY
RA + GBA = _____
UA (MIN.) + GBA = _____
UA (MAX.) + GBA = _____

FACTOR FOR MULTI-TENANT USER
RA + UA(MAX.) = _____

DEFINITIONS

Gross Building Area (GBA): Area of floor with perimeter limits defined by the outside face of the exterior wall.

Gross Interior Area (GIA): Area of floor with perimeter limits defined by the inside face of the most dominant exterior wall surface.

Rentable Area (RA): Gross interior area less:
1. Strairways except where contained in a lobby area used exclusively by the tenant.
2. Elevators and enclosed pipe and duct shafts at each floor level through which they pass.
3. Fire towers and penthouses.

Usuable Area-Max. (UA-Max.) The rentable area less toilets, minimum corridors, lobbies, janitor's closets, electrical, mechanical, and communications rooms (all used in common with each tenants in the building).

Usuable Area-Min. (UA-Min.) The usuable area (maximum) less the difference between the minimum and maximum corridor configuration.

Form 7–1 Square footage calculation form.

## Chapter 8

Crunching the Numbers to Determine Financial Feasibility

The calculation of a project's economic estimates is first completed on a preliminary basis and then refined repeatedly until final costs are obtained. These calculations are run manually or by computer. The use of the personal computer has not only shortened this process but made it rather enjoyable to experiment with different cost assumptions.

The initial estimates are "ballpark" figures for each line item. These estimates are based on "educated guesses" from past experiences, rules of thumb, or estimates from contracting professionals.

Prior to formulating the numbers on paper, the developer should first outline the various line item categories which he will encounter. Most errors result from the developer in the project economics by overlooking necessary items than by underestimating costs.

Since developers measure their success based on original profit and absorption calculations, it is wise to add safety factors to assumptions. It is better to be surprised with profit at the end of the deal than to be disappointed because the project comes in late and over the budget.

The two types of financial forecasting which will be reviewed in this chapter are the development proforma and the property operating proforma. To better assist the reader in understanding this process a case study (Sutton Place Apartments) of an apartment property will be included at the end of this chapter.

HOW TO PREPARE A DEVELOPMENT PROFORMA

The development proforma includes the proceeds and costs of the project. The two types of development costs are direct and indirect costs. Direct costs, also known as hard costs, are those costs which result from building construction and improvements costs. Indirect costs, or soft costs, include the architectural and engineering costs, all financing costs, and those costs not directly related to the construction of the improvements. Each of these costs can be broken down into multiple subcategories as follows.

Proceeds and Incomes

The proceed categories include those items where money will flow into the developer's checkbook.

Equity

This is the amount of cash equity that the developer will contribute into the development. This amount will either be determined by the developer up front or required by the lender, based on the shortfall of the construction or permanent loan.

- Partners
- General partner
- Limited partner
- Joint venture partners

Loan Financing Proceeds

These are the proceeds generated by the various loans obtained by the developer. They will include the construction, permanent, and any additional loans placed on the property.

- Land acquisition loan
- Construction loan
- Permanent loan—first mortgage
- Permanent loan—second mortgage
- Interim loan
- Partner loan

Rental Income

This income includes all the base rent and additional charges made to the tenants.

- Base rent
- Percentage rent

- Common area maintenance (CAM) charges
- Operating expense pass through
- Parking

Fees

This is additional income derived by the tenants for late fees, cleaning charges, pet fees, application fees, credit check fees, and bad check charges.

Deposit Income

This is funds for various tenant deposits. All or part of these funds may be returned to the tenant at the end of their lease.

- Rental security
- Cleaning security
- Sales deposits
- Pet deposits

Interest Income

This is income on any funds that are left in the bank.

- Partnership account
- Escrow account
- Operating account

Vending Income

This is income from any vending machines on the property.

- Laundry
- Telephone
- Food/drinks

Sale Proceeds

This is income generated by either selling part of the development (residential housing) or the total property; it is called buyer sales income.

Association Fees

This income is paid by the tenants for their share of any association fees.

Miscellaneous Income

This is the category to include any other proceeds not included in the above items.

Applications of the Proceeds

The applications of the proceeds include those items which are paid out by the developer.

Hard or Direct Costs

Land

     This is the cost of the land, the land closing costs, and the cost of carrying the land. Since the developer has already contracted for the land, he should be able to estimate these costs. The developer should contact the attorney for estimating potential closing costs.

- Tracts
- Interest carry
- Closing costs
- Real estate commission
- Real estate taxes
- Insurance
- Utilities
- Zoning fees
- Neighborhood agreements
- Legal
- Title policy
- Engineering fees

Site Costs

     These are the costs pertaining to developing the site. They begin with clearing the land and end with the costs of final landscaping. Preliminary cost estimates are based on the total land area, either per square footage or per acre. Since each site is different, these estimates tend to be unreliable.

- Survey and testing
- Land improvements
- Landscaping
- Entrance, fencing, and signage
- Punch out
- Site contingency

Building Construction Costs

     These are the costs for the building. These costs are first estimated as per square foot or per unit costs. When estimating, ensure that you have a clear definition of each line item and the assumptions used in its derivation. Many general contractors will give a price per gross square footage but this price may include the roof overhang, which is not calculated by the developer when thinking of the square footage. In addition, when obtaining this preliminary estimate, the developer should ensure that he is using a general contractor who has recently constructed a similar type property. These costs will include the following:

- Concrete
- Waterproofing
- Carpentry
- Fireplace
- Roofing
- Mechanical
- Electrical
- Plumbing
- Interior finish
- Doors, windows, glass
- Exterior finish
- Flooring
- Finishes
- Appliances
- Specialties
- Tenant improvements
- Amenities
- Punch out
- Warranty
- Contingency

Construction Overhead

The overhead costs of the project include the insurance, bonds, permits, security, vehicle expense, blueprints, and fees for the contractor and developer. Typically the general contractor's fee is a percentage of the construction costs and the developer's fee is a percentage of the total costs or a flat fee. The developer's administration fees may include the costs for construction management. The following costs should be included as overhead costs.

- Field office
- Utilities
- Deposits
- Permits

- Insurance
- Bonds
- Tools
- Labor
- Security
- General and administrative
- Vehicle expenses
- Signage
- Blueprints
- General contractor's fee

Professional Fees

The professional fees include the legal, accounting, architectural, engineering, and any other professional fees involved with the development of the property. A sampling are as follows.

- Legal
- Accounting
- Architectural
- Land planner
- Engineering
- Landscape architecture
- Interior space designer
- Interior decorator
- Estimator
- Tax service
- Property management
- Consultant
- Appraiser
- Market researcher
- Construction management
- Developer's fee

Furniture, Fixtures, and Equipment (F, F, & E)

If the planned project has furniture or equipment, especially if the property is a hotel, there will be expenses for millwork and artwork which must be included in the estimate.

- Common area furniture and accessories
- Office

- Maintenance
- Pool

Soft or Indirect Costs

Marketing

The marketing costs include the agency and production costs for marketing brochures, setting up the model room and the marketing office, media placement, promotions, market research, general and administrative marketing office costs, and displays, including architectural models. These costs are initially based on a percentage of the total budget or a flat dollar amount. It should be remembered that for longer leasing or selling periods, larger marketing budgets will be required.

- Agency fee
- Production costs
- Brochures
- Stationary, business cards, etc.
- Signage
- Media placement
  Newspaper
  Magazine
  Radio
  Television
  Billboards
  Direct mail
- Mailing lists
- Public relations
- Promotions
- Entertainment
- Travel
- Models
  Furniture
  Accessories
  Signage
  Plants and maintenance
  Built-ins
  Interior finish
  Security system
  Music system
- Office
  Furniture
  Accessories

Signage
Plants and maintenance
Built-ins
Supplies
- Salaries
  Receptionist
  Maid
  Manager
  Assistant manager
  Sales
  Security
  Valet
  Maintenance

Sales Expenses

These are the costs associated with selling or leasing the property. These costs are based on salaries or percentages of the sale or lease. The payroll taxes and employee benefits are also included in this category.

- Sales draws
- Sales/leasing commissions—residential
- Sales/leasing commissions—commercial
- Sales/leasing commissions—agents
- Sales office staff
- Payroll taxes
- Employee benefits

Financing Costs

These are the costs associated with obtaining the various loans to acquire and develop the property. The construction loan and permanent loan points are usually based on a percentage of the proposed loan. The interest costs are calculated on the outstanding balance on a monthly basis. Some developers use a simplified approach to calculating the interest carry. They multiply the total loan amount by 60 percent (the average outstanding balance) and then divide by the number of months to build the project. The computer can be programmed to calculate these exact interest cost based per the assumptions of the projected loan and its terms. Typical financing costs are as follows.

- Land acquisition loan fee
- Land acquisition loan closing costs
- Land acquisition debt service
- Construction loan fee
- Construction loan closing costs

- Construction debt service
- Permanent loan fee
- Permanent loan closing costs
- Permanent debt service
- Miscellaneous loan fee
- Miscellaneous loan closing costs
- Miscellaneous loan debt service
- Loan mortgage broker

Unit Closing Costs

If the property is going to be sold in total or in pieces (such as residential housing), this category will project the sale costs.

- Deed tax
- Mortgage tax
- Recording tax
- Mortgage buy down
- Commitment fee
- Private mortgage insurance
- FNMA/FHLMC fees
- Title insurance
- Title exam
- Survey
- Pest inspection
- Appraisal
- Legal fees
- Loan discount fees
- Assignment fee
- Amortization schedule
- Tax service fee
- Credit report

Deposits

This category includes the deposits which will be required for the development. Assuming that all of the deposits are refunded at the end of the construction phase, this category should be zeroed out.

- Gas
- Electricity
- Water/sewer
- Telephone

- Furniture
- Equipment

General and Administrative

This category includes all of the development office costs or a portion of the developer's home office costs.

- Bank account
- Accounting
- Postage
- Travel
- Entertainment
- Petty cash
- Office supplies
- Equipment rental
- Home office charges

Taxes

This expense includes the real estate, personal property, and any sales tax due during the development phase. Typically, the local real estate tax assessor will assess the value of the property as of the first day of the year. If the development began in January and was completed in July, the property will more than likely be taxed as land for that year. Various taxes which may be applicable are as follows.

- IRS taxes
- Real estate taxes
- Personal property taxes
- Sales taxes

Property Operating Costs

These costs include all of the property operating costs once the tenant has taken possession of his or her space or the premises. Typically these expenses are offset by the rental revenue received from the tenant. The estimating of these costs will be explained in the property operating costs section later in this chapter.

- Salaries and wages
- Repairs and maintenance
- Utilities
- Taxes
- Insurance
- General and administrative
- Management fees

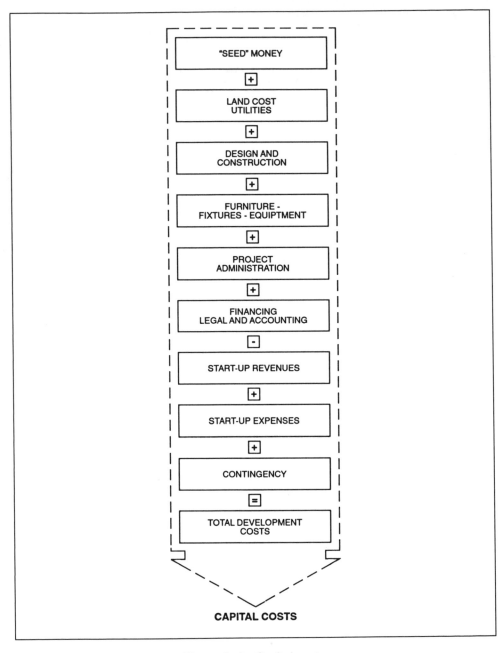

CAPITAL COSTS

Figure 8-1 Capital costs.

- Marketing
- Contract services
- Supplies
- Unit maintenance
- Deposits and bonds
- Banking
- Reserves and replacements
- Capital expenditures
- Developer's subsidy to Owner's Association

Contingency Category

It is imperative that the developer have a contingency fund which can be used for unexpected expenses. This amount is usually based on a percentage of the total development costs.

CASH FLOWS AND PREPARING THE OPERATING PROFORMA

In completing the preliminary operating proforma, the developer should prepare a "quick and dirty" calculation of revenues and expenses. The objective of these calculations is to find the net operating income (NOI). Knowing the NOI will provide the developer and lender with a number for calculating potential value and the actual cash flows of the development. To find cash flows, the interest, taxes, debt service, and participation payments are subtracted from the NOI. A more complete and detailed analysis of this process is provided in Chapter 11. The following will provide the types of revenues and expenses that comprise the operating proforma.

Revenues

Gross Potential Income (GPI)

The initial step of this analysis is to calculate the gross potential income (GPI) of the property. The GPI is calculated by multiplying the total available rentable square footage or the total number of units available times the proposed market rental rates. For example:

$$100 \text{ units} \times \$500 \text{ per month} \times 12 \text{ months} = \$\ \ 600,000 \text{ GPI}$$

or

$$100,000 \text{ sq. ft.} \times \$12.00 \text{ per sq. ft.} = \$1,200,000 \text{ GPI}$$

Miscellaneous Income

For purposes of the developer's operating proforma, miscellaneous income should be based on either square footage amount or number of units times a specified dollar amount.

$$100 \text{ units} \times \$5 \text{ per month} \times 12 \text{ months} = \$\ 6,000$$

or

$$100,000 \text{ sq. ft.} \times \$.10 \text{ per sq. ft.} = \$10,000$$

Vacancy or Uncollectible Factor

The vacancy or uncollectible factor is that percentage of the GPI which will not be collected. Most developers use a 5 (5%) vacancy factor for apartments, office and retail developments. Lodging proforma might use a 30 (30%) to 35 (35%) percentage vacancy factor. The developer should carefully review the current occupancy level for the selected product type.

$600,000	GPI
6,000	Miscellaneous income
606,000	Total potential income
5%	Vacancy factor
$ 30,300	Vacancy

Effective Gross Income (EGI)

The effective gross income (EGI) is the sum of the rental income plus all the miscellaneous income less the vacancy factor.

Gross potential income (GPI)
+ Miscellaneous income
− Vacancy or uncollectible factor (%)
= Effective gross income (EGI)

$600,000	GPI
6,000	Miscellaneous income
606,000	Total potential income
5%	Vacancy or uncollectible factor
$ 30,300	Vacancy
= $575,700	Effective gross income

Operating Expenses

The following three methods are used by developers to project operating expenses: percentage of effective gross income (% EGI), dollars per unit, and dollars per square foot.

Percentage of Effective Gross Income (% EGI)

In this method, the total operating expenses are divided by the effective gross income. The results can be distorted when a property has low rental rates due to an over supplied rental market. In addition, newer properties tend to have lower percentage rates due to lower maintenance costs.

$$\frac{\text{Operating expenses}}{\text{Effective gross income}} = \% \text{ EGI}$$

Dollars per Unit

Many apartment properties use this method. The total operating expenses are divided by the total number of units. This method can give distorted results because smaller properties usually have higher dollar per unit costs because of a smaller number of units over which to spread the costs.

$$\frac{\text{Operating expenses}}{\text{Number of units}} = \text{Dollars per unit}$$

The dollars per unit method can be further divided between fixed and variable expenses.

Fixed Expenses

These expenses are more predictable and tend not to vary with the properties' occupancy; they include:

- Utilities—common area
- Real estate taxes
- Insurance
- Contract services

Variable Expenses

These are the expenses which vary with the occupancy of the property, for example:

- Salaries and wages
- Repairs and maintenance
- Utilities—if landlord paid
- General and administrative
- Management fees
- Professional fees
- Marketing
- Supplies
- Unit maintenance
- Deposits and bonds

- Banking
- Reserves and replacements

Dollars per Square Foot

This method divides the total operating expenses by the gross or net square footage in the property.

$$\frac{\text{Operating expenses}}{\text{Total square footage (gross or net)}} = \text{Dollars per foot}$$

Net Operating Income (NOI)

Once the operating expenses are determined, the developer can obtain the net operating income for the property.

$$
\begin{array}{l}
\text{Effective gross income (EGI)} \\
\underline{- \text{Operating expenses}} \\
= \text{Net operating income (NOI)}
\end{array}
$$

Debt Service

The debt service is the amount of money which is paid on a periodic basis to service the loan. This payment will include both interest on the outstanding loan balance as well as a principal loan reduction payment.

Before-Tax Cash Flow

From the net operating income (NOI), the developer can then subtract the property debt service. This new figure will give the investor the before-tax cash flow (BTCF) for the property (see Figure 8–2).

$$
\begin{array}{l}
\text{Net operating income (NOI)} \\
\underline{- \text{Debt service}} \\
= \text{Before-tax cash flow}
\end{array}
$$

Below the Bottom Line Expenses

The below the bottom line expenses are the following items:

- Leasing commissions
- Tenant improvements
- Capital expenditures

After-Tax Cash Flow

The after-tax cash flow is calculated by subtracting the taxes due from the before-tax cash flow and the below line expenses (see Figure 8–2).

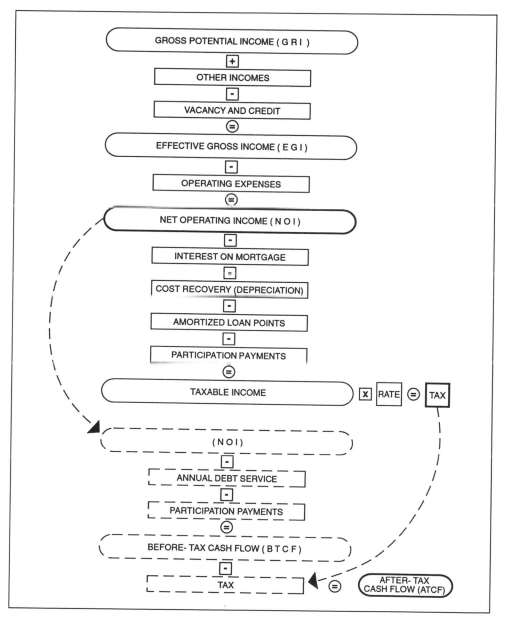

Figure 8–2   Cash flow calculations.

> Before-tax cash flow
> − Leasing commissions
> − Tenant improvements
> − Capital expenditures
> − Taxes due
> ―――――――――――――
> = After-tax cash flow

FIVE-TO-TEN YEAR OPERATING FORECASTS

Once the developer has calculated the beginning year operating expenses, future forecasts should be made. These forecasts should consider concessions such as free rent, tenant design, and construction costs. In addition, they should reflect lease-up schedules along with escalations of rent in the future. They must also take into account expenses for capital improvements and escalations of operating costs. The following will discuss these concepts.

Space Absorption

During the lease-up or rent-up phase, the developer should project how the space will be absorbed, based on that portion of the market which he thinks can be captured within the development. Since it is very unlikely that all of the space will be occupied at construction completion, the developer must make assumptions based on the marketing team's recommendation as to how long it will take to lease up the space. Projections must be based on a specified number of units or square footage per month. See Chapter 13 for a more thorough analysis in determining your market share absorption.

Inflation Increases

The developer will start with the beginning year and then increase the revenue and expenses by an inflation factor. This inflation factor is estimated by reviewing the past history of the market. The inflation increase can be the same for both the revenue and expense side of the equation or it can vary per year. In addition, the developer can choose to base this factor on a percentage of consumer price index (CPI).

Commercial Forecasting Idiosyncrasies

Commercial forecasting differs from residential forecasting because of the long terms of commercial leases. Since commercial properties usually have multiple year leases, a projection for current market rents should be made when the lease expires. For example, a commercial tenant has signed a five (5) year lease at $10.00 per square foot, with a five (5%) rent escalation per year.

Year 1 $10.00 per sq. ft.
Year 2 $10.50 per sq. ft.
Year 3 $11.03 per sq. ft.
Year 4 $11.58 per sq. ft.
Year 5 $12.16 per sq. ft.

As can be seen, the rental in the fifth year is at $12.16 per square foot. If the developer makes the assumption that a strong market will exist when this lease expires, the market rental will be projected at $14.00 per square foot in the fifth or sixth years.

Assuming the existing tenant has a desire to renew the lease, the developer has two options: to negotiate a new lease with the existing tenant or to find a new tenant. To complete this evaluation, the developer will probably spend minimal dollars in tenant improvements to satisfy the existing tenant as opposed to the extensive expenditure in finding a new tenant and providing new tenant construction.

Lease Turnover Costs

Lease turnover costs are more critical with commercial properties than residential properties. When the tenant vacates the residential property, the cost for refurbishment is usually minimal and included in the operating expenses. When a commercial tenant vacates, there will be additional costs which usually occur below the net operating income (NOI) bottom line. These costs include tenant improvements (which are usually capitalized—not expensed for accounting purposes) and real estate leasing commissions. When projecting the costs for the tenant improvements, an inflation factor should be added to today's costs for forecasting into the future. In addition, other costs can include rental concessions. Frictional vacancy can occur. Frictional vacancy includes the time in months from when the old tenant moves out until a new tenant is found and moves in.

Capital Expenditure Items

Since all assets eventually wear out, the developer should make allowances for these items. During the first few years of operations, few items will need to be replaced. As time passes, items such as the roof, appliances, and paving will need either minor or major repairs. The developer should project these items and their current cost for replacement. An amount should then be set aside every year as reserve in an interest-bearing account to be used at a later date as needed. This projected dollar amount can be based on today's actual cost, a specified dollar amount per unit (apartments), square footage (commercial), or on a percentage of total income.

PROCESS OF REFINEMENT

The process of refinement within the development process is all encompassing. With the planning and decision making occurring within each discipline and the gathering of new knowledge about government regulations, design ideas, construction costs, market need, site planning, and financing arrangements, the process is like a series of funnels which become smaller and smaller until the project is leased up and operating for a number of years. Even though the refining will continue to occur on a much smaller basis, knowledge of the complete proforma will be almost complete. Figure 8–3 diagrams the refinement process.

Massaging the Preliminary Numbers

Once all of the preliminary numbers have been completed, the developer should continue to update and massage the numbers. This process will continue right up to the completion of the property. The developer should always try to obtain the most reliable numbers from the sources that have the answers. For example, in reviewing the utility costs, the developer should first contact the local utility departments with a set of the plans. Based on experience, the utility company will be able to project the potential cost for their services. Additionally, the developer should contact local management companies who should have a good grasp on the potential operating costs.

Massaging the Final Numbers

To formulate the preliminary numbers, a large number of assumptions will have to be made. The process of finalization will simply be the process of eliminating assumptions and substantiating the estimates. In addition, through the sensitivity analysis, creative financing, and consideration of sales prices and rental rates, proforma calculations will change. Constantly exploring ways for decreasing costs and increasing revenues over time will not only increase net operating incomes, but also increase the value of the property at a sale in the future.

APPROACHES TO FINANCIAL FEASIBILITY

Once the developer has completed the formulation of the financial assumptions, and performed all of the necessary analysis, his calculations will reveal the rental rate or sales price needed for the development's project economics to "pencil out." This rental rate can be established by the known market rate or through project economic's calculations. If his calculations equate to a rental rate above the market, the developer must massage the number, or change his assumptions.

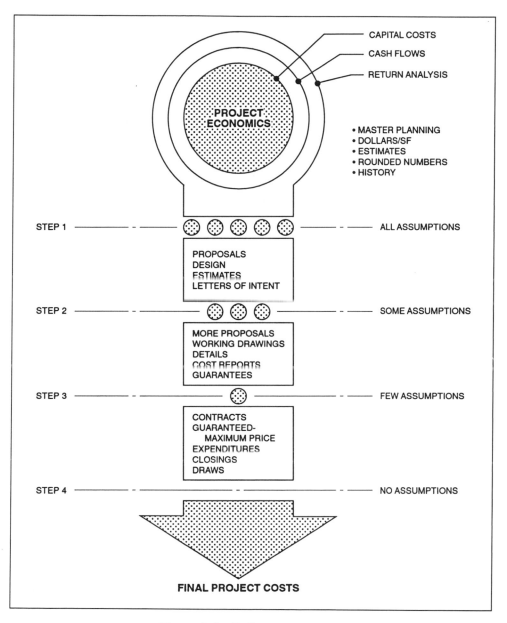

Figure 8–3 Refinement process.

This process is described as either the "Frontdoor or Backdoor Approaches" to financial feasibility of the development.

Frontdoor Approach to Financial Feasibility

The frontdoor approach (Figure 8–4) defines the development's physical characteristics and their costs. Then calculations determine what rates or prices must be

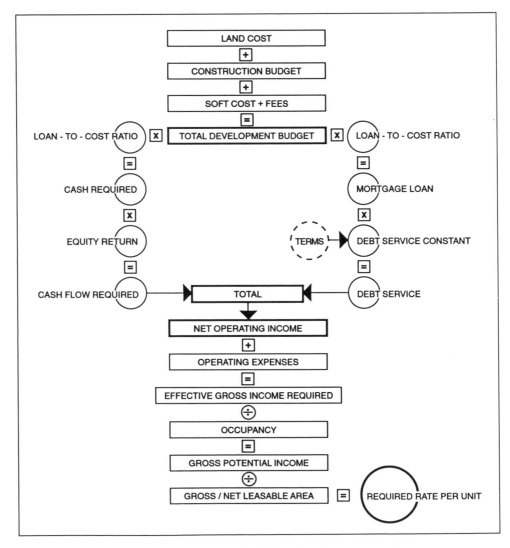

Figure 8–4   Financial feasibility: frontdoor approach.

charged to justify the cost of the development. This approach just takes into consideration the first year costs of the development.

Using the Sutton Place Apartments example, the developer will add the cost of the land ($750,000), the construction costs ($35 × 96,000 sq. ft.), and the indirect costs and development fee ($789,808). The total cost for the development is $4,899,808. It should be noted that there is another $217,600 in rent-up income plus $800 in miscellaneous income not included in this analysis to offset the development costs.

The lender will require that the developer put in about 10 percent of the development costs or $500,000 in equity. The developer is requiring at least a 14.35 percent return on the equity investment. This will equate to $72,500 in the first year after lease up.

The lender will provide a loan for 85 percent of the development costs ($4,200,000). The monthly debt service payment is $36,858.01 or $442,296 per year.

In order to service the debt and meet the developer's required equity return the property must throw off at least $514,796.12. This amount represents the net operating income (NOI) that must be achieved.

$$\text{Debt service (per year)} = \$442,296.12$$
$$\text{Equity return @ } 14.35\% = \$\ 72,500.00$$
$$\text{Dollars required to service} \quad \$514,796.12$$

The developer then adds the operating costs of $264,000 ($2,200 per unit per year) to the net operating income to arrive at the required effective gross income (EGI) or dollars collected after reducing for vacancies. This amount totals $778,796. This amount is then divided by the occupancy rate of 95 percent (1 less the 5 percent vacancy rate). This calculates into a $816,000 gross potential income (GPI) required by the developer for financial feasibility. This equates to $8.50 per gross leasable area (GLA) or $.71 per square foot per month.

In reviewing the market study, the developer finds that he can obtain between $480 to $510 per month for the one-bedroom unit and $595 to $615 for the two-bedroom unit. Assuming that he fixes his preliminary rental rates at:

# Units	Type Unit	Sq.Ft.	Rent/Mo.	Rent/Sq.Ft.
40	1 BR, 1 BA	600	$ 500	$ .83
80	2 BR, 2 BA	900	$ 600	$ .66
120		96,000	$816,000	$8.50

It appears from this approach that the developer can make the numbers work. In addition, the debt coverage ratio and the break-even point required by the lender are met.

Debt coverage ratio

$$\frac{\$514,796}{\$442,296} = 1.16 \text{ (Acceptable)}$$

Break-even cash flow ratio

$$\frac{\$264,000 + \$442,296}{\$816,000} = 86.6\% \text{ (Acceptable)}$$

BACKDOOR APPROACH TO FEASIBILITY

The backdoor approach (Figure 8–5) considers the flow of dollars in and out of the development. The final analysis of this approach shows the developer how much he can spend for project costs.

Using the previous example, the developer takes the cash flow proforma and analyzes the equity and lender requirements:

Gross potential income (GPI)	816,000
+ Miscellaneous income	3,000
− Vacancy @ 5%	(40,950)
= Effective gross income (EGI)	$778,050
− Operating expenses	$264,000
= Net operating income	$514,050

The developer then subtracts the projected yearly debt service of $442,296 to obtain the available cash flow of $71,754. His required equity return of 14.35 percent calculates to a $500,028 equity requirement.

Taking the $514,051 net operating income and dividing by the 1.15 debt coverage ratio results in $447,000. This number is then divided by the debt constant of .105309 (10 percent interest at a 30-year amortization), which then calculates to a potential loan amount of $4,244,651.

The developer then calculates the sum of the required equity of $500,028 plus the potential loan of $4,244,651 to arrive at $4,744,679. From this amount he adds $218,400 (the rent-up income of $217,600 and the rent-up miscellaneous income of $800) and then subtracts the land and the indirect development costs of $1,539,808 from this amount to arrive at $3,423,271. This figure calculates to a $35.66 per square foot, giving the developer a $.66 per square foot gap to build the project.

SENSITIVITY ANALYSIS: "WHAT IF" SCENARIOS

A sensitivity analysis (Figure 8–6) is an economic projection which demonstrates a range of assumptions showing the developer both the potential downside or upside of the development's project economics. The variables which can affect this analysis are:

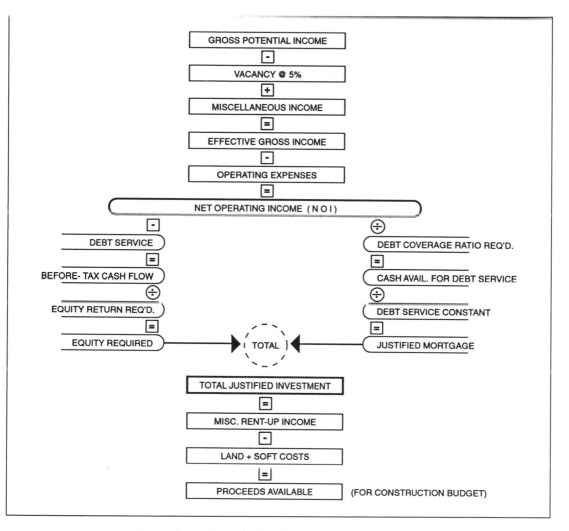

Figure 8–5 Financial feasibility: backdoor approach.

- Rental rates
- Operating expenses
- Mortgage terms
    Interest rate
    Amortization period
- Increases of the revenue and expenses
- Development costs

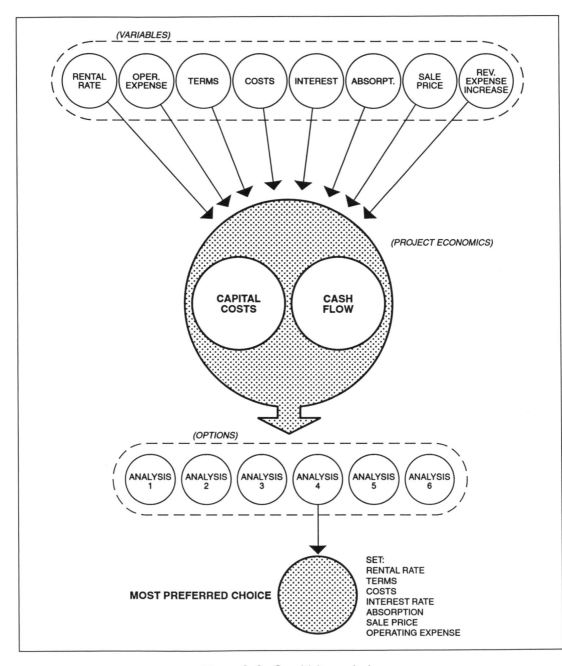

Figure 8–6   Sensitivity analysis.

- Leveraged or all cash
- Absorption projections
- Projected sale price

By changing these variables, the developer can visualize and realize how each will impact the total profitability of the development. The sensitivity analysis is the "what if" game, which the developer can play. By using the personal computer, the developer can set up a model for the development and then easily change these variables with the "touch" of a key.

VALUE AND THE REAL ESTATE DEVELOPMENT

After completing all of the monumental work necessary for the completion of a real estate development, the developer's perception of its value may be different than the market's perception of its value. To ascertain its real value, the developer should obtain an appraisal. An appraisal is an expert opinion of the value of the property by someone who is qualified to make such an opinion. The appraiser in determining an opinion of value will use one of three types of methods or a combination of each to confirm conclusions (see Figure 8–7). They are as follows:

- Cost approach
- Sales or market comparison approach
- Income or capitalization of income approach

The developer is looking for the appraiser to provide a recommendation as to fair market value. Prior to contracting with the appraiser, the developer should review the basic development and operating assumptions which he has projected with the potential appraiser candidate. If the appraiser does not feel comfortable with the developer's assumptions, the developer should reassess his projections for error or find another new appraiser to confirm his projections one way or another. It should be noted that without an appraisal which lies within the developer's projected value, the developer will never be able to obtain financing per his assumptions.

The previously used 120-unit apartment case study is used as an example for illustrating how an appraiser will determine value using the three appraisal methods.

Sales or Market Comparison Approach

The sales or market approach is based on a concept that suggests that the value of a property tends to be set by the cost of acquiring an equally desirable substitute property. The value estimate is based on prices which are paid for similar properties in "arms length" market transactions over a time period which reasonably

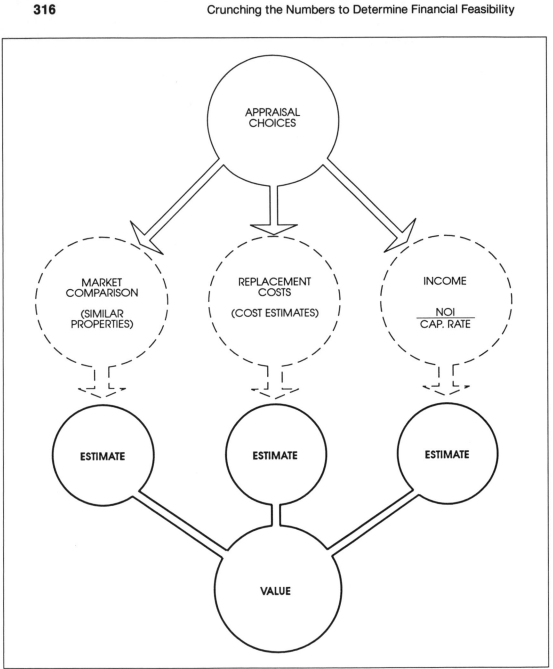

Figure 8–7 Appraisals.

reflects market conditions. This approach depends on the existence of recent sales of properties with similar location, size, utility, construction and overall market appeal. This method is also used in valuating the land portion of the development.

Comparable Sales and Market Information

Property	Sale Date	Gross Rent Multiplier (GRM)	Price/ sq.ft.	Price/Unit
1	Jan 1990	6.4	$56.80	$45,000
2	Feb 1990	6.5	$58.00	$47,300
3	Dec 1989	6.7	$57.35	$46,600
4	Feb 1990	6.8	$57.25	$45,000

Value
Based on a 6.6 gross rent multiplier = $816,000 × 6.6 = $5,385,600
    Approximately $5,400,000

Cost Approach

The cost approach is based on a concept which suggests that the value of a property tends to be set by the cost of producing (constructing) a substitute property of equal utility. The value estimate is predicated on the cost of acquiring the vacant land plus the cost of constructing the improvements.

Replacement Costs

Constructions costs @ $35/sq. ft.	$3,360,000
Architect	25,000
Financing costs	126,000
Interest carry	132,000
Marketing	15,000
Miscellaneous costs	150,000
Replacement cost new	$3,808,000
+Profit @ 25%	$ 952,000
+Land value	$ 750,000
=Indicated value by cost approach	$5,510,000
Approximately	$5,500,000

Income or Capitalization of Income Approach

The income capitalization approach is based on a concept which suggests that the value of a property is set by the cost of acquiring an equally desirable substitute property offering similar economic benefits. The value estimate is predicated on discounting these benefits (including cash flows and reversion), using one of several capitalization processes employing market derived investment return rates.

$$\text{Capitalization rate} = \frac{\text{Net operating income}}{\text{Value}}$$

or

$$\text{Value} = \frac{\text{Net operating income}}{\text{Capitalization rate}}$$

In addition to return rates, every element of the cash flow is market derived or supported. These include rents, expenses, and vacancy rates. Therefore, as with the other two approaches to value, the validity of this approach depends on adequate market data.

For example:

Unit Information

40 1 BR, 1 BA units @ 600 sq.ft.	=	24,000 sq.ft.
80 2 BR, 2 BA units @ 900 sq.ft.	=	72,000 sq.ft.
Total		96,000 sq.ft.

Operating Statement

40 1 BR, 1 BA units @ $500 per month =	$ 20,000
80 2 BR, 2 BA units @ $600 per month =	$ 48,000
Total	$ 68,000
	× 12 Mo.
Gross potential income	$816,000
−Vacancy @ 5%	($ 40,800)
+Miscellaneous income @ $25 per unit	$ 2,850
=Effective gross income	$778,050
−Operating expenses @ $2,200 per unit	($264,000)
=Net operating income	$514,050

Comparable Sales and Market Information

Property	Sale Date	Cap Rate	Gross Rent Multiplier (GRM)	Price/ sq.ft.	Price/ Unit
1	Jan 19XX	9.25%	6.4	$56.80	$45,000
2	Feb 19XX	9.30%	6.5	$58.00	$47,300
3	Dec 19XX	9.25%	6.7	$57.35	$46,600
4	Feb 19XX	9.20%	6.8	$57.25	$45,000

Value
Based on 9.5% capitalization rate = $5,411,053
                Approximately $5,400,000

Discounted Cash Flow

Since this appraisal is of a proposed new development, the appraiser will have to discount the projected cash flow to include the rent-up process. The appraiser will complete a five (5) to seven (7) year cash flow projection of the property and then discount the cash flow based on a net present value. This net present value is determined by local market conditions.

Based on the above example, the appraiser has calculated a $5,200,000 value. For a review of the discounted cash flow analysis which is used in appraisal process, please refer to page 350.

Summary of the Appraisal Approaches

In correlation of the four appraisal approaches to value, the appraiser has indicated the following:

Sales or marketing approach	$5,400,000
Cost approach	$5,500,000
Income capitalization approach	$5,400,000
Discounted cash flow	$5,200,000

In reviewing these figures, the appraiser placed the most value on the income capitalization approach and has placed the value at $5,400,000.

Cost versus Market Value

In reviewing exactly what the value of the development is worth, the difference between the development cost and the market value should be discussed. The cost is exactly what the development will cost to produce, while the market value is the price which a "ready and willing" buyer will pay for the property. The market value will fluctuate based on market conditions. Although a property might originally cost $4,000,000 to develop, its current value may be only $3,500,000. Since property valuation is weighted more heavily on the income approach, it does not matter what the actual costs are or will be to a potential lender or buyer. Income property's value is based on the income stream and the potential return to the investor.

PROJECTING TAXABLE INCOME

One aspect of the "go" "no go" decision is the effect of taxes on the development and the developer. A thorough understanding of tax implications will benefit the development bottom line cash flow. In projecting taxable income, the developer will use depreciation over time, tax schedules and rates, interest on the principle of the loan. Because the regulations are ever changing, the developer must be constantly aware of new implications caused by new law and make decisions appropriately. Prior to making final decisions, it is imperative that the developer seek counsel from his attorney, financial planner, and accountant. The following will discuss some of the concepts related to tax matters.

Taxable Income (Loss) Schedule

The taxable income (loss) schedule is determined by taking the net operating income and subtracting the interest paid on the mortgage loan, the depreciation taken on the improvements, the amortized costs of any fees or points paid on the mortgage, and then adding back any replacement reserves.

> Net operating income
> − Interest on the permanent mortgage
> − Depreciation deduction
> − Amortization of the closing costs
> − Amortized points on the permanent mortgage
> − Amortization of the leasing commissions
> − Capital expenditures/tenant improvements depreciation
> = Taxable income (loss)

From this amount, the developer will then use this amount (taxable income) times a multiplier to calculate the appropriate tax.

Interest Calculation

The formula for calculating the interest paid during a period is based on the debt service payments less the beginning and ending loan constant multiplied by the original loan amount.

$$\text{Interest Paid} = (\text{PI payments}) - \text{Constant (beginning)}$$
$$- \text{constant (end)}$$
$$\times \text{Original loan amount}$$

Depreciation

Depreciation is an expense which reflects the loss in value of the improvements to real estate. To calculate depreciation, take one (1) less the percentage of salvage value and divide this by the useful life of the asset.

$$\text{Straight line depreciation rate} = \frac{1 - \% \text{ of salvage value}}{\text{Useful life}}$$

To arrive at the depreciable basis, the developer should take the cost of the development less the land (land is not depreciable) and divide by the number of years the current IRS Tax Code allows.

DEPRECIATION TABLES

CLASS	ASSETS	METHOD	CONVENTIONAL
3 Year	ADR midpoints of 4 years or less, except automobiles and light trucks	200% decling balance	Half–year (a)
5 Year	ADR midpoints of more than 4 years and less than 10 years, and adding automobiles, light trucks, semiconductor manufacturing equipment, and research and experimentation property	200% decling balance	Half–year (a)
7 Year	ADR midpoints of 10 years or more, but less than 16 years; property with no ADR midpoint not classified elsewhere	200% decling balance	Half–year (a)
10 Year	ADR midpoints of 16 years or more, but less than 20 years	200% decling balance	Half–year (a)
15 Year	ADR midpoints of 20 years or more, but less than 25 years; municipal wastewater treatment plants, certain distribution plant equipment	150% decling balance	Half–year (a)
20 Year	ADR midpoints of 25 years or more, other than real property with ADR midpoints of 27.5 years or more; municipal sewers	150% decling balance	Half–year (a)
27.5 Year	Residential rental and manufactured housing	Straight–line	Mid–month
31.5 Year	Nonresidential real property that either has no ADR midpoint or midpoint of 27.5 years or more.	Straight–line	Mid–month

NOTES:

(a) Mid–quarter convention applies to all personal property where more than 40% of such property is placed in service during the last three months of a tax year.

Figure 8–8 Depreciation tables.

27.5 YEAR TABLE FOR RESIDENTIAL REAL ESTATE

RECOVERY YEAR	JAN	FEB.	MAR.	APR.	MAY	JUN.	JUL.	AUG.	SEP.	OCT.	NOV.	DEC.
1	3.48	3.18	2.87	2.57	2.27	1.96	1.66	1.36	1.06	0.75	0.45	0.15
2 THRU 27	3.63	3.63	3.63	3.63	3.63	3.63	3.63	3.63	3.63	3.63	3.63	3.63
28	2.14	2.44	2.75	3.05	3.35	3.63	3.63	3.63	3.63	3.63	3.63	3.63
29	0.00	0.00	0.00	0.00	0.00	0.03	0.33	0.63	0.93	1.24	1.54	1.84

31.5 YEAR TABLE FOR NONRESIDENTIAL REAL ESTATE

RECOVERY YEAR	JAN	FEB.	MAR.	APR.	MAY	JUN.	JUL.	AUG.	SEP.	OCT.	NOV.	DEC.
1	3.04	2.77	2.51	2.24	1.98	1.71	1.45	1.19	0.92	0.66	0.39	0.13
2 THRU 31	3.17	3.17	3.17	3.17	3.17	3.17	3.17	3.17	3.17	3.17	3.17	3.17
32	1.86	2.13	2.39	2.66	2.92	3.17	3.17	3.17	3.17	3.17	3.17	3.17
33	0.00	0.00	0.00	0.00	0.00	0.02	0.28	0.54	0.81	1.07	1.34	1.60

PERSONAL PROPERTY PLACED IN SERVICE AFTER JANUARY 1, 1987

If Recovery Year Is:	-Year	5-Year	7-Year	10-Year	15-Year	20-Year
1	33.00%	20.00%	14.00%	10.00%	5.00%	4.00%
2	45.00%	32.00%	25.00%	18.00%	10.00%	7.00%
3	22.00%	16.00%	13.00%	14.00%	9.00%	7.00%
4		16.00%	12.00%	12.00%	8.00%	6.00%
5		16.00%	12.00%	12.00%	7.00%	6.00%
6			12.00%	8.00%	7.00%	5.00%
7			12.00%	8.00%	6.00%	5.00%
8				8.00%	6.00%	5.00%
9				7.00%	6.00%	5.00%
10				7.00%	6.00%	5.00%
11					6.00%	5.00%
12					6.00%	5.00%
13					6.00%	5.00%
14					6.00%	5.00%
15					6.00%	5.00%
16						4.00%
17						4.00%
18						4.00%
19						4.00%
20						4.00%

STRAIGHT-LINE

If Recovery Year Is:	-Year	5-Year	7-Year	10-Year	15-Year	20-Year
1	16.70%	10.00%	7.10%	5.00%	3.30%	2.50%
2	33.30%	20.00%	14.30%	10.00%	6.60%	5.00%
3	33.30%	20.00%	14.30%	10.00%	6.60%	5.00%
4	16.70%	20.00%	14.30%	10.00%	6.60%	5.00%
5		20.00%	14.30%	10.00%	6.60%	5.00%
6		10.00%	14.30%	10.00%	6.60%	5.00%
7			14.30%	10.00%	6.60%	5.00%
8			7.10%	10.00%	6.60%	5.00%
9				10.00%	6.60%	5.00%
10				10.00%	6.60%	5.00%
11				5.00%	6.60%	5.00%
12					6.60%	5.00%
13					6.60%	5.00%
14					6.60%	5.00%
15					6.60%	5.00%
16					3.30%	5.00%
17						5.00%
18						5.00%
19						5.00%
20						5.00%
21						2.50%

Figure 8-8 Depreciation tables. (*Cont'd*)

+ Site costs
+ Construction hard costs
+ Project overhead
+ Professional fees
+ Marketing
+ Construction interest
+ General and administrative
+ Contingency
= Basis of the development

Amortization of the Closing Costs

The various costs associated with the closing of the property should be amortized over five years.

Amortization of Points on the Permanent Mortgage

The loan points paid to obtain the various loans will need to be amortized and spread over the term of the mortgage.

$$\text{Amortization of permanent loan points} = \frac{\text{Total loan points}}{\text{Term of the mortgage}}$$

Amortization of the Leasing Commissions

The leasing commissions paid out should be amortized over the length of the tenant's lease unless a cash out is requested by the broker.

$$\text{Amortization of leasing commissions} = \frac{\text{Leasing commissions}}{\text{Term of the lease}}$$

Capital Expenditures/Tenant Improvement Depreciation

The costs of any capital expenditures or tenant improvements should also be deducted. The advice of a tax accountant should be sought to verify whether these expenses are expenses or capital cost items.

Projecting Taxable Income on Sale

The taxable income on the sale is determined by taking the sales price less any costs of the sale less the adjusted basis. This calculation equals the capital gains due. From this capital gains figure the investor's marginal tax rate is multiplied to arrive at the taxes due on sale.

Sales price
− Sales expense
= Amount realized
− Adjusted basis
= Capital gains on sale
× Investor's marginal tax rate
= Taxes due on sale

Adjusted Cost Basis

The adjusted cost basis represents the tax payer's property cost for tax purposes, not what the investor originally paid for the property.

Original basis
+ Capital expenditures
− Property sold
− Depreciation taken
= Adjusted cost basis

Excess Depreciation: Excess depreciation is the amount of depreciation taken on a property less that amount of depreciation that was available under the straight-line depreciation rules. Since residential and nonresidential properties use straight-line depreciation, there will not be any excess depreciation.

Total depreciation taken
− Straight-line depreciation allowed to date
= Excess depreciation

Capital Gain

A gain on the sale takes place when the property is sold for more than the investor's adjusted cost basis. This capital gain is then taxed at the investor's marginal tax rate.

Sales price
− Adjusted cost basis
= Gain on the sale
− Excess depreciation
= Capital gain

Taxes Due on the Resale

The tax due on the sale calculated by multiplying the investor's marginal tax rate by the capital gain.

Capital gain
× Investor's marginal tax rate
= Taxes due on the resale

After-Tax Equity Reversion

The after-tax equity reversion is figured by subtracting the mortgage balance and the taxes due on the sale from the net sales price. This calculation tells the investor the amount of money left over after the sale is complete.

$$
\begin{array}{l}
 \text{Net sales price} \\
- \text{Mortgage balance} \\
\underline{- \text{Taxes due on the sale}} \\
= \text{After-tax equity reversion}
\end{array}
$$

Profit

The profit is calculated by adding the total after-tax cash flow to the after-tax equity reversion and then subtracting the equity investment.

$$
\begin{array}{l}
 \text{Total after-tax cash flow} \\
\underline{+ \text{After-tax equity reversion}} \\
= \text{Total cash return} \\
\underline{- \text{Equity investment}} \\
= \text{Profit}
\end{array}
$$

LENDER FINANCIAL RATIOS AND OTHER MEASUREMENT TOOLS

Debt Service Coverage Ratio (DSCR)

The potential lender will review how much cash flow coverage his loan will have at any time. This formula is calculated by dividing the net operating income by the debt service.

$$
\text{Debt service coverage} = \frac{\text{Net operating income}}{\text{Debt service}}
$$

Loan-to-Value Ratio (LVR)

Many lenders will only provide loans based on a percentage of the appraised value. This formula is calculated by dividing the potential loan amount by the appraised value.

$$
\text{Loan-to-value ratio} = \frac{\text{Potential loan amount}}{\text{Appraised value}}
$$

Break-Even Cash Flow Ratio

The lender will also desire to know at any given time period, the development's break-even point or stabilization. This formula is calculated by the sum of the operating expenses and the debt service and dividing by gross potential income.

$$\text{Operating expenses} + \text{Debt service} = \text{Break-even rental income}$$

$$\text{Break-even point cash flow} = \frac{\text{Break-even income}}{\text{Gross potential income (GPI)}}$$

Operating Expense Ratio

The operating expense ratio is calculated by dividing the total operating expenses by the effective gross income (EGI).

$$\text{Operating expenses ratio} = \frac{\text{Total operating expenses}}{\text{Effective gross income (EGI)}}$$

FINANCIAL RULES OF THUMB

Payback Period

The payback period is the number of years which is needed to recover the initial equity investment from future cash flows. It is calculated by dividing the investment cost or value by any of the five levels of income.

1. Gross potential income (GPI)
2. Effective gross income (EGI)
3. Net operating income (NOI)
4. Before-tax cash flow (BTCF)
5. After-tax cash flow (ATCF)

$$\text{Payback period} = \frac{\text{Investment cost or value}}{\text{Various types of income}}$$

The payback method is broken down into two categories: multipliers or its reciprocal rates of return. Once these calculations are completed, the developer should compare these figures to other comparable properties.

Multipliers

Gross Rent Multiplier (GRM):   The gross rent multiplier is the investment cost or value divided by the gross potential income.

$$\text{Gross rent multiplier (GRM)} = \frac{\text{Investment cost or value}}{\text{Gross potential income (GPI)}}$$

Effective Gross Income Multiplier (EGIM): The effective gross income multiplier is the investment cost or value divided by the effective gross income.

$$\text{Effective gross income multiplier (EGIM)} = \frac{\text{Investment cost or value}}{\text{Effective gross income (EGI)}}$$

Net Income Multiplier (NIM): The net income multiplier is calculated by dividing the investment cost or value by the net operating income.

$$\text{Net income multiplier (NIM)} = \frac{\text{Investment cost or value}}{\text{Net operating income (NOI)}}$$

Before-Tax Cash Flow Multiplier: The before-tax cash flow multiplier is calculated by dividing the before-tax cash flow by the equity investment.

$$\text{Before-tax cash flow multiplier} = \frac{\text{Equity investment}}{\text{Before-tax cash flow (BTCF)}}$$

After-Tax Cash Flow Multiplier: The after-tax cash flow multiplier is calculated by dividing the after-tax cash flow by the equity investment.

$$\text{After-tax cash flow multiplier} = \frac{\text{Equity investment}}{\text{After-tax cash flow (ATCF)}}$$

Rates of Return

Overall Capitalization Rate (OR)

The overall capitalization rate (OR) is calculated by dividing the net operating income by the investment cost or value.

$$\text{Overall capitalization rate} = \frac{\text{Net operating income (NOI)}}{\text{Investment cost or value}}$$

Equity Dividend Rate (EDR) (Cash on Equity)

The equity dividend rate (EDR) is calculated by dividing the before-tax cash flow by the equity investment.

$$\text{Equity dividend rate} = \frac{\text{Before-tax cash flow (BTCF)}}{\text{Equity investment}}$$

After-Tax Rate (ATR) (After Cash on Equity)

The after-tax rate (ATR) is calculated by dividing the after-tax cash flow by the equity investment.

$$\text{After-tax rate} = \frac{\text{After-tax cash flow (ATCF)}}{\text{Equity investment}}$$

Average Rates of Return

Average Rate of Return on Net Operating Income

The average rate on net operating income is calculated by dividing the average net operating income by the investment costs or value.

$$\text{Average rate on NOI} = \frac{\text{Average net operating income}}{\text{Investment costs or value}}$$

Average Rate of Return on Before-Tax Cash Flow

The average rate on before-tax cash flow is calculated by dividing the average rate on before-tax cash flow by the equity investment.

$$\text{Average rate on before-tax cash flow} = \frac{\text{Average rate on before-tax cash flow}}{\text{Equity investment}}$$

Average Rate of Return on After-Tax Cash Flow

The average rate on after-tax cash flow is calculated by dividing the average after-tax cash flow by the equity investment.

$$\text{Average rate on after-tax cash flow} = \frac{\text{Average after-tax cash flow}}{\text{Equity investment}}$$

Average Rate of Return on After-Tax Cash Flow, Adjusted for Reversion

The average rate on after-tax cash flow, adjusted for reversion (the sale) is calculated by dividing the sum of the average after-tax cash flow and the net sales proceeds by the equity investment.

$$\genfrac{}{}{0pt}{}{\text{Average rate on}}{\genfrac{}{}{0pt}{}{\text{after-tax cash flow,}}{\text{adjusted for reversion}}} = \frac{\genfrac{}{}{0pt}{}{\text{Average after-tax cash}}{\text{flow} + \text{Net sales proceeds}}}{\text{Equity investment}}$$

Time-Value Methods of Return

Internal Rate of Return (IRR)

The internal rate of return is a rate of return model where a rate is calculated such that the present value of the inflow equals the present value of the outflows. One of the problems with the IRR analysis is that it assumes that all the outflow (cash flow) money is reinvested at the same rate that it is presently returning. Many times the investor will be unable to achieve this high of a return when these funds are reinvested.

$$\text{Zero net present value} = \frac{\text{Cash Flow 1}}{(1+1)^1} + \frac{\text{Cash Flow 2}}{(1+1)^2}$$

$$+ \frac{\text{Cash Flow } n}{(1+1)^n} + \frac{\text{Reversion}}{(1+1)^n}$$

$$- \text{Original Equity Investment}$$

Financial Management Rate of Return (FMRR)

The financial management rate of return is a rate of return model that is similar to the internal rate of return in that it calculates the investor's return based on cash in and the timing of the cash flow out. The basic difference is that the internal rate of return calculates the reinvestment rate at the same rate as the return, while the financial management rate of return calculates this reinvestment at a predetermined rate.

$$\text{Zero net present value} = \text{Equity} - \text{future value (FV) of equity benefits} \times \frac{1}{(1+1)^n}$$

Net Present Value (NPV)

The net present value of an investment is equal to the present value of the inflows minus the present value of the outflows. Stated another way, the net present value is the difference between what an investment is worth and its costs.

Development Ratios

Appraised Value to Total Cost Ratio

The appraised value to total cost ratio is calculated by dividing the appraised value by the total development costs of the project.

$$\text{Appraised value to total cost ratio} = \frac{\text{Appraised value}}{\text{Total development cost}}$$

Equity to Total Cost Ratio

The equity to total cost ratio is calculated by dividing the equity investment by the total development costs of the project.

$$\text{Equity to total cost ratio} = \frac{\text{Equity investment}}{\text{Total development costs}}$$

Equity to Value Ratio

The equity to value ratio is calculated by dividing the equity investment by the projected value of the project.

$$\text{Equity to value ratio} = \frac{\text{Equity investment}}{\text{Projected value}}$$

Development Yield

To understand the relationship between projected profits and the total costs of the development.

Developer's projected profits = Appraised value $(-)$ Total development costs

$$\frac{\text{Developer's projected profits}}{\text{Total development costs}} = \text{Development yield}$$

Property Measurements

The price paid or the appraised value of various property types is another useful benchmark to be used by the investor to determine property values.

Price per Square Foot

The price per square foot is derived by dividing the sales price or the appraised value by the total square footage of the property.

$$\frac{\text{Sales price or appraised value}}{\text{Square footage (gross or net)}} = \text{Price per square foot}$$

It should be noted by the investor that square footage measurements should be on an equal basis. Some properties are measured by the:

Gross Square Footage: This is the total square footage of the property. It includes all of the tenant space, the lobby area, hallways, stairways, elevator shafts, restroom facilities, and the mechanical areas.

Net Square Footage: This is the square footage of the building less the square footage that is not leased to the tenant. It excludes the hallways, stairways, elevator shafts, restroom facilities, and the mechanical areas.

Example: A property just sold for $250,000. It has 5000 square feet of gross building area and 4500 net building area. Its price per square footage cost is $50.00 (gross) and $55.55 (net).

$$\frac{\$250,000}{5000 \text{ (gross)}} = \$50.00/\text{sq. ft. (gross)}$$

$$\frac{\$250,000}{4500 \text{ (net)}} = \$55.55/\text{sq. ft. (net)}$$

When using this benchmark and comparing it to other properties in the market, the investor should take into consideration that typically smaller properties have higher square footage costs than larger properties. This is because there is an economy of scale when constructing larger properties.

Price per Unit

The price per unit is calculated by dividing the sales price or appraised value by the number of units in the property. This benchmark is typically used for residential multi-family properties.

$$\frac{\text{Sales price or appraised value}}{\text{Number of units}} = \text{Price per unit}$$

It should be noted that since properties do not have the same unit mix (the number of units in each bedroom category), that this benchmark can be deceptive when comparing to other properties of the same size.

Price per Room

The price per room is the investment cost or value divided by the total number of rooms in the unit.

$$\text{Price per room} = \frac{\text{Investment cost or value}}{\text{Total number of rooms}}$$

USING COMPUTERS TO ASSIST THE DEVELOPER

The complexity of today's economic's projections and the magnitude of scenarios which the developer must consider demand that the developer acquire and learn to use a personal computer. Not only does the personal computer speed up calculations, but they provide a filing system for later reference and modification of formats to suit each individual project. The following four computer software development companies provide programs for real estate development problems.

The Refine Group, Inc.
P. O. Box 194
Blacksberg, VA 24063
(703) 552-3000

H. B. Pascall Co., Inc.
251 W. 59th St.
New York, NY 10024
(212) 496-2323

Real Projections Inc.
2945 Harding St., Suite 110
Carlsbad, CA 92008
(619) 434-2180

Realdex Corporation
1100 Coddington Center, Suite A
Santa Rosa, CA 95418
(707) 579-1914

In addition, the National Association of Realtors has developed a book entitled *Software Directory,* which is available upon request. The book provides a complete listing of the software available for real estate development applications.

HOW TO MAKE THE DEVELOPMENT VALUE JUDGMENT

When evaluating the development's potential, the developer should review the appropriate ratios for the project economics as well as completing sensitivity analysis illustrating the upside and downside potentials. Each ratio should be viewed individually as well as how they relate to the total project numbers. From this analysis, the developer will be able to evaluate the projected returns relative to his expected risk-reward ratios. In addition, the developer must ensure that he has minimum assumptions and that these assumptions are the most up-to-date for the marketplace. It is extremely important that contingency funding for any unforeseen expenditures is provided.

CASE STUDY: SUTTON PLACE APARTMENTS

For review, this chapter will analyze the ten (10) acres which were purchased for $750,000 in Chapter 4. In our example, the developer intends to develop a 120-unit apartment complex. The following are the assumptions used by the developer.

Projected Development Costs

Land costs	$750,000
Building costs	$35 per square foot
Architect	$25,000
Taxes	$12,000: $6000 at closing and $6000 in the tenth month

Insurance	$3000
Construction loan fee	1%
Mortgage broker fee	1%
Permanent loan fee	1%
Miscellaneous closing costs	$10,000
Appraisal	$5000
Marketing	$15,000: $5000 in the fifth month $10,000 in the sixth month
Developer's fee	2% of the loan: Paid over the first six months
Operating expenses	Based on $264,000 per year ($22,000 per month) 60% in fifth month, 70% in the sixth month, 80% in the seventh month, 90% in the eighth month, thereafter full $22,000 per month
Interest	10% interest only on the outstanding loan balance until rent up is completed
	The new permanent loan will fund at the end of the first year. It will be a $4,200,000 first mortgage, 10%, 30-year amortization
Inspection fees	$500 per month during the construction period (six months)
Legal	$5000 in the first month
Accounting	$700 per month during the construction period, $1000 in the twelfth month
Contingency	$36,000: $6000 per month over the first six months

Projected Unit Information

	40-1BR, 1BA	600 sq. ft.
	80-2BR, 2BA	900 sq. ft.
Total units	120 units	96,000 sq. ft.

The preliminary market study reveals that the developer can receive between $480 to $510 per month for the one-bedroom units and $595 to $615 for the two-bedroom units.

Projected Operating Assumptions

Vacancy and Uncollectible	5% per year
Miscellaneous income	$25 per unit per year
Operating expenses	$2200 per unit per year
Debt service	$36,858.01 per month: based on $4,200,000 at 10%, 30-year amortization (.105309 constant)
Capital expenditures	$100 per unit, starting in Year 3
Revenue increases	2.5% in Year 2, thereafter 5%
Expense increases	2.5% in Year 2, thereafter 5%

Absorption Lease-Up

1 BR, 1 BA	6 units per month: months 1–5 8 units per month: month 6
2 BR, 2 BA	12 units per month: months 1–5 16 units per month: month 6

Financing Assumptions

Construction loan to cost ratio	90%
Permanent loan to value ratio	77%
Debt coverage ratio	1.15 minimum
Minimum break-even point	85% minimum

Sale Assumptions

Capitalization rate (on current NOI)	9.5%
Sale costs (of sales price)	2%

Projected Equity Assumptions

Equity requirement	$500,000
Equity return (cash on equity)	14.35%

Projected Development Costs

The projected development costs and operating figures are:

Direct costs:

Land	$ 750,000
Building Costs	3,360,000

Indirect costs:

Architect	25,000
Taxes	12,000
Insurance	3,000
Miscellaneous closing costs	10,000
Appraisal	5,000
Marketing	15,000
Developer's overhead fee	84,000
Inspection fees	3,000
Legal	5,000
Accounting	5,200
Contingency	36,000

Financing costs:

Construction loan fee	12,000
Permanent loan fee	42,000
Mortgage broker	42,000
Construction loan interest	328,548

Lease-up costs:

Rental income	(217,600)
Miscellaneous income	(800)
Operating expense	132,000
Permanent debt service	$ 0
Total	**$4,681,348**

Projected Operating Costs

Salaries and wages	$ 40,000
Real estate taxes	27,000
Insurance	18,000
Repairs and maintenance	55,000
Utilities	23,000
Management (% of EGI)	39,902
Reserve replacement	15,000
Legal and accounting	12,000
Advertising	18,000
General and administrative	$ 17,098
Total	**$ 264,000**

Case Study Calculations

The following computer sheets will illustrate how the following are calculated. These are based on the aforementioned assumptions for Sutton Place Apartments.

- General assumptions
- Rental assumptions
- Rental absorption
- Operating expenses—during rent-up
- Key variables
- Project cost summary
- Stabilized operating proforma
- Development cash flow proforma
- Ten year cash flow proforma
- Taxable income
- Depreciation
- Sale analysis
- Refinancing potential
- Debt service analysis
- Lender financial ratios
- Financial ratios
- Debt service analysis
- Discounted cash flow analysis

PROPERTY NAME: SUTTON PLACE APT.
LOCATION: Atlanta, Ga.

GENERAL ASSUMPTIONS

	ASSUMP.	INFORM.		ASSUMP.	INFORM.
UNIT MIX			**CONSTRUCTION UNDERWRITING**		
One Bdrm, One Bath	40		Construction Loan Amount	$4,200,000	
Two Bdrm, Two Bath	80		Interest Rate	10.00%	
Total Units		120	Loan Fee	1.00%	$42,000
			Month Construction Loan Repaid	12	
RENTAL RATES (PER MONTH)			Const. Loan–To–Cost Ratio		88.09%
One Bdrm, One Bath	$500				
Two Bdrm, Two Bath	$600		**PERMANENT UNDERWRITING**		
Total Rental Per Month		$68,000	Debt Coverage Ratio	1.15	
			Available For Debt Service		$514,051
SQUARE FOOTAGE			Interest Rate	10.00%	
One Bdrm, One Bath	600		Amortization Period (Yrs)	30	
Two Bdrm, Two Bath	900		Term (Yrs)	10	
Total Units		96,000	Loan Constant (Yr)		10.53%
			Maximum Loan Amount		$4,244,672
OPERATING ASSUMPTIONS			Actual Loan Amount	$4,200,000	
Vacancy Factor	5.00%		Loan to Cost Ratio (%)		89.72%
Miscellaneous Income (Per Unit)	$25		Loan to Appraised Value (%)		77.62%
Operating Expenses (Per Unit)	$2,200		Loan Fee (%)	1.00%	$42,000
Management Fee	5.00%		Monthly Payment		$36,858
Utilities (Paid by Tenant)	Electric		Annual Payment		$442,296
Capital Expenditures (Per Unit)	$100.00		Net Cash Flow After Debt Service		$71,754
Starting in Year	3		Mortgage Broker Fee	1.00%	$42,000
Revenue Increases	2.50%		Misc. Closing Costs	$10,000	
Starting in Year	2				
Thereafter	5.00%		**REFINANCING**		
Expense Increases	2.50%		Debt Coverage	1.15	
Starting in Year	2		Interest Rate	10.00%	
Thereafter	5.00%		Amortization Period (Yrs)	30	
			Term (Yrs)	10	
EQUITY SUMMARY			Constant	10.53%	
Equity To Be Contributed	$500,000		Closing Costs (% of loan)	1.00%	
APPRAISAL			**LAND**		
Capitalization Rate	9.50%		Cost	$750,000	
Stabilized NOI	$514,051		Acres	10	
Appraised Value–Stabilized		$5,411,058	Square Feet of Land		435,600
Present Worth Factor	14.30%		Floor Area Ratio		22.04%
			Cost Per Acre		$75,000
DEPRECIATION/AMORTIZATION			Cost Per Foot of Land		$1.72
Depreciation (Yrs)	27.5		Units Per Acre		12
Mortgage Fees (Yrs)	10				
Capital Expenditures (Yrs)	27.5		**CONSTRUCTION COSTS**		
			Cost (Per Sq.Ft.)	$35.00	$3,360,000
SALE					
Capitalization Rate	9.50%		**INDIRECT COSTS**		
Based on NOI (Year)	Current		Developers Fee:		
Sales Cost	2.00%		% of the Construction Loan	2.00%	$84,000
TAXES					
Tax Rate	28.00%				

PROPERTY NAME: SUTTON PLACE APT.
LOCATION: Atlanta, Ga.

KEY VARIABLES

TIMING LEGEND:

A — All Cost is month entered
B — First Month of ratable spread
C — Number of months spread
D — Specific amounts and months
    Enter in table to right

DESCRIPTION	AMOUNT	A	B	C	D
DIRECT COSTS:					
Land	$750,000	1			
Building Cost	$3,360,000				10%—Mo. 1, 15%—Mo. 2 20%—Mos.3–5, 15%—Mo.6
INDIRECT COSTS:					
Architectural	$25,000	1			
Taxes	$12,000				50%—MO.1, 50%—MO.10
Insurance	$3,000	1			
Misc. Closing Costs	$10,000	1			
Appraisal	$5,000	1			
Marketing	$15,000				33%—MO.5, 67%—MO.6
Developer's Fee	$84,000		1	6	
Inspection Fee	$3,000		1	6	
Legal	$5,000		1		
Accounting	$5,200				$700/Mo.—6 Mo., $1000—12th Mo.
Contingency	$36,000		1	6	
FINANCING COSTS:					
Construction Loan Fee	$42,000	1			
Permanent Loan Fee	$42,000	1			
Mortgage Broker Fee	$42,000	1			

NOTES

1. Equity goes into project when construction loan is funded.
2. Construction Interest—paid last day of month
3. Space is available for rent in 7th Month.

PROPERTY NAME: SUTTON PLACE APT.
LOCATION: Atlanta, Ga.

PROJECT COST SUMMARY

DIRECT COSTS:	TOTAL	COST/UNIT	% OF TOTAL COSTS	COST/S.F.
Land	$750,000	$6,250.00	16.02%	$7.81
Building Cost	$3,360,000	$28,000.00	71.77%	$35.00
TOTAL DIRECT COSTS	$4,110,000	$34,250.00	87.80%	$42.81
INDIRECT COSTS:				
Architectural	$25,000	$208.00	0.53%	$0.26
Taxes	$12,000	$100.00	0.26%	$0.13
Insurance	$3,000	$25.00	0.06%	$0.03
Misc. Closing Costs	$10,000	$83.33	0.21%	$0.10
Appraisal	$5,000	$41.67	0.11%	$0.05
Marketing	$15,000	$125.00	0.32%	$0.16
Developer's Fee	$84,000	$700.00	1.79%	$0.88
Inspection Fee	$3,000	$25.00	0.06%	$0.03
Legal	$5,000	$41.67	0.11%	$0.05
Accounting	$5,200	$43.33	0.11%	$0.05
Contingency	$36,000	$300.00	0.77%	$0.38
TOTAL INDIRECT COSTS	$203,200	$1,693.33	4.34%	$2.12
FINANCING COSTS:				
Construction Loan Fee	$42,000	$350.00	0.90%	$0.44
Permanent Loan Fee	$42,000	$350.00	0.90%	$0.44
Mortgage Broker Fee	$42,000	$350.00	0.90%	$0.44
Construction Loan Interest	$328,548	$2,737.90	7.02%	$3.42
TOTAL FINANCING COSTS	$454,548	$3,787.90	9.71%	$4.73
TOTAL COSTS PRIOR TO LEASE–UP	$4,767,748	$39,731.23	101.85%	$49.66
LEASE–UP COSTS:				
Rental Income	($217,600)	($1,813.33)	−4.65%	($2.27)
Miscellaneous Income	($800)	($6.67)	−0.02%	($0.01)
Operating Expense	$132,000	$1,100.00	2.82%	$1.38
Permanent Debt Service	$0	$0.00	0.00%	$0.00
NET DURING LEASE–UP	($86,400)	($720.00)	−1.85%	($0.90)
TOTAL PROJECT COSTS	$4,681,348	$39,011.23	100.00%	$48.76

PROPERTY NAME: SUTTON PLACE APT.
LOCATION: Atlanta, Ga.

RENTAL ASSUMPTIONS

TYPE UNIT	# UNITS	RENT/ MONTH	TOTAL RENT/ MONTH	TOTAL RENT/ YEAR	SQ.FT.	TOTAL SQ.FT.	RENT/ SQ.FT.
1 Br, 1 Ba	40	$500	$20,000	$240,000	600	24,000	$0.83
2 Br, 2 Ba	80	$600	$48,000	$576,000	900	72,000	$0.67
TOTAL	120		$68,000	$816,000		96,000	
AVERAGE			$566.67				$0.71

RENTAL ABSORPTION

MONTH	1,1 RENTED	2,2 RENTED	TOTAL RENTED	CUMM. TOTAL RENTED	% OCCUP.	GROSS RENT/ MONTH	CUMM. GROSS RENT/ MONTH
1							
2							
3							
4							
5							
6							
7	6	12	18	18	15.00%	$10,200	$10,200
8	6	12	18	36	30.00%	$10,200	$20,400
9	6	12	18	54	45.00%	$10,200	$30,600
10	6	12	18	72	60.00%	$10,200	$40,800
11	6	12	18	90	75.00%	$10,200	$51,000
12	8	16	24	114	95.00%	$13,600	$64,600
TOTAL	38		114				$217,600

OPERATING EXPENSES—DURING RENT—UP

MONTH	% OF TOTAL	AMOUNT
1		
2		
3		
4		
5		
6	60.00%	$13,200
7	70.00%	$15,400
8	80.00%	$17,600
9	90.00%	$19,800
10	100.00%	$22,000
11	100.00%	$22,000
12	100.00%	$22,000
TOTAL		$132,000

PROPERTY NAME: SUTTON PLACE APT.
LOCATION: Atlanta, Ga.

STABILIZED OPERATING PROFORMA

	TOTAL	PER UNIT	PER SQ.FT.	% of EGI
Gross Potential Income	$816,000	$6,800.00	$8.50	104.88%
Plus: Miscellaneous Income	$3,000	$25.00	$0.03	0.39%
Less: Vacancy	($40,950)	($341.25)	($0.43)	−5.26%
	-----	-----	-----	-----
Effective Gross Income	$778,050	$6,484	$8.10	100.00%
Operating Expenses:				
Salaries & Wages	$40,000	$333.33	$0.42	5.14%
Real Estate Taxes	$27,000	$225.00	$0.28	3.47%
Insurance	$18,000	$150.00	$0.19	2.31%
Repairs & Maintenance	$55,000	$458.33	$0.57	7.07%
Utilities	$23,000	$191.67	$0.24	2.96%
Management	$38,903	$324.19	$0.41	5.00%
Reserve Replacement	$15,000	$125.00	$0.16	1.93%
Legal & Accounting	$12,000	$100.00	$0.13	1.54%
Advertising	$18,000	$150.00	$0.19	2.31%
General & Administrative	$17,097	$142.48	$0.18	2.20%
	-----	-----	-----	-----
Total Operating Expenses	$264,000	$2,200.00	$2.75	33.93%
Net Operating Income (NOI)	$514,051	$4,283.75	$5.35	66.07%
Less: Debt Service	($442,296)	($3,685.80)	($4.61)	−56.85%
	-----	-----	-----	-----
Before Tax Cash Flow	$71,754	$597.95	$0.75	9.22%
	=====	=====	=====	=====

PROPERTY NAME: SUTTON PLACE APT.
LOCATION: Atlanta, Ga.

DEVELOPMENT CASH FLOW PROFORMA

MONTHLY COST SPREAD	1	2	3	4	5	6	7	8	9	10	11	12	TOTAL
DIRECT COSTS:													
Land	$750,000												$750,000
Building Cost	$336,000	$504,000	$672,000	$672,000	$672,000	$504,000							$3,360,000
TOTAL DIRECT COSTS	$1,086,000	$504,000	$672,000	$672,000	$672,000	$504,000	$0	$0	$0	$0	$0	$0	$4,110,000
INDIRECT COSTS:													
Architectural	$25,000												$25,000
Taxes	$6,000									$6,000			$12,000
Insurance	$3,000												$3,000
Misc. Closing Costs	$10,000												$10,000
Appraisal	$5,000												$5,000
Marketing					$5,000	$10,000							$15,000
Developer's Fee	$14,000	$14,000	$14,000	$14,000	$14,000	$14,000							$84,000
Inspection Fee	$500	$500	$500	$500	$500	$500							$3,000
Legal	$5,000												$5,000
Accounting	$700	$700	$700	$700	$700	$700						$1,000	$5,200
Contingency	$6,000	$6,000	$6,000	$6,000	$6,000	$6,000							$36,000
TOTAL INDIRECT COSTS	$75,200	$21,200	$21,200	$21,200	$26,200	$31,200	$0	$0	$0	$6,000	$0	$1,000	$203,200
FINANCING COSTS:													
Construction Loan Fee	$42,000												$42,000
Permanent Loan Fee	$42,000												$42,000
Mortgage Broker Fee	$42,000												$42,000
Construction Loan Interest	$6,615	$11,084	$17,003	$22,971	$29,031	$33,883	$34,211	$34,475	$34,673	$34,855	$34,903	$34,845	$328,548
TOTAL FINANCING COSTS	$132,615	$11,084	$17,003	$22,971	$29,031	$33,883	$34,211	$34,475	$34,673	$34,855	$34,903	$34,845	$454,548
TOTAL COSTS PRIOR TO LEASE–UP	$1,293,815	$536,284	$710,203	$716,171	$727,231	$569,083	$34,211	$34,475	$34,673	$40,855	$34,903	$35,845	$4,767,748
LEASE–UP COSTS:													
Rental Income – 1 Bd, 1 Ba							($3,000)	($6,000)	($9,000)	($12,000)	($15,000)	($19,000)	($64,000)
Rental Income – 2 Bd, 2 Ba							($7,200)	($14,400)	($21,600)	($28,800)	($36,000)	($45,600)	($153,600)
Miscellaneous Income							($36)	($75)	($113)	($150)	($188)	($238)	($800)
Operating Expenses						$13,200	$15,400	$17,600	$19,800	$22,000	$22,000	$22,000	$132,000
Permanent Debt Service													$0
NET DURING LEASE–UP	$0	$0	$0	$0	$0	$13,200	$5,163	($2,875)	($10,913)	($18,950)	($29,188)	($42,838)	($86,400)
TOTAL PROJECT COSTS	$1,293,815	$536,284	$710,203	$716,171	$727,231	$582,283	$39,374	$31,600	$23,760	$21,905	$5,715	($6,993)	$4,681,348
EQUITY	$500,000												$500,000
CONSTRUCTION LOAN BALANCE	$793,815	$1,330,099	$2,040,302	$2,756,472	$3,483,703	$4,065,986	$4,105,360	$4,136,960	$4,160,720	$4,182,625	$4,188,341	$4,181,348	

PROPERTY NAME: SUTTON PLACE APT.
LOCATION: Atlanta, Ga.

TEN YEAR CASH FLOW PROFORMA

YEAR	1	2	3	4	5	6	7	8	9	10
AVERAGE RENT/MONTH PER UNIT–1BR, 1 BA	$500	$513	$538	$565	$593	$623	$654	$687	$721	$757
AVERAGE RENT/MONTH PER UNIT–2BR, 2 BA	$600	$615	$646	$678	$712	$748	$785	$824	$865	$909
GROSS POTENTIAL INCOME	$408,000	$836,400	$878,220	$922,131	$968,238	$1,016,649	$1,067,482	$1,120,856	$1,176,899	$1,235,744
PLUS: MISC. INCOME	$1,500	$3,075	$3,229	$3,390	$3,560	$3,738	$3,925	$4,121	$4,327	$4,543
LESS: VACANCY	($191,100)	($41,666)	($43,911)	($46,107)	($48,412)	($50,832)	($53,374)	($56,043)	($58,845)	($61,787)
EFFECTIVE GROSS INCOME	$218,400	$797,809	$837,538	$879,415	$923,385	$969,555	$1,018,032	$1,068,934	$1,122,381	$1,178,500
LESS: OPERATING EXPENSES	($132,000)	($270,600)	($284,130)	($298,337)	($313,253)	($328,916)	($345,362)	($362,630)	($380,761)	($399,799)
NET OPERATING INCOME	$86,400	$527,209	$553,408	$581,078	$610,132	$640,639	$672,671	$706,304	$741,619	$778,700
DEBT SERVICE–PERMANENT LOAN		($442,296)	($442,296)	($442,296)	($442,296)	($442,296)	($442,296)	($442,296)	($442,296)	($442,296)
DEBT SERVICE–CONSTRUCTION LOAN	($207,961)									
LESS: CAPITAL EXPENDITURES	$0	$0	($12,000)	($12,600)	($13,230)	($13,892)	($14,586)	($15,315)	($16,081)	($16,885)
BEFORE TAX CASH FLOW (BTCF)	($121,561)	$84,913	$99,112	$126,182	$154,606	$184,451	$215,788	$248,693	$283,242	$319,519
LESS: TAXES	($4,166)	$0	$0	($4,182)	($13,017)	($22,341)	($32,181)	($42,568)	($164,254)	($174,465)
AFTER TAX CASH FLOW (ATCF)	($125,727)	$84,913	$99,112	$122,000	$141,589	$162,110	$183,608	$206,124	$118,988	$145,054

NOTES

1. YEAR 1 DEBT SERVICE IS CONSTRUCTION INTEREST ONLY (STARTING MONTH 7)

2. ASSUME THAT THE PASSIVE LOSS LIMITATIONS DO NOT APPLY

3. ASSUME THAT ANY TAX SAVINGS GENERATED FROM TAXABLE LOSS (YEAR 2 & 3) ARE NOT CONSIDERED
   CONTRIBUTIONS TO CASH FLOW

PROPERTY NAME: SUTTON PLACE APT.
LOCATION: Atlanta, Ga.

DEBT SERVICE ANALYSIS

PRINCIPAL	$4,200,000
INTEREST RATE	10.00%
NO. PAYMENTS (MO.)	360
MONTHLY PAYMENT	$36,858.01
BEG. OF MONTH	1
MONTHS REMAINING	12
LOAN CONSTANT (MONTH)	0.008776
LOAN CONSTANT (YEAR)	0.105309

	12 MONTHS YEAR 1	YEAR 2	YEAR 3	YEAR 4	YEAR 5
FIRST MORTGAGE					
BEGINNING BALANCE	$4,200,000	$4,176,653	$4,150,861	$4,122,369	$4,090,893
INTEREST	$418,949	$416,504	$413,804	$410,820	$407,524
PRINCIPAL	$23,347	$25,792	$28,492	$31,476	$34,772
TOTAL DEBT SERVICE	$442,296	$442,296	$442,296	$442,296	$442,296
ENDING BALANCE	$4,176,653	$4,150,861	$4,122,369	$4,090,893	$4,056,121

	YEAR 6	YEAR 7	YEAR 8	YEAR 9	YEAR 10
BEGINNING BALANCE	$4,056,121	$4,017,709	$3,975,273	$3,928,394	$3,876,606
INTEREST	$403,883	$399,861	$395,417	$390,509	$385,086
PRINCIPAL	$38,413	$42,435	$46,879	$51,788	$57,210
TOTAL DEBT SERVICE	$442,296	$442,296	$442,296	$442,297	$442,296
ENDING BALANCE	$4,017,709	$3,975,273	$3,928,394	$3,876,606	$3,819,396

PAYMENT NUMBER	INTEREST PAID	PRINCIPAL PAID	BALANCE REMAINING	SUM OF YEARLY INTEREST	SUM OF YEARLY PRINCIPAL	SUM OF YEARLY PAYMENTS
1	$35,000.00	$1,858.01	$4,198,141.99	$0.00	$0.00	$0.00
2	$34,984.52	$1,873.49	$4,196,268.50	$0.00	$0.00	$0.00
3	$34,968.90	$1,889.10	$4,194,379.40	$0.00	$0.00	$0.00
4	$34,953.16	$1,904.84	$4,192,474.56	$0.00	$0.00	$0.00
5	$34,937.29	$1,920.72	$4,190,553.84	$0.00	$0.00	$0.00
6	$34,921.28	$1,936.72	$4,188,617.12	$0.00	$0.00	$0.00
7	$34,905.14	$1,952.86	$4,186,664.25	$0.00	$0.00	$0.00
8	$34,888.87	$1,969.14	$4,184,695.12	$0.00	$0.00	$0.00
9	$34,872.46	$1,985.55	$4,182,709.57	$0.00	$0.00	$0.00
10	$34,855.91	$2,002.09	$4,180,707.48	$0.00	$0.00	$0.00
11	$34,839.23	$2,018.78	$4,178,688.70	$0.00	$0.00	$0.00
12	$34,822.41	$2,035.60	$4,176,653.10	$418,949.17	$23,346.90	$442,296.07

PROPERTY NAME: SUTTON PLACE APT.
LOCATION: Atlanta, Ga.

TAXABLE INCOME

YEAR	1	2	3	4	5	6	7	8	9	10
NET OPERATING INCOME	$86,400	$527,209	$553,408	$581,078	$610,132	$640,639	$672,671	$706,304	$741,619	$778,700
−INTEREST	$0	($418,949)	($416,504)	($413,604)	($410,820)	($407,524)	($403,883)	($399,861)	($395,417)	($390,509)
−DEPRECIATION (27.5 YRS.)	($71,523)	($143,045)	($143,045)	($143,045)	($143,045)	($143,045)	($143,045)	($143,045)	($143,045)	($143,045)
−CAPITAL EXPENDITURES (27.5 YRS.)	$0	$0	($436)	($695)	($1,378)	($1,881)	($2,411)	($2,968)	($3,553)	($4,187)
−AMORT. OF PERM./MTG. BROKER FEE (10 YRS.)	$0	($8,400)	($8,400)	($8,400)	($8,400)	($8,400)	($8,400)	($8,400)	($8,400)	($8,400)
TAXABLE INCOME (LOSS)	$14,877	($43,186)	($14,978)	$14,834	$46,491	$79,788	$114,931	$152,030	$191,204	$232,579
TAXES @ 28% TAX RATE (SAVINGS)	$4,166	($12,092)	($4,194)	$4,132	$13,017	$22,341	$32,181	$42,568	$53,537	$65,122

345

PROPERTY NAME: SUTTON PLACE APT.
LOCATION: Atlanta, Ga.

DEPRECIATION

DESCRIPTION	TOTAL
BUILDING COSTS	$3,360,000
INDIRECT COSTS	$203,200
CONSTRUCTION LOAN FEE	$42,000
CONSTRUCTION INTEREST	$328,548
DEPRECIABLE BASIS	$3,933,748

YEAR	1	2	3	4	5	6	7	8	9	10
DEPRECIABLE BASIS	$71,523	$143,045	$143,045	$143,045	$143,045	$143,045	$143,045	$143,045	$143,045	$143,045
CAPITAL EXPENDITURES (2)		$0	$436	$458	$481	$505	$530	$557	$585	$614
CAPITAL EXPENDITURES (3)			$0	$436	$458	$481	$505	$530	$557	$585
CAPITAL EXPENDITURES (4)				$0	$436	$458	$481	$505	$530	$557
CAPITAL EXPENDITURES (5)					$0	$436	$458	$481	$505	$530
CAPITAL EXPENDITURES (6)						$0	$436	$458	$481	$505
CAPITAL EXPENDITURES (7)							$0	$436	$458	$481
CAPITAL EXPENDITURES (8)								$0	$436	$458
CAPITAL EXPENDITURES (9)									$0	$436
CAPITAL EXPENDITURES (10)										$0
TOTAL	$71,523	$143,045	$143,482	$143,940	$144,421	$144,926	$145,457	$146,013	$146,598	$147,212

PROPERTY NAME: SUTTON PLACE APT.
LOCATION: Atlanta, Ga.

SALE ANALYSIS

YEAR	1	2	3	4	5	6	7	8	9	10
SALES PRICE – BASED										
ON CURRENT NOI	$5,411,058	$6,590,109	$6,917,597	$7,263,477	$7,626,651	$8,007,983	$8,408,382	$8,828,801	$9,270,241	$9,733,753
LESS: SALES COST	($108,221)	($131,802)	($138,352)	($145,270)	($152,533)	($160,160)	($168,168)	($176,576)	($185,405)	($194,675)
LESS: ORIGINAL EQUITY	($500,000)	($500,000)	($500,000)	($500,000)	($500,000)	($500,000)	($500,000)	($500,000)	($500,000)	($500,000)
LESS: OUTST. LOAN BAL.	($4,200,000)	($4,176,653)	($4,150,861)	($4,122,369)	($4,090,893)	($4,056,121)	($4,017,709)	($3,975,273)	($3,975,273)	($3,975,273)
BEFORE TAX EQUITY REV.	$602,837	$1,781,654	$2,128,383	$2,495,838	$2,883,224	$3,291,702	$3,722,506	$4,176,952	$4,609,563	$5,063,805
LESS: TAXES DUE ON SALE	($403,371)	($766,956)	($896,993)	($1,032,206)	($1,172,299)	($1,317,516)	($1,468,113)	($1,624,360)	($1,786,538)	($1,954,945)
AFTER TAX EQUITY REV.	$199,465	$1,014,698	$1,231,390	$1,463,632	$1,710,926	$1,974,186	$2,254,393	$2,552,592	$2,823,025	$3,108,860

TAXES DUE ON SALE:

	1	2	3	4	5	6	7	8	9	10
SALES PRICE – BASED										
ON CURRENT NOI	$5,411,058	$6,590,109	$6,917,597	$7,263,477	$7,626,651	$8,007,983	$8,408,382	$8,828,801	$9,270,241	$9,733,753
LESS: SALES COST	($108,221)	($131,802)	($138,352)	($145,270)	($152,533)	($160,160)	($168,168)	($176,576)	($185,405)	($194,675)
AMOUNT REALIZED	$5,302,837	$6,458,307	$6,779,245	$7,118,207	$7,474,118	$7,847,823	$8,240,215	$8,652,225	$9,084,837	$9,539,078
LESS: ADJUSTED BASIS	($3,862,225)	($3,719,180)	($3,575,698)	($3,431,758)	($3,287,337)	($3,142,411)	($2,996,954)	($2,850,941)	($2,704,343)	($2,557,130)
CAPITAL GAINS ON SALE	$1,440,612	$2,739,127	$3,203,547	$3,686,449	$4,186,780	$4,705,413	$5,243,260	$5,801,284	$6,380,494	$6,981,948
TAXES DUE @										
MARGINAL TAX RATE – 28%	$403,371	$766,956	$896,993	$1,032,206	$1,172,299	$1,317,516	$1,468,113	$1,624,360	$1,786,538	$1,954,945

PROPERTY NAME: SUTTON PLACE APT.
LOCATION: Atlanta, Ga.

LENDER FINANCIAL RATIOS

YEAR	1	2	3	4	5	6	7	8	9	10
DEBT SERVICE COVERAGE RATIO	1.16	1.19	1.25	1.31	1.38	1.45	1.52	1.60	1.68	1.76
LOAN TO VALUE RATIO (END OF YEAR)	77.62%	63.38%	60.00%	56.75%	53.64%	50.66%	47.78%	45.03%	42.98%	40.84%
BREAK EVEN CASH FLOW RATIO	0.00%	86.23%	84.08%	81.66%	79.40%	77.22%	75.15%	73.18%	71.30%	69.51%
OPERATING EXP. RATIO (W/O CAP. EXP.)	33.93%	33.92%	33.92%	33.92%	33.92%	33.92%	33.92%	33.92%	33.92%	33.92%

FINANCIAL RATIOS

	1	2	3	4	5	6	7	8	9	10
VALUE MULTIPLIERS:										
GROSS RENT MULTIPLIER (GRM)	6.63	7.88	7.88	7.88	7.88	7.88	7.88	7.88	7.88	7.88
EFFECTIVE GROSS INCOME MULT. (EGIM)	6.95	7.85	7.85	7.85	7.85	7.85	7.85	7.85	7.85	7.85
NET INCOME MULT. (NIM) (W/O CAP. EXP.)	10.53	12.50	12.50	12.50	12.50	12.50	12.50	12.50	12.50	12.50
BEFORE TAX CASH FLOW MULTIPLIER	6.97	5.89	5.04	3.98	3.23	2.71	2.32	2.01	1.77	1.56
AFTER TAX CASH FLOW MULTIPLIER	N/A	5.89	5.04	4.10	3.53	3.08	2.72	2.43	4.20	3.45
VALUES (PER UNIT):										
PRICE PER UNIT	$45,092	$54,918	$57,647	$60,529	$63,555	$66,733	$70,070	$73,573	$77,252	$81,115
PRICE PER SQUARE FOOT	$56.37	$68.85	$72.06	$75.66	$79.44	$83.42	$87.59	$91.97	$96.57	$101.39
PRICE PER ROOM (BEDROOM)	$27,056	$32,951	$34,588	$36,317	$38,133	$40,040	$42,042	$44,144	$46,351	$48,669
RATES OF RETURN:										
CASH ON EQUITY RATIO	N/A	16.98%	19.82%	25.24%	30.92%	36.86%	43.16%	49.74%	56.65%	63.90%
AVERAGE RATE ON NET OPERATING INCOME	9.50%	8.00%	7.81%	7.63%	7.45%	7.27%	7.11%	6.94%	6.79%	6.63%
AVERAGE RATE ON BEFORE TAX CASH FLOW	14.35%	16.98%	18.40%	20.68%	23.24%	25.97%	28.84%	31.82%	34.92%	38.14%
AVERAGE RATE ON AFTER TAX CASH FLOW	N/A	16.98%	18.40%	20.40%	22.39%	24.39%	26.44%	28.59%	27.98%	28.08%

TIME VALUE METHODS OF RETURN:										
YEAR	1	2	3	4	5	6	7	8	9	10
INTERNAL RATE OF RETURN (PRE TAX)	120.57%	64.12%	52.86%	46.86%	42.99%	40.24%	38.18%	36.72%	35.30%	34.26%

	1	2	3	4	5	6	7	8	9	10
INITIAL CASH INPUT	($500,000)	($500,000)	($500,000)	($500,000)	($500,000)	($500,000)	($500,000)	($500,000)	($500,000)	($500,000)
1	$1,102,837	$0	$0	$0	$0	$0	$0	$0	$0	$0
2		$1,346,834	$84,913	$84,913	$84,913	$84,913	$84,913	$84,913	$84,913	$84,913
3			$1,857,088	$99,112	$99,112	$99,112	$99,112	$99,112	$99,112	$99,112
4				$1,998,093	$126,182	$126,182	$126,182	$126,182	$126,182	$126,182
5					$2,357,708	$154,608	$154,608	$154,608	$154,608	$154,608
6						$2,737,023	$184,451	$184,451	$184,451	$184,451
7							$3,137,208	$215,798	$215,798	$215,798
8								$3,599,504	$248,693	$248,693
9									$4,005,236	$283,242
10										$4,475,820

DEVELOPMENT PROFIT

STABILIZED NET OPERATING INCOME	$514,051
CAPITALIZATION RATE	9.50%
APPRAISED VALUE	$5,411,058
LESS: DEVELOPMENT COSTS	($4,681,348)
DEVELOPMENT PROFIT	$729,710
DEVELOPMENT PROFIT %	15.59%

PROPERTY NAME: SUTTON PLACE APT.
LOCATION: Atlanta, Ga.

REFINANCING POTENTIAL									

YEAR	2	3	4	5	6	7	8	9	10
POTENTIAL LOAN AMOUNT	$4,353,679	$4,570,030	$4,796,531	$5,038,458	$5,290,381	$5,554,900	$5,832,645	$6,124,277	$6,430,491
LESS: OUTSTANDING LOAN BAL.	($4,150,861)	($4,122,369)	($4,090,893)	($4,056,121)	($4,017,709)	($3,975,273)	($3,928,394)	($3,876,606)	($3,819,396)
LESS: REFINANCING COSTS	($43,537)	($45,700)	($47,965)	($50,385)	($52,904)	($55,549)	($58,326)	($61,243)	($64,305)
	-----	-----	-----	-----	-----	-----	-----	-----	-----
NET PROCEEDS	$159,281	$401,960	$659,653	$931,952	$1,219,768	$1,524,077	$1,845,924	$2,186,428	$2,546,789
LESS: EQUITY	($500,000)	($500,000)	($500,000)	($500,000)	($500,000)	($500,000)	($500,000)	($500,000)	($500,000)
	-----	-----	-----	-----	-----	-----	-----	-----	-----
OUTSTANDING EQUITY BALANCE	($340,719)	($98,040)	$159,653	$431,952	$719,768	$1,024,077	$1,345,924	$1,686,428	$2,046,789
NEW REFINANCING									
LOAN-TO-VALUE RATIO (LTV-%)	78.45%	78.45%	78.45%	78.45%	78.45%	78.45%	78.45%	78.45%	78.45%
GROSS POTENTIAL INCOME	$836,400	$878,220	$922,131	$968,238	$1,016,649	$1,067,482	$1,120,856	$1,176,899	$1,235,744
OPERATING EXPENSES	$270,600	$284,130	$298,337	$313,253	$328,916	$345,362	$362,630	$380,761	$399,799
DEBT SERVICE @ .1053 - K	$458,442	$481,224	$505,285	$530,550	$557,077	$584,931	$614,177	$644,886	$677,131
	-----	-----	-----	-----	--===		=-==-	-----	-----
OPERATING EXPENSES + DEBT SERVICE	$729,042	$765,354	$803,622	$843,803	$885,993	$930,293	$976,807	$1,025,648	$1,076,930
BREAK-EVEN (% OF GPI)	87.16%	87.15%	87.15%	87.15%	87.15%	87.15%	87.15%	87.15%	87.15%

NOTES:

1. NET OPERATING INCOME IS BASED ON CURRRENT YEAR

2. THE TOTAL $500,000 EQUITY INVESTMENT CANNOT BE FULLY RECAPTURED UNTIL DURING YEAR 4

PROPERTY NAME: SUTTON PLACE APT.
LOCATION: Atlanta, Ga.

DISCOUNTED CASH FLOW ANALYSIS										

YEAR	1	2	3	4	5	6	7	8	9	10
GROSS POTENTIAL INCOME	$816,000	$836,400	$878,220	$922,131	$968,238	$1,016,649	$1,067,482	$1,120,856	$1,176,899	$1,235,744
PLUS: MISC. INCOME	$3,000	$3,075	$3,229	$3,390	$3,560	$3,738	$3,925	$4,121	$4,327	$4,543
LESS: VACANCY	($40,950)	($41,666)	($43,911)	($46,107)	($48,412)	($50,832)	($53,374)	($56,043)	($58,845)	($61,787)
EFFECTIVE GROSS INCOME	$778,050	$797,809	$837,538	$879,415	$923,385	$969,555	$1,018,032	$1,068,934	$1,122,381	$1,178,500
LESS: OPERATING EXPENSES	($264,000)	($270,600)	($284,130)	($298,337)	($313,253)	($328,916)	($345,362)	($362,630)	($380,761)	($399,799)
NET OPERATING INCOME	$514,050	$527,209	$553,408	$581,078	$610,132	$640,639	$672,671	$706,304	$741,619	$778,700
PRESENT WORTH FACTOR (14.30%)	0.87489	0.76543	0.66967	0.58589	0.51259	0.44846	0.39235	0.34327	0.30032	0.26275
DISCOUNTED PRESENT WORTH	$449,738	$403,543	$370,601	$340,447	$312,747	$287,300	$263,924	$242,450	$222,723	$204,601
CUMMULATIVE PRESENT WORTH	$449,738	$853,281	$1,223,882	$1,564,329	$1,877,076	$2,164,376	$2,428,300	$2,670,749	$2,893,472	$3,098,073

REVERSION–YEAR 10		NOI–1ST YEAR	
NET OPERATING INCOME	$778,700	$514,050	
CAPITALIZATION RATE	9.50%	9.50%	
VALUE	$8,196,845	$5,411,053	
LESS: SALES COST	($163,937)		
PROCEEDS OF SALE	$8,032,908		
P.W. FACTOR (14.30%)	0.2627		
P.W. REVERSION	$2,110,622		
CUMMULATIVE P.W. CASH FLOW	$3,098,073		
INDICATED VALUE	$5,208,696		
SAY	$5,200,000		

ADDITIONAL CASE STUDIES

Four additional case studies are provided for review in Chapter 16 as follows.

Case No. 1   Retail
Case No. 2   Industrial Building—Build to Suit
Case No. 3   Corporate Summit Office Building
Case No. 4   Residential Subdivision—Land Development

FINANCIAL FORMS

Development Proforma Form (8–1)

This form is to be used to calculate the total development costs.

DEVELOPMENT PROFORMA FORM

FORM 8-1

PROPERTY TYPE _____

NO. UNITS _____

TOTAL SQ.FT. _____

DESCRIPTION	COST	COST./ UNIT	COST./ SQ.FT.	PERCENT OF TOTAL COSTS
REVENUE:				
RENTAL INCOME	$_____	$_____	$_____	_____%
SALES INCOME	$_____	$_____	$_____	_____%
MISCELLANEOUS INCOME	$_____	$_____	$_____	_____%
TOTAL REVENUE	$_____	$_____	$_____	_____%
DIRECT COSTS:				
LAND	$_____	$_____	$_____	_____%
SITEWORK & DEMOLITION	$_____	$_____	$_____	_____%
PERMITS & FEES	$_____	$_____	$_____	_____%
UTILITY CONNECTION FEES	$_____	$_____	$_____	_____%
SHELL	$_____	$_____	$_____	_____%
PARKING STRUCTURE	$_____	$_____	$_____	_____%
TENANT IMPROVEMENTS	$_____	$_____	$_____	_____%
DIRECT CONTINGENCY COSTS	$_____	$_____	$_____	_____%
TOTAL DIRECT COSTS	$_____	$_____	$_____	_____%
INDIRECT COSTS:				
ARCHITECTURAL	$_____	$_____	$_____	_____%
SPACE PLANNING	$_____	$_____	$_____	_____%
ENGINEERING	$_____	$_____	$_____	_____%
INSPECTION FEES	$_____	$_____	$_____	_____%
INSURANCE	$_____	$_____	$_____	_____%
MARKETING	$_____	$_____	$_____	_____%
LEASE COMMISSIONS	$_____	$_____	$_____	_____%
PROPERTY TAXES	$_____	$_____	$_____	_____%
LEGAL	$_____	$_____	$_____	_____%
ACCOUNTING	$_____	$_____	$_____	_____%
CLOSING COSTS	$_____	$_____	$_____	_____%
FURNITURE, FIXTURES & EQUIPMENT	$_____	$_____	$_____	_____%
OPERATING EXPENSES	$_____	$_____	$_____	_____%
INDIRECT CONTINGENCY COSTS	$_____	$_____	$_____	_____%
TOTAL INDIRECT COSTS	$_____	$_____	$_____	_____%
FINANCING COSTS:				
CONSTRUCTION LOAN FEE	$_____	$_____	$_____	_____%
PERMANENT LOAN FEE	$_____	$_____	$_____	_____%
INTEREST	$_____	$_____	$_____	_____%
TOTAL FINANCING COSTS	$_____	$_____	$_____	_____%
TOTAL DEVELOPMENT COSTS	$_____	$_____	$_____	_____%

Form 8-1   Development proforma form.

Operating Proforma Form (8–2)

This form is to be used to calculate the projected operating proforma.

OPERATING PROFORMA FORM

FORM 8–2

PROPERTY NAME _____
PROPERTY TYPE _____
NO. UNITS _____
TOTAL SQ. FT. _____

DESCRIPTION	COST	COST./ UNIT	COST./ SQ.FT.	PERCENT OF GPI	PERCENT OF EGI
REVENUE:					
GROSS POTENTIAL INCOME	$_____	$_____	$_____	_____%	_____%
PLUS: MISCELLANEOUS INCOME	$_____	$_____	$_____	_____%	_____%
LESS: VACANCY & UNCOLLECTIBLE INCOME	$_____	$_____	$_____	_____%	_____%
EFFECTIVE POTENTIAL INCOME	$_____	$_____	$_____	_____%	_____%
OPERATING EXPENSES:					
SALARIES & WAGES	$_____	$_____	$_____	_____%	_____%
REPAIRS & MAINTENANCE	$_____	$_____	$_____	_____%	_____%
UTILITIES	$_____	$_____	$_____	_____%	_____%
TAXES	$_____	$_____	$_____	_____%	_____%
INSURANCE	$_____	$_____	$_____	_____%	_____%
GENERAL & ADMINISTRATIVE	$_____	$_____	$_____	_____%	_____%
MANAGEMENT FEES	$_____	$_____	$_____	_____%	_____%
PROFESSIONAL FEES	$_____	$_____	$_____	_____%	_____%
MARKETING	$_____	$_____	$_____	_____%	_____%
CONTRACT SERVICES	$_____	$_____	$_____	_____%	_____%
SUPPLIES	$_____	$_____	$_____	_____%	_____%
UNIT MAINTENANCE	$_____	$_____	$_____	_____%	_____%
DEPOSITS & BONDS	$_____	$_____	$_____	_____%	_____%
BANKING	$_____	$_____	$_____	_____%	_____%
RESERVES & REPLACEMENTS	$_____	$_____	$_____	_____%	_____%
TOTAL OPERATING EXPENSES	$_____	$_____	$_____	_____%	_____%
NET OPERATING INCOME	$_____	$_____	$_____	_____%	_____%
DEBT SERVICE:					
1ST MORTGAGE	$_____	$_____	$_____	_____%	_____%
2ND MORTGAGE	$_____	$_____	$_____	_____%	_____%
TOTAL DEBT SERVICE	$_____	$_____	$_____	_____%	_____%
TENANT IMPROVEMENTS	$_____	$_____	$_____	_____%	_____%
LEASING COMMISSIONS	$_____	$_____	$_____	_____%	_____%
CAPITAL EXPENDITURES	$_____	$_____	$_____	_____%	_____%
BEFORE-TAX CASH FLOW	$_____	$_____	$_____	_____%	_____%

Form 8–2   Operating proforma form.

## Chapter 9

Financing for the
Real Estate Development

Since the construction of real estate developments usually require much more money than the developer's own resources, additional financing must be secured from other sources. These sources provide loans which are usually made in the form of mortgages as instruments of debt secured by real property for a specified period of time. Sometimes lenders will provide funds to the developer for the construction of the development and then convert these short-term loans into a long-term permanent loan. The developer will make regular monthly payments to the lender as payment for this debt. Upon repayment of the loan, the debt is paid, collateral is released, and the developer or partners become the owner of the property, realizing all of the benefits of cash flows and depreciation.

Financing is the lifeblood of the real estate development process (assuming the developer does not finance the development costs from his own resources), for without these funds from an outside source, regardless of the planned development's location, design, and pre-leases, it cannot proceed. In today's real estate finance market it is becoming more difficult to find reliable sources at the right price to finance new development ventures, due to the current tightening of the lender market.

The right financing package is similar to a good recipe. Not only must the loan rate and terms fit the product but all the terms and conditions must give the developer the flexibility needed to successfully build, market, manage, and ultimately sell the property.

Some borrowers have properties which are 95 percent occupied with expenses meeting the proforma, but are experiencing losses because of excessive debt service requirements from loans which have no flexibility in prepayment, subordinate financing, or due on sale clauses. In addition, these terms prevent a potential sale because the property cannot be refinanced in the current marketplace.

To find and secure financing, the developer must understand how to identify potential lenders, how to present the financing proposal, how to negotiate and close the loan.

The first step in finding lenders is to compile a list of potential lending sources. Sources can be found in the local yellow pages, through mortgage brokers or local banking institutions, and industry newsletters, such as:

Novick's Financial Newsletter
    Novick Income Property Finance Report
    IPFR Publishing, Inc.
    111 John Street
    Penthouse
    New York, NY 10038
    (212) 233-7360

Crittenden Newsletter
    Crittenden Financing
    Crittenden Publishing Company
    Box 1150
    Navato, CA 94948
    (415) 382-2400

Fleet's Guide
    Fleet's Press
    3337 Duke Street
    Alexandria, VA 23314
    (703) 370-3246

These newsletters publish the names of various lenders and report on their size and the types of deals which they are currently financing. The list should be long, with 20 to 50 names, because the process is like finding a "needle in a haystack."

In searching for the perfect loan, the developer should negotiate with more than one lender at a time. Therefore identify a number of available lenders and consider them all together. Even though the loan officer informs you that your loan appears to be acceptable, the loan terms may completely change by the time the final commitment is approved by the loan committee. Since "time is of the essence," negotiating with more than one lender can prove to your advantage.

When preparing your loan proposal, attempt to have a complete submission. This will decrease the loan processing time and give you the best possible probability for acceptance. It is also important to consider the sophistication of the lender to whom you are submitting your proposal. For the more sophisticated lenders, you will use all of the items outlined in this chapter. For other lenders, who are smaller, and with whom you have existing relationships, your presentation may be abbreviated. In addition, if the lender is not very sophisticated, too much or too polished a presentation may be intimidating. You may want to make your presentation piecemeal giving only what is requested. If they ask for the other information later, you will have it and can submit at that time. We will discuss the loan package in more detail later in this chapter.

Using Mortgage Brokers or Mortgage Bankers

If the developer does not have the time nor the contacts to locate the best available financing, he may choose to use the services of outside professionals, such as a mortgage broker or a mortgage banker. As will be mentioned in Chapter 10, the Mortgage Broker finds financing for a percentage of the loan.

A mortgage banker is an individual or company that can originate and service the mortgage loan. Many of these companies put together mortgage pools of either their own funds or funds of other investor participants. To find the names of local mortgage brokers, begin with your local association of mortgage bankers/brokers.

Mortgage Brokers

Mortgage brokers will charge a fee for their services. This fee usually ranges from one-half to one percent of the mortgage loan amount. A good broker can put the initial loan proposal together and use his list of relationships in the financial community for finding the best possible loan. In addition, the broker can help structure the business terms and can offer sophistication within the process which the borrower may not possess. Remember, if you decide to use a mortgage broker, choose a qualified one who is experienced with the type of financing for which you are searching.

Mortgage Bankers

A mortgage banker is an individual or firm which underwrites, closes, or services loans in their own name and then sell the loans to the secondary mortgage market. Many mortgage bankers will act as a correspondent:

> **Correspondent:** Many mortgage bankers will act as loan correspondents for a pool of life insurance companies and pension funds. These institutions will rely on the local knowledge of their correspondent to protect their interests.

MAXIMIZING FINANCIAL RETURNS

The developer will not only construct the components of the development to function efficiently, and seek to lease the property at above market rate faster than the proforma schedule, but he must select financing vehicles for constructing the development which will fit within his investment strategy, as discussed in Chapter 1. Depending upon his attitude toward risk and his financial resources, the developer may choose to develop a property with leveraged or non-leveraged financing. Obviously, non-leveraged financing is not financing at all and the funds for development are from available cash. This can usually occur only on small projects or with developers which are very liquid. Consider the following.

The Use of Leverage

The majority of real estate developers will look to increase their potential investment return by using "Other People's Money" (OPM). The more debt placed on a property, the higher the potential return (assuming the property is not overburdened with debt). For example: A developer can develop an apartment property for $5,000,000 with a net operating income of $520,000. It is projected that at the end of three years he will sell the property for $6,200,000 with one percent in sales costs. The developer is able to obtain the following loans at 10.5 percent interest rate for a 30-year amortized loan. Plan 1: Financed with a 70 percent loan for $3,500,000, Plan 2: Financed with a 80 percent loan for $4,000,000, and Plan 3: Financed with a 90 percent loan for $4,500,000.

Leverage Case Study			
Operations	Plan 1	Plan 2	Plan 3
Effective gross income	$900,000	$900,000	$900,000
– Operating expenses	($380,000)	($380,000)	($380,000)
= Net operating income	$520,000	$520,000	$520,000
– Debt service	($384,191)	($439,075)	($493,959)
= Cash flow	$135,809	$ 80,925	$ 26,041
Average rate on BTCF (Before-tax cash flows)	9.05%	8.09%	5.21%
Break-even ratio	84.91%	91.01%	97.11%
Debt coverage ratio	135.35	118.43	105.27
Resale: (numbers in 1000s)			
Sales price	$ 6,200	$ 6,200	$ 6,200
– Sales costs	($ 62)	($ 62)	($ 62)
– Mortgage balance	($ 3,441)	($ 3,933)	($ 4,424)
– Original equity	($ 1,500)	($ 1,000)	($ 500)
= Before-tax equity reversion	$ 1,197	$ 1,205	$ 1,214
Profit (3 years)	79.77%	120.49%	242.66%
Profit (per year)	26.59%	40.16%	80.89%

You will note from the previous example that Plan 3 achieves the best returns, but it should be noted that it has a break-even ratio of 97.11 percent.

The developer should be sure to not overleverage the property. If a property has too much debt, it can create "reverse leverage." Reverse leverage occurs when the net operating income of a property decreases, and due to the high monthly debt service, the property will start to have a reduced or negative cash flow.

Borrowing to Reduce the Equity in the Development

The majority of developers cannot afford to pay all cash for their developments. Even if they could, they would be limited to the number of purchases that could be made. By financing property, the developer can structure a loan to suit his needs. Depending upon the availability of the developer's cash and the current market rates for loans, the developer can structure the overall investment needs by borrowing more or less. The developer should understand that with leveraged financing, a project which fails to perform as projected, will be in danger of foreclosure and he may lose all of his equity invested, participation in cash flows and residuals, as well as damaging his reputation.

Nonleverage for Risk Aversion

In nonleveraged real estate transactions, no financing occurs. Therefore there is no debt and the pressures to repay that debt are not present. Consequently, cash flows are greater and the returns on the cash are higher and quicker if the project performs on schedule. Long-term, extremely high profits can result. Unfortunately, the cash is tied up for a long period of time in the physical asset limiting any other investment which the developer may wish to pursue. The risk is in the limitations of the investor to follow other transactions. Land purchased for cash to be developed at a future date is a wise transaction. These investments are of a smaller nature, and with the absence of monthly principle and interest payments due, the developer is free to follow the cycles of the market until the timing for the development of the site is just right, assuming he has other financial resources by which to live and conduct business. Another advantage for non-leveraged real estate on properties which are leased to multi-tenants is that a smaller percentage of leased space is necessary for a break-even position. A break-even position being one where one's cash had been invested in a safe vehicle like a savings account or a Treasury Bill.

FINANCING FOR THE DEVELOPMENT PHASE

In the first phase of the development process, the developer must obtain financing to acquire the land, construct the site improvements, and construct the building.

To obtain this financing, the developer must find a lender who is willing to make these types of loans.

Sources of Development Loans

Due to the risky nature and the experience level required for these types of loans, the field will be much smaller than those lenders who will make the permanent loan on the property. The main sources for this type of financing are listed below.

Commercial Banks

Local or regional banks are a good source for short term financing. Since their costs of funds is not tied to the same rates as the savings institutions, they can offer more competitive rates. Their loans are usually made on a short-term basis only. Banks usually will make construction loans. Traditionally, banks are not as aggressive as savings and loans and usually will have stricter loan procedures.

Savings and Loans

An advantage of dealing with savings and loans institutions is their knowledge of the community. Usually they have more flexible terms than other lenders, but this flexibility comes with higher costs, in the form of higher up-front fees.

Current market and governmental conditions play a large part in the availability of their funds, since they are dependent on a stream of incoming funds from depositors. Savings and loans are regulated by governmental agencies, to ensure that the institution is following prudent lending procedures.

Local Development and Housing Authorities

Local development and housing agencies issue both taxable and tax-exempt financing to help stimulate new development activity in a local market area. These loans usually have very restrictive lending criteria.

The development agency will issue an inducement letter to the borrower who will, in turn, obtain a credit enhancement, such as an insurance policy or a letter of credit, to guarantee the bonds. Due to the status as tax-exempt bonds, a potential lender can offer the borrower a reduced interest rate and still be able to meet its yield requirements.

Small Business Administration (SBA)

The Small Business Administration is a governmental agency which will insure a percentage of the loan that is made by a local lender. These loans can be made on real property for business use, when a business owner desires to purchase the building which is currently being rented. These loans have many restrictions and take a long time to process. The interest rate is usually lower than the current market because the government is guaranteeing a portion of the loan.

Insurance Companies

Financing in this arena comes with strict loan criteria. Unfortunately, most transactions are very large. These lenders can often become partners with the developer and participate in the advantages therein. Advantages of this type of financing come in lower rates, lower up-front fees, and sometimes the absence of personal guarantees.

Pension Funds

Pension funds usually have large amounts of cash which must generate a return. Many times, institutions will make loans and market these loans to pension funds while continuing to service these loans.

Mortgage Real Estate Investment Trusts (REIT)

Because of problems in the 1970s, there are very few of these lenders available today. Most have been absorbed into other institutions. In meeting the needs of potential borrowers, they will generally lend high amounts, but require a participation in cash flows, refinancing, and resale proceeds.

Types of Development Loans

The following are the loans that may be required during the construction phase of the development.

Land Acquisition Loan

A land acquisition loan is used to secure the purchase of raw land. Such a loan can be negotiated for up to 100 percent of the purchase price or a certain percentage of the appraised value. Some lenders will also commit additional dollars for future interest carry. The borrower's track record and ability to secure the debt with collateral will weigh heavily on the lender's decision to provide for this financing.

Construction Loan

Construction loans are the riskiest type of real estate loans a lender can make. This is because at this stage of the development, the construction costs, the schedule and the forecasted rental absorption are just good estimates. Many problems can be incurred by the developer during this stage that translate into extra risk for the construction lender.

The construction loan is used to finance erection of buildings. The loan can be structured as individual loans for condominiums or as a large blanket loan on a large building. These loans are usually for a short period of time (nine to 36 months) depending on the type of property. Most require interest-only payments based on a fixed or a floating interest rate. Figure 9–1 illustrates how a typical construction loan increases over the course of the construction cycle.

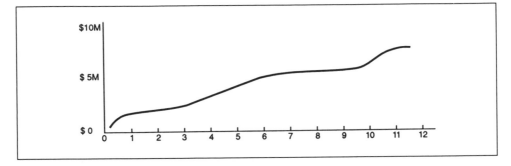

Figure 9-1   Construction loan.

When making a construction loan, most lenders will require that the borrower have a source of permanent financing secured, before agreeing to provide this financing. In some instances, the construction lender may not require that the developer (depending on financial strength and development experience) have a permanent loan to repay their construction loan. This type of construction loan is called an:

> **Open-Ended Mortgage:**   A mortgage which gives the borrower additional mortgage funding over the term of the loan and is based upon achievement. If the developer increases the net operating income or reaches set goals, the lender may increase the loan's funding.

In other situations, the developer may be able to negotiate a

> **Piggyback Mortgage:**   This type of loan automatically converts from construction or temporary financing to permanent financing through the same lender, hence the term "piggyback."

In order to reduce risk, the construction lender might require the developer to obtain a permanent loan from an outside source. This can be in any of the following type loans:

> **Standby or Take-Out Loan:**   When a construction lender requires the developer to obtain a permanent loan to pay off his loan prior to closing the construction loan, the developer might obtain a standby commitment. This loan is obtained by the borrower with the intention that it be used, if a more favorable loan is not available when the construction loan matures. Most standby lenders charge fees for issuing their loan commitment.
>
> **Forward Commitment:**   In a loan with a forward commitment a borrower will pay a fee in advance to ensure that funds will be available at a predetermined rate and date in the future. Oftentimes developers of housing projects

will purchase a forward commitment of permanent mortgage funds to ensure that potential buyers will have adequate mortgage funds to finance their homes.

In order for the construction lender to gain comfort that he will indeed be taken out by the new permanent lender, he might require that this new lender enter into a:

Buy-Sell Agreement: A buy-sell agreement is a tri-party agreement in which the construction lender, the permanent lender, and the developer all agree that when all parties have met their predetermined obligations, the permanent lender will buy the loan from the construction lender. The benefits to this type of agreement are that the construction lender has a contractual purchase agreement that he will be taken out of his loan, the permanent lender has comfort that the borrower will not go shopping for another cheaper loan, and the developer has peace of mind that both lenders are obligated to the deal. If the developer is not able to obtain a construction loan for all the hard and soft costs, he might seek funding for this shortfall rather than picking up the cost himself. The following is an example of this type of loan.

Gap Loan: When the developer cannot acquire all of the financing needed for construction from a particular lender, this type of loan may be used. The developer must find other financing to fill the gap of funds needed until the original construction lender releases additional financing. Usually, these funds are tied to milestones of achievement of break-even or occupancy levels. When a developer with an open-ended construction loan is unable to obtain a permanent loan that meets his terms and conditions, a bridge loan may be used.

Bridge Loan: The term bridge is used because the loan does just that. It bridges from one loan to another. An example would be from construction which is short-term to permanent which is long-term. It is another tool which the developer can use to buy time while searching for better terms. The bridge loan could be used to pay off the construction financing, and the permanent loan would be used to pay off the bridge loan.

Loan Participation

In situations where the lender desires to reduce risk or is unable to fund a construction loan the size required by the lender, the lender may assemble a syndication of other lenders to fund the construction loan. Usually in this situation, the lead lender will take a larger share of the up-front fees for putting the deal together as well as a monthly servicing fee to service the loan.

Construction Loan Issues

Once the list of potential lenders is compiled, the developer should consider the following issues relative to lender response.

- Type of property you need on which financing is needed
- Location of the property
- Magnitude of loans which lender normally provides
- Lender's quoted interest rate

If the answers to these issues are positive, then the following should be considered.

- Percentage of total development cost on which the lender will provide financing
- Funding of development fees
- Terms of the construction loan
- Rate for the construction loan
- Interest payment schedule
- Construction loan personal liability
- Prepayment penalty
- Points to be charged for the construction loan
- Estimate of loan closing costs
- Reimbursement of predevelopment costs at closing
- Construction loan closing attorney
- Time for underwriting the loan
- Time funding the loan
- Submissions necessary for the underwriting of this loan
- Construction draw schedule
- Stored materials funding schedule
- Any holdback?
- Letters of credit or bonding of contractor
- Inspecting architect fees and schedule of visits
- Phasing of property funding
- Approved appraisers
- Will all loans for building, site costs, or land costs be funded together?
- Loan extensions costs and terms
- Equity required
- Can a letter of credit be used instead of cash?

- Can the borrower get a sample copy of the loan documents prior to closing the loan?

Construction Loan Commitment

Once the potential construction lender is prepared to do the construction financing, a construction loan commitment is prepared. This commitment is issued to outline all of the agreed upon terms and conditions of the loan. Document 9–1 is a sample construction/permanent loan commitment letter.

Document 9–1   Loan commitment.

December 1, 19_____

Name
Address

Gentlemen:

    We are pleased to advise you that we have approved your application for a $_____ loan subject to all of the terms and conditions which follow herein. For simplicity, _____ will be referred to as the "Bank," you as "Borrower," the foregoing loan as the "Loan" and the security hereinafter mentioned as the "Security Property."

    Upon receipt of your acceptance of this commitment, we will then advise the closing attorney to prepare the loan instruments.

    We appreciate the opportunity to serve you. If you have any questions relating to this commitment, please contact us.

TERMS

BORROWER: _____

Amount of Loan: $_____

Purpose: The proceeds of the loan shall be used to pay the costs of constructing, fixturing, and equipping a _____ square foot _____ story office building all in accordance with plans and specifications to be approved by Bank.

Security: First Deed to Secure Debt on _____ acres of land which will be developed with _____ square feet. A true legal description to be provided by the closing attorney.

Completion Date: _____ (_____) months from the date of initial disbursement of the loan funds.

(Cont'd)

Document 9–1   Loan commitment. *(Cont'd)*

Maturity: _____ (_____) months from the date of the initial disbursement of the loan funds. Borrower shall have the option to extend the loan for an additional _____ months upon payment of a _____% fee ($_____).

Construction Interest Rate: An interest rate which is _____ percent (_____%) above the Bank's prime rate in effect from time to time. The interest shall be charged and calculated on a 360/365-day year applied to actual days, and shall be payable monthly.

Construction Loan Fee: $_____. $_____ payable upon execution of this commitment with the balance due and payable at closing.

Conversion to the Permanent Loan: The permanent loan will close within 30 days after the execution of the Certificate of Completion (signed by the approved Architect).

Permanent Loan Interest Rate: A fixed interest rate of _____ percent (_____%) will be charged to the borrower. The interest shall be charged and calculated on a 360/365-day year applied to actual days, and shall be payable monthly in arrears.

Permanent Loan Fee: $_____. $_____ payable upon execution of this commitment with the balance due and payable at closing.

Permanent Loan Amortization: The permanent loan will be amortized over _____ years.

Permanent Loan Maturity: The permanent loan will be due and payable _____ (_____) years from the date of funding.

Closing Attorney: _____
_____
_____
_____

Requirements

Prior to the disbursement of any portion of the Loan proceeds, the Borrower shall have satisfied the documentation requirements and other conditions:

Note and Deed to Secure Debt

The loan is to be evidenced by a promissory note of Borrower and secured by a first deed to secure debt conveying the Security Property, the form and substance of each of which is subject to approval by the Bank. The deed to secure debt shall be submitted to and revised by the Bank prior to execution and recordation. Upon approval and recordation, in lieu of the original deed to secure debt

Document 9-1 Loan commitment. *(Cont'd)*

which should be forwarded to the Bank as soon as available, the Bank is to be furnished with a copy with the original recording receipt attached.

Guarantee

The Borrower shall furnish a guarantee agreement in form and substance acceptable to Bank, and consistent with the terms thereof, executed by _____.

Security Interest

The Bank shall be afforded a first security interest in all fixtures, equipment, and other non-realty items now or hereafter placed in or used in connection with the Security Property perfected by filing, in the required filing offices, of the Bank form financing statement, the substances of which must be acceptable to the Bank and submitted and reviewed by the Bank prior to execution and filing. Upon approval and filing, receipted copies of the original filed financing statements are to be furnished by the Bank.

Title Evidence

The Borrower shall furnish to the Bank a policy of title insurance issued by a company acceptable to and insuring the Bank in the amount of the loan (or the certificate of an attorney acceptable to the Bank, certifying to the Bank that the deed to secure is a first lien on the Security Property), each without exception for possible filed mechanic's and material man's liens and containing only such title exceptions as are acceptable to the Bank. Should a binder be issued, the term of said binder shall not be less than the term of the Loan. The title insurance policy or binder on the title certificate must be submitted to and reviewed by the Bank prior to the Loan closing. If the original title policy is not available at Loan closing, a marked-up binder initialed by the title company will be acceptable, providing the original policy is promptly forwarded to the Bank.

Easements

Borrower shall furnish evidence that all easements for parking, ingress and egress, and any other easements deemed necessary, are in place for the benefit of the subject property.

Hazard Insurance

Borrower shall furnish to the Bank a standard fire insurance policy issued by a company acceptable to the Bank (together with the paid premium invoice) in an amount which is the greater of the amount of the loan or 100 percent of the insurable value of the Security Property, with extended coverage, vandalism and

(Cont'd)

malicious mischief insurance. Said policy shall contain standard mortgage loss payable clause in favor of the Bank.

General Liability Insurance

The Borrower shall furnish a general liability insurance policy issued by a company acceptable to the Bank with limits of $_____ per accident or occurrence for personal injury and $_____ per accident or occurrence for injury to property. The general liability insurance policy shall name the Bank as additional insured.

Workman's Compensation Insurance

The Borrower and all contractors performing work on the Security Property shall carry Workman's Compensation insurance with statutory coverage limits.

Loss of Rents Insurance

The Borrower shall furnish a loss of rents insurance policy, acceptable to the Bank, in an amount sufficient to pay at least _____ (____) month's debt service on the loan.

Other Insurance

The Borrower shall furnish such other insurance as may be required by the bank and bank counsel.

Certificate of Insurance

The Borrower shall furnish a certificate or letter in form satisfactory to the Bank and Bank counsel from a person acceptable to the Bank and knowledgeable in insurance matters stating that he has read the insurance requirements contained in the Loan Documents and that the insurance carried by the Borrower fully complies with the requirements thereof.

Construction Loan Agreement

The Bank shall furnish to the Borrower a construction loan agreement.

Permanent Loan Agreement

The Bank shall furnish to the Borrower a permanent loan agreement.

Appraisal

The Borrower shall furnish to the Bank an appraisal made by an MAI appraiser approved by the Bank, and which appraisal must be in an amount not less than $_____ and otherwise acceptable to the Bank.

Document 9-1   Loan commitment. *(Cont'd)*

Authority to Borrow

The Borrower shall furnish to the Bank a copy of the corporate resolution and any existing future amendments thereto, a certificate of good standing and such other documents as the Bank may require.

Due-on-Sale Clause

The loan documents will provide that, in the event Borrower transfers any portion of its ownership in the property which is security for this loan or in the event the Borrower ceases to be a stockholder or substantially dilutes his/her interest, the Bank shall, at its sole discretion, have the right to accelerate the loan and declare that then unpaid principal balance and all accrued interest due and payable.

Current Survey

The Borrower shall furnish to the Bank a current survey showing no encroachments and otherwise acceptable to the Bank, prepared and certified by a certified land surveyor, which survey shall designate, without limitation, (i) the dimensions of the Security Property, (ii) the dimensions and location of the buildings and other improvements constructed thereon, (iii) the location of all easements of record affecting the Security Property, specifying the holder of each such easement and the pertinent recordation information, (iv) any and all building restriction and/or setback lines, and (v) means of ingress and egress. The Borrower shall furnish to the Bank within _____ (_____) days after being requested to do so updated surveys of the Security Property acceptable to the Bank.

Soils Testing

The Borrower shall furnish to the Bank a certified test of the soil conditions to the lender. This report is to include information on all soil conditions, rock formations, and any chemical contaminations found in the soil.

Parking

The Borrower must provide the Bank with satisfactory evidence that the Security Property has, and will have, adequate parking at all times during which the Loan is outstanding.

Building Permits

The Borrower shall provide the Bank certified true copies of the building permits for construction of improvements.

(Cont'd)

Document 9–1   Loan commitment. *(Cont'd)*

Independent Consultant

The Bank shall employ an independent consultant to review and approve the plans, specifications, soil reports and projected costs prior to construction, and to review and recommend for payment all progress payments during construction, which services shall be at Borrower's expense.

Construction Contracts

The Borrower shall deliver to the Bank for approval an executed copy of the construction contract, which contract shall be unconditionally assigned to the Bank. The Bank shall also have the right to approve the Borrower's general contractor. No change orders to the hereinabove referenced contract shall be issued without the prior written approval of the Borrower, the Bank, permanent lender (if any), and requisite lessees.

Architectural Contracts

The Borrower shall deliver to the Bank an executed copy of the architect's contract, which shall be unconditionally assigned to the Bank. Such assignment shall provide that the Bank will have the unconditional right to use of the plans and specifications at no additional cost and to architectural services as contracted in the event of a default of this loan.

Costs and Contracts

The Borrower shall furnish to the Bank a detailed cost breakdown (soft and hard costs) in a form and substance acceptable to the Bank, and periodic updates thereof as the Bank may, from time to time, require, together with copies of supportive bids and executed contracts and subcontracts. The cost breakdown and all updates thereof shall be certified by a design architect or engineer as fair and reasonable and that the cost breakdown and all updates thereof include all items necessary to fully complete the improvements in accordance with the final approved plans and specifications. At the request of the Bank, the Borrower shall assign as additional collateral for the Loan any contract designated by the Bank.

General Contractor's Completion Bond

The Borrower shall furnish to the Bank, an acceptable completion bond in an amount no less than the contract amount. This bond will also be assigned to the Bank, in case of a default under the loan obligations.

General Contractor's Reserve

The Bank will have a loan holdback in the amount of _____% of the hard construction costs from each construction loan draw request. Upon receipt of the certificate of completion from the architect and/or engineer, this final holdback will be disbursed to the Borrower.

Document 9-1   Loan commitment. *(Cont'd)*

Certificate of Completion

Upon completion of the construction of the Security Property and related improvements, the Borrower shall furnish to the Bank a certificate of completion relative to the Security Property and related improvements, executed by the supervising architect and/or engineer, Borrower and Borrower's general contractor evidencing that the improvements have been completed in accordance with the approved plans and specifications. The aforesaid certificate shall be furnished to and approved by the Bank prior to the final loan disbursement.

Certificate of Occupancy

The Borrower shall furnish to the Bank a certificate of occupancy issued by the appropriate governmental authority having jurisdiction and/or such other assurances required by, and which shall be acceptable to the Bank, evidencing that the Security Property and the occupancy thereof comply with all applicable zoning ordinances, building codes and all other applicable local, state, and federal laws, rules, regulations, and/or requirements. The aforesaid certificate shall be furnished to and approved by the Bank prior to the final loan disbursement.

Assurance of Utility Availability

The Borrower shall furnish evidence acceptable to the Bank that all utilities (including drainage both on-site and off-site) necessary for the development, operation, or occupancy of the Security Property are available to the Security Property, that the Security Property is connected thereto, and that all requisite tap-on or connection fees have been paid.

Plans and Specification-Assignment Thereof

The Borrower shall furnish to the Bank a complete and final set of working plans and specifications in respect of the Security Property initialed for identification by the Borrower, contractor, if any, and the design architect. Any and all subsequent changes to said plans and specifications must be approved by the Bank. The Borrower shall also furnish to the Bank a letter from the design architect/engineer allowing for use of the plans and specifications by the Bank without cost or expense to the Bank. The Borrower shall also furnish to the Bank evidence acceptable to the Bank that all plans and specifications have been approved by all necessary governmental agencies.

Compliance with Governmental Regulations

Prior to the commencement of construction and the initial loan disbursement, the Borrower shall furnish evidence acceptable to the Bank that the Security Property and the improvements to be constructed thereon comply with all

(Cont'd)

Document 9-1 Loan commitment. *(Cont'd)*

applicable zoning ordinances, building codes, and all other applicable local, state, and federal laws, rules, regulations, and/or requirements.

Preleasing Requirement

The Borrower shall furnish to the Bank fully executed leases for _____ square feet of the Security Property, which shall be in all respects satisfactory to the Bank.

Assignment of Leases

The Borrower shall by instrument in form and substance acceptable to the Bank assign unto the Bank as additional security for the loan all leases now or hereafter existing on the Security Property and all rents, issues and profits derived therefrom. All leases shall be in form and substance satisfactory to the Bank. The Bank reserves the right to require the Borrower to record any and all of such leases and/or the assignment thereof.

Additional Collateral

In order to make this Loan, the Bank shall require the Borrower to keep as a deposit in the Bank, a Certificate of Deposit in the amount of $_____. This additional collateral will be released to the Borrower when the Security Property has obtained satisfactory leases in the amount of _____% of the total gross leasable area.

Tenant Estoppel Certificates

The Borrower shall furnish acknowledgments, satisfactory to the Bank, signed by all tenant(s) immediately prior to the initial disbursement of the loan stating that the leases are in full force and effect, that the tenants are in occupancy, doing business, and paying rent on a current basis with no rental offsets or claims, that there has been no repayment of rent other than that provided for in the leases, and that there are no actions, whether voluntary or otherwise, pending against any of the tenants under the bankruptcy laws of the United States or any state thereof. The Borrower shall furnish such other documents which may be required by the Bank to carry out the above intent. At the time of disbursements subsequent to the initial disbursement, the Bank may require from the Borrower, in addition to the estoppel certificates for the newer tenants, evidence satisfactory to the Bank that the tenants from whom the estoppel certificates were received at the prior disbursement are still in occupancy under the previously reviewed lease(s).

Subordination of Leases

The Bank may, at its sole option, require that any and/or all of the leases affecting the real property be made subject and subordinate to the lien of the

Document 9-1   Loan commitment. *(Cont'd)*

Bank's mortgage or trust deed. The Bank may similarly require that any and/or all leases be made superior and prior to the Bank's lien, or that a Subordination Non-Disturbance and Attornment Agreement in form satisfactory to the Bank be executed by any and/or all tenants.

Signage and Publicity

If it is not prohibited by any applicable law, the Bank reserves the right to erect signs on the Security Property identifying all participating lenders, and to include the Security Property, its name and photograph or artistic rendering, in the Bank's promotional literature and communications.

Secondary Financing

Any secondary financing to be secured by the Security Property shall not be permitted without the consent of the Bank. The loan documents will provide that, in the event the Borrower obtains secondary financing without the approval of the Bank, the Bank shall have the right, at its sole option, to accelerate the loan and declare the then unpaid principal balance and all accrued interest due and payable.

Further Encumbrances

The Borrower agrees that it shall not pledge, transfer, convey, or otherwise encumber the security, including any of the improvements, furniture, fixtures, and equipment now or hereafter located on the Security Property or grant any rights or easements affecting the Security Property without the prior written consent of the Bank.

Related Agreements

The Borrower shall furnish the Bank with executed copies of all agreements of any nature whatsoever to which the Borrower is a party affecting or relating to the use, operation, development, or construction of the improvements on the Security Property.

Other Documents

The Borrower shall furnish such other instruments, documents, opinions, and/or assurances as the Bank may require.

Financial Statements

For as long as the Loan shall remain outstanding, the Borrower, at his expense, agrees to deliver to the Bank an income statement, balance sheet, and other financial information reasonably required by the Bank as soon available but in no event more than _____ days after the end of each of its fiscal years. The

(Cont'd)

Borrower is also responsible for providing the Bank with annual personal financial statements of all endorsers and/or guarantors of this Loan.

Legal Opinions

The Borrower shall deliver to the Bank an opinion of counsel for the Borrower to the effect that:

1. The Security Property as improved and to be improved for its use conforms with the applicable zoning ordinances, and that it has not discovered any federal, state, or municipal laws, restrictions, regulations, or requirements including, but not limited to, those relating to environmental matters which would be violated by the Security Property as improved or to be improved and its use.

2. The Borrower and all Guarantors have full power and authority to enter into this Loan, to execute and deliver all documents related thereto, and to carry out all the terms and conditions of the Loan.

3. The Note, the Deed to Secure Debt, and other loan documents constitute the valid and legally binding obligation of the borrower and Guarantors and, upon the filing and recording of the Deed to Secure Debt and other documents related thereto, the Bank will have a fully perfected first lien and security interest in the Security Property.

No Adverse Change

No part of the Security Property shall be damaged and not repaired to the satisfaction of the Bank, nor taken in condemnation or other like proceeding, nor shall any such proceeding be pending. Neither the Borrower nor any tenant under any assigned lease, nor any guarantor on the Loan, or of any such lease, shall be involved in any bankruptcy, reorganization, dissolution, or insolvency proceeding.

Bank's Right to Waive

The Bank reserves the right to waive, in whole or in part, any of the terms and conditions hereunder or in any of the documents referenced herein. The Bank further reserves the right to reinstate any such term or condition so waived subsequent to any such waiver.

Loan Disbursement Procedure

Upon the receipt and approval by the Bank of all requisite Loan documents, and/or provided and so long as the Borrower complies with all obligations imposed upon the Borrower in the Loan documents in accordance with the General Contractor's Requisition for Payment, which must be approved and certified by the supervising architect or engineer of the work performed, and be the Bank's independent consultant, the requisition and certification (it is suggested

Document 9-1 Loan commitment. *(Cont'd)*

that the American Institute of Architect's standard form be used) must be in a form satisfactory to the Bank and all items included under the requisition shall be subject to the Bank's final approval, and further subject to the following terms:

1. Advances shall be conditioned upon requisitions submitted by the Borrower stating the costs of materials in place and the labor performed, with such requisitions to be properly certified and executed by the contractor, architect, and Borrower. At the Bank's request, all such costs shall be verified by paid receipts, invoices, and lien waivers.

2. Advances shall not exceed the amount projected in each category as submitted by the Borrower and approved by the Bank pursuant to the cost breakdown required above. Any excess funds in any costs category may be transferred to another category only at the Bank's option. Any costs or anticipated costs in excess of the amount projected in each cost category must be immediately paid in cash into the project by the Borrower at the Bank's request. In no event shall the aggregate amount of all advances exceed the loan amount.

3. No advances will be made for stored materials except at the sole and absolute discretion of the Bank.

4. Advances shall be made no more than _____ times per month. All inspection fees shall be paid by the Borrower.

5. Prior to each advance, the title to the Security Property shall be examined to the date of each advance and the Bank shall be furnished with an endorsement to its mortgage title insurance increasing the amount of insurance thereunder to the cumulative total of all advances, including the advance made at the date of the endorsement, with no change in the status of the title.

6. The Bank may withhold payment of any requisition or any part thereof on account of:

   A. Defective work or work not performed in a good and workmanlike fashion in strict accordance with the approved plans and specifications

   B. Claims or liens filed or evidence indicating the probable filing of claims or liens

   C. Failure or inability of the contractor to make payments to subcontractors for materials or labor

   D. In the sole and absolute opinion of the Bank, the improvements as described herein cannot be fully completed and all projected related expenses paid with the funds committed but not yet advanced hereunder.

(Cont'd)

Document 9-1   Loan commitment. *(Cont'd)*

Approval of Loan Documentation and Fees and Expenses

The Loan shall be made without cost to the Bank. The Borrower shall pay for all costs and expenses incurred in connection with this Loan whether or not the Loan is closed, including, but not limited to, title insurance premiums, surveyor's fees, appraiser's fees and legal fees. All requisite Loan documents and related instruments shall, at the option of the Bank, be submitted to the Bank's attorney for review and approval, and by acceptance of this commitment as hereinafter set forth, the Borrower shall be deeded to have expressly agreed to pay all legal fees incurred by the Bank in connection herewith.

Warranties by the Bank

The approval of the Bank of the plans and specifications and any subsequent inspection of the Security Property conducted by the Bank during construction shall in no way constitute a warranty as to the technical sufficiency, or adequacy of any such construction nor shall it constitute a warranty as to the soil conditions involved in the Security Property.

In connection with the aforementioned disbursement procedure, at no time shall the Bank be required to disburse Loan proceeds which in the sole determination of the Bank would result in the balance of the Loan proceeds being insufficient to pay for the complete cost of the construction of the Security Property according to the plans and specifications thereof.

Funds shall be disbursed in accordance with the following schedule:

Description	Cost	Equity	Loan
Land	$_____	$_____	$_____
Sitework	$_____	$_____	$_____
Building shell costs	$_____	$_____	$_____
Tenant costs	$_____	$_____	$_____
Soft costs	$_____	$_____	$_____
Architectural/engineering	$_____	$_____	$_____
Closing costs	$_____	$_____	$_____
Inspection fees	$_____	$_____	$_____
Leasing commissions	$_____	$_____	$_____
Marketing	$_____	$_____	$_____
Taxes	$_____	$_____	$_____
Insurance	$_____	$_____	$_____
Interest reserve	$_____	$_____	$_____
Operating costs	$_____	$_____	$_____
Contingency	$_____	$_____	$_____
Totals	$_____	$_____	$_____

Document 9–1   Loan commitment. *(Cont'd)*

Representations of the Borrower

The validity of this commitment is subject to the accuracy of all the information, representations, and materials submitted with, and in support of, the Borrower's application for the Loan. In the event the Bank determines that any information or representations contained in the Loan application are not accurate or correct, the Bank shall have the right to terminate this commitment, whereupon the Bank shall have no further obligations hereunder.

Assignment or Modification

Neither this commitment nor the Loan can be modified or assigned without prior written consent of the Bank.

Acceptance of Commitment

In order for this commitment to remain effective the acceptance copy of this commitment must be executed by the Borrower and returned to the Bank on or before the expiration of the _____ (_____) day from the date hereof. Any extension of such time for acceptance must be in writing and signed by the Bank.

Expiration of Commitment

To cause this commitment to remain in effect, the Loan must be closed and the Bank must disburse Loan proceeds prior to _____, 19_____, and any extension of such date must be in writing and signed by the Bank.

The terms and conditions of this commitment shall survive settlement and any violation of said terms and conditions will constitute a default under the note and deed to secure debt.

Termination of Commitment

The Bank may terminate this commitment if:

1. Any material adverse change shall occur with respect to the Security Property, Borrower, Permanent Lender, or any Guarantor or with respect to any other person or entity connected with the Loan or the Security Property for the Loan or other source of repayment of the Loan at any time prior to the closing of the Loan

2. Any part of the Security Property shall have been taken in condemnation or other like proceeding, or any such proceeding is pending at the time of closing, except a taking for road widening which is intended to facilitate the use of the improvements

(Cont'd)

Document 9-1 Loan commitment. *(Cont'd)*

The terms and conditions of this commitment shall survive settlement and any violation of said terms and conditions will constitute a default under the note and deed to secure debt.

Very truly yours,

THE AMERICAN BANK

By:

The undersigned hereby accepts the foregoing commitment and the terms and the requirements herein set forth, and agrees to be bound thereby.

_____

By: _____ Attest: _____

Tax I.D. Number _____ Guarantor: _____

Terms of the Loan

- Name of the borrowing entity
- Amount of the loan
- Purpose of the loan
- The security for the loan
- The number of months for the construction loan
- Construction interest rate—describe the index used, how many days in a month, the floor and ceiling available
- Fee for the construction loan and when it is paid
- Who will pay for the closing costs

  If applicable:

- If the loan has a permanent loan conversion feature:
  When it will be exercised
  What is the interest rate?
  Amortization period
  Maturity date
  Prepayment penalty formula
  Permanent loan fees—how much and when are they due?
- If the loan requires a release provision
  Pay down provision formula

Items to Be Signed by the Borrower at Closing

- Construction (permanent, if applicable) note and deed to secure debt
- The borrower will guarantee (personally or corporately) the Note

- Assignment of lease agreement
- Assignment of additional collateral (if applicable)
- Uniform Commercial Code Financing statement
- Signed closing statement

Items Required by the Lender

- Copy of a title insurance policy acceptable to the lender
- Copy of a letter that parking, ingress and egress, and any other easements necessary are in place for the benefit of the property
- Copy of a paid hazard insurance policy
- Copy of the general liability insurance policy with limits approved by the lender
- Copy of a Workman's Compensation insurance policy for all contractors within the statutory coverage limits required by law
- Copy of a rent loss insurance policy (if applicable) in an amount determined by the lender
- Copy of a current appraisal completed by an approved MAI Appaiser
- Copy of a letter that the borrower (if applicable) has the authority to borrow for the corporate entity
- Copy of a current survey
- Copy of a soils report
- Copy of a letter from the zoning department that the property can accommodate the necessary parking as required by law
- Copy of the development and building permits
- Copy of all construction documents: plans, specifications, cost breakdowns, schedules
- Copy of all architectural and engineering agreements and final working drawings
- Copy of the general contractor completion bond or letter of credit
- Copy of all utility letters from the proper authorities: gas, electricity, water, sewer, telephone, cable TV
- Copy of a letter from the zoning department stating that the proposed development meets all local zoning regulations
- Copies of all signed leases and credit file (if applicable)
- Copies of all tenant estoppel certificates (if applicable)
- Copies of all environmental letters that state that the property does not violate any local, state, or federal environmental laws
- Copies of all major subcontractor's contracts
- Copies of all geo-technical studies

- Copies of the construction contract
- Copy of the lender approval letter of the general contractor
- Copy of the architectural contract

Miscellaneous Items Required by Lenders

- Payment by the borrower for an independent consultant to review the plans and specifications for the property
- Holdback for the general contractor

Items to Be Supplied at the Closing

- Release of first draw proceeds

Items Required upon Competition of Construction

- Copy of the certificate of competition by the certifying architect
- Copy of all certificates of occupancy
- Copy of the as-built survey
- Copies of all lien waivers
- Copy of the final general contractor's competition affidavit

Clauses to Be Inserted into the Documents

The following clauses are typical clauses that are inserted into construction loan documents.

Permanent Loan Take-Out Requirements: This clause will specify the terms and conditions under which the construction lender will approve a permanent loan take-out.

Interest Payment Clause: This clause defines the interest rate and on that which it is based. It can be a fixed rate or a floating rate based on a specified index.

Reimbursable Items at Closing Clause: Since the developer will have a substantial amount of predevelopment funds spent prior to the actual closing, he will need to state and list in the construction loan exactly which amount of these funds will be reimbursable to him at closing.

Line Item Expense Clause: This clause specifies how much money is available in each line item. The developer should be comfortable with the amounts that are available in each category because many lenders will not fund out of the contingency account once a particular account has been fully funded.

Draw Request Clause: This clause will specify the number of monthly draw requests available to the developer, the procedure to follow, and the cost for the draw request inspection. This clause will also specify who will certify this draw request as well as the requirement of signed waivers of mechanics liens from each subcontractor.

General Contractor Holdback Clause: This clause will specify what amount of each construction loan request will be held in reserve for construction items pending the certified completion of the development.

Tenant Improvement Holdback Clause: This clause will specify the amount of funds which will be held in reserve by the lender for construction of the tenant improvements.

Contingency Account Clause: This clause specifies the amount of funds held in a separate contingency account and how these funds can be dispersed.

Plans and Specification Clause: This clause specifies that the borrower must complete the development according to the approved plans and specifications and that any changes must be approved by the lender.

Final Disbursement Clause: This clause specifies what is required by the lender to obtain the final draw request. This usually requires a certification of completion from the architect, a final title policy, a certificate of occupancy, and an "as-built" survey.

Default and Acceleration Clause: The default and acceleration clause specifies under what conditions the construction loan can be called into default. It will specify the proper notices which will be given prior to accelerating the outstanding balance of the loan. The cause for this default can include:

- Failure to comply with the construction loan agreement
- Disapproval of the quality of construction as it conforms with plans and specifications
- Delay or suspension of construction
- Bankruptcy or insolvency by the developer or general contractor
- Default in the loan documents
- The loan out of balance
- Default or loss of the permanent loan commitment

Release of Personal Liability Clause: Many construction loans can be negotiated with a full or partial release of personal liability once the development is complete or has achieved an occupancy level or net operating income level.

Subordination of Leases Clause: This clause gives the lender (at his option) the right to require that any leases affecting the real property be made subject and subordinate to the lien of the lender's mortgage or trust deed.

Signage Clause: This clause gives the lender the right (if not prohibited by local law) to place a sign on the property identifying them as the lender. This clause might require that the borrower pay for this expense item.

Default Clause: This clause defines what monetary and nonmonetary events will trigger a default in the construction loan documents and cause a loan acceleration. Nonpayment of the construction interest due is a monetary default, while a stoppage of the construction activity or a material change in the financial condition of the borrower or guarantor will trigger a nonmonetary default.

Secondary Financing Clause: This clause may prohibit or allow for secondary financing to be placed on the property. If it is allowed, typically the lender will want to approve (not to be unreasonably withheld) and to be made aware of when it is placed on the property.

Further Encumbrance Clause: This clause prohibits the borrower from pledging, transfering, conveying, or otherwise encumbering the security without the prior written consent of the lender.

Financial Statement Clause: This clause gives the lender the right to require that the borrower submit up-to-date financial statements on a periodic basis.

No Adverse Change Clause: This clause states that:

- No part of the Security Property shall be damaged and not repaired to the satisfaction of the lender.
- The lender shall be notified if there is any material financial change with the borrower, guarantor, or tenants.

Lender's Right to Waive Clause: This clause gives the lender the right to waive any of the clauses in the documents (in whole or part), without giving up the right to reinstate said clause in the future.

Warranties by the Bank Clause: This section gives the lender a waiver of responsibility for his approvals of the plans, specifications, and construction inspection he will conduct.

Representations of the Borrower Clause: This clause gives the lender the right to terminate this commitment in the event that the accuracy of all the information, representations, and materials submitted by the borrower contains information that is not accurate or correct.

Assignment or Modification Clause: This clause states that neither this commitment nor the loan can be modified or assigned without prior written consent of the lender.

Acceptance of Commitment Clause: This clause states that the borrower has a pre-determined number of days to execute this commitment letter before it expires.

Termination of Commitment Clause: This clause defines the reasons why the lender may terminate this commitment.

Legal Opinions Required from the Borrowers Attorney

The following legal opinions are typically a requirement by the lender.

- The borrowing entity exists and has the right to carry on its business and enter this transaction.
- The borrower is not in violation of any securities laws.

- The loan documents will be fully enforceable according to their provisions.
- The deed of trust, when recorded, will be a valid lien on the property.
- The financing statement, when recorded, will perfect a security interest in the personal property identified therein.
- The borrower has obtained all of the legal permits and licenses required to carry on their business and the operation of the property.
- The property may be used for the purposes which it is being used.
- Any provisions of any agreements between the borrower and lender do not violate any known law.
- There are no pending legal matters which may adversely affect the lender's interest in the borrower's property or inhibit the ability of the borrower to repay the funds.
- No form of rent control, or proposed rent control, is in effect or is pending.

FUNDING THE PERMANENT LOAN

A permanent first mortgage loan is made with the intention of being placed on the property for a long period of time. Most savings institutions make these loans for 5 to 30 years. Frequently, savings institutions make the loans and then sell them in the secondary market to long-term investors. In addition life insurance companies make permanent loans at lower rates (their cost of funds is usually lower) and for longer periods of time. These loans can be made at a fixed or adjustable rates of interest, or they can be tied to a specific index. Some lenders will lend more than others, depending on how aggressive they are and how much cash is available. The developer must consider all of the various sources of financing in finding the permanent loan.

Sources of Permanent Financing

Since this type of loan requires less risk on the part of the lender, there are many more sources of financing than the construction loan. The following are potential lending sources of financing (see Figure 9–2).

Credit Companies

These lenders provide short-term financing for construction or short-term permanent loans. Because they have large sums of money to lend, they usually have a higher minimum loan limit.

Mortgage Limited Partnerships

Some large syndication companies form public pools for lending. These partnerships are either all-cash or low leverage vehicles, designed to produce

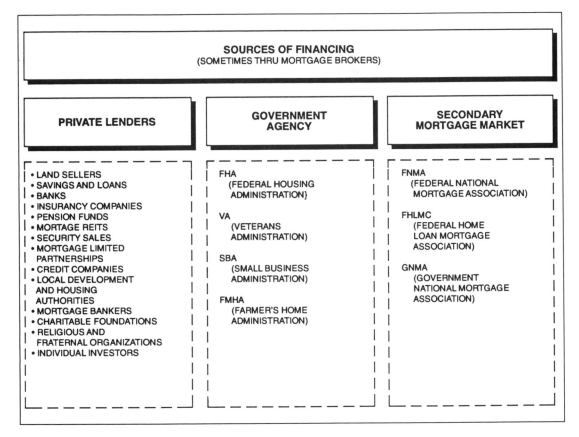

Figure 9–2   Sources of financing.

income for the investors. The target markets for these partnerships are the public and pension funds.

The lending policies of these pools are based on fixed criteria. They will usually lend the borrowers more than they can borrow from traditional banking sources. For this increased loan amount, these partnerships will take a participation in the investment's current cash flow, as well as future resale proceeds.

Charitable Foundations

Usually these foundations will invest only in high-grade, quality investments.

Religious and Fraternal Associations

These sources make loans to members at below market rates. Contact these associations to ascertain the availability of funds.

Individual Investors

This source of funds can be from family or friends. Lending options, since not governmentally regulated are very flexible.

Securities Sold by Wall Street Brokerage Firms

Some major Wall Street brokerage companies raise large sums of money for real estate mortgage financing, which come from securities which are sold to the general public. Both Government National Mortgage Association (GNMA) and Federal National Mortgage Association (FNMA) trade packages of mortgage loans in the secondary mortgage market as securities through Wall Street firms.

Real Estate Mortgage Investment Conduit (REMIC): Prior to 1986, mortgage-backed securities were available to investors, but such securities were only backed by residential mortgages. Through REMICs, investors for the first time had an option to invest in securities backed by commercial mortgages. The investment is backed by a pool of mortgages, and are therefore referred to as "mortgage-backed securities." This interest is issued to investors in the form of pass-through certificates, bonds, or other legal forms.

Mortgage-Backed Securities: There are two types of mortgage-backed securities which serve as an alternative source of financing.
1. A certificate that evidences ownership of an interest in a mortgage loan or pool of mortgage loans
2. An obligation that is secured by a mortgage loan or a pool of mortgage loans

These type of securities can be issued and purchased by the following:

> Government National Mortgage Association (GNMA)
> Federal National Mortgage Association (FNMA)
> Federal Home Loan Mortgage Corporation (FHLMC)
> Homebuilders
> Multi-builder issuers
> Investment bankers
> Banks
> Savings and loans
> Private mortgage insurance companies
> Arbitragers

Collateralized Mortgage Obligations (CMO):   CMOs use the cash flow from the various types of underlying securities to repay the bond classes in the order of their priority. Because each bond class has a different maturity date, the cash flow can be structured to pay out at the stated maturity date of that particular bond class.

Government Guaranteed Loans

Federal Housing Administration (FHA): The FHA was formed to encourage an increase in home ownership, improve the standard of housing, and to create a better method of financing. This financing is made by lenders which must comply with criteria and is guaranteed by the U.S. Government. The following are provided:

TITLE I-Mobile Homes: Mobile homes as primary place of residence.

TITLE II-Sec. 203(b): For one to four family dwellings

TITLE II-Sec. 203(b): Veterans

TITLE II-Sec. 207: Mobile homes, and rental housing

TITLE II-Sec. 221(d)(2): Low-cost, one to four family dwellings for displaced or dwellings for low-income family units.

TITLE II-Sec. 221(d)(4): Five or more dwelling units.

TITLE II-Sec. 222: Owner occupied homes for service personnel.

TITLE II-Sec. 223(f): Refinancing of existing multifamily dwellings.

TITLE II-Sec. 234(c): Individually owned condominium units

TITLE II-Sec. 234(d): Condominiums and condominium conversions.

TITLE II-Sec. 235: Lower-income families mortgage interest payments on low-cost homes, duplexes, or condominiums.

TITLE II-Sec. 245: Graduated payment mortgage (GPM)

Veterans Administration (VA): The VA supervises loans exclusively for qualified veterans of military service. The origins of this type of financing were created to provide governmental loan guarantees for home ownership. This financing can be provided to the borrower of up to 100 percent financing.

Secondary Mortgage Markets

The secondary mortgage markets are comprised by Federal National Mortgage Association (FNMA), the Government National Mortgage Association (GNMA), and the Federal Home Loan Mortgage Corporation (FHLMC).

Federal National Mortgage Association (FNMA): In 1938, the Federal National Mortgage Association, or "Fannie Mae," was created. The principal function of FNMA is to purchase FHA insured mortgages from private lenders in the secondary mortgage market. These purchases replenish the residential housing market with a new supply of mortgage capital. It is considered a quasi-governmental agency due to its long established ties to the government, even though it is a private corporation.

Federal Home Loan Mortgage Corporation (FHLMC): The Federal Home Loan Mortgage Corporation, or "Freddie Mac," was formed during the 1969 credit crunch by the Federal Home Loan Bank Board (FHLBB).

They sell bonds on the open market to provide additional funds for purchasing mortgages from savings institutions.

Government National Mortgage Association (GNMA): The Government National Mortgage Association, or "Ginnie Mae," was established as a new corporation by the Housing Act of 1968. Its purpose is to execute FNMA functions which were left with the Department of Housing and Urban Development.

Types of Permanent Loans

There are three basic types of permanent loans.

1. Fixed payment mortgage
2. Variable rate mortgage
3. Participating mortgage

The following are descriptions of these various types of permanent first mortgages:

Fixed Payment Mortgages

Self-Amortizing or Level Payment Mortgage: Self-amortizing mortgages require level monthly payments each month over the amortization period. Each month's interest is charged on the outstanding balance.

Fixed Payment Rate with an Accrual: An accrual mortgage with a fixed payment rate is originally set up with a fixed payment rate but with a higher accrual rate. The payment rate is determined by what the borrower or property can afford to pay, and the accrual rate is the rate currently charged in the marketplace. This type of loan is used during periods of high interest rates. The accrued interest on the principal balance plus the accrued interest due on the accrued interest is all due at a specified date in the future.

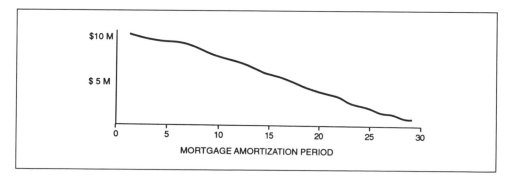

Figure 9–3 Self-amortizing loans.

Pledged Account Mortgage (PAM):   A pledged account mortgage is typically found in residential lending. In this mortgage the lender requires that the borrower pledge a specific amount of money into an escrow account. These funds will then be used in the initial years to supplement the periodic monthly mortgage payments.

Variable Rate Mortgages

Due to the uncertainty of the current mortgage market, many lenders will protect themselves by offering variable rate mortgages that have interest rates that float on a pre-determined index. Typically, these loans will have the following:

- Base pay rate
- Periodic interest rate cap
- Lifetime interest rate cap
- Ability to convert to a fixed-rate loan

Advantages of these types of loans include:

- A lower initial pay rate than might be available with a fixed rate loan
- Assumable
- The ability to convert to a lower fixed rate loan in the future when rates head downward.

The major disadvantage of this type of loan is:

- The potential increases in the monthly debt service when rates head upward.

The following are the various types of these loans.

Adjustable Rate or Renegotiated Rate Mortgage: Adjustable rate mortgages were authorized in 1981 by the Comptroller of the Currency. The interest rate in this type mortgage is adjusted on a periodic basis and is based on a specified point spread over a specified rate index. These loans typically will have a yearly and a lifetime ceiling on the rate adjustment. Some of these indices are as follows:

Interest rate on three-, six-, or twelve-month Treasury bills
The yield on a one-, two-, three-, or five-year Treasury securities
The average cost of funds to the lending institution
Prime rate
Libor prime rate

For example, a loan rate can be set at 1 percent over the current six-month Treasury bill rate and would be adjusted every six months. Many of these loans have a "floor" and a "ceiling"—that is, the interest rates below which or above which the rate on the loan cannot go.

Negative or Accelerated Amortization Mortgage: Negative or accelerated amortization mortgages are based on a pre-determined index. Depending on how this index fluctuates over the time period, the loan balance will either amortize more quickly or will accrue interest which will be added to the original loan balance. In some extreme cases, the borrower can even end up owing more than he originally borrowed. This is called negative amortization. Usually, the lender will place a cap on the amount of negative loan amortization. If the borrower hits this cap, he will usually be required to pay any of this accrual on a current basis with his usual monthly mortgage payment.

Graduated Payment Mortgage (GPM): A graduated payment mortgage is designed to start at a specified interest rate and then graduate to a higher specified interest rate over a specified time period.

Growing Equity Mortgage (GEM): In a growing equity mortgage there is a set interest rate, but the monthly debt service payment is increased over a specific time period. This increased payment can be pre-determined or it can be based on a spread over a specified index. This increased funding is then applied toward the principal loan balance and will help amortize the loan at a much faster pace.

Reverse Annuity Mortgage (RAM): A reverse annuity mortgage is typically designed for elderly homeowners who have substantial equity in their home. The lender will periodically pay an amount of money back to the homeowner for bills which are needed to be paid. Because of these payments the loan can increase over time and thus creating negative amortization.

Interest Only Mortgage: Interest only mortgage loans will have a monthly payment based on interest only for a short period of time. This loan will be due in a short period of time. After a specified date it will start amortizing over a scheduled term. Since the borrower is not repaying principal during this time period, the monthly mortgage payments will be lower than those loans that amortize the principal.

Participating Mortgages

Many times, in order for lenders to increase their yield, they choose to participate in the cash flow and future property appreciation. The following are two methods to achieve their goals.

Shared Appreciation Mortgage (SAM): A shared appreciation mortgage is a mortgage in which the lender will reduce the interest rate to a below market rate in return for a specified share of future cash flow and resale profits.

Convertible Mortgage: A convertible mortgage is a first mortgage which contains a clause that in a specified time, the lender has the right to convert the loan to an ownership position.

Miscellaneous Types of Mortgages

Mini-Permanent (Bullet or Balloon) Mortgage: A mini-permanent mortgage can be a permanent loan with a long amortization period but will have a short maturity due date. This type of loan can be interest only. Careful planning should be used when obtaining this type of loan. Due to the short-term of the loan, the borrower will have to refinance within a three- to five-year period. In many cases, the financing market can take a ride upwards and this will reduce the chances of refinancing the loan. In addition, new market conditions may even decrease the developer's chances of obtaining a loan for the same dollar amount. An example of this type of loan is one which is made for a three- to five-year period, is interest-only or amortized over a long term, and due after those three to five years, as specified in the loan.

Blanket Mortgage: A blanket mortgage is a single mortgage which covers more than one piece of property. Oftentimes an owner will obtain a loan on a number of smaller properties under one mortgage.

Leasehold Mortgage: A leasehold mortgage is a mortgage with a lease that acts as the primary security rather than the real estate itself. This loan is based on the income that is generated from the property per the lease. The lender usually requires that the rental income cover the debt service as well as the other expenses. The lender evaluates the credit of the tenant. The lender will require an assignment of this lease and possibly an insurance policy that will guarantee payment. The lender may have the right to approve any cancellation or changes in the lease. Great care will be taken by the lender in such a transaction. The lender does not want the loan to appear as a lease as opposed to a financing transaction. This type of loan should be structured as a loan, and not as giving the lender an economic interest in the property.

Chattel Mortgage: When there is a desire to finance furniture for hotels or apartments, a chattel mortgage can be used. They are placed only on movable personal property.

Buy Down Mortgage: These are used primarily in residential lending. They are a common practice to assist the lender in qualifying for the loan. It is financing in which the borrower advances funds to the lender to reduce some of the interest rate. In residential lending, the builder may use this technique to help a purchaser qualify for a loan. Buy downs are more common during periods of high interest rates. For example, a builder may prepay the lender to reduce the interest rate from 11 to 9 percent for a specified number of years. The lender will calculate the interest rate spread during this time period and then discount this amount to be paid in cash at the loan closing.

Private Mortgage Insurance (PMI)

In instances where the borrower has borrowed in excess of 80 percent of the appraised value of the property, this insurance is required by the lender. Should the borrower default in repayment of the loan, this insurance will guarantee the lender that he will eventually receive his money back. This insurance is used in residential lending and gives the lender the incentive to lend in areas where financing is usually not provided.

Permanent Loan Questions and Issues

In choosing the most qualified lender from your list of potential lenders, consider the following issues:

- Will the lender finance this type of property?
- Will the lender finance this type of property in this location?
- Will the lender finance the amount needed?
- Will the lender's interest rate work within your projected economics?

If the answer to these four questions is "yes," then proceed to consider the following issues.

- Will the lender lend on a percentage of the appraised value or on a certain debt service coverage ratio?
- Debt coverage ratio to be used
- Will the lender project out the rents?
- Loan rate to be charged
- Can accrual loans with lower pay rates be used?
- Rates to be used (fixed or tied to an index)
- Are interest only loans available?
- Loan term
- Loan amortization period
- Loan extensions
- Loan extension terms
- Points charged at commitment
- Points charged at closing
- Who pays closing costs?
- What are the closing costs?
- Whose attorney will close the loan?
- Appraisals required?
- Approved appraisers
- Loan funding date
- Prepayment of loan
- Can the loan be funded with an earn-out based on a higher net operating income?
- Loan lock-in period

- Prepayment penalty
- Are any personal guarantees required for this loan?
- Can these guarantees be for less than the total amount of the loan, and can they be released based on the property performance?
- Escrows for taxes and insurance
- Borrower's interest on escrow funds
- Is there a dragnet clause in the loan documents?
- Assignment at resale
- Transfer fee at loan assumption
- Will the loan rate or terms change upon resale?
- Will the new borrower have to qualify for the loan?
- What items will the new borrower have to submit to the lender?
- Reduction of interest rate
- Price for buying down the rate
- Does the loan require any cash flow or future resale profit participation by the lender?
- Requirements prior to underwriting
- Response time for a firm commitment
- Commitment extensions and cost
- Can the borrower obtain a copy of the loan documents prior to closing?
- Requirements for monthly, quarterly, or yearly operating statements

The Permanent Loan Commitment

The loan commitment issued by the permanent lender will be very similar to the one issued by the construction lender. If the construction loan is combined with the permanent loan, then the commitment will include those terms of the permanent loan.

Permanent Loan Clauses

The borrower and his attorney should carefully read each and every clause in the loan commitment and loan documents. There will be many clauses the borrower will have no problem with, while other clauses may have to be negotiated totally out or partially stricken. Other than residential permanent home loans, the borrower will usually be able to negotiate with the lender. The following are the most common clauses that the borrower will encounter.

Due-on-Sale Clause: This clause provides that, in the event that the borrower transfers any portion of its ownership in the property which is security for the loan or in the event the borrower ceases to be a stockholder or substantially dilutes his interest, the lender shall, at its sole discretion, have the right to accelerate the loan and declare that the unpaid principal balance and all accrued interest due and payable. Since low interest rate financing might be attractive upon resale, the borrower should not avoid having this clause in the documents.

Right-to-Transfer Clause: A right-to-transfer clause in the mortgage documents will give the borrower the right to transfer the property to another party. Usually, if the borrower is able to have a right-to-transfer clause in his documents, the lender will have the right to approve the new purchaser. This right to approve should have the language "not to be unreasonably withheld."

Acceleration Clause: The acceleration clause in the mortgage documents gives the lender the right to accelerate the total unpaid principal balance in case of default. The borrower should negotiate a grace period during which he can cure any default.

Lock-In Clause: Many mortgages have a lock-in clause providing that the loan cannot be prepaid for a specified period of time for any reason. The borrower should try to negotiate to remove the lock-in period for the maximum flexibility.

Prepayment Clause: Many lenders require a specified prepayment penalty for early loan payment. If a borrower obtained a mortgage during a period of high interest rates, he may desire to refinance this mortgage when rates come down. The borrower will have to evaluate the cost of this penalty and the closing costs on a new loan as opposed to the savings in the interest rate under a new loan.

Escrow Clause: Many lenders will require the borrower to escrow funds monthly for the real estate taxes and the insurance policy. If this is a requirement of the lender, the borrower should make sure that any interest earned on these funds will accrue to him. The interest earned on these escrow funds is a major source of revenue for most lenders.

Foreclosure and Right of Redemption Clause: Foreclosure is the last option by a lender to recover payment on a property that is in default. The borrower should know the foreclosure regulations and any redemption laws.

Defeasance Clause: A defeasance clause gives the borrower the right to redeem the property after a default if the borrower pays off the total indebtedness to the lender.

Subordination Clause: Many lenders insist that no secondary financing be allowed on the property, or they may require the right to approve any junior financing. Lenders want to make sure that the property is not burdened with too much monthly debt. If there is a total prohibition of any junior debt, this could preclude the borrower from reselling the property and providing any seller financing.

Release Clause: A release clause in a mortgage stipulates that upon paying a specified amount of money, the borrower can release a portion of the property which the lender has been holding as collateral for the loan.

Exculpatory Clause: An exculpatory clause pertains to the personal liability of the borrower in case of a default. If possible the borrower should negotiate all of the personal liability out of the mortgage or at least liability for only a small portion of the loan amount.

Dragnet Clause: A dragnet clause is an open-ended clause in which the property stands as security for all of the obligations that the borrower has to that lender—the note contemplated in the deed to secure debt, as well as any other indebtedness to the lender.

Cross-Default Clause: A cross-default clause is a provision in a mortgage that pledges several pieces of properties to the lender as collateral. If one of these loans is in default, it will trigger a default in the other properties.

Default Clauses: This section outlines what monetary and nonmonetary events will trigger a default in the loan documents. Upon this default, the borrower will usually have a predetermined time period to clear up the defaulted item. Typically these clauses favor the lender and gives the lender the right to accelerate the mortgage upon the default. Upon a nonmonetary default, the lender will usually notify the borrower of the defaulted item and the specific time period to cure the default. Typical monetary defaults are nonpayment of the monthly debt service payment, nonpayment of the real estate taxes, or other property assessments. Nonmonetary defaults are failure to maintain the property's insurance premium, bankruptcy or insolvency of the borrower, or nonperformance of rebuilding property that was destroyed by fire.

HOW TO PREPARE A LOAN PACKAGE

When requesting a loan from an institution, the borrower is required to submit a loan proposal with all the necessary personal and property information required. Each lender will have their unique requirements, but the following outline can be used in preparing this package.

I.   Borrower's name, address, telephone number, social security number

II.   Resume of borrower(s)

III.   Financing statements: If this information is confidential, simply state that these financial statements are available upon request

IV.   Description of Property: Type, location, size acreage, zoning, and topographical information:
        A. Unit information:
           1. Residential
              a. Unit mix
              b. Rental rates

        c. Type units

        d. Size units (number of bedrooms/bath)

        e. Square footage

        f. Who pays utilities?

     2. Commercial

        a. Rental rates

        b. Square footage per floor

        c. Bay widths and depths

        d. Expense pass through

        e. Who pays utilities?

  B. Interior features

  C. Amenities

  D. Management facilities

  E. Parking (on-site, off-site, covered)

  F. Type of construction

  G. Type of utilities

  H. Landscaping

V. Development team credentials

  A. Developer

  B. Equity partner

  C. Architect

  D. Engineer

  E. Landscape architect

  F. General contractor

  G. Appraiser

  H. Management company

  I. Marketing company

  J. Construction management company

  K. Attorney

  L. Accountant

  M. Interior decorator

  N. Advertising agency

  O. Public relations agency

VI. Marketing plan

  A. Target market

  B. Media used to advertise the property

  C. Real estate commissions

VII.   Property management plan
    A. Description of management/maintenance employees
    B. Salary levels
    C. Office hours
VIII. Construction
    A. Schedule of construction (to include starting and completion dates)
    B. Late penalties
    C. Phasing
IX.   Illustrations
    A. Aerials
    B. Site plan
    C. Floor plans
    D. Elevations
    E. Renderings/pictures
    F. Topography map
X.   Maps
    A. State
    B. City
    C. County
    D. Neighborhood
XI.   Zoning Letter from governmental authorities
XII.   Utility letters from local utilities: (capacities and availability)
XIII. Construction drawings and specifications
XIV.   Development proforma
    A. Sources and uses of funds
    B. Month-by-month cost analysis showing all line items
    C. Notes to line-item analysis
XV.   Operating proforma
    A. Month-by-month revenue and expense budget showing leasing schedules
      1. Notes to line-item analysis
    B. Month-by-month capital expenditure budget
      1. Notes to line-item analysis
XVI.   Market study illustrating comparable market data: A market study of the area comparables, including the following information
    A. Name and address of comparable property
    B. Rental rates

        C. Expense pass through

        D. Who pays utilities?

        E. Type of units

        F. Unit mix

        G. Year property built

        H. Type of utility system

        I. Unit features

        J. Amenities

        K. Current rental concessions

        L. Security deposit

        M. Current occupancy

        N. Leasing commission

XVII. Executive summary appraisal

XVIII. Contracts: This section can include the following agreements with some available upon request

        A. Land purchase contract

        B. Architectural/engineering contracts

        C. General contractor contract

        D. Management contract

        E. Marketing contract

        F. Condominium documents/by-laws

        G. Joint venture documents

        H. Partnership documents

        I. Ground lease

        J. Covenants, conditions, and restrictions (C, C & R's)

XIX. Developer's references

XX. Loan Request

        A. Construction loan

            1. Type of loan

            2. Loan amount

            3. Loan rate

            4. Loan term

            5. Loan points

            6. Closing costs

            7. Loan closing date

            8. Frequency of draws

            9. Dollars funded at first draw

           10. Draw holdback

           11. Loan guarantor

    B. Permanent loan

       1. Type of loan

       2. Loan amount

       3. Loan security

       4. Loan recourse

       5. Loan closing date

       6. Loan rate

       7. Loan term/maturity

       8. Loan amortization

       9. Escrows

       10. Assignability

       11. Transfer fee

       12. Prepayment penalty

       13. Closing costs

       14. Loan points

       15. Due-on-sale clause

       16. Secondary financing

       17. Grace period and late charges

       18. Fire and insurance proceeds

       19. Borrowing entity

XXII. Exhibits

    A. Working drawings/specifications

    B. Appraisal

    C. Feasibility study

    D. Boundary and topographic survey

    E. Environmental impact study

    F. Development and building permits

    G. Construction costs/subcontractor's bids

    H. Soils test

    I. Contractor's bond or letter of credit

    J. FMLMC, FHA, FNMA, VA approval letter

HOW THE APPRAISAL PROCESS WORKS

Along with the financing loan package, the developer must submit an updated appraisal for the proposed development. This appraisal will be used by the lender to complete their financial analysis and a proposed offer to the developer. Upon refinancing of the property, the developer will also be required to obtain an updated appraisal. Detailed information about the different procedures for determining value, which appraisers use, can be found in the Value and Real Estate Developments section of Chapter 8. That information and the following will give a complete picture of the process.

Appraisals can be provided in response to information needed for the following:

- Loan value
- Insurance value
- Tax values
- Estate values
- Condemnation awards
- Exchange value
- Lease value
- Book value

The following appraisal outline is designed so that the developer and the lender can choose the areas which they need for the financing transaction.

Appraisal Outline

I. Cover letter with appraised value
II. Certification of appraisal
III. Underlying assumptions and limiting conditions
IV. Table of contents
V. Introduction
    A. Identification of the property
    B. Legal description
    C. Purpose of the appraisal
    D. Definition of market value
    E. Property rights appraised
    F. Current ownership
    G. Current zoning/proposed zoning
    H. Date of appraisal
VI. Property plat
VII. Regional data
    A. Location
    B. Demographics

  C. Climate
  D. Topography
  E. Soil and subsoil
  F. Employment
  G. Economic base
  H. Retail trade
  I. Tourism
  J. Military
  K. Utilities
  L. Municipal services
  M. Transportation
  N. Government
  O. Religious institutions
  P. Recreation
  Q. Educational facilities
  R. Regional conclusion
  S. Regional map
 VIII. Neighborhood Data
  A. Location
  B. Demographics
  C. Area development trends
  D. Transportation
  E. Access
  F. Utilities
  G. Neighborhood conclusion
  H. Map
 IX. Property Description
  A. Location
  B. Site description
  C. Site plan
  D. Site improvement description
  E. Building improvement description
  F. Unit mix
  G. Floor plans
  H. Elevation of buildings
  I. Amenity description

       J.   Pictures of property
          1. Entrance
          2. Front elevation
          3. Side elevations
          4. Rear elevation
          5. Aerial
          6. Amenities
          7. Typical neighborhood

X.   History of the property

XI.   Highest and best use of the property
       A. If vacant
       B. If built

XII.   Real estate market
       A. Residential
          1. Building permits
             a. For sale housing
             b. Rental
          2. Area vacancy rates
          3. Absorption history
          4. Pricing averages
       B. Commercial
          1. Building permits
             a. Office
             b. Retail
             c. Lodging
             d. Industrial
          2. Area vacancy rates
          3. Absorption history
          4. Pricing averages

XIII. Valuation
       A. Methodology
          1. Cost approach
             a. Land comparables
             b. Replacement costs
             c. Depreciation
             d. Cost approach value

2. Market approach
   a. Improvement sale comparables
3. Income approach
   a. Market rental rates
   b. Operating expenses
   c. Stabilized income and expense statement
   d. Overall capitalization rate technique
   e. Development of interest and capitalization rate through utilizing mortgage equity analysis
   f. Rent-up analysis projections
   g. Rent loss analysis valuation
   h. Discounted cash flow analysis
4. Reconciliation
   a. Final valuation
   b. Final valuation after construction and absorption

XIV. Addenda
   A. Accelerated cost recovery system (ACRS)
      1. History of accelerated cost recovery system
      2. Definition of personal property/estimated value
         a. Itemized value
         b. Depreciation schedule
      3. Class of property
   B. Real estate tax comparables
      1. Millage rate
         a. Breakdown—two-year history
      2. Comparables
         a. Name and location of property
         b. Taxes per unit/square foot
         c. Ownership
         d. Number of units, square footage
         e. Last tax bill
         f. Comments
   C. Market Study
      1. Comparables
         a. Name and location of property
         b. Current occupancy
         c. Total units/square footage

        d. Unit type

        e. Unit mix

        f. Unit size

        g. Square footage (gross/net)

        h. Rental rate and term

        i. Who pays utilities

        j. Rent per square foot

        k. Parking

        l. Security deposits/earnest money

        m. Real estate leasing/sales commissions

        n. Unit features and amenities

        o. Absorption history

        p. Quality of property

        q. Condition of property

    2. Summary of comparable pricing

    3. Projected subject pricing schedule

    4. Absorption projection

    5. Comparable map

  XV. Qualifications of appraiser

NEGOTIATING THE TERMS AND CONDITIONS OF THE LOAN

As in all types of negotiations, the borrower should first understand how a lender functions.

Lender's Decision-Making Process

Being conservative by nature, lenders normally have rigid lending policies and parameters which are determined by a loan policy committee. Typical parameters include: (1) the types of properties which they will provide financing, (2) location where they will lend, and (3) the amount of financing which they will provide. When submitting a loan proposal, it is essential that the borrower understand that there will be regular meetings to develop and redevelop these policies and to approve or disapprove loan submissions. Before the committee will review your loan proposal, along with any of their staff recommendations, the loan officer will screen the borrower and the structure of the transaction to ensure that the committee can act expeditiously.

Borrower Screening

The lender will review and verify the borrower's credit history, personal, and business references, and track record. When analyzing the borrower's credit, the lender will review the four "Cs" of credit; they are character, capacity, collateral, and capital. The lender will also look very carefully at the borrower's record of past loan repayments. No lender wants to take back the property and then pursue borrower for the deficiency on the loan.

Evaluating the Loan: Five Formulas Used by the Lender

The lender will review all of the market conditions in the area local to the subject property. The lender is lending funds based on a future income stream. Consequently, the lender wants to ensure that the property will be able to support these monthly payments not only now, but in the future. The lender will require an appraisal of the property. From that appraisal and a determined net operating income, a loan amount will be set. This loan amount will be based on the total development costs or on the value of the development. The following are ways of determining this loan amount (see also Figure 9–4).

Loan-to-Construction Cost Ratio: Many construction lenders will loan based on a percentage of the total costs of the development. Included in this cost calculation will be the land, direct and indirect costs. Additionally, many lenders will advance developments fees to the developer during the construction period.

$$\text{Total construction costs} \times \text{Ratio} = \text{Construction loan}$$

Debt Coverage Ratio (DCR): The debt coverage ratio is a formula which shows the lender the coverage left after all the expenses and the debt service is paid. The formula is as follows:

$$\frac{\text{Net operating income}}{\text{Annual debt service}} = \text{Debt coverage ratio}$$

Example: If the property has a net operating income of $200,000, and its annual debt service payment is $160,000, the debt coverage ratio is 1.25. This means that there is 25 percent coverage over and above the total expenses of the property.

Annual Loan Constant (ALC): By using a loan constant table, the lender can look up the loan constant for the current loan terms which he is offering. This loan constant is then multiplied by the loan amount and divided by 1200 to get the monthly debt service payment.

$$\text{Annual loan constant} = \frac{1200 \times \text{Monthly payment}}{\text{Loan amount}}$$

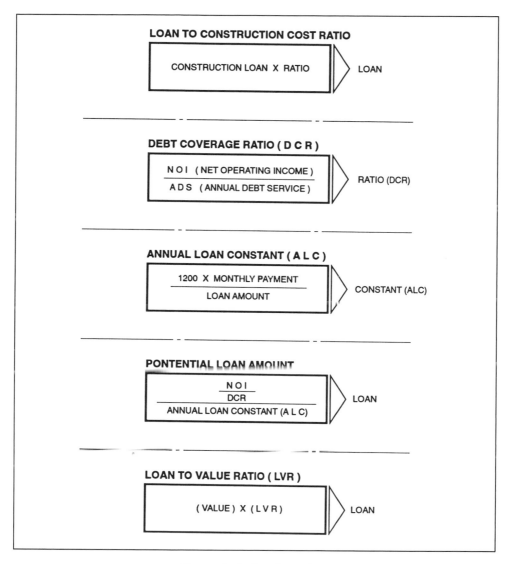

Figure 9-4 Lender ratios.

Potential Loan Amount (PLA): The lender will divide the net operating income by the debt coverage ratio and then divide that number by the annual loan constant to get the loan amount he would loan.

$$\frac{\dfrac{\text{Net operating income (NOI)}}{\text{Debt coverage ratio}}}{\text{Annual loan constant}} = \text{Loan amount}$$

Example: A property has a net operating income of $2,000,000, and the lender is currently using a 1.15 debt coverage ratio. Current loans are made at 10 percent for thirty years.

$$\frac{\$2,000,000 \ (NOI)}{1.15 \ (DCR)} = \$1,666,667$$

$$\frac{\$1,666,667}{.1053 \ (\text{Loan constant})} = \$ \ 15,827,797$$

$$\$ \ 15,827,797 = \text{Potential loan amount}$$

Loan-to-Value Ratio (LVR):   Many lenders use the loan to value ratio to arrive at their lending decisions. This method involves lending funds based upon a maximum predetermined percentage of the appraised value of the property. Many lenders use different percentages determined by the various types of property and the credit worthiness of the borrower. For example, a lender might make an 80 percent loan to value loan on an apartment property. If the property is appraised at $3,000,000, the lender will then lend a maximum of $2,400,000 on the property.

$$\text{Appraised value} \times \text{Loan to value ratio (LVR)}$$
$$= \text{Loan amount}$$
$$\$3,000,000 \times 80\% = \$2,400,000 \ (\text{loan amount})$$

How a Lender Prices the Loan

Before a lender can determine the price which will be charged for the loan, he must consider the credit history of the borrower and all of the information provided on the proposed property. Other lender's offerings within the market and the risks associated with the development will also be considered in this pricing effort. The risk is usually based on:

- Type of project
- Type of tenancy (length of lease and the credit worthiness of the tenant)
- Predictability of future income streams to repay the loan
- Financial strength of the borrower
- Track record of the borrower

The following will discuss the various terms and conditions which the lender will propose.

Interest Rate

Since the use of money has a cost, lenders must review their costs of funds and determine the profit margin which they must receive on the use of these funds. The profit margin is based on the risk which is taken by the lender, the length of time which the funds will be outstanding, and the repayment schedule.

If the borrower is a good customer and has a substantial balance in the lender's institution, this profit margin may be reduced.

Loan Fees

Another term for these fees is points. These fees are in addition to the interest rate charged by the lender and provide another way for the lender to increase his profits. They, generally, range from 1 to 4 percent and this percentage is determined by the magnitude of the risk.

Construction Loan Period

The construction loan period is usually determined by the amount of time necessary to construct. Many times lenders will include additional time for the property to achieve a stabilized occupancy, which will allow the developer to receive a larger permanent loan.

Permanent Loan Amortization Period

Since every loan has to be repaid, the lender will determine the amount of time he will give the borrower in which to repay the loan. The time period will be based on the type of property. Certain properties, such as mini-warehouses, will have shorter loan amortization periods than Class A office buildings.

Maturity Period

To reduce the monthly debt service payment, the lender may give the borrower a greater amortization period but require that the loan be repaid at an earlier date. This not only gives the borrower a lower payment, but will allow the lender to receive his funds at an earlier date than amortized. An example is a 20-year loan with a 15-year maturity date.

Conditions Stipulated in the Loan Agreement

The lender may add extra stipulations into the loan documents. These may require the borrower to collateralize the loan, either through securing the property with a mortgage or even by adding the borrower's personal guarantee of the loan repayment. An escrow account may be required to fund projected negative cash flows during the lease-up period. Each lender's requirement will vary relative to problems which they have experienced in the past. The borrower must negotiate carefully in this area to ensure that the most favorable terms are accepted.

Financial Guarantees

In some financing transactions, further security may be required by lenders to minimize their risk if default should occur. This security, or guarantees can take various forms. This section will consider aspects of some of the more common types.

Recourse Versus Nonrecourse Guarantees

Most lenders today will require a personal guarantee from the developer or his corporation during the construction loan phase of financing. In addition, full or partial financial guarantees will be required for the permanent loan. The developer should reduce these financial guarantees as much as possible. Many developers have lost their fortunes due to personal guarantees which they have made on properties which they developed, but which failed. Some methods to minimize these risks are as follows:

- Finding substitute or additional guarantors to reduce risk. These additional guarantors will reduce the developer's risk exposure by reducing his guarantee portion. By using this method, the developer will probably have to share the ownership of the transaction.
- Negotiating a burn-off of the personal guarantee relative to the achievement of a predetermined net operating income for a specified time period.
- Negotiating a guarantee for only the upper portion of the loan balance. For example, a $1,000,000 loan might only have the top 10% or $100,000 personally guaranteed by the borrower.

Jointly and Severally

When more than one borrower is involved in borrowing funds for a development, the lender will usually require that the borrowers sign the personal guarantees both personally and jointly and severally with the other borrowers. Each borrower should be made aware that if these loans are ever called early or if they are in default of the loan terms then not only is each borrower responsible for his own share of the loan but is also responsible for the other borrowers should they not be able to honor the financial commitment to the lender.

Letters of Credit

As additional collateral, many lenders require the developer to post letters of credit during construction and rent-up phases of the development. These letters of credit can be called by the lender if the developer fails to achieve specified income objectives.

Additional Collateral

Often, the lender will not only require the developer to sign the loan with a personal guarantee, but will require that additional collateral of other property or assets (stock, bonds, etc.) be provided as security. Upon default, the developer may lose these other assets.

Credit Enhancements

Credit enhancements are guarantees of bonds by institutions who are rated by a national rating service, such as Moody's or Standard and Poor's. The guarantees are usually made by life insurance companies or major banking institutions. The developer will pay a fee for these guarantees.

Credit Tenants

In order to reduce financial exposure as much as possible, in office, industrial, and retail developments, the developer may need preleased tenants to sign lease guarantees. These guarantees will assist the lender in underwriting the financing.

Points to Remember When Negotiating for a Loan

As you have started to short list your lenders, you should start ranking each loan offering. The developer should begin narrowing down his options to the best two or three proposals. Remember, each loan will be somewhat different and should be analyzed carefully. Once you have decided on the best offering, request a written commitment from the lender. The lender will most likely request a nonrefundable binder to be paid upon acceptance of this commitment. At this point you should request that your attorney be given copies of all the loan closing documents.

When reviewing the mortgage documents presented by the lender, the borrower should take special care to analyze his obligations. An attorney who specializes in this area of the law will be of great assistance. Typically, most lenders fashion these documents to their benefit. Many of these clauses will not be subject to negotiation, while others can be reworded to the benefit of the borrower. In addition, some clauses can be totally removed. It is more common to negotiate these clauses in commercial transactions than it is in residential home loans. As in any negotiation, if you find a problem clause, ask that it be removed. It must be remembered and understood that when borrowing money the "Golden Rule" applies—that rule states, "He who has the gold rules."

Know Your Lender's Position on Issues (Positives And Negatives)

Develop a sense of whether your lender is lending on the property or on the experience and integrity of the borrower. The key to obtaining a loan is to develop a lasting relationship with the lender. Lenders are conservative individuals who must have the utmost confidence in the borrower's ability to pay back the loan.

Be Creative About Structuring Your Financial Needs

Be creative when structuring your financing needs. Since there are many options, the borrower must refine the loan to meet his needs. Each party has its own desires, and with good, creative thinking each party can reach its objectives. A knowledgeable mortgage banker/broker along with your accountant and attorney can prove helpful at this time. The basic tenet of creativity is that nothing is carved in stone. Just because 80 percent financing is the norm, does not mean that 100 percent financing is not possible. Remember that lenders are in the business of lending money and they desire to make loans. If one structure on their "menu" does not work, another might. Remember, if you don't ask, you don't receive. If one proposal doesn't work, search for other possibilities with the lender, until you find the one that meets the needs of both parties.

Plan to "Unwind" Your Loan

Probably one of the most important things to remember when structuring your loan is how you will unwind the loan. It is easier to plan this strategy in advance. If the loan's lock-in provisions, prepayment penalty, subordinate financing, and the due-on-sale clauses are determined at the beginning, the borrower can better control the loan when it needs to be assumed, or the property resold. Without these favorable provisions, the borrower will have a difficult time using his own loan in future opportunities. You may be on good terms with your lender today, but tomorrow he might be gone or the policies of the lending institution may change.

CLOSING THE LOAN

Once the developer has submitted all of the information requested, the lender will, if interested, issue a loan commitment letter. This letter will outline the basic terms and conditions under which the lender will make the loan. If all of these points are agreeable to the borrower, he should sign the commitment letter and return it with the required deposit. This fee is used to pay the lender's costs associated with the underwriting of the loan as well as to show the lender that the borrower intends to finalize the loan.

Once the lender's commitment letter is signed, the developer's attorney should contact the lender's attorney to prepare the closing documents. The attorney will review all of the mortgage documents, and then negotiate the language in the documents. The attorney will coordinate the survey work and the title insurance that is needed for the closing. The attorney will then schedule the closing of the loan and will notify all the parties concerned of the time and place of the closing. At the closing, the attorney will review the closing statement. Once all of the documents have been signed, the attorneys will disburse the funds. The developer should then request copies of all the documents and a copy of the permanent loan amortization schedule be sent to his place of business.

PERMANENT LENDER'S CLOSING CHECKLIST

After the loan has been approved by the lender, the developer's attorney and the lender's attorney should compile a closing checklist of all the items required to complete the transaction. The developer should then schedule and delegate the work to his team so that the transaction can be complete as soon as possible. The following is a sampling of the types of items needed prior to closing.

General Information

- Lender
- Borrower(s)
- Guarantor(s)
- Property description
- Purpose of development
- Loan amount
- Proposed closing date
- Lender's attorney
- Borrower's attorney

Permanent Loan Preclosing Items

- Legal description
- Commitment for title insurance
- Copy of all recorded title exceptions
- Easements receipt and approved by lender
- Insurance certification
- Certificate of approval of insurance
- Permanent loan commitment
- Appraisal
- Feasibility study
- Articles of incorporation and by-laws of borrower-certified copy (if applicable)
- Certificate of existence of borrower
- Survey, surveyor's inspection report, and certificate to lender's title insurer
- Borrower's certificate of corporate resolution and incumbency
- Parking letter (if applicable)
- Utility's availability letters
- Zoning letter
- Copies of all executed leases
- Certification of environmental concerns compliance
- Tenant estoppel certificates
- Copies of service contracts

- Borrower(s) financial statements
- Pest report (if applicable)
- Evidence of land ownership

Loan Documents Signed at the Permanent Loan Closing

- Closing statement
- Note
- Guaranty
- Deed to secure debt
- Assignment of leases and rents
- Loan agreement
- Assignment of borrower's interest in documents
- Consents to assignments of borrower's interest
- Uniform Commercial Code financing statements
- Borrower's certificate-No Adverse Change
- Tenant estoppel certificate
- Lease subordination, nondisturbance and attornment agreements
- Affidavit of title
- Title binder
- Mortgage title policy (after closing)
- Opinions of borrower's and guarantor's counsel

  Borrowing entity exists and has the right to carry on its business and enter this transaction

  Borrower is not in violation of any securities laws

  Loan documents will be fully enforceable according to their provisions

  Deed of trust, when recorded, will be a valid lien on the property

  Financing statement, when recorded, will perfect a security interest in the personal property identified therein

  Borrower has obtained all of the legal permits and licenses required to carry on their business and the operation of the property

  Property may be used for the purposes which it is being used

  Any provisions of any agreements between the borrower and lender do not violate any known law

  There are no pending legal matters which may adversely affect the lender's interest in the borrower's property or inhibit the ability of the borrower to repay the funds

  No form of rent control, or proposed rent control is in effect or is pending

REFINANCING THE PROPERTY

During the course of the ownership of the property, the developer may decide to refinance the property. Reasons for this refinancing may include:

- A maturity of the existing loan
- A better loan environment that will allow a new mortgage with better terms and conditions, which may create a larger cash flow for the property
- Consolidate the various underlying loans into a new loan with better terms and conditions
- The need to pull out some profits by refinancing with a larger loan, these funds will be "tax-free" to the developer
- Increasing the chance of a resale for the property by having a new mortgage on the property with better terms and conditions

Second Mortgages

If the developer faces a situation where there is a lock-in provision or a prepayment penalty that is usually large, he may decide to place a second mortgage on the property. The proceeds of this second mortgage will generate tax-free proceeds that can be used for renovating the property or for other ventures. It should be noted that typically the rate for a second mortgage is higher than that of a first mortgage.

Wraparound Mortgage (All-Inclusive Trust Deed)

A wraparound mortgage is subordinate (junior) to the existing first or second mortgages. This type of loan will "wraparound" the current debt and will include all new funds advanced. For example, a developer with an existing loan for $900,000 with interest at 10 percent, may secure a new wraparound mortgage for $1 million with an interest rate at 11 percent. In this example, the new lender is only lending $100,000 of "new" funds, but he is also receiving the interest rate "point spread" (the difference between 10 percent and 11 percent) on the original $900,000.

FINANCING FORMS

Lender Checklist Form 9–1

This lender checklist form is to be used to qualify various loans.

LENDER CHECKLIST FORM

FORM 9-1

PREPARED BY _____
DATE ____/____/____

LENDER INFORMATION

LENDER'S NAME _____	SPECIALIZATION:	DEAL SIZE	LOAN TYPE:
CONTACT _____	RESIDENTIAL:		LAND ACQUISTION _____
ADDRESS _____	SINGLE–FAMILY _____ $_____		DEVELOPMENT _____
_____	MULTI–FAMILY _____ $_____		CONSTRUCTION _____
TEL. NO. (__)_____	CONDOMINIUM/TOWNHOME _____ $_____		STANDBY _____
	ADULT CONGREGATE CARE _____ $_____		PERMANENT _____
LENDING AREA:	NURSING HOME _____ $_____		
_____	COMMERCIAL:		
_____	OFFICE _____ $_____		
_____	RETAIL _____ $_____		
	INDUSTRIAL _____ $_____		
	LODGING _____ $_____		

TYPICAL DEAL

CONSTRUCTION:	PERMANENT:	RECOURSE: NO ____ YES ___ % ___
LOAN AMOUNT $_____	TYPE LOAN _____	DUE-ON-SALE CLAUSE: NO ____ YES ___
LOAN-TO-VALUE RATIO _____%	LOAN-TO-VALUE RATIO _____%	JUNIOR FINANCING PROHIBITION: NO ___ YES ___
LOAN RATE _____%	LOAN CONSTANT USED _____%	DATE LOAN DELINQUENT _____
LOAN TERM (MONTHS) _____	LOAN AMORTIZATION PERIOD (YEARS) _____	LATE CHARGE _____%
POINTS _____%	LOAN MATURITY (YUEARS) _____%	GRACE PERIOD (DAYS) _____ _____
CLOSING COSTS _____%	LOAN PAYMENT RATE _____%	ASSIGNABILITY: NO ____ YES ___
FREQUENCY OF DRAWS (PER MONTH) _____	LOAN ACCRUAL RATE _____%	TRANFER FEE (% OF LOAN) _____%
DRAW HOLDBACK $_____	INDEX USED _____	NEW INTEREST RATE _____%
PERSONAL LIABILITY: YES ___ NO ___	LOAN BUYDOWN COST _____%	PREPAYMENT PENALTY: NO ___ YES ___ _____%
TAKE-OUT LOAN REQUIRED: YES ___ NO ___	POINTS _____%	LOCK-IN (YEARS) _____
	CLOSING COSTS _____%	
	ESCROWS REQUIRED: INSURANCE ___ TAX ___	

COMMENTS

_____
_____
_____
_____
_____
_____
_____
_____
_____
_____
_____
_____
_____
_____
_____
_____
_____
_____
_____
_____
_____

Form 9-1 Lender checklist form.

## Chapter 10

Raising the Equity

If the developer is unable to structure the financing for 100 percent of the needed funds, he must find some cash equity for the complete financing of the development. Typically, the lender will require the cash equity in the development deal on the front end, either by purchasing the land or part of the land, or by the placing of escrow cash or a cash equivalent with the lender. Depending on the cash position of the developer, he might contribute the equity himself, borrow funds, or have other individuals contribute the equity needed to close.

Assuming that the developer decides that he cannot put in all the equity himself, he must raise the necessary capital from other sources. This chapter provides guidelines for the developer to follow in this endeavor. If in finding these resources the developer must go into partnership with others, he will usually become the "managing partner" with the new partners becoming limited partners.

What Is Equity?

Equity is normally that cash at risk from either the developer or his partners which bridges the gap between the mortgage loan and the total costs of the development. By definition, it is also that interest or value remaining in the property after payment of all liens or other charges on the property. An owner's equity in property is normally the monetary interest the owner retains over and above the mortgage indebtedness. If the property is encumbered with a long-term mortgage, the developer's equity in the property increases with each monthly principal mortgage payment not including the increased value through appreciation.

Why Does the Lender Require Equity?

By the developer investing his own cash in the deal either for the land or the gap between the costs and the loan will focus the developer's attention on the transaction to such a degree that there is a higher probability for success and for the lender to achieve his projected return. Typically, lenders use loan-to-value ratios (LTV) to determine the amount of equity which will be required. The reason why lenders use loan-to-value ratios is to place the borrower at a certain level of risk and to avoid having the total risk for the transaction.

HOW TO FIND SOURCES OF EQUITY

Once the amount of equity is determined, the developer should list potential equity investors, such as the sources below.

- Friends
- Business associates
- Money raisers
    Broker/dealers who specialize in real estate
    Financial planners who specialize in real estate
    Wholesalers who have contacts with money raisers
- Accountants who have clients who desire to invest in real estate
- Attorneys who have clients who desire to invest in real estate
- Real estate brokers who know of potential investors
- Bankers who have clients who may be potential investors
- Insurance agents who have clients who might be potential investors
- Real estate investment firms
- Institutional joint venture partners
    Banks
    Savings and loans
    Insurance companies
    Pension funds

DETERMINATION OF THE REQUIRED EQUITY

To determine the amount of equity needed for the acquisition, the developer should review all the areas where funds will be needed. They can include the following:

- Lender equity requirements
- Fees paid to money raiser

- Negative cash flow funding
- Working capital reserves for future negative cash flow or capital expenditures
- Up front "seed money" for predevelopment costs

Working Capital Reserves: The Dollars Needed for Staying Power

Working capital is one of the most important aspects of the whole transaction. Since real estate is normally held for a relatively long period of time, it will go through many economic cycles. Financial problems occur in real estate deals when there is a cash flow problem due to loss of potential rents and increased costs of operating expenses including unforeseen repairs.

The amount of working capital raised should be determined by the developer's calculations of a worst case scenario—that is, how much money should be raised to carry the property in the worst situation. There are no hard and fast rules on the exact amount needed, either on a per-unit or percent of income basis. This amount of money will be a function of the length of time the developer will be holding the property and his property management philosophies.

Most deals run into trouble when they no longer have working capital. Oftentimes, limited partnerships have an initial funding of this working capital account and only to be reluctant to ask the investment partners for additional funding to replenish the account. The determination and replenishment of the account should be annual and include annual projections of operating budgets.

FINDING EQUITY AND THE OFFERING

Types of Investor's Needed

In many types of real estate transactions, the managing partner is in need not only of equity but expertise in areas in which he is lacking. In many cases, the developer (the individual or individuals who will oversee the daily operations of the property) will seek an active joint venture partner to not only contribute the necessary equity for the transaction, but to play an active role in the development, management, or leasing of the property.

If the developer is capable of handling all of the facets of the transaction, he is probably going to look for a passive money partner, typically a limited partner. If the developer is capable of handling the deal but desires a partner to share the financial risks over and above the partner's contribution, he should search for this type of partner and structure the transaction accordingly, giving this new partner incentives as required.

PREPARING THE INVESTOR PACKAGE

Once the project economics are complete, and acceptable financing is found, the developer should begin to create an investor package. This package will include all the information regarding the property. It will detail the terms of the transaction, the financial projections, the mortgage information, and other information needed to raise the equity for which the developer is searching. The following is an outline for this package. Once again, this outline is generic listing both items which can be included in residential and commercial properties. The developer should customize the outline according to his particular product type.

Investor Information Package Outline

    I.   Introduction to the property
        A. Brief summary of the property
        B. Brief summary of the transaction
        C. Proposed closing date of the transaction
    II. Area Overview
        A. State information
            1. Population
            2. Income
            3. Employment
            4. Industry
            5. Retail buying power
            6. Government
            7. Map
        B. City information
            1. Population demographics
            2. Income
            3. Employment
            4. Industry
            5. Retail buying power
            6. Government
            7. Map
        C. County information
            1. Population demographics
            2. Income
            3. Employment
            4. Industry
            5. Retail buying power

      6. Government

      7. Map

   D. Neighborhood information (by census tract)

      1. Population demographics

      2. Income

      3. Employment

      4. Industry

      5. Retail buying power

      6. Residential housing

      7. Traffic count

      8. Map

   E. Building permits (number of properties, dollar value)

      1. Commercial

      2. Residential

III. Property description

   A. Location

      1. State

      2. City

      3. County

      4. Neighborhood

      5. Street address

   B. Property type

      1. Commercial

         a. Number of buildings

         b. Number of floors

         c. Square footage per building (gross/net)

         d. Square footage per floor (gross/net)

         e. Number of parking spaces

      2. Residential

         a. Number of buildings

         b. Number of floors

         c. Number of units

         d. Unit information

         e. Number of parking spaces

   C. Site description

      1. Acreage

      2. Zoning

      3. Density

      4. Topography description

5. Legal description

6. Plat

D. Construction

   1. Type of construction used

   2. Type of roof

   3. Type of exterior facade

   4. Utility system

   5. Insulation factors (R-factors)

   6. Landscaping

E. Unit features

   1. Commercial tenant finish (allowance)

   2. Residential

F. Furniture

   1. List inventory (room location, manufacturer, model number, color)

G. Property amenities

   1. Commercial

   2. Residential

      a. Management office

      b. On-site maintenance staff

      c. Clubhouse

      d. Laundry facilities

      e. Pool

      f. Tennis court

      g. Racquetball court

      h. Playground area

      i. Picnic area

      j. Mail pick-up

H. Leasing information

   1. Commercial

      a. Minimum/maximum floor area

      b. Rental rate per square foot (gross/net)

      c. Lease terms

      d. Rent escalations

         (1) Flat rate

         (2) Consumer Price Index (CPI)

         (3) Operating expense pass through

         (4) Percentage rents

    e. Common area charges

    f. Tenant allowances

    g. Rent concessions

    h. Security deposit policy

    i. Real estate commission policy

    j. Rent schedule

    k. Occupancy

    l. Tenant profile

2. Residential

    a. Rental schedule per unit type/location

         (1) Utilities

         (2) Parking

    b. Lease term

         (1) Option period

    c. Rent escalations

    d. Rent concessions

    e. Security deposit policy

    f. Pet Policy

    g. Fees

         (1) Application

         (2) Cleaning

         (3) Pet

    h. Rental profile

    i. Real estate commission policy

    j. Occupancy

    k. Tenant profile

I. Visual descriptions

  1. Property photographs

  2. Rendering

  3. Site plans

  4. Floor plans

J. Property players (name, address, telephone number, contact)

  1. Current owner

  2. Proposed new ownership

  3. Property management company

  4. Leasing company
  5. Architect
  6. Landscape architect
  7. Engineers
  8. General contractor
  9. Construction manager
  10. Attorney
  11. Title company
  12. Accountant
  13. Money raiser
  14. Real estate broker
  15. Mortgage broker
  16. Lenders
      a. Construction
      b. Permanent
      c. Investor note
         (1) Surety
  17. Appraiser
  18. Tax consultant
  19. Insurance agent
K. Construction dates
  1. Estimated date permitted
  2. Estimated date final certificate of occupancy issued
L. Construction information
  1. Copy of construction contract
  2. Line-item costs
  3. Critical path
  4. Projected construction draw schedule
  5. Construction penalties
      a. Date due
M. Investment summary
  1. Estimate value
  2. Price yardsticks
      a. Price per unit
      b. Price per square foot
      c. Gross rent multiplier

d. Capitalization rate

e. Internal rate of return

N. Fees schedule

1. Development fee

2. Construction management fee

3. Management fee

4. Leasing fee

5. Resale fee

O. Offering summary

1. Investment unit size (number of investment units)

2. Projected yearly write-offs

3. Allocation of benefits

a. Cash flow

(1) General partners

(2) Limited partners

(3) Special limited partners

b. Taxable income (loss)

(1) General partners

(2) Limited partners

(3) Special limited partners

c. Refinancing/resale

(1) General partners

(2) Limited partners

(3) Special limited partners

4. Proposed closing date

5. Proposed managing/general partners

P. Financial summary

1. Forecast of investment performance

2. Sources and sources of proceeds

3. Forecast of cash flow

4. Forecast of taxable income (loss)

5. Forecast of resale

6. Back-up exhibits

a. Summary of transaction

b. Operating expenses

(1) Line-item analysis

    c. Capital expenditure budget
       (1) Line-item analysis
    d. Summary of financing
       (1) Lender
       (2) Original loan closing date
       (3) Original loan amount
       (4) Current loan balance
       (5) Interest rate
       (6) Monthly payment
       (7) Loan amortization
       (8) Loan maturity
       (9) Loan extension
           (a) Extension fees
           (b) Rate increase
           (c) Term
      (10) Prepayment penalty
           (a) Lock-in period
      (11) Security for loan
      (12) Escrows
           (a) Real estate taxes
           (b) Insurance
      (13) Loan transferability
           (a) Assumption fee
      (14) Loan points
      (15) Closing costs
      (16) Loan buy down
      (17) Due on sale clause
      (18) Loan guarantees
      (19) Lender reporting requirements
    e. Surety bond (if required by note lender)
       (1) Points
       (2) Guarantor
    f. Fees to seller
       (1) Name of fee
       (2) Amount of fee
       (3) Payment date
       (4) Explanation of fee

g. Fees to general partner
    (1) Name of fee
    (2) Amount of fee
    (3) Payment of fee
    (4) Explanation of fee
h. Tax allocation of closing costs and fees
    (1) Items to expense
    (2) Items to add to the basis
    (3) Items to capitalize
    (4) Items to amortize
        (a) Number of years
i. Depreciation schedule
    (1) Real property
    (2) Personal property
j. Debt service amortization schedules
k. Construction period interest schedule (if to-be-built)
l. Sales tax schedule (if to-be-built)

Q. Inventory
  1. Office
  2. Maintenance shop
  3. Model
  4. Laundry room
  5. Pool equipment
  6. Amenities
R. Appraisal cover letter
S. Comparable market study
T. Feasibility study
U. Seller warranties
V. Copy of land purchase agreement
W. Copy of development agreement
X. Copy of management agreement
Y. Copies of engineering studies
  1. Soils tests
  2. Environmental impact study
Z. Resume of the general partner

The developer should also gather information on the potential investment group to which the package will be sent. This information should include the investor's investment experience, net worth, yearly salary history, and banking references. Not only will this information provide the developer with insight into how the investor package should be customized for a particular investor's needs, but knowing in-depth knowledge about the investor and his past business association may prevent the developer from beginning a partnership which would later prove disastrous. The developer after expending a tremendous amount of time does not need to realize that he has inexperienced investors or investors who are not capable of the financial requirements.

PROFESSIONAL RAISING OF EQUITY

Unless your company has established working relationships with equity sources, this aspect of the financial need will require assistance of professionals. Options which are available in the marketplace include wholesalers, brokers, or underwriters. The developer should identify these professionals during the acquisition process in much the same way that other team members are selected based on their qualifications and experience. These professionals work on a "best effort" basis, making no guarantee that all of the funds will be raised. As a caution, the developer should also identify other sources. Wholesalers will coordinate the fund raising for a fee. He will either market the deal to individual money raisers or to a group of these money raisers who have a stable of retail clients. The Underwriter is an individual or corporation who represent a group of clients who are searching for quality real estate investments.

HOW TO SELECT POTENTIAL INVESTORS

In the search for potential investors, the developer can make the best choice by considering the following:

- Investor interest in this type of property
- Investor interest in location of the property

If the response to the first two issues is positive, the developer should then narrow down the list.

- Passive or active investors
- Typical holding period
- Investing motivation
    Capital appreciation
    Cash flow
    Tax benefits

- Required projected rates of return by investors
    Cash flow
    Tax losses
    Internal rate of return
- Profit and tax benefit splits desired
    Cash flow
    Tax losses
    Refinancing proceeds
    Resale proceeds
- Allocation of preferred proceeds among investors
- Payment of fees
    Development fees
    Property management fees
    Partnership management fees
    Leasing fees
    Refinancing fees
    Resale brokerage fees
- Magnitude of money raiser fees
- Money raiser participation
    If the money raiser will stay in the deal, will it be an active or passive role?
- Passive or active investor group
- Form of investment vehicle
    Corporation
    Subchapter S
    General partnership
    Limited partnership
    Joint venture
    Tenants in common
    Joint tenancy with right of survivorship
- Equity by investor group (cash or finance)
    If the group finances the equity, over what period of time will they pay off the loan?

CHECKING OF REFERENCES

Obviously, it would be very foolish for investors to enter a business transaction with a developer without getting to know him better either personally or through previous business contacts. The developer should submit a complete set of references to the potential investment group. These references should include his track record in these type of transactions, past educational and business background, net worth, and personal and business references. This investor should be supplied with a complete investment package as discussed previously. The developer should require the same from the investors.

STRUCTURING THE EQUITY TRANSACTION

To structure a deal with equity investors, knowing that all have their uniqueness, it is important to consider the following issues.

- Types of ownership vehicle which is most advantageous for the transaction
- Fees, which will be paid to the developer, when he acts as a managing partner in this new ownership entity

There are many types of ownership vehicles. The investor's attorney and accountant should evaluate the alternatives and decide which vehicle is the most appropriate for this new association. The following are various aspects of a joint venture relationship which should be considered.

Establishing a Joint Venture

A joint venture is an ownership arrangement between the developer and another party. This party might be an experienced working partner or an inexperienced money partner. Once the business terms of this arrangement have been negotiated, the developer should prepare the final joint venture documents. The following are the main topics that should be negotiated between the developer and the joint venture partner.

Venture Purpose: This section should outline the purpose of the venture— that is, will the venture develop the property to hold or sell?

Percentages of Ownership: The section will define what percentage of the deal each partner will receive. Typically these deals are structured as 50 percent to each partner, but they can be allocated in any way which the partners desire.

Venturer Capital Contributions: This section will set the initial capital contribution made by each partner and how future capital contributions will be made.

Loan Guarantees: This section will define which party will personally endorse the construction and permanent loans.

Default in Capital Calls: This section will deal with the possibility that one party cannot honor their commitment to fund a capital call when due.

Defaulting Venturer's Loss of Rights: This section will define the loss of rights by the defaulting party.

Timing of Distributions: This section will outline when distributions will be made to the partners.

Management of Venture: This section will outline responsibilities of the partners for daily management decisions.

Compensation for Services: This section will list the various fees paid to the partners and define the scope of their services.

Duration of Venture: This section will define how long the venture will last.

Termination of Venture: This section will outline under what circumstances the venture can and will be terminated.

Buy/Sell Agreement: This section will outline action to take in case one or both parties to the venture want to buy the other party's interest.

Bookkeeping of Venture Records: This section will define who will handle the daily accounting of the venture and how this accounting should be reported for income tax purposes.

Tax Allocation: This section will deal with how the tax allocations will be allocated to each partner.

PARTNERSHIPS

Partnerships are comprised of general and limited partnerships. The main benefit to limited partnerships, as opposed to a corporation is that they avoid double taxation of profits. Limited partnerships per federal tax provisions were created to encourage oil exploration. They pay no income tax, but instead, all bottom line profits are distributed to the limited partners who file the tax individually. In addition to profits, all tax advantages are passed on to the investors. The following are definitions of players in limited partnerships.

General Partners

The person or group which manage a limited partnership's day-to-day affairs. Within the limited partnership relationships, the general partner has the greatest liability and is paid by fee for this responsibility.

Limited Partnerships

Limited partnerships have become very popular over the past 15 years because they enable investors to pool their funds to purchase larger and more sophisticated properties than they could have acquired individually. Unless the partnership agreement states otherwise, the limited partners are only liable for their contribution. The following are two types of offerings.

Private Placement Limited Partnerships

These can have no more than 35 investors. They are not registered with the Securities and Exchange Commission (SEC) or state security administrations. These partnerships are designed to have a limited number of investors who meet certain knowledge, net worth, and liquidity requirements.

Interstate Offerings: Interstate offerings are deals which may be sold to investors in any of the 50 states. It does not matter in which state the property is located or where the managing general partner is based. Each investor has to meet certain suitability requirements to invest.

Intrastate Offerings: Intrastate offerings are deals that are only sold to a specified number of investors who reside in the same state in which the managing general partner and the property are located.

Public Limited Partnerships

These must be registered in the states where they are sold as well as with the SEC. These can be offered to an unlimited number of investors. They are not publicly traded and like private limited partnerships, they have limited liquidity.

Master Limited Partnerships

These partnerships are registered with state agencies and with the SEC. They are traded securities and listed with an exchange and can be offered to an unlimited number of investors.

CHECKLIST FOR ESTABLISHING A LIMITED PARTNERSHIP

Step 1: The Preparation of the Memorandum

In preparing the memorandum, the managing partner, or in our case the developer, should hire an attorney which specializes in not only real estate law but in security law as well. This is because in the act of raising cash for the transaction, the managing partner is not selling real estate, but is selling a security. Because a security is being sold, a whole new group of rules and regulations imposed by the government must be followed.

Limited Partnership Memorandum

1. Cover page including the name of the partnership, the size of the offering, the number of units to be sold, and other information
2. Qualifications of investors
3. Offering description and summary

4. Risk description
5. Capitalization
6. Use of proceeds
7. Plan of offering
8. Cash flow distribution
9. Property Description
10. Property Acquisition
11. General partner compensation
12. General partner's credentials and net worth statements
13. General partner's previous offerings
14. General partner fiduciary responsibilities
15. General partner's conflict of interest
16. Land purchase agreement
17. Development agreement
18. Property management agreement
19. Federal tax consequences
20. State and local taxes
21. Transfer of partnership interest restrictions
22. Limited partnership agreement summary
23. Current general partner litigation
24. Definition of terms
25. Partnership balance sheet
26. Accounting forecasts
    A. Cash flow forecasts
    B. Taxable income (loss) forecasts
    C. Resale forecasts
27. Exhibits
    A. Amended and restricted certificate and agreement of limited partnership
    B. Prior performance of the general partner
    C. Draft of the tax opinion from the law firm

Outline of a Subscription Booklet

The following is an outline of what should be included in a Subscription Booklet:

1. Subscription instructions
2. Investor questionnaire
3. Representative questionnaire

4. Copy of the amendment and restated certificate and agreement of limited partnership
5. Subscription agreement
6. Promissory note
7. Financial statement
8. Banking references
9. Indemnity agreement

Step 2: Evaluation of the Selling Agreement

The selling agreement is the agreement between the managing general partner and the underwriter that defines the duties of the parties as well as the fee structure to be paid to the selling group.

Step 3: Creation of the Offering Brochure

To help expedite the marketing program, the managing partner should prepare a simple, one-to-four page brochure that includes the facts on the proposed offering. This circular should include the following information:

- Picture or rendering of the property
- Purchase price and terms of the deal
- Financing
- Use of proceeds
- Description of the property
- Location map
- Rental schedule and unit mix
- Financial schedules
    Cash flow projections
    Taxable income (loss) projections
    Resale projections
- The unique advantages of this investment
- Marketing contact/telephone number

Step 4: Blue Sky Law Compliance

Each of the 50 states has different rules and regulations governing the sale of real estate securities. Once all of the home states of the potential investors have been determined, the securities attorney should then apply to these states for blue sky clearance. Each state has different requirements and a different fee structure. An official offer cannot be made to any investor until blue sky clearance has been obtained in his state.

Step 5: Securities Marketing

Since the selling of a limited partnership is a security it is highly regulated by governmental agencies. Care should be taken that all rules and regulations are followed to the letter. Noncompliance with these regulations can cause future problems, potential litigation with investors, and other serious consequences, such as fines or jail sentences. You should be certain that you are not misrepresenting or omitting any material facts in the transaction. To market these securities, do the following:

1. Identify the potential investors
2. Confirm that investors meet deal suitability requirements
3. Inform the investors of the benefits of the deal
4. Acquaint the investors with this type of ownership vehicle
5. Review the track record of the general partner with the potential investor
6. Close the deal

The following methods could be used to identify potential investors:

- Seminars on the benefits of real estate ownership
- Advertising
- Researching the state records for investors who have invested in other partnerships
- Contacting attorneys, accountants, bankers, or insurance agents who have clients looking for real estate investments
- Contact broker/dealers or financial planners

Step 6: Review the Investor Subscription Package

As the units are sold, each investor should send in the copy of the subscription booklet and a check for the unit purchased. The managing general partner should carefully review the subscription booklet to make sure that all the information requested is completed and that the investor meets the suitability requirements of the transaction. If any of this information is not correct, the managing general partner should notify the investor to correct the information or notify the investor that he does not meet the suitability requirements. After a careful review of this package, the managing general partner should sign off on the various documents in this package.

Step 7: The Escrow Account: Setting It Up

Prior to any investor contributions being collected, the managing general partner should establish an escrow account with a local bank. The bank should have a set of instructions as to how and when to break escrow and to distribute these collected funds.

As these funds are collected, the managing general partner should compile a list with the names of the investors and the monies collected. Once this transaction is completely subscribed, the managing general partner should contact the bank to disburse the collected funds.

HOW TO TERMINATE A PARTNERSHIP

Everything around us is in a constant state of flux. Investor needs and desires change. Therefore, it is imperative that any partnerships that are formed not only have detailed agreements for their management, but also have detailed agreements for their dissolution. One partner can buy the other's interests, or the partnership can be sold if possible. These agreements should consider the death, default, bankruptcy, or incompetence of the managing partner.

Another way to change the ownership structure without a termination is called a "cram down." This usually occurs when the members of a joint venture fail to perform as agreed. As one partner makes additional contributions, the other loses a proportional share of his ownership and their ownership is crammed down.

RESPONSIBILITIES OF PARTNERS

Managing General Partner (The Developer)

The managing general partner (managing partner) is the individual or entity who controls and oversees the daily operations of the property, as well as the partnership's affairs. If there are a number of general partners, one individual might be appointed managing partner.

Special Limited Partner

The special limited partner is an individual or entity who is considered a limited partner, but has a different profit split from the other limited partners.

Limited Partner

Limited partners are those individuals or entities whose liabilities are limited only to their original contribution. An accredited investor is a limited partner who does not count as one of the 35 investors in an interstate offering. To qualify this investor must have a net worth of at least $1,000,000, or an annual income of at least $200,000, or must invest at least $150,000 in the offering. This investment

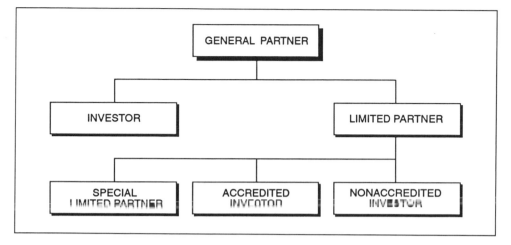

Figure 10-1 Limited partnership organizational chart.

should not be more than 20 percent of the investor's total net worth. Nonaccredited investors are the opposite of accredited. Figure 10-1 shows the organizational chart of a limited partnership.

FEES PAID TO THE DEVELOPER FOR SERVICES RENDERED

Obviously, for the responsibility of performing the managing partner duties, the developer deserves some type of compensation. There are many different types of fee revenues which can be received, the majority of which are defined below.

Syndication Fees

These fees are for services rendered for the new partnership for negotiating of the transaction, the placement of the financing, the guaranteeing of any leases or loans, and the setting up of the property and management accounting systems. The managing partners could take a small fee and a larger share of the deal. They may be a flat fee or a fee based on a percentage of the equity raised in the range of from 1 to 12 percent.

Property Management Fee

In some cases, the managing partner has his own management company and will charge a fee which is competitive with other management firms in the area. This fee is usually based on a percentage of the gross rental income of the property and ranges between 3 percent and 6 percent.

Partnership Management Fee

The managing partner or developer will usually charge a fee for the responsibility of managing the partnership accounting, tax preparation, and investor correspondence. This fee is usually a flat monthly fee or is based on a percentage of the collections from the property.

Leasing Commissions

Whether the developer or managing partner uses in-house staff or a local broker, a leasing commission fee will be required. This fee is usually based on a flat rate per tenant or a percentage of the total volume of the lease. This fee is usually competitive with the local market and ranges between 4 percent to 5 percent of the total lease value.

Refinancing Fee

If the existing debt on the property is refinanced during the ownership period, the managing partner may take a fee for this service. The managing partner would search for and negotiate a new loan when the current financing becomes due or when the timing is right to obtain a new loan with better terms and conditions. This fee can either be based on a flat rate or on a percentage of the new loan. Similar to the leasing commission, all or a portion of this fee may be paid to an outside mortgage broker. This fee will range between one-half to one percent of the new loan amount.

Sale Brokerage Fee

To execute a sale, the managing partner will have to search for a new buyer, formulate the structure of the transaction, and supervise the communication between attorneys, accountants, and the investment group to close the transaction. The fee for this service is in the range of 1 to 5 percent or can be a set flat fee at closing.

Mortgage Servicing Fee

If the sale includes any financing which is taken back by the partnership, the managing partner will have to service this loan for the remaining time period. When these payments are received, the managing partner must deposit these funds in a bank and then disburse them to the investment group as they are received. A fee may be charged to the partnership for this service. This fee can be either a set monthly fee with an escalation over time or a percentage of the dollars collected.

PROFIT AND TAX LOSSES: STRUCTURING THE BENEFITS

When investors invest in real estate, they carefully analyze their rate of return on equity relative to cash flows and residuals received. In addition, due to depreciation and various types of tax losses, these rates of return can be enhanced. Usually, the investor with the greatest investment will receive a preferred return with subsequent remaining funds split between the other partners. These splits can be established in any number of ways. They can be equal or not. In addition, many partnerships are structured on a sliding scale with changes in ownership percentages occurring at the time various key objectives in construction, lease up, or operations are met. The following will discuss the various types of benefits which the partners can receive.

Cash Flow

Cash flows result essentially from the difference between the gross rent, expenses, debt service, and taxes. This cash flow must be distributed to the various partners. Depending on the partnership agreements, this cash flow can flow to one on a preferred basis or can be divided equally. A common arrangement at this point divides this cash flow by allocating 75 percent to the investment partners and 25 percent to the managing partner or developer.

Tax Benefits

The source of these tax benefits is the depreciation taken on the existing assets. The 1986 tax revision will only allow the passive investor to offset the income generated by the property from operations and sale, although upon sale of a property, any unused losses from the property may be used against other income. Due to this factor, investors will place greater emphasis on the economics of the transaction than on the tax benefits received. These tax benefits should be looked upon as the extras in the transaction which have future benefits.

Refinancing Proceeds

When refinancing property, funds can be generated by increased cash flow or from the difference between the existing and new mortgages, which may result in tax-free dollars. The developer, or investors can use these funds to up-grade finishes and systems, fund capital accounts, or for distribution. Investor's original capital shall be returned first with the remainder split between the partners.

Sale Proceeds

After sale, former partnership transactions are normally terminated. At termination, the investor receives the amounts of their original investment remaining plus any funds due per their preferred cash flow agreement. The balance is then split between the developer and the investors. In determining these splits, the developer and the investment group or joint venture partner should negotiate a deal which meets the needs and desires of each party. The equity side of the deal should remember that the developer makes his living from real estate and he should have a vested interest in the deal, as well as a future incentive for good management.

## Chapter 11

The Construction Process

Nowhere in the total development process is the real estate developer more exposed for such a magnitude of liability than during the construction of the project. Even if the developer has labored diligently in selecting the site, in choosing and managing the architect, and in securing financing, the whole structure of the deal can become unraveled if during the construction process, the management of time and resources (budgets and schedules) is faulty. The developer must select a construction team that is seasoned, knowledgeable, creative, diligent, experienced, and careful in all that they do. The following is a list of reasons why developments suffer because of a poor construction process.

- Problems due to casualty, delays, or even problems with unions and governmental agencies, give the community a negative perception of the development and the developer.

- Cost overruns on the construction side of the equation can affect marketing by reducing the contingencies available for negative cash flows during the lease-up period.

- Schedule overruns can prevent tenant construction and delays for which penalties in space leases may be enormous.

- Poor workmanship in systems and finishes can haunt a development for years and cause additional expenditures.

- Litigation from actions due to construction can consume time and resources.

- Wasted time will be expended in selecting another contractor. This time could be used in marketing and "deal making."
- The confidence of lenders in your ability as a developer can be lost preventing financing of further transactions.
- Your project can be fined or "shut down" due to failure to comply with codes and ordinances.
- In general, your business life can become miserable.

This chapter will provide information concerning the overall role of the contractor, his selection, strategies in the construction process, agreements and negotiations, insurance, and management. A knowledge of these issues, along with the selection of an outstanding construction project manager for your team will give the developer a foundation for avoiding the pitfalls he may encounter.

THE ROLE OF THE GENERAL CONTRACTOR

When the developer does not have the in-house staff to construct the development, he should hire a general contractor to perform this service. The general contractor will be an asset to the development process because of his experience, his purchasing power for labor and materials, his organization, and ability to guarantee the construction costs. The contractor will become insurance to shield the developer from the liabilities of construction. The experienced contractor will know how to schedule work efforts, price effectively, and assemble and manage the construction team. In the development process, the general contractor will provide many types of services. The following will describe his different roles.

Predevelopment

The contractor's role in predevelopment is one of construction planner and estimator. He should be brought into the team at the same time as the architect. This will provide the developer with a complete design and construction team. Most contractors will provide this service prior to their selection, as long as the developer clearly states his intentions. The contractor will perceive this as an opportunity to know the project in more detail and to demonstrate his abilities and service. If a contractor is used in a construction management capacity, he will commonly require a fee for predevelopment. The following are key tasks which the developer can perform during predevelopment.

- Advise architects on the practical consequences of their decisions
- Prepare periodic cost evaluations and estimates for the overall budget and on various systems

- Recommend early purchase items in equipment and materials
- Advise on the prepackaging of bid documents for the awarding of separate construction contracts if once predevelopment has finished, the developer wishes to bid to confirm price
- Develop overall and detail schedules for the project

Deal Making, Financing, and Risk Containment

Often in the initial proposal for a deal, the contractor can be included on the team for his financial strength and particular product experience. The developer is usually not selected for his contractor, but the contractor's presence and experience only strengthen the developer's position. In addition, because of the contractor's contacts within the marketplace, the developer may find opportunities through contractor relationships.

Once the lender has decided to finance your development, he will require, prior to closing, that you have a negotiated construction contract with adequate pricing. The lender will be interested in your contractor's financial strength and experience to assure him that his investment is protected. He will also require various bonding and insurance to protect from loss during this process. This bonding and insurance will also provide risk containment for the developer and should be evaluated carefully.

Building and Lease-Up

Once mobilized, the contractor becomes the general officer who is responsible for all activities on the site. He will hire subcontractors of all types, assemble a staff, organize on-site offices, and coordinate with all local authorities for utilities and permits. He must consider rain delays and plan contingencies to overcome them. He must be prepared for material delays in shipping and must make sure that the project is built per the quality specified. Everything which goes under and within the physical product of the development will bear his mark. His failure will become the developer's challenge. The buyer of space, merchandise, rooms or units will be affected by the quality of his work. He will be responsible for the finishes and systems within the tenant's space and the tenant's perception of the development will be directly proportional to the comfort derived from the way in which all the pieces fit and function together.

Substantial Completion and Certificate of Occupancy

On or about the time of substantial completion of the project, the contractor will be responsible to the owner for providing various information for the developer's ongoing use and property management. In addition the contractor must ensure that all the work has been completed per construction documents. The following is a list of key items which must be addressed.

- Operating manuals giving operating instructions for various installed systems and their maintenance (normally provided in a bound notebook at completion)
- Warranties, which are normally included in the purchase of various equipment and systems (normally provided in a bound notebook at completion)
- Mechanical equipment—complete with flow arrows, tags and control schematics, chillers charged and operable, test and balance reports, and air handling units cleaned with permanent filters
- Electrical equipment—transformers and primary cables complete and signed off by utility companies, labeled panels, labeled circuiting, and all fixtures installed
- Fire safety equipment complete, tested and approved by local fire marshal
- All site work complete including sanitary and storm sewers, domestic water, site lighting, paving, and parking lot stripping.
- All quality assurance/quality control test inspections are complete and work approved—more on this subject is found later in this chapter
- Generally all surfaces cleaned and all debris removed

SELECTING THE GENERAL CONTRACTOR

In Chapter 6, in the section entitled Selecting the Team, we discussed evaluation procedures for the total predevelopment team. An abbreviated contractor's evaluation sheet was included. The purpose of that evaluation was for the selection of the contractor in the preliminary phases of the process. Once the development has reached a "go" status, the developer may wish to reconsider his decision, because of the importance of its magnitude. This section will focus solely on the contractor's selection in detail and be an addition to the information found in that chapter. This section will assume that the program for the development has been completed and is the backbone for the interview with the contractor. The following listings will provide data for formulating a custom evaluating procedure per the developer's unique program.

Representative or Relevant Project Data

The developer may require that the contractor provide data on specific projects. This listing will give an outline for the presentation of that data and should refer to representative projects exactly like the one which the developer intends to develop and relevant projects with characteristics similar to the new development.

Contractor name _____

Project type _____

Representative _____

General:

I. Location
   Personnel
      Project manager
      Job superintendent
   Description
      Size
      Construction type (structure, facade, systems, unique)
   Client
      Name:
      Contact:
      Phone:
   Architect
      Name:
      Contact:
      Phone:

II. Contract type
      Bid/negotiated
      Fee
      Savings split
      Liquidated damages/bonuses

III. Costs
      Original budget
      Original contract
      Change order costs
      Type of change orders
      Actual costs
      Savings overages
      Involved in feasibility/value engineer/results?

IV. Schedule
      Start date
      Projected completion date
      Completion date
      Schedule change orders extension

        Show schedules used on job

        Show schedule updates

        Schedule consultant

        Were there liquidated damages/bonuses collected

V. Quality

        Punch list (type and number of items)

        Major subcontractors

          Mechanical

          Electrical

          Forming/precast

          Glass and glazing

          Roofing

          Sitework

Evaluation Considerations

The strength of the contractor is measured by his liquidity, net worth and management team depth. These considerations are stressed in this section. The developer should look for the contractor's ability to function and perform. The following is an outline to use in developing questions for evaluation.

1. Financial information

    Financial statement required
    Differences between assets and liabilities
    Bonding company letter, bonding capacity?
    Dollar value of work logged against capacity
    Average value of work done yearly
    References from banking, accounting, insurance, and legal

2. Management Organization and Procedures

    Method of updating cost on projects . . . computer
    Any special or unique management systems
    Proposed project manager and resumes
    Key management resumes
    Size of company
    Time in business

3. Cost Control

    Method of estimating a job
    Keeping cost records and updating
    Representative invoicing procedures
    Project manager and superintendent involvement in cost control
    Systems for approving and paying invoices

4. Schedule control

   Experience with other schedule consultants
   Scheduling of jobs . . . systems and methods
   Updating of schedules
   Job schedule meetings procedures
   Collecting of liquidated damages

5. Quality control

   Location of projects presently under construction
   Project manager
   Superintendent
   Punch list copy

6. Contracts (subcontract, fees, percentage bid versus negotiated, any collect liquidated damages)

   Percentage of work bid or negotiated
   Fee on negotiated work and percent of overhead versus profit
   Fee on change orders
   Percentage fee on bid work, on change orders
   Items of overhead included?
   Types of subcontracts—bid or negotiated
   Supply typical owner/contractor contract

7. Development team involvement

   Familiarity with square footage cost of building systems
   Full disclosure of cost on estimate
   Involvement in development teams reasoning
   Feasibility involvement without fee
   Percentage of total work started in predevelopment

8. Project review

   Location of most representative project under construction
   Knowledge of MEP and structural systems
   Type contracts
   Punch list copy and projected completion
   Percentage of total work completed for private developers
   Percentage of total work completed for the government
   Percentage of total work industrial
   Percentage of total work commercial
   Percentage work load, projects and their dollar value

Numerical Evaluation System

When evaluating a number of contractors with such a complexity of data, other than an intuitive approach, a grading or evaluation system is recommended. The following is an example of one possible system. Because the weighing numbers total 100, the rating can be any grouping of numbers as long as they are consistent for all contractors being evaluated.

Evaluation System					
Contractor Name _____					
Considerations	Weight	×	Rating	=	Score
Financial stability	.15	×			
Management organization/procedures	.05	×			
Cost control	.10	×			
Schedule control	.10	×			
Quality control	.10	×			
Development team ability	.05	×			
Representative experience	.25	×			
Relevant experience	.20	×			

Data Checklist

The following has been developed as a checklist not only for the contractor to be interviewed but for the developer to schedule and collect all pertinent data for the process. Details for each section can be found on the previous pages.

Contractor Name _____

I.   AIA document: Contractor's qualifications statement
II. Firm brochure
III. Representative projects packages
     General information
     Photographs
     Construction schedules . . . projected versus actual
     Construction costs . . . projected versus actual
     Change orders
     Punch lists
     Type contract
IV. Relevant projects
     (same information as item no. III)
V.   Management structure and procedures
VI. Project manager and superintendent resumes
     (interview required)
VII. Financial status information

VIII. Major subcontractor recommendations
IX.   Fee structure

CONSTRUCTION STRATEGIES

In addition to selecting the contractor, the developer must decide on the type of relationship wanted. Depending on the project type, the developer's staff, and the nature and location of the work to be completed, the developer has a number of choices from which to choose. It is recommended that the matter be considered carefully with both the architect and contractor prior to beginning work. The following will review various methods which can be used (see Figure 11–1).

Design-Build

This method, also known as the "turnkey contract," gives the contractor total responsibility for the design and construction of the project. Using this method, the developer benefits by relating to only one entity and the contractor has total control of the work created by the designers. The major disadvantage is that the developer is totally dependent on the financial stability, management controls, and operating effectiveness of this contractor for all phases of design and construction.

General Contractor

This method is the most traditional method used by developers. The difference between design-build and this method is that the design functions are performed by others. As a general rule, the contractor awards subcontracts to other contractors for the accomplishment of the work. The general contractor becomes the clearinghouse for many other contractor's work. He negotiates all the contractors and manages all billing and invoicing.

Few Primes

In this method, the developer contracts with more than one prime (general) contractor. There can be one contractor designated as the general contractor, but all the other contractors are not necessarily subcontracted to him. The developer will avoid paying the mark up on this other contractor's work but he must have more administrative and coordination time to manage the process.

Multiple Primes

This approach uses no dominant general contractor to handle the total construction job. The developer would act as the general contractor and then subcontract the many construction work tasks to individual subcontractors.

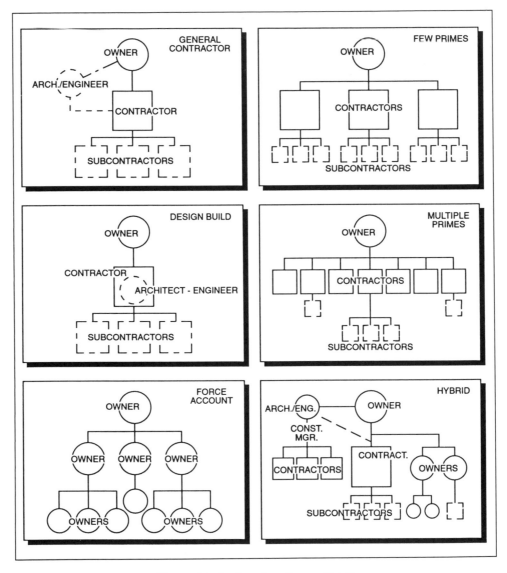

Figure 11–1 Construction methods.

Force Account

In the force account method, the developer not only performs the general contracting in house but also the design functions as well. The developer uses his own employees and construction equipment to handle the various construction work tasks.

Joint Venture

On projects of substantial magnitude, and because of some unique construction requirements, two or more contractors may joint venture mixing staff from each company. They, as one entity, will function as a general contractor.

CONTROLLING COSTS

There are different agreements which the developer can negotiate with the contractor for controlling costs. Each one has a unique process to follow. Consequently, the decision to follow one of these paths must be made early in the process. We will discuss the bid award system, the fast track guaranteed maximum—negotiated price and the cost plus contracts because they are most widely used.

Bid Award Contracts

The bid award process entails soliciting bids for the work from a selected contractor's list and awarding the job to the lowest bidder or the bidder which the developer believes has the most accurate costs. Along with each bid, the general contractors must provide a breakdown of their costs for review to insure that all items are included. Additionally, each bidder should include bank references and a letter from his bonding company stating their bonding capacity for the job. In this situation, construction documents by the designers and architects will be complete and ready for construction, and the bid will be based on the construction documents. If required, the architect may assist the developer in the process. It should be noted that before the developer receives these guaranteed costs which will be used in his project economics, he will have risk in his predevelopment budget for major design work prior to financing and be at risk for these expenditures should the project be "no go." If the developer uses this method of cost control, he will follow the following procedure.

1. Prepare a list of potential bidders
2. Finalize bidding package (including plans and specifications)
3. Review drawings and specifications

4. Prepare a draft request for proposal (RFP), which includes the instructions to the bidders, the bid proposal form, and the proposed contract documents
5. Review and approval of RFP
6. Approve the final bidder list
7. Finalize RFP and issue to the bidders
8. Conduct the pre-bid conference
9. Bidders prepare their bids
10. Receives and evaluates the bids
11. Reviews and make a preliminary recommendation
12. Developer conducts a pre-award meeting and negotiates the contract
13. Contract is awarded and construction agreement is drafted, approved, and signed
14. General contractor mobilizes for construction
15. Construction begins

Fast Track —Guaranteed Maximum —Negotiated Contract

This method of cost control was developed to allow the developer to obtain financing before major expenditures of predevelopment funds, and to save on interest costs by shortening the development process. Previously, the developer was at risk for construction documentation costs until the project was financed. Using this method, these costs were reduced along with the total time for completing the project. The contractor, based on pricing drawings produced by the architect and other designers, using his experience provides a guaranteed maximum/not to exceed price which the developer can use in his project economics. Armed with this price and the contractor's agreement, the developer can obtain financing. The design and construction team fast track the process by finishing designs, drawings, specification for long lead items first as schematics, then gradually adding the missing pieces until the total set of drawings is complete. The big difference with this process and the bid award process is that the building is 50 percent complete before the drawings are complete. In the bid award process all the drawings are complete before the contractor begins. Needless to say, this process requires mature and experienced contractors and architects working closely with a schedule consultant and a developer who has a bias for action in decision making.

Cost-Plus Contract

The contractor performs for a set fee regardless of how much the project finally costs, but he bills the developer for the costs plus this fee. When the bid-award or the fast track system is used, the contractor's overhead and fees are a percentage of the costs and if the project costs rise, so do the fees.

Lump-Sum Contract

A lump-sum contract includes a fixed price which is agreed upon by both parties. This price stays fixed for the term of the contract and is subject to changes only in cases of additional work required or certain specified unknown construction items, such as rock or poor soil conditions. This type of contract places the burden of risk on the contractor. Contractors will usually inflate their costs to include this additional risk factor.

Unit Pricing Contract

The unit pricing method is a variation of the lump-sum method. The lump-sum contract fixes the total price, whereas the unit price method will fix the price of specified items. The total contract is determined by multiplying the unit pricing by the quantity of items used. This method can be used effectively for tenant development work.

Lump-Sum with Escalation Contract

This method is used to eliminate any unwarranted price increases to cover contingencies in the general contractor's bid.

Fixed Price Incentive Contract

This method allows the fee portion of the price to be adjusted either upward or downward depending on certain factors which are controlled by the general contractor. This price adjustment is typically based on actual construction costs incurred by the general contractor during the work. The following factors are agreed upon by both parties:

- Target cost of the work
- Target fee for the work
- Target price (cost plus fee)
- Ceiling price that will limit the owner's responsibility for any cost overruns
- Formula for establishing the final general contractor's fee

Fixed Price Prospective Price Redetermination

This method fixes a price for a portion of the work, and makes provisions for a price redetermination for future work of the same type.

AGREEMENTS TO CONSTRUCT

The cost control methods previously discussed will be the basis for all agreements between the contractor and developer and will form the foundations for negotiations. The completeness of the drawings will always influence the adding or deletion of standard clauses. In addition, a very difficult site with many unknowns or a very complex building type with inherent liabilities will also create extensive negotiations. This section will include an outline of a standard contract and a listing of some key items which should be included in the developer's contract.

Scope of Work

The scope of work will describe the work which the general contractor will be performing, by referring to the plans and specifications.

Start Date of Construction

This section will specify how the notice to proceed with construction will be given.

Construction Scheduling

This section will outline the schedule which will be followed during construction.

Construction Completion Date

This section will specify the time when construction must be complete.

Rain Days Extension

This section will specify the definition of a "rain day" and how construction duration may be altered.

Bonus and Penalty Fee Clause

This clause determines the bonus and penalty. The formula for these items will be based on scheduling of construction. Since the interest charges increase the longer it takes to build the project, the general contractor should pay a penalty for not performing per the agreed upon time schedule. On the other hand, if the general contractor delivers the project early he should share in the reduction of the interest costs. This fee is usually based on the daily interest costs for the development.

Cost Saving Split

Depending on the type of contract which was negotiated, a savings in any construction costs may be split between both parties.

Change Orders

This section will detail the procedures to be used for any change orders required.

Guarantees

This section will state exactly what guarantees the general contractor is making.

Draw Schedule

This section will specify the procedures for draw requests.

Reserve

This section will outline the composition of the construction reserve and when it will be released to the general contractor.

Lien Waivers

This section will detail which lien waivers will be required by the general contractor from the subcontractors and material suppliers prior to funding draw requests

Backcharges

During the course of the construction project, it may be necessary for the developer to contract for certain work operations performed by others. In these instances, the developer will backcharge the general contractor for the cost of this work.

Punch Out

This section will define the procedure for the final punch-out of the property. A specified time period will be agreed upon to complete these punch out items. If after this time period expires and the work is not complete, the developer should be able to have this work completed by others and then reduce the contractor's reserve (or sometimes called retainage).

Warranty

This section will define the warranties of construction which the general contractor will give to the developer.

Broom Clean Condition

This section will define how the project is turned over to the developer.

Staging of Phases

If the development consists of more than one development phase, the contract should spell out the construction timing of each phase.

Arbitration or Litigation Clause

The contract should include a clause which sets procedures for disputes between both parties.

Construction Contract Outline

The following will give the developer insight concerning the overall issues addressed in the construction contracts.

    Article 1—The Contract Documents
    Article 2—Work
    Article 3—The Contractor's Duties and Status
    Article 4—Time of Commencement and Substantial Completion
    Article 5—Cost of the Work and Guaranteed Maximum Cost
    Article 6—Contractor's Fee
    Article 7—Changes in the Work
    Article 8—Costs to be Reimbursed
    Article 9—Cost Not to be Reimbursed
    Article 10—Discounts, Rebates, and Refunds
    Article 11—Subcontracts, Purchase Orders, and Other Agreements
    Article 12—Accounting, Cost Control, and Records
    Article 13—Applications for Payment
    Article 14—Payments to the Contractor
    Article 15—Stored Materials
    Article 16—Insurance

Article 17—Notices

Article 18—Assignment, Governing Law, and Subordination

Article 19—Termination

Article 20—Indemnification

Article 21—Miscellaneous Provisions

Exhibits:
  Listing of all drawings, specifications and revisions
  Alternatives, clarifications, and exclusions
  Clarifications and qualifications
  Exclusions
  Allowances
  Tenant work allowance cost breakdown
  Construction cost analysis
  General conditions (AIA Document A201)
  Copy of construction schedule
  Typical equipment rental schedule
  Copy of AIA G702 application and certification for payment
  Daily report format
  Form for inventory of stored materials
  Insurance requirements
  Legal description
  Definition of substantial completion
  Subcontractor (or vendor's) consent
  Subcontractor's subordination agreement
  Contractor's affidavit regarding subcontractors and vendors
  Subordination agreement
  Letter of guaranty
  Consent of general contractor
  Equal opportunity clause
  Equal opportunity clause (handicapped workers)

INSURANCE AND RISK CONTAINMENT

The developer should establish a risk containment program to minimize risk because of the unexpected. He should seek counsel with professionals within the insurance industry to consider the various risks that may be encountered during construction and property management of the development. The following lists possible risks and containment measures that can be used. Since this is a section on construction, we will address the contractor's insurance in detail.

Risks and Exposure Identification (Form 11–8)

Natural types
- Abnormal weather
- Earthquake and earth movement
- Flood and tidal wave
- Meteorites and unexplained phenomenon
- Fire, collapse, etc.

Utilities, Government, and Quasi Government
- War, nuclear explosion
- Civil commotion, riots
- Failure to deliver
    Traffic access
    Water and sewer
    Electricity, gas, and telephone
    Certificates of occupancy

Design
- Errors and omissions
- Documentation release delays
- Architect's financial failure

Construction
- Financial failure of general contractor or subcontractor
- Performance failure of general contractor or subcontractor
- Labor disputes

Damage Containment

The following insurance may be provided to protect the developer for the above-referenced loss.

- Bodily injury
- Physical damage
    Abnormal weather
    Earthquake and earth movement
    Flood and tidal wave
    Meteorites and unexplained phenomena
    Fire, collapse, etc.
    Civil commotion, riot
    War, nuclear explosion

- Consequential damage
    Additional construction interest
    Additional construction cost or demolition of ruined structure
    Loss of cash flow at 95 percent occupancy
    Loss of tenants
    Tenant furnishings storage charges
    Tenant's loss due to late occupancy
    Loss of permanent financing
    Failure to deliver access and utilities
    General contractor's performance and financial failure
    Labor disputes
    Physical damages consequences
- Architect's error's and omissions

Contractor's Insurance

The following is a listing of the various types of insurance which the contractor may carry at the developer's request to protect the project from loss. In addition, some of the reasoning behind the coverage will be discussed.

Liability Insurance

Workman's Compensation

  This type of insurance protects employers from claims arising from injuries sustained by employees in the course of employment

Comprehensive General (Public) Liability

  This type of insurance protects against legal liability from the public.

Property Insurance

Standard Builder's Risk

  Builder's risk insurance protects against physical damage to the insured property during the construction period which results from any of the perils named in the policy. This coverage provides reimbursement based on the actual loss or damage, rather than any legal liability which may have occurred. There are four methods used to establish the proper amount of coverage and to determine the policy premium.

  Completed Value: This method is based on the assumption that the project's value increases at a constant rate during the course of construction. When the policy is written for the value of the completed project, the premium is based on a reduced or average value. The dollar coverage is the actual value of the completed work and stored materials at any given time. This type of insurance must be taken out at the start of the construction. It is recommended that this method be used for most projects.

Reporting Basis: This method requires that the general contractor periodically notify the insurance carrier during construction of the increase in the value of the project. The coverage and premiums are based on this reported value. This method is most advantageous when the completed value is low during most of the project, but increases rapidly toward the end. Failure to report an increase in value may result in a lack of proper coverage.

Automatic Builder's Risk: This method gives the general contractor temporary protection automatically, pending the issuance of a specific policy for each project.

Ordinary Builder's Risk: This seldom used type of policy is written for a fixed value. The coverage may be increased by endorsement at the request of the insured.

Miscellaneous Insurance

Fire and Explosion Legal Liability

This type of insurance protects against legal liability from damage caused to property of others (building or contents) which is owned, rented, or under the contractor's control, and which is excluded from the regular liability policy.

Water Legal Liability

This insurance protects against legal liability from claims due to water damage to other's property from the use or escape of water on property owned, rented, or under the contractor's control.

Multi-Peril Crime

This coverage is available through several types of policies designated as "crime" policies.

Types of Bonds

Surety Bonds

If the bonded contractor fails to complete the job, the surety of a completion bond will step in and guaranty satisfactory completion.

Bid or Proposal Bonds

These bonds guarantee that when the contract is awarded the contractor will execute the contract documents and will furnish the required performance and payment bonds, if requested.

Performance Bonds

These bonds provide for the performance of the agreement by the general contractor and payment by the Surety of the developer's loss up to the bond penalty if the general contractor defaults.

Labor and Material Payment Bonds

These bonds provide that the vendors providing labor and materials for the project shall be promptly paid.

Maintenance Bonds

These bonds protect the developer, usually for a period of 12 months, against defects in workmanship and materials.

Special Indemnity Bonds

In some cases, a special indemnification is required against injury to persons or property.

Release of Lien Bonds

These bonds are given to obtain payment from the developer when a mechanic's lien or other lien is placed against the property or on the unpaid contract price. This bond assures the developer that he will not suffer loss or damage from the lien claim.

Letters of Credit

Sometimes, letters of credit supplied by the general contractor's bank will replace a performance bond. Be sure that the letter of credit is not issued by the construction lender. If the general contractor defaults under the terms and conditions of the contract, the developer can call the letter of credit and use it to finish the project.

CONSTRUCTION MANAGEMENT PROCESS

In Chapter 6, we discussed the managing of the process from the developer's point of view during the predevelopment period using his staff or consultants to coordinate and initiate action from the total team, including the contractor. Because of the myriad of work tasks of the contractor and the size of his staff, it is imperative that he have a well-organized team with systems for controlling ordering, deliveries, storage, installation, safety, and expenditures. This section will focus on the management of the contractor's team.

Preconstruction Meeting

Prior to the start of construction, the developer or his representatives should set up a meeting with all the team members involved in the construction of the project.

This meeting will establish team interaction procedures to follow. The following is an outline of an agenda which lists issues to consider.

I.   Construction coordination
    A. Participants
    B. Time required for the conference
    C. Topics of discussion
    D. Minutes of the meeting
II. Identification of key personnel
    A. Names and 24-hour telephone numbers
    B. Define authority and responsibility
    C. Designate sole contact for administration of contract
III. Authority and responsibility
    A. Methods of construction
    B. Rejection of work by inspector
    C. Stopping the work
    D. Safety on the site
    E. Authority of the inspector
IV. Conformance with the plans and specifications
    A. Call attention to areas of special concern
    B. Answer any contractor questions
V.   Contract administration
    A. Notice to proceed
    B. Time of the contract
    C. Liquidated damages
    D. Insurance requirements and bonds
    E. Record drawings (procedure, responsibility for)
    F. Mobilization (identify scope)
    G. Contractor submittal procedure
    H. Survey and staking
    I. Environmental requirements
    J. Change orders and extra work procedures
    K. Unforeseen underground condition procedures
    L. Coordination with utilities
    M. Progress payments and retainage procedures
    N. Closeout procedures
VI. Material and equipment
    A. Substitutions of "or equal" items
    B. Long lead prepurchase items

      C. Assignments of procurement contracts to general contractor

      D. Owner furnished materials or equipment

      E. Storage and protection

      F. Concealed shipping damage

      G. Payment for materials not yet used

  VII. Contractor's schedule

      A. Owner rights to approve

      B. Submittal requirements

      C. Owner can set milestones

 VIII. Change orders and extra work

      A. Who has the authority to issue

      B. The effect on time and cost

      C. Field order versus change orders

      D. Emergency changes

      E. Cumulative change orders

   IX. Subcontractors and suppliers

      A. Contractual relationship

      B. Submittal requirements

    X. Coordination with other agencies and contractors

      A. Interface requirements

      B. Testing and validation of systems

      C. Highway departments

      D. Code enforcement agencies

      E. Other regulatory agencies of government

   XI. Handling of disputes, protests, and claims

      A. Must exhaust all contractual means

      B. Resolution by the engineer

      C. Arbitration versus litigation

  XII. Labor requirements

      A. Davis-Bacon Act

      B. Documentation and audit requirements

      C. Federal, state, and local requirements

 XIII. Right-of-way and easements

      A. Permanent easements for the project

      B. Temporary easements for construction

      C. Dumping sites and storage areas

      D. Access to the site by heavy equipment

XIV. Owner protection
  A. Warranties and guarantees
  B. Bond protection during guarantee
  C. Security
  D. Extended maintenance of landscaping

XV. Punch list procedures
  A. Contractor certification of completion
  B. Punch list inspection procedures
  C. Final acceptance inspection
  D. Remaining punch list items

Contractor's Team and Responsibilities

The following chart (Figure 11–2) will illustrate all of the various personnel involved in the key management tasks within the contractor's organization. Obviously for smaller projects, the contractor will handle most of the tasks himself.

COST MONITORING

For the contractor and the developer to be aware of the exact status of project and construction costs, systems must be used which reveal the targeted budget, the costs to date, and expected costs to complete the work. In addition, in the normal process of construction, changes will occur due to desired or overlooked items. A new innovation which will make the development more competitive in the marketplace or a failure to specify particular items are examples of changes that can occur, which can negatively affect the development.

Obviously, the prudent developer will not give direction for modifications to the general contractor without being aware of costs or savings to date, the cost of the change and any time implications which will affect the construction schedule. This knowledge for effective decision making will not be available unless the developer has programmed the contractor to provide the data and the developer has developed systems for analysis of that data. The developer must direct the contractor to provide periodic reports of costs and savings. Armed with this information and the other needs of the project, the developer can plan strategy for the overall management of the project expenditures. For instance, if savings occur, the developer has the option of using these savings for the desired changes. The following series of forms is a "monitoring system" designed to assist the developer in making effective decisions. The "monitoring system" is comprised of a number of information gathering components.

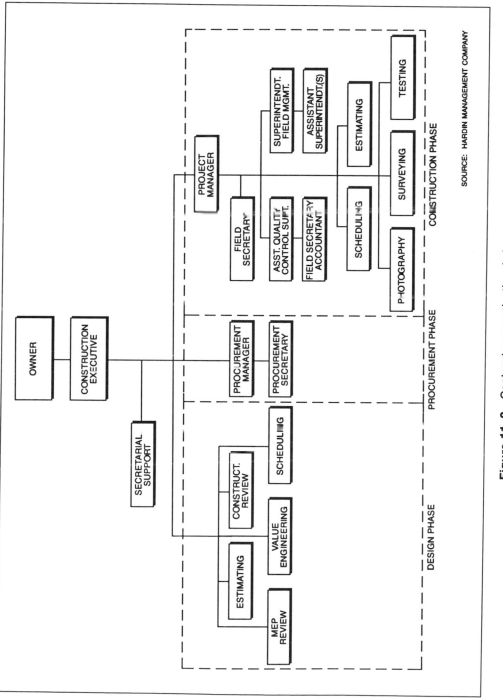

Figure 11–2 Contractor organizational chart.

SOURCE: HARDIN MANAGEMENT COMPANY

461

Schedule Summary

This component will list the key contractual dates during the construction development sequence (see Form 11–1).

Commitment Dates Summary

From the detailed schedule for construction, all of the key dates for work activities should be listed sequentially by date with corresponding work tasks (see Form 11–2).

Unresolved Issues

From the normal process of design and construction, various alternatives, problems, and questions will arise. Until they are answered, they are unresolved. This sheet will provide an ongoing list of these items (see Form 11–3).

Cost Summary

From the project economics, the overall costs of the predevelopment, land, design, construction, and F, F & E costs will be known. This form will give the manager a "broad brush" look at how they change over time (see Form 11–4).

Design Costs

Due to additional services and savings realized in design proposals, the costs of the production of construction documents will change. This form will provide details to all consultants on the costs relative to billings and be backup for items in the cost summary (see Form 11–5).

Construction Costs

This will provide the same function as for the design cost, but for construction. The same can be used for all items mentioned in the cost summary (see Form 11–6).

Exposure Items

As items are listed as unresolved for decision making and before a decision can be made, they must be priced. If the item has a cost and is not included within the contractual price, then it is a potential exposure (see Form 11–7).

All of these forms can be kept in a notebook or logged into the manager's computer. After filling out the following forms during the predevelopment process, the project manager can revise them on a biweekly or monthly basis to have the most up-to-date set of criteria for decision making. The summary schedule will keep him ever aware of the key dates toward which the whole team is moving. If the contract is revised, then these dates should be revised. The commitment sheet will give the key dates on a daily or weekly basis of work which must begin or be completed. Obviously, if a certain aspect of the work did not begin in a timely manner, it will not be finished in a timely manner. Knowing this, the manager can initiate action for the team to get back on schedule. Unresolved issues keep the manager's focus on problems which must be resolved and allow the developer to know potential problems ahead of time. The Cost Sheets give a biweekly or monthly view of the progress of the work and give indications of problem areas. They also help in the decision making by revealing savings which can be spent elsewhere or contingency remaining. The exposure sheet will provide cost information which requires planning and for problems in the future or cost information for items which need decisions.

THE ART OF CONSTRUCTION SCHEDULING

In Chapter 6, the various types of schedules which can be used in the process were listed and those related to design and construction documentation were described in detail. This section will describe the detailed Foundations and Superstructure Schedule, the Detailed Construction Schedule, and the Near-Term (during construction) Schedules, which occur during construction.

Detailed Foundations, Superstructure, and Skin Schedule

Working closely with the contractor and the subcontractor, this schedule is developed with a summary of the most up to date design schedule. Commitments are made and the process is monitored on a biweekly basis. Figure 11–3 shows the detailed foundation and superstructure schedule.

Detailed Construction Schedule

Using activity information sheets produced by subcontractors, this schedule is developed using the chronologic system to illustrate the total work efforts to be monitored and completed per determined time sequences. This schedule can cover time periods from six months to three years depending upon the building type (see Figure 11–4).

Near-Term Scheduling During Construction

Once the detailed construction schedule for three years is complete, another method of scheduling is needed to monitor week to week activities. If in the biweekly meetings, an activity which is behind continues for three or four weeks without being addressed, the domino effect can be so substantial that the delay can multiply into months, greatly affecting the economics of the development. To

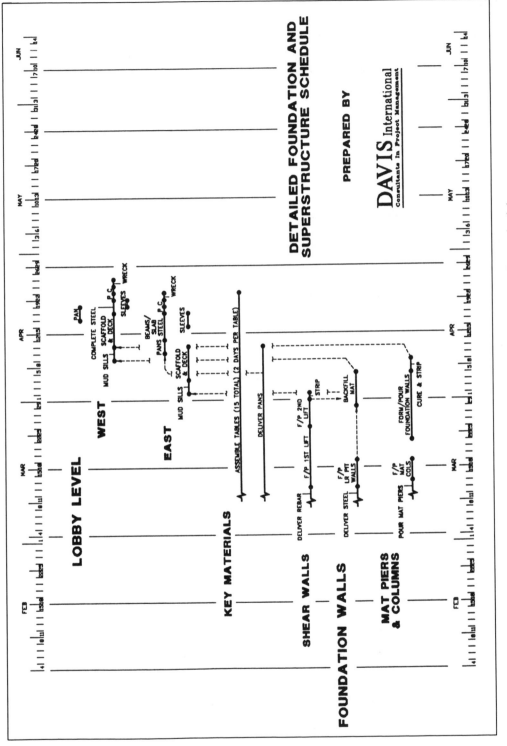

Figure 11-3 Detailed foundation and superstructure schedule.

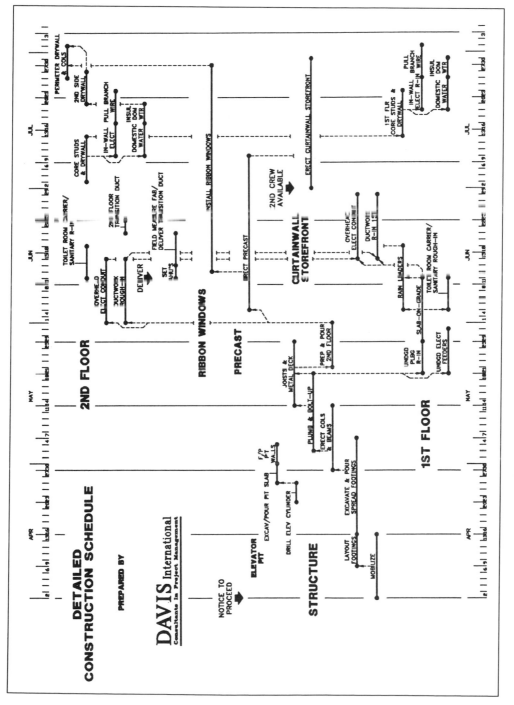

Figure 11-4 Detailed construction schedule.

465

prevent this, near-term scheduling (see Figure 11–5) has been developed as an alarm and preventive maintenance system. On a biweekly basis over a 90-day period, mini-schedules are developed for distribution so that the subcontractors can focus on these work tasks and their response in accomplishing these work tasks can be monitored. They are constantly changing and have proved useful for reporting the progress in the near term.

In summary, when scheduling, the contractor must develop a master listing of all of the work tasks necessary to build the project. He must take that list and organize it in terms of durations, priorities, similar work tasks, disciplines of work, normal construction procedures, and the ordering of materials. Then he must place that information on some device to illustrate the most efficient process for completing it. Graphs and diagrams, using either drawing or computed illustrations, are most commonly used. Then day by day and week by week, the contractor must use this schedule to monitor and report on the progress of the work. It should remind him of his successes and his failure to meet projected objectives and provide incentives to take action to bring delayed items back in line with the originally planned schedule.

In very complex projects, the developer or contractor may choose to use a scheduling consultant to manage the scheduling process. This consultant will gather data from the development team, provide schedules and reports, and give developers an impartial view of the status of the work.

QUALITY ASSURANCE—QUALITY CONTROL

To assure that the contractor is building the project as planned and those items which are covered over by construction will not become liabilities or issues for litigation in the future, the developer should establish a quality assurance/quality control program. Essentially, it is a "watch dog" program to reveal weaknesses within construction, promptly giving time for remedy. Its sophistication can vary from the project manager's observations, to the architect's and engineer's observations, to inspection and testing companies checking on compaction, welding, concrete settling, and reinforcing bar placement. Obviously, using all of the techniques will provide the very best program, but the developer must decide on that which is best for the development size and that which may be required by the lender. The following are various methods used in the management of the construction project.

- Developer's project manager constantly visiting and observing the installation of the various elements of the project. He should be knowledgeable of scheduling of work for involving property management personnel at key installations.

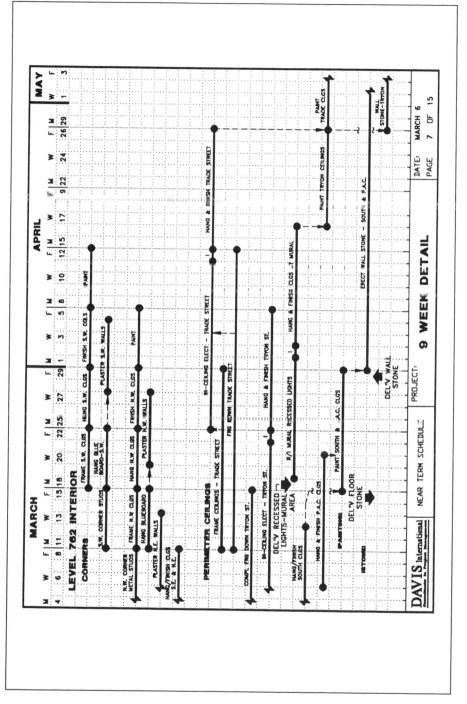

Figure 11-5 Near term schedules.

- The architects contractual agreement requires that the architect visit the site periodically in an inspection-only capacity. He or she will observe and provide the developer and contractor with items to be considered. When the contractor declares substantial completion, the architect will provide punch listing services and follow up after their completion.

- Quality assurance/quality control testing program can be accomplished by a number of testing and engineering services depending on the project's location and the services required. The following are the issues to be considered in proposals for these services.

  Sitework, paving, and earthwork

  Concrete

  Masonry

  Structural steel frame and other steel members

  Metals

  Roofing and roofing sheet metal

  Curtain walls, window framing

PROPOSALS FOR QUALITY ASSURANCE-QUALITY CONTROL PROGRAMS

When requesting proposals for quality assurance-quality control (QAQC) programs, the following checklist and description will prove helpful in concluding that all of the pertinent information for your QAQC program has been considered and is covered. The proposals, after a general description of the services, testing facilities, procedures, insurance coverage, and indemnities are addressed should refer to that particular aspect of the work, how it will be performed, and the cost for the quality control program. Usually, testing companies and geo-technical engineers provide this type of service.

Outline for Quality Assurance-Quality Control Proposals

    I.   General

        A. Professional services (observations, samplings, tests, verifications, inspections, and other technical services offered)

        B. Certifications of the technicians providing the service

    II.   Testing laboratory facilities

        A. National Bureau of Standards compliance in the handling of specimen and sampling storage as well as handling, curing, preparation, and testing)

III. Procedures
   A. Procedures in following the standards set by the American Society of Testing Materials
IV. Insurance
   A. Coverages
      1. Workman's Compensation
      2. Comprehensive general liability
      3. Professional liability (errors and omissions)
   B. Limits of coverages
   C. Carriers
   D. Cancellation
V. Indemnity
   A. Holding developer harmless for losses, damages, expenses, costs (including reasonable attorney's fees), claims, demands, injuries, deaths, or suits
VI. Equal opportunity
   A. Affirmative action
   B. Indemnity
VII. Services
VIII. Time for performance
IX. Reports
X. Project description
XI. Division two: Sitework, paving, and earthwork
   A. Systems and material review of materials, thickness, depth and construction process
      1. Sub-base preparation
      2. Base course
      3. Wearing surfaces
   B. Advising owner about the suitability or unsuitability of the material, thickness, depth or construction processes
   C. Fee for these services individually
XII. Division three: Concrete
   A. Material and Mix review
   B. Sampling and testing of concrete
   C. Concrete floor flatness
   D. Concrete reinforcement placing

     E. Precast concrete
       1. Mix design and review
       2. Reinforcement steel placing
       3. Spot measurements and surveys
     F. Fee for these services
XIII. Division four: Masonry
     A. Fee for these services
XIV. Division five: Metals
     A. Precast concrete connections
     B. Structural steel
     C. Steel decking
     E. Fee for these services
XV. Division seven: Moisture protection
     A. Sealants and caulking
       1. Visual inspections
       2. Joint construction
       3. Installation procedures
     B. Sprayed on fireproofing
       1. Inspections
     C. Waterproofing
       1. Inspections of systems
     D. Fee for these services
XVI. Division eight: Curtain walls and window framing
     A. Visual inspections of frames and glass
     B. Report format
     C. Certification of work
     D. Curtain wall connections
     E. Skylights
     F. Fee for these services

CONSTRUCTION PHASE INSIGHTS

The final two sections of this chapter will provide miscellaneous information about various issues heretofore not covered to complete the picture of the construction.

Obtaining the Necessary Development and Building Permits

Just prior to closing the construction loan, the general contractor will visit the local building department to obtain land disturbance, and or special development and building permits. These permits must be posted in a conspicuous place on the job site.

Mobilization

Once the notice to proceed with construction has been given, the general contractor will start mobilizing crews and equipment at the job site for commencing construction.

Construction Draws

As established by the contract, the general contractor will prepare his construction draw request. This request will then be sent to both the developer and the architect or the party who will be inspecting for the lender. Along with the construction draw request there will be copies of the required lien waivers.

Change Order Requests

Since most developments usually have construction changes, change orders will document the change with appropriate approvals. These changes can either be made by the general contractor or the developer, but if they change the contract amount or the intent of the contract documents, they must be approved by the developer and the architect.

Construction Management Progress Reports

On a periodic time basis, the construction manager will complete a progress report. This report along with the scheduling consultant's report should give the developer a total picture of the status of the project.

- Meeting minutes
- Executive summary
- Problems/recommendations
- Action item list
- Near term schedule
- Trend chart

- Key item procurement schedule-critical items
- Key item procurement schedule-full look ahead
- Pictures

Punching Out the Building

Once the construction project is declared complete, the developer must completely "punch out" the property. He will then direct his team along with the architect to inspect every square inch of the property for uncompleted and defective items. This list will then be submitted to the general contractor to complete within a specified time period.

Final Inspection

Once all of the work is completed, the general contractor will request that the lender's architect inspect the property and certify the job complete. Once this has been completed, the general contractor should be paid in full, unless the contract specified that certain reserve funds be reimbursed at a later date.

Final As-Built Survey

Along with this final inspection, an as-built survey should be completed and recorded with local governmental agencies.

Warranties Callback Period

Since there will undoubtedly be future warranty calls by the developer to the general contractor, a procedure should be established between the parties to respond to callbacks. Just prior to the expiration of the warranty callback period, the developer should conduct a complete inspection of the property. Other than unseen latent structure deficiencies, this will usually be the developer's last chance to have the general contractor repair problems.

Owner's Operation and Material Manual

Upon completion of the construction project, the general contractor should prepare an Owner's Operation and Material Manual. This manual will contain all the information for the developer to maintain the property. The following is an outline of this manual.

   I.   List of construction players: Company names, contacts, addresses, telephone numbers

    A. General contractor

    B. Subcontractors

        1. Foundations

        2. Framing

        3. Electrical

        4. Mechanical

        5. Plumbing

        6. Painting

        7. Exterior facade

        8. Roofing

        9. Elevator

        10. Windows

        11. Doors

        12. Window coverings

        13. Landscaping

        14. Paving

        15. Pool installation

II.   Mechanical information

    A. Manufacturer: Company name, contact, address, telephone number

    B. Warranty period

    C. Serial numbers

III.   Appliance information

    A. Manufacturer: Company name, contact, address, telephone number

    B. Warranty period

    C. Serial numbers

IV.   Lighting information

    A. Manufacturer: Company name, contact, address, telephone number

    B. Warranty period

    C. Model numbers

V.   Paint information

    A. Manufacturer: Company name, contact, address, telephone number

    B. Warranty period

    C. Color chart numbers

   VI.   Wall covering
       A. Manufacturer: Company name, contact, address, telephone number
       B. Warranty period
       C. Model numbers
  VII. Floor covering
       A. Manufacturer: Company name, contact, address, telephone number
       B. Warranty period
       C. Model numbers
 VIII. Window and door information
       A. Manufacturer: Company name, contact, address, telephone number
       B. Model numbers
   IX. Roofing information
       A. Manufacturer: Company name, contact, address, telephone number
       B. Warranty period
    X. Elevators and escalators
       A. Manufacturer: Company name, contact, address, telephone number
       B. Warranty period
       C. Model numbers
   XI. Operating manuals
       A. Mechanicals
       B. Elevators and escalators
       C. Appliances

CONSTRUCTION PHASE FORMS

Schedule Summary Form 11–1

This form will list the key contractual dates during the construction development sequence for monitoring.

SCHEDULE SUMMARY FORM

PROJECT _____   FORM 11–1
DATE ___/___/___

DESCRIPTION	DATE
SCHEDULED COMPLETION OF PRICING SCHEMATICS	___/___/___
SCHEDULED COMPLETION OF CONSTRUCTION DOCUMENTS	___/___/___
PROJECTED COMPLETION OF CONSTRUCTION DOCUMENTS	___/___/___
CONTRACTOR'S NOTICE TO PROCEED (PRE–CLOSING)	___/___/___
CONTRACTOR'S NOTICE TO PROCEED (CONSTRUCTION)	___/___/___
CONTRACTS DATE FOR SUBSTANTIAL COMPLETION	___/___/___
TARGETED DATE FOR SUBSTANTIAL COMPLETION WITH SLIPPAGE	___/___/___
RECOVERY PLAN DATE OF SUBSTANTIAL COMPLETION	___/___/___

DAYS LOST TO DELAYS/LOST DAYS
  WEATHER _____
  OTHER _____

POTENTIAL NEW CONTRACTORS COMPLETION DATE (ASSUMING LOST DAYS ARE ACCEPTED)	___/___/___

Form 11–1   Schedule summary form.

Commitment Dates Form 11-2

This form will be used to list all of the key dates for committed work activities for monitoring.

COMMITMENT DATES FORM

PROJECT _____   FORM 11-2

DATE ____/____/____

DESCRIPTION*	DATE
	___/___/___
	___/___/___
	___/___/___
	___/___/___
	___/___/___
	___/___/___
	___/___/___
	___/___/___
	___/___/___
	___/___/___
	___/___/___
	___/___/___
	___/___/___
	___/___/___
	___/___/___
	___/___/___
	___/___/___
	___/___/___
	___/___/___
	___/___/___
	___/___/___
	___/___/___
	___/___/___
	___/___/___
	___/___/___
	___/___/___
	___/___/___
	___/___/___
	___/___/___
	___/___/___
	___/___/___
	___/___/___
	___/___/___
	___/___/___

NOTE *:
THE DESCRIPTIONS ARE TAKEN OFF OF SCHEDULES SIMILAR TO THOSE
ILLUSTRATED IN FIGURES 6-8, 6-9, 6-10, 11-3, 11-4, AND 11-5

Form 11-2   Commitment dates form.

Unresolved Issues Form 11-3

This form will be used to provide a list of all unresolved issues to be addressed in construction management meetings. (Essentially a "thing to do" list).

UNRESOLVED ISSUES FORM

PROJECT _____   FORM 11-3

DATE ___/___/___

DESCRIPTION	DATE*
_____	___/___/___
_____	___/___/___
_____	___/___/___
_____	___/___/___
_____	___/___/___
_____	___/___/___
_____	___/___/___
_____	___/___/___
_____	___/___/___
_____	___/___/___
_____	___/___/___
_____	___/___/___
_____	___/___/___
_____	___/___/___
_____	___/___/___
_____	___/___/___
_____	___/___/___
_____	___/___/___
_____	___/___/___
_____	___/___/___
_____	___/___/___
_____	___/___/___
_____	___/___/___
_____	___/___/___
_____	___/___/___
_____	___/___/___
_____	___/___/___
_____	___/___/___
_____	___/___/___
_____	___/___/___
_____	___/___/___
_____	___/___/___
_____	___/___/___
_____	___/___/___

NOTE: *:
THE DATES ARE SHOWH TO INDICATE WHEN THE ISSUES MUST BE RESOLVED

Form 11-3 Unresolved issues form.

Summary Cost Form 11–4

This form will be used to compile up-to-date development "hard cost" and compare these costs to the original budgets.

COST SUMMARY FORM

PROJECT _____   FORM 11–4

DATE ___/___/___

DESCRIPTION	PROJECT DEVELOPMENT PLAN	REVISIONS	CURRENT	COMMITED	DIFFERENCE
PREDEVELOPMENT	$_____	$_____	$_____	$_____	$_____
LAND	$_____	$_____	$_____	$_____	$_____
DESIGN	$_____	$_____	$_____	$_____	$_____
CONSTRUCTION	$_____	$_____	$_____	$_____	$_____
F, F & E	$_____	$_____	$_____	$_____	$_____
TOTAL	$_____	$_____	$_____	$_____	$_____

ALLOWANCES:	ALLOCATED	ACTUAL	REMARKS
_____	$_____	$_____	_____
_____	$_____	$_____	_____
_____	$_____	$_____	_____
_____	$_____	$_____	_____
_____	$_____	$_____	_____
_____	$_____	$_____	_____
_____	$_____	$_____	_____
_____	$_____	$_____	_____
_____	$_____	$_____	_____
_____	$_____	$_____	_____
_____	$_____	$_____	_____
_____	$_____	$_____	_____
_____	$_____	$_____	_____
_____	$_____	$_____	_____
_____	$_____	$_____	_____
_____	$_____	$_____	_____
_____	$_____	$_____	_____
_____	$_____	$_____	_____
_____	$_____	$_____	_____
_____	$_____	$_____	_____
_____	$_____	$_____	_____
_____	$_____	$_____	_____
_____	$_____	$_____	_____
_____	$_____	$_____	_____
TOTAL	$_____	$_____	

Form 11–4   Summary costs form.

Design Costs Form 11-5

This form will be used to compile up-to-date design costs to be compared to the original budgets.

DESIGN COSTS FORM

PROJECT _____   FORM 11-5
DATE ___/___/___

DESCRIPTION	PROJECT DEVELOPMENT PLAN	REVISIONS	CURRENT	COMMITED	DIFFERENCE
ARCHITECT/ENGINEER	$_____	$_____	$_____	$_____	$_____
LANDSCAPE ARCHITECT	$_____	$_____	$_____	$_____	$_____
INTERIOR DESIGNER	$_____	$_____	$_____	$_____	$_____
CIVIL ENGINEER	$_____	$_____	$_____	$_____	$_____
SCHEDULING CONSULTANT	$_____	$_____	$_____	$_____	$_____
KITECHEN CONSULTANT	$_____	$_____	$_____	$_____	$_____
GRAPHICS CONSULTANT	$_____	$_____	$_____	$_____	$_____
SURVEYOR	$_____	$_____	$_____	$_____	$_____
GEO-TECHNICAL ENGINEER	$_____	$_____	$_____	$_____	$_____
ELEVATOR CONSULTANT	$_____	$_____	$_____	$_____	$_____
ENVIRONMENTAL CONSULTANT	$_____	$_____	$_____	$_____	$_____
ENERGY CONSULTANT	$_____	$_____	$_____	$_____	$_____
SKIN CONSULTANT	$_____	$_____	$_____	$_____	$_____
SECURITY CONSULTANT	$_____	$_____	$_____	$_____	$_____
_____	$_____	$_____	$_____	$_____	$_____
_____	$_____	$_____	$_____	$_____	$_____
_____	$_____	$_____	$_____	$_____	$_____
_____	$_____	$_____	$_____	$_____	$_____
_____	$_____	$_____	$_____	$_____	$_____
_____	$_____	$_____	$_____	$_____	$_____
_____	$_____	$_____	$_____	$_____	$_____
_____	$_____	$_____	$_____	$_____	$_____
_____	$_____	$_____	$_____	$_____	$_____
_____	$_____	$_____	$_____	$_____	$_____
_____	$_____	$_____	$_____	$_____	$_____
_____	$_____	$_____	$_____	$_____	$_____
_____	$_____	$_____	$_____	$_____	$_____
_____	$_____	$_____	$_____	$_____	$_____
_____	$_____	$_____	$_____	$_____	$_____
_____	$_____	$_____	$_____	$_____	$_____
_____	$_____	$_____	$_____	$_____	$_____
_____	$_____	$_____	$_____	$_____	$_____
_____	$_____	$_____	$_____	$_____	$_____
_____	$_____	$_____	$_____	$_____	$_____
_____	$_____	$_____	$_____	$_____	$_____
_____	$_____	$_____	$_____	$_____	$_____
_____	$_____	$_____	$_____	$_____	$_____
_____	$_____	$_____	$_____	$_____	$_____
TOTAL	$_____	$_____	$_____	$_____	$_____

Form 11-5   Design costs form.

Construction Costs Form 11–6

This form will be used to compile up-to-date allowance costs relative to the original budget.

CONSTRUCTION COSTS FORM

PROJECT _____   FORM 11–6

DATE ___/___/___

DESCRIPTION	PROJECT DEVELOPMENT PLAN	REVISIONS	CURRENT	COMMITED	DIFFERENCE
BUILDING SHELL	$_____	$_____	$_____	$_____	$_____
SITEWORK	$_____	$_____	$_____	$_____	$_____
LANDSCAPING	$_____	$_____	$_____	$_____	$_____
ADDITIONAL SCOPEWORK	$_____	$_____	$_____	$_____	$_____
ALLOWANCES (SPECIFIC)	$_____	$_____	$_____	$_____	$_____
1. _____	$_____	$_____	$_____	$_____	$_____
2. _____	$_____	$_____	$_____	$_____	$_____
3. _____	$_____	$_____	$_____	$_____	$_____
4. _____	$_____	$_____	$_____	$_____	$_____
5. _____	$_____	$_____	$_____	$_____	$_____
6. _____	$_____	$_____	$_____	$_____	$_____
7. _____	$_____	$_____	$_____	$_____	$_____
8. _____	$_____	$_____	$_____	$_____	$_____
9. _____	$_____	$_____	$_____	$_____	$_____
10. _____	$_____	$_____	$_____	$_____	$_____
_____	$_____	$_____	$_____	$_____	$_____
_____	$_____	$_____	$_____	$_____	$_____
_____	$_____	$_____	$_____	$_____	$_____
_____	$_____	$_____	$_____	$_____	$_____
MISCELLANEOUS	$_____	$_____	$_____	$_____	$_____
_____	$_____	$_____	$_____	$_____	$_____
_____	$_____	$_____	$_____	$_____	$_____
_____	$_____	$_____	$_____	$_____	$_____
_____	$_____	$_____	$_____	$_____	$_____
_____	$_____	$_____	$_____	$_____	$_____
_____	$_____	$_____	$_____	$_____	$_____
_____	$_____	$_____	$_____	$_____	$_____
_____	$_____	$_____	$_____	$_____	$_____
_____	$_____	$_____	$_____	$_____	$_____
_____	$_____	$_____	$_____	$_____	$_____
_____	$_____	$_____	$_____	$_____	$_____
_____	$_____	$_____	$_____	$_____	$_____
_____	$_____	$_____	$_____	$_____	$_____
_____	$_____	$_____	$_____	$_____	$_____
_____	$_____	$_____	$_____	$_____	$_____
_____	$_____	$_____	$_____	$_____	$_____
_____	$_____	$_____	$_____	$_____	$_____
_____	$_____	$_____	$_____	$_____	$_____
_____	$_____	$_____	$_____	$_____	$_____
TOTAL	$_____	$_____	$_____	$_____	$_____

Form 11–6 Construction costs form.

Exposure Items Form 11-7

This form will be used to compile the costs of any exposure items which occur unexpectedly.

EXPOSURE ITEMS FORM

PROJECT _____

DATE ___/___/___

FORM 11-7

DESCRIPTION*	COST	ALLOCATION/ SOURCE
	$_____	
	$_____	_____
	$_____	_____
	$_____	_____
	$_____	_____
	$_____	_____
	$_____	_____
	$_____	_____
	$_____	_____
	$_____	_____
	$_____	_____
	$_____	_____
	$_____	_____
	$_____	_____
	$_____	_____
	$_____	_____
	$_____	_____
	$_____	_____
	$_____	_____
	$_____	_____
	$_____	_____
	$_____	_____
	$_____	_____
	$_____	_____
	$_____	_____
	$_____	_____
	$_____	_____
	$_____	_____
	$_____	_____
	$_____	_____
TOTAL	$_____	

NOTE*:
TO IDENTIFY AND MONITOR THOSE COSTS, IDENTIFY WHICH ARE NOT INCLUDED
IN THE INITIAL CONTRACTOR COSTS AND MUST BE INCLUDED IN CHANGE ORDERS OR
TAKEN OUT OF THE ALLOWANCES

Form 11-7   Exposure items form.

Risk Identification-Damage Containment Form 11-8

This form is to be used to identify the risk for which insurance is needed.

RISK IDENTIFICATION – DAMAGE CONTAINMENT FORM

FORM 11-8

PROJECT _____
DATE ____/____/____

RISK IDENTIFICATION	BODILY INJURY	PHYSICAL DAMAGE	CONSEQUENCES	COMMENTS
Natural				
Abnormal Weather	_____	$_____	_____	_____
Earthquake	_____	$_____	_____	_____
Flood	_____	$_____	_____	_____
Phenomenon	_____	$_____	_____	_____
Fire	_____	$_____	_____	_____
Government				
War, Nuclear	_____	$_____	_____	_____
Civil	_____	$_____	_____	_____
Failure to Del.:	_____	$_____	_____	_____
(Traffic Access)	_____	$_____	_____	_____
(Water/Sewer)	_____	$_____	_____	_____
(Electric/Gas/Telephone)	_____	$_____	_____	_____
(Certif. of Occupancy)	_____	$_____	_____	_____
Design				
Errors & Ommissions	_____	$_____	_____	_____
Doc. Rel. Delay	_____	$_____	_____	_____
Arch. Fin. Failure	_____	$_____	_____	_____
Construction				
Fin. Failure	_____	$_____	_____	_____
Performance Failure	_____	$_____	_____	_____
Labor Disputes	_____	$_____	_____	_____
	_____	$_____	_____	_____
TOTAL		$_____		

COMMENTS

_____
_____
_____
_____
_____
_____
_____
_____
_____
_____

Form 11-8   Risk identification-damage containment form.

RISK IDENTIFICATION – DAMAGE CONTAINMENT FORM

FORM 11–8

PROJECT _____

DATE ____/____/____

RISK IDENTIFICATION	BODILY INJURY	PHYSICAL DAMAGE	CONSEQUENCES	COMMENTS
Physical Damage				
Weather	_____	$_____	_____	_____
Earthquake	_____	$_____	_____	_____
Flood	_____	$_____	_____	_____
Phenomenon	_____	$_____	_____	_____
Fire	_____	$_____	_____	_____
Civil Commotion	_____	$_____	_____	_____
War, Nuclear	_____	$_____	_____	_____
Consequential Damage				
Failure to Del.:	_____	$_____	_____	_____
(Traffic Access)	_____	$_____	_____	_____
(Water/Sewer)	_____	$_____	_____	_____
(Electric/Gas/Telephone)	_____	$_____	_____	_____
(Certif. of Occupancy)	_____	$_____	_____	_____
Design				
Construction Interest	_____	$_____	_____	_____
Construction Cost	_____	$_____	_____	_____
Demolition	_____	$_____	_____	_____
Cash Flow–95% Occupancy	_____	$_____	_____	_____
Tenant Finish Storage	_____	$_____	_____	_____
Tenant Rent Loss	_____	$_____	_____	_____
Loss Of Permanent Financing	_____	$_____	_____	_____
Failure To Deliver Access	_____	$_____	_____	_____
G.C. Perm. Failure	_____	$_____	_____	_____
G.C. Finish Failure	_____	$_____	_____	_____
Labor Disputes	_____	$_____	_____	_____
Architect's E & O	_____	$_____	_____	_____
TOTAL		$_____		

COMMENTS

_____

_____

_____

_____

_____

_____

_____

Form 11–8 Risk identification-damage containment form. (*Cont'd*)

Application and Certification for Payment Form 11–9

This is a sample form which can be used when requesting payment of construction costs.

APPLICATION AND CERTIFICATION FOR PAYMENT FORM

FORM 11–9

PROPERTY _____
ADDRESS _____
ADDRESS _____

ARCHITECT _____
PROJECT NO. _____
CONTRACTOR _____

LENDER _____
ADDRESS _____
ADDRESS _____
ATTENTION _____

APPLICATION DATE ___/___/___
APPLICATION NO. _____
PERIOD FROM ___/___/___ TO ___/___/___

CHANGE ORDER SUMMARY	ADDITIONS	DEDUCTIONS
Change Orders approved	$_____	$_____
in previous months by	$_____	$_____
Owner	$_____	$_____
	$_____	$_____
TOTAL	$_____	$_____

SUBSEQUENT CHANGE ORDERS

Number	Approved Date		
		$_____	$_____
_____	___/___/___	$_____	$_____
_____	___/___/___	$_____	$_____
_____	___/___/___	$_____	$_____
_____	___/___/___	$_____	$_____
	TOTAL	$_____	$_____
NET CHANGE ORDERS		$_____	$_____

State of _____ County of _____

The undersigned Contractor certifies that the work covered by this Application For Payment has been completed in accordance with the Contract Documents, that all amounts have been paid by him for Work for which previous Certificates For Payment were issued and payments received from the Owner, and that the current payment shown is now due.

Contractor _____
By _____
Date ___/___/___

Application is made for payment, as shown below in connection with the Contract.

The present status of the account for the Contract is as follows:

ORIGINAL CONTRACT SUM $_____

NET CHANGE BY CHANGE ORDER $_____

CONTRACT SUM TO DATE $_____

TOTAL COMPLETED & STORED TO DATE $_____

RETAINAGE (___%) $_____

TOTAL EARNED LESS RETAINAGE $_____

LESS PREVIOUS CERTIF FOR PAYM'TS $_____

CURRENT PAYMENT DUE $_____

Subcribed and sworn to before this _____
day of _____, 19___
Notary Public:

My Commission expires ___/___/___

In accordance with the Contract and this Application For Payment the Contractor is entitled in the amount shown above.

Architect _____
By _____
Date ___/___/___

Form 11–9   Application and certification for payment form.

Draw Request Letter Form 11-10

This form can be used when making draw requests.

DRAW REQUEST LETTER FORM

FORM 11-10

PROJECT NAME _____
BORROWER'S NAME _____
ADDRESS _____
ADDRESS _____

ACCOUNT NO. _____
NOTE NO. _____
DUE DATE ___/___/___

LENDER'S NAME _____
ADDRESS _____
ADDRESS _____
TEL. NO. (___)_____

TO: _____

    THE UNDERSIGNED OWNER HEREBY REQUESTS A PAYMENT IN THE SUM OF
$_____ COVERING THE ADVANCE PROVIDED FOR BY THE LOAN
AGREEMENT HERETO EXECUTED ON THE _____ DAY OF _____,
19___ AS INDICATED BY THE TOTAL AMOUNT OF THE INDIVIDUAL PAYMENTS
SET FORTH IN THE SCHEDULE BELOW. YOU ARE AUTHORIZED TO ADD TO
THIS ADVANCE AN AMOUNT EQUAL TO THE INTEREST DUE ON THE CONSTRUCTION
LOAN UP TO THIS DATE OF THE ADVANCE REQUESTED HEREIN.

    THE UNDERSIGNED FURTHER DIRECTS AND AUTHORIZES YOU TO
CREDIT THE ABOVE AMOUNT TO THE ACOUNT OF _____.

    THE UNDERSIGNED OWNER FURTHER CERTIFIES THAT THEY WILL USE THE
LOAN PROCEEDS TO PAY THE ITEMS LISTED ON EXHIBIT "A" IN THE ATTACHED
PROJECT COST REPORT FORM, AND THAT THERE HAS BEEN NO CHANGE IN THE PROJECT
COSTS AS ORIGINALLY SUBMITTED, AVAILABLE PROCEEDS OF THE CONSTRUCTION
LOAN ARE SUFFICIENT TO FULLY COMPLETE AND PAY FOR THE CONSTRUCTION OF
THE PROJECT.

OWNER _____
TITLE _____
DATE ___/___/___

Form 11-10 Draw request letter form.

Change Order Request Form 11–11

This form can be used when requesting change orders.

CHANGE ORDER REQUEST FORM

FORM 11–11

PROJECT _____   CONTRACTOR _____
ADDRESS _____   ARCHITECT _____
_____

CONTRACT DATE ___/___/___
CHANGE ORDER NO. _____
CHANGE ORDER DATE ___/___/___

THE FOLLOWING ITEMS ARE ADDED AS CHANGE ORDERS

DESCRIPTION	AMOUNT	#DAYS
_____	$ _____	_____
_____	$ _____	_____
_____	$ _____	_____
_____	$ _____	_____
_____	$ _____	_____
_____	$ _____	_____
_____	$ _____	_____
_____	$ _____	_____
TOTAL	$ _____	_____

NOTE:

1. COPIES OF ALL DRAWINGS ARE ATTACHED AS EXHIBITS

THE ORIGINAL (CONTRACT SUM)(GUARANTEED MAXIMUM COST) IS $ _____
NET CHANGE BY THE PREVIOUS AUTHORIZED CHANGE ORDER $ _____
THE (CONTRACT SUM)(GUARANTEED MAXIMUM COST) PRIOR TO THIS CHANGE WAS $ _____
THE (CONTRACT SUM)(GUARANTEED MAXIMUM COST) WILL BE (INCREASED/DECREASED/UNCHANGED)
  BY THIS CHANGE ORDER $ _____
THE NEW (CONTRACT SUM(GUARANTEED MAXIMUM COST) INCLUDING THIS CHANGE ORDER WILL BE $ _____
THE CONTRACT TIME WILL BE (INCREASED/DECREASED/UNCHANGED) BY (DAYS)   _____
THE DATE OF SUBSTANTIAL COMPLETION AS OF THE DATE OF THIS CHANGE ORDER THEREFORE IS ___/___/___

AUTHORIZED BY:

_____   _____   _____
OWNER   ARCHITECT   CONTRACTOR

_____   _____   _____
TITLE   TITLE   TITLE

_____   _____   _____
ADDRESS   ADDRESS   ADDRESS
                       _____   _____

___/___/___   ___/___/___   ___/___/___
DATE   DATE   DATE

THIS DOCUMENT IS NOT VALID UNTIL ALL PARTIES HAVE REVIEWED AND SIGNED.

Form 11–11   Change order request form.

Project Cost Report Form 11–12

This form can be used when reviewing project costs.

PROJECT COST REPORT FORM

FORM 11–12

PROJECT ____________

DEVELOPER ____________

LENDER ____________

DESCRIPTION	AMOUNT BUDGETED	PREVIOUS PAYMENTS	CURRENT PAYMENTS	BALANCE TO COMPLETE
________	$______	$______	$______	$______
________	$______	$______	$______	$______
________	$______	$______	$______	$______
________	$______	$______	$______	$______
________	$______	$______	$______	$______
________	$______	$______	$______	$______
________	$______	$______	$______	$______
________	$______	$______	$______	$______
________	$______	$______	$______	$______
________	$______	$______	$______	$______
________	$______	$______	$______	$______
________	$______	$______	$______	$______
________	$______	$______	$______	$______
________	$______	$______	$______	$______
________	$______	$______	$______	$______
________	$______	$______	$______	$______
________	$______	$______	$______	$______
________	$______	$______	$______	$______
________	$______	$______	$______	$______
________	$______	$______	$______	$______
CONSTRUCTION LOAN	$______	$______	$______	$______
LETTER OF CREDIT	$______	$______	$______	$______
EQUITY	$______	$______	$______	$______
TOTAL	$______	$______	$______	$______

OWNER ____________

TITLE ____________

DATE ___/___/___

I HEREBY CERTIFY THAT THE ABOVE ANALYSIS OF THE PROJECT COSTS AND EXPENSE REQUIREMENTS IS, TO THE BEST OF MY KNOWLEDGE AND BELIEF TRUE AND COMPLETE.

Form 11–12 Project cost report form.

Lien Release Form 11-13

This form can be used to insure that after contractors receive payment they can not place a lien on the project for that amount.

LIEN RELEASE FORM

FORM 11-13

SUBMITTED BY _____
DATE ___/___/___   JOB NAME _____
REQUEST NO. _____   JOB NO. _____

To: _____

   We hereby request payment for work completed during the period from _____ to _____ in accordance with the terms of our Contract with you for the above referenced project, as shown in detail on the attached schedule and summarized as follows:

Original Contract Amount	$_____
Approved Change Orders through No. _____	$_____
Total Contract Amount	$_____ *
Value of Work Completed to Date	$_____ *
Stored Materials to Date	$_____ *
Total Completed & Stored to Date	$_____
Less: Amount Retained	$_____
Total to Date Less Retainage	$_____
Less: Amount Previously Paid	$_____
Amount Due This Request	$_____

* Must agree with attached detail.

AFFIDAVIT AND RELEASE OF LIEN

   The Contractor hereby certifies that the above summary and attached schedule represent an accurate accounting of the status of payments to date and the value of Work performed and materials supplied to date under the terms of the Contract between _____ and the undersigned relating to the above referenced project.

   The Contractor further certifies that all materials, labor, and services furnished by him through the above mentioned pay period have been fully applied for or will be paid from the proceeds of this draw (except as listed on the attached schedule) and the premises of the above named job cannot be made subject to any valid liens or claim by anyone who furnished materials, labor, or services to the Contractor for use in said job. The Contractor hereby releases _____, its affiliates, and subsidiaries, and its affiliates from any futher liaiblity in connection with all materials, labor, and services furnished by the Contractor through the above mentioned pay period.

   This Release is given in order to induce payment in the amount of $_____ and, on receipt of said payment by the Contractor, this Release becomes in full force and effect.

Sworn to and subscribed before me this _____ day of _____, 19___

_____
Notary Public

_____
Contractor

By: _____
Title: _____
Date ___/___/___

Form 11-13 Lien release form.

## Chapter 12

The Marketing Process: Selling the Product

To excel in real estate development, the developer should be totally market oriented. His every decision should consider the context of the market and the potential users of his selected product. From the inception of the development's concept, the selection of the site, the design of the building, rental rates, and financing, the developer should be fashioning every aspect of the development for the time when he will be convincing the potential user to lease or buy. In addition, he must know his competition and have strategies for winning over them.

This chapter will discuss all the issues the real estate developer must address during the marketing process and give insights into each. We will consider the market study, the marketing team, leasing and sales criteria, advertising and public relations, budgets, and the marketing campaign. In addition, we will discuss the agreements used for closing the lease or sale and provide examples of these agreements for your review.

Thus far, we have discussed market research, feasibility, and market studies. The market study has only been referenced briefly. In this chapter, we will provide more complete explanations concerning this study, referring specifically to its preparation.

At this stage of the cycle, the developer has determined the product type and location of the proposed development. To make these decisions, the developer should have completed various levels of the market study. Initial market research should have given direction in planning overall strategy, and when the buildings were master planned and designed, markcting strategy should have provided criteria for that design. In addition, some lenders will require that a market study be included in the loan package, providing additional statistical data.

Once the project is financed and construction is under way, the developer should bring together all of the marketing data he has used to date and develop a marketing business plan. Depending on the developer's organization, this may be done in house or contracted out with a marketing research company.

PREPARING THE MARKET STUDY

To effectively lease or sell within the marketplace, it is essential to know one's competition. An evaluation of that competition in comparison to the property to be marketed in a market analysis is often used to plot strategy for the sale. In evaluating a potential property, the current market comparables should be carefully studied. Those who complete this study should first compile a list of properties that are competitive with the subject property. These properties should be of a similar building type, marketed toward a similar target market, and in locations similar to the subject property. Because each market has its own particular set of characteristics and location boundaries, some comparables may be five miles from the subject property while others may be just down the street. In addition, two-story garden apartment properties should not be compared with high-rise luxury properties, and Class A office properties should not be compared with Class C office properties.

To obtain a list of potential comparables, the individual completing the market analysis should begin by driving the area adjacent to the subject property and listing those properties which appear similar. Additional properties can be obtained through interviews with property managers. The yellow pages, local real estate boards, banks, and appraisers are other sources which can be used in completing the list. Using this list as a basis, data can be compiled and analyzed on each competitive piece of property. The market study comparable forms located at the end of this chapter can be used in completing this task.

Since no two properties are exactly alike, certain adjustments must be made for accurate comparisons. These can include adjustments for utilities, features, and amenities. Since some properties have the tenant paying for all or some of the operational costs, while others do not, this adjustment figure is needed for a better comparison between properties. These adjustment factors are often available at the local utility companies. In addition, some properties have more "bells and whistles," or features and amenities. A cost factor should be added or subtracted for these items. These cost figures are very subjective and sometimes leave room for error in analysis.

The completed study should contain photographs of each comparable property. These photographs can be used when rating each property as well as for future reference. The following will address various issues and information which should be included in this market study.

What Information to Include in the Market Study

Depending on the developer's specific product type, the market study should provide information as per the following listing.

Residential

- Name of property
- Address
- Telephone number
- Age of the property
- Type construction
- Number and mix of units
- Current monthly rental rate or purchase price
- Current monthly parking rental price
- Number of bedrooms, bathrooms
- Basement area
- Type of parking
- Square footage (heated and non-heated)
- Utility costs payment responsibilities
- Unit features
- Property amenities
- Lease term
- Rent/sale concessions
- Date of last rent or sale price increase
- Current occupancy or number of units sold (time period)
- Distance to the subject property
- Property owner/telephone number
- Managing agent/telephone number

Commercial

- Type property
  office
  retail
  industrial

- Name of property
- Address
- Telephone number
- Age of the property
- Type construction
- Current rental rate per square foot (gross/net)
- Type rent escalation used
- Type of parking
- Tenant improvement (TI) allowance
- Utility costs payment responsibilities
- Unit features
- Property amenities
- Lease term
- Rent concessions
- Leasing commission—how paid
- Current occupancy rate
- Distance to the subject property
- Property owner/telephone number
- Managing agent/telephone number
- Marketing agent/telephone number

Tips on Verifying Occupancy and Rental Rates

Finding accurate information about existing occupancies and rental rates is often the most difficult data to find because some owners refuse to provide the information. If the information is unavailable, try some of the following.

- Contact the local postal clerk who can verify the number of tenants within the property.
- Check with the local utility companies. These companies include the electric, gas, and water companies. They should have current knowledge of units which are occupied.
- Walk or drive by each unit and observe occupied dwellings.
- Have a business associate or friend contact the manager or property owner to inquire about renting space. Since all managers and property owners need to rent their vacant or soon-to-be vacant space, they will provide a summary on the rental rates and concessions. Sometimes this process may need to be repeated two to three times to gather the necessary information.
- Review the real estate classified section of the local newspaper. Many times properties advertise their rates and concessions to the public.

In addition to the conventional property comparables, the study should also include those "for sale" residential properties that are purchased by investors for rental and subleases of commercial space. All of these will add additional available inventory to a market area.

How to Obtain Information on the Unit Mix, Square Footage, and the Property's Age

If the information regarding the unit mix, square footage, and age of the property is not known by the manager, the following methods can be used to obtain this information:

- Contact the local building department. Many times they file the original building plans for the property. These files will show the unit mix as well as the date of construction.
- Contact the local tax assessment department. In order to assess the property properly, this information should be in the files.

Comparative Analysis of the Competition

To excel in your property's leasing, operations and management, it is important to understand the competition. Adjacent or neighboring properties within the community should be studied and rated relative to your development and other competition. Consistency in rating can be achieved by using a set of standards by which all are compared. The following are some areas of comparison to consider:

- Appearance
- Architectural design style
- Expertise of the property management team
- Location and ease of access
- Amenities
- Special features and interior design
- Terms and conditions of transaction
- Expertise of marketing and public relations
- Tenant or buyer profile
- Financing
- Allowances and concessions
- Tenant improvement allowance

In gathering the data required, call the various properties and inform them of your intent to complete a market study and request information on their property specific. In addition, offer the property manager of that property a copy of your completed study if he or she provides information about the project.

How Graphing Can Help You Analyze Market Data

In order to better analyze this data, the information should be graphed for a visual picture of the market conditions. The information to be plotted will include the square footage and the current adjusted rental rate. Once the data is plotted, a line should be drawn which intersects the average of this data. The properties which are above this line will show the LOW SIDE of the market while the properties which are below this line are the HIGH SIDE of the market. Table 12–1 demonstrates this process when analyzing a one-bedroom, one-bathroom apartment property.

Based on the market data shown in the above example, it can be seen that the subject property is on the low side of the market. This example gives three other properties with the same "5" rating but they are located on the high side of the market. Interpretation of this graph demonstrates that the subject property has room to increase rents by up to $20 per month without going over the average line in the graph. It can also be seen from this graph that Meadow Creek, with a "4" rating, should reduce its rental rates to be in line with the market. Meadow Creek's adjusted rental rate is $.45 per square foot while the average adjusted rate is $.49 per square foot. It appears that due to the "4" rating, this property should reduce its rent to increase its occupancy level.

The same graphing technique can be used to illustrate various unit types. The graphing of this data will show the relative strengths and weaknesses of the various unit types in that particular market.

This graphing and analysis process can also be used when searching for undervalued properties. This is the same process which can be used to analyze total markets and individual segments. This analysis process can demonstrate to an investor which properties have a better chance of increasing their rental rates and consequently their value.

Reviewing the Demographics, Area Trends, and Occupancy Rates

In conjunction with analyzing the comparable data, the area demographics, area trends, and occupancy rates must be carefully reviewed. This information will show the character and make-up of the market area as well as market equilibrium. This data will show whether the market area is on an uptrend, downtrend, or simply stagnant.

MARKETING PROFESSIONALS — CHOOSING THE TEAM

In preparing marketing strategy, the developer must decide to use the very best available team to assist in marketing the property. He may already have that team in house or he may have to contract with other professionals whose primary business is the marketing of buildings, land, or space. If using outside marketing

Table 12-1   Sample Market Study Summary
MARKET STUDY SUMMARY

PROPERTY   FOX DOWNS
LOCATION   ATLANTA, GEORGIA
TYPE PROPERTY   GARDEN APARTMENT
TYPE UNIT   ONE BEDROOM, ONE BATH

CODE/RATING	NAME	DISTANCE TO SUBJECT (MILES)	AGE	RENTAL RATE	SQ.FT.	UTILITIES PAID BY TENANT	UTILITY ADJUSTMENT *	FEATURES **	AMENITIES ***	FEATURES/AMENITIES ADJUSTMENT	ADJUSTED RENT	ADJUSTED RENT/SQ.FT.	NO. UNITS	OCCUPIED UNITS	% OCCUPIED
NP-5	NOTTINGHAM PINE	2.5	4	$300.00	550	+E	$0.00	WP,UC,DW,C,P/B	SP/TC	$5.00	$305.00	$0.55	48	42	87.50%
OP-5	OAKS PLACE	4	5	$320.00	620	+E	$0.00	WP,UC,DW,C,P/B	SP/TC,CH	$0.00	$320.00	$0.52	36	35	97.22%
SP-5	SUTTON PLACE	5	2	$325.00	650	+E	$0.00	WP,UC,DW,C,P/B	SP/TC,CH	$0.00	$325.00	$0.50	40	38	95.00%
ML-6	MILL LAKE	1.5	5	$290.00	575	NONE	$23.00	WP,UC,DW,C,P/B	SP/TC,CH	$0.00	$313.00	$0.54	28	26	92.86%
MC-4	MEADOW CREEK	2.5	2	$325.00	725	+E	$0.00	WP,UC,DW,C,P/B	SP/TC,CH	$0.00	$325.00	$0.45	32	24	75.00%
TA-8	THE AMBERS	3	4	$330.00	620	+E	$0.00	WP,UC,DW,C,P/B	SP/TC	$5.00	$335.00	$0.54	12	12	100.00%
PC-3	PEBBLE CREEK	1.5	6	$300.00	680	+E	$0.00	WP,UC,DW,C,P/B	SP/TC,CH	$0.00	$300.00	$0.44	52	46	88.46%
TV-3	THE VILLAGE	2	1	$295.00	585	+E	$0.00	WP,UC,DW,C,P/B	SP/TC,CH	$0.00	$295.00	$0.50	24	20	83.33%
SUB-5	FOX DOWNS			$300.00	650	+E	$0.00	WP,UC,DW,C,P/B	SP/TC,CH	$0.00	$300.00	$0.46	28	28	100.00%
AVG.				$308.27	630.20						$311.41	$0.49	300	271	90.33%
TOTAL					189,060						$93,424.00				

ADJUSTMENTS

* UTILITY ADJUSTMENT	$0.04 /FT.
** FEATURES:	
WP–WALLPAPER	$5.00
UC–UTILITY CONNECTIONS	$10.00
C–CARPET	$30.00
P/B–PATIO/BALCONY	$10.00
DW–DISHWASHER	$10.00
*** AMENITIES:	
SP–SWIMMING POOL	$10.00
TC–TENNIS COURT	$5.00
CH–CLUBHOUSE	$5.00

ADJUSTED RENT/SQ.FT.
ONE-BEDROOM, ONE-BATH APARTMENT UNITS

expertise, the developer must carefully check the references and track record of those being considered. Enthusiasm and sales oriented individuals are best for sales agents, while technicians who love details are best for completing studies. Professionals who know what is going on in the community and love to be around other people seem to be best for advertising and public relations.

A detailed agreement should be prepared between the parties to outline the scope of duties as well as outline the fees and payment schedules. The following team members can be selected to assist your marketing efforts.

Marketing Consultants

Marketing consultants are individuals who for a flat fee or a percentage of the gross sales will consult with the developer or marketing agent to position the development for marketing.

Advertising Agencies

Advertising agencies will prepare the marketing materials, such as the brochures, project stationery, business cards, fliers, and media advertising. Depending on the size of these agencies, they may execute the total package or subcontract parts of their assignment to other professionals. These agencies will usually charge a flat rate based on the production time as well as a media placement fee for placing the advertising in the media.

Public Relations Agencies

Public relations agencies work toward setting an image of your development in the community by managing the message which is placed in local media and creating events which announce, demonstrate, or celebrate the story which the developer desires for the public to hear. These individuals usually work on a fee per assignment or on a monthly retainer.

Brokers, Leasing, or Sales Agents

Once the developer is familiar with the market, he must decide who will market the property. The developer who has the staff, experience, and financial resources may decide to market the property in house to obtain more control of the marketing process and costs. It should be noted that he will have additional office overhead due to the increased staff.

If the developer decides that he should contract for this service, he should make a list of potential marketing companies or real estate brokerage companies and from this list, interview and check references. Once he has made a decision, he should then negotiate and prepare a marketing agreement.

Eight Items to Require of Marketing Agents

1. Thorough knowledge of the market area
2. Thorough knowledge of the subject property
3. Communication and listening skills
4. Good negotiating skills
5. Broad contact base of potential users

6. Acceptance in the local brokerage community
7. Knowledge of financing techniques and potential lenders
8. Ability to close the deal

Points to Consider When Negotiating the Marketing Agreement

When negotiating the marketing agreement, the developer must ensure that he clearly defines the duties between both parties. When negotiating the fee schedule, the developer should make sure that he knows the competition's offerings to ensure that his marketing agents have all the highest incentives to continue to sell the property effectively. The following will consider some of the issues which must be considered.

Scope of Broker's Duties

This section outlines the responsibilities of the agent.

Owner's and Broker's Expenses

These two sections detail which expenses are to be paid by both parties.

Budget

This section outlines when and who should prepare and approve the marketing budget.

Disbursement of Funds

This section details how and when the funds will be disbursed.

Employees

This section details whose responsibility it is to hire and dismiss employees.

Compensation of the Broker for Services

This section describes in detail which fees are to be paid for various services rendered by the broker.

Fees: The payment for services can be structured as a flat fee for each sale or lease or as a percentage of the total sale or lease. The developer may structure a draw against commission or a flat monthly retainer which will be offset by future commissions.

Bonuses: As an incentive to the broker, the developer may offer a bonus based on performance. This performance can be tied into a specified dollar volume of sales for a specified time period.

Golden Handcuffs: To protect his interest, the developer may have a clause which states that if the agent leaves prior to the completion of the marketing effort, the agent will lose all or a portion of fees and bonuses.

Term of Agreement

This section states the starting and ending dates of the agreement. It may also contain language regarding any extensions.

Termination

Due to the possibility of a lawsuit with the agent, the developer should be sure to document the events of early termination with the broker and clearly define the circumstances for termination.

Accounting

This section defines who will manage the accounting process on an ongoing basis in the case of early termination.

Purchaser or Tenant Deposits

This section directs where the deposits are placed. The developer should require that any deposits placed in a separate escrow account not be comingled in the broker's day-to-day operating accounts.

Insurance

This section requires the broker to have a certain amount of liability insurance.

MARKETING STRATEGIES—CREATING THE MARKETING BUSINESS PLAN

The marketing agent should develop with the approval of the developer a complete marketing strategy. This strategy should be followed and updated periodically when conditions in the market change or when it appears that the strategy must be revised. This strategy should consider all issues to be addressed and set procedures for sales and reporting. The market plan outline can be used in developing marketing plans. Following this outline, various issues are presented which are paramount in the implementation of the successful marketing for the development.

Marketing Plan Outline

I.   Purpose and scope
II.   Project description
    A. Number units
    B. Type units
    C. Unit mix
    D. Square footage (gross/net)
    E. Rent

      F.   Utility payment responsibilities

      G. Rent per square foot

      H. Location

      I.   Unit features

      J.   Project amenities

      K. Location map

III.   Area demographics (city, county, census tract)

      A. Population

      B. Household income

      C. Renters versus owners

      D. Traffic counts

IV.   Area information

      A. Employment

      B. Schools

      C. Utilities

      D. Shopping

      E. Transportation

      F.   Patterns of growth

      G. Building permits

V.   Market study

      A. Number units

      B. Type units

      C. Unit mix

      D. Square footage (gross/net)

      E. Street rent

      F.   Utility payment responsibilities

      G. Rent per square foot

      H. Location

      I.   Unit features

      J.   Project amenities

      K. Location map

      L. Rating

      M. Conclusion

          1. Potential pricing per unit

             a. Price per unit

             b. Price per square foot

             c. Price per floor

             d. Price per location

VI.   Target market
VII. Marketing
    A. Advertising media
        1. Newspaper
        2. Magazines
        3. Radio
        4. Television
        5. Billboards
        6. Direct mail
        7. Fliers
    B. Signage
        1. Entrance
        2. Office
        3. Model
        4. Directional
    C. Brochures
        1. Site plan
        2. Floor plans
        3. Project information
        4. Financial sheet
    D. Stationary, envelopes
    E. Business cards
    F. Public relations
        1. Initial announcement
        2. Groundbreaking
        3. First sales
        4. Final sales
        5. Sell-out
    G. Promotions
    H. Sales office
        1. Furnishings
        2. Equipment
        3. Supplies
    I. Model
        1. Furnishings
    J. Marketing budget
        1. By line item/month

    K. Unit pricing
        1. Options/pricing
    L. Current resident profiles
        1. Name
        2. Unit number
        3. Type unit
        4. Current rent
        5. Male/female
        6. Age
        7. Income bracket
        8. Occupation
        9. Education
        10. Summary of current tenants
VIII. Renovation budget (item and cost) (if condominium conversion)
    A. Site
    B. Building exterior
    C. Unit interior
        1. Clean
        2. Paint
        3. Wallpaper
        4. Appliances
        5. Punch-out
    D. Amenities
    E. Narrative
IX. Project documentation
    A. Reservation agreement
    B. Purchase agreement
    C. Condominium documents
    D. Bylaws
    E. Articles of incorporation
    F. Condominium association
X.   Critical path
    A. Project documentation
    B. Engineering and survey
    C. Sales office
    D. Model
    E. In-house sales

  F. Outside sales

  G. Pre-sale closings

  H. Site work

   1. Entrance

   2. Paving

   3. Landscaping

   4. Fencing

  I. Exterior building renovations

  J. Interior unit renovation

  K. Amenities renovation

   1. Clubhouse

   2. Tennis court

   3. Pool

 XI. Conversion budget

  A. Revenue

  B. Expenses

  C. Capital expenditures

  D. Narrative

 XII. Association budget

  A. Income

  B. Expenses

  C. Reserve account

 XIII. Reserve account

 XIV. Developer's warranty

 XV. Conclusions

Developing the Theme and Image for the Product

When conceptualizing the development, the developer should plan special characteristics or features which make his development unique within the scope of market demand. From this uniqueness, a theme can be created. The development's marketing strategy should focus on this theme. Apartments can be positioned with a theme toward the "good life" or to appeal to various age groups. Commercial properties can stress location, appearance, sophistication or quality of services.

Creating the Proper Name for the Development

The name of the development should create a visual image within the mind of the prospect. The name should be easy to understand and remember. Many names are based on the location (such as One Peachtree Building), a historical fact about the property (such as Battle Run Apartments), or a unique amenity (such as Tennis Club Apartments).

LEASING AND SALES CRITERIA

Once the project economics are completed, the developer should develop what is known as leasing and sales criteria. The purpose of this criteria is to summarize the parameters within which marketing personnel must function in the act of the sale. For instance, how low or how high can they go in making the sale? What maximum concessions or enhancements to the deal can be offered to interested prospects and what commissions will be paid to associated brokers? In addition, for the various type units and associated amenities, how are each priced?

How to Determine the Pricing Schedule

In preparing the pricing schedule, the developer must remember that pricing must reflect that which the customer will pay for the product. The process of determining the pricing for the product will begin with the initial pricing based on the market comparables and then be revised based on the absorption of the product. If the marketing effort is ahead of schedule and there appears to be a demand for the product, the price schedule can be revised upwardly in response to demand. Similarly, if marketing efforts are slower than anticipated, the prices may have to be reduced or concessions added to increase buyer demand. The developer should consider these possibilities in his sensitivity studies when completing project economics.

How to Determine the Market Share and Absorption

In determining market share and projected absorption schedules, the marketing agent must obtain and analyze the following information:

- Total existing product inventory in the market area
- Total inventory under construction
- Total proposed inventory (to be built)
- Current occupancy of this inventory
- Past absorption levels of existing inventory

This information should then be broken down into ranking or class of properties. For example, Class A office buildings should be separated from Class B and Class C type properties. Once this information is compiled, it should be analyzed and compared to the development's property. Based on his past history of annual leasing, and the strength of his staff, the developer should then make a prediction concerning the share of the available market which he can capture. This prediction will be used in cash flow projections. If he fails to capture this share of the market on schedule and has no contingency plan, the development will suffer financially. The following example is a simplified method for analyzing this information and making market projections.

Case Study

A local market contains 1,000,000 square feet of Class A office space; a developer is proposing to construct an office building with 100,000 square feet. Currently under construction are two smaller office developments of 50,000 square feet each. Past history demonstrates a yearly absorption of 100,000 square feet per year. The existing Class A office market is 95 percent occupied. From reviewing the existing market and the two new competitors, it is decided that the proposed development is superior to the two other properties because of location, floor sizes, and building amenities. The marketing agent then projects that although the proposed project is only 50 percent of this new inventory, he should be able to capture a minimum of 60 percent of the year's proposed absorption.

By taking the total building absorption per year and dividing it by 95 percent of the total building square footage, the marketing agent can obtain the number of months it should take to absorb this new inventory.

Determining the Fee Structure for Outside Brokers

Often, brokers will bring users to the development. Consequently, the developer and marketing agent should determine a fair fee structure to compensate them for their services. Some properties offer a referral fee of 10 percent of the total sale, while other properties offer a full-market commission. To obtain a full-market commission, the marketing agent should survey the competition. In situations of oversupply, developers tend to pay full-market commissions, while in a sellers' market, this rate tends to drop. This fee and incentives should be fashioned to

Case Study

Table 12–2

Building	Total Sq.Ft.	Percentage of New Space	Projected Mkt. Share	Sq.Ft. Absorption Per Year	Rent-up # Months
Subject	100,000	50	60%	60,000	19.0
Bldg. #2	50,000	25	20%	20,000	28.5
Bldg. #3	50,000	25	20%	20,000	28.5
Total	200,000	100	100%	100,000	

encourage activity within your development and make it easier for the broker to receive his commission.

LEGAL AGREEMENTS

When the marketing effort culminates in a sale, whether it be a lease or a purchase, the terms of the sale should be documented with a legal agreement. These agreements should be reviewed by a real estate attorney prior to their signing. They should be very thorough and include all terms and conditions. Future problems can be avoided by well-prepared documents and excellent counsel. The following types of documents are used to consummate the deal.

Reservation Agreement

A reservation agreement will be used when preleasing or preselling a development. It might be used before the final documents are completed.

Sales Agreement

The sales agreement is used when selling property. It outlines all of the business terms and conditions under which the sale takes place.

Condominium Documents

Condominium documents include the declaration of covenants, conditions, and restrictions of the condominium property. These documents are given to the prospect prior to making his purchasing decision. Most states have condominium laws which guide the formulation of these documents.

Bylaws

The bylaws govern the association. This association can be for a condominium, subdivision, or cooperative development.

Warranty Agreements

Warranty agreements are used by the developer to define the extent of his legal obligations after purchase or lease.

Leasing Agreements

Leasing agreements are used by all types of rental properties. They define the terms and conditions between the owner and the tenant.

Workletters

These agreements are used to formalize the agreement between the landlord and the tenant. They describe leasehold improvements for which the landlord is responsible. The completion of the workletter is essential for lease negotiations.

Document 12–1   Sample tenant work letter.

October 10, 19_____

Mr. Steve Robbins
Robbins Engineering Co.
1010 Stonehaven Rd.
Cleveland, Ohio 44121

RE: Overlook Building

Dear Mr. Robbins:

The following terms and conditions are offered to you regarding your space requirements in the above referenced building.

Landlord:	HZ Partners, Ltd.
Tenant:	Robbins Engineering Co.
Square footage:	10,500 sq. ft. (gross)
Base rental rate:	$20.00 per square foot (gross)
Rent escalations:	Five (5%) percent per year
Area of premises:	4th Floor
Total rental area of building:	105,000 sq. ft. (gross)
Tenant's percentage share:	10%
Lease term:	10 years
Free rent period:	Six (6) months after move-in
Commencement date:	February 1, 19_____
Expiration date:	January 31, 19_____
Renewal option:	2 to 5 year options
Commitment deposit:	Refundable $5,000.00 paid upon acceptance of this agreement
Security deposit:	Two months rental, payable upon lease execution
Use of premises:	Office
Design fee allowance:	$.25 per square foot (gross)

Document 12–1 Sample tenant work letter. *(Cont'd)*

Landlord tenant improvement allowance:	$15.00 per square foot (gross)
Space design:	See Exhibit A

If these terms and conditions are acceptable to you, please acknowledge at the bottom of this page and return this agreement within five (5) business days to the undersigned. Upon receipt of the executed letter, I shall instruct my attorneys to draft a formal lease agreement.

Sincerely,

Alan Garber
Marketing Representative

AG/kf

Enc.

Accepted and agreed upon this _____ day of _____, 19_____

Robins Engineering Co.

BY: _____

Exhibits

A. Sample lease
B. Tenant design
C. Building rules and regulations

MARKETING FILES

Two types of files should be kept in the marketing process: project files and prospecting files. Prospecting files should be ongoing until the prospect becomes a tenant. At that point in time, the prospect files should become a part of the project file. The following listing can be used for the major categories of the project files.

- Correspondence
- Market analysis/market feasibility studies
- Strategic planning
- Budgets/statute reports
- Competition reports
- Advertising/public relations
    Groundbreaking/topping out/grand openings
    Signage/billboards

Media coverage
Visual aids
Direct mail
- Broker relations
- Marketing center
- Monthly status reports
- Leasing or sales development
Prospect status reports
Proposals/leases
Other

Prospecting Files

Since the marketing agent must keep track of his prospects, he should have an organized set of files to track his sales progress and the documents which the prospect has received. The following is a list of items that should be contained in these files:

I. Prospect card
   A. Name
   B. Address
   C. Telephone numbers (home, office, car, fax)
   D. Person information (family size)
   E. Type space required
   F. Date of contact
   G. How they found out about the property
   H. Follow-up dates and comments
II. Checklist of documents and items prospect received
   A. Reservation agreement
   B. Lease agreement
   C. Sales agreement
   D. Condominium/association documents
   E. Bylaws
   F. Space design
III. Prospect credit history
IV. Checklist of documents and items received at closing
   A. Closing documents
   B. Warranty
   C. Keys
   D. Security cards/numbers

FINANCING AND CONCESSIONS

For the developer to secure financing, and to price the development effectively, certain key assumptions must be made. A wise developer will have included the input of marketing professionals in formulating these assumptions and their subsequent refinements. Usually, these assumptions will have included the following:

- Market absorption rate
- Concessions offered
- Commission fees
- Budgets
- Operation's costs
- Share of the market
- Expenses in advertising and public relations
- Marketing and sales offices
- Projected overhead expenses

The developer should clearly explain the parameters of the deal so that all marketing personnel are working within the same limitations. As a proposal is presented to a prospect, the information concerning the offer must be accurate and within the project economics. To make a sale only to find that it was below your projections will have a domino effect throughout the total development and affect future deal making.

MEDIA PLACEMENT

To create an image and to make the development known, marketing personnel must use every available media opportunity. The following is a list of publications in which the marketing agent can advertise. The placement of these ads should relate directly to the development's target market.

Newspapers

Newspapers contain two types of advertising: classified and display. The proper section of the newspaper should be reviewed as to the profile of the reader. For example, office space advertising should be in the business or classified section (under office space for rent) and not in the women's section of the Sunday paper.

Trade Journals

Local real estate related trade journals, such as apartment, home, or commercial guides are another source of advertising. These journals not only go to potential prospects, but to local real estate brokers as well. Depending on the type and budget of the development, both regional or national trade journals can offer excellent exposure to the consumer or real estate broker.

Local Magazines

Depending on the marketing budget of the project, local business or city magazines can help market to the potential consumer. Once again, only those magazines which your prospects read should be used.

Television

Television can offer great exposure for the development, but must be tailored for your market segment in time and presentation. Television is more expensive than most advertising and is usually reserved for larger developments.

Radio

The best times to use radio advertisement are in the early morning and late afternoon. This is when most prospects are sitting in traffic, listening to the radio. Each radio station has regularly updated demographics of their listeners. A study of these should give an indication of the right station to use.

Billboards

Local billboards with high traffic counts and excellent visibility can assist in getting the word out to the public. Many times these contracts are on a month-to-month basis or longer. Many billboard companies sell packages which include rotating the messages to other locations. These locations should be carefully reviewed to ensure that they meet your marketing criteria.

Signage

Local directional signage can assist the consumer in finding the development. These signs can be placed on vacant property with the owner's approval.

Yellow Pages

Certain types of properties, such as mini-warehouses, require placement of advertising in the yellow pages. Plan ahead since the yellow pages typically are published once a year. Depending on the size and ad placement, the cost can range from $100 per to over $1000 per month.

Specialty Advertising

Specialty advertising is advertising on pens, pencils, matchbook covers and other similar "give away" items. These items are given away to "suspects" in the hope that they will be a constant reminder of the product.

REPORTING PROCEDURES

The developer should require that a reporting system be established to monitor leasing and sale progress, to measure and evaluate results. Complete systems of reporting consist of the following elements.

- An internal report in which the marketing agents record the mailing, the contacts and the nature of their responses. The purpose of this report is to measure effectiveness. If the marketing efforts failed with a particular prospect, questions should be asked to prevent this occurrence in the future. With this information, marketing plans can be changed and strategies altered. In addition, if shifts in the market are observed, sales techniques can be changed.
- A monthly leasing status report can also be used to keep the developer informed if he is using outside professionals for marketing. In addition, this report can be used to keep investors and joint-venture partners apprised of the status of activity. This report should summarize the previous month's activity. It can list all of the prospects and where they are in the total marketing process: active, proposal, lease, or signed lease. The status report should also give explanations as to the reasons for changes in the report from month to month.
- Monthly changes to occupancy levels in the building should be given in a monthly summary report complete with diagrams of the master plan or floor plan showing exactly where the new buyers or tenants are located. Sometimes these reports are placed on the walls of the marketing office so everyone can observe progress.
- Quarterly update of the marketing study should be an ongoing activity to ensure that the developer and his marketing staff are up to date on the ever-changing market.

VISUAL AIDS AND COLLATERAL MATERIALS

Once the developer has financed the development and the designed buildings are under construction, he must create ways to explain the benefits of this new environment to prospective buyers. The tools used for these explanations should be designed carefully, to evoke a strong positive response. There are a lot of visual techniques which can be used. Explanations of various options available are as follows.

Brochures

Brochures can range from expensive four-color pieces to a simple one-page, black-and-white piece. The brochure should touch on all the property facts. Obviously, sophisticated developments require sophisticated brochures for sophisticated buyers.

Fliers

Fliers are usually one- or two-page mini-brochures which either will be given to the potential user or mailed as a direct mail piece.

Stationary

Since this is a small expense in the total picture, quality should be used with the consistency of the development's logo. The use of a graphic designer will generally provide an outstanding product.

Business Cards

All marketing agents should have business cards which are project specific. They should have a similar quality to your stationery and be designed by a graphics designer for the best effect. The business card should also be included with most letters or fliers.

Presentation Drawings

When standing before the prospect, the marketing professional should be prepared to clearly and concisely explain the benefits, functions, and aesthetics of the development. This can be achieved with finely presented drawings and illustrations. Figures 12–1 through 12–5 show different drawings that could be presented as visual-aid materials. Remember that the sale can be directly related to the prospect's understanding of your development and whether or not all of his questions were answered. If there are unique features of your development, then show them. The following are examples of visual aids which can be used.

- Colored renderings
- Computerized renderings onto existing photographs

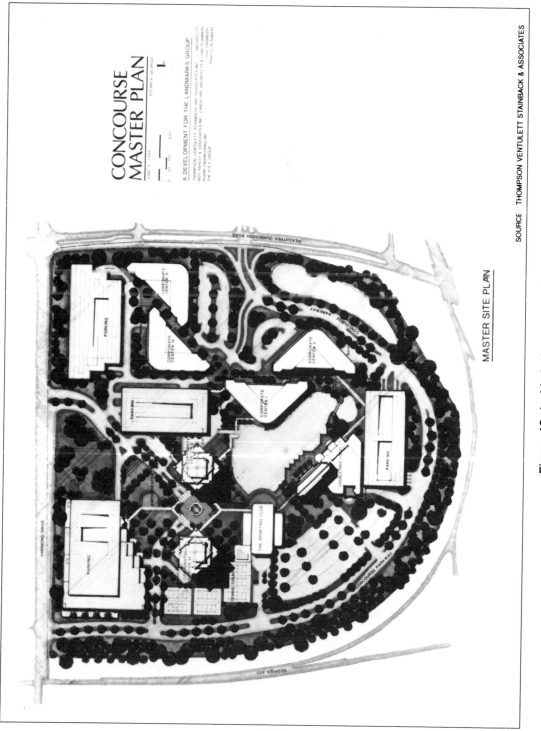

Figure 12–1 Marketing presentation.

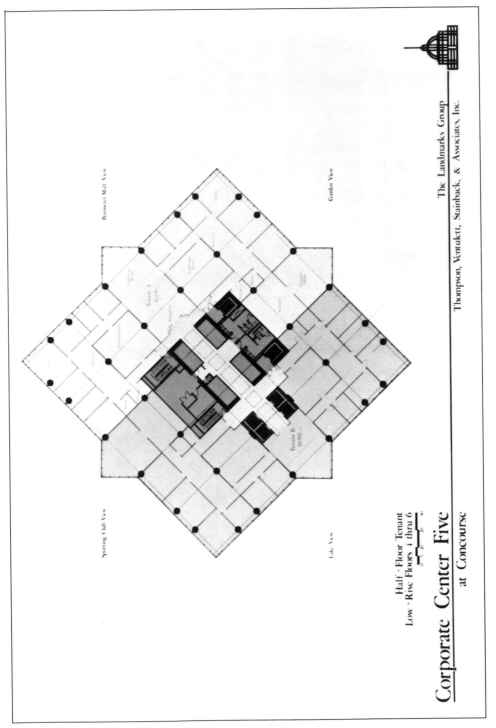

Figure 12–2 Marketing presentation.

514

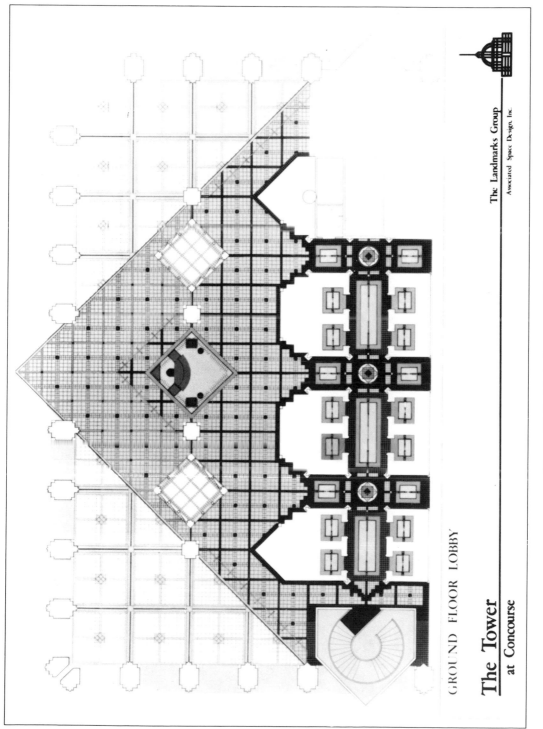

GROUND FLOOR LOBBY

The Tower
at Concourse

The Landmarks Group
Associated Space Design, Inc.

Figure 12-3   Marketing presentation.

515

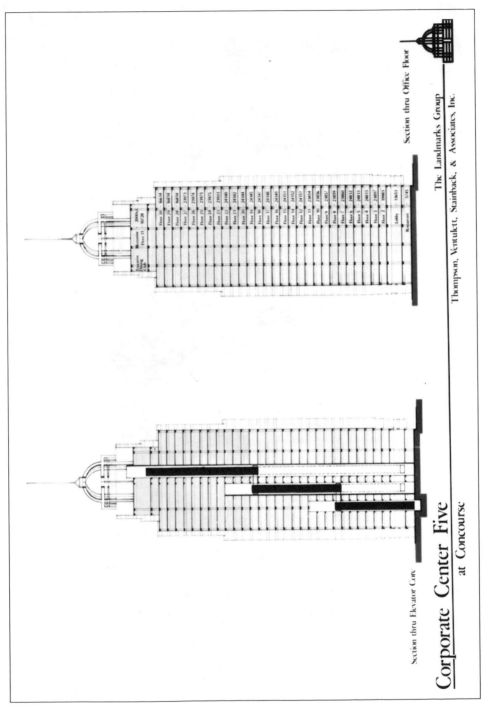

Corporate Center Five
at Concourse

Section thru Elevator Core

The Landmarks Group

Thompson, Ventukett, Stainback, & Associates, Inc.

Section thru Office Floor

Figure 12-4 Marketing presentation.

516

SOURCE: THE LANDMARKS GROUP

Figure 12-5 Marketing presentation.

- Colored master plans
- Sketches of features
- Landscaping drawings
- Rendered floor plans illustrating core layouts and potential layouts for prospective tenants
- Listings of features
- Circulation drawings showing vehicular and pedestrian circulations
- Interior design materials and finishes boards
- Systems of the building
- Market study information
- Location maps for ease of access
- Photographs of similar features in other buildings not in your market

Audio-Visual Presentations

Music and mood photography can raise the emotions and enthusiasm of a sale as nothing else can. Along with presentation drawings and with the right timing, audio-visual presentations can have a positive effect. Specialists can be commissioned to produce these, customized to the development's needs. The length of these presentations should be managed very carefully, ensuring that they do not interfere with one-on-one, person-to-person contact which is critical for the sale. The following are some types which can be used.

- Television monitors with video cassettes
- Multi-projector programmed slides and music
- Simple slide show with a live narrator

Architectural Models

Usually, these aids are most effective in illustrating the three-dimensional character of projects. With the finishes of the buildings, trees, lakes, and automobiles, the prospect can begin to live within the development. These can be simple cardboard models to highly sophisticated plastic models which rise out of the floor in the middle of presentations complete with dynamic lighting and music. Interiors of buildings which have very unique spaces like shopping centers usually are very successful models. Costs can range from $5000 to $200,000.

SALES OR LEASING OFFICES

Depending on the size and budget of the development, a separate sales or leasing office may be required. This office will house the marketing personnel and provide the home base for all marketing efforts. Conference rooms should be provided for presentations and for closing the sale. These sales offices can be elaborate monuments to the project or simple trailers in the center of construction projects.

Office Location

The sales/leasing office's location is extremely important, because it is the first glimpse of the product for the public, and since it will be operational prior to the project's completion, its function is critical to the overall marketing campaign's success. It should be located adjacent to the new development, possibly with a view to or over the site. It should provide easy access from local freeway systems. Ease of access and parking must be provided and finding it must be simple for the potential buyer. Once the project is complete, the office should be relocated into the project.

Office Design

The design should include a reception area, seating area, display area or a listening room, closing or conference room, kitchenette, and office space for the marketing agents. Depending on the project's size and budget, this can be one room or a series of separate areas. It is recommended that an interior designer or architect be employed in the creation of this office so that the imagery is appropriate. The imagery should set the stage for understanding what the development will be.

Furnishing the Office

The furnishings and the artwork should be chosen to be contextual with the design of the project. An interior designer should be employed for maximum effect. The prospect should leave either remembering that the experience was extremely comfortable or remember that working with the developer's marketing agents was so positive that the office has no meaning.

Staffing the Office

Once again, depending on the marketing budget, the staff can consist of a single marketing agent who will handle all the marketing functions or separate individuals who will handle positions, such as a receptionist, hostess, financing coordinator, space designer, and marketing agent.

Use of the Office

Once all the office and all the visual presentations are complete, procedures for its use should be established. With many different people using the space, it should always be left ready for the next presentation complete with the full complement of visual aids. The functions of the office should be planned to allow complete privacy during presentations. In addition, its layout should provide ease of service for serving meals prior to or during presentations and complete privacy during closings.

THE MODEL SUITE

When the prospect is considering potential housing, lodging, or office suites, the model room has proven effective for a number of reasons. First, it becomes a full-scale test for the development team to review for approval prior to building it over and over again. Second, it becomes a full-scale model for prospective users to experience prior to buying or leasing rooms of space. Colors and finishes can be checked prior to the ordering of materials and the tenant will have a complete picture of the standard tenant finishes to be selected. In housing, the future tenant can see the possibilities of furniture layout and understand how his or her furniture will fit in this new home.

Where to Locate

The model could either be located within the sales or leasing office and placed where the potential tenant or buyer can envision all of the amenities of the project. The model suite should become a part of the total marketing presentation and be easily accessible. It should give the marketing agent another tool to use in making the sale.

Model Theme and Decor

The model should feature all of the standard items which are offered and its appearance should represent the tastes of the target market. It should be complete and have the appearance of being lived in. Furniture can be rented to minimize costs. In selecting the appearance, an interior designer should be used. Since this space must be available to be viewed by the public at any time, it should be kept neat and clean.

DESCRIPTION PACKAGES

The developer should ensure that the marketing professionals have a complete package of information on the property. This information will answer many of the questions that are asked of the marketing agent by the potential user. This package should include the following:

    I.   Name of property/address/telephone number
    II.   Developer information
        A. Company name
        B. Address
        C. Telephone number
        D. Track record
        E. List of references
    III.   List of development players
        A. Marketing company
        B. Management company
        C. Architect
        D. Land planner
        E. Engineers
            1. Civil
            2. Structural
            3. Mechanical
            4. Plumbing
            5. Environmental
        F. General contractor
        G. Construction lender
        H. Permanent lender
        I. Interior decorator
        J. Attorney
        K. Accountant
    IV.   Physical description of the development
        A. Land area
        B. Construction specifications
            1. Exterior material
            2. Roof
    V.   Unit information
        A. Number of units
        B. Unit sizes and square footage
        C. Rental/sale prices
        D. Utility information
    VI.   Unit features
    VII. Property amenities

VIII. Financing terms (if applicable)
   A. Lender(s)
   B. Loan-to-value ratio
   C. Current interest rates and terms
   D. Closing costs
   E. Loan qualifications
   F. Items required by lender for loan submittal

IX. Association information (if applicable)
   A. Monthly fee breakdown

X. Move in information
   A. Utility
      1. Names, telephone numbers
      2. Deposit requirements
      3. Cost schedule
   B. Moving brochure

XI. Area information
   A. Schools
   B. Shopping
   C. Transportation
   D. Cultural
   E. Employment centers
   F. Real estate taxes

XII. Exhibits
   A. Brochure
   B. Site plan
   C. Floor plan
   D. Elevations
   E. Wall sections
   F. Area maps
   G. Sales/lease agreement

PREPARATION OF MARKETING BUDGETS

During the predevelopment phase of the project, estimates of marketing budgets will be prepared. Normally, they will be based on dollars-per-square-foot or on percentage of costs, with special considerations for unusual items. As project planning matures, so will the marketing budget. It will be constantly refined based on the design and marketing program of the development, until the project is financed and the loan is approved. Knowing that this budget is the fuel which propels the marketing campaign, its accuracy, in response to the marketing plan is essential.

Scheduling and Marketing Budgets

Along with estimating the expenditures of the marketing strategy, the developer and marketing professional must plan the timing of the expenditures and provide a cash flow analysis. A schedule can be used for total project planning of marketing activities. Cash flows can then be projected based on the expenditures for the activities on a month-by-month basis. This schedule can also be used by marketing personnel for work task assignments and by the developer for follow-up.

Preparing the Marketing Budget

The marketing budget should include both the potential uses of funds as well as the timing of these funds. This budget should be updated every week, month, quarter, or year, depending on the type and size of development. The marketing budget money may be spent to draw the "suspect" to the development. If it appears that the projected number of "suspects" is not being drawn to the development, the marketing agent should try another alternative and modify expenditures within the budget. The following is a sample list of broad categories that will be included in the marketing budget.

Advertising Agency and Public Relations

- Fees
- Commissions
- Production
- Expenses

Model

- Temporary lease
- Utilities
- Interior designer fee
- Set-up
- Freight charges
- Built-ins
- Furniture lease/purchase
- Accessories
- Window coverings
- Painting
- Wall coverings

- Appliance upgrades
- Upgraded flooring
- Upgraded lighting fixtures
- Off-site landscaping
- Security system
- Maid service
- Plant purchase/rental
- Maintenance
- Salvage value—resale

Leasing/Sales/Management Office

- Temporary lease
- Utilities
- Interior designer fee
- Set-up
- Freight charges
- Built-ins
- Furniture lease/purchase
- Accessories
- Window coverings
- Painting
- Wall coverings
- Appliance upgrades
- Upgraded flooring
- Upgraded lighting fixtures
- Off-site landscaping
- Security system
- Maid service
- Plant purchase/rental
- Maintenance
- Special equipment (appliances, computers, etc.)
- Supplies
- Salvage value—resale

Media and Visual Aids

- Brochures
- Fliers
- Newspaper

- Magazines
- Radio
- Television
- Billboard
- Signage
- Telemarketing
- Special drawings and illustrations
- Architectural models
- Audio-visual presentations

Promotions

Promotions items pertain to putting on any special promotion-oriented activities.

- Invitations
- Food and parties
- Entertainment, parties
- Clean-up
- Gifts

Marketing Research

- Prospect lists
- Broker lists
- Multi-listing fee
- Demographics
- Sales/leasing data

General and Administrative

- Telephone
- Answering service
- Postage
- Equipment purchase/rental
- Equipment maintenance
- Stationary/envelopes
- Business cards
- Office supplies
- Travel and entertainment
- Membership dues
- Donations

- Document printing
- Photography
- Courier
- Seminars
- Signage

Displays

- Built-ins
- Frames
- Renderings/plans/elevations
- Aerials
- Maps

MARKETING CAMPAIGNS: MATCHING PRODUCT WITH PROSPECT

A key aspect of the marketing plan will be the planning of the marketing campaign. This campaign may begin some time prior to financing, sometimes prior to construction completion, and be ongoing into property management. The campaign begins with preselling of the development and changes with the trends of the market. This campaign will include prospecting, presentations, and the development of relationships after the target market has been identified.

FINDING THE USERS

Using the defined target market, the marketing professional must find the users to whom he can deliver his message. The first step is to identify where and who they are, prior to making a personal contact. If he can identify a specific need, the initial contact will be easier. If there is no specific need, the marketing professional should develop the relationship hoping that the contact will become a prospect in the future. Potential users are initially called "suspects." After they have been qualified by the marketing agent, they become "prospects." The following are a listing of methods used to find users.

Mail List Companies

Mail list companies sell lists of names. These lists are broken down by various categories. The marketing agent should purchase lists of companies which fit the target market description. Many times these companies also will supply mailing labels and mailing services.

Criss-Cross Directories

Criss-cross directories include the names, addresses, and telephone numbers of local residences and businesses. This is an invaluable tool when trying to get "suspect" information.

Business Directories

Business directories are available for local and national type businesses. These directories include the name of the company, company officers, telephone number, address, number of employees, standard industrial code (SIC), and name of the potential contacts of the various departments.

Retail User Directories

Retail users can be found in retail user directories which feature the names, addresses, telephone numbers, contact names, areas of interest, demographic criteria, and site or size requirements. The following publications are available for use:

Directory of Leading Chain Stores in the United States
Business Guides, Inc.
425 Park Ave.
New York, NY 10022
(212) 371-9400

Leasing Opportunities
International Council of Shopping Centers
665 Fifth Ave.
New York, NY 10022
(212) 421-8181

Retail Leasetrac
Retail Leasetrac, Inc.
3125 Presidential Parkway
Suite 330
Atlanta, GA 30340
(404) 452-8452

Retail Tenant Directory
Monitor Publishing Co.
2535 Landmark Dr., No. 207
Clearwater, FL 34621
(813) 725-7250

Yellow Pages

The local yellow pages can give the marketing agent information on locations of potential retail "suspects" as well as a complete listing of the local brokers in the area.

Real Estate Research Companies

Many larger cities have real estate companies which specialize in gathering and selling data on tenants in commercial buildings. This information includes the building name, tenant name, address, telephone number, contact person, lease dates, and lease rate. This information will assist the marketing agent in quickly penetrating potential "suspects" before the competition finds these individuals.

Real Estate Brokers and Agents

Real estate agents are a prime source of potential users. Most cities have agents who specialize in certain product types. The marketing agent should contact the local Board of Realtors to obtain this list of brokerage companies. By contacting these companies the marketing agent can compile a list of those agents which specialize in his type of product. The marketing agent should then spread the word through the local and regional brokerage community. This can be done by periodic fliers or by individual contacts with the brokers and their weekly sales meeting.

For a comprehensive listing of these brokers and agents, please call the local Board of Realtors, or acquire a copy of the following:

National Roster of Realtors Directory
Stamats Communications, Inc.
427 Sixth Ave., SE
Cedar Rapids, IA 52406
(319) 364-6032

Cold Calling

Cold calling is a technique of either just knocking on a potential "suspect's" door or calling him on the telephone. This technique can be extremely frustrating to the marketing agent due to the fact that it is extremely difficult to get in touch with the "decision maker" the first time. Typically, the marketing agent has to go through a number of individuals before finding the right person.

Referrals

The marketing agent should network through friends, business associates, and past clients to obtain the names of other potential "suspects." It makes it a lot easier to make contact with these "suspects" when you are able to use the name of someone they know as an introduction.

Advertising

Advertising in the various types of media mentioned above can be a valuable tool. The marketing agent must be able to get the word out to the consumer about the product being marketed. Often, this notice in the media will result in calls requesting additional information.

Public Relations

Public relations articles can be worth extra sales if properly positioned and timed, especially if they are a catalyst for users requesting more information.

Direct Mail

Direct mail campaigns are directed to groups of potential prospects. Fliers, letters, or post cards are mailed to selected target groups. Receiving a message which is informative and interesting can create interest in your product.

Telemarketing

Telemarketing is similar to direct mail campaigns, except rather than mailing information, the marketing is done by telephone. If there appears to be an interest from a "suspect," a follow-up direct mail piece will be sent.

PRESELLING THE MARKET

Preselling of the product to the market is extremely difficult. Preselling is typically a requirement of the construction lender. These lenders will only lend if they can be shown that there is a market for the product. They will typically predetermine a specified percent of the development that must have bona fide presale/leasing commitments prior to funding the loan.

During the preselling phase, the marketing agent will secure signed agreements for leasing space or reservations for buyers to purchase. Typically, these deals will include a reduced price or extra concessions to induce the user to commit prior to seeing the completed project. Preselling or preleasing can occur in residential, office and industrial type developments, depending on the economy and the number of buyers in the market. Obviously, there is more security for the lender with this type of leasing schedule for the development. An effective presale marketing campaign will include various public relations events and articles about the progress of the development along with mailings to interested parties concerning the construction and sales/leasing progress.

Promotions

Marketing promotions should be an integral part of the ongoing marketing strategy. These promotions include public relations announcements and events or parties aimed at the potential user.

The Grand Opening

At the grand opening stage, the development is ready to be viewed by the public. During this stage, the prices will usually increase (assuming the market demand is there) over the original presale prices. The grand opening will also include extra marketing dollars from the budget to promote this event. A grand opening will not be included in preselling the property.

Broker Parties

Broker parties are designed to solicit the local real estate brokerage community in marketing of the property. Typically, this is their first presentation and impression of the development. These events are set up at times which are convenient to the brokers and are usually catered.

VIP Parties

VIP parties include local dignitaries, such as the mayor, council persons, or other influential individuals. These types of events usually create good public relations articles within local media.

Tenant/Buyer Parties

These events bring together the committed and prospective users in a social setting.

Neighborhood Parties

Neighborhood parties are initiated to gain good will with local neighbors, hopefully leading to referral business.

Close Out Parties

The close out parties are to announce to the world that the property is now sold out and there has been a successful marketing campaign.

THE PRESENTATION — OR THE SALE

The presentation of the product is as good as the first impression made by the marketing agent. The following are the phases in the presentation to the user. The majority of the time spent in the presentation should be spent listening to the user. Only in this way can the marketing professional customize the presentation to meet all the needs of the prospect.

The Initial Meeting and Qualifying the Prospects

At the initial meeting, first impressions are made of the product and the marketing agent. The marketing agent should welcome the prospect to the property and then introduce himself. The marketing agent should make the prospect as comfortable as possible.

After the introductions are completed, the marketing agent should prequalify the "suspect" to determine if his needs fit the product. This qualifying stage will reduce time wasted by both parties. The following five basic questions should be asked by the marketing agent:

1. What size space is desired?
2. What is his schedule for needing the space?
3. What is his desired price range?
4. What features will they require?
5. What amenities will you require?

Presentation of Features and Benefits

The presentation should include all of the pertinent information about the development presented in such a way that the user can see his needs met. The prospect should be walked through the development carefully, clearly, and concisely pointing out all of its features. The presentation should include pictures, renderings, property information, terms, models and, if possible, conclude with a visit to the space specific within the project and the model suite. The prospect should always leave with some type of collateral material. In addition, a wise marketing professional will have another meeting scheduled for follow-up.

Follow-Up

Follow-up should be used by the marketing professional to answer any additional questions. Responsiveness to questions and creativity in proposals should be presented in each contact with the prospect.

CLOSING THE SALE—LEASING AND SALES AGREEMENT

Once the prospect indicates that a decision in favor of your property has been reached, the marketing agent should seek to have a letter of understanding prepared or a contract signed. In order to expedite this process, the marketing agent should have all the necessary documents prepared in advance. The idea at this stage is to get the prospect to commit as quickly as possible.

Postclosing Follow-Up

After the documents have been signed, the marketing agent should stay in touch with the customer. The easier the move-in by the user, the better impression of the property and the marketing agent. Consequently, additional referrals may bring additional business. The user also may be a future prospect in another development or at least will have to renew the lease at some future time.

THE LEASING AGREEMENT

The preparation of the sales or leasing documents should require careful attention to detail. These agreements should be prepared by experienced professionals and reviewed by the developer and marketing agent prior to finalizing. The lease document is a binding document between the owner (lessor) and the tenant (lessee) which spells out the exact terms and conditions for the tenant occupying the rental space. The negotiations of these agreements will begin with a working document which outlines the terms and conditions of the agreements and then is finalized with a formal legal document.

Types of Leases

The basic type of lease is when the tenant pays a predetermined rental payment on a monthly basis. Many commercial properties who have long-term tenants might use any of the following type leases.

Flat Rental

A flat rental lease stipulates the exact monthly rental that the tenant will pay. The tenant will then know exactly what the rental obligation is for a given time period. The landlord will then be exposed to any increases in expenses over this time period. For example:

> Year 1 $10.00 per sq. ft.
> Year 2 $10.00 per sq. ft.

Step-Up Rental

This type of lease stipulates that on a predetermined date in the future the monthly rental rates will increase. For example,

> Year 1 $10.00 per sq. ft.
> Year 2 $11.00 per sq. ft.

Year 3 $12.00 per sq. ft.
Year 4 $13.00 per sq. ft.
Year 5 $14.00 per sq. ft.

Escalation

An escalation lease contains language that will increase the monthly rental payment based on a tenant's prorata share of increases in the following three items:

1. **Real estate taxes:** Typically, this language will include the
   A. Selection of a base year
   B. Date when payment is due
   C. Ability of the tenant to contest any tax increase
2. **Operating expenses:** Typically, this language will include sections on the following operating expenses increases that are exempt or pro rated
   A. Mortgage debt service
   B. Ground rent
   C. Capital expenditures
   D. Marketing expenses
   E. Vacant space, common area maintenance charges
3. **Extra services:** Many tenants will require services over and above the standard services offered by the landlord. These services can include:
   A. Additional HVAC time
   B. Excess water usage
   C. Excessive trash removal
   D. Additional janitorial services

Cost-of-Living Index

The cost-of-living index lease will base the yearly rental increases on a predetermined cost-of-living index. In many cases this index may have a floor and a ceiling rate.

Percentage Lease

Many retail leases base their increases of the yearly rental on a percentage of the gross income of the tenant over a specified dollar amount. This method enables the landlord to share in the success of the tenants. Careful screening should be used to verify the actual collections of these tenants, because an understatement of these revenues can cost the investor lost revenue. For example, a clothing shop might have a $12.00 per square foot rental rate plus 5 percent of revenue over $100,000 per year in gross revenue.

Terms and Conditions of Leases

The terms and conditions will include the following. Please note that the items included in the sales agreement will be reviewed in detail in Chapter 14.

Description of Premises

This description will include the building number, suite number, and number of gross or net square footage. An exhibit to the lease will include a copy of the space plan and the tenant improvement specifications. The exhibit should be initialed by both the owner and the tenant.

Base Rental Rate

This will include the initial rental rate for the lease as well as any rental charged for parking.

Rental Escalations

Rental escalations are increases in the base rental rate at the yearly anniversary date of the lease. The following are methods used for additional rent increases.

Additional Rental

This will include any additional rental due by the tenant, such as:

Common Area Maintenance (CAM) Charges: Most retail leases have a common area maintenance fee which is charged to each tenant. This charge is based on a set rate per square foot. CAM charges may include the following:

- Janitorial
- Common area utility costs
- Landscaping
- Security

Operating Cost Pass Through: This method will pass on the cost of any increases in operating expenses over a specified amount. For example, the lease might say that all costs over a $3.00 per square foot base rate will be passed on to the tenant.

Tenants Percentage of the Total Building Area

In leases that require the tenant to pay for a prorata share of operating expenses, it is important to list both the total square footage of the building and the total square footage of each tenant. The following formula is used to calculate this ratio:

$$\frac{\text{Total tenant space (gross or net)}}{\text{Total building space (gross or net)}} = \text{Tenant's prorata percentage (gross or net)}$$

Lease Term

The lease term will define the term of the lease. It will include both the starting and the ending dates.

Renewal Options

Renewal options will include the number and the length of the renewal periods.

Expansion Options

Expansion options will define the amount of option space available in the future to the tenant, the cost of this space, and when the option must be exercised by the tenant.

First Right of Refusal

In lieu of an option, the lease might contain language which the tenant has a "first right of refusal" on certain predetermined space. This right will then contain language about how much time the tenant has to decide to exercise this right.

Commencement Date

Although a tenant might have possession at an earlier date, this date may specify the actual date the rent is due.

Deal Concessions

Depending on local market conditions, the developer might offer various deal concessions to the potential tenant. Typically, developers will offer concessions in lieu of a reduction in the base rental rate for the following reasons:

- There is pressure from the lender to have leases at the proforma rental rate.
- It is easier to increase the tenant's rental rate to the market rate when the lease expires by starting at the current market rate.
- The developer is able to keep the appraisal value of the property at a higher level than if the base rental rate is dropped.

Typical concessions offered by developers are listed below.

Free Rent

Free rent is based on a predetermined number of months in which the tenant will either pay no rent or a reduced rental rate. Many developers choose to put this concession in a side letter with the tenant. Because many leases are recorded in the local courthouse, many developers do not want their business dealings publicized.

Extra Parking

Extra parking spaces might be in the deal as a tenant inducement.

Increased Tenant Improvement (TI) Allowance

Commercial properties have specified tenant improvement allowances. As an inducement, this allowance might be increased.

Cash Payment Up Front

Depending on the developer's financial resources or the structuring of the construction loan, an up-front cash payment might be offered to the tenant. This cash can be used by the tenant for moving expenses or for plain business working capital.

Moving Expenses

Since the cost of moving is very expensive, the developer may pay for all or part of this expense. This expense includes cost of moving material, moving van rental, additional moving insurance, change of stationery, new telephone systems, additional furniture, and decorating costs.

Free Memberships

As an additional rental inducement, many developers will offer free memberships to local business or health club facilities.

Ownership of Building

To assist in potential financing, the developer might offer to large space users a percentage of the building ownership.

Lease Buyout

As an inducement to get a tenant to move prior to his current lease expiration, many developers will buy out the remaining lease of the tenant. This can be done by paying the tenant's current landlord an amount equal to the present value of the remaining lease value or by the developer assuming the remaining lease. If the developer assumes the balance of the lease, he will then try to re-market this space to a potential user.

Interior Architectural and Interior Design Fees

As further inducement the developer might offer to include the cost for architectural and interior design of the tenant's space.

Commitment Deposit

Due to the cost of designing the tenant space and preparing the lease, many developers require a commitment deposit by the tenant. This deposit is used to defray these expenses if the tenant does not sign a lease. If the tenant signs the lease, this deposit can be applied against the security deposit or the first month's rental.

Security Deposit

The security deposit is to be used as additional rental security or can be applied to the last month's rental. It is also used to offset any tenant damage at the end of the lease.

Termination Fee

If the tenant moves out early, the landlord can either sue to collect the balance of the rental or can negotiate an early termination fee.

Use of Premise

This section of the lease defines how the premises may be used.

Design Fee Allowance

This allowance is for the space planning of the tenant space. It is usually based on a flat dollar amount per lease square footage. The reason for this allowance is because many potential tenants change their design criteria several times and the developer does not want to pay for their indecisiveness.

Tenant Improvement (TI) Allowance

Each building will usually specify a predetermined allowance for tenant improvements. This allowance will be a function of the market and the type of property.

Paying for Increases in the Tenant Improvements

If the tenant exceeds the allotted tenant improvement allowance, the following are three methods of paying for this expense.

1. Negotiate for the tenant to pay for this cost upfront.
2. The developer will amortize this cost over the term of the lease. There should be a penalty provision in case the tenant moves out early.
3. Split this cost between the tenant and the developer.

If the developer must pay for all or a portion of this expense, he may have to pay for this out of his own pocket or he might be able to negotiate a bank loan (using the lease as collateral) to obtain these funds.

Types of Operating Leases

Depending on the type of property or tenant, the developer can pay for all or only some of the operating expenses.

Gross Lease

The landlord pays the real estate taxes, maintenance of the common area, and the insurance.

Net Lease

The tenant pays only the real estate taxes.

Net Net Lease

The tenant pays the real estate taxes and maintenance of the common area. The landlord is responsible for paying the insurance.

Net Net Net Lease

The tenant pays for the real estate taxes, the maintenance of the common area, and the insurance (commonly referred to as triple net lease).

MARKETING FORMS

Residential Data Form (12-1)

This form is to be used when gathering information on comparable residential properties.

RESIDENTIAL DATA FORM

FORM 12-1

GENERAL INFORMATION

PROPERTY NAME _____
ADDRESS _____
ADDRESS _____
DATE PREPARED ___/___/___
MAP # _____

TYPE PROPERTY:
SINGLE-FAMILY _____
MULTI-FAMILY _____
MOBILE HOME _____
  LOT RENTAL _____

ARCHITECTURAL STYLE:
TRADITIONAL _____
CONTEMPORARY _____
OTHER _____

BUILDING TYPE:
ONE LEVEL _____
TOWNHOME _____
GARDEN _____
MID-RISE _____
HIGH-RISE _____

TYPE CONSTRUCTION:
WOOD FRAME _____
STEEL _____
CONCRETE _____
MASONRY _____

UTILITIES PAID BY: LANDLORD TENANT
GAS _____ _____
ELECTRICITY _____ _____
WATER _____ _____

NO. UNITS _____
NO. BUILDINGS _____
TOTAL SQ. FT. _____
LAND (ACREAGE) _____
DENSITY (UNITS/ACRE) _____
LAND EFFICIENCY _____%

ELEVATORS: NO ____ YES ____ # ___
SPRINKLERS: NO ____ YES ___

UTILITY SYSTEM: GAS   ELECTRIC
HVAC _____ _____
HOT WATER _____ _____
COOKING _____ _____
DRYER _____ _____
FIREPLACE _____

INDIVIDUAL METERS ____ MASTER METER ___

PARKING: COVERED ___ # SPACES ___ MONTHLY FEE $___
PARKING: SURFACE ___ # SPACES ___ MONTHLY FEE $___

YEAR BUILT

LEASE INFORMATION

LEASE TERM (MONTHS) _____
SECURITY DEPOSIT $____
REFUNDABLE DEPOSIT $____
NON-REFUNDABLE DEP $____
PET POLICY: NO ___ YES ___ HT. ___ WT. ___
LAST RENT INCREASE ___/___/___
  PERCENTAGE INCREASE _____%
CURRENT RENT CONCESSION _____

TARGET MARKET

ALL ADULT ____ MARRIED WITH KIDS ___
SENIOR CITIZENS ____ STUDENTS ___
MILITARY ___   OTHER _____

UNIT FEATURES

FLOORING: CARPET ___ VINYL ___ WOOD ___
WALL: PAINT ___ WALLPAPER ___
WINDOWS: BLINDS ___ DRAPES ___ SHADES ___ RODS ___
FIREPLACE: NO ___ YES ___
PATIO ___ BALCONY ___ SCREEN PORCH ___ SUNROOM ___
APPLIANCES: REFRIGERATOR ___ FF ___ ICE MAKER ___
OVEN ___ SC ___ CC ___ MICROWAVE ___
DISHWASHER ___ DISPOSAL ___ TRASHMASHER ___
WASHER ___ DRYER ___ W/D CONNECTIONS ___

AMENITIES

SWIMMING POOL: ADULT ___ KIDS ___ INSIDE ___
EXERCISE ROOM ___ SAUNA ___ BAR ___
TENNIS COURT: LIGHTED ___ # ___
JOG TRAIL ___ TOT LOT ___ PICNIC AREA ___
PLANNED ACTIVITIES ___ SECURITY ___ DOORMAN __
LAUNDRY ROOM ___ OTHER _____
CABLE TV ___ INCLUDED ___ NOT INCLUDED ___

RENTAL INFORMATION

UNIT TYPE	#UNITS	MONTHLY RENT RATE	SQ.FT.	RENT/ SQ.FT.	OCCUPANCY
_____	_____	$_____	_____	$_____	_____%
_____	_____	$_____	_____	$_____	_____%
_____	_____	$_____	_____	$_____	_____%
_____	_____	$_____	_____	$_____	_____%
_____	_____	$_____	_____	$_____	_____%
_____	_____	$_____	_____	$_____	_____%
_____	_____	$_____	_____	$_____	_____%
_____	_____	$_____	_____	$_____	_____%
TOTAL		$_____	_____		_____%
AVERAGE		$_____	_____	$_____	

Form 12-1 Residential data form.

Commercial Data Form (12–2)

This form is to be used when gathering information on comparable commercial properties.

COMMERCIAL DATA FORM

FORM 12–2

GENERAL INFORMATION

PROPERTY NAME _____
ADDRESS _____
ADDRESS _____
DATE PREPARED __/__/__
MAP # _____

TYPE PROPERTY:
OFFICE _____
 BUSINESS PARK _____
RETAIL: CONVENIENCE _____
 RETAIL: NEIGHBORHOOD _____
 RETAIL: COMMUNITY _____
 RETAIL: REGIONAL _____
 RETAIL: THEME _____
INDUSTRIAL: OFFICE/WAREHOUSE _____
 INDUSTRIAL: BULK _____
 INDUSTRIAL: MINI–WAREHOUSE _____

ARCHITECTURAL STYLE:
TRADITIONAL _____
CONTEMPORARY _____
OTHER _____

BUILDING TYPE:
ONE LEVEL _____
TOWNHOME _____
GARDEN _____
MID–RISE _____
HIGH–RISE _____

OFFICE % _____
WAREHOUSE % _____
TYPE CONSTRUCTION:
 WOOD FRAME _____
 STEEL _____
 CONCRETE _____
 MASONRY _____

UTILITIES PAID BY:	LANDLORD	TENANT
GAS		
ELECTRICITY	_____	_____
WATER	_____	_____
TRASH	_____	_____

JANITORIAL SERVICE: NO ____ YES ____ # DAYS/WK ____

NO. BUILDINGS _____
TOTAL SQ. FT. (GROSS) _____
TOTAL SQ. FT. (NET) _____
NO. FLOORS _____
LAND (ACREAGE) _____
DENSITY (UNITS/ACRE) _____
LAND EFFICIENCY _____%

ELEVATORS: NO ____ YES ____ # ____
 SERVICE ELEVATORS: NO ____ YES ____ #
SPRINKLERS: NO ____ YES ____

UTILITY SYSTEM:
 TOTAL ELECTRIC ____
 SPLIT SYSTEM ____
 INDIVIDUAL METERS ____
 MASTER METER ____
 HEAT PUMPS ____
 SPACE HEATER ____

YEAR BUILT _____

PARKING: COVERED ____ # SPACES ____ MONTHLY FEE $____
PARKING: SURFACE ____ # SPACES ____ MONTHLY FEE $____

LEASE AND RENTAL INFORMATION

LEASE TERM (MONTHS) _____
SECURITY DEPOSIT $____
REFUNDABLE DEPOSIT $____
NON–REFUNDABLE DEP. $____
OPTIONS (NO./YRS.) __/__
RENT ESCALATIONS: FIXED ____ STEP–UP ____ CPI INCREASE ____% PASS THRU ____
TENANT IMPROVEMENT ALLOWANCE ($/SQ. FT.) $____
REAL ESTATE BROKERAGE COMMISSION ____%
CURRENT RENT CONCESSION _____
RENT PER SQ.FT (GROSS) $_____ TO $_____
RENT PER SQ.FT (NET) $_____ TO $_____

SPACE FEATURES

SPRINKLER ____ REAR LOADING DOCK ____
SIGNAGE ____
BAY DEPTH ____ BAY WIDTH ____ CEILING HEIGHT ____
SMALLEST SPACE (SQ.FT.) _____
LARGEST SPACE (SQ.FT.) _____

TARGET MARKET

LOCAL ____ REGIONAL ____ NATIONAL ____

ANCHOR TENANT:
 TENANT _____ SQ.FT. _____
 TENANT _____ SQ.FT. _____
 TENANT _____ SQ.FT. _____

AMENITIES

SECRETARIAL SERVICE ____ CONFERENCE ROOM ____
EXERCISE ROOM ____ SAUNA ____
TENNIS COURT: LIGHTED ____ # ____
RESTAURANT ____ MAIL ROOM ____
SECURITY ____

Form 12–2 Commercial data form.

Lease Checklist Form (12–3)

This form is to be used as a checklist when leasing property.

LEASE CHECKLIST FORM

FORM 12-3

TENANT INFORMATION

TENANT NAME	_____	IMPORTANT DATES	
CONTACT	_____	LEASE COMMENCEMENT	___/___/___
ADDRESS	_____	LEASE ANNIVERSARY	___/___/___
	_____	FIRST MONTH RENT DUE	___/___/___
TEL. NO	(___)_____	LEASE TERM	_____
		OPTIONS (#/YRS)	_____/_____

DESCRIPTION OF EVENT	LEASE SECTION	DATE DUE	DATE COMPLETE	LETTER	COMMENTS
APPLICATION	____	__/__/__	__/__/__	____	_____
LEASE	____	__/__/__	__/__/__	____	_____
RENTAL GUARANTEE	____	__/__/__	__/__/__	____	_____
KEY LETTER	____	__/__/__	__/__/__	____	_____
BROKER AGREEMENT	____	__/__/__	__/__/__	____	_____
1ST MONTH RENT	____	__/__/__	__/__/__	____	_____
SECURITY DEPOSIT	____	__/__/__	__/__/__	____	_____
FINANCIAL STATEMENT	____	__/__/__	__/__/__	____	_____
LEASE RECORDED	____	__/__/__	__/__/__	____	_____
SIGN APPROVAL LETTER	____	__/__/__	__/__/__	____	_____
TENANT'S BUILDERS RISK INSURANCE POLICY	____	__/__/__	__/__/__	____	_____
LANDLORD APPROVE OF PLANS & SPECS	____	__/__/__	__/__/__	____	_____
SUBCONTRACTOR LETTER	____	__/__/__	__/__/__	____	_____
ROOF LETTER	____	__/__/__	__/__/__	____	_____
TENANT'S ACCEPTANCE LETTER	____	__/__/__	__/__/__	____	_____
CERTIFICATE OF OCCUPANCY	____	__/__/__	__/__/__	____	_____
TENANT'S INSURANCE POLICY	____	__/__/__	__/__/__	____	_____
LANDLORD'S CONSTRUCTION ACCEPTANCE LETTER	____	__/__/__	__/__/__	____	_____
TENANT COLOR OUT FORM	____	__/__/__	__/__/__	____	_____
LANDLORD HVAC LETTER	____	__/__/__	__/__/__	____	_____
EMPLOYEE LICENSE TAG #'S	____	__/__/__	__/__/__	____	_____
HVAC MAINTENANCE AGREEMENT	____	__/__/__	__/__/__	____	_____
_____	____	__/__/__	__/__/__	____	_____
_____	____	__/__/__	__/__/__	____	_____
_____	____	__/__/__	__/__/__	____	_____
_____	____	__/__/__	__/__/__	____	_____
_____	____	__/__/__	__/__/__	____	_____
FINANCIAL STATEMENT–YEAR 2	____	__/__/__	__/__/__	____	_____
FINANCIAL STATEMENT–YEAR 3	____	__/__/__	__/__/__	____	_____
FINANCIAL STATEMENT–YEAR 4	____	__/__/__	__/__/__	____	_____
FINANCIAL STATEMENT–YEAR 5	____	__/__/__	__/__/__	____	_____
WORK ORDERS	____	__/__/__	__/__/__	____	_____
WORK ORDERS	____	__/__/__	__/__/__	____	_____
WORK ORDERS	____	__/__/__	__/__/__	____	_____
WORK ORDERS	____	__/__/__	__/__/__	____	_____

COMMENTS

_____

_____

_____

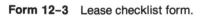

Form 12-3 Lease checklist form.

Commercial Lease Summary Form (12–4)

This form is to be used as a summary for the commercial lease terms of each lease.

COMMERCIAL LEASE SUMMARY FORM

FORM 12–4

PROPERTY _____
LESSEE _____
SUITE NO. _____
TEL. NO. (____)_____

LEASE INFORMATION

LEASED REVIEWED BY _____ LEASE TERM _____	BEG. LEASE DATE ___/___/___	DIRECTORY LISTING _____
LEASED APPROVED BY _____ DATE LEASE SIGN ___/___/___	END LEASE DATE ___/___/___	PARKING PERMITS _____
MOVE–IN DATE ___/___/___	ANNIVERSARY DATE ___/___/___	KEYS ISSUED _____

SQUARE FOOTAGE:

GROSS SQUARE FOOTAGE _____

NET SQUARE FOOTAGE _____

RENTAL RATE:

RENTAL (/SQ.FT./MO.) $_____

UTILITIES PAID BY LESSEE:

OPERATING EXPENSE PASSTHRU:

BASE YEAR _____

TAXES $_____

INSURANCE $_____

PERCENTAGE RENT:

PERCENTAGE _____%

BREAKPOINT $_____

PARKING:

NO. SPACES–FREE _____

NO. SPACE–PAID _____

RATE/CAR/MO. $_____

GAS _____

ELECTRICITY _____

WATER _____

SEWER _____

RENT ESCALATIONS:

FIXED _____%

CPI (BASE YR>) _____

STEP–UP _____

RENEWAL/EXPANSION NOTICE:

NOTIFICATION DATE ___/___/___

NO. OPTIONS _____

TERM _____

RATE (SQ.FT.) $_____

SQ.FT. _____

SERVICES PROVIDED BY LESSOR:

JANITORIAL _____

NO. DAYS/WK _____

SECURITY DEPOSIT:

DEPOSIT $_____ __

HELD BY _____

INTEREST @ _____%

TERMINATION CLAUSE:

DATE ___/___/___

PENALTY _____

REAL ESTATE COMMISSION

BROKER _____   ADDRESS _____

AGENT _____   ADDRESS _____

TEL. NO. (____)_____

COMMISSION STRUCTURE:

FIRST MONTH $_____   PERCENTAGE _____%

THEREAFTER $_____   LEASE VALUE $_____

LESSEE CREDIT CHECK

BANK REFERENCE:

BANK _____

CONTACT _____

TEL. NO. (____)_____

CREDIT RATING _____

TRADE REFERENCE:

FIRM _____

CONTACT _____

TEL. NO. (____)_____

CREDIT RATING _____

TRADE REFERENCE:

FIRM _____

CONTACT _____

TEL. NO. (____)_____

CREDIT RATING _____

ESTIMATED CONSTRUCTION COSTS

ALLOWANCE $_____   COST/SQ/FT/ $_____

TOTAL COST $_____   COST/SQ/FT/ $_____

DIFFERENCE $_____   COST/SQ/FT/ $_____

LESSEE TO PAY EXTRA COST OF $_____

BY CASH $_____

AMORTIZED PER SQ.FT. $_____

TERM _____ RATE _____%

Form 12–4   Commercial lease summary form.

Leasing Status Report Form (12–5)

This form is to be used to review the leasing status.

LEASING STATUS REPORT FORM

FORM 12–5

PROPERTY _____
WEEK ENDING ___/___/___
PREPARED BY _____
PROPERTY TYPE _____

TENANT NAME	SUITE #	UNIT SIZE (SQ.FT.)	QUOTED RATE	TENANT IMPROVEMENT ALLOWANCE (PER SQ.FT.)	LEASE TERM QUOTED	BROKER	STATUS
_____	____	_____	$_____	$_____	_____	_____	_____
_____	____	_____	$_____	$_____	_____	_____	_____
_____	____	_____	$_____	$_____	_____	_____	_____
_____	____	_____	$_____	$_____	_____	_____	_____
_____	____	_____	$_____	$_____	_____	_____	_____
_____	____	_____	$_____	$_____	_____	_____	_____
_____	____	_____	$_____	$_____	_____	_____	_____
_____	____	_____	$_____	$_____	_____	_____	_____
_____	____	_____	$_____	$_____	_____	_____	_____
_____	____	_____	$_____	$_____	_____	_____	_____
_____	____	_____	$_____	$_____	_____	_____	_____
_____	____	_____	$_____	$_____	_____	_____	_____
_____	____	_____	$_____	$_____	_____	_____	_____
_____	____	_____	$_____	$_____	_____	_____	_____
_____	____	_____	$_____	$_____	_____	_____	_____
_____	____	_____	$_____	$_____	_____	_____	_____
_____	____	_____	$_____	$_____	_____	_____	_____
_____	____	_____	$_____	$_____	_____	_____	_____
_____	____	_____	$_____	$_____	_____	_____	_____
_____	____	_____	$_____	$_____	_____	_____	_____
_____	____	_____	$_____	$_____	_____	_____	_____
_____	____	_____	$_____	$_____	_____	_____	_____
_____	____	_____	$_____	$_____	_____	_____	_____
_____	____	_____	$_____	$_____	_____	_____	_____
_____	____	_____	$_____	$_____	_____	_____	_____

STATUS KEY
1. LEASE HAS A GOOD CHANCE OF BEING SIGNED
2. ACTIVE DIALOGUE
3. SHOWS SOME INTEREST

Form 12–5 Leasing status report form.

Chapter *13*

Maximizing the Returns Through Property Management

To realize the maximum return on investment in real estate development, the real estate developer must have effective property management. Effective property management means that the property is 90 to 100 percent leased, the tenant's needs are paramount in the manager's mind, rents are collected on time, vendor billings are paid and up to date, there is an ongoing preventative maintenance program, the systems are operating efficiently within operating budget forecasting, and the cash flow from the development is equal to or better than predicted within the project proforma.

For a project to perform in this manner, it is essential that the real estate developer consider the implications of property management from the early conceptual stages of the project. To have completed the project without considering the implications of property management will have programmed the development for failure. Property management is not something that happens after the fact. It is the secret of long-term profitability for the development even if the development is sold in the future. Incompetent property management can result in loss of value and possible foreclosure.

Property management's responsibilities are very similar to the developer's activities in the creation of the project. The developer must make all decisions based on market demand. The same is true for the property manager. The developer's objective is to create a product that will lease well. The property manager's objective is to maintain a product that will stay leased. The developer must design the product so that it appeals to future tenants. The property manager must re-design the product, estimate the costs, and manage the construction, on a smaller scale, so that it satisfies the needs of the tenants. The developer must make creative decisions which appeal to the tenant. The property manager must make operational decisions which do not create negative impressions. The developer must estimate the rents, while the property manager must collect the rents. The developer must select the materials and systems, while the property manager must maintain those same systems and materials. Consequently, it is easy to understand why unilateral decision making without property management input can create an enormous amount of problems. The performance of the property manager is an extension of the proforma for the development and the only insurance which the developer possesses that can guarantee that the development will perform as intended.

The most important issue to remember in property management is service to the customer. If any business must be customer oriented, it is property management. The customer (tenant) must feel that his or her needs are paramount to the building developer, owner, or property manager. Each person on the property's management staff must be educated to perform and respond in the same manner. Each time an operational manager enters a tenant's space, his demeanor and offers to help must be thought of as the single most important link in that tenant's renewal. In addition, if the service is outstanding to the tenants, it will become the project's best advertising, bringing new tenants and additional revenues to the project's bottom line.

This chapter will paint a picture of the property management function. We will discuss the team, management agreements, policies and procedures, operating budgets, accounting, tenant leases and many other aspects of property management. In addition, many different forms are included to assist in the performance of this function.

WHO WILL MANAGE THE PROPERTY?

To successfully perform the property management function, the developer must exercise care in personnel selection. The developer can either choose to have an in-house management staff or to contract for this service with third-party companies. If he chooses to perform this function in-house, he must select his team from personnel who understand his philosophy of service as well as being market sensitive and customer driven. If he selects a company to manage the property, he must know that their management of the property will enhance his investment.

In-House Management

Increased financial and management control as well as having an additional profit center (management fees) are the advantages of managing developments in-house. The drawbacks are increased overhead expenses and the increased time necessary for the management of personnel. With this route, the developer should be committed to spending the money and time to oversee the operation. Depending on the size of the operation, many developers will hire a director of property management to oversee the daily operations of the various properties and report directly to the developer on the weekly and monthly status. Usually, in-house property management staff are necessary and cost effective when the developer has multiple properties within a given area.

Third-Party Companies

If the developer desires to contract with a management company, he should search for firms specializing in his property type. This selection process should include personal interviews with the firm's principals, checking of references (both past and present clients), and a personal visit to current properties under management. This personal visit should include interviews with on-site personnel and a thorough review of on-site and home office reporting and filing systems. In addition, plan on a few meetings with the project's tenants to confirm the service level.

Management Philosophies

In order to ensure a long-term relationship between the developer and the management company, the developer should fully define his objectives and philosophy in property management. He should then spend as much time as necessary to make sure that this philosophy of management will be followed by the management company. In addition, once the management company has taken over the property, the developer should follow up with surveys of tenants, spot checking for evidence that his directions are being followed.

Property Management Staffing

Regardless of the method the developer uses to manage the property, the following types of personnel will be employed. Figure 13–1 shows the various relationships of the personnel.

Property Manager (Building Manager)

The property manager is responsible for the overall daily operations of the property. The property manager may have multiple properties to supervise.

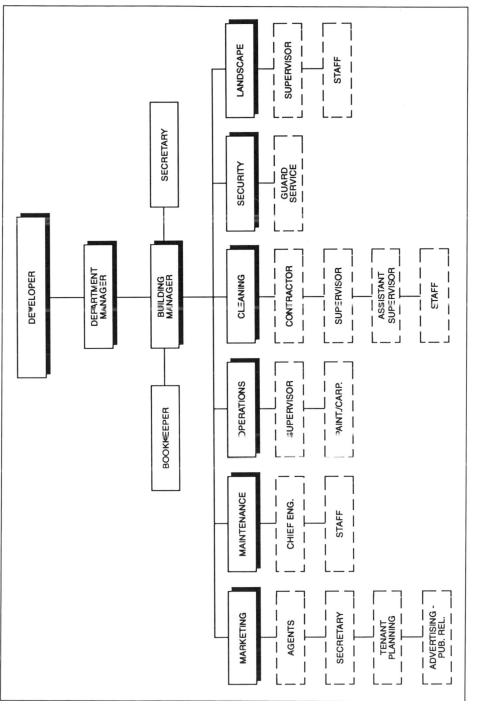

Figure 13-- Property management staff diagram.

547

Resident Manager (For Residential)

The resident manager is located on the premises. This individual oversees revenue collections, tenant relations, and refers maintenance problems to the maintenance department. They have similar responsibilities as building managers.

Assistant Resident Manager

This individual assists the resident manager in all property management tasks.

Bookkeeper

Accounting and the payment of all invoices to vendors or contractors are the bookkeeper's responsibility.

Office Receptionist (or Secretary or Administrative Assistant)

If the project's size warrants this position, the office receptionist will welcome guests and handle all incoming telephone calls.

Leasing Agent

The leasing agent will coordinate the showing and negotiating of leases for the tenant spaces.

Advertising and Public Relations

Their responsibility can include developing an image of the property, strategic placement of newspaper articles, and tenant relations through special events.

Space Planner

They are responsible for taking a new tenant's program for his office functions and creating a layout of space which will be constructed as their premises.

Tenant Development Manager

They are responsible for the space planning and construction of all tenant space. They can also be responsible for renovations to the base building.

Operations Manager

The operations manager coordinates all the daily work orders including the scheduling of deferred maintenance programs. Depending on the size of the project and the operations manager's experience level, this individual might respond to work orders. Additionally, this individual can order supplies and inventory.

Chief Engineer

They are usually responsible for the mechanical, electrical, fire protection, and plumbing systems of the building.

Assistant Operations Manager

If the project's size warrants an assistant, this individual assists the maintenance supervisor in daily routines.

Maids, Janitors, Porters, and Laborers

Again, depending on the size of the development, these positions can be for full-time or part-time employees. They help to fill the gap when maintenance repairs are backlogged. They may be used to help clean up or respond to tenant requests.

Security

This position can be full-time in a large development or part-time in smaller properties. Many residential properties employ local off-duty police officers for this position.

Amenity Workers

These workers can be full time, part-time, or even seasonal personnel. They assist in areas such as the pool, exercise rooms, or special sporting areas.

Landscape Supervisor

Depending on the size of the development, this person can oversee all landscape installation and maintenance. In addition, ongoing maintenance of sprinkler systems can be their responsibility.

THE MANAGEMENT AGREEMENT

Long before the project is completed, and just prior to financing, a property management agreement must be executed. Once the team is selected, the developer should negotiate the terms of this agreement, including fees and the services to be performed. Once these terms and conditions are negotiated, they should be placed in a formal agreement by an attorney. The following are issues to negotiate during this preliminary phase of the relationship.

Fee Structure

Essentially, how the management company will be paid comprises the fee structure. Typically, this fee is based on a percentage of the collected rental income and is paid to the management company monthly. During lease-up periods this monthly fee is negotiated as a flat rate. Once this collected income reaches a specified amount, the flat rate converts to the specified percentage. This section should detail the formula used to determine what collected monthly income is. Fee percentages for different properties vary as follows:

Apartments	3.5% to 6.0% of collections
Office buildings	3.0% to 5.0% of collections
Retail	3.0% to 5.0% of collections
Industrial	3.0% to 5.0% of collections
Mini-warehouses	4.0% to 6.0% of collections
Lodging	3.0% to 7.0% of collections

Term of the Agreement

This section determines that time period for the agreement. This period can vary from a month-to-month to over five-year contracts.

Scope of Responsibilities of the Management Firm

This section lists all of the duties of the management firm. To avoid future conflict between the parties this section should be clearly defined.

Collection of Monies

This section defines who will collect the rental and where the funds will be deposited.

Expenses of the Management Firm

This section will outline what expenses the owner will pay for and what expenses the management firm is expected to pay for.

Employees

This section will determine who will be employees of the management firm and the property owner.

Authorization to Sign Service Documents

This section defines who will sign service contracts.

Major Repairs

This section outlines the procedure for the management firm to take when requesting, bidding, and making purchase orders for major items. This section will typically have to determine the amount of money that the management firm can spend without authorization by the owner.

Insufficient Income

This section defines how the property owner will fund all property negative cash flows.

Reporting Systems

This section will list all of the weekly, monthly, quarterly, and yearly accounting and management reports which will be required by the developer or lender. Many developers will require the management company to submit these reports per predetermined formats.

Operating and Capital Expenditure Budget

This section will determine when the annual operating and capital expenditure budgets are to be completed and how often they are to be updated.

Compliance with Legal Requirements

This section will require that the management firm comply with all local, state, and federal laws.

Assignment of Contract

This section will define the rights of the management firm to assign their interest in the management contract.

Termination Clause and Penalty

The termination section will list any reasons for an early termination of the agreement and what, if any, penalty will be paid by the developer for exercising this clause. In addition, it will define the obligations of both parties after the notice has been given to the management firm.

MANAGEMENT COMPANY RESPONSIBILITIES

The developer should request that the management company prepare a property management business plan prior to assuming responsibilities for property management. This plan should discuss the following topics:

- Operating budget projections
- Capital expenditures projections
- Tenant service center (if needed)

- Operational plan to provide job descriptions and responsibilities for each member of the property management staff for the following:
  Management team
  Operations department
  Day cleaning department
  Landscape department
  Tenant development department
  Security department
  Tenant service center
- Mission, goals, and objective statements
- Space utilization
- Inspection procedures
- Policies and procedures
- Hiring practices
- Complete analysis of the property

Analysis of the Property

A well-qualified management company, whether owned by the developer or a third-party management firm, should completely analyze the physical and financial aspects of the proposed development. As the property matures, this outline should be revised to reflect the current information.

Property Management Business Plan

    I.   Property
        A. Name/address/telephone
        B. Current management (resident manager address/telephone)
        C. Leasing company (leasing agent/address/telephone)
        D. Building data
            1. Any phasing
            2. Age of buildings
            3. Floors in each building
            4. Number of units or total gross and net square footage
        E. Specific unit data
        F. Site information
            1. Acreage
            2. Zoning
            3. Density of the property
            4. Parking spaces
        G. Amenities

H. Construction description
  1. Type of construction
  2. Utilities
  3. Roof
  4. Facade
  5. Landscaping
  6. Floor system
  7. Elevators
  8. Foundations
  9. Security
  10. Restrooms
  11. Interiors
  12. Framing
  13. Fire protection
II. Property location
  A. Neighborhood
  B. Demographics
  C. Traffic patterns
  D. Support facilities
    1. Schools
    2. Shopping
    3. Churches
  E. Area's growth trends
  F. Local government
  G. Area employment trends
III. Location maps
  A. State
  B. City
  C. County
  D. Neighborhood
  E. Site plan of property
IV. General tenant data
V. Tenant profile
  A. Residential
    1. Length of occupancy
    2. Type of employment
      a. White collar
      b. Blue collar

        3. Size of family

        4. Marital status

        5. Number of children

        6. Age of adults

        7. Age of children

        8. Income of household

        9. Rental payment history

    B. Commercial

        1. Type of business

        2. Length of occupancy

        3. Rental payment history

VI.   Rental policies

    A. Deposits

    B. Animals

    C. Parking

    D. Management office and building hours

VII.   Security of property

VIII.   Exterior and interior building inspection

IX.   Utility deposits

    A. List, address, and amount of each deposit

X.   Insurance coverage

XI.   Taxes

    A. Current assessments

    B. Rates

XII.   Service contracts

XIII.   Occupancy history

    A. History by month (2 to 3 years)

    B. Occupancy percentages

    C. Projected absorption

XIV.   Budget forecasts

    A. Month-by-month budget projections until 95 percent occupancy is achieved

XV.   Capital expenditure budget

XVI.   Deferred maintenance programs

XVII.   Staff description, records, and procedures

XVIII.   Inventory

    A. Listing of all current inventory

    B. Proposed new inventory, timing, and cost estimates

XIX.   Photographs of property
XX.   Floor plans
XXI.   Market comparables

PROPERTY MANAGEMENT POLICIES AND PROCEDURES

Prior to the actual opening of the development, the various management operating policies and procedures should be established. These policies and procedures will give structure to the management program.

Rental Rates and Collections

The rental rates and collection policy and procedure is one of the main management functions. The rental rates should be established prior to the opening of the development. These rates should fall within the range of the comparable type properties in the marketplace.

The collection policy will define when the rent is due by the tenant and penalties assessed for late payment or returned checks. This policy will also establish the eviction process to be used in cases where the tenant will not pay the rent. This eviction process must follow the local state laws.

Maintenance Service: Handling of Work Orders

The tenant or tenants of the development are not only paying for the use of their space but for the continued maintenance of that space. The management company should have an established policy for work orders. After the tenant registers a complaint, these requests should then be turned into work orders by the maintenance staff. Items which cannot be handled in-house should be promptly turned over to subcontractors. The management company must respond to the tenants' needs immediately. The only reason for a delay in completing work orders should be the back ordering of a part.

Deferred Maintenance Schedule

A planned maintenance schedule should be prepared by the management company to include physical items to be reviewed on a regular basis. The concept of a deferred maintenance program is to spend as little money as possible on a regular basis to prevent major expenditures in the future. Areas to include in a deferred maintenance program are the following:

- Mechanical systems
- Plumbing
- Electrical

- Roof
- Paving

Employee Schedules and Benefits

The benefits to the employees should be determined prior to hiring the employees. These benefits should include:

- Salary
- Bonus schedules
- Vehicle and mileage allowances
- Insurance of all types
- Work schedule
- Paid holidays

Tenant Record Keeping: How to Keep Organized Files

In order to make the management office flow smoothly, a system should be set up to record all tenant rental activity and tenant service calls. The following is a sample of how this file system should be established.

Tenant Files

    The tenant files should include copies of the following information:

- Tenant lease application
- Credit check
- Lease reservation application (if applicable)
- Lease agreement
- Work orders performed in tenant space
- Correspondence between landlord or managing agent and the tenant

Work Orders

    Work orders should be made in triplicate, one for the tenant, one for the maintenance staff, and one for the tenant file. The maintenance staff's copy will be used to keep a history of service calls and problems.

SERVICE CONTRACTS

Depending on the capabilities of in-house maintenance personnel, management companies may choose to contract for services. An agreement is negotiated and these services are performed on a regular basis. All service contracts should include the following items:

- Current monthly or annual fee
- Term of the contract
- Escalations in the monthly fee
- Scope of work to be performed
- Termination clause
- Early termination fee

Examples of these types of service contracts are listed below.

Types of Contracts

- Pest control
- Trash removal
- Landscaping
- Elevator
- Janitorial
- Maid service
- Window washing
- Parking lot cleaning
- Snow removal
- Elevator and lobby music
- Security
- Laundry
- HVAC (heating, ventilating, and air conditioning)
- Special events

PREPARING THE OPERATING BUDGETS

An operating budget is a financial statement which lists the income and the expenses for an income property. These income and expenses for the year are combined into a cash flow statement which predicts how much net operating income the property will produce annually. If the operating budget is prepared after the building is leased-up, the individual tenants and their rents are listed. The expenses are listed per their various categories projected.

Preparing the Revenue Calculations

The first part of an operating statement is to obtain the current revenue items. The management company will need to prepare a forecast of rent collections. The projected rental revenues are calculated by multiplying the total square footage or number of units by the total annualized rent per square foot or per unit.

Total rental square footage or total number of rental units

×

Total annualized rental/sf or unit

=

Total rental income

+

Additional rental

+

Miscellaneous income

=

Gross potential income (GPI)

Additional Rental

Commercial properties will include additional items to be added to the GPI. These include:

- Rent escalations
- Percentage rents
- Common area maintenance (CAM) charges
- Operating expenses pass through

Miscellaneous Income

Miscellaneous income includes the following items:

- Late fees
- Forfeited deposits
- Vending income
- Laundry income
- Parking income
- Charges to tenants for transfers, insufficient funds
- Interest on bank accounts and security deposits (depending on state security deposit escrow laws)
- Application fees
- Commitment fees
- Cleaning fees
- Pet fees

Vacancy Allowances

Vacancy allowance is the percentage of the gross potential income that will be uncollectable due to the space being either unoccupied or occupied but under a free rental period.

Uncollectable Income

Uncollectable income is income that is uncollectable due to tenants which move out early or are unable to pay the rent or rental income.

Preparing the Operating Expenses

Once the management company has thoroughly reviewed all of the income which the property can generate and projected it over time, they must forecast the operating expenses. To provide support for each estimate, they should verify as many of these expenses as possible. This will entail detailed research with utility companies, vendors, and subcontractors to develop costs per square feet or per unit. Obviously, the past history of the property's operational costs can be used if the project is completed. Having completed this forecast of expenses, these costs should be compared with other management companies in the area with similar building types as a check for accuracy. In addition, the following reference books may prove helpful:

- Institute of Real Estate Management's (IREM) books on operating costs.

  Expense Analysis: Condominiums, Cooperatives and Planned Unit Developments

  Income-Expense Analysis Conventional Apartments

  Income-Expense Analysis: Office Buildings, Downtown and Suburban

  Institute of Real Estate Management
  430 North Michigan Avenue
  Chicago, IL 60611-4090
  (312) 661-1930

- Building Owners and Managers Association's (BOMA) book on office building operating costs.

  BOMA Experience Exchange Report

  Building Owners and Managers Association International
  1250 Eye St., NW, Suite 200
  Washington, DC 20005
  (202) 289-7000

- Urban Land Institute's (ULI) book on retail operating costs.

  Dollars and Cents of Shopping Centers

  Urban Land Institute
  1090 Vermont Avenue, N.W.
  Suite 300
  Washington, DC 20005-4962
  (202) 289-8500

Once the estimates for operating expenses are complete, the management company can obtain the net operating income for the property. From this figure, the debt service can be subtracted. This new figure will give the cash flow before taxes.

Operating Expense Items to Consider

The following will provide an explanation of the different types of expenses (see also Figure 13–2).

Salaries for All Personnel

- Staff
  Managers
  Temporary help
  Accounting
  Clerical
  Groundskeeping
  Maintenance
  Pool control and maintenance
  Porters and attendants
  Security guards
  Housekeeping
  Contract labor
  Leasing agents
- Staff cash disbursements
- Commissions and bonuses
- Employment benefits
- Profit sharing
- Benefits
- Unemployment tax
- Payroll tax

Maintenance and Repairs

- Mechanical, electrical, and plumbing
- Door lock upkeep
- Fixtures and appliances
- Exterior and roof repairs
- Window repairs
- Window treatment repairs
- Finishes (exterior and interior)
- Parking lots (paving and lighting)
- Signage and graphics

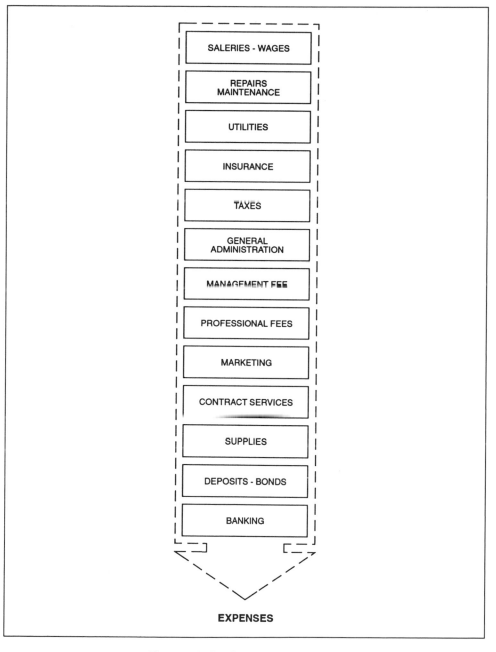

Figure 13–2 Operating expenses.

- Floor coverings
- Millwork and carpentry
- Mirrors
- Playgrounds and tennis courts
- Masonry
- Clubhouse
- Clubhouse furniture and fixtures
- Landscaping

Public Utilities

- Electric
- Gas
- Water
- Sewer

All Taxes

- Property taxes
- Personal property taxes
- Vehicle taxes

Liability Protection (Insurance)

- Property
- Liability
- Contents
- Fidelity
- Boiler/machinery
- Vehicle
- Flood
- Rent loss
- Errors and omissions
- Health
- Workman's Compensation
- Life

Administrative Costs

- Attorney's fees
- Accounting
- Dues, donations and subscriptions
- Petty cash

- Office equipment and supplies
- Travel and entertainment
- Entertainment
- Fixtures, furniture, and equipment (F, F, & E) rental
- Telephone
- Copier lease
- Postage
- Interior plants rental
- Printing
- Contract maintenance
- Janitorial
- Equipment maintenance
- Utilities
- Pagers and answering services
- Deliveries
- Licenses
- Uniforms and cleaning
- Fees
- Artwork
- Credit bureau
- Training seminars
- Professional society memberships
- Computer and processing expenses

Indirect Property Management Fees

Expenses paid to the property management company or to the managing partner as a partnership management fee, are usually based on a percentage of the collected income.

Professional Fees

- Attorneys
- Accounting
- Architectural engineering
- Additional property management
- Landscape design
- Appraisals
- Feasibility studies
- Specialty consultants

- Construction project management
- Brokers (real estate or mortgage)
- Tax consultant

Marketing

Expenses associated with the leasing of the property, including:

- Agency fees
- Newspaper and magazine advertising
- Business cards, brochures, fliers, and printing
- Postage and direct mail
- Signage and graphics
- Photography (project and aerial)
- Visual aids (renderings and plans)
- Special events (parties)
- Prospect files
- Gifts
- Advertising (billboards, television, radio)
- Parties
- Gifts
- Marketing aids
- Prospect lists
- Public relations in general
- Project models and displays
- Tenant relations
- Marketing data

Contract Services

- Pest control
- Trash
- Landscaping
- Elevator maintenance
- Janitorial
- Maid service
- Window cleaning
- Parking lot maintenance and control
- Snow removal
- Background music
- Security and guards

- Laundry
- Service of heating and cooling equipment

Inventory of Supplies

Expenses for supplies needed for maintaining the property, including:

- HVAC
- Plumbing
- Electrical
- Appliances
- Cleaning
- Pool
- Painting
- Fire safety

Renewal or Tenant Unit Maintenance

Expenses associated with making a space ready for a new tenant, including:

- Cleaning
- Carpet
- Painting
- Wallpaper
- Sheetrock
- Drapery cleaning
- Turnkey

Deposits and Bonds

Expenses for deposits or bonds that the property must post, including:

- Electric
- Gas
- Water/sewer
- Telephone
- Equipment

Banking

Expenses for banking charges, including:

- Open bank account
- Checks
- Returned checks
- Wire charges
- Service charges

Reserves and Replacements

- Flooring
- Appliances
- Landscaping
- Cabinets
- Plumbing
- Signage

Net Operating Income (NOI)

The income received less all operating expenses not including debt service incurred by the property is considered net operating income.

Debt Service

The cost of servicing any loans on the property, including all mortgages is debt service. This category can also include any ground lease payments.

Before-Tax Cash Flow

The money available after the debt service but prior to taxes is before-tax cash flow.

Capital Expenditures

Capital expenditure costs are items which are nonrecurring. These items should be capitalized and not expensed currently. An accountant should make this determination. Examples are:

- Commercial tenant improvements
- New roof
- New parking lot
- Appliance purchases

Tenant Improvements (TI)

Tenant improvement costs are those incurred to make the space ready for the tenant. Typically, these costs are associated with commercial properties.

Leasing Commissions

The cost of the commissions paid for leasing the space is typically for commercial properties. This commission can either be paid up front or over the term of the lease. This item is negotiated with the leasing agent prior to leasing. The leasing commission might also include future space expansion or lease options by the tenant.

Net Spendable Cash Flow Prior to Taxes

Net spendable cash flow prior to taxes is calculated by taking the cash flow after debt service and subtracting any costs for capital expenditures and leasing commissions. Capital expenditures and leasing commissions are usually not included in the operating expenses of the property so that they will not affect the value of the property.

REAL ESTATE TAXES

Prior to taking over a property, the manager must carefully review all real estate taxes. Because of the burden which they create especially when one considers their magnitude and implications, constant monitoring is required. Without a clear indication concerning taxes, project economics can be severely affected. Appraisers and tax consultants can help review these matters for a new or newly purchased development. In order to understand the development's tax situation, the following issues should be considered:

- Current tax assessments and bills
- Last three year's tax assessments and tax bills
- Will the personal property be taxed separately?
- Current personal property tax assessment and bills
- Current land assessment and tax bills
- Assessment ratios used by the local tax department
- Taxing of residential and commercial properties
- Homestead exemptions which are allowed
- Timing of property assessments
- Past and current millage rates
- Breakdown of millage rate
- Projected increases in the millage rate
- Dates for receiving tax bills
- Tax bill's due date and can it be paid in installments?
- Penalties for late payment and starting date
- Discounts for early payment
- Tax appeal procedures
- Tax consultants used

INSURANCE COVERAGE

Prior to the completion of the development, the management company should obtain quotes for the various types of insurance coverage required by the development. The following types of insurance coverage will be considered.

Types of Insurance Coverage

Permanent Coverage

This insurance will cover the property improvements. Usually, the value of the property is determined and then the value of the site improvements, such as the foundations, are deducted. The assumption here is that if the property is totally destroyed due to fire or weather, the foundation should still be in place. In addition, the coverage should increase to cover additional value due to inflation.

Contents

Contents insurance covers the furniture and equipment of the development.

Liability

Liability insurance covers the loss involved from any accidents on the property. Usually, this coverage will pay for the legal fees to defend any lawsuits against the property, the owner, and the management company.

Rent Loss

Rent loss insurance covers the loss of rent during the period that the property is under reconstruction due to fire or other weather conditions. The premium for this coverage is based on the time period in which the rent loss will occur.

Riders

Many insurance policies offer additional riders to cover other areas not covered in the general policy.

Flood: This covers any damage to the property during flood.

Glass Breakage: This covers any damage of glass due to weather or vandalism.

Earthquake: In certain parts of the country, earthquake insurance is available.

Boiler: Boiler insurance is available for properties using these types of systems.

Employee Theft: Employee theft insurance covers any loss of property due to property employees.

Workman's Compensation

Workman's Compensation insurance covers any losses incurred by employees when injured on the job.

Vehicle

Vehicle insurance covers any vehicles owned by the development. This insurance will include: damage and liability coverage.

Board of Directors

Board of directors liability insurance is usually required by owner's associations.

What Is the Proper Amount of Deductible?

The deductibility of each type of coverage should be carefully analyzed. The lower the deductibility, the higher the yearly premium and conversely, the higher the deductibility, the lower the yearly premium. The amount of deductible is a function of the budget available and the amount of risk which the owner desires to take in partially self-insuring himself.

How to Get the Best Pricing

The best pricing available is found with insurance agents who constantly shop the market for the best rates. Additionally, the amount of insurance in place and the past amount of claims may affect insurance pricing.

Insurance Coverage: Issues to Consider

There are a few key issues to consider prior to researching for the best insurance policy.

1. Companies which cover this type of property
2. Companies which insure in this location
3. Companies which have the amount of coverage desired
4. Data required by these companies for an accurate quote

After items one through four have been satisfied, continue to consider the following in selecting the best company and policy to use.

- Recommendations for coverage
- Select amounts which will totally replace the property or pay off the mortgage
- Premiums

- Terms
- Deductibles
- Recommended deductible amounts
- Content's coverage, amounts, and premiums
- Rent loss insurance
- Payment schedule
- Projected increases and decreases in the premiums
- Appraisals required
- Boiler/machinery coverages
- Vehicle insurance
- Workman's Compensation insurance
- Fidelity insurance availability
- Property manager's errors and omissions insurance availability
- Utility bond coverage availability
- Tenant security deposit bonds availability
- Group life and hospitalization insurance availability for the property employees
- Flood insurance availability
- All who should be included on the policy

THE ACCOUNTING SYSTEM

In order to properly account for all of the receipts and disbursements, the management company should prepare monthly accounting statements for the property owner. In this section we shall note the types of accounting methods to use. In the beginning of property management, the manager, with the counsel of his accountant and IRS should determine the method to be used. Once decided, the method cannot be changed without IRS approval. The two basic types are cash method and accrual method.

Cash Method of Accounting

The cash method recognizes revenue when cash is received and recognizes expenses when they are paid out.

Accrual Method of Accounting

The accrual method recognizes revenue and expenses when they occurred, even though they may not have been received or paid.

Management of Accounting

To manage accounting, systems should be devised which result from the unique needs of the project and standard accounting procedures. The following types of records should be established and monitored regularly. At the end of this section will be examples of the completed forms used.

Accounting Chart of Accounts

Every management company will use a different set of accounting chart of accounts. The chart of accounts will include the broad categories as well as the subcategories. See Figure 13–3.

Monthly Accounting Reports

The following monthly accounting reports should be generated by the management company to the property owner every month.

Monthly Rent Rolls

The monthly rent roll report shows each tenant, listed by name, unit number, unit type, current monthly rent, miscellaneous income, past due rental, and security deposit.

Profit and Loss Statement

The overall operating performance by categories and subcategories for all the revenue and expenses is tracked. It shows these figures for the current month, year-to-date, as well as budget variance categories. See Figure 13–4.

Balance Sheet

The balance sheet shows the overall financial position of each category at the end of each reporting period (monthly, quarterly, or yearly). See Figure 13–5.

Trial Balance

The trial balance is a monthly report of all the general ledger account balances. It shows the previous month's ending balance, the current month's activity, and the new ending balance for each category. See Figure 13–6.

General Ledger

The general ledger is a detailed monthly listing of all the transactions posted to each general ledger account during the property's current fiscal year. All cash disbursements, cash receipts, and journal entries are shown by general ledger account code. The year-to-date totals will tie these figures into the trial balance.

CHART OF ACCOUNTS
SEVILLE COMPANIES
Court Ridge Apartments

Account	Description	Account	Description
01030-000	Land	05025-000	NSF Charge
01041-000	Building Additions	05030-000	Credit Check Charge
01042-000	Building Retirements	05035-000	Pet Damages
01061-000	Building Improvements	05040-000	Laundry/Vending
02000-000	Cash Operating Account	05045-000	Interest Income
02010-000	Certificate of Deposit	05050-000	Other Property Income
02020-000	Petty Cash	06010-000	Real Estate Taxes
02045-000	Tenant Security Deposit	06020-000	Utilities
03000-000	Tenant Rent Receivable	06030-000	Insurance
03020-000	Other Tenant Receivables	06035-000	Drywall Repair
03025-000	Other Receivables	06036-000	Electrical Repair
03060-000	Organizational Costs	06037-000	Elevator Maintenance
03061-000	Accumulated Amortization	06038-000	Grounds Maintenance
04020-000	Accounts Payable	06041-000	Supplies & Materials
04030-000	Federal Income Tax Withheld	06042-000	Services
04040-000	FICA Tax Liability	06043-000	Maintenance Payroll
04050-000	State Income Tax Withheld	06044-000	Casual Labor
04060-000	State Unemployment Tax	06050-000	Contracted Labor
04070-000	Federal Unemployment Tax	06060-000	Cleaning
04080-000	City Tax Withheld	06070-000	Leasing Commissions
04140-000	Accrued Improvements	06080-000	Management Fees
04180-000	Security Deposits	06090-000	Administration
04190-000	Accrued Liabilities	06100-000	Promotion & Marketing
04260-000	Mortgage Note Payable	06510-000	Depreciation Expense
04420-000	Begin. Capital General Partner	06520-000	Amortization
04421-000	Begin. Capital Limited Partner	06530-000	Accrued Improvements
04430-000	Cash Distributed General Partner	06600-000	Mortgage Interest
04431-000	Cash Distributed Limited Partner	07060-000	Mortgage Principal
04440-000	Share of Income-General Partner	07070-000	Additions to Property
04441-000	Share of Partnership Income Ltd.	07075-000	Discounts Lost
04445-000	YTD Net Income	07080-000	Freight Charges
04446-000	YTD Net Income Contra	07085-000	Sales Tax
05001-000	Gross Potential Income	08010-000	Depreciation Expense
05002-000	Delinquent Rent Current Month	08020-000	Amortization
05003-000	Vacancy Loss Current Month	08030-000	Accrued Improvements
05004-000	Rental Discount/Concessions	08040-000	Cash Flow Offset
05005-000	Prior/Next Month Collections	08050-000	Net Income Offset
05010-000	Deposits Collected	09006-000	Cash Flow Contra
05011-000	Deposits Disbursed	09010-000	Contra to Other Distrib.
05020-000	Utility Reimbursement	09020-000	Contra to Non-Cash Expense
		09030-000	Contra Net Income

Figure 13-3 Chart of accounts.

572

PROFIT AND LOSS STATEMENT (VARIABLE BUDGET)
For the One Month Ended January 31, 19__
SEVILLE COMPANIES
Court Ridge Apartments

	Current Period Actual	Current Period Budget	Variance %	Year-to-Date Actual	Year-to-Date Actual	Variance %
Revenues						
Rental Income	$170,847.31	$175,000.00	−2.37%	$170,847.31	$175,000.00	−2.37%
Deposit Income	$3,375.00	$2,800.00	20.54%	$3,375.00	$2,800.00	20.54%
Other Income	$6,013.07	$2,780.00	116.30%	$6,013.07	$2,780.00	116.30%
Total Revenues	$180,235.38	$180,580.00	−0.19%	$180,235.38	$180,580.00	−0.19%
Cash Operating Expenses						
Real Estate Taxes	$29,550.00	$27,500.00	7.45%	$29,550.00	$27,500.00	7.45%
Utilities	$1,366.81	$1,500.00	−8.88%	$1,366.81	$1,500.00	−8.88%
Insurance	$100.00	$100.00	1.01%	$100.00	$100.00	1.01%
Repairs & Maintenance						
Drywall Repairs	$230.75	$250.00	−7.70%	$230.75	$250.00	−7.70%
Electrical Repair	$1,593.00	$1,600.00	−0.44%	$1,593.00	$1,600.00	−0.44%
Elevator Maintenance	$6,631.00	$7,500.00	−11.59%	$6,631.00	$7,500.00	−11.59%
Grounds Maintenance	$6,317.56	$7,000.00	−9.75%	$6,317.56	$7,000.00	−9.75%
Plumbing	$1,273.66	$1,400.00	−9.02%	$1,273.66	$1,400.00	−9.02%
Supplies & Materials	$9,344.78	$10,000.00	−6.55%	$9,344.78	$10,000.00	−6.55%
Services	$4,239.00	$5,000.00	−15.22%	$4,239.00	$5,000.00	−15.22%
Maintenance Payroll	$3,563.30	$3,700.00	−3.69%	$3,563.30	$3,700.00	−3.69%
Casual Labor	$924.75	$1,000.00	−7.53%	$924.75	$1,000.00	−7.53%
Contracted Labor	$6,764.55	$7,100.00	−4.72%	$6,764.55	$7,100.00	−4.72%
Cleaning	$1,599.23	$2,000.00	−20.04%	$1,599.23	$2,000.00	−20.04%
Leasing Commissions	$200.00	$200.00	0.00%	$200.00	$200.00	0.00%
Management Fees	$4,417.00	$4,480.00	−1.41%	$4,417.00	$4,480.00	−1.41%
Administration	$563.00	$700.00	−19.57%	$563.00	$700.00	−19.57%
Promotion & Marketing	$103.99	$150.00	−30.67%	$103.99	$150.00	−30.67%
Total Operating Expenses	$78,864.38	$81,270.00	−2.96%	$78,864.38	$81,270.00	−2.96%
Net Funds Flow From Operations	$101,371.00	$99,310.00	2.08%	$101,371.00	$99,310.00	2.08%
Non Operating Expenses						
Amortization	$1,000.00	$1,000.00	0.00%	$1,000.00	$1,000.00	0.00%
Mortgage Interest	$900.00	$900.00	0.00%	$900.00	$900.00	0.00%
Financial Net Income	$99,471.00	$97,410.00	2.12%	$99,471.00	$97,410.00	2.12%
Other Disbursements						
Mortgage Principal	$75.00	$75.00	0.00%	$75.00	$75.00	0.00%
Additions to Property	$128,065.27	$128,065.27	0.00%	$128,065.27	$128,065.27	0.00%
Total Other Disbursements	$128,140.27	$128,140.27	0.00%	$128,140.27	$128,140.27	0.00%
Non-Cash Expenses						
Amortization	$1,000.00	$1,000.00	0.00%	$1,000.00	$1,000.00	0.00%
Total Non-Cash Expenses	$1,000.00	$1,000.00	0.00%	$1,000.00	$1,000.00	0.00%
Net Cash Flow	($29,669.27)	($31,730.27)	−6.50%	($29,669.27)	($31,730.27)	−6.50%
Net Income	$99,471.00	$97,410.00	2.12%	$99,471.00	$97,410.00	2.12%

Figure 13-4 Profit and loss statement (variable budget).

BALANCE SHEET
For the Month Ended January 31, 19__
SEVILLE COMPANIES
Court Ridge Apartments

	Assets		
Property			
Land	$1,418,400.00		
Building Additions	$128,065.27		
Total Building Assets		$1,546,465.27	
Improvements			
Building Improvements	$19,380.00		
Total Building Improvements		$19,380.00	
Total Property & Improvements			$1,565,845.27
Cash & Receivables			
Cash Operating Accpunt	$8,940.77		
Certificates of Deposit	$67,979.60		
Petty Cash	$850.00		
Tenant Security Deposits	$23,925.00		
Total Cash & Receivables		$101,695.37	
Tenant Rent Receivable	$93,522.09		
Other Tenant Receivables	$5,128.03		
Other Receivables	$742.00		
Total Receivables		$99,392.12	
Total Cash & Receivables			$201,087.49
Other Assets			
Organizational Costs	$16,250.00		
Accumulated Amortization	($3,165.00)		
Total Other Assets			$13,085.00
Total Assets			$1,780,017.76
			==========

	Liabilities and Capital		
Accrued Liabilities & Payables			
Accounts Payable	$88,796.32		
Payroll Taxes Payable	$1,544.13		
Security Deposits	$23,305.00		
Accrued Liabilities	$16,425.00		
Total Liabilities & Payables		$130,070.45	
Mortgage Note Payable		$161,325.00	
Total Liabilities			$291,395.45
Partnership Capital			
Beginning Partner's Capital		$4,330,000.00	
Cash Distributions		($2,940,848.69)	
Partnership Income (Loss)		$99,471.00	
Total Partnership Capital			$1,488,622.31
Total Liabilities and Capital			$1,780,017.76
			==========

Figure 13–5   Balance sheet.

TRIAL BALANCE
For the One Month Ended January 31, 19__
SEVILLE COMPANIES
Court Ridge Apartments

Account	Description	Debit	Credit	Account	Description	Debit	Credit
01030–000	Land	$1,418,400.00		06070–000	Leasing Commissions	$200.00	
01041–000	Building Additions	$128,065.27		06080–000	Management Fees	$4,417.00	
01061–000	Building Improvements	$19,380.00		06090–000	Administration	$563.00	
02000–000	Cash Operating Account	$8,940.77		06100–000	Promotion & Marketing	$103.99	
02010–000	Certificate of Deposit	$67,979.60		06520–000	Amortization	$1,000.00	
02020–000	Petty Cash	$850.00		06600–000	Mortgage Interest	$900.00	
02045–000	Tenant Security Deposit	$23,925.00		07060–000	Mortgage Principal	$75.00	
03000–000	Tenant Rent Receivables	$93,522.09		07070–000	Additions to Property	$128,065.27	
03020–000	Other Tenant Receivables	$5,128.02		09020–000	Amortization	$1,000.00	
03025–000	Other Receivables	$742.00		09001–000	Cash Flow Offset	$37,237.94	
03060–000	Organizational Costs	$16,250.00		09003–000	Net Income Offset		$166,378.21
03061–000	Accumulated Amortization		$3,165.00	09006–000	Cash Flow Contra Acct.		$37,237.94
04020–000	Accounts Payable		$88,796.32	09010–000	Contra to Other Distrib.		$128,140.27
04030–000	Federal Income Tax W/H		$856.33	09020–000	Contra to Non–Cash Exp.		$1,000.00
04040–000	FICA Tax Liability		$132.99	09030–000	Contra Net Income	$166,378.21	
04050–000	State Income Tax W/H		$483.13				
04060–000	State Unemployment Tax		$35.90			$2,216,556.94	$766,130.60
04070–000	Federal Unemployment Tax		$0.06				
04080–000	City Tax Withheld		$27.53				
04180–000	Security Deposits		$23,305.00				
04190–000	Accrued Liabilities		$16,425.00		Current Period Net Income		$99,471.00
04260–000	Mortgage Note Payable		$161,325.00		Year-to-Date Net Income		$99,471.00
04420–000	Begin. Capital General Partner		$330,000.00				
04421–000	Begin. Capital Limited Partner		$4,000,000.00				
04430–000	Cash Distributed Gen. Partner	$2,940,848.69					
05001–000	Gross Potential Income		$224,202.40				
05002–000	Delinquent Rent Current Month	$8,514.11					
05003–000	Vacancy Loss Current Month	$35,948.46					
05004–000	Rental Discount/Concessions	$14,757.79					
05005–000	Prior/Next Month Collections		$5,865.27				
05010–000	Deposits Collected		$3,500.00				
05011–000	Deposits Disbursed	$125.00					
05020–000	Utility Reimbursement		$2,500.00				
05025–000	NSF Charge		$250.00				
05030–000	Credit Check Charge		$300.00				
05035–000	Pet Damages		$350.00				
05040–000	Laundry/Vending		$239.60				
05045–000	Interest Income		$450.00				
05050–000	Other Property Income		$1,923.47				
06010–000	Real Estate Taxes	$29,550.00					
06020–000	Utilities	$1,366.81					
06030–000	Insurance	$182.00					
06035–000	Drywall Repair	$230.75					
06036–000	Electrical Repair	$1,593.00					
06037–000	Elevator Maintenance	$6,631.00					
06038–000	Grounds Maintenance	$6,317.56					
06039–000	Plumbing	$1,273.66					
06041–000	Supplies & Materials	$9,344.78					
06042–000	Services	$4,239.00					
06043–000	Maintenance Payroll	$3,563.30					
06044–000	Casual Labor	$924.75					
06050–000	Contracted Labor	$6,764.55					
06060–000	Cleaning	$1,599.23					

Figure 13–6 Trial balance.

GENERAL LEDGER
For the One Month Ended January 31, 19__
SEVILLE COMPANIES
Court Ridge Apartments

Scr Date	Ref	Description	Beginning Balance	Current	Year-to-Date	Ending Balance
01030-000		Land	$1,257,000.00			
gj 01/01/__		Purchase Tract No. 1192		$161,400.00		

				$161,400.00		$1,418,400.00
01041-000		Building Additions	$0.00			
cd 01/03/__		Roofing		$128,065.27		

				$128,065.27		$128,065.27
01061-000		Building Improvements	$0.00			
cd 01/08/__		Upgrade Hallway		$19,380.00		

				$19,380.00		$19,380.00
02000-000		Cash Operating Account	$82,546.23			
cd 01/02/__		Roofing		($128,065.27)		
cd 01/03/__		Upgrade hallway		($19,380.00)		
cd 01/04/__		Cash investment		($10,000.00)		
cd 01/05/__		Replenish petty cash		($100.00)		
cd 01/20/__		Dep. Ref. Week of 01/13		($125.00)		
cr 01/02/__		Rents received		$70,230.89		
cr 01/03/__		Rents received		$27,680.25		
cr 01/04/__		Rents received		$21,493.10		
cr 01/20/__		Dep. Rec. Week of 01/13		$3,500.00		
cr 01/20/__		Laundry room		$239.60		
cr 01/30/__		Month end receipts		$1,350.00		
cr 01/30/__		Special svc.		$1,123.47		
gj 01/15/__		Pay period ending 01/15		($3,103.16)		
gj 01/30/__		Refunds		($620.00)		
gj 01/30/__		January-Debt Svc.		($975.00)		
os 01/25/__		Activity Reconcil.		($53,355.09)		

				($90,106.21)	($7,559.98)	
02010-000		Certificates of Deposits	$57,979.60			
cd 01/04/__		Cash investment		$10,000.00		

				$10,000.00	$67,979.60	
02020-000		Petty Cash	$750.00			
cd 01/05/__		Replenish petty cash		$100.00		

				$100.00	$850.00	
02045-000		Tenant Security Deposits	$22,950.00			
gj 01/06/__		Dep. rec. week of 01/6		$975.00		

				$975.00	$23,925.00	
03000-000		Tenant Rent Receivable	$5,224.68			
cr 01/04/__		Rent Received		($135,904.99)		
gj 01/01/__		January rent charges		$224,202.40		

				$88,297.41	$93,522.09	

Figure 13-7 General ledger.

The end-of-the-year totals are then used as the beginning-of-the-year totals for the following year. See Figure 13–7.

Cash Deposits

The cash deposit report is a detailed listing of all of the monthly deposits. They are grouped together and listed in chronological order by transaction date within each bank account. See Figure 13–8.

Weekly Distribution

The weekly distribution report shows a detailed weekly listing of all the transactions posted to each general ledger account code.

CASH DEPOSITS
Month–To–Date Deposit Recap–January 19__
SEVILLE COMPANIES
Court Ridge Apartments

CRJ No.	Date Opened	Date Closed	Rent	Utility	Deposit	Other	Total	Corrected	Verification Number
220	01/02/	01/02/__	$70,230.89	$0.00	$0.00	$0.00	$70,230.89	N	_____
221	01/03/__	01/03/__	$27,680.25	$0.00	$0.00	$0.00	$27,680.25	N	_____
222	01/04/__	01/04/__	$21,493.10	$0.00	$0.00	$0.00	$21,493.10	N	_____
223	01/05/__	01/05/__	$16,500.75	$0.00	$0.00	$0.00	$16,500.75	N	__
TOTAL DEPOSITS			$135,904.99	$0.00	$0.00	$0.00	$135,904.99		
Less: Current Period NSF's			($500.00)	$0.00	$0.00	$0.00	($500.00)		
DEPOSIT SUBTOTAL			$135,404.99	$0.00	$0.00	$0.00	$135,404.99		
Less: Previous Period NSF's			$0.00	$0.00	$0.00	$0.00	$0.00		
NET MTD DEPOSITS			$135,404.99	$0.00	$0.00	$0.00	$135,404.99		

Figure 13–8 Cash deposits.

Miscellaneous Reports

- Payroll register
- W-2 wage and tax statement
- 1099 forms
- Deposit liability summary
- Employee summary
- Payroll register
- Payroll deposit liability to date
- Tax accrual reports

The Use of the Computer

Today's personal computers can be used for both the home office accounting and the on-site reporting. There are numerous software companies that sell both methods of accounting systems. The use of computers provides the management company and owner with quicker and more reliable calculations of financial information, enabling quicker reaction time to potential management and financial problems. In addition, many properties have on-site computers which prepare tenant information; this information is then retrieved by modem by the home office. There are also many software programs designed to monitor the systems of the buildings to minimize operational costs and to account for all rents received and expenses paid. Here is one software sales organization:

Proven Solutions
1303 Hightower Trail
Suite 201
Atlanta, GA 30350
(770) 399-1993

In addition, the National Association of Realtors has developed a book entitled *Software Directory,* which is available upon request. The book provides a complete listing of the software available for real estate development applications.

INVENTORY AND SUPPLIES

Prior to the opening or assuming responsibility for a development, property management personnel should prepare a proposed inventory. This inventory will vary depending on the type and the size of the property and its status. Obviously, a new property will not have any inventory. The amount of inventory should be based on the required need and should be planned carefully. Excess inventory is unnecessary and results in additional carrying charges. In addition, proper security measures should protect from loss.

Office

The office should be supplied with items such as computers, typewriters, copy, and fax machines. In addition, after-hours service lines and the telephone system should connect all departments. This equipment can either be purchased, leased, or leased with an option to purchase. Maintenance service contracts should be considered

Maintenance Shop

The maintenance shop inventory will include both tools and large pieces of equipment as well as an inventory of parts for appliances, mechanical, plumbing, and electrical items. These can also include carpentry and landscape items.

Vehicles

Depending on the type and size of the property, various types of vehicles might be required, such as trucks, vans, buses, or golf carts.

Amenities

Various types of amenities will require a parts inventory. Examples are tennis court nets or pool equipment or parts.

Supplies

Janitor's closets or maintenance rooms should be stocked with chemicals for cleaning and specialty supplies for bathrooms.

TENANT LEASES

In residential type properties, the management company will handle both the management and the leasing of the property. A recommended process to be followed is:

- Prospect filling out application for residency
- Prospect filling out employment references

- Prospect filling out credit check and character references and other information required
- Checking out all references
- Accepting tenant as a potential resident and reviewing the lease agreement with them
- Selecting the unit and walk through inspection with tenant, noting all problem areas to be addressed and the condition of the unit
- Signing the lease agreement and collecting all deposit checks in addition to turning over all keys to that unit to the new tenant.

THE OWNER'S ASSOCIATION

If the property under development is a "for sale" type property that will have an owner's association, the management company should coordinate the drafting of these documents. These documents will include the covenants, conditions, and restrictions, the bylaws of the association, and the association operating budget. Typically, the developer will retain control of this association until a specified percentage of the units or space has been sold. At that point the association will be turned over to the group of owners.

A well-planned set of documents and accounting records will avoid potential problems upon transferring over the control.

PROPERTY MANAGEMENT FORMS

Budget Forecast Form (13-1)

This form is to be used when preparing the budget forecasts.

BUDGET FORECAST FORM

FORM 13-1

PROPERTY NAME _____

YEAR _____

DESCRIPTION/MONTH	JAN	FEB	MAR	APR	MAY	JUN	JUL	AUG	SEP	OCT	NOV	DEC	TOTAL
REVENUE													
GROSS POTENTIAL INCOME	$	$	$	$	$	$	$	$	$	$	$	$	$
MISCELLANEOUS INCOME	$	$	$	$	$	$	$	$	$	$	$	$	$
VACANCY & UNCOLLECTIBLE INCOME	$	$	$	$	$	$	$	$	$	$	$	$	$
EFFECTIVE GROSS INCOME	$	$	$	$	$	$	$	$	$	$	$	$	$
OPERATING EXPENSES													
SALARIES & WAGES	$	$	$	$	$	$	$	$	$	$	$	$	$
REPAIRS & MAINTENANCE	$	$	$	$	$	$	$	$	$	$	$	$	$
UTILITIES	$	$	$	$	$	$	$	$	$	$	$	$	$
TAXES	$	$	$	$	$	$	$	$	$	$	$	$	$
INSURANCE	$	$	$	$	$	$	$	$	$	$	$	$	$
GENERAL & ADMINISTRATIVE	$	$	$	$	$	$	$	$	$	$	$	$	$
MANAGEMENT FEES	$	$	$	$	$	$	$	$	$	$	$	$	$
PROFESIONAL FEES	$	$	$	$	$	$	$	$	$	$	$	$	$
CONTRACT SERVICES	$	$	$	$	$	$	$	$	$	$	$	$	$
SUPPLIES	$	$	$	$	$	$	$	$	$	$	$	$	$
UNIT MAINTENANCE	$	$	$	$	$	$	$	$	$	$	$	$	$
DEPOSITS & BONDS	$	$	$	$	$	$	$	$	$	$	$	$	$
BANKING	$	$	$	$	$	$	$	$	$	$	$	$	$
RESERVES & REPLACEMENTS	$	$	$	$	$	$	$	$	$	$	$	$	$
TOTAL OPERATING INCOME	$	$	$	$	$	$	$	$	$	$	$	$	$
NET OPERATING INCOME	$	$	$	$	$	$	$	$	$	$	$	$	$
DEBT SERVICE-1ST MORTGAGE	$	$	$	$	$	$	$	$	$	$	$	$	$
DEBT SERVICE-2ND MORTGAGE	$	$	$	$	$	$	$	$	$	$	$	$	$
GROUND LEASE	$	$	$	$	$	$	$	$	$	$	$	$	$
TENANT IMPROVEMENTS	$	$	$	$	$	$	$	$	$	$	$	$	$
LEASING COMMISSIONS	$	$	$	$	$	$	$	$	$	$	$	$	$
CAPITAL EXPENDITURES	$	$	$	$	$	$	$	$	$	$	$	$	$
BEFORE-TAX CASH FLOW	$	$	$	$	$	$	$	$	$	$	$	$	$

Form 13-1 Budget forecast form.

Residential Lease Summary Form (13–2)

This form is to be used when summarizing the residential leases.

RESIDENTIAL LEASE SUMMARY FORM

FORM 13–2

PROPERTY _____
ADDRESS _____
ADDRESS _____

TENANT PAYS: UNFURNISHED   _____
 GAS   _____   FURINISHED   _____
 ELECTRICITY   _____
 WATER   _____
 SEWER   _____
 CABLE TV   _____

UNIT TYPE	UNIT MIX	SQ.FT.	STREET RENT	RENT/ SQ.FT.	# OCCUPIED	% OCCUPIED	
_____	_____	_____	$_____	$_____	_____	_____%	
_____	_____	_____	$_____	$_____	_____	_____%	
_____	_____	_____	$_____	$_____	_____	_____%	
_____	_____	_____	$_____	$_____	_____	_____%	
_____	_____	_____	$_____	$_____	_____	_____%	
TOTAL	_____	_____			_____	_____%	

DATE OF LAST RENT INCREASE ___/___/___ PERCENTAGE OF RENT INCREASE _____%

TENANT	SUITE #	UNIT TYPE	LEASE TERM	END DATE	SECURITY DEPOSIT	RENTAL RATE	FURN./ UNFURN.
_____	_____	_____	_____	_____	$_____	$_____	$_____
_____	_____	_____	_____	_____	$_____	$_____	$_____
_____	_____	_____	_____	_____	$_____	$_____	$_____
_____	_____	_____	_____	_____	$_____	$_____	$_____
_____	_____	_____	_____	_____	$_____	$_____	$_____
_____	_____	_____	_____	_____	$_____	$_____	$_____
_____	_____	_____	_____	_____	$_____	$_____	$_____
_____	_____	_____	_____	_____	$_____	$_____	$_____
_____	_____	_____	_____	_____	$_____	$_____	$_____
_____	_____	_____	_____	_____	$_____	$_____	$_____
_____	_____	_____	_____	_____	$_____	$_____	$_____
_____	_____	_____	_____	_____	$_____	$_____	$_____
_____	_____	_____	_____	_____	$_____	$_____	$_____
_____	_____	_____	_____	_____	$_____	$_____	$_____
TOTAL	_____	_____	_____	_____	$_____	$_____	$_____

Form 13–2 Residential lease summary form.

## Chapter 14

The Sale of the Development (The Developer's Final Reward)

In Chapter 1, we discussed the real estate developer's investment strategy. In some cases, one aspect of the developer's business plan may be the sale or resale. In fact, to achieve the developer's required return, the sale may be essential. If the development is completed, leased-up, and has an ongoing program of property management, it is now positioned for realizing the maximum value and the timing for a sale is now. This chapter will consider the reasons for selling, value determination, methods of sale, sales presentation packages, and sale procedures.

REASONS FOR SELLING

There are many reasons for selling property. Pressure of some type is usually the main reason. The developer may have self-imposed pressure to reach a preset objective. The project may not be performing and the lenders may be applying pressure. Low absorption rates, downturns in the economy, and saturation of a need may create pressure. Other reasons for selling include the following:

- Cash infusion is needed quickly
- Dissolution of a partnership

- Working capital is needed
- Paying off debt service
- Receiving outstanding offer
- Investor pressure for profit
- Lease expiration of a major tenant
- Local environment deterioration
- Changing development diversification
- Business operations change or bankruptcy

There may be other reasons for selling but the developer should make it his objective to sell only when his profit yield is at its greatest.

SALE PRICING—TERMS AND CONDITIONS

After the developer has made the decision to sell, the first decisions to make are the asking price and the terms required for the sale. This asking price must be market based and not emotion based. It must also be higher than expected to give room for negotiations, but it must be set to generate enough interest so that negotiations with the future buyer will begin.

In addition, the terms must have a degree of flexibility for these negotiations. This is due to the fact that some buyers are term buyers and will pay a higher price if these terms are to their satisfaction. Some examples of this are lower or phased down downpayment, owner financing, or deductible fees paid to the owner in place of downpayments. Other ideas may include guarantees on cash flows.

Ultimately, in the decision concerning price and terms, the developer must analyze the market conditions before reaching a conclusion. The current market conditions may dictate, due to vacancy rates, competing construction, and interest rate, a specific asking price. If after reviewing the most recent sales, the developer realizes that recently sold properties were sold only after a long period of time and at much lower prices than originally asked, he may have to adjust the price or remove the project from the market until more favorable conditions exist.

For information concerning national comparative sales criteria, the following publication may prove useful in establishing the sales price.

National Real Estate Index
Liquidity Fund
1900 Powell St.
7th Floor
Emeryville, CA 94608
(800) 992-7257

SALE TRANSACTIONS

To respond to his investment strategy, the developer may have to try a number of ways to divest himself of interest in the property and in so doing realize his rewards differently than originally intended. The following are possibilities for consideration.

Cash Sale

This simply occurs when the purchaser pays all cash at closing and becomes the owner of the property with all of ownership's rights and privileges.

Presale with Earn-Out

Many times, developers will sell their property prior to total rent-up. In situations like this, in order for the developer to realize the full value of the property he may close the property at one price and then be able to get increases in the overall sales price by reaching predetermined rental achievements.

Installment Sales

Sellers of property may use installment sales for either realizing gain over a number of years or when the market dictates that the downpayment be divided into a number of payments over a few years. This recognized gain is spread over the life of the debt in the same proportion in which the payments are received.

Tax-Free Exchange

A "tax-free" exchange is used to sell property which avoids paying taxes upon resale. For detailed information on these tax free exchanges, refer to Section 1031 of the Internal Revenue Service Code. The key to having these exchanges lies in the definition of "like kind." The properties exchanged must be of a same use and character regardless of the quality. Hotel or an office building may be exchanged because they are income producing property where profits are derived from rents.

Exchanges may also involve cash or nonqualifying property. This nonqualifying property is commonly referred to as "boot." The gain on the sale is recognized to the extent of any boot received. To prevent the seller from converting a nonrecognizable loss by the transfer of boot, the IRS disallows the recognition of any loss, notwithstanding the receipt of boot. The transfer of boot in the form of nonqualifying property whose fair market value exceeds its adjusted basis will cause a taxable gain to be recognized.

Sale of the Partnership Interest

In situations where "due-on-sale clauses" in financing documents prevent a sale unless the total debt is paid off or restructured, this type of sale may be used, unless the lender has also prevented this type of sale within the agreements.

Using this type of sale requires all liens to be satisfied or removed from the property along with any other obligations attached to existing partnerships. Indemnification against any unknown obligations will probably also be required.

Donations

The seller may choose to donate the property for tax purposes. It should be noted that properties which are highly leveraged sometimes trigger recognition of the same amount of gain and depreciation recapture as the sale. This would be especially true if the property were held in a partnership and the partnership interest was donated. Another donation possibility is giving the property to a family member in a lower tax bracket. These gifts can be subject to gift taxes. This can be offset by donating the property subject to indebtedness which is forgiven later on an annual basis.

Incorporation of Interests

Tax free transfer of real estate interest to a corporation is permitted by the IRS. This is accomplished by assuring that the person making the transfer owns at least 8 percent of issued and outstanding stock right after the transfer is concluded.

Foreclosures

When a foreclosure occurs, it is treated as an involuntary sale, and the developer's resultant tax is the same as a regular sale of the property. Gains or losses are a function of liability for short falls or deficiencies or if the developer has a right of redemption.

At this foreclosure, the developer will realize gains or losses which are equal to the difference of the basis in the property and any amounts realized by the sale type transaction. Because in most instances the developer realizes a loss, tax consequences can be quite severe because of the gain generated and the lack of cash flows to offset the tax payments.

Deed-in-Lieu of Foreclosure

When the lender does not want to foreclose upon the developer, deed-in-lieu of foreclosure can be used. This is an option when the developer is planning on filing bankruptcy. Using this method will keep the lender from going through a long, protracted period of trying to foreclose on the property. The developer simply deeds over the title to the property to the lender in lieu of any foreclosure.

Sale Leaseback

A sale leaseback is a sale in which the developer sells his property to an investor and simultaneously leases the property back from the investor. Many larger corporations execute this type of transaction to free up their capital for other purposes.

PREPARING SUCCESSFUL SALE PACKAGES

After the developer has made a decision concerning the asking price and proposed terms of the sale, it is important that a sales package be developed with key information which will entice prospective purchasers and generate interest. Two components are necessary for these packages to be successful. The first is a summary type form which can be easily read and create additional interest in the property. The second is a more detailed component which gives all the specifics necessary for the buyer to formulate an offer. Having the information in this form will allow the developer to focus only on those prospects which are genuinely interesting. The following is an outline of the information that should be in this presentation package.

Sales Package Outline

I. Name, address, and general description
II. Property data
    A. Unit mix
    B. Square footage (gross/net)
    C. Rent per month
       1. Common area maintenance (CAM) charges
       2. Lease options
          a. Terms
    D. Who pays utilities?
    F. Lease terms
    G. Security deposit
    H. Pet policy
III. Profiles of tenants
    A. Tenant name
    B. Tenant profile

IV.   Demographics of the area

V.   Financial proforma

VI.   Financing details

   A. Lender

   B. Balance

   C. Rate

   D. Amortization

   E. Maturity date

   F. Monthly payment

   G. Loan extension

      1. Extension fees

      2. Interest rate

      3. Loan term

   H. Prepayment penalty

      1. Prepayment fee

   I. Escrows

   J. Loan transferability

      1. Assumption fee

   K. Due-on-sale clause

   L. Loan guarantees

VII.   Site and floor plans

VIII.   Location maps

IX.   Visual aids (photographs and renderings)

X.   Market comparables

   A. Name/address

   B. Number units/total square footage

   C. Type units

   D. Rent/month

   E. Rent/square foot/month

   F. Payment of utilities

   G. Percentage rents if applicable

   H. Rent escalations

   I. Common area maintenance charges

XI.   Seller's price and associated terms

XII.   Broker representation (name, telephone, etc.)

TEN STEPS OF A PROFITABLE SALE (Figure 14–1)

Step 1: Will a Real Estate Broker's Services Be Required?

Developers who are active within the various disciplines of the real estate business can sometimes sell their own property, but generally, more traffic will be generated through the use of brokers. To select this broker, interview various

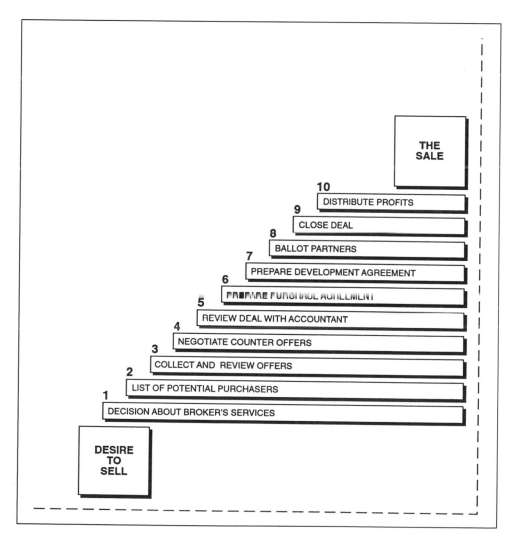

Figure 14–1 Sale process.

brokers in the community which specialize in your type of property. The better qualified brokers will possess the following type skills.

- Specific product experience and knowledge
- Experience in the markets
- Network of broker contacts
- Financing expertise
- Lender relationships
- Stable of contacts with potential purchasers
- Credential of integrity within the community
- Drive and ambition to make sales

After or during the selection process, the amount of the commission should be established. The commission can be added to the asking price or come out of the current asking price. The markets will determine the best method to use.

Step 2: Listing Potential Purchasers

Before distributing the sales package, potential purchasers should be identified. The list can be formulated by listing potential purchasers which meet the following criteria.

- Adjacent property owners
- Property owners within the community which own similar properties
- Contacts who have made earlier inquiries
- Those purchasers who advertise interest in your type property be they regional or national.

The following publications can be purchased when you are looking for information concerning investors of particular product types.

Crittenden Real Estate Buyers
Crittenden Publishing, Inc.
P.O. Box 1150
Novato, CA 94948
(800) 421-3483
(415) 382-2400

Directory of Real Estate Investors
National Register Publishing Co.
3004 Glenview Rd.
Wilmette, IL 60091
(312) 441-4020

National Real Estate Investor Directory
Communications Channels, Inc.
6255 Barfield Rd.
Atlanta, GA 30324
(404) 256-9800

Real Estate Source Book
Macmillan Publishers-Directory Division
3004 Glenview Rd.
Wilmette, IL 60091
(800) 621-9669

Navaro Real Estate Buyers
Box 22728
San Diego, CA 92192
(619) 552-0802

Step 3: Reviewing the Offers

The developer should collect as many offers as possible. Each offer will most likely be different, and many buyers may not be real buyers which are capable of closing on the transaction. The offers which have been collected should be reviewed by accountants or analyst staff. The present value of the sales price is important and should be reviewed carefully. Comparatively, the following factors would be considered in selecting the best offer.

- Price offering
- Downpayment
- Closing date
- Seller guarantees to the buyer
    Rental rate milestones
    Occupancy stabilizations
    Cash flow short falls
- Financing guarantees
    Amount
    Accrued or paid interest rate
    Maturity of loan
- Potential buyer credibility in financial strength or qualifications

Step 4: Counteroffer Negotiations

After identifying a few prospective qualified buyers, negotiation should proceed with at least three. Proposing a counteroffer is the best way to reduce the amount of qualified buyers and to begin negotiations.

Step 5: Making the Deal

After negotiations, and an informal verbal agreement relative to price and terms, produce and sign a letter of intent with the purchaser which outlines the transaction. The developer's attorney and accountant should review this letter prior to signing. This will ensure that no transaction is begun which will adversely affect the developer or his investment group.

Step 6: Purchase Agreement Preparation

From the letter of intent, the attorney can formulate documentation necessary for the purchase agreement. Drafts should be sent to the buyer, seller, and their respective attorneys for review. Generally, additional negotiations are necessary to resolve questions and conflicts. After resolving these issues, all parties should sign the agreement and the purchaser should deliver any funds or earnest money required.

Purchase Agreement
- Sale of the property
- Price
- Allocation of purchase price
- Closing
    Warranty deeds
    Lien affidavit
    Lender affidavits
    Plans and specifications
    Documents affecting title and business operations
    ALTA policy of title insurance
    Termite treatment guarantee
    Zoning letter
    Opinion of counsel concerning status of documents
- Taxes
- Title examination
- Default
- Survey
- Prorations at closing
- Representations and warranties
    Seller's right to execute purchase agreement
    Conveyance of property
    Pending litigation
    Availability of utility services
    Vehicular access

Seller's compliance at closing
Existing insurance policies
Compliance with local building and zoning ordinances
Condition of building improvements

- Damage, destruction, and eminent domain
- Survival
- Notices
- Captions
- Entire agreement; modification
- Binding effect
- Controlling law
- Construction of terms
- Effective date
- Exhibits
    Legal
    Plans and specifications
    Utility letters
    Insurance policies
    Zoning letter

Step 7: Development Agreement Preparation When Selling Prior to Construction Completion

If the purchaser is buying a property which will be constructed or is currently under construction, and he will take title prior to its completion, a development agreement will be needed. This document will define all the rights and obligations of the parties. The following areas should be addressed.

Definition of Terms

This section will define the various terms to be used in the document. These terms will include the following:

- Completion of the property
- Construction loan
- General contractor
- Loan documents
- Plans and specifications
- Permanent loan

Developer Fees

This section will outline the fees the developer is due and when they are due.

Obligations of the Developer

This section will outline all of the obligations of the developer.

Project Financing

This section will define who is responsible for obtaining and paying for the construction and permanent loan financing.

Change Orders by the Purchaser

This section will define the change order process.

Insurance

This section will outline what insurance coverage will be placed on the development during construction and after completion. It will also define who will pay for this expense and whose name will be on the policy.

Penalties

This section will list the penalties for late completion and when they are due.

Reports to Purchaser

This section will outline what reports will be supplied by the developer to the purchaser and when they will be due.

Inventory

This section will list all the inventory that will be sold along with the real estate.

Punch-Out

This section will outline the process for making and completing the punch-out list.

Developer Warranties

This section will define what items the developer will warrant and for what time period.

Step 8: Soliciting Partner Response

If there is an investment partnership that must approve this resale, the managing partner should prepare an investor letter and ballot outlining the following facts.

- Sale highlights
- Information on the purchaser
- Reason for the sale
    Price and terms

  Diminished tax benefits
  Market conditions
  Financing
- Detailed outline of the sale price and terms
- Exhibits
  Estimated sources and applications of funds at closing
  Distribution of cash in subsequent years
  Summary of cash flow and tax benefits per investment unit
- Sale ballot
- Investor certificate

Step 9: Deal Closing

To expedite the closing, the seller (developer) should assist the purchaser in finding any information required to make decisions. In addition, no action by the purchaser should interrupt the normal day-to-day operations of the property. Employees should be notified that a sale is pending. On the day of the closing, all income and expenses should be pro rated and a closing statement prepared. The attorneys should manage the efforts for signing of documentation.

Step 10: Distribution of Profits

After sales proceeds are distributed by the attorneys, the developer will distribute all profits to the partners and investors who are involved in the transaction. If any seller financing was taken back in the transaction, the managing partner must coordinate receiving these payments and the distribution split with other partners. For an understanding about how sale proceeds are distributed, see Figure 14–2.

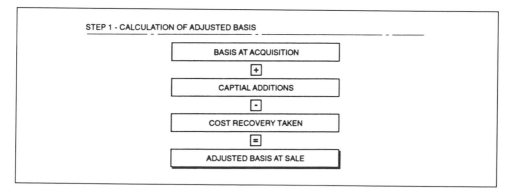

Figure 14–2 Calculation of sale proceeds. (*Cont'd on pg. 596*)

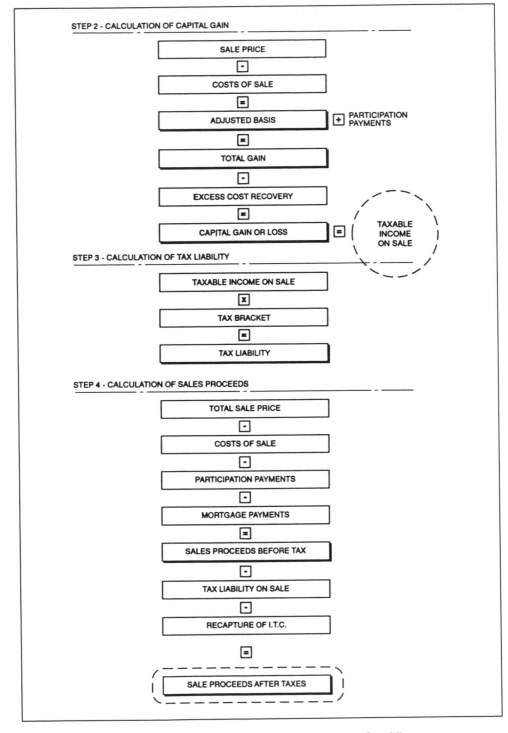

Figure 14–2 Calculation of sale proceeds. (*Cont'd*)

SALE FORMS

Sale Prospect Form (14-1)

This form is to be used to keep track of the various sale offers.

SALE PROSPECT FORM

FORM 14-1

PROPERTY NAME _____

WEEK OF ___/___/___

PROSPECT NAME	TEL. NO.	BROKER	TEL. NO.	DATE CONTACTED	OFFERED PRICE	TERMS

Form 14-1 Sale prospect.

## Chapter 15

Responding to Changing Cycles
of the Real Estate Industry

Historically, we see ever-ending cycles of growth followed by downturns in the market where many developers' projects and businesses fail. We see products developed which were poorly constructed, poorly financed, poorly conceived, poorly managed, and poorly marketed. We see lenders taking back properties and eventually selling them for a loss. We read many articles which question our practices and look for solutions to what seems to be a problem which continues to repeat itself. If the solutions to these problems were simple, all developers would be successful. The solution to surviving during downturns of the market and building healthy, thriving developments and development firms cannot be found in one answer alone. The problems that cause these failures are varied. They may be found in the developer's values, knowledge, work ethic, philosophy, ability to manage a team, ability to manage resources, ability to structure a successful deal, or even ability to second-guess the market fluctuations.

It is unfortunate that there is an absence of literature available for the real estate developer to overview the last 50 years in real estate development and observe the cycles of real estate change and the reasons for those changes. It seems that memory of the last downturn in the cycle is the only key on which new decisions for development are made. Sadly enough, lenders have short memories and developers make too many "gut decisions." Consequently, the industry as a whole continues to be cyclic. The names of the players and the vehicles for lending and developing change, but the same problems create the cycles and continue to plague the industry. It is interesting to follow the mid 1970s and 1980s downturns, because we see similarities in each period. The symptoms which created these cycles were inflated land values, easily available loans, land banking, projections with twisted logic, large bureaucratic developer organizations, failure to meet lease-up schedules, oversupply in the market, and the lack of experience of new developers. In addition, because of closeness of the international community in which we live today and its interdependence of economies, a war, change of governments, or a natural disaster can send rippling effects throughout the lending and corporate communities which are, in turn, felt by the developer. The developer who is not sensitive to all of these factors in his decision-making process will be placing his business and future wealth in jeopardy.

Too often, it is the only image of the developer and the dream of great wealth which draws one into the business—not whether or not the potential developer has the experience or skills necessary to build a successful business. This potential developer, after he has "made the deal," may lack the patience or "know how" to "manage the deal." The reality of real estate development requires strong players able to execute all of the activities and procedures required for a successful business. Wealth can be acquired, but only after much effort and persistence. When we begin a real estate development venture, we must think sensibly, and build a foundation of strength, so that the traps can be avoided along our path to success. The reality traps are over-extravagant lifestyle, get-rich-quick schemes, growing too fast, and failure to observe the past (history).

The probability of getting rich quick in the real estate business is phenomenally low. Unfortunately, our newspapers carry the accounts of the successful broker or developer and even though this person has been in business for 20 years, we overlook that fact and set out to be as successful in just six months. When one considers the education required just to gain knowledge about financing, business, design and construction, and marketing, that alone should dispel any notion that someone can get rich quick in real estate development. The get-rich-quick concept is so absurd within real estate development because work on projects can take from one to three years just to begin construction and another one to three years to complete construction and lease-up. Then, after lease-up, the tenants must be satisfied so that leases are renewed. Only after that period of time do we get a clear picture of whether or not our proforma is working. In a generation of "fast food addicts," who watch solutions to life's problems resolved in the 30 minutes of television programming, it is difficult to come in touch with this reality. We want it and we want it now! The reality is that it takes time.

After the developer's first development is under way and he has found a niche where additional development opportunities exist, the biggest challenge will be to control company growth. If he allows it to grow too fast or tries to complete more projects than he is capable of, even though things will seem like they are booming, his direction may be failure. A frenzy of activity does not guarantee profits. Major spurts of growth in response to demand must be studied carefully, and the personnel added must fit the organization's puzzle as well as possible. If he allows his growth to be out of control, his standard operating procedures in business can be a setting where market studies are not studied carefully, financial planning is overlooked, inexperienced and incompatible staff are hired, schedules are not met, too many meetings occur and the excuse that there is not enough time for planning is accepted. In an effort to take advantage of what seems like an opportunity, the developer begins to take more risk, which is like crawling out on a very long limb where getting there is very easy, but once there, climbing back is more difficult. Especially in major growth periods, the developer must exercise discipline and search for wisdom in building his business. He must exercise care and develop sound business principles of values and belief concerning leadership, procedural systems, organization, personnel, and resources. If there is a lack of experience, then it can only be found through study of other businesses and from the wise counsel of other professionals. Even though it seems like there is not time to grow carefully, if he wants to survive in the future, the developer must control this growth even to the point of saying no to some ventures.

Getting started is the largest single challenge in the real estate development business. Surviving when faced with adversity is a close second. This chapter will consider the problems of the current real estate development market, warning signs about which to be aware, and potential ideas which will help the developer survive during troubled times—on project development, corporate, or personal levels.

CAUSES OF THE REAL ESTATE DECLINE IN THE 1980s

The main reason for this decline is that the forces of supply and demand were out of equilibrium. Oversupply of product type was caused by two very significant reasons: The deregulation of the savings and loan industry and the spin-off effect of easy money and excessive tax benefits.

Deregulation of the Savings and Loan Industry

In October of 1986 Congress deregulated the savings and loan industry and allowed these institutions to vary from their original intended functions, that is, to lend to the residential housing market. With this deregulation came fierce competition by these institutions to increase profitability. Many institutions began increasing their payout rates to depositors. In order to maintain this flow of cash, they entered into the commercial financing arena. As history has proved, they were ill-equipped to manage these types of loans. Loans were made to unqualified developers for properties which should never have been approved. Loans were made on the basis of faulty appraisals and were fee-driven. Only the potential upside was reviewed and not the consequences of the downside possibilities within the transaction. In addition, many lenders became extremely aggressive and started making loans which were not only approaching 100 percent of total costs, but were in excess of these costs. With little if any real equity in their deals, many developers were walking when the project failed. Without any real expertise in working out these problems, lenders were caught holding nonfunctioning, nonprofitable investments.

Tax Reform Act of 1986

Tax laws during the early 1980s enabled investors to take large tax write-offs based on deductions for depreciation, interest, and other accounting items. These write-offs became the main force for the creation of developments, and not a return on investment. Because of these "paper" tax write-offs, the development market became driven by the combination of "easy money" and the motivation of investors to play the real estate game. Unfortunately, with the Tax Reform Act of 1986, the tax game came to an abrupt halt and investors were no longer motivated to invest in real estate developments.

Bond Financing for the Housing Market

During the 1980s, the federal government offered tax-exempt bond financing to residential developers to promote new construction for low- and moderate-income housing. The final outcome of many of these programs was that many projects ended up being targeted to higher income tenants instead of the lower- to moderate-income market. In addition, many projects designed for the elderly housing market were projected to rent up to ten units per month but ended up only renting two to three units per month, thus causing many properties to default on their financing obligations.

World Economy

During the early 1980s, world economies were experiencing rapid growth. With the price of oil increasing, many cities experienced rapid expansion in office space requirements caused by new energy company expansion and the creation of new companies within the fuel industry. With this increased need for office space, many developers began large projects to provide for these needs. Unfortunately, during this time the price of oil dropped and the requirements of these energy-based companies changed. No longer did they require all this space. These changes created a ripple effect within the real estate market which, in turn, affected the need for residential and retail product which had been developed.

In addition, other companies were merging and consolidating to reduce overhead to become more competitive. Additionally, with the creation of "junk bond" financing, many firms were restructuring with leveraged buy outs (LBO). In the early days of these LBOs, companies restructured their work force to economize and oftentimes reduced their office requirements. When the economy began to slow down, original financial projections were not achieved. Consequently, these companies began facing severe financial pressure because of the excessive debt caused by the leveraged buy out. This pressure then caused ripple effects for less demand of office space placing a burden on the developer, his investors, the lender, and ultimately the tax payer.

Furthermore, during this period, interest rates began fluctuating and for protection, lenders began floating interest rates to their borrowers resulting in greater costs for the projects or unanticipated costs if the developer was foolish enough not to have locked in his interest rates for construction and permanent financing.

The Spinoff Effect Caused by Easy Money and Excessive Tax Benefits

Overbuilding

Because of the "easy money" available to developers and the influx of tax-driven equity dollars, more and more developers entered the business. In many cases, the only entrance fee into the development business was a piece of land under control (and in many cases the price paid was too high), an inflated developer's financial statement and a flimsy feasibility study or appraisal. Many developers were either unqualified as developers or unqualified to develop their intended product type. Together with this financing and the inflated tax benefits, excess development has resulted in most every product type.

Aggressive Financial Proformas

During this time period, many developers were projecting healthy rent increases and stable operating expenses. In reality, with the overdeveloped situation, rent concessions were eating into profitability and property values. Additionally, expenses were increasing due to the floating debt service payments. Add to these problems the increase in the debt service carry due to longer rent-up absorption periods and one can easily see why project economics begin registering shortfalls eventually resulting in a financing crisis.

Credit Crunch

Due to many of the problems caused by the excesses of the 1980s, new banking rules and regulations have been enacted to help curb the lending practices of the 1980s. The Financial Institutions Reform, Recovery and Enforcement Act of 1989 (FIRREA) as well as other rules imposed by the Office of Thrift Supervision (OTS) have created new and stricter capital requirements on the thrift industry. These rules required that thrifts increase their capital based for any new construction lending. This increase has caused many healthy thrifts to reduce or totally stop making any new loans. In addition, many thrifts have imposed requirements on many of their outstanding borrowers that will cause outstanding loans to be paid down or paid off. The thrifts hope that these funds will then help them meet the new capital base requirements.

Additionally, the federal agencies that regulate the banking agencies are trying to prevent a crisis in the banking industry similar to the savings industry. New rules have also been imposed on banks to increase their capital base. Due to the extreme scrutiny that the banks have been put under regarding their existing real estate loan portfolios, many banks have also sharply reduced their lending business.

Resolution Trust Corporation (RTC)

On August 9, 1989, President Bush signed into law the Financial Institution Reform, Recovery and Enforcement Act of 1989 (FIRREA). This law dissolved the Federal Saving and Loan Insurance Corporation (FSLIC) and transferred the responsibility of liquidating insolvent savings and loan assets prior to January 1, 1989, to the Federal Deposit Insurance Corporation's (FDIC)'s Division of Liquidation. This law provides for a major restructuring of the thrift industry, as well as a reorganization of the federal regulatory agencies that oversee that industry. The Resolution Trust Corporation (RTC) was established to resolve these thrift problems and to dispose of the assets within those institutions.

Unfortunately, as of the writing of this section, the RTC is having great difficulty in trying to rid itself of its various properties and other financial institutions it must dispose of. The longer it takes the RTC to liquidate its portfolio, the possibility exists that the value of these properties will be decreased even further. In addition, if the RTC ends up dumping properties at "fire sale" prices, the net effect will be that other healthy properties will lose value while trying to compete with these properties that can now afford to offer greater concessions to the rental market.

Deflation of Real Estate Values

The final outcome of all of the problems of the 1980s is that property values have decreased rather dramatically, in some instances from 25 to 50 percent of the original costs. The economics of supply and demand have reduced the real estate industry as a whole into, if not a depression, then surely a recession that may take to the end of this decade to recover.

ANALYSIS OF THE SITUATION
OR
THE DIAGNOSIS OF POTENTIAL PROBLEM AREAS

If after the ground breaking, the beginning of construction or during preleasing or sales periods of the project, reports on expected performance relative to proforma reveal that there are shortfalls in cash flow, cost overruns, and schedule problems, the developer must act quickly to solve these problems to avoid an erosion of his potential profits. This reaction will be based proportionally on his ability to recognize warning signs well ahead of time and his ability to react with action to these warning signs in ways to neutralize these problems and reposition the development for continued success. Too often, symptoms occur, go unrecognized and are allowed to continue without action being taken which will ensure that the problems are solved. The following checklist can be used to identify symptoms of potential problem areas. Later in this chapter we will describe ways the developer can respond with action within these problem areas.

Diagnosis of Project Development

Shortfalls in Cash Flow Projections

- Property management failures
  (excessive tenant relocations)
  (escalating operational expenses)
- Marketing problems
  (absence of market studies)
  (preleasing and presales)
  (concessions expectations)

Failure in Design

- Lack of expansion possibilities
- Dated appearance
- Poorly functioning space
- Behind the competition
- Failure of systems
- Safety problems
- High maintenance expenses

Failures in Construction

- Construction cost overruns
- Construction schedule failures
- Bankruptcy of contractors

Failure in Financing

- Cannot meet debt service payments
- Cannot comply with other aspects of the financing agreements

Legal Action by Development Team, Joint Venture Partners, or Tenants

Diagnosis of Development Business Practices

Inability to Obtain Financing Too Often

Inability to Use Predevelopment Seed Money Effectively

- Not winning competitions
- Not closing on potential deals
- Nonproductive use of capital

Inability to Retain Staff

- Dissatisfaction expressed with status quo
- Leadership development
- Commitment of team

Loss of Operating Capital

- No funds to pursue new deals
- No growth in net worth
- Absence of reserves

Inability to Make It Happen

- Too long to make decisions
- Time management
- Sloppy work

Lack of Business Growth

- No new business
- No new ideas
- Development market is saturated

Loss of Business Due to Legal Action

- Too much time spent in court
- Too much money spent for attorney's fees

Diagnosis of Personal Life

Burnout

- Lack of interest in work
- Excessive fatigue
- Change of attitude

Family Problems

- Tension with wife and children

Legal Problems

- Loss of personal possessions from project failure
- Too much productive time spent in litigation

PRESCRIPTIONS AND SOLUTIONS FOR PROBLEM AREAS

Knowing fully that there is a myriad of problems that the developer will face on each one of the different types of products which he can develop, this section is written to give a broad brush perspective of action which can be taken in response to particular symptoms described in the previous section. The developer should never wait until the last minute to create contingencies for potential problems. If this happens, it is typically too late. The developer should be able to react instinctively to any situation based on his study and experience. It should be noted that no property, corporation, or person is alike and the solutions presented are to be used only as guidelines. Some properties may have only one potential problem while others may have a combination of problems. Some corporations may just need some fine tuning while others need a complete overhaul. In addition, a developer must be able to change his personal and professional life if he finds that he is successful but miserable due to personal family and financial pressures.

PROJECT DEVELOPMENT PRESCRIPTIONS

Shortfalls in Cash Flow Projections

If this problem surfaces, its solution depends on the status of the project. If there are shortfalls during development, it is usually due to some type of marketing failure. If there are shortfalls after construction completion and lease-up, then the solution to shortfalls will be found in the discipline of property management. In addition, the shortfalls in marketing may be more serious if there have been cost overruns in other line items of the capital cost budget. The following are ways to respond to problems with the marketing discipline of the process.

Market Studies

If market studies were not used to create the program in the beginning of the development for setting leasing schedules and concessions, then have one completed as soon as possible. Decisions about how to solve your immediate problems and new direction that may be necessary will be based upon these new studies.

Market and Marketing Repositioning

Because the rental income is the "life blood" of the property, during preleasing and lease-up after construction completion, the product's positioning within the market should be monitored carefully. Obviously, this should have been the catalyst of the project's origin even before construction started, but as in any effort, mistakes are made and new direction is sometimes required to adjust and fine tune the developer's efforts. With change continually occurring in markets, analysis and evaluation should be occurring weekly combined with review of leasing or selling reports to date. The following issues must be considered in marketing repositioning when proforma expectations are not being met.

Missing the Target Market

Is the product missing the intended market? If so, determine what is a better fit for the completed product and how can it reach that market. The following are some ideas.

- Change the "theme" of the property: This can often be achieved through changes in the marketing collateral pieces, paint, graphics, and signage.
- Readjustment in the marketing mix of tenants: Add a new retail tenant that will help increase the shopping traffic.
- Pinpoint advertising precisely to that market.

Inept Marketing Team

The developer should determine if the original marketing team (whether his own or an outside firm) is aggressive enough. Many times they need redirection or motivation. Other times, their tools for marketing may be inadequate. If the developer decides that a change is needed, he should interview and contract with a new marketing team and ensure they have the proper motivation (financially) and direction. He should then continue to communicate with them regularly to keep up-to-date on their progress. In addition, the developer should encourage marketing by the local brokerage community to broaden his range of prospects. To increase the participation of the real estate brokerage community, the developer can offer the following:

- Increases in the leasing commission rate schedule
- Acceleration of the leasing payout: up-front versus over the lease term
- Special incentives to the brokers: free trips or prizes

Wrong Pricing Schedule

As soon as the developer becomes aware that either his absorption rate is lower than projected or that his competition is using concessions or lower rental rates, the developer should determine whether or not his property's offering needs adjustment to meet the market conditions. This adjustment can be completed by:

- Lowering the rental rate
- Offering free rent, either at the front or back of the lease term or spread over the term of the lease
- Offering increases in the tenant allowance
- Moving allowances
- Buy-out of existing leases

Unrealistic Absorption Period

By watching the monthly leasing absorption schedule and the weekly traffic and activity reports, the developer can see if he is on target or falling behind in expectations. Since the development process can occur over a long period of time, original projections made many months or years previously, may need to be reworked to respond to the current market conditions. By adjusting this time period, the property may have changes which can result in shortfalls. Contingencies created specifically for this situation should have been included within the original proforma economics.

Too Small Marketing Budget

Many marketing budgets completed early in the development process were based on absorption periods. If these periods change, additional funds may be required to keep the marketing efforts moving. If this occurs, consider the following.

- Calculate the total marketing budget and rework the line items, decreasing them as required.
- Allocate additional contingency funds to the marketing budget line item.
- Value engineer other line items within the total capital costs of the project economics so that additional funds can be allocated to that activity which produces the "life blood" of the development.

When the project is completed and being managed either by in-house or third-party property management, the following are solutions to problems that may be occurring and affecting cash flow. Since property management controls the operating expenses and has constant interaction with the tenants, they should be monitored carefully. Two primary duties should be the comfort and satisfaction of the existing tenants and the controlling of operational expenses. How well they maintain the property will play a major role in successfully reaching these goals. Happy tenants will renew leases and save a lot of time and effort in marketing and negotiating with new tenants.

Paper Work Trail

If the management company is supplying the developer with either late, incorrect, or poorly organized reports or paper work, this should raise a flag that there is a problem. The developer should meet with the management team and set standards which must be met.

Excessive Loss of Tenants

If there appears to be an excessive number of tenants relocating, the developer should closely monitor the situation as to the exact reasons for these changes. It may be that the competition is offering a better proposition or that the management team is failing in their efforts to serve the tenants. The following are possible solutions to better communications:

- Monthly newsletters from property management to the building occupants which are friendly and helpful.
- Personal meetings prior to rent increases to discuss these increases.

Controlling Increases in Operating Expenses

By reviewing the monthly operating statements, the developer should be able to spot trends in the various line items. To prevent these increases the developer should:

- Require the management team to update the operating budget on a monthly or quarterly basis.
- Reassess the need and cost of the various service contracts.
- Reassess the real estate tax bill. Have the management review the tax bills for the competing properties. Contact a company that specializes in the reduction of real estate property taxes.
- Bid insurance policies. Review if a higher deductible is acceptable.
- Reevaluate the staffing requirements. Can less staff manage the property needs without lowering service to the tenants?
- Decide if outside contract services can lower costs by reducing the current property staffing.
- Decide if another management company would do a better job for a lower management fee.

Renegotiating Current Leases

The developer should have a way to review the status of the tenants with long-term leases. If a tenant begins to experience financial difficulty, the developer will be well-suited to know this earlier rather than later so that some type of contingency planning can occur. There is nothing worse than to come to work on Monday morning only to learn that the tenant has vacated the premises for destinations unknown. Reworking of organizations can also create problems and these should be monitored carefully. In some instances, the developer might be able to renegotiate a new lease with a tenant to give the tenant a better deal over the long term by increasing the lease rate up-front. If the developer is successful in negotiating this situation, he might be able to use this extra income to help refinance the property. In other situations, the developer might be able to negotiate a buy-out by the tenant of his lease (with a cash payment) and then be able to turn and re-lease this space and a better lease rate. Ultimately, it is better to initiate action before the situation worsens and maintain the cash flows into the project.

Understanding the Market

As a final note to this section on problem solving, the following is a list of questions which the developer should be asking about the product and its relation to the market regardless of whether he is within the marketing phase or the property management phase of the project. To survive as a real estate developer, it is imperative that market sensitivity be a single-minded goal and one which is pursued daily. Unfortunately, this requires a tremendous amount of time, but in proportion to having to take the time to solve problems created by not paying attention to the market, it is proportionately small. Asking the following questions will provide insight into the information necessary to understand the market.

- What problems exist which must be fixed?
- Is this a real problem or only a perceived one?
- Is there a product which will satisfy the need?
- Can the product be produced more inexpensively and marketed more effectively?
- What is the competition doing to solve this problem?
- How will my solution rate with the competition?
- How effective are my marketing solutions?
- How long will it take for my product to be absorbed into the market?
- What effect will others copying my product near my location have on my projected economics?
- How long should I stay in the business of producing this product when others begin copying my success?
- What contingencies do I have if my projections of market absorption are inaccurate?
- Are the needs for my product changing and how can I measure this change and modify what I am doing?
- Do I need to offer concessions or incentives for the customers to buy my product?
- Do I need to scale back my development plans or build in phases?
- Should I diversify my product type and location?
- Should I presell my product versus speculating on the market?

Failures in Design

Another reason why developments fail is because of faulty design. Since design is intended to be the physical demonstration of execution of the project economics, it is imperative that the developer spend careful time selecting the designers and engineers and programming the design. Often, the developer tends to work in a vacuum, when creating the product. It is necessary that the developer uses his total team in the programming and evaluation of the design for the following reasons:

- By using all the team members, each person managing or selling the product will have ownership and be motivated to a higher degree.
- Using this master mind of knowledge, the project should perform to a higher degree.

Lack of Expansion Possibilities

Since the need to expand or modify a development may affect its growth or future response to the market, it is best to master plan the project giving the development options for change in the future. The following should be considered from the project's inception:

- Program the site where additional buildings or parking can be added at a future date.
- Program the floor plans for changes in the market by giving large spans between columns as possible should today's design become obsolete.

Dated Appearance

There are many buildings all around us which are from another period of time and are not preferred by the market. To prevent this problem, choose designers who can give you a timeless design, that is, a design which is good today and will be good tomorrow. It is imperative that the very best designers be used. In addition, select materials which are not trendy in color and texture. If your project appearance is dated, then hire a Class A designer to renovate your project to bring its look up to date. Both interior design and architecture should be planned accordingly. Project economics should consider the re-working of interior design periodically because of normal wear and tear.

Poorly Functioning Space

A few symptoms which indicate that a project is not functioning effectively are as follows:

- Turn-around for truck and drop-off are not large enough
- Not enough parking spaces, distances are too far, and spaces are too small
- Modulation of exterior mullions does not respond to efficient tenant layouts

- Too many columns in tenant spaces
- Layout of spaces leads to disorientation
- Lobbies too crowded because of the size of the spaces
- Security is too difficult to control
- Too much square footage is used for circulation
- Lack of covered walkway between building and covered garage

Behind the Competition

If your project is not being selected by buyers and tenants on a consistent basis, it is possible that many of its features are inferior. To avoid this problem or renovate to solve this problem, consider the following:

- Parking (walking distances, covered parking, secure parking, available parking)
- Eating and dining options
- Amenities provided to the buyer or tenant (athletic facilities or clubs, retail proximity, public transportation, conference centers, water features, views to the exterior, corner offices or rooms, lakeside locations, limousine services)
- Ease of access from transportation arteries
- Flexibility in layouts

Failure of Systems

After the project is completed, some of the problems which occur as a result of system's failure are the following:

- Elevator waiting times are too great
- Environmental systems fail to provide comfort in changing weather conditions (Air Conditioning)
- Roof leaks which damage interior spaces
- Exterior wall leaks due to failure of window systems
- Cracks in walls due to expansion and contraction of structural systems
- Blackouts in power supply systems

Elevator problems can be resolved by adding additional cabs or by increasing the speed of the machinery. In addition, the timing of door openings and use of computers to control response to call requests usually provides fine tuning of these systems. It is best to hire an elevator consultant to assist you in these matters. The best way to solve environmental system failure is to hire experienced engineers in the very beginning. If the system is in trouble, then hire these engineers to provide ways to upgrade the systems. Usually, these problems will be resolved by upgrading the equipment or by additional equipment. Other times, computer systems for control may resolve the problem. Roof leak problems are best resolved by having warranties which cover future problems. It is best to minimize value engineering with the quality of the roof. Wall leak problems should be prevented by testing during the design phase or evidence that testing has been performed. When there is a leak in a roof or wall, immediately hire a consultant to identify the problems and suggest solutions to be corrected immediately. If the structural design has failed to take into account movement and cracks are appearing, consider the connections of materials and provide for movement within acceptable tolerances. Blackout can be prevented by proper planning for power uses. Additional service may be needed or if the blackout problem is external to the site, an uninterrupted power system (UPS) may be required. Consult your electrical engineer for a precise solution to the problem.

Safety Problems

To avoid litigation and loss of life the developer should have the project reviewed regularly to ascertain unsafe situations. Potential problems are lack of adequate access during fires and failure of the security or fire safety systems. In addition, all guardrails or handrails should be inspected as to their integrity. Changes of level should be marked carefully and speed should be controlled through the development.

High Maintenance Expenses

If the property management expenses are out of alignment with projected proforma, it is possible that some design modification may be necessary to control this problem long term. The best way to respond to this problem is to identify the problem area and identify alternatives to resolve the issue. Initial costs and payback period analysis over 10 years should be studied prior to the decision to use any available reserves. In addition, consultants can help resolve this problem.

Failure in Construction

Sometimes, after the project economics have been completed, the loan closed, and construction underway, the developer finds that there are overruns in projected construction costs and that the project is behind schedule through failures in construction management. Often these problems are caused by the following:

- "Low balling" of construction costs by the contractor to get the job. With appropriate contracts, these costs should be the contractor's responsibility. It is possible that if the general contractor develops financial problems, his bonding company may have to bear this financial burden. In many cases, the developer may have to pursue legal action with the bonding company to pay for these costs. If this is the case, the developer might have to cover the shortfall and hope to get repaid when the dust settles.

- Change orders brought on by changes desired by the developer. The developer might have changed his mind on various design and construction ideas after the construction began or he might have been forced to make some changes caused by market conditions or tenant requests.
- Unforeseen underground site work, caused by poor soil conditions, rock, or underground water conditions, not originally anticipated.
- Labor problems with subcontractors and shortages of supplies by the material suppliers.

Construction Overruns

The best way to respond to all of these potential problems is to provide contingencies of funds within design and construction budgets including some contingency of interest payments on the construction loan. Once these potential costs are encountered, the developer can value engineer some items and create savings to pay for cost overruns or use some of the contingency to pay for overtime to get the project back on schedule. These problems are usually not encountered with the proper selection of the contractor and his staff and being responsive to the advice which that particular trusted contractor provides. Various ways to respond to cost overrun problems are as follows:

- Value engineer other items on the capital cost budget to make up for the overruns.
- If the construction contract has a guaranteed construction cost, then refuse to pay for the overruns and if this affects the construction process, seek legal advice.
- Conduct an inventory of the work completed and, in addition, have the contractor accounting records reviewed by professional accountants.
- Negotiate a settlement with the contractor either through a loan or by giving him ownership in the project. Another idea is to guarantee some portion of the cash flows over time or a preferred return on the residual at sale.
- Request additional funds from the lender and re-work all proforma economics to reflect this change to the capital cost budget.
- Set up new systems of contracting, managing and accounting which prevent and ensure these overruns from occurring in any future construction within this project.
- Consider changing the staff of the contractor or the construction management team if there is evidence of negligence or lack of monitoring and supervision of expenditures.

Construction Scheduling

Since the failure to meet schedules can affect move-in dates, interest payments, reputation, and other capital cost budget projections, it is best to react to the slightest schedule problems immediately. The following methods can be used to get the project back on schedule.

- If a schedule consultant is not involved with the project, hire one. His or her wealth of experience and ability to know of ways to expedite various work procedures can be a project's salvation.

- Conduct regular meetings with all consultants and contractors and develop a plan to make up the lost time. Never let an item go longer than two weeks behind schedule before looking for contingencies about how to make it up.

- Evaluate whether the cost for overtime, depending on your contract, is less than the interest costs and late penalties. If so, it is probably wise to devise shifts to work around the clock until the time is made up.

- If the construction contract is tied to a schedule and penalties for failure to meet that schedule, then penalize the contractor and use those funds to meet shortfalls. If the failure to meet schedule is severe enough to affect the projected profits of the project, seek legal action.

Construction Omission and Errors

Once it becomes evident that some type of construction deficiency must be corrected, the following guidelines should be followed. First, ascertain if the problem is in violation of a warranty which has been provided. If so and the item has been installed as per the construction documents per the manufacturer guidelines, then the solution to the problem is simple and the contractor has the responsibility to correct it by contract. If he refuses, then the construction retainage can be held, and the developer can have someone else fix the problem and sue the contractor for the difference. Usually, these are the remedies for which a construction contract provides. As long as the contract is solid and followed, the developer is usually protected. This is why it is wise to have legal counsel in the formulation and production of these contracts. The construction costs of the project inherently carry the greatest liability for the developer because of their magnitude. Additionally, the bonding of the contractor is of utmost importance and should be carefully considered. In legal action, the developer may have to take legal action against not only the general contractor, but his subcontractors, material suppliers or installers as well as his bonding company to recover losses.

Failure to Meet Debt Service Payments

Debt Service Restructuring

If for any number of the aforementioned reasons, the property is not producing the projected cash flows, then the developer should consider finding ways to rework his debt service till the shortfalls can be satisfied. Since current financing affects the profitability of the property, the developer should always keep current on the financing market.

When preparing a debt servicing restructuring, the developer should prepare a complete financial plan for the lender and any other creditors who might be involved. This plan should include:

- Current financial statements for the property
- Projections of the "most likely case scenario" of the property, including:
  Assumptions used
  Market comparables
  Changing demographics
- Plan of how each creditor will be paid back
  Sales of assets
- Federal and state tax liabilities owed
- Financial statements of the guarantors

This plan should then be presented to all creditors involved at the same time. The developer must show all concerned that he is still in control of the situation and that he is the best person to implement this plan. This is the one and only time that the developer will be able to convince creditors that he has thought out the situation very carefully and that this is the best solution to a bad problem. The lender and other creditors, if convinced of this matter should then give the developer the leeway he needs to maximize the potential payback and viability of the project.

Refinancing: Refinancing can bring in either new "tax free" money or can be used to reduce the monthly debt service. A reduction in this debt service can be caused by:

Reduction in the current interest rate
Longer amortization period with the same interest rate as currently on the property

If the property cannot be refinanced, it is probably due to one or more of the following factors:

No lenders are willing to finance that property type in that location
Net operating income does not justify a new loan
Interest rates too high to justify a refinance

If this is the case, the developer should seek to negotiate some type of loan modification with the lender to help alleviate the cash flow problem.

Request Modification of the Monthly Debt Service Payment from the Lender by the Following:

- Reducing the current interest rate for a specified time period
- Reducing the interest rate and accruing the difference and adding this amount to the current loan balance
- Keep the same interest rate, but increase the loan amortization period

- Instituting a cash flow mortgage, that is paying all excess cash flow as paying the expenses to the lender
- Offering the lender a participation in future cash flow and resale profits for providing a lower interest rate today
- Getting a debt service moratorium for a specified time period—this will then enable the developer to use this cash for property renovations, increases in the marketing budget or other property carrying costs

Renegotiate the Other Terms of the Loan: Since the developer is going to try to cut a better deal with the lender, he might as well try to renegotiate some other terms he does not like, but had to accept originally.

- Modifying loan guarantees. Try to reduce financial exposure on the loan. The developer might have to put up additional collateral on this loan but might get a reduction in all or some of the loan guarantee he has signed.
- Increasing the loan amount to provide new capital. It might be possible that with a well thought-out plan, the lender might be willing to advance additional capital if its use would position the property for better and more promising marketability.
- Allowing secondary financing. It might be possible that the developer can obtain a second mortgage on the property even though it will add new debt service; it may also provide new tax free dollars that can be used by the developer.

Methods to Raise Money to Help Fund the Debt Service: Unless it has been decided by the developer that "putting good money after bad" is a fruitless effort to bring the property to profitability, the developer should have a plan to bring in new partner equity. This plan could include:

- The developer's own funds: Although not an attractive thought, this will allow the developer to retain ownership position. In order to obtain these funds the developer can:

  Fund out of existing cash flow from other properties
  Refinance other properties
  Sell other properties
  Fund from existing lines of credit (assuming they have no takedown restrictions)

- Having to call for new funds from his existing financial partners. Depending on the original ownership structure the financial partners might have or not have any legal obligation to fund cash calls. If they have an obligation to fund, they probably will have a rate of interest on their new funding and a priority of repayment.

  If the financial partners are not legally obligated to make cash calls, they will have to evaluate what the potential consequences are of not assisting the developer financially. They may, if new investors come in, include a dilution of their original interest and loss of priority or a possible tax problem if the property is lost through foreclosure. They will have to be comfortable that their new money has a reasonable chance of repayment in a reasonable time period.

- Selling off part of his equity to a new investment group: If the developer and current financial partners determine that they would rather not invest their own money (for whatever reason), they might try to bring in a new partner. Chances are this new partner will require:

    Higher rate of return
    Priority or repayment over the existing partners
    No personal loan obligations
    Depending on the ownership structure, they might want some management control

Other Options Which Can Be Used by the Developer to Deal with the Lender and Creditor: Once the developer has tried the methods described above, there still may be a problem and other ideas must be initiated. It could be that there is no market, or that it is just too overbuilt, or that he has been unable to make any progress in renegotiating with the lender. If the developer finds this to be true, then he will have the following options:

Nonpayment of Monthly Debt Service: If the developer is not getting anywhere in negotiations with the lender, he can stop paying his monthly debt service. Although this procedure will not help his credit rating, it will get the attention of the lender. Most lenders think that as long as the developer is paying his debt service on time, nothing is wrong. Once the debt service payments are discontinued, the lender will take notice and even action.

Change the Use of the Property: Depending on the market demand and the type of property, the developer might be able to alter the use of the property. For example, an apartment property might have a problem, due to a oversupply of apartments, but there could possibly be a demand for ownership housing. In this case, the developer might convert the property over to condominium ownership. The reverse situation might also take place, that is, converting a condominium property over to a rental property until there is a demand for condominiums.

Sell the Property: If the developer is unable to fund the current and projected negative cash flows, he might decide or be forced by the lender to sell the property. This sale could be made at a break even, possible loss, or even a potential profit. If there is a loss on the sale, the developer must negotiate a payback schedule with the lender. The developer should seek to negotiate a low interest rate over a long term with an interim grace period and a discount for early repayment.

Give the Property Back to the Lender or Face Foreclosure: If the market does not produce a ready, willing, and able purchaser in the time period required by the lender, the developer might try to negotiate a "deed in lieu of foreclosure." In this situation, the developer would be willing to forego whatever equity he has in the property (if any) to be able to just hand back the keys to the property to the lender and walk away from the problem. Although no developer wants this situation, it is better than a foreclosure on his track record. In addition, the developer should review how his time and resources are best spent. In many cases the developer will spend great sums of both time and money only to come to the conclusion that nothing short of a miracle can help and it is better to move on to another objective.

If the lender is willing to take back the property, but there will be a shortfall between the mortgage balance and the current value, the developer may need to negotiate terms to pay back the lender for this deficit.

Put the Property or Ownership Entity into Bankruptcy: If the developer has a large equity stake in the property or if he wants to move the tax consequences of a foreclosure into another tax year, he can decide to place the property into bankruptcy. Once the property is put into bankruptcy, the lender is unable to complete the foreclosure process. During this period, the developer can then prepare a plan of reorganization. If prior to the actual filing of the bankruptcy, the developer is able to convince at least 50 percent of his creditors (this must total at least two-thirds of the total dollar amount owed) to approve a repayment plan, he might be able to secure a prepackage bankruptcy plan. This plan will help reduce the legal cost of the bankruptcy and the time it takes to complete the proceedings.

Suffer the Consequences of a "Cram Down":   Often in the documentation of financing and joint venture agreements, cram down provisions are included. Essentially a cram down is a preset dilution of partnership interest relative to failures to perform. If negative cash flows are not funded by one party, then the party failing to perform loses a percentage of his interest to the other when the other person covers the other responsibility.

Options Available to the Lender: During the period of financial renegotiations, the developer must do his best to convince the lender that the financial difficulties of the property were due to the local market conditions and that time is needed to work it out. The lender can then make the decision to allow the developer to work his new game plan or force him to pay off the loan, if the loan is in default.

Due to the recent changes and interpretation of the accounting rules, lenders today are more restricted than in the past in how they can restructure troubled loans. The borrower must be able to show that he has substantial equity in the property or else the lender might run the risk of having the restructuring treated as an "in-substance foreclosure," which will for accounting purposes have the same effect as a foreclosure on the lender's books. This will then force the lender to add substantially to his capital reserve requirements.

The developer should be aware of the following options which the lender has in this situation:

Assignment of Rents and Leases: As part of the loan documents signed by the developer, the lender will most likely to able to get an assignment of the rents as paid. This will protect the lender from the developer taking these funds for his own personal use.

Require Additional Collateral or a Partial Loan Paydown: If the developer is having financial problems, the lender may be able to extract additional collateral be put up to secure the property or have the developer paydown the current loan balance to reduce the monthly break-even point.

Accelerate the Mortgage: If the developer goes into default under any of the monetary or nonmonetary terms of the loan, the lender can be able to accelerate the mortgage balance.

Mortgagee in Possession: Under certain circumstances, it is possible for a lender to acquire possession of the property without foreclosing. The lender will then control the property until the borrower has either satisfied the default or foreclosure has occurred. During this period, the lender is entitled to the rents but is held to strict responsibilities with respect to the management functions and can possibly be personally liable to third parties.

Appointment of a Receiver: Depending on the language in the mortgage documents and the local state laws, many lenders can ask the court to provide a receiver to enforce the rights and interests of the lenders. To obtain this appointment, the lender must be able to demonstrate that:

- The borrower is insolvent
- The security for the loan is shown to be inadequate
- There is a serious impairment of the property

Start Foreclosure Proceeding: Once the developer goes into technical default under the terms of the mortgage, the lender can start the foreclosure process. Since each state has different foreclosure laws, the developer should carefully review how this process works.

Sue on Personal Loan Guarantees: Many lenders would rather sue on the mortgage note (assuming that there are personal guarantees which have net worth). In this situation, the lender might not foreclose on the property (due to the potential foreclosure problems in many states). By using this tactic, the lender will try to get the developer to the table to offer them a better deal.

Sue on the Mortgage Deficiency: Assuming that the property has gone to foreclosure and that there were personal guarantees, the lender can then proceed to sue the borrower for any loan losses incurred by the lender.

Legal Action by a Member of the Development Team, Joint Venture Partner, or Lender

As in every type of business transaction, the possibility of poor communication or conflict can occur between the developer, his partners, team members, tenants, or the public. Typically, the tell-tale symptoms of a problem are phone calls not returned, partners requesting that conversations be taped, mail sent certified, and heated conversations.

When these symptoms occur, the developer should first review his legal agreements with his attorney to fully understand the original terms and conditions of the agreements. Using his attorney's counsel, he should meet with the other party without his attorney present to peacefully settle the disagreement. If this proves to be a fruitless effort, he should turn the issue over to his legal counsel. Prior to beginning the flow of legal paper work, he should again meet with his attorney to predict the required probability of success, the time to resolve the issue with litigation, and the cost for the process. Based on this knowledge, the developer must decide whether he will (1) cave in to the other party's request, (2) negotiate a compromise, (3) stall for time, or (4) go the distance through the courts as far as necessary.

If possible, the developer should avoid legal confrontation because it always is an expensive use of time and strength and always prevents productivity in the core of the business.

DEVELOPMENT BUSINESS PRESCRIPTIONS

Inability to Obtain Financing

If in the process of trying to get projects started, the developer finds that financing is almost an impossibility, the following guidelines should be followed.

- Give the lender more participation in the cash flows and potential residual at sale.
- Rework cash flow analysis and carefully check all calculations to find ways to increase yield and reduce costs. If your staff for project finance and analysis has run out of ideas, hire advisors to help in the effort.
- Have an advisor review your lender presentation and seek to find ways to additional interest in your project.
- Broaden your scope of potential lenders to find additional interest.

- Seek equity partners and be willing to surrender ownership for the sake of getting the project off the ground. As a last resort surrender all ownership if you have no equity investment, but seek to have contracts for a development fee, leasing, and management fee.

Inability to Use Predevelopment Seed Money Effectively

It is quite a disappointment for the developer to use his resources to fund early studies about the feasibility of a project only to arrive at a point where no deal can be made for any number of reasons. The following will describe ways to use this seed money to its maximum. All projects which are pursued do not close, but the ones which do must make up for the expenditures of the ones which don't.

- Never place money down on a property without a "free look." This will reduce your monetary risk and give you time to check it out.
- Whenever possible, especially in a joint-venture situation, have the other partner fund the predevelopment costs and you do all of the work. If this is not acceptable, offer a token not to exceed 50 percent sharing of the costs.
- Do not land bank without strong financial partners taking the financial burden or get terms that will not overburden current cash flow.
- Never overpay for land to be developed.
- During the "free look" period, have as many as possible of your consultants "spec" their fees and become a part of the team seeking to find potential work. Often this can be done with guarantees that once the project becomes reality, a bonus will be paid.
- Budget and monitor all "seed money" expenditures from the very start and hire no consultants without a guaranteed maximum agreement.
- Keep personnel and travel costs to a minimum, traveling only on a "must go" basis.
- Use local consultants when possible for speed and ease of communications even when the project is "out of town."
- Always prepare winning proposals in competition so that the potential client senses a "spirit of excellence" beyond that of the competition. This can be seen in the professionalism of the team selected, the careful project economic's analysis, and the offering.

In Preparing Winning Proposals

Whether the real estate developer is being considered for development, leasing, or management opportunities, it is essential that outstanding proposals be submitted. The proposals must be prepared to communicate clearly not only the ideas which the developer has for the potential project, but about his skills to accomplish those ideas and work tasks. They must be easy to read and their very format and presentation should clearly indicate that the reader is dealing with professionals who have the expertise needed. To win the deal, it is imperative that the developer set himself apart from the others who are being considered. To win in these types of situations, there are four ingredients necessary. They are as follows:

- Outstanding relationships with the future client.
- Outstanding ideas which can help the client achieve his goals (in service, design, or management).
- Outstanding economics.
- An outstanding presentation of the first three items.

The following outline provides a sequence which can be used in these formal written presentations and list the various ingredients to be included. Essentially we are suggesting that three packages of information be included. These can be packaged in volumes, notebooks, or simply labeled sections one, two, or three, depending upon the magnitude of the information to be presented. The three sections that must be included, unless requested otherwise, are (1) the project or work task, (2) the developer credentials, and (3) an appendix (with the team's credentials).

Proposal Outline

I. The project or work tasks
   A. Contents
   B. Statement of mission
   C. Objectives
   D. Program components
      1. Master plan
      2. Component characteristics
      3. Total project photographs
   E. Environmental considerations
      1. Site and surroundings
      2. Transportation
      3. Parking
      4. Special surrounding features
      5. Utilities
      6. Zoning and permitting
   F. Building features
      1. Architecture
      2. Parking deck
      3. Space descriptions

4. Space planning
5. Square footage
6. Floor plan photographs
7. Systems
   a. Structural
   b. HVAC
   c. Plumbing
   d. Fire protection
   e. Security
8. Construction cost estimates
9. Synopsis

G. Benefits
1. Location
2. Community
3. Expansion and flexibility
4. Reward versus risk
5. Team
6. Commitments

H. Project ownership and economics
1. Proposed ownership
2. Risk reward summary
3. Capital cost projections
4. Projections of net operating income
5. Operating expenses
6. Financing
7. Summary of cash flows
8. Project value
9. Qualifications
10. Exhibits

I. Services
1. Marketing and leasing
2. Property management

J. Delivery schedule and specifications
1. Summary schedule
2. Outline construction specifications

K. Development team
1. Owner-developer
2. Management and leasing

  3. Retail management and leasing
  4. Hotel management (if required)
  5. Retail consultant (if required)
  6. Architecture and construction
II. Developer credentials
  A. Contents
  B. Implementation (generally, how will the project be implemented by the developer)
  C. Leadership
     (Provide an organizational diagram)
     (List the leaders/biographical sketches)
  D. Responsibilities
     (List the many service tasks which the various team disciplines will provide)—that is, development, financing, design, construction, marketing, property management
  E. Management
     1. Project development plan
     2. Architectural programming
     3. Team selection criteria
     4. Master planning and pricing documentation
     5. Proforma of financial projections
     6. Energy consultant analysis
     7. Scheduling
     8. Coordination and interface
     9. Cost control reports
     10. Provide process diagram
  F. History
     (Provide a brief historic summary of the company and its early beginnings)
  G. Projects
     (List all the projects completed to date including their location, square footage, number of units, and total costs)
     (Provide photographs or a brochure of a sampling of the projects which have been completed)
  H. Relationships
     1. Joint venture and investment partners
     2. Corporate clients
     3. Banking
     4. Leasing and property management

    I. Resources

       (Provide listing of those financial institutions who are providing financing for existing projects)

    J. References

       (List only those with whom outstanding relationships exist including attorneys, CPAs, lenders, partners, and government officials)

   III. Appendix (team members)

     A. Include key team member brochures or

     B. Include short summary descriptions (one page) of each team member (the idea is to sell not only yourself but the strength of your team)

Inability to Retain Staff

Not only must the developer be in touch with who he is and act and perform as a leader, but he must understand the people he is leading. In the highly charged atmosphere of real estate development, often it is difficult to know the people with whom we are working because of the images each is trying to project. In addition, everyone is so focused on the project, that the actual time spent in just being friends is often very small. The developer must become a student of understanding that which motivates his staff and then devise ways in which he can learn about each individual in detail as much as possible. The effort must be sincere and come from a desire to show genuine care and concern. We must come to understand them through their physical, social, and psychological needs. In essence, each person is motivated uniquely and only as we become students of their behavior will we understand this. Our reactions and responses must always be in the context of the big picture of building a business of associates who are highly motivated to develop real estate. It has been observed that in the real estate sales business some factors influence the retention of staff and other factors influence the performance on the job. They are as follows.

Retention Factors

- Policies and administration
- Supervision
- Working conditions
- Interpersonal relationships
- Money, status, and security

Performance Factors

- Achievement
- Recognition for accomplishment
- Challenging work

- Increased responsibility
- Growth and development

To expedite the understanding of staff and to scrutinize the team to ensure that its chemistry composition is positioned for maximum effectiveness, behavioral testing is suggested. If psychological tests are not administered prior to the hiring of personnel, it is suggested. All of us have developed behavioral patterns or distinct ways of thinking, feeling, and acting. The core of this behavior will reflect our individual identities. By knowing the behavioral styles of the team, the developer can learn to appreciate each person as a unique individual, see where conflicts with others have the potential for occurring and structure interactions and tasks to avoid these weaknesses, thereby creating a motivational environment most conducive to the success of the team. A system which has been developed to help in this effort is called the "Personal Profile System" and was developed by Dr. John Geier of Performax Systems International, Inc. This system has been tested and proven effective in the following areas:

- Training and development of personnel
- Coaching and counseling
- Hiring and placement
- Performance appraisals
- Career path planning
- Team building
- Conflict resolution
- Executive development

After we understand those items which motivate and the unique characteristics of our team, the developer must provide financial incentives for his associates. These incentives must not reward for attendance, but they must reward for achievement and for achievement of the total team. These can be in the form of a yearly bonus, limited partnerships, benefits, and recognition. The yearly bonus must be tied to the increase of net worth of the total company. Each person must realize that without growth, there is no reward. Limited partnerships should be given to those leaders who have excelled to provide incentive for retention with the firm. Incentives must be provided so that the developer recruits the best, keeps the best, and motivates the best.

Another aspect of team management is for the leader to control the environment in such a way as to avoid employee burnout. Obviously, this is only a one-way street and the employee must also manage himself. Regardless, the developer can protect his resources of people by creating an environment which will prevent this burnout as much as possible. If the developer observes "what's the use" attitudes verbally or in body language, constant lateness, extreme absenteeism, sloppy work, or antagonism, there are probably work related environmental problems which should be changed. The following ideas might help.

- Compliment sincerely.
- Set reasonable goals with the team, and help them reach them, (dream with the team).
- Be fair and reasonable in your expectation.
- Express a sense of joy in what the team is doing.
- Have an open-door policy.
- Give team members quiet times.
- Communicate effectively.
- Demonstrate excellence by example.
- Have regular conversations with staff and initiate those conversations.
- Evaluate the team regularly.
- Help the team broaden their knowledge and expand into other areas of expertise.
- Give more solutions and less problems.
- Give understanding and learn to express concern.
- Pay based on performance rather than set rules.
- Give directions with dignity (never yell).
- Value and evaluate team's input.
- Lean on the team and delegate effectively.
- Have a good follow-up system.

Finally, one key issue which must be addressed is "chain of command" or hierarchy of leadership. Nothing can stifle an organization more than hesitation in decision making. This usually occurs when there is no clear indication about what decisions can be made and who can make them. Lines of communication become confused and there are no clear lines of authority. These problems sometimes occur when the developer experiences success and staff growth and the number of personnel increases. Unless the developer establishes a clear hierarchy of leadership and gives authority to those whom he trusts through experience, he will greatly weaken his organization through the inefficiencies that will be created and decrease his chances for survival when the inevitable changes in the economy occur.

In Loss of Operating Capital

When beginning a development, the object is to build wealth and not to lose it. If the developer does not plan for the inevitable down side and protect his existing as well as potential resources, he is doomed to failure both personally and professionally. He must tactically have a preventive maintenance plan which does everything to avoid the worst case scenario and a contingency plan which takes into account ultimate failure. This section will suggest ideas to consider to protect business and personal resources.

Protect Business Resources Through Outstanding Performance

- Perform on schedule.
- Minimize assumptions in capital costs and cash flow analysis.
- Carefully monitor the construction, leasing, and property management process.
- Have the right kind of personnel doing the right kind of job.
- Maintain a "lean" organization with minimum overhead.
- Focus on the customer.
- Check and double-check.
- Maintain excellent follow-up.

Protect Business Resources Through Excellent Financing

- Have the financing of every project stand on its own (avoid cross collateralizing and cross default).
- Avoid personal guarantees or set out formulas for the release of personal guarantees through performance (avoid recourse financing as much as possible).
- Make sure the lender must give advanced verbal and written warning for default notices.
- Make sure financing isn't a "band aid" and will work for the long-term of the project.
- Joint venture the risk.
- Carefully consider the downside risk possibilities.
- Don't be afraid to walk away from bad financing.
- Plan for renegotiations with the lender or vender should the project get into trouble (i.e., reduced interest rate, cash flow mortgage, accrual of liability to future date).
- Maintain positive relationships with the lenders.
- Pay cash for land purchases or tie-up land without cash downpayments.

Protect Business Resources Through Contingency Planning

- Plan by accumulating reserves to cover overhead during down turns in the economy.
- Plan for accumulating reserves to pay debt service and maintenance during a slow down in lease-up or sales.
- Have contingency plans for reducing office overhead by reducing the organization and the physical plant.

- Maintain a sensitivity within the office organization concerning the conservation of resources through minimum overhead expense unless its expense is imperative to the success of the project.
- Allocate as much as possible of office overhead expense to projects.
- Manage existing cash reserves to assure that they are liquid and maintained in vehicles which are receiving the highest return with minimum risk.

Effective Management of Business Resources

To be able to take advantage of opportunities which occur and to expedite the decision-making processes, the developer must have systems and procedures which not only give an accurate accounting on the status of his projects, but allow all the aspects of the process to proceed as predictably as possible. Systems are communicators which not only tell how something should be accomplished, but indicate to us when it has not been accomplished. These systems should be characterized by the following:

- They are designed where they complete a full cycle of process activity; only in this way can activities be checked and doubled-checked.
- They function best when based on a set of accepted standards and clear procedural directives.
- They allow evaluation of activities against understood standards allowing the setting of clear objectives and abilities for monitoring.
- They are fully integrated within the disciplines of the organization—that is, development systems work with finance and accounting as well as marketing, property management and design and construction.
- They allow for maximum creativity by managing the predictable elements of the business and allowing focus on the unpredictable.

For the developer to function in the most efficient way, systems must be developed so that the work efforts are organized, productive, orderly, efficient, in harmony, consistent, and stable. These systems must embody the rules and procedures which the company adopts for its functioning. If in the process of creating these systems, efficiency is paramount, then the development company should be able to function with the least amount of overhead. Surviving during downturns in the economy are much more possible when the total team is overhead sensitive. In addition, these systems should provide more time for the pursuit of new opportunities which would have otherwise been missed. The following is a list of various systems to be developed and integrated among the disciplines of the development team.

- Management systems
- Communication systems
- Personnel systems
- Production systems

- Financial systems
- Administrative systems
- Research systems
- Marketing systems

Inability to Make It Happen

There are volumes and volumes of books written about time management. Therefore, this section will not spend a great amount of space preaching about how survival depends on how one uses and organizes time. Obviously, we all have the same 24-hour day and our success relative to others largely depends on how we use that time. If we are too busy enjoying the success rather than creating the success, it will not be too long before the enjoyment comes to an end. In the everyday work place there are enormous pressures to be involved in all types of unproductive activities. How and what we choose to do with our time will either strengthen or weaken our chance for survival in a downturn of economy. A few thoughts which will help are given below.

Use a Day-Timer

This simple tool will enable you to not only schedule your time, but review and plan activities which are imperative for your success. There are a multitude of options available from a small wallet to a larger book type. For more information concerning the availability of these products, contact the following and request a catalog:

Day-Timers, Inc
One Day-Timer Plaza
Allentown, PA 18195-1551
(215) 395-5884

Another thought concerning the management of time is the suggestion that you begin your day the night before and have predetermined the schedule for the new day ahead of time. This will do wonders when your alarm fails to go off tomorrow and your day is already planned.

Use a Computer

Without going into an extensive treatise about the merits of computers, consider the options of how a computer will expedite your complete development operation.

- Gathering and storing of networking data
- Marketing and leasing status reports
- Calculating capital costs and cash flow analysis
- Monitoring of construction costs

- Monitoring of building systems
- Accounting procedures
- Producing cost control reports
- Developing proposals
- Day-to-day production of memos, letters, and reports

Learning how to be literate in computer semantics and operations will not only broaden your expertise but provide a tool for your personal use and allow more self-sufficiency and independence. It will also allow you to manage your time without waiting for someone else's availability.

Other Items to Consider

Mark H. McCormack, in his book, *What They Don't Teach You in Harvard Business School* by Bantam Books has a chapter entitled "Getting Things Done." In this chapter he develops a list of time wasters and gives insight into ways we can "make it happen" in the least possible time. The issues which he considers are as follows: (note that just reading over this list alone makes one more sensitive to areas which must be disciplined).

- Being conscious of the time factor
- Maintaining one's predetermined schedule
- Understanding how to be most effective with different personalities
- Handling phone calls
- Running and participating in internal meetings
- Participating in external meetings
- Understanding yourself and your own work habits
- Learning to know how and when to say no
- Learning effective decision-making procedures
- Expeditious inter-office communications
- Knowing what needs to be written or filed
- Learning effective ways to read correspondence and mail
- Keeping a neat, well-planned office

Another book that provides some interesting insights is *How to Work the Competition into the Ground and Have Fun Doing It* by John T. Molly, published by Warner Books. Within this book, the reader can find valuable insight into monitoring one's time and finding ways to make our efforts more efficient.

In Lack of Business Growth

To survive as a real estate developer, we must view the development of projects with a long-term perspective. In other words, when beginning the first development, plan as if you are building a business and not simply completing a project. As in the growth of any business, each small step, if calculated carefully, becomes a foundation for each future step. To be able to make these decisions effectively requires that strategic and tactical planning be used. If you desire to be a real estate developer, then plan to be one. Take the time to set objectives and to plot strategy. Numerous books can be used to develop this plan. The following three books can be used as needed. They are not real estate oriented, but their insight can be valuable. One of the main reasons that a business does not grow is that there is no plan for growth.

Business Plan Workbook
by Gary A. Cooper
Prentice Hall Publishing Co.
Prentice Hall Building
Englewood Cliffs, NJ 07632

Develop Your Business Plan
by Richard L. Leza and Jose F. Placencia
The Oasis Press
300 North Valley Drive
Grants Pass, OR 97526

Total Business Planning
by E. James Burton, Ph.D. and W. Blan McBride
John Wiley & Sons
60 Third Avenue
New York, NY 10016

In addition, the following outline can be used in the development of business planning. Please observe that the outline can be modified depending on the status of your business at this time or if you are already involved in real estate development. Business plans should be used during start-up, yearly as a checking and monitoring device, and when the marketplace indicates that a new direction should be taken. In a full-service real estate development company, business plans should include planning for corporate long-range and short-range planning. In addition, the developer should require staff participation in the process along with any key management consultants who are team members. The business plan should illustrate planning for development, marketing, design and construction, finance and accounting, and property management. Each discipline's leader should have specific missions to be accomplished and evaluated. Not only will this give direction to your team, but the planning will pull the whole team together and allow your development business to have a greater chance for survival during the changes of the marketplace as well as allow you to take advantage of the growth periods to the maximum. Not only should companies have business plans, but projects as well. An aspect of this project planning was discussed in Chapter 6 under the Project Development Plan.

Business Plan Outline

I. Overview . . . Introduction
  A. Objectives
    1. Short range
    2. Long range
  B. The Market
    1. Summary
    2. Market studies
    3. Feasibility studies
  C. Research, networking, and public relations
    1. Research
    2. Networking
    3. Public relations
  D. Development
  E. Marketing
  F. Finance and accounting
  G. Property management
  H. Responsibilities and reporting
  I. Corporate office interface
  J. Product types
  K. Projects
  L. Management team and staffing
  M. Office planning
  N. Schedules
  O. Budgets

Planning for the Worst Case Scenario

Since sometimes the inevitable happens rather quickly, the developer should have a game plan on how to survive and react to adversity. This game plan will include:

- Staffing: Who is really needed and can their salary be readjusted?
- Office space requirements: Is all the office space needed or can some be subleased out?
- Corporate operating expenses: Can certain items be reduced or cut out completely? For example, is the corporate plane really necessary?
- Outside consultants: Can outside consultants replace in-house staffing? It might cost more per hour for the consultant but there is a reduction in office

space and benefits. Additionally, when a project is complete, the consultant is not an overhead expense.

- Reduce any corporate debt if possible.
- Make sure that all properties are in separate entities: If one property has problems this will not hinder other properties financially.

Networking for Future Growth

Networks of relationships with other professionals who are associated within the business is an essential ingredient in the long-term survival and growth within the real estate development business. It is these relationships where we find creativity, strategic information, counsel, help, joint-venture partners, equity investors, professional staff, and ideas. Recently, in a local magazine, an article featured a very successful developer who has gone through some severe changes in his business over the past 10 years. Over this period he had reorganized and reworked his operation. Presently in a large metropolitan area, he is the one developer in a downturned economy who is building the super large projects which are preleased at 65 to 75 percent and this is in the down cycle of real estate development. The one key thought of the article was the fact that he had phenomenally good relationships within the community and this fact was presented as the reason his business was thriving. This example illustrates the importance of building these networks of friends in all disciplines of the business. Over and over again, we are reminded that other people want to do business with people they trust and respect and with whom they are friends. Therefore, make it a priority to build networks of contacts with whom you befriend. Over the years and in the long run, these very people will help you survive during the changes of the economy. The following businesses represent various areas where relationships with individuals on different levels will prove helpful. Another way to visualize this quest is to ask the question: What kind of people do I need to know to understand real estate development and who are the people who are involved in real estate on the decision-making levels?

- Brokers and marketing agents
- Other developers
- Financial planners or certified public accountants
- Investors of all types
- Politicians
- Government officials
- Architects, contractors, and engineers
- Attorneys
- Corporate executives (especially those involved in planning for growth and decision making)
- Leaders of local and national associations

- Decision makers of all types of companies
- Mortgage brokers
- Long-term corporate relationships
- Tenants as partners

Diversify in Your Development Direction for Continued Growth

The real estate developer usually selects a product and masters its production in design, marketing, financing, and management. Then once he has mastered that product and understands when to develop and when not to develop, he should take his profits and diversify into another product type in a similar way. There is one shortfall to avoid. The developer must not try to immediately diversify into another product type without first testing the new product on a smaller scale of production. The reason for this recommendation is that each product type has idiosyncrasies in marketing, costs, and property management which can be only learned through experience. Sometime the learning curve is steep and to pursue a project of significant magnitude, prior to understanding that product thoroughly, can cause substantial failure.

By plowing his profits into the development of new product over time and gradually with patience developing systems and procedures for the development and management of the new product, the developer will eventually find that he has developed expertise in residential, retail, office, and industrial developments. It is unlikely that all areas of real estate development will be affected severely during downturns of the economy. Therefore the developer can focus on those areas which are in a growth mode and stabilize and manage in those areas which are not. The developer should always be on the lookout for "niche properties," such as infill apartment properties or specialized retail centers. In order to better prepare for these new opportunities, the developer should always be reviewing new product types. This review process should include:

- Visits to these properties
- Collect property brochures, floor plans, pictures of the elevations, etc.
- Discuss with the tenants, developers, and lenders involved in this new product type

Other methods to increase cash flow that the developer should consider are:

- Renovate and reposition existing owned properties to bring up to current market conditions. If justified expand the properties.
- Acquire existing properties that need the developer's expertise to bring out their financial potential.
- Establish relationships with the real estate brokerage and corporate community to develop "build-to-suit" transactions or developments in which the tenant will get a piece of the ownership by becoming a lead tenant.

- Seek ground lease opportunities in which less equity is required by the lender.
- Establish relationships with large investment groups in which the developer will take a development fee for putting the project together and a negotiated piece of the future profits.
- Look into purchasing other businesses outside the real estate business that are countercyclical to the real estate industry. This cash flow can then be used to plow back into future real estate deals.

In addition, the diversification should also be applied to the service-oriented segments of the business so the developer can diversify sources of income. The best scenario is to have income from the following sources:

- Development fees
- Property cash flows
- Residuals (profits at sale)
- Sale and leasing brokerage commissions
- Property management fees
- Consulting and training
- Mortgage brokerage
- Workout consulting with lenders or the Resolution Trust Corporation

The developer who has diversified into brokerage and property management not only enters an arena which provides him with greater development opportunities, but also provides him with income sources when development possibilities do not exist. Properties must always be managed, sold, or leased.

Experience Growth Because of Continued Education

The best possible persons should be hired and then they should receive the best possible training on an ongoing basis to accomplish and sustain long-term growth potential. In our ever-changing business environment, we should continue training because there is no such thing as too much training. Education and new experiences expose the individual to new ideas and increase their sensitivity and creativity. Through education, performance is usually enhanced. A company which is operating with alert motivated people, understanding the latest ideas within the marketplace and using them for an ultimate in efficiency will have by far a better chance for survival and sustained growth during the downturns of the business. Everything is changing around us, and the best preventive medicine for change is to be equipped to respond positively as quickly as possible.

Continuing education will reap benefits in efficiency also if we are equipped to be successful more often than not. Having the proper knowledge to negotiate the construction contract for opportunities of savings, or to know how to prospect for tenants more effectively, or to understand how to be sensitive to tenant and customers needs, will allow the developer to generate new and repeat business and to increase wealth and store reserves that may be needed in the future.

To stay on the cutting edge of the real estate development business, it is imperative for the developer and his staff to possess the skills necessary for success. The following is a list of the skills which development, design and construction, marketing, finance, accounting, and property management will need to excel during the good and bad times.

- Psychological skills
- Social skills
- Physical skills
- Managerial skills
- Technical skills
- Organizational skills

As the developer considers continuing education for himself and his staff, he should fashion educational programs to strengthen his knowledge and constantly keep him abreast of latest knowledge within the industry. In addition, he should consider motivational and character building seminars for the overall health of his organization. From his analysis of the team, including their strengths and weaknesses, along with his business objectives, a program for each of his team members can be planned and included within his yearly business plan. The Institute of Real Estate Management (IREM), the Realtors National Marketing Institute, and your local or state Board of Realtors can provide this type of information as well as certifications available.

In Potential Losses of Business Due to Legal Action

If the developer finds that his business growth is stymied and in the process of evaluating the situation finds that inordinate amounts of time were spent in litigation during the past year, it is obvious that in order to experience growth in the future, this must change. Because of this situation, he will long-term experience the following:

- Loss of reputation because others are always suspicious of the business man who spends a lot of time in court even if innocent.
- Loss of time that otherwise could be used productively.
- Loss of resources which could be used as "seed money" in exploring other profitable ideas.

The developer must establish convictions and procedures with which to operate his business and help avoid legal action at all costs whenever possible because litigation is usually not profitable.

PRESCRIPTIONS FOR PERSONAL LIFE

Protecting Yourself

A common occurrence in the work place among professionals who strive for excellence and who are possessed with a great deal of ambition is burnout. After giving our all to be successful, suddenly we find that our desire and care for our work has diminished. We find that we are fatigued more often and the people around us would rather we leave. If this occurs when adversity reaches our business, the results in our lives can be devastating. We will find that when we need all of our strength to survive, it will not be there. The following are symptoms of burnout. These should be sign posts warning us that something must change and change quickly.

Burnout Symptoms

- Chronic fatigue and emotional exhaustion
- Increase in negative emotions (antagonistic, depressed, helpless empty feeling, anger, and frustration)
- Sense of giving more than we are receiving
- Poor attitude, diminished interest, sloppy in our work, but busy and accomplishing little
- Development of intestinal problems (ulcers, indigestion)
- Headaches
- Disturbed sleep, lack of ability to slow the mental thought processes down
- Desire to be somewhere other than work on a daily basis
- Reduced interest in physical activity and exercise
- Reduced interest in social interactions

Obviously, one will not have all of these symptoms at one time, but if in a regular evaluation of ourself, we find that there is a 25 to 50 percent occurrence, it is time to initiate some action to change our trend toward burnout. The following are ways to avoid burnout. It is good advice whether we are experiencing these symptoms or not to follow this preventive medicine, simply because it makes sense.

Burnout Avoidance

- Allow more time to complete work tasks (relieve pressure).
- Set reasonable career expectations.
- Set limits on how much you will give or take.
- Start each day with a positive goal (identify regularly your mission).
- Think about the past but work toward the future.
- Take a vacation daily (5 to 15 minutes to stop and "smell the roses").

- Introduce yourself to new ideas and skills (learn about new things not directly related to real estate development; develop new hobbies).
- Accomplish things which are not desirable to do (to have the feeling of overcoming adversity and being victorious).
- Evaluate yourself regularly; compliment yourself and reward yourself with celebrations.
- Maintain a healthy attitude by not overreacting to issues.
- Improve and maintain a healthy self image (lose weight gradually, dress better, communicate more effectively, focus on the positive points and compliment yourself).
- Develop disciplines of physical exercise (golf, tennis, racquetball, and jogging).
- Develop a sense of humor, laugh more, put yourself in a position to laugh more through movies, books, etc.
- Develop habits of stress management.
- Seek professional assistance.

Protecting Your Family

The real estate development business is such an exciting business. It allows you to be involved in the total fabric of our society, but too often in our desire to excel, it can squeeze out everything else in our lives. Consequently, our spouses, children, and health can be negatively affected. The developer or his staff can experience burnout; children can become disoriented and distant, experimenting with drugs, alcohol, and crime; and the lack of a healthy relationship with our spouses can result in divorce. This section is included because it is believed that if we have a stable family, we can survive the adversities which will eventually come in a far better way. When there is confusion at the office and we can retreat to the safety of our homes and loved ones, it is much easier to get up the next morning and try again. A parent who spends all his time away from home creating deals and building monuments to himself will find that the returns on his investment of a quantity of quality time with his children will be directly proportional to the magnitude of time he has spent with them. When serious problems occur, he will then spend great amounts of quality time which could have been invested in his business trying to solve those problems. One way to solve this problem is to become a student at being a parent. Read a number of books about how to relate to your children and apply the ideas which you read, and above all, spend time with them. Even make them a part of your development activities.

Protect Your Mate

Unfortunately, today divorce in all businesses is fairly commonplace. Thousands and thousands of books and articles are written about the subject, with various opinions, based on reactions to experiences and sociological or psychological studies. This section is not meant to be a platform for marital counseling. Therefore, it will be brief. Its briefness does not mean that the subject is not extremely important. How we relate to our mate can have significant impact on our business success. If we have an intimate friend and companion with whom we can share our disappointments, deepest thoughts, and desires and needs, it allows us to relate and respond to our business associates in the most mature way. Unfortunately, many of the management principles which we follow in business are forgotten when we arrive home in the evenings. Our behavior toward our mates will go a long way toward making our marriages successful. The main reason we have included this subject is that it has been our aim to illustrate as many keys as possible that will give the developer a greater probability for success. Having marital problems just when everything else in business is going wrong may be the final aspect in failure. Conversely, marital support at that special time can be the one piece of the puzzle that can lead to greater success. The following are a few ways in which we can protect our partner by maintaining our relationships with our mate.

- Spend regular quality time.
- Developing the capacity to sincerely listen.
- Spend time planning together and setting goals.
- Develop common interests where special time can be spent together.
- Make your mate your business partner.
- Leave nagging problems at work.
- Avoid nagging about anything.
- Develop positive memories.
- Establish traditions.
- Give full acceptance.
- Minimize expectations.
- Avoid selfishness.
- Be individuals but yet part of one team.
- Plan for your eventual death.

Protecting Your Personal Resources

Initially, the developer should consult his attorney and CPA to devise legal ways to protect the accumulated assets. The objective will be to place assets where they cannot be attacked by creditors.

- Place your home and other key possessions in your spouse's name or in another family member's name.
- Place funds set aside for children's education in trusts in their name.
- Place all other assets in similar trusts with other family members.
- Have reserve funds set aside for "a rainy day."

Additionally, the developer should have a basic understanding of the tax strategy and how the bankruptcy codes work. Although this is the last thing that he would ever want to do, he might one day be in a position where he has no choice but to file bankruptcy.

THE 1990s AND ECONOMIC FACTORS ABOUT WHICH THE DEVELOPER SHOULD BE AWARE

Based on the fact that we are now entering a global economy and the excesses of the 1980s are over, it appears that the future role of the developer will still be entrepreneurial but that he must align himself with strong capital bases. Due to the oversupply of most product types, the first part of the 1990s will be one of reorganizing internally to meet these financial and market challenges.

Developers will also need to spend more time on the basics of streamlining their properties to meet market demand. In order to meet this demand, the developer will need to research the market and to see what makes it tick. This research will need to be backed up by extensive data collection and interpretation.

Other items that the developer will face during this period are:

- The tightening of credit for anyone involved in the real estate business
- Increases in the amount of equity that will be required by lenders
- Increases in the time and cost to obtain entitlements
- A changing demographic market, that is, the advancing in age of the "baby boom generation," the numbers of individuals who will be working at home, the consolidation of business into more streamlined machines, the fact that more companies will use less space per person, and that many people will have offices in their homes
- Reduction in property values due to the dumping of properties into an already oversaturated market by dissatisfied owners, lenders, and the Resolution Trust Corporation (RTC)

To meet this new challenge, the developer will need to have patience, financial staying power, and a willingness to change with the times.

As mentioned in Chapter 1, the time to build is during the upside of the market cycle. During this period, any oversupply in product type is or has been absorbed and it is time to plan new product to meet future demand. Since no developer has a crystal ball allowing him to know his competitor's plans, he should carefully review not only his market in the light of the general economy. Some suggestions are as follows:

- Read the local and national business periodicals.
- Review interest rate trends.
- Understand the local and national unemployment figures.

- Analyze local rental rates, concessions given, rent expiration dates, and future projected space demand.
- Understand new credit demands required by lenders.
- Be on top of operating expenses and understand how to lower expenses without sacrificing quality of the services to the tenant.
- Constantly update the financial situation of current long-term tenants.
- Make sure that as soon as a problem or even the slightest hint of a potential problem arises that he not "stick his head in the sand" and hope that the problem will go away, but he must aggressively try to correct that problem.

In summary, during the 1990s and beyond, because of the cycles of history, the new developer or the developer who desires to grow and continue in business must unlearn the patterns of the past and follow the successful patterns of those who have had "staying power" during the various cycles of the 1970s and 1980s. The following are characteristics after which one's business should be fashioned.

- There must be an honest appraisal of the development company's market position, recognizing its strengths and weaknesses—for example, the developer must prepare realistic proformas, and accurate forecasts of rent projections based on reality and not on presupposition. In addition, he must reduce operating costs to the minimum, while having organizational structures created specifically for focusing on the key services which are provided to the customer. Finally, new developments should begin only after all costs are fully considered and these costs are reinforced by rents rather than some magic appreciation which may occur in the future.
- The developer must adopt simple strategies and focus on those strategies with commitment. This will be evident when one's focus reveals that the projects initiated have increased value at the end above which they cost. Also, this focus on strategy will mean that in each venture, the development company will only participate in ventures where they bring value to the transaction. Simple strategies will also force the development company to place the customer, the tenant, or the client's interest above its own, thereby following basic axioms for business success. This focus will also give the development company the reason to walk away from marginal deals.
- The developer must maintain financial discipline in all decision making— in other words, maintain strict control on one's capital and time and consider the alternatives available. Also, it must mean that the development company keeps abreast of the requirements of the financial markets, in terms of returns, support for fee structures, and appreciation.
- The developer must continually have an orientation to the basics of business fundamentals relative to the customer, the service provided, staff, objectives to build net worth, projects and organizations, and have a well-developed system for control at all levels of the organization.

- Above all, the developer must maintain entrepreneurial flexibility rather than becoming encumbered by large, lethargic bureaucratic organizations. The developer can maintain a large organization, but that organization must be capable of being easily reduced to adjust to changing market realities and must be able to grow quickly to take advantage of new opportunities. Both of these needs can be satisfied if the entrepreneurial company is governed by values and attitudes which breed success.

As the cycles occur and the real estate industry matures, the successful developers will be forced to think and plan strategically to be able to understand how all the pieces of the development puzzle fit together. Their focus will be on their strengths and what they do best to carefully position themselves in the competitive markets. This strategy will force them to get back to the basics of serving the customer, calculating costs and rents, controlling costs, and managing overhead and profits as well as their staff.

Chapter *16*

Project Economics for
Various Product Types

To give the reader a better understanding of the development process, four product types are presented in this chapter. These give insight into how to prepare the development proforma and the operating proforma for the different product types. Although this workbook mentions many types of real estate investments, this chapter will focus on the following:

- Retail
- Industrial Building (Build to Suit)
- Corporate Summit Office Building
- Residential Subdivision—Land Development

The same due-diligence process and analytical tools which are used in these product types can be easily applied to other types of real estate. The process of running these numbers is the same for all types of properties; the only difference will be in the line items used and the absorption period to rent-up or sell the product.

PRODUCT TYPE NO. 1: RETAIL

PROPERTY NAME: MARKETPLACE
LOCATION: Atlanta, Ga.

GENERAL ASSUMPTIONS

	ASSUMP.	INFORM.		ASSUMP.	INFORM.
SQUARE FOOTAGE/EFFICIENCY			**SALE**		
Gross Square Feet	100,000		Capitalization Rate	9.00%	
Net Square Feet	100,000		Based on NOI (Year)	Current	
Building Efficiency		100.00%	Sales Cost	2.00%	
PARKING			**LAND**		
# of Surface Parking Spaces	500		Cost	$3,145,000	
Ave. Monthly Rent per Space	$0.00		Acres	15	
Total Parking per 1,000 SF NRA		5.00	Square Feet of Land		653,400
			Floor Area Ratio		15.30%
RENTAL INCOME			Cost Per Acre		$209,667
Lease Term—Anchor (Yrs)	15		Cost Per Foot of Land		$4.81
Options (Number/Years)	3/5				
Lease Term—Locals (Yrs)	5		Land Sale:		
Options (Number/Years)	1/5		Parcel 1 (1 Acre)	$400,000	
			Parcel 2 (1.5 Acre)	$550,000	
OPERATING ASSUMPTIONS					
Op. Cost—Leased Space (/SF/YR)	NET		Net Land Cost	$2,195,000	
Op. Cost—Vacant Space (/SF/MO)	$0.10		Net Land Acres	12.5	
Vacancy Factor	6.00%		Square Feet of Land		544,500
Management Fee	3.00%		Floor Area Ratio		18.37%
Reserves (Per Sq.Ft. NRA)	$0.15		Cost Per Acre		$175,600
Rent Increases (Per Year)	5.00%		Cost Per Foot of Land		$4.03
Expense Increases (Per Year)	5.00%				
Starting in Year	3		Land—% of Total Costs (Net)		28.18%
CONSTRUCTION UNDERWRITING			**CONSTRUCTION COSTS**		
Construction Loan Amount	$7,800,000		Hard Costs (Site & Shell) (Per S.F.)	$33.00	$3,300,000
Interest Rate	9.00%		Tenant Allowance (Excl. Grocery) (Per S.F.)	$3.20	$320,000
Loan Fee (%)	1.00%	$78,000	Plyon Sign	$0.25	$25,000
Month Construction Loan Repaid (End of)	12		Landscaping (Per S.F.)	$0.85	$85,000
			Total Construction Costs	$37.30	$3,730,000
PERMANENT UNDERWRITING					
Debt Coverage Ratio	1.10		**DIRECT COST CONTINGENCY**		
Available For Debt Service		$913,307	Total Constuction Costs	$37.30	$3,730,000
Interest Rate	9.50%		Enter Percentage	5.00%	
Amortization Period (Years)	30		Contingency Amount	$1.87	$186,500
Loan Constant (Yr)		10.09%			
Maximum Loan Amount		$8,228,526	**LEASING COMMISSIONS**		
Actual Loan Amount	$7,800,000		Percentage of Lease	4.00%	
Loan to Cost Ratio		100.15%	Paid for Lease Term (Yrs)	5	
Permanent Loan Fee	2.00%	$156,000	Paid Upon	Move–in	
Monthly Payment		$65,587	Paid Upon Renewal	No	
Annual Payment		$787,040			
Net Cash Flow After Debt Service		$126,267	**DEVELOPER'S FEE**		
			Total Square Footage	100,000	
EQUITY SUMMARY			Enter Per Square Footage	$3.60	
Equity Required		$0	Developer's Fee	$360,000	
Actual Equity To Be Contributed	$0				
			INDIRECT COST CONTINGENCY		
APPRAISAL			Total Square Footage	100,000	
Capitalization Rate	9.00%		Enter Per Square Footage	$0.90	
Stabilized NOI	$913,307		Contingency Amount	$90,000	
Appraised Value—Stabilized	$10,147,853				

PROPERTY NAME: MARKETPLACE
LOCATION: Atlanta, Ga.

KEY VARIABLES

TIMING LEGEND:

A — All Cost is month entered
B — First Month of ratable spread
C — Number of months spread
D — Specific amounts and months
Enter in table to right

DESCRIPTION	AMOUNT	A	B	C	D
DIRECT COSTS:					
Land	$2,195,000	1			
Hard Costs (Site & Shell)	$3,000,000		1	9	
Tenant Allowance (Excl. Grocery)	$320,000		7	3	
Pylon Sign	$25,000		8	1	
Landscaping	$85,000		8	2	
Contingency	$186,500		1	9	
INDIRECT COSTS:					
Architecture & Engineering	$150,000	1			
Soils Tests	$50,000	1			
Survey	$10,000	1			
Testing and Inspection	$45,000		1	9	
Pre Constr. Project Mgmt.	$42,000	1			
Title and Closing Costs	$15,000	1			
Legal, Accounting and Adm.	$63,000		1	9	
Insurance	$12,000	1			
Appraisal	$8,000	1			
Construction Administration	$54,000		1	9	
Permits and Fees	$35,000	1			
Development Foo	$360,000		1	9	
Marketing	$24,000		6	7	
Property Taxes	$5,000	1			
Lease Commissions	$205,200	1			
Contingency, Indirect Cost	$90,000		1	9	
FINANCING:					
Construction Loan Fee	$78,000	1			
Permanent Loan Fee	$156,000	1			

NOTES:

1. Numbers are rounded.
2. Proforma rents are increased 5% at year end anniversary date during the rent—up period.
3. Profroma expenses are increased 5% starting year 3
4. Construction interest is paid at the end of the month
5. Space available for rent in 10th month.
6. Permanent Loan is funded in 13th month.

PROPERTY NAME: MARKETPLACE
LOCATION: Atlanta, Ga.

PROJECT COST SUMMARY

	TOTAL	COST/SF	% OF TOTAL COSTS
DIRECT COSTS:			
Land	$2,195,000	$21.95	28.17%
Hard Costs (Site & Shell)	$3,300,000	$33.00	42.35%
Tenant Allownace (Excl. Grocery)	$320,000	$3.20	4.11%
Pylon Sign	$25,000	$0.25	0.32%
Landscaping	$85,000	$0.85	1.09%
Contingency	$186,500	$1.87	2.39%
TOTAL DIRECT COSTS	$6,111,500	$61.12	78.44%
INDIRECT COSTS:			
Architecture & Engineering	$150,000	$1.50	1.93%
Soils Tests	$5,000	$0.05	0.06%
Survey	$10,000	$0.10	0.13%
Testing and Inspection	$45,000	$0.45	0.58%
Pre Constr. Project Mgmt.	$42,000	$0.42	0.54%
Title and Closing Costs	$15,000	$0.15	0.19%
Legal, Accounting and Adm.	$63,000	$0.63	0.81%
Insurance	$12,000	$0.12	0.15%
Appraisal	$8,000	$0.08	0.10%
Construction Administration	$54,000	$0.54	0.69%
Permits and Fees	$35,000	$0.35	0.45%
Development Fee	$360,000	$3.60	4.62%
Marketing	$24,000	$0.24	0.31%
Property Taxes	$5,000	$0.05	0.06%
Lease Commissions	$205,200	$2.05	2.63%
Contingency, Indirect Cost	$90,000	$0.90	1.16%
TOTAL INDIRECT COSTS	$1,123,200	$11.23	14.42%
FINANCING COSTS:			
Construction Loan Fee	$78,000	$0.78	1.00%
Permanent Loan Fee	$156,000	$1.56	2.00%
Construction Loan Interest	$544,211	$5.44	6.98%
TOTAL FINANCING COSTS	$778,211	$7.78	9.99%
TOTAL COSTS PRIOR TO LEASE−UP	$8,012,911	$80.13	102.84%
LEASE−UP COSTS:			
Rental Income	($234,000)	($2.34)	−3.00%
Management Fee	$7,020	$0.07	0.09%
Reserves	$3,750	$0.04	0.05%
Operating Cost−Vacant	$1,800	$0.02	0.02%
Permananet Debt Service	$0	$0.00	0.00%
NET DURING LEASE−UP	($221,430)	($22.14)	100.00%
TOTAL PROJECT COSTS	$7,791,481	$77.91	100.00%

PROPERTY NAME: MARKETPLACE
LOCATION: Atlanta, Ga.

		UNIT MIX, RENTAL, SQUARE FOOTAGE					

TENANT	#	(NRA) SQ. FT.	MO. RENT/ SQ.FT.	GROSS RENT/ MONTH	MONTHS VACANT	MONTHS FREE	AMOUNT OF FREE RENT
DRY CLEANERS	1	1,500	$1.25	$1,875	0	0	$0
VIDEO	2	3,000	$1.25	$3,750	0	0	$0
CARD SHOP	3	1,500	$1.25	$1,875	0	0	$0
GROCERY STORE	4	50,000	$0.50	$25,000	0	0	$0
DRUG STORE	5	8,000	$1.00	$8,000	0	0	$0
CRAFT SHOP	6	1,500	$1.25	$1,875	0	0	$0
MEN'S CLOTHING	7	3,000	$1.25	$3,750	0	0	$0
WOMEN'S CLOTHING	8	3,000	$1.25	$3,750	0	0	$0
TOY SHOP	9	3,000	$1.25	$3,750	0	0	$0
ELECTRONIC SHOP	10	1,500	$1.25	$1,875	0	0	$0
WALLPAPER SHOP	11	3,000	$1.25	$3,750	0	0	$0
PAINT SHOP	12	1,500	$1.25	$1,875	0	0	$0
FRAME SHOP	13	1,500	$1.25	$1,875	0	0	$0
WOMEN'S SHOES	14	1,500	$1.25	$1,875	0	0	$0
BOOK SHOP	15	1,500	$1.25	$1,875	0	0	$0
SIGN SHOP	16	1,500	$1.25	$1,875	0	0	$0
COMPUTER SHOP	17	4,500	$1.25	$5,625	0	0	$0
JEWELRY SHOP	18	1,500	$1.25	$1,875	0	0	$0
KITCHEN & BATH SHOP	19	1,500	$1.25	$1,875	0	0	$0
VACANT	20	1,500	$1.25	$1,875	0	0	$0
VACANT	21	1,500	$1.25	$1,875	0	0	$0
VACANT	22	1,500	$1.25	$1,875	0	0	$0
VACANT	23	1,500	$1.25	$1,875	0	0	$0
		------		------			
TOTAL		100,000		$85,500			
		=====		=====			
OCCUPIED		94,000		$78,000			
VACANT		6,000		$7,500			
TOTAL		100,000		$85,500			
		=====		=====			

PROPERTY NAME: MARKETPLACE
LOCATION: Atlanta, Ga.

TENANT IMPROVEMENT ASSUMPTIONS

TENANT	#	SQ. FT.	T.I./ SQ.FT.	T.I. AMT.	MOVE–IN MO.
DRY CLEANERS	1	1,500	$6.40	$9,600	1
VIDEO	2	3,000	$6.40	$19,200	1
CARD SHOP	3	1,500	$6.40	$9,600	1
GROCERY STORE	4	50,000	$0.00	$0	1
DRUG STORE	5	8,000	$6.40	$51,200	1
CRAFT SHOP	6	1,500	$6.40	$9,600	1
MEN'S CLOTHING	7	3,000	$6.40	$19,200	1
WOMEN'S CLOTHING	8	3,000	$6.40	$19,200	1
TOY SHOP	9	3,000	$6.40	$19,200	1
ELECTRONIC SHOP	10	1,500	$6.40	$9,600	1
WALLPAPER SHOP	11	3,000	$6.40	$19,200	1
PAINT SHOP	12	1,500	$6.40	$9,600	1
FRAME SHOP	13	1,500	$6.40	$9,600	1
WOMEN'S SHOES	14	1,500	$6.40	$9,600	1
BOOK SHOP	15	1,500	$6.40	$9,600	1
SIGN SHOP	16	1,500	$6.40	$9,600	1
COMPUTER SHOP	17	4,500	$6.40	$28,800	1
JEWELRY SHOP	18	1,500	$6.40	$9,600	1
KITCHEN & BATH SHOP	19	1,500	$6.40	$9,600	1
VACANT	20	1,500	$6.40	$9,600	
VACANT	21	1,500	$6.40	$9,600	
VACANT	22	1,500	$6.40	$9,600	
VACANT	23	1,500	$6.40	$9,600	
		–––––		–––––	
TOTAL		100,000		$320,000	
		–––––		–––––	

PROPERTY NAME: MARKETPLACE
LOCATION: Atlanta, Ga.

LEASE COMMISSION ASSUMPTIONS

LEASE (MO) TENANT	60 #	MONTHS PAYING RENT	COMMISSION RATE	 AMOUNT	100% PAID @ MOVE—IN
DRY CLEANERS	1	60	4.00%	$4,500	1
VIDEO	2	60	4.00%	$9,000	1
CARD SHOP	3	60	4.00%	$4,500	1
GROCERY STORE	4	60	4.00%	$60,000	1
DRUG STORE	5	60	4.00%	$19,200	1
CRAFT SHOP	6	60	4.00%	$4,500	1
MEN'S CLOTHING	7	60	4.00%	$9,000	1
WOMEN'S CLOTHING	8	60	4.00%	$9,000	1
TOY SHOP	9	60	4.00%	$9,000	1
ELECTRONIC SHOP	10	60	4.00%	$4,500	1
WALLPAPER SHOP	11	60	4.00%	$9,000	1
PAINT SHOP	12	60	4.00%	$4,500	1
FRAME SHOP	13	60	4.00%	$4,500	1
WOMEN'S SHOES	14	60	4.00%	$4,500	1
BOOK SHOP	15	60	4.00%	$4,500	1
SIGN SHOP	16	60	4.00%	$4,500	1
COMPUTER SHOP	17	60	4.00%	$13,500	1
JEWELRY SHOP	18	60	4.00%	$4,500	1
KITCHEN & BATH SHOP	19	60	4.00%	$4,500	1
VACANT	20	60	4.00%	$4,500	
VACANT	21	60	4.00%	$4,500	
VACANT	22	60	4.00%	$4,500	
VACANT	23	60	4.00%	$4,500	
				— — — —	
TOTAL				$205,200	
				=====	

PROPERTY NAME: MARKETPLACE
LOCATION: Atlanta, Ga.

STABILIZED OPERATING PROFORMA

	TOTAL	PER S.F.	% OF EGI
Gross Potential Income	$1,026,000	$10.26	106.38%
Less: Vacancy	($61,560)	($0.62)	−6.38%
	-----	-----	-----
Effective Gross Income	$964,440	$9.64	100.00%
Less: Common Area Maint.	NET	$0.00	0.00%
Less: Real Estate Taxes	NET	$0.00	0.00%
Less: Insurance	NET	$0.00	0.00%
Less: Management Fee	($28,933)	($0.29)	−3.00%
Less: Operating Expenses (Vacant Space)	($7,200)	($0.07)	−0.75%
Less: Reserves	($15,000)	($0.15)	−1.56%
	-----	-----	-----
Net Operating Income	$913,307	$9.13	94.70%
	-----	-----	-----
Less: Debt Service	($787,040)	($7.87)	−81.61%
	-----	-----	-----
Before−Tax Cash Flow	$126,267	$1.26	13.09%
	=====	=====	=====

PROPERTY NAME: MARKETPLACE
LOCATION: Atlanta, Ga.

DEVELOPMENT CASH FLOW PROFORMA

MONTHLY COST SPREAD	1	2	3	4	5	6	7	8	9	10	11	12	TOTAL
DIRECT COSTS:													
Land (Net of Parcel Sales)	$2,196,000												$2,196,003
Hard Costs (Site & Shell)	$366,667	$366,667	$366,667	$366,667	$366,667	$366,667	$366,667	$366,667	$366,667				$3,300,003
Tenant Allowance (Excl. Grocery)							$106,667	$106,667	$106,667				$320,001
Pylon Sign									$26,000				$26,000
Landscaping							$42,500	$42,500					$85,000
Contingency	$20,722	$20,722	$20,722	$20,722	$20,722	$20,722	$20,722	$20,722	$20,722				$184,498
TOTAL DIRECT COSTS	$2,582,389	$387,389	$387,389	$387,389	$387,389	$367,389	$494,056	$436,556	$561,556				$6,111,802
INDIRECT COSTS:													
Architecture & Engineering	$150,000												$150,000
Soils Test	$5,000												$5,000
Survey	$10,000												$10,000
Testing & Inspection		$5,000	$5,000	$5,000	$5,000	$5,000	$5,000	$5,000	$5,000				$45,000
Pre Construction Project Mgmt.	$42,000												$42,000
Title and Closing Costs	$15,000												$15,000
Legal Accounting and Adm.	$7,000	$7,000	$7,000	$7,000	$7,000	$7,000	$7,000	$7,000	$7,000				$63,000
Insurance	$12,000												$12,000
Appraisal	$6,000												$6,000
Construction Administration		$6,000	$6,000	$6,000	$6,000	$6,000	$6,000	$6,000	$6,000				$54,000
Permits and Fees	$35,000												$35,000
Development Fee	$40,000	$40,000	$40,000	$40,000	$40,000	$40,000	$40,000	$40,000	$40,000				$360,000
Marketing							$4,000	$4,000	$4,000	$4,000	$4,000	$4,000	$24,000
Property Taxes	$5,000												$5,000
Lease Commissions	$205,200												$205,200
Contingency, Indirect Costs	$10,000	$10,000	$10,000	$10,000	$10,000	$10,000	$10,000	$10,000	$10,000				$90,000
TOTAL INDIRECT COSTS	$555,200	$68,000	$68,000	$68,000	$68,000	$68,000	$72,000	$72,000	$72,000	$4,000	$4,000	$4,000	$1,123,200
FINANCING COSTS:													
Constr. & Perm. Loan Fee	$78,000												$78,000
Permanent Loan Fee	$156,000												$156,000
Construction Loan Interest	$26,478	$29,112	$32,773	$36,462	$40,179	$43,923	$48,633	$53,498	$58,690	$58,606	$58,521	$58,436	$544,211
TOTAL FINANCING COSTS	$259,478	$29,112	$32,773	$36,462	$40,179	$43,923	$48,633	$53,498	$58,690	$58,606	$58,521	$58,436	$778,211
TOTAL COSTS PRIOR TO LEASE-UP	$3,397,067	$484,501	$488,162	$491,851	$495,568	$499,312	$614,689	$562,054	$692,246	$62,606	$62,521	$62,436	$8,012,911
LEASE-UP COSTS:													
Rental Income										($78,000)	($78,000)	($78,000)	($234,000)
Management Fee										$2,340	$2,340	$2,340	$7,020
Reserves										$1,260	$1,260	$1,260	$3,750
Operating Cost—Vacant										$600	$600	$600	$1,800
Permanent Debt Service													$0
NET DURING LEASE-UP	$0	$0	$0	$0	$0	$0	$0	$0	$0	($73,810)	($73,810)	($73,810)	($221,430)
TOTAL PROJECT COSTS	$3,397,067	$484,501	$488,162	$491,851	$495,568	$499,312	$614,689	$562,054	$692,246	($11,204)	($11,289)	($11,374)	$7,791,481
CONSTRUCTION LOAN BALANCE	$3,397,067	$3,881,568	$4,369,729	$4,861,580	$5,357,148	$5,856,460	$6,471,048	$7,133,102	$7,825,348	$7,814,144	$7,802,855	$7,791,481	
CONSTRUCTION INTEREST	$26,478	$29,112	$32,773	$36,462	$40,179	$43,923	$48,633	$53,498	$58,690	$58,606	$58,521	$58,436	

PROPERTY NAME: MARKETPLACE
LOCATION: Atlanta, Ga.

	FIVE YEAR CASH FLOW PROFORMA

	(3 MO.)				
YEAR	1	2	3	4	5
GROSS POTENTIAL INCOME	$248,936	$1,038,825	$1,090,766	$1,145,305	$1,202,570
LESS: VACANCY	($14,936)	($62,330)	($65,446)	($68,718)	($72,154)
	-----	-----	-----	-----	-----
EFFECTIVE GROSS INCOME	$234,000	$976,495	$1,025,320	$1,076,586	$1,130,416
OPERATING EXPENSES:					
LESS: OPER. EXPENSES (VACANT SPACE)	($1,800)	($7,200)	($7,560)	($7,938)	($8,335)
LESS: MANAGEMENT FEE	($7,020)	($29,295)	($30,760)	($32,298)	($33,913)
LESS: RESERVES	($3,750)	($15,000)	($15,750)	($16,538)	($17,364)
	-----	-----	-----	-----	-----
TOTAL OPERATING EXPENSES	($12,570)	($51,495)	($54,070)	($56,773)	($59,612)
NET OPERATING INCOME	$221,430	$925,000	$971,251	$1,019,813	$1,070,804
DEBT SERVICE	($175,124)	($787,040)	($787,040)	($787,040)	($787,040)
CASH FLOW PRIOR TO RELEASING EXP.	$46,306	$137,960	$184,211	$232,773	$283,764
RELEASING EXPENSES:					
LESS: COMMISSIONS					
LESS: TENANT IMPROVEMENTS					
LESS: VACANCY & FREE RENT					
	-----	-----	-----	-----	-----
TOTAL RELEASING EXPENSES	$0	$0	$0	$0	$0
NET PROJECT CASH FLOW	$46,306	$137,960	$184,211	$232,773	$283,764
	=====	=====	=====	=====	=====

NOTES:

1. THE LEASES ESCALATE EVERY 12 MONTHS FROM THE ANNIVERSARY DATE
2. DEBT SERVICE IN YEAR 1 IS BASED ON 3 MONTHS ($58,288/MO.) CONSTRUCTION INTEREST
3. RESERVES ARE BASED ON 100% OCCUPANCY

PROPERTY NAME: MARKETPLACE
LOCATION: Atlanta, Ga.

DEBT SERVICE ANALYSIS

PRINCIPAL	$7,800,000
INTEREST RATE	9.50%
NO. PAYMENTS (MO.)	360
MONTHLY PAYMENT	$65,586.63
BEG. OF MONTH	1
MONTHS REMAINING	12
LOAN CONSTANT (MONTH)	0.008409
LOAN CONSTANT (YEAR)	0.100895

	12 MONTHS YEAR 1	YEAR 2	YEAR 3	YEAR 4	YEAR 5
FIRST MORTGAGE					
BEGINNING BALANCE	$7,800,000	$7,751,902	$7,699,030	$7,640,911	$7,577,024
INTEREST	$738,942	$734,168	$728,921	$723,152	$716,812
PRINCIPAL	$48,098	$52,872	$58,119	$63,887	$70,228
TOTAL DEBT SERVICE	$787,040	$787,040	$787,040	$787,040	$787,040
ENDING BALANCE	$7,751,902	$7,699,030	$7,640,911	$7,577,024	$7,506,796

PAYMENT NUMBER	INTEREST PAID	PRINCIPAL PAID	BALANCE REMAINING	SUM OF YEARLY INTEREST	SUM OF YEARLY PRINCIPAL	SUM OF YEARLY PAYMENTS
1	$61,750.00	$3,836.63	$7,796,163.37	$0.00	$0.00	$0.00
2	$61,719.63	$3,867.00	$7,792,296.37	$0.00	$0.00	$0.00
3	$61,689.01	$3,897.62	$7,788,398.76	$0.00	$0.00	$0.00
4	$61,658.16	$3,928.47	$7,784,470.28	$0.00	$0.00	$0.00
5	$61,627.06	$3,959.57	$7,780,510.71	$0.00	$0.00	$0.00
6	$61,595.71	$3,990.92	$7,776,519.79	$0.00	$0.00	$0.00
7	$61,564.12	$4,022.51	$7,772,497.28	$0.00	$0.00	$0.00
8	$61,532.27	$4,054.36	$7,768,442.92	$0.00	$0.00	$0.00
9	$61,500.17	$4,086.46	$7,764,356.47	$0.00	$0.00	$0.00
10	$61,467.82	$4,118.81	$7,760,237.66	$0.00	$0.00	$0.00
11	$61,435.21	$4,151.41	$7,756,086.25	$0.00	$0.00	$0.00
12	$61,402.35	$4,184.28	$7,751,901.97	$738,941.51	$48,098.03	$787,039.54

PROPERTY NAME: MARKETPLACE
LOCATION: Atlanta, Ga.

SALE ANALYSIS

	(3 MO.)				
YEAR	**1**	**2**	**3**	**4**	**5**
SALES PRICE–BASED ON CURRENT NOI	$9,841,333	$10,277,785	$10,791,674	$11,333,008	$11,901,478
LESS: SALES COST	($196,827)	($205,556)	($215,833)	($226,660)	($238,030)
LESS: ORIGINAL EQUITY	$0	$0	$0	$0	$0
LESS: OUTSTANDING LOAN BALANCE	($7,800,000)	($7,751,902)	($7,699,030)	($7,640,911)	($7,577,024)
	– – – – –	– – – – –	– – – – –	– – – – –	– – – – –
BEFORE TAX EQUITY REVERSION	$1,844,507	$2,320,327	$2,876,810	$3,465,436	$4,086,425

NOTE:

1. Permanent loan is funded at beginning of the second year.

PROPERTY NAME: MARKETPLACE
LOCATION: Atlanta, Ga.

LENDER FINANCIAL RATIOS

	(3 MO.)				
YEAR	1	2	3	4	5
LENDER FINANCIAL RATIOS:					
DEBT SERVICE COVERAGE RATIO	1.26	1.18	1.23	1.30	1.36
LOAN–TO–VALUE RATIO (END OF YEAR)	79.17%	75.42%	71.34%	67.42%	63.66%
BREAK–EVEN (PRIOR TO RELEAS. EXP.) (%)	75.47%	80.72%	77.11%	73.68%	70.40%
OPERATING EXPENSES RATIO (W/O CAP. EXP.)	5.07%	5.27%	5.27%	5.27%	5.27%

FINANCIAL RATIOS

VALUE MULTIPLIERS:					
GROSS RENT MULTIPLIER (GRM)	9.88	9.89	9.89	9.90	9.90
VALUES (PER UNIT):					
PRICE PER SQUARE FOOT (NET)	$98.41	$102.78	$107.92	$113.33	$119.01
AVERAGE RATE OF RETURN:					
CASH ON EQUITY RATIO	N/A	N/A	N/A	N/A	N/A

TIME VALUE METHODS OF RETURN:
INTERNAL RATE OF RETURN: SINCE THERE IS NO EQUITY CONTRIBUTION FOR THIS DEVELOPMENT THE IRR IS INFINITE.

DEVELOPMENT PROFIT

STABILIZED NET OPERATING INCOME	$913,307
CAPITALIZATION RATE	9.00%
APPRAISED VALUE	$10,147,856
LESS: DEVELOPMENT COSTS	($7,791,481)
DEVELOPMENT PROFIT	$2,356,375
DEVELOPMENT PROFIT (%)	30.24%
	=====

PRODUCT TYPE NO. 2: INDUSTRIAL BUILDING
(Build-to-Suit)

PROPERTY NAME: ABC INDUSTRIAL BUILDING (BUILD–TO–SUIT)
LOCATION: Atlanta, Ga.

GENERAL ASSUMPTIONS

	ASSUMP.	INFORM.		ASSUMP.	INFORM.
BUILDING DESCRIPTION			**APPRAISAL**		
Footprint: (600' x 200')	120,000		Capitalization Rate	9.00%	
Floor: 5" 4,000 psi slab on grade			Stabilized NOI	$349,200	
Walls: concrete tilt–up panels			Appraised Value–Stabilized		$3,880,000
Frame: structural steel, 24' clear					
Roof: single–ply EPDM			**SALE**		
(10lb. ballasted R–10)			Capitalization Rate	9.00%	
Rear load with 21 dock high truck			Based on NOI (Year)	Current	
doors, 50' (28,000 Sq.Ft.) concrete			Sales Cost	2.00%	
truck apron, 4,461 Sq.Yd. heavy duty					
asphalt paving			**DIRECT COSTS**		
Aluminumm store front (2,600 Sq.Ft.)			Land (Acreage)	6	
with 4 entrance doors			Land (Per S.F.)	$2.50	$653,400
Surface parking (# spaces)	150		Building Contingency (% of Shell)	5.00%	
(3,500 Sq.Yd. light duty asphalt)			Interior Contingency (% of Interior)	5.00%	
Class III building sprinkler			Shell (S.f.)	114,000	
Pre–graded site			Interior Finish Building Costs (Per S.F.)	$0.97	
			Interior (S.F.	6,000	
LEASE SUMMARY			Interior Tenant Costs (Per S.F.)	$20.00	
ABC Company (AAA–Credit Tenant)					
Lease Rate (Per Yr.)	$3.00		**INDIRECT COSTS**		
Lease Payment (Per Year)		$360,000	Permits		$10,000
Type Lease	Triple Net		Legal & Title		$18,000
Lease Term (Yrs)	15		Architectural/Engineering		$50,000
Options (Number/Yrs)	2/5		Leasing Commission (Paid at move–in)	3.00%	$108,000
			Developer's Fee (% of Construction Loan)	3.00%	$89,997
OPERATING ASSUMPTIONS			Contingency (% of Permits, Legal, A/E)	10.00%	$7,800
Vacancy	0.00%				
Management Fee	3.00%				
Rent Increases (Per year)	5.00%				
Expense Increases (Per year)	5.00%				
CONSTRUCTION UNDERWRITING					
Construction Loan Fee	1.00%	$29,999			
Construction Loan Rate	10.00%				
Construction Loan Amount	$2,999,908				
PERMANENT UNDERWRITING					
Permenant Loan Fee	1.00%	$29,999			
Debt Coverage Ratio	1.10				
Loan Interest Rate	9.00%				
Loan Amortization Period (Yrs)	30				
Loan Constant		9.66%			
Debt Service Payment (Yearly)		$289,655			
Maximum Loan Amount		$3,287,820			
Permanent Loan Amount		$2,999,908			
Loan to Value Ratio		77.32%			

PROPERTY NAME: ABC INDUSTRIAL BUILDING (BUILD−TO−SUIT)
LOCATION: Atlanta, Ga.

CONSTRUCTION COSTS		

DESCRIPTION	$/SQ.FT.	AMOUNT
SHELL:		
Sitework (including site utilities, curb & gutter, paving, sidewalks)	$2.52	$302,400
Foundations & Floor Slab	$2.41	$289,200
Structure (including structural steel, joists, metal deck)	$2.55	$306,000
Building Skin (including tilt−up concrete walls, coating, and caulking)	$2.18	$261,600
Doors, Canopies, Soffits	$0.49	$58,800
Storefront	$0.41	$49,200
Roof Systems	$1.72	$206,400
Plumbing	$0.14	$16,800
Sprinklers	$0.54	$64,800
Electrical	$0.28	$33,600
Contingency	$0.66	$79,440
TOTAL SHELL	$13.90	$1,668,240
INTERIOR:		
Warehouse finish @ 114,000 Sq.Ft. (Heat, light, sealed, concrete)	$0.92	$110,400
Standard office finish @ 6,000 Sq.Ft.	$1.00	$120,000
Contingency	$0.10	$11,520
TOTAL INTERIOR	$2.02	$241,920
TOTAL CONSTRUCTION COSTS	$15.92	$1,910,160

PROPERTY NAME: ABC INDUSTRIAL BUILDING (BUILD—TO—SUIT)

LOCATION: Atlanta, Ga.

KEY VARIABLES

TIMING LEGEND:

A — All Cost is month entered
B — First Month of ratable spread
C — Number of months spread
D — Specific amounts and months
    Enter in table to right

DESCRIPTION	AMOUNT	A	B	C	D
DIRECT COSTS:					
Land	$653,400	1			
Hard Costs (Site & Shell)	$1,668,240		2	5	
Hard Costs (Interior)	$241,920		5	2	
INDIRECT COSTS:					
Permits	$10,000	1			
Legal & Title	$18,000	1			
Architectural/Engineering	$50,000	1			
Leasing Commission (Paid at move—in)	$108,000	1			
Developer's Fee	$89,997		1	6	
Contingency (% of Permits, Legal, A/E)	$7,800		1	6	
FINANCING:					
Construction Loan Fee	$29,999	1			
Permanent Loan Fee	$29,999	1			

NOTES

1. Permanent Loan is funded in 7th month.

PROPERTY NAME: ABC INDUSTRIAL BUILDING (BUILD–TO–SUIT

LOCATION: Atlanta, Ga.

PROJECT COST SUMMARY

DIRECT COSTS:	TOTAL	% OF TOTAL COSTS	COST/S.F.
Land	$653,400	21.78%	$5.45
Shell Building	$1,668,240	55.61%	$13.90
Interior Building	$241,920	8.06%	$2.02
	-----	-----	-----
TOTAL DIRECT COSTS	$2,563,560	85.45%	$21.36
INDIRECT COSTS:			
Permits	$10,000	0.33%	$0.08
Legal & Title	$18,000	0.60%	$0.15
Architectural/Engineering	$50,000	1.67%	$0.42
Leasing Commission	$108,000	3.60%	$0.90
Developer's Fee	$89,997	3.00%	$0.75
Contingency	$7,800	0.26%	$0.07
	-----	-----	-----
TOTAL INDIRECT COSTS	$283,797	9.46%	$2.36
FINANCING COSTS:			
Construction Loan Fee	$29,999	1.00%	$0.25
Permanent Loan Fee	$29,999	1.00%	$0.25
Construction Loan Interest	$92,552	3.09%	$0.77
	-----	-----	-----
FINANCING COSTS	$152,550	5.09%	$1.27
LEASE–UP COSTS:			
Rental Income	N/A	N/A	N/A
Management Fee	N/A	N/A	N/A
Permanant Debt Service	N/A	N/A	N/A
	-----	-----	-----
NET DURING LEASE–UP	N/A	N/A	N/A
TOTAL PROJECT COSTS	$2,999,908	100.00%	$25.00
	=====	=====	=====

PROPERTY NAME: ABC INDUSTRIAL BUILDING (BUILD−TO−SUIT)
LOCATION: Atlanta, Ga.

DEVELOPMENT CASH FLOW PROFORMA

MONTH	1	2	3	4	5	6	7	8	9	10	11	12	TOTAL
DIRECT COSTS:													
Land	$653,400												$653,400
Shell Building		$333,648	$333,648	$333,648	$333,648	$333,648							$1,668,240
Interior Building					$120,960	$120,960							$241,920
TOTAL DIRECT COSTS	$653,400	$333,648	$333,648	$333,648	$454,608	$454,608							$2,563,560
INDIRECT COSTS:													
Permits	$10,000												$10,000
Legal & Title	$18,000												$18,000
Architectural/Engineering	$50,000												$50,000
Leasing Commission	$108,000												$108,000
Developer's Fee	$15,000	$15,000	$15,000	$15,000	$15,000	$15,000							$99,997
Contingency	$1,300	$1,300	$1,300	$1,300	$1,300	$1,300							$7,800
TOTAL INDIRECT COSTS	$202,300	$16,300	$16,300	$16,300	$16,300	$16,300							$283,797
FINANCING COSTS:													
Construction Loan Fee	$29,999												
Permanent Loan Fee	$29,999												
Construction Loan Interest		$7,631	$10,547	$13,463	$16,380	$20,304	$24,228						$92,552
TOTAL FINANCING COSTS	$59,998	$7,631	$10,547	$13,463	$16,380	$20,304	$24,228						$92,552
LEASE−UP COSTS:													
Rental Income							($30,000)	($30,000)	($30,000)	($30,000)	($30,000)	($30,000)	($180,000)
Management Fee							$900	$900	$900	$900	$900	$900	$5,400
Permanent Loan Debt Service							$24,138	$24,138	$24,138	$24,138	$24,138	$24,138	$144,828
TOTAL LEASE−UP COSTS	$0	$0	$0	$0	$0	$0	($4,962)	($4,962)	($4,962)	($4,962)	($4,962)	($4,962)	($29,772)
TOTAL PROJECT COSTS	$915,698	$349,948	$349,948	$349,948	$470,908	$470,908	($4,962)	($4,962)	($4,962)	($4,962)	($4,962)	($4,962)	$2,907,355
CONSTRUCTION LOAN BALANCE	$915,698	$1,265,645	$1,615,593	$1,965,540	$2,436,448	$2,907,355	$2,907,355						

NOTE:

1. Permanent Loan Debt Service−starts in month 7

PROPERTY NAME: ABC INDUSTRIAL BUILDING (BUILD–TO–SUIT)
LOCATION: Atlanta, Ga.

STABILIZED OPERATING PROFORMA

	TOTAL	PER S.F.	% OF EGI
Gross Potential Income	$360,000	$3.00	100.00%
Less: Vacancy	$0	$0.00	0.00%
Effective Gross Income	$360,000	$3.00	100.00%
Expenses:			
Less: Management Fee	($10,800)	($0.09)	−3.00%
Net Operating Income	$349,200	$2.91	97.00%
Less: Debt Service	($289,655)	($2.41)	−80.46%
Cash Flow	$59,545	$0.50	16.54%

PROPERTY NAME: ABC INDUSTRIAL BUILDING (BUILD–TO–SUIT)
LOCATION: Atlanta, Ga.

FIVE YEAR CASH FLOW PROFORMA

	(6 MO)				
YEAR	1	2	3	4	5
GROSS POTENTIAL INCOME	$180,000	$369,000	$387,450	$406,823	$427,164
LESS: MANAGEMENT FEE	($5,400)	($11,070)	($11,624)	($12,205)	($12,815)
NET OPERATING INCOME	$174,600	$357,930	$375,827	$394,618	$414,349
DEBT SERVICE	($144,828)	($289,655)	($289,655)	($289,655)	($289,655)
CASH FLOW	$29,772	$68,275	$86,171	$104,963	$124,693

NOTE:

1. THE LEASE ESCALATES EVERY 12 MONTHS FROM THE ANIVERSARY DATE

PROPERTY NAME: ABC INDUSTRIAL BUILDING (BUILD−TO−SUIT)
LOCATION: Atlanta, Ga.

DEBT SERVICE ANALYSIS

PRINCIPAL	$2,999,908
INTEREST RATE	9.00%
NO. PAYMENTS (MO.)	360
MONTHLY PAYMENT	$24,137.94
BEG. OF MONTH	7
MONTHS REMAINING	6
LOAN CONSTANT (MONTH)	0.008046
LOAN CONSTANT (YEAR)	0.096555

	6 MONTHS YEAR 1	YEAR 2	YEAR 3	YEAR 4	YEAR 5
FIRST MORTGAGE					
BEGINNING BALANCE	$2,999,908	$2,989,890	$2,968,455	$2,945,009	$2,919,364
INTEREST	$134,810	$268,220	$266,209	$264,010	$261,604
PRINCIPAL	$10,018	$21,435	$23,446	$25,645	$28,051
TOTAL DEBT SERVICE	$144,828	$289,655	$289,655	$289,655	$289,655
ENDING BALANCE	$2,989,890	$2,968,455	$2,945,009	$2,919,364	$2,891,313

PAYMENT NUMBER	INTEREST PAID	PRINCIPAL PAID	BALANCE REMAINING	SUM OF YEARLY INTEREST	SUM OF YEARLY PRINCIPAL	SUM OF YEARLY PAYMENTS
1	$22,499.31	$1,638.63	$2,998,269.08	$0.00	$0.00	$0.00
2	$22,487.02	$1,650.92	$2,996,618.17	$0.00	$0.00	$0.00
3	$22,474.64	$1,663.30	$2,994,954.87	$0.00	$0.00	$0.00
4	$22,462.16	$1,675.77	$2,993,279.09	$0.00	$0.00	$0.00
5	$22,449.59	$1,688.34	$2,991,590.75	$0.00	$0.00	$0.00
6	$22,436.93	$1,701.01	$2,989,889.74	$134,809.65	$10,017.97	$144,827.62
7	$22,424.17	$1,713.76	$2,988,175.98	$0.00	$0.00	$0.00
8	$22,411.32	$1,726.62	$2,986,449.37	$0.00	$0.00	$0.00
9	$22,398.37	$1,739.57	$2,984,709.80	$0.00	$0.00	$0.00
10	$22,385.32	$1,752.61	$2,982,957.19	$0.00	$0.00	$0.00
11	$22,372.18	$1,765.76	$2,981,191.43	$0.00	$0.00	$0.00
12	$22,358.94	$1,779.00	$2,979,412.43	$0.00	$0.00	$0.00
13	$22,345.59	$1,792.34	$2,977,620.09	$0.00	$0.00	$0.00
14	$22,332.15	$1,805.79	$2,975,814.30	$0.00	$0.00	$0.00
15	$22,318.61	$1,819.33	$2,973,994.97	$0.00	$0.00	$0.00
16	$22,304.96	$1,832.97	$2,972,162.00	$0.00	$0.00	$0.00
17	$22,291.21	$1,846.72	$2,970,315.28	$0.00	$0.00	$0.00
18	$22,277.36	$1,860.57	$2,968,454.71	$268,220.19	$21,435.04	$289,655.23

PROPERTY NAME: ABC INDUSTRIAL BUILDING (BUILD−TO−SUIT)
LOCATION: Atlanta, Ga.

SALES ANALYSIS

YEAR	1	2	3	4	5
SALES PRICE−BASED ON CURRENT NOI	$3,880,000	$3,977,000	$4,175,850	$4,384,643	$4,603,875
LESS: SALES COSTS	($77,600)	($79,540)	($83,517)	($87,693)	($92,077)
LESS: ORIGINAL EQUITY	$0	$0	$0	$0	$0
LESS: OUTSTANDING LOAN BALANCE	($2,989,890)	($2,968,455)	($2,945,009)	($2,919,364)	($2,891,313)
	-----	-----	-----	-----	-----
BEFORE TAX EQUITY REVERSION	$812,510	$929,005	$1,147,324	$1,377,586	$1,620,484
	=====	=====	=====	=====	=====

PROPERTY NAME: ABC INDUSTRIAL BUILDING (BUILD−TO−SUIT)
LOCATION: Atlanta, Ga.

LENDER FINANCIAL RATIOS

YEAR	1	2	3	4	5
DEBT SERVICE COVERAGE RATIO	1.21	1.24	1.30	1.36	1.43
LOAN TO VALUE RATIO (END OF YEAR)	77.06%	74.64%	70.52%	66.58%	62.80%
BREAK EVEN CASH FLOW RATIO	83.46%	81.50%	77.76%	74.20%	70.01%

FINANCIAL RATIOS

VALUE MULTIPLIER:

GROSS RENT MULTIPLIER (GRM)	10.78	10.78	10.78	10.78	10.78

VALUE (PER UNIT):

PRICE PER SQUARE FOOT	$32.33	$33.14	$34.80	$36.54	$38.37

AVERAGE RATE OF RETURN:

CASH ON EQUITY RATIO	N/A	N/A	N/A	N/A	N/A

TIME VALUE METHODS OF RETURN:
 INTERNAL RATE OF RETURN: SINCE THERE WAS NO EQUITY REQUIREDMENT,
THE IRR IS INFINITE.

DEVELOPMENT PROFIT

STABILIZED NET OPERATING INCOME	$349,200
CAPITALIZATION RATE	9.00%
APPRAISED VALUE	$3,880,000
LESS: DEVELOPMENT COSTS	($2,999,908)
DEVELOPMENT PROFIT	$880,092
DEVELOPMENT PROFIT %	29.34%
	=====

PRODUCT TYPE NO. 3: CORPORATE SUMMIT OFFICE BUILDING

PROPERTY NAME: MAIN STREET OFFICE BUILDING
LOCATION: Atlanta, Ga.

GENERAL ASSUMPTIONS

	ASSUMP.	INFORM.		ASSUMP.	INFORM.
SQUARE FOOTAGE/EFFICIENCY			**CONSTRUCTION UNDERWRITING**		
Gross Square Feet	215,054		Construction Loan Amount	$25,939,994	
Net Square Feet	195,000		Interest Rate	9.50%	
Building Efficiency		90.68%	Loan Fee (%)	0.50%	$129,700
PARKING			**PERMANENT UNDERWRITING**		
# of Surface Parking Spaces	655		Debt Coverage Ratio	1.20	
# of Parking Structure Spaces	125		Available For Debt Service		$2,693,117
Ave. Monthly Rent per Space	Free		Interest Rate	9.00%	
Parking Structure Sq. Ft.	38,750		Amortization Period (Years)	30	
Total Parking Structure Cost	$813,750		Loan Constant (Yr)		9.66%
Structure Cost per Space		$6,510.00	Maximum Loan Amount		$25,939,994
Structure Cost per Foot		$21.00	Actual Loan Amount	$25,939,994	
Total Parking per 1,000 SF NRA		4.00	Loan to Cost Ratio		85.46%
			Loan Fee (%)	1.00%	$259,400
RENTAL INCOME			Month Loan Funded	13	
Lease Term (Yrs)	5		Monthly Payment		$208,719
Free Rent (Months)	6		Annual Payment		$2,504,626
OPERATING ASSUMPTIONS			**EQUITY SUMMARY:**		
Op. Cost—Leased Space (/SF/YR)	$6.00		Equity Required		$5,000,000
Op. Cost—Vacant Space (/SF/YR)	$3.60		Actual Equity To Be Contributed	$5,000,000	
Assume Constant (Years 1 – 3)			Equity Put In At	Closing	
Vacancy Factor	5.00%		Equity (% of Dev. Costs – Incl. Lease – Up Exp)		16.47%
Management Fee	3.00%		Equity (% of Dev. Costs – Excl. Lease – Up Exp)		17.73%
Base Fee (Until 3% Hit) (Per Month)	$8,000		Equity (% of Appraised Value)		13.31%
Reserves (Per Sq.Ft. NRA) – 4th Yr.	$0.15				
Revenue Increases	5.00%		**APPRAISAL**		
Starting in Year	2		Capitalization Rate	8.00%	
Expense Increases	5.00%		Stabilized NOI	$3,005,554	
Starting in Year	4		Appraised Value – Stabilized	$37,569,425	
LEASING COMMISSIONS			**SALE**		
Fee	4.00%		Capitalization Rate	8.00%	
Paid At	Move – In		Based on NOI (Year)	Current	
No. Months Paid On	54		Sales Cost	2.00%	
RELEASING TENANT IMPROVEMENTS					
T.I. – New Tenants (Per S.F.)	$15.00				
T.I. – Existing Tenants (Per S.F.)	$2.00				
Increases in T.I. – Starting Year	6				
Expense Increase (Per Year)	5.00%				
% of Existing Tenants Needing T.I.	25.00%				
RELEASING					
% of Net S.F. Released (Per Year)	10.00%				
Concessions	None				
# Months of Downtime Vacancy	4				
CAPITAL EXPENDITURES					
Capital Expenditures (Per S.F. – Net)	$0.50				
Starting Year	4				
Expense Increase (Per Year)	5.00%				

PROPERTY NAME: MAIN STREET OFFICE BUILDING
LOCATION: Atlanta, Ga.

COST ASSUMPTIONS		

	ASSUMP.	INFORM.
LAND		
Cost	$7,655,670	
Acres	9.25	
Square Feet of Land		402,930
Bldg./Land Area Ratio		48.40%
Cost Per Acre		$827,640
Cost Per Foot of Land		$19.00
SITE IMPROVEMENTS & DEMOLITION	$150,000	
SHELL COSTS		
Shell Square Feet		215,054
Cost per Sq.Ft.	$46.50	
Total Shell Cost		$10,000,000
PARKING STRUCTURE COSTS		
Cost per Sq.Ft.	$21.00	$813,750

TENANT IMPROVEMENTS	PER SQ.FT.	TOTAL
Gross Square Feet		215,054
Total Cost per Sq. Ft.	$19.04	$4,095,000
Net Retable Sq.Ft.		195,000
Total Cost per Net Sq.Ft.	$21.00	$4,095,000

	ASSUMP.	INFORM.
DIRECT COST CONTINGENCY		
Applied to Site, Demo, Shell		
and T.I. built with Shell		$15,058,750
Enter Percentage	5.00%	
Contingency Amount		$752,937
INDIRECT COSTS		
Developer's Fee:		
% of Construction Loan		$25,939,994
Enter Percentage	2.50%	
Developer's Fee		$648,500
INDIRECT COST CONTINGENCY		
Applied to All Indirect Costs		
(Except DEveloper's Fee)		$2,269,704
Enter Percentage	5.00%	
Contingency Amount		$113,485

PROPERTY NAME: MAIN STREET OFFICE BUILDING
LOCATION: Atlanta, Ga.

KEY VARIABLES

TIMING LEGEND:

A – All Cost is month entered
B – First Month of ratable spread
C – Number of months spread
D – Specific amounts and months
    Enter in table to right

DESCRIPTION	AMOUNT	A	B	C	D
DIRECT COSTS:					
Land	$7,655,670	1			
Sitework and Demolition	$150,000	1	2		
Shell Costs	$10,000,000		3	9	
Parking Structure	$813,750		6	6	
T.I. done with Shell (100%)	$4,095,000				50% OF T.I. PAID THE MONTH PRIOR TO MOVE–IN,
					50% OF T.I. PAID THE MONTH OF MOVE–IN,
Contingency, Direct Cost	$752,937		1	12	
INDIRECT COSTS:					
Engineering	$20,000		3	6	
Soils Tests	$10,000	1			
Survey	$10,000	1			
Testing and Inspection	$25,000		6	12	
Government Reports, Consultants	$15,000		6	12	
Title and Closing Costs	$15,000	1			
Legal, Accounting and Adm.	$75,000		1	32	
Insurance	$18,000		6	12	
Architecture	$500,000				$250K – MO.1, BAL. – OVER 11 MOS.
Permits and Fees	$200,000	1			
Utility Connection	$157,250		11		
Marketing	$200,000		10	20	
Property Taxes	$153,114				50% – MO.4, 50% – MO.12
Space Planning	$50,000		12	18	
Developer's Fee	$648,500		1	12	
Contingency, Indirect Cost	$113,485		1	30	
Lease Commissions	$821,340				50% PAID UPON MOVE–IN OF TENANT
					50% PAID WHEN RENT COMMENCES
FINANCING:					
Construction Loan Fee	$129,700	1			
Permanent Loan Fee	$259,400	1			

NOTES:

1. Free rent is outside the lease.
2. Space is available for rent in the 12th Month.

PROPERTY NAME: MAIN STREET OFFICE BUILDING
LOCATION: Atlanta, Ga.

PROJECT COST SUMMARY

	TOTAL	COST/SF	% OF TOTAL COSTS
DIRECT COSTS			
Land	$7,655,670	$39.26	25.22%
Sitework and Demolition	$150,000	$0.77	0.49%
Shell Cost	$10,000,000	$51.28	32.94%
Parking Structure	$813,750	$4.17	2.68%
Tenant Improvements	$4,095,000	$21.00	13.49%
Contingency, Direct Cost	$752,937	$3.86	2.48%
TOTAL DIRECT COSTS	$23,467,357	$120.35	77.31%
INDIRECT COSTS			
Engineering	$20,000	$0.10	0.07%
Soils Tests	$10,000	$0.05	0.03%
Survey	$10,000	$0.05	0.03%
Testing and Inspection	$25,000	$0.13	0.08%
Government Reports, Consultants	$15,000	$0.08	0.05%
Title and Closing Costs	$15,000	$0.08	0.05%
Legal, Accounting and Adm.	$75,000	$0.38	0.25%
Insurance	$18,000	$0.09	0.06%
Architecture	$500,000	$2.56	1.65%
Permits and Fees	$200,000	$1.03	0.66%
Utility Connection	$157,250	$0.81	0.52%
Marketing	$200,000	$1.03	0.66%
Property Taxes	$153,114	$0.79	0.50%
Space Planning	$50,000	$0.26	0.16%
Developer's Fee	$648,500	$3.33	2.14%
Contingency, Indirect Cost	$113,485	$0.58	0.37%
Lease Commissions	$821,340	$4.21	2.71%
TOTAL INDIRECT COSTS	$3,031,689	$15.55	9.99%
FINANCING COSTS			
Construction Loan Fee	$129,700	$0.67	0.43%
Permanent Loan Fee	$535,650	$2.75	1.76%
Construction Loan Interest	$1,031,347	$5.29	3.40%
TOTAL FINANCING COSTS	$1,696,697	$8.70	5.59%
TOTAL COSTS PRIOR TO LEASE–UP	$28,195,743	$144.59	92.89%
LEASE–UP COSTS:			
Rental Income	($5,303,130)	($27.20)	−17.47%
Management Fee	$229,701	$1.18	0.76%
Operating Cost—Occupied	$1,901,255	$9.75	6.26%
Operating Cost—Vacant	$321,747	$1.65	1.06%
Reserves	$0	$0.00	0.00%
Permanent Debt Service	$5,009,256	$25.69	16.50%
NET LEASE–UP COSTS	$2,158,829	$11.07	7.11%
TOTAL PROJECT COSTS	$30,354,571	$155.66	100.00%

NOTE:

1. T.I. AND LEASING COMMISSIONS– BASED ON 100% OCCUPANCY

PROPERTY NAME: MAIN STREET OFFICE BUILDING
LOCATION: Atlanta, Ga.

RENTAL ASSUMPTIONS

TENANT	(NRA) SQ. FT.	% OCCUP.	MONTH RENT/ SQ.FT.	GROSS RENT/ MONTH	MONTHS VACANT	MONTHS FREE	MONTH RENT STARTS	AMOUNT OF FREE RENT
OFFICE #1	39,000	20.00%	$1.95	$76,050	0	6	18	$456,300
OFFICE #2	14,182	27.27%	$1.95	$27,655	1	6	19	$165,929
OFFICE #3	14,182	34.55%	$1.95	$27,655	2	6	20	$165,929
OFFICE #4	14,182	41.82%	$1.95	$27,655	3	6	21	$165,929
OFFICE #5	14,182	49.09%	$1.95	$27,655	4	6	22	$165,929
OFFICE #6	14,182	56.36%	$1.95	$27,655	5	6	23	$165,929
OFFICE #7	14,182	63.64%	$1.95	$27,655	6	6	24	$165,929
OFFICE #8	14,182	70.91%	$1.95	$27,655	7	6	25	$165,929
OFFICE #9	14,182	78.18%	$1.95	$27,655	8	6	26	$165,929
OFFICE #10	14,182	85.46%	$1.95	$27,655	9	6	27	$165,929
OFFICE #11	14,182	92.73%	$1.95	$27,655	10	6	28	$165,929
OFFICE #12	4,430	95.00%	$1.95	$8,639	11	6	29	$51,831
VACANCY	9,750		$1.95	$19,013				$0
TOTAL	195,000			$380,250				$2,167,425

TENANT IMPROVEMENT ASSUMPTIONS

TENANT	SQ. FT.	T.I./ SQ.FT.	T.I. AMOUNT	MOVE–IN MONTH	CONST. PERIOD	CONST. START
OFFICE #1	39,000	$21.00	$819,000	18	2	17
OFFICE #2	14,182	$21.00	$297,822	19	2	18
OFFICE #3	14,182	$21.00	$297,822	20	2	19
OFFICE #4	14,182	$21.00	$297,822	21	2	20
OFFICE #5	14,182	$21.00	$297,822	22	2	21
OFFICE #6	14,182	$21.00	$297,822	23	2	22
OFFICE #7	14,182	$21.00	$297,822	24	2	23
OFFICE #8	14,182	$21.00	$297,822	25	2	24
OFFICE #9	14,182	$21.00	$297,822	26	2	25
OFFICE #10	14,182	$21.00	$297,822	27	2	26
OFFICE #11	14,182	$21.00	$297,822	28	2	27
OFFICE #12	4,430	$21.00	$93,030	29	2	28
VACANCY	9,750	$21.00	$204,750			
TOTAL	195,000		$4,095,000			

PROPERTY NAME: MAIN STREET OFFICE BUILDING
LOCATION: Atlanta, Ga.

LEASE COMMISSION ASSUMPTIONS

LEASE (MO)   60

TENANT	SQ. FT.	MONTHS PAYING RENT	COMMISSION RATE	AMOUNT	50% PAID @ MOVE–IN	50% PAID @ RENT START
OFFICE #1	39,000	54	4.00%	$164,268	12	18
OFFICE #2	14,182	54	4.00%	$59,735	13	19
OFFICE #3	14,182	54	4.00%	$59,735	14	20
OFFICE #4	14,182	54	4.00%	$59,735	15	21
OFFICE #5	14,182	54	4.00%	$59,735	16	22
OFFICE #6	14,182	54	4.00%	$59,735	17	23
OFFICE #7	14,182	54	4.00%	$59,735	18	24
OFFICE #8	14,182	54	4.00%	$59,735	19	25
OFFICE #9	14,182	54	4.00%	$59,735	20	26
OFFICE #10	14,182	54	4.00%	$59,735	21	27
OFFICE #11	14,182	54	4.00%	$59,735	22	28
OFFICE #12	4,430	54	4.00%	$18,659	23	29
VACANCY	9,750	54	4.00%	$41,067		
	-----			-----		
TOTAL	195,000			$821,340		
	=====			=====		

PROPERTY NAME: MAIN STREET OFFICE BUILDING
LOCATION: Atlanta, Ga.

LEASE ANALYSIS (RENT INCREASES DURING RENT-UP)

ASSUMPTIONS:

	TENANT 1	TENANT 2	TENANT 3	TENANT 4	TENANT 5	TENANT 6	TENANT 7	TENANT 8	TENANT 9	TENANT 10	TENANT 11	TENANT 12	TOTAL
SQUARE FOOTAGE	39,000	14,182	14,182	14,182	14,182	14,182	14,182	14,182	14,182	14,182	14,182	4,430	185,250
RENT PER MONTH	$1.95	$1.95	$1.95	$1.95	$1.95	$1.95	$1.95	$1.95	$1.95	$1.95	$1.95	$1.95	
MOVE-IN MONTH	12	13	14	15	16	17	18	19	20	21	22	23	
RENT COMMENCE MONTH	18	19	20	21	22	23	24	25	26	27	28	29	
NUMBER OF MONTHS FREE	6	6	6	6	6	6	6	6	6	6	6	6	

MONTH-MONTH	POT. BLDG. OCCUP. (PHYS.)	POT. TOTAL SQ.FT. RENTED	TENANT 1	TENANT 2	TENANT 3	TENANT 4	TENANT 5	TENANT 6	TENANT 7	TENANT 8	TENANT 9	TENANT 10	TENANT 11	TENANT 12	TOTAL	TOTAL PER YR.
1	0.00%	0													$0	$0
2	0.00%	0													$0	
3	0.00%	0													$0	
4	0.00%	0													$0	
5	0.00%	0													$0	
6	0.00%	0													$0	
7	0.00%	0													$0	
8	0.00%	0													$0	
9	0.00%	0													$0	
10	0.00%	0													$0	
11	0.00%	0													$0	
12	20.00%	39,000	FREE												$0	
13	27.27%	53,182	FREE	FREE											$0	
14	34.55%	67,364	FREE	FREE	FREE										$0	
15	41.82%	81,546	FREE	FREE	FREE	FREE									$0	
16	49.09%	95,728	FREE	FREE	FREE	FREE	FREE								$0	
17	56.36%	109,910	FREE	FREE	FREE	FREE	FREE	FREE							$0	
18	63.64%	124,092	$76,050	FREE	FREE	FREE	FREE	FREE	FREE						$76,050	
19	70.91%	138,274	$76,050	$27,655	FREE	FREE	FREE	FREE	FREE	FREE					$103,705	
20	78.18%	152,456	$76,050	$27,655	$27,655	FREE	FREE	FREE	FREE	FREE	FREE				$131,360	
21	85.46%	166,638	$76,050	$27,655	$27,655	$27,655	FREE	FREE	FREE	FREE	FREE	FREE			$159,015	
22	92.73%	180,820	$76,050	$27,655	$27,655	$27,655	$27,655	FREE	FREE	FREE	FREE	FREE	FREE		$186,670	
23	95.00%	185,250	$76,050	$27,655	$27,655	$27,655	$27,655	$27,655	FREE	FREE	FREE	FREE	FREE	FREE	$214,325	$1,113,103
24	95.00%	185,250	$76,050	$27,655	$27,655	$27,655	$27,655	$27,655	$27,655	FREE	FREE	FREE	FREE	FREE	$241,979	
25	95.00%	185,250	$76,050	$27,655	$27,655	$27,655	$27,655	$27,655	$27,655	$27,655	FREE	FREE	FREE	FREE	$269,634	
26	95.00%	185,250	$76,050	$27,655	$27,655	$27,655	$27,655	$27,655	$27,655	$27,655	$27,655	FREE	FREE	FREE	$297,289	
27	95.00%	185,250	$76,050	$27,655	$27,655	$27,655	$27,655	$27,655	$27,655	$27,655	$27,655	$27,655	FREE	FREE	$324,944	
28	95.00%	185,250	$76,050	$27,655	$27,655	$27,655	$27,655	$27,655	$27,655	$27,655	$27,655	$27,655	$27,655	FREE	$352,599	
29	95.00%	185,250	$76,050	$27,655	$27,655	$27,655	$27,655	$27,655	$27,655	$27,655	$27,655	$27,655	$27,655	$8,639	$361,238	
30	95.00%	185,250	$79,853	$27,655	$27,655	$27,655	$27,655	$27,655	$27,655	$27,655	$27,655	$27,655	$27,655	$8,639	$365,040	
31	95.00%	185,250	$79,853	$29,038	$27,655	$27,655	$27,655	$27,655	$27,655	$27,655	$27,655	$27,655	$27,655	$8,639	$366,423	
32	95.00%	185,250	$79,853	$29,038	$29,038	$27,655	$27,655	$27,655	$27,655	$27,655	$27,655	$27,655	$27,655	$8,639	$367,807	
33	95.00%	185,250	$79,853	$29,038	$29,038	$29,038	$27,655	$27,655	$27,655	$27,655	$27,655	$27,655	$27,655	$8,639	$369,139	
34	95.00%	185,250	$79,853	$29,038	$29,038	$29,038	$29,038	$27,655	$27,655	$27,655	$27,655	$27,655	$27,655	$8,639	$370,572	
35	95.00%	185,250	$79,853	$29,038	$29,038	$29,038	$29,038	$29,038	$27,655	$27,655	$27,655	$27,655	$27,655	$8,639	$371,954	
36	95.00%	185,250	$79,853	$29,038	$29,038	$29,038	$29,038	$29,038	$29,038	$27,655	$27,655	$27,655	$27,655	$8,639	$373,337	$4,190,025

PROPERTY NAME: MAIN STREET OFFICE BUILDING
LOCATION: Atlanta, Ga.

TENANT IMPROVEMENTS

TOTAL MONTH	TENANT 1	TENANT 2	TENANT 3	TENANT 4	TENANT 5	TENANT 6	TENANT 7	TENANT 8	TENANT 9	TENANT 10	TENANT 11	TENANT 12	VACANCY	TOTAL	TOTAL PER YR.
1														$0	
2														$0	
3														$0	
4														$0	
5														$0	
6														$0	
7														$0	
8														$0	
9														$0	
10														$0	
11	$409,500													$409,500	
12	$409,500	$148,911												$558,411	$967,911
13		$148,911	$148,911											$297,822	
14			$148,911	$148,911										$297,822	
15				$148,911	$148,911									$297,822	
16					$148,911	$148,911								$297,822	
17						$148,911	$148,911							$297,822	
18							$148,911	$148,911						$297,822	
19								$148,911	$148,911					$297,822	
20									$148,911	$148,911				$297,822	
21										$148,911	$148,911			$297,822	
22											$148,911	$46,515		$195,426	
23												$46,515		$46,515	
24													$204,750	$204,750	$3,885,500
25														$0	
26														$0	
27														$0	
28														$0	
29														$0	
30														$0	
TOTAL	$819,000	$297,822	$297,822	$297,822	$297,822	$297,822	$297,822	$297,822	$297,822	$297,822	$297,822	$93,030	$204,750	$4,095,000	

PROPERTY NAME: MAIN STREET OFFICE BUILDING
LOCATION: Atlanta, Ga.

LEASE COMMISSIONS

TOTAL MONTH	START MONTH	TENANT 1	TENANT 2	TENANT 3	TENANT 4	TENANT 5	TENANT 6	TENANT 7	TENANT 8	TENANT 9	TENANT 10	TENANT 11	TENANT 12	VACANCY	TOTAL
1															$0
2															$0
3															$0
4															$0
5															$0
6															$0
7															$0
8															$0
9															$0
10															$0
11															$0
12	1	$82,134													$82,134
13	2		$29,867												$29,867
14	3			$29,867											$29,867
15	4				$29,867										$29,867
16	5					$29,867									$29,867
17	6	$82,134					$29,867								$112,001
18	7		$29,867					$29,867							$59,734
19	8			$29,867					$29,867						$59,734
20	9				$29,867					$29,867					$59,734
21	10					$29,867					$29,867				$59,734
22	11											$29,867	$9,330		$39,197
23	12						$29,867								$29,867
24	13							$29,867							$29,867
25	14								$29,867						$29,867
26	15									$29,867					$29,867
27	16										$29,867				$29,867
28	17											$29,867	$9,330		$39,197
29	18													$41,067	$41,067
30	19														$0
31	20														$0
32	21														$0
33	22														$0
34	23														$0
35	24														$0
36	25														$0
TOTAL		$164,268	$59,735	$59,735	$59,735	$59,735	$59,735	$59,735	$59,735	$59,735	$59,735	$59,735	$18,659	$41,067	$821,340

PROPERTY NAME: MAIN STREET OFFICE BUILDING
LOCATION: Atlanta, Ga.

DEVELOPMENT CASH FLOW PROFORMA—YEAR 1

MONTHLY COST SPREAD	1	2	3	4	5	6	7	8	9	10	11	12	TOTAL
DIRECT COSTS:													
Land	$7,665,870												$7,665,870
Sitework and Demolition	$75,000	$75,000											$150,000
Shell Cost			$1,111,111	$1,111,111	$1,111,111	$1,111,111	$1,111,111	$1,111,111	$1,111,111	$1,111,111	$1,111,111		$10,000,000
Parking Structure								$135,626	$135,626	$135,626	$135,626	$135,626	$813,760
Tenant Improvements												$409,500	$967,911
Contingency, Direct Cost	$62,745	$62,745	$62,745	$62,745	$62,745	$62,745	$62,745	$62,745	$62,745	$62,745	$62,745	$62,745	$752,937
TOTAL DIRECT COSTS	$7,793,615	$137,745	$1,173,856	$1,173,856	$1,173,856	$1,309,481	$1,309,481	$1,309,481	$1,309,481	$1,309,481	$1,718,981	$831,186	$20,340,398
INDIRECT COSTS:													
Engineering	$10,000												$20,000
Soils Tests	$10,000												$10,000
Survey			$3,333	$3,333	$3,333	$3,333	$3,333	$3,333					$14,663
Testing and Inspection													$9,750
Gov't Reports, Consultants	$18,000												$18,000
Title and Closing Costs	$2,344	$2,344	$2,344	$2,344	$2,344	$2,083	$2,083	$2,083	$2,083	$2,083	$2,083	$2,083	$28,135
Legal, Accounting and Adm.						$1,260	$1,260	$1,260	$1,260	$1,260	$1,260	$1,260	$10,000
Insurance		$2,344	$2,344	$2,344	$2,344	$2,344	$2,344	$2,344	$2,344	$2,344	$2,344	$2,344	$10,000
Architecture	$250,000	$62,727	$22,727	$22,727	$22,727	$1,800	$1,800	$1,800	$1,800	$1,800	$1,800	$1,800	$400,000
Permits and Fees	$200,000					$22,727	$22,727	$22,727	$22,727	$22,727	$22,727	$62,727	$200,000
Utility Connection													$167,250
Marketing									$10,000	$10,000	$10,000	$10,000	$20,000
Property Taxes				$76,557								$76,557	$153,114
Space Planning												$2,776	$2,776
Developer's Fee	$64,042	$64,042	$64,042	$64,042	$64,042	$64,042	$64,042	$64,042	$64,042	$64,042	$64,042	$64,042	$768,500
Contingency, Indirect Cost	$3,783	$3,783	$3,783	$3,783	$3,783	$3,783	$3,783	$3,783	$3,783	$3,783	$3,783	$3,783	$45,394
Lease Commissions												$62,134	$62,134
TOTAL INDIRECT COSTS	$648,166	$62,998	$68,229	$162,786	$86,229	$81,062	$91,062	$91,062	$97,729	$97,729	$654,979	$699,198	$1,936,126
FINANCING COSTS:													
Construction Loan Fee	$129,700												$129,700
Permanent Loan Fee	$269,400												$526,680
Construction Loan Interest	$0	$29,611	$31,491	$41,716	$62,628	$83,020	$74,607	$99,096	$109,094	$109,094	$121,904	$278,280	$947,709
TOTAL FINANCING COSTS	$399,100	$29,611	$31,491	$41,716	$62,628	$83,020	$74,607	$99,096	$109,094	$109,094	$121,904	$135,496	$1,612,989
TOTAL COSTS PRIOR TO LEASE—UP	$8,727,883	$230,161	$1,291,676	$1,379,357	$1,312,713	$1,453,564	$1,476,160	$1,499,296	$1,517,103	$1,517,103	$2,095,864	$1,266,100	$23,789,244
LEASE—UP COSTS:													
Rental Income	$0	$0	$0	$0	$0	$0	$0	$0	$0	$0	$0	$278,280	$0
Management Fee													$9,000
Operating Cost—Occupied												$18,500	$18,500
Operating Cost—Vacant												$46,800	$46,800
Reserves													$0
Permanent Debt Service													$0
NET DURING LEASE—UP	$0	$0	$0	$0	$0	$0	$0	$0	$0	$0	$0	$74,300	$74,300
TOTAL PROJECT COSTS	$8,727,883	$230,161	$1,291,676	$1,379,357	$1,312,713	$1,453,564	$1,476,160	$1,499,296	$1,517,103	$1,617,103	$2,095,864	$1,389,400	$23,863,664
LESS: EQUITY CONTRIBUTION	$6,000,000												
CONSTRUCTION LOAN BALANCE	$3,727,883	$3,977,994	$5,269,410	$6,647,767	$7,960,480	$9,451,044	$10,899,194	$12,396,422	$13,681,286	$15,366,391	$17,494,255	$18,863,654	

PROPERTY NAME: MAIN STREET OFFICE BUILDING
LOCATION: Atlanta, Ga.

DEVELOPMENT CASH FLOW PROFORMA—YEAR 2

MONTHLY COST SPREAD	13	14	15	16	17	18	19	20	21	22	23	24	TOTAL
DIRECT COSTS:													
Land													$0
Sitework and Demolition													$0
Shell Cost													$0
Parking Structure													$0
Tenant Improvements	$297,822	$297,822	$297,822	$297,822	$297,822	$297,822	$297,822	$297,822	$297,822	$196,428	$46,815	$204,780	$3,127,099
Contingency, Direct Cost													$0
TOTAL DIRECT COSTS	$297,822	$297,822	$297,822	$297,822	$297,822	$297,822	$297,822	$297,822	$297,822	$196,428	$46,815	$204,780	$3,127,099
INDIRECT COSTS:													
Engineering													$0
Soils Tests													$0
Survey													$0
Testing and Inspection	$2,083	$2,083	$2,083	$2,083	$2,083								$10,417
Gov't Reports, Consultants	$1,250	$1,250	$1,250	$1,250	$1,250								$6,250
Title and Closing Costs													$0
Legal, Accounting and Adm.	$2,344	$2,344	$2,344	$2,344	$2,344	$2,344	$2,344	$2,344	$2,344	$2,344	$2,344		$28,125
Insurance	$1,500	$1,500	$1,500	$1,500	$1,500								$7,500
Architecture													$0
Permits and Fees													$0
Utility Connection													$0
Marketing	$10,000	$10,000	$10,000	$10,000	$10,000	$10,000	$10,000	$10,000	$10,000	$10,000	$10,000	$10,000	$120,000
Property Taxes	$2,778	$2,778	$2,778	$2,778	$2,778	$2,778	$2,778	$2,778	$2,778	$2,778	$2,778	$2,778	$33,333
Space Planning	$3,783	$3,783	$3,783	$3,783	$3,783	$3,783	$3,783	$3,783	$3,783	$3,783	$3,783	$3,783	$45,394
Developer's Fee	$29,667	$29,667	$29,667	$29,667	$29,667	$59,735	$59,735	$59,735	$59,735	$59,735	$59,197	$29,667	$569,340
Contingency, Indirect Cost													$0
Lease Commissions			$1,500	$1,500	$1,500	$112,001	$17,018	$112,783	$4,264	$4,264	$39,187	$48,771	
TOTAL INDIRECT COSTS	$63,905	$63,905	$63,905	$63,905	$63,905	$130,905	$78,639	$78,639	$78,639	$78,639	$58,101	$48,771	$820,359
FINANCING COSTS:													
Construction Loan Fee													$0
Permanent Loan Fee													$0
Construction Loan Interest	$163,738												$163,738
TOTAL FINANCING COSTS	$163,738	$0	$0	$0	$0	$0	$0	$0	$0	$0	$0	$0	$163,738
TOTAL COSTS PRIOR TO LEASE-UP	$636,165	$361,427	$361,427	$361,427	$361,427	$428,727	$376,461	$376,461	$376,461	$274,065	$104,616	$253,821	$4,131,196
LEASE-UP COSTS:													
Rental Income		$(8,000)	$(8,000)	$(8,000)	$(8,000)	$(78,060)	$(103,705)	$(131,380)	$(159,015)	$(186,670)	$(214,325)	$(241,979)	$(1,113,104)
Management Fee	$6,000	$6,000	$6,000	$6,000	$6,000	$6,000	$6,000	$6,000	$6,000	$6,000	$6,000	$6,000	$66,000
Operating Cost—Occupied	$26,591	$33,692	$40,773	$47,884	$54,955	$62,046	$69,137	$76,228	$83,319	$90,410	$62,625	$62,625	$770,265
Operating Cost—Vacant	$42,546	$35,291	$34,098	$29,782	$26,527	$21,272	$17,018	$12,783	$8,509	$4,254	$2,925	$2,925	$239,847
Reserves													$0
Permanent Debt Service	$208,719	$208,719	$208,719	$208,719	$208,719	$208,719	$208,719	$208,719	$208,719	$208,719	$208,719	$208,719	$2,604,626
NET DURING LEASE-UP	$286,856	$286,692	$291,528	$294,365	$297,201	$223,987	$199,169	$174,350	$149,532	$124,713	$97,944	$70,290	$2,497,625
TOTAL PROJECT COSTS	$821,000	$640,119	$642,955	$646,792	$648,628	$652,714	$676,630	$650,811	$626,993	$398,778	$202,560	$323,811	$6,628,812
LESS: EQUITY CONTRIBUTION	$0												$0
CONSTRUCTION LOAN BALANCE	$19,684,674	$20,324,793	$20,967,748	$21,613,639	$22,262,167	$22,914,881	$23,490,512	$24,041,323	$24,567,316	$24,986,095	$25,188,655	$25,492,497	

PROPERTY NAME: MAIN STREET OFFICE BUILDING
LOCATION: Atlanta, Ga.

DEVELOPMENT CASH FLOW PROFORMA – YEAR 3

MONTHLY COST SPREAD	25	26	27	28	29	30	31	32	33	34	35	36	TOTAL	GRAND TOTAL
DIRECT COSTS:														
Land													$0	$7,655,870
Sitework and Demolition													$0	$150,000
Shell Cost													$0	$10,000,000
Parking Structure													$0	$813,750
Tenant Improvements													$0	$4,095,000
Contingency, Direct Cost													$0	$752,937
TOTAL DIRECT COSTS	$0	$0	$0	$0	$0	$0	$0	$0	$0	$0	$0	$0	$0	$23,467,357
INDIRECT COSTS:														
Engineering													$0	$20,000
Soils Tests													$0	$10,000
Survey													$0	$10,000
Testing and Inspection													$0	$25,000
Gov't Reports, Consultants													$0	$15,000
Title and Closing Costs													$0	$15,000
Legal, Accounting and Adm.	$2,344	$2,344	$2,344	$2,344	$2,344	$2,344	$2,344	$2,344					$18,750	$75,000
Insurance													$0	$18,000
Architecture													$0	$500,000
Permits and Fees													$0	$200,000
Utility Connection													$0	$157,250
Marketing	$10,000	$10,000	$0,000	$10,000	$10,000								$50,000	$200,000
Property Taxes	$2,778	$2,778	$2,778	$2,778	$2,778								$13,899	$153,114
Space Planning													$13,899	$650,000
Developer's Fee													$0	$848,500
Contingency, Indirect Cost	$3,783	$3,783	$3,783	$3,783	$3,783	$3,783							$22,597	$113,485
Lease Commissions	$29,867	$29,867	$9,861	$29,867	$20,330	$41,067							$199,866	$821,340
TOTAL INDIRECT COSTS	$48,771	$48,771	$8,771	$48,771	$28,235	$47,194	$2,344	$2,344	$0	$0	$0	$0	$275,202	$3,031,699
FINANCING COSTS:														
Construction Loan Fee													$0	$129,700
Permanent Loan Fee													$0	$535,650
Construction Loan Interest													$0	$1,031,347
TOTAL FINANCING COSTS	$0	$0	$0	$0	$0	$0	$0	$0	$0	$0	$0	$0	$0	$1,696,697
TOTAL COSTS PRIOR TO LEASE–UP	$48,771	$48,771	$8,771	$48,771	$28,235	$47,194	$2,344	$2,344	$0	$0	$0	$0	$275,202	$28,195,742
LEASE–UP COSTS:														
Rental Income	($209,634)	($297,269)	($324,944)	($362,596)	($361,236)	($365,040)	($366,423)	($367,807)	($369,189)	($370,572)	($371,954)	($373,337)	($4,190,026)	($6,303,130)
Management Fee	$8,099	$8,919	$9,746	$10,578	$10,837	$10,961	$11,034	$11,034	$11,076	$11,117	$11,159	$11,200	$126,701	$229,701
Operating Cost – Occupied	$92,626	$92,626	$92,626	$92,626	$92,626	$92,626	$92,626	$92,626	$92,626	$92,626	$92,626	$92,626	$1,111,500	$1,901,265
Operating Cost – Vacant	$2,926	$2,926	$2,926	$2,926	$2,926	$2,926	$2,926	$2,926	$2,926	$2,926	$2,926	$2,926	$35,100	$321,747
Reserves													$0	$0
Permanent Debt Service	$208,719	$208,719	$246,719	$208,719	$208,719	$208,719	$208,719	$208,719	$208,719	$208,719	$208,719	$208,719	$2,504,628	$5,009,266
NET DURING LEASE–UP	$58,523	$4,972	($8,876)	($63,894)	($95,952)	($100,981)	($103,395)	($106,348)	($109,030)	($111,712)	($114,394)	($470,965)	($1,745,732)	$2,158,829
TOTAL PROJECT COSTS	$107,394	$53,743	$92	($35,113)	($67,717)	($63,787)	($101,321)	($104,004)	($109,030)	($111,712)	($114,394)	($470,965)	($2,020,933)	$30,354,571
LESS: EQUITY CONTRIBUTION	$0													
CONSTRUCTION LOAN BALANCE	$25,599,881	$25,653,604	$25,663,697	$25,618,584	$25,550,867	$25,497,080	$25,395,759	$25,291,754	$25,182,724	$25,071,012	$24,956,618	$24,485,653		$24,485,653

PROPERTY NAME: MAIN STREET OFFICE BUILDING

LOCATION: Atlanta, Ga.

STABILIZED CASH FLOW PROFORMA

	TOTAL	PER/SQ.FT	% OF EGI
Gross Potential Income (GPI)	$4,563,000	$23.40	105.26%
Less: Vacancy	($228,150)	($1.17)	−5.26%
	—————	—————	—————
Effective Gross Income (EGI)	$4,334,850	$22.23	100.00%
Operating Expenses:			
Less: Operating Expenses	($1,170,000)	($6.00)	−26.99%
Less: Management Fee	($130,046)	($0.67)	−3.00%
Less: Reserves	($29,250)	($0.15)	−0.67%
	—————	—————	—————
Total Operating Expenses	($1,329,296)	($6.82)	−30.67%
Net Operating Income (NOI)	$3,005,554	$15.41	69.33%
Less: Debt Service	($2,504,629)	($12.84)	−57.78%
	—————	—————	—————
Before−Tax Cash Flow	$500,925	$2.57	11.56%
	=====	=====	=====

PROPERTY NAME: MAIN STREET OFFICE BUILDING
LOCATION: Atlanta, Ga.

CASH FLOW PROFORMA (YEARS 4–10)

YEAR	4	5	6	7	8	9	10
AVERAGE RENT PER YEAR	$24.83	$26.05	$27.38	$28.75	$30.18	$31.69	$33.28
GROSS POTENTIAL INCOME	$4,842,112	$5,084,218	$5,338,428	$5,605,350	$5,885,617	$6,179,898	$6,488,893
LESS: VACANCY	($242,106)	($254,211)	($266,921)	($280,267)	($294,281)	($308,995)	($324,445)
EFFECTIVE GROSS INCOME	$4,600,006	$4,830,007	$5,071,507	$5,325,082	$5,591,337	$5,870,903	$6,164,449
OPERATING EXPENSES:							
LESS: OPERATING EXPENSES	($1,228,500)	($1,289,925)	($1,354,421)	($1,422,142)	($1,493,249)	($1,567,912)	($1,646,307)
LESS: MANAGEMENT FEE	($138,000)	($144,900)	($152,145)	($159,752)	($167,740)	($176,127)	($184,933)
LESS: RESERVES	($29,250)	($30,713)	($32,248)	($33,861)	($35,554)	($37,331)	($39,198)
TOTAL OPERATING EXPENSES	($1,395,750)	($1,465,538)	($1,538,815)	($1,615,755)	($1,696,543)	($1,781,370)	($1,870,439)
NET OPERATING INCOME	$3,204,256	$3,364,469	$3,532,692	$3,709,327	$3,894,793	$4,089,533	$4,294,010
LESS: DEBT SERVICE	($2,504,629)	($2,504,629)	($2,504,629)	($2,504,629)	($2,504,629)	($2,504,629)	($2,504,629)
CASH FLOW PRIOR TO RELEASING EXP.	$699,627	$859,840	$1,028,063	$1,204,698	$1,390,164	$1,584,904	$1,789,381
RELEASING EXPENSES:							
COMMISSIONS			$106,769	$112,125	$117,702	$123,591	$129,792
TENANT IMPROVEMENTS–NEW			$368,550	$368,550	$368,550	$368,550	$368,550
TENANT IMPROVEMENTS–EXISTING			$82,875	$82,875	$82,875	$82,875	$82,875
DOWNTIME VACANCY			$177,948	$186,875	$196,170	$205,985	$216,320
TOTAL RELEASING EXPENSES	$0	$0	$736,142	$750,425	$765,297	$781,001	$797,537
LESS: CAPITAL EXPENDITURES	$97,500	$102,375	$107,494	$112,868	$118,512	$124,437	$130,659
NET PROJECT CASH FLOW	$699,627	$859,840	$291,921	$454,273	$624,867	$803,903	$991,844

681

PROPERTY NAME: MAIN STREET OFFICE BUILDING
LOCATION: Atlanta, Ga.

DEBT SERVICE ANALYSIS

PRINCIAPAL	$25,939,994
INTEREST RATE	9.00%
NO. PAYMENTS (MO.)	360
MONTHLY PAYMENT	$208,719.06
BEG. OF MONTH	1
MONTHS REMAINING	12
LOAN CONSTANT (MONTH)	0.008046
LOAN CONSTANT (YEAR)	0.096555

	12 MONTH YEAR 1	YEAR 2	YEAR 3	YEAR 4	YEAR 5
FIRST MORTGAGE					
BEGINNING BALANCE	$25,939,994	$25,762,773	$25,568,927	$25,356,897	$25,124,978
INTEREST	$2,327,407	$2,310,783	$2,292,599	$2,272,709	$2,250,953
PRINCIPAL	$177,221	$193,846	$212,030	$231,920	$253,675
TOTAL DEBT SERVICE	$2,504,629	$2,504,629	$2,504,629	$2,504,629	$2,504,629
ENDING BALANCE	$25,762,773	$25,568,927	$25,356,897	$25,124,978	$24,871,302

PAYMENT NUMBER	INTEREST PAID	PRINCIPAL PAID	BALANCE REMAINING	SUM OF YEARLY INTEREST	SUM OF YEARLY PRINCIPAL	SUM OF YEARLY PAYMENTS
1	$194,549.96	$14,169.10	$25,925,824.90	$0.00	$0.00	$0.00
2	$194,443.69	$14,275.37	$25,911,549.52	$0.00	$0.00	$0.00
3	$194,336.62	$14,382.44	$25,897,167.09	$0.00	$0.00	$0.00
4	$194,228.75	$14,490.31	$25,882,676.78	$0.00	$0.00	$0.00
5	$194,120.08	$14,598.98	$25,868,077.80	$0.00	$0.00	$0.00
6	$194,010.58	$14,708.48	$25,853,369.32	$0.00	$0.00	$0.00
7	$193,900.27	$14,818.79	$25,838,550.54	$0.00	$0.00	$0.00
8	$193,789.13	$14,929.93	$25,823,620.61	$0.00	$0.00	$0.00
9	$193,677.15	$15,041.90	$25,808,578.70	$0.00	$0.00	$0.00
10	$193,564.34	$15,154.72	$25,793,423.98	$0.00	$0.00	$0.00
11	$193,450.68	$15,268.38	$25,778,155.61	$0.00	$0.00	$0.00
12	$193,336.17	$15,382.89	$25,762,772.71	$2,327,407.42	$177,221.29	$2,504,628.70

PROPERTY NAME: MAIN STREET OFFICE BUILDING
LOCATION: Atlanta, Ga.

SALE ANALYSIS

YEAR	4	5	6	7	8	9	10
RESALE ASSUMPTIONS:							
SALES PRICE—BASED ON CURRENT NOI	$40,053,2?8	$42,055,861	$44,153,654	$46,366,5?6	$48,684,916	$51,119,161	$53,675,119
LESS: SALES COST	($801,0?4)	($841,117)	($883,173)	($927,3?2)	($973,698)	($1,022,383)	($1,073,502)
LESS: OUTSTANDING LOAN BALANCE	($25,356,8?7)	($25,124,978)	($24,871,302)	($24,593,8?0)	($24,290,329)	($23,958,358)	($23,595,246)
LESS: EQUITY	($2,556,9?3)	($2,556,943)	($2,555,943)	($2,556,9?3)	($2,556,943)	($2,556,943)	($2,556,943)
	-----	-----	-----	-----	-----	-----	-----
BEFORE TAX EQUITY REVERSION	$11,338,3?4	$13,532,823	$15,847,236	$18,288,4?1	$20,863,946	$23,581,477	$26,449,428
	=====	=====	=====	=====	=====	=====	=====

PROPERTY NAME: MAIN STREET OFFICE BUILDING
LOCATION: Atlanta, Ga.

LENDER FINANCIAL RATIOS

YEAR	4	5	6	7	8	9	10
DEBT SERVICE COV. RATIO (EXCL. RELEASING EXP.)	1.28	1.34	1.41	1.48	1.56	1.63	1.71
LOAN–TO–VALUE RATIO (END OF YEAR)	63.31%	59.74%	56.32%	53.04%	49.89%	46.87%	43.96%
BREAK–EVEN (PRIOR TO RELEASING EXPENSES)	80.55%	78.09%	75.74%	73.51%	71.38%	69.35%	67.42%
BREAK–EVEN (AFTER TO RELEASING EXPENSES)	80.55%	78.09%	89.53%	86.89%	84.38%	81.99%	79.71%
BREAK–EVEN (AFTER CAPITAL EXPENDITURES)	82.56%	80.10%	91.55%	88.91%	86.40%	84.01%	81.73%
OPERATING EXPENSES RATIO (W/O CAP. EXP.)	30.34%	30.34%	30.34%	30.34%	30.34%	30.34%	30.34%

FINANCIAL RATIOS

VALUE INDICATORS:

	4	5	6	7	8	9	10
SALES PRICE/SQ.FT. (NRA)	$205	$216	$226	$238	$250	$262	$275
GROSS RENT MULTIPLIER (GRM)	8.27	8.27	8.27	8.27	8.27	8.27	8.27
EFFECTIVE GROSS INCOME MULTIPLIER (EGIM)	8.71	8.71	8.71	8.71	8.71	8.71	8.71

AVERAGE RATES OF RETURN:

	4	5	6	7	8	9	10
CASH ON EQUITY RATIO	13.99%	17.20%	5.84%	9.09%	12.50%	16.08%	19.84%

TIME VALUE METHODS OF RETURN:

YEAR	4	5	6	7	8	9	10
PRE TAX IRR	30.71%	28.99%	26.93%	25.41%	24.24%	23.30%	22.54%
INITIAL CASH IMPUT	($5,000,000)	($5,000,000)	($5,000,000)	($5,000,000)	($5,000,000)	($5,000,000)	($5,000,000)
1	$0	$0	$0	$0	$0	$0	$0
2	$0	$0	$0	$0	$0	$0	$0
3	$0	$0	$0	$0	$0	$0	$0
4	$14,594,874	$699,628	$699,628	$699,628	$699,628	$699,628	$699,628
5		$16,949,606	$859,840	$859,840	$859,840	$859,840	$859,840
6			$18,696,101	$291,922	$291,922	$291,922	$291,922
7				$21,299,746	$454,321	$454,321	$454,321
8					$24,045,726	$624,840	$624,840
9						$26,942,305	$803,885
10							$29,998,253

DEVELOPMENT PROFIT

	WITH LEASE–UP COSTS	WITHOUT LEASE–UP COSTS
STABILIZED NET OPERATING INCOME	$3,005,555	$3,005,555
CAPITALIZATION RATE	8.00%	8.00%
APPRAISED VALUE	$37,569,438	$37,569,438
LESS: DEVELOPMENT COSTS	($30,354,571)	($28,195,742)
DEVELOPMENT PROFIT	$7,214,867	$9,373,696
DEVELOPMENT %	23.77%	33.25%

PRODUCT TYPE NO. 4: RESIDENTIAL SUBDIVISION — LAND DEVELOPMENT

PROPERTY NAME: PINEHURST AT RIVER'S PLANTATION
LOCATION: Atlanta, Ga.

GENERAL ASSUMPTIONS

# Acres	50
Land Price Per Acre	$21,000
# Lots	120
Land Cost	$1,050,000
Investor's Equity	$100,000
Investor's Profit Percentage	25.00%
Loan Proceeds	$1,750,000
Loan Fees	2.00%
Loan Closing Costs	0.50%
Lot Discharge	100.00%
Developer's Fee (Per Lot) – (Paid Qtrly)	$500
Interest Rate	10.00%
Sales Commissions	5.00%
Amenity Membership Payments (Per Lot)	$1,000

Lot Prices:	QTR 3	QTR 4	QTR 5	QTR 6	QTR 7	QTR 8	QTR 9	QTR 10	TOTAL
11,250 sq.ft. Lots									
–Interior	$20,000	$20,000	$21,000	$21,000	$21,000	$21,000	$22,000	$22,000	
–Golf	$24,000	$24,000	$25,000	$25,000	$25,000	$26,000	$26,000	$26,000	
–Lake	$28,000	$28,000	$29,000	$29,000	$29,000	$30,000	$30,000	$30,000	
–Golf/Lake	$32,000	$32,000	$33,000	$33,000	$34,000	$34,000	$34,000	$35,000	
18,000 sq.ft. Lots									
–Interior	$28,000	$28,000	$29,000	$29,000	$29,000	$30,000	$30,000	$30,000	
–Golf	$36,000	$36,000	$37,000	$37,000	$38,000	$38,000	$39,000	$39,000	
–Lake	$42,000	$43,000	$43,000	$44,000	$44,000	$45,000	$45,000	$46,000	
–Golf/Lake	$49,000	$50,000	$50,000	$51,000	$51,000	$52,000	$53,000	$53,000	
Lot Sales Absorption:									
11,250 sq.ft. Lots									
–Interior	11		11	11	12	11	15	6	77
–Golf									
–Lake	3		3	3	3	5			17
–Golf/Lake									
18,000 sq.ft. Lots									
–Interior	1	12	1	1	11				26
–Golf									
–Lake									
–Golf/Lake									
TOTAL	15	12	15	15	26	16	15	6	120

PROPERTY NAME: PINEHURST AT RIVER'S PLANTATION
LOCATION: Atlanta, Ga.

SITE DEVELOPMENT & AMENITY COST BREAKDOWN

DESCRIPTION	UNIT	QUANTITY	PRICE	TOTAL	GRAND TOTAL
CLEARING AND GRADING					
Clearing	LF	5,920	$2.75	$16,280.00	
Grading	LF	5,920	$5.00	$29,600.00	
Entrance Pad Stone	TN	80	$18.00	$1,440.00	
Mass Rock (ripped)	CY	150	$6.00	$900.00	
Mass Rock (shot)	CY	0	$25.00	$0.00	
Back Fill Curb	LF	11,808	$0.16	$1,889.28	
Seed Shoulders & Easements	LF	15,300	$0.40	$6,120.00	
Silt Fence	LF	2,000	$1.40	$2,800.00	
Bury Misc. Timber Piles	LF	100	$4.00	$400.00	
SUB TOTAL					$59,429.28
PAVING					
Paving 6 inches & 2 inches	SY	17,623	$6.50	$114,549.50	
Stabilization	SY	0	$50.00	$0.00	
SUB TOTAL					$114,549.50
CURB & GUTTER					
24 inch Highback	LF	11,808	$4.00	$47,232.00	
Throats	EA	22	$300.00	$6,600.00	
Tops	EA	22	$300.00	$6,600.00	
Slot Construction	LF	95	$40.00	$3,800.00	
SUB TOTAL					$64,232.00

PROPERTY NAME: PINEHURST AT RIVER'S PLANTATION
LOCATION: Atlanta, Ga.

SITE DEVELOPMENT & AMENITY COST BREAKDOWN

DESCRIPTION	UNIT	QUANTITY	PRICE	TOTAL	GRAND TOTAL
SANITARY SEWER					
Tie In to EX. M.H.	EA	3	$100.00	$300.00	
8 inch Pipe 0 – 10	LF	5,482	$9.75	$53,094.00	
8 inch Pipe 10 – 12	LF	1,460	$10.55	$15,403.00	
8 inch Pipe 12 – 14	LF	1,051	$12.10	$12,717.10	
8 inch Pipe 14 – 16	LF	459	$13.50	$6,196.50	
8 inch Pipe 16 – 18	LF	120	$14.75	$1,770.00	
8 inch Plugs	EA	4	$35.00	$140.00	
8 inch DIP (extra)	LF	670	$15.60	$10,452.00	
8 inch Fernco	EA	18	$40.00	$720.00	
48 inch MH Riser	VF	305	$85.00	$25,925.00	
Rings and Covers	EA	28	$170.00	$4,760.00	
Inverts	EA	28	$100.00	$2,800.00	
8 inch Boots	EA	51	$35.00	$1,785.00	
Adjust MH in streets	EA	22	INCLUDED	$0.00	
8 inch x 6 inch connections	EA	121	$40.00	$4,840.00	
6 inch Pipe	LF	3,879	$8.00	$31,032.00	
6 inch Plugs	EA	121	$20.00	$2,420.00	
4 in x 4 in service markers	EA	121	$15.00	$1,815.00	
6 inch DIP (extra)	LF	0	$11.00	$0.00	
8 in x 6 in DIP T's (extra)	EA	0	$140.00	$0.00	
Pipeline Clearing	LF	940	$1.80	$1,692.00	
Trench Rock (Blasted)	LF	81	$47.11	$11,199.99	
SUB TOTAL					$158,810.10
STORM SEWER					
18 inch CMP	LF	1,182	$11.00	$13,002.00	
18 inch BCCMP	LF	192	$11.70	$2,246.40	
18 inch RCP	LF	0	$21.50	$0.00	
24 inch CMP	LF	452	$13.75	$6,215.00	
24 inch BCCMP	LF	80	$14.40	$1,152.00	
30 inch CMP	LF	780	$15.50	$12,090.00	
30 inch BCCMP	LF	64	$16.00	$1,024.00	
18 inch Headwalls	EA	5	$200.00	$1,000.00	
30 inch Headwalls	EA	2	$400.00	$800.00	
48 inch MH Riser	VF	160	$86.00	$13,760.00	
WI Tops	EA	2	$125.00	$250.00	
JB Tops	EA	2	$125.00	$250.00	
Ring and Covers	EA	4	$170.00	$680.00	
Round to Square adapter	EA	4	$150.00	$600.00	
Inverts	EA	26	$100.00	$2,600.00	
Tail Ditching	LF	650	$1.50	$975.00	
Pipeline Clearing	LF	1,685	$1.80	$3,033.00	
Rip Rap	TN	64	$25.00	$1,600.00	
SUB TOTAL					$61,277.40

PROPERTY NAME: PINEHURST AT RIVER'S PLANTATION
LOCATION: Atlanta, Ga.

SITE DEVELOPMENT & AMENITY COST BREAKDOWN

DESCRIPTION	UNIT	QUANTITY	PRICE	TOTAL	GRAND TOTAL
WATER					
CCWA Payment	LS	98	$649.00	$63,602.00	
SUB TOTAL					$63,602.00
ENTRANCE					
Entrances	LS	100	$200.00	$20,000.00	
Signs	LS	100	$80.00	$8,000.00	
Maintenance	LS	100	$80.00	$8,000.00	
SUB TOTAL					$36,000.00
POWER & STREET LIGHTING					
Cowetta Fayette EMC Payment	LS	100	$93.00	$9,300.00	
SUB TOTAL					$9,300.00
AMENITIES					
Planning & Engineering	LS	100	$48.00	$4,800.00	
Clearing & Grading	LS	100	$50.00	$5,000.00	
Pool (30 x 60)	LS	100	$390.00	$39,000.00	
Pool deck	SF	4,000	$2.00	$8,000.00	
Fencing	LS	400	$12.00	$4,800.00	
Pool Furnishings & Equip	LS	100	$40.00	$4,000.00	
Tennis courts (3)	LS	100	$380.00	$38,000.00	
Curb & Gutter	LF	580	$4.00	$2,320.00	
Catchbasin	EA	1	$1,800.00	$1,800.00	
Sidewalks	SF	1,280	$1.50	$1,920.00	
Paving	SY	1,400	$10.00	$14,000.00	
Playscape	LS	100	$30.00	$3,000.00	
Entryway	LS	100	$20.00	$2,000.00	
Landscaping	LS	100	$250.00	$25,000.00	
Irrigation	LS	100	$20.00	$2,000.00	
Clubhouse/Sales	SF	1,290	$65.00	$83,850.00	
Contingency	LS	100	$305.10	$30,510.00	
SUB TOTAL					$270,000.00
CONTINGENCY					
Contingency	LS	100	$350.00	$35,000.00	
SUB TOTAL					$35,000.00
TOTAL SITE DEVELOPMENT					$872,200.28

PROPERTY NAME: PINEHURST AT RIVER'S PLANTATION
LOCATION: Atlanta, Ga.

DEVELOPMENT PROFORMA

REVENUE:

# LOTS	QTR 1	QTR 2	QTR 3	QTR 4	QTR 5	QTR 6	QTR 7	QTR 8	QTR 9	QTR 10	TOTALS	PER LOT
11,250 sq.ft. Lots												
—Interior			11		11	11	12	11	15	6	77	
—Golf											0	
—Lake											0	
—Golf/Lake			3		3	3	3	5			17	
18,000 sq.ft. Lots											0	
—Interior											0	
—Golf			1	12	1	1	11				26	
—Lake											0	
—Golf/Lake											0	
TOTAL # LOTS SOLD	0	0	15	12	15	15	26	16	15	6	120	
TOTAL REVENUE	$0	$0	$352,000	$432,000	$367,000	$387,000	$772,000	$401,000	$330,000	$132,000	3,153,000	$26,275
(—) SALES COMMISSIONS @ 5%	$0	$0	($17,600)	($21,600)	($18,350)	($18,350)	($38,600)	($20,050)	($16,500)	($6,600)	(157,650)	($1,314)
(+)AMENITY MEMBERSHIP PAYMENTS			$15,000	$12,000	$15,000	$15,000	$26,000	$16,000	$15,000	$6,000	120,000	$1,000
NET REVENUE	$0	$0	$349,400	$422,400	$363,650	$363,650	$759,400	$396,950	$328,500	$131,400	3,115,350	$25,961

LOT VALUE MATRIX

LOT PRICES:

11,250 sq.ft. Lots								
Interior	$20,000	$20,000	$21,000	$21,000	$21,000	$21,000	$22,000	$22,000
—Golf	$24,000	$24,000	$25,000	$25,000				$28,000
—Lake	$28,000	$28,000	$29,000	$29,000	$29,000	$30,000	$30,000	$30,000
—Golf/Lake	$32,000	$32,000	$33,000	$33,000	$34,000	$34,000	$34,000	$35,000
18,000 sq.ft. Lots								
—Interior	$28,000	$28,000	$29,000	$29,000	$29,000	$30,000	$30,000	$30,000
—Golf	$36,000	$36,000	$37,000	$37,000	$38,000	$38,000	$39,000	$39,000
—Lake	$42,000	$43,000	$43,000	$44,000	$44,000	$45,000	$45,000	$46,000
—Golf/Lake	$49,000	$50,000	$50,000	$51,000	$51,000	$52,000	$53,000	$53,000

PROPERTY NAME: PINEHURST AT RIVER'S PLANTATION
LOCATION: Atlanta, Ga.

DEVELOPMENT PROFORMA

	QTR 1	QTR 2	QTR 3	QTR 4	QTR 5	QTR 6	QTR 7	QTR 8	QTR 9	QTR 10	TOTALS	PER LOT
REVENUE												
Developer's Equity	$100,000										$100,000	$833
Net Revenue	$0	$0	$349,400	$422,400	$363,650	$363,650	$759,400	$396,950	$328,500	$131,400	$3,115,350	$25,961
Total Revenue	$100,000	$0	$349,400	$422,400	$363,650	$363,650	$759,400	$396,950	$328,500	$131,400	$3,215,350	$26,795
COSTS												
Land	$1,050,000										$1,050,000	$8,750
Loan Fees & Closing Costs	$43,750										$43,750	$365
Interest		$34,594	$42,526	$40,193	$34,769	$26,853	$18,740	$0	$0	$0	$197,975	$1,650
Site Development:												
Clearing & Grading	$59,429										$59,429	$495
Paving		$114,550									$114,550	$955
Curb & Gutter		$64,232									$64,232	$535
Sanitary Sewer	$158,810										$158,810	$1,323
Storm Sewer	$61,277										$61,277	$511
Water		$63,602									$63,602	$530
Entrance			$36,000								$36,000	$300
Power & Street Lighting		$9,300									$9,300	$78
Amenity			$135,000	$135,000							$270,000	$2,250
Contingency	$35,000										$35,000	$292
Engineering:											$0	$0
Design	$37,500										$37,500	$313
Layout		$18,750									$18,750	$156
Misc.		$6,250									$6,250	$52
Taxes & Insurance	$3,000	$3,000	$3,000	$3,000							$12,000	$100
Legal & Closing Costs	$13,000										$13,000	$108
Appraisal	$5,000										$5,000	$42
Marketing & Advertising			$12,250	$12,250	$12,250	$12,250	$12,250				$61,250	$510
County Fees	$2,000										$2,000	$17
Development Fees	$15,000	$15,000	$15,000	$15,000							$60,000	$500
Total Costs	$1,483,767	$329,278	$244,076	$205,443	$47,019	$39,103	$30,990	$0	$0	$0	$2,379,676	$19,831
Net Proceeds	($1,383,767)	($329,278)	$105,324	$216,957	$316,631	$324,547	$728,410	$396,950	$328,500	$131,400	$835,674	$6,964
CONSTRUCTION LOAN PROCEEDS												
Beg. Loan Balance	$0	$1,383,767	$1,713,044	$1,607,721	$1,390,764	$1,074,133	$749,586	$0	$0	$0		
(+) Draws	$1,383,767	$329,278	$244,076	$205,443	$47,019	$39,103	$30,990	$0	$0	$0		
(−) Lot Discharge @ 100%	$0	$0	($349,400)	($422,400)	($363,650)	($363,650)	($780,576)	$0	$0	$0		
End Loan Balance	$1,383,767	$1,713,044	$1,607,721	$1,390,764	$1,074,133	$749,586	$0	$0	$0	$0		
CASH FLOW BALANCE (PROFIT)												
Beg. Cash Flow	$0	($100,000)	($100,000)	($100,000)	($100,000)	($100,000)	($100,000)	($121,176)	$275,774	$604,274		
Development Cash Flow	$0	$0	$0	$0	$0	$0	($21,176)	$396,950	$328,500	$131,400		
Less: Developer's Equity	($100,000)										($100,000)	
Cum. Cash Flow	($100,000)	($100,000)	($100,000)	($100,000)	($100,000)	($100,000)	($121,176)	$275,774	$604,274	$735,674	$735,674	$6,131
Investor's Profit @ 25%											$183,919	
Developer's Profit @ 75%											$551,756	

PROPERTY NAME: PINEHURST AT RIVER'S PLANTATION
LOCATION: Atlanta, Ga.

DEVELOPMENT SUMMARY

		TOTAL	PER LOT	% OF COSTS
REVENUE:				
Lot Sales		$3,153,000.00	$26,275	132.50%
Less: Sales Commissions		($157,650.00)	($1,314)	−6.62%
Plus: Amenity Membership Payments		$120,000.00	$1,000	5.04%
		− − − − −	− − − −	− − − − −
NET REVENUE		$3,115,350.00	$25,961	130.91%
DEVELOPMENT COSTS:				
Land		$1,050,000.00	$8,750	44.12%
Site Development:				
Clearing & Grading	$59,429.28		$495	2.50%
Paving	$114,549.50		$955	4.81%
Curb & Gutter	$64,232.00		$535	2.70%
Sanitary Sewer	$158,810.10		$1,323	6.67%
Storm Sewer	$61,277.40		$511	2.58%
Water	$63,602.00		$530	2.67%
Entrance	$36,000.00		$300	1.51%
Power & Street Lighting	$9,300.00		$78	0.39%
Amenity	$270,000.00		$2,250	11.35%
Contingency	$35,000.00	$872,200.28	$292	1.47%
Engineering:				
Design	$37,500.00		$313	1.58%
Layout	$18,750.00		$156	0.79%
Misc.	$6,250.00	$62,500.00	$52	0.26%
Taxes & Insurance		$12,000.00	$100	0.50%
Legal & Closing Costs		$13,000.00	$108	0.55%
Appraisal		$5,000.00	$42	0.21%
Marketing & Advertising		$61,250.00	$510	2.57%
County Fees		$2,000.00	$17	0.08%
Development Fees		$60,000.00	$500	2.52%
Financing Costs:				
Points		$40,100.00	$334	1.01%
Interest		$197,975.35	$1,650	8.32%
		− − − − −	− − − −	− − − − −
TOTAL DEVELOPMENT COSTS		$2,379,675.63	$19,831	100.00%
PROFIT		$735,674.37	$6,131	30.91%

RETURN ON COST (%)   30.91%
                                    = = = = =

RETURN ON EQUITY (%) – INVESTOR   183.92%
                                    = = = = = =

RETURN ON EQUITY/YR (%) – INVESTOR 73.57%
                                    = = = = =

Real Estate Development
Procedural Matrix Diagram

The mega-diagram behind the cover has been created to move the reader through the complete real estate development process while relating the various work tasks to the different disciplines of the real estate business (i.e., development, marketing, design and construction, finance and accounting, and property management). The best way to use the diagram is to read the central shaded spine from left to right through each page, observing the key activities of the process. Then, following the parallel lines projected by development, marketing, property management, finance and accounting, and design and construction, observe vertically how each discipline influences or reacts to that work task or activity along the shaded central horizontal spine. In addition, the numbers which will be found refer to the chapters within this book where additional information and other figures and diagrams can be found.

Glossary

A

Abandonment A voluntary surrender of owned or leased property without naming a successor as an owner or a tenant.

Absentee owner A property owner who does not personally manage or reside at the property.

Absorption rate An estimated time period in which a property will be leased.

Abstract of title A historical summary of all of the recorded instruments and legal proceedings that affect title to a property.

Acceleration clause A clause in a mortgage document which gives the mortgagee the right to accelerate full repayment of the debt if the mortgagor defaults on any of the obligations.

Accelerated cost recovery system (ACRS) A method of depreciation introduced by the Economic Recovery Act of 1981 which determines the useful life of various types of property.

Accelerated depreciation A method of depreciation in which the asset is written off more quickly than under the straight line method.

Acceptance The act of agreeing to accept an offer.

Access right The right of ingress and egress to a property.

Accredited investor Under the Securities and Exchange Commission Regulation D, a wealthy investor who does not count as one of the 35 investors allowed to invest in a private limited partnership. To qualify the investor must have a net worth of at least $1,000,000 or an annual income of at least $200,000 or must have invested at least $150,000 into the deal, and the investment must not be more than 20 percent of the investor's net worth.

Accrual basis An accounting method in which income and expenses are recognized as they are earned or incurred, even though they might not have been received or paid.

Accrued interest Interest which is owed but has not been currently paid.

Accumulated depreciation The sum total of all depreciation taken to date.

Acknowledgement A declaration by an individual stating that he has signed a document voluntarily.

Acquisition The process of acquiring property.

Acquisition cost The total cost of acquiring a piece of property including all fees, closing costs, and expenses of renovation.

Acquisition fee A fee paid to a syndicator for services in acquiring a property.

Acre A measurement of land that contains 43,560 square feet, 160 square rods, 10 square chains, or 4840 square yards.

Adjustable rate mortgage (ARM) A mortgage in which the rate of interest is tied to a floating index. The interest rate is adjusted at specified time periods.

Adjusted average rate of return method A modified rule of thumb which results in using an average income or cash flow figure taking into account the expected sales price or equity reversion.

Adjusted tax basis The price on which a capital gain or a loss is based, sales price less costs and commissions.

Administrator An individual appointed by a court to administer the estate of a person who died intestate.

Administrator's deed A deed that conveys property of an individual who died without a will.

Ad valorem tax (Latin) A tax on property based on the current value of the property.

Adverse possession Acquisition of title to property in which an occupant has been in actual, open, notorious, and continuous use of such property for a period specified by state law.

After-tax cash flow (ATCF) Amount of money that is available after all expenses, including taxes are paid.

After tax cash flow multiplier A payback method that is equal to the equity divided by the after-tax cash flow.

After-tax equity reversion (ATER) The net selling price less any unpaid outstanding mortgages less the taxes due on sale.

After-tax rate (ATR) A rate of return measure equal to the after-tax cash flow divided by the equity.

After-tax real rate of return Amount of money the investor can keep after paying any taxes from a sale, adjusted for inflation.

Agency Legal relationship between a principal and agent arising from a contract in which the principal engages the agent to perform certain acts on the principal's behalf.

Agent Individual who is authorized by another person (principal) to act in the latter's behalf in a transaction involving a third party.

Agreement of sale Written agreement between a buyer and a seller of a piece of property.

Air rights The right to use, occupy, or control the space above a designated property. These rights can be sold, leased, or donated to another party.

Alternative minimum tax Flat rate tax that applies to individual taxpayers at certain income levels.

Amenities Attractive improvement features of a piece of property.

Amortization The gradual repayment of debt through systematic payment of the principal over a specific period of time. The loan will be fully amortized when the loan balance is zero.

Amortization schedule Table which shows the periodic principal and interest payments on a mortgage loan. This schedule will also show the remaining balance due on this loan as the loan is being paid off.

Anchor tenant Key tenant in a shopping center that will attract other businesses and shoppers.

Annual debt service The sum total of the monthly debt service payments required by a lender.

Annual percentage rate (APR) The actual cost of borrowing on an annual basis.

Apartment A dwelling unit within a multi-family structure.

Appraisal An estimated value of a piece of property by a qualified person.

Appraiser A qualified individual who conducts appraisals.

Appreciation The increase in the value of a property, resulting from an increase in the performance of the property through management or inflation.

Approaches to value Three appraisal techniques employed by an appraiser to estimate the value of real estate: market data, income, and the cost approach.

Appurtenance Something that is outside the property lines but is considered a part of the property and adds to its greater enjoyment.

Architect An individual who functions as a creator, coordinator, and author of the drawings and specifications used in the development design phase.

Arrears Denotes a payment at the end of a term. Most mortgage interest payments are made in arrears.

Arm's-length transaction A transaction which takes place between unrelated parties.

Articles of partnership A document describing the terms and conditions of a partnership, including the nature of its business and the rights and responsibilities of the partners.

As is A condition of property without guarantees.

Asking price The amount of value a property owner sets as the selling price.

Assemblage The combination of two or more properties to sell as one.

Assessed value The value placed on a property by the local taxing authority.

Assessment A special payment or tax on a property by a local taxing authority.

Assessment ratio The ratio of assessed value to market value.

Assessor An official who determines property taxes for a local government.

Assignment of contract or lease The transfer of all title, right, and interest that a lease possesses in certain real property.

Assignee One to whom a transfer of interest in property is made.

Assignor One who makes an assignment of interest in property.

Assets Everything owned by a person or other entity which can be used to make payments on a debt.

Assumable loan Loan which can be taken over by a new borrower when property is resold. The new borrower will assume all the liabilities of the original borrower.

Assumption fee A fee charged by a lender to permit the transfer of a mortgage.

At risk Those dollars that are exposed to the danger of loss. Investors in a limited partnership can claim tax deductions only if they can prove to the IRS that there is a chance that they will never realize a profit and that they can lose their investment.

At-risk rules The tax law that limits tax losses to the amount of money that an investor can lose.

Attachment A legal taking of a property to force payment of a debt.

Attornment A tenant's formal agreement to be a tenant of a new landlord.

Auction A public sale of a property to the highest bidder.

Automatic renewal clause A lease clause that automatically renews the lease unless both tenant and landlord notify each other of a desire to terminate.

Average rate of return Rules of thumb which will result in an average income or cash flow figures as percentages of the total or equity cost.

Average rate on after-tax cash flow The average rate of return measure which equals the average after-tax cash flow divided by the equity costs.

Average rate on before-tax cash flow The average rate of return measure which equals the average before-tax cash flow divided by the equity costs.

Average rate on net operating income The average rate of return measure which equals the average net operating income divided by the investment costs.

B

Backup contract A contract to buy property which becomes effective if a prior contract fails to perform.

Bad debt allowance An allowance used to reduce the potential gross income; it is based on the probability that some of the rental income will be uncollectable.

Balance sheet A financial statement which lists all assets, liabilities, and equity, where the assets must be equal to the liabilities and equity.

Balloon loan A debt repayment in which the outstanding principal balance is due at a specified time.

Band of investment An appraisal technique in which the overall interest rate is derived from weighing mortgage and equity rates.

Bank A financial institution which is authorized to provide a variety of financial services.

Bankruptcy A condition one seeks through the courts when one cannot pay debts.

Base rent The minimum rent due under a lease that has a participation requirement.

Base year The year of a lease term which is used as the standard when implementing the escalation clause. The operating costs are judged either higher or lower during the next year when compared to the base year.

Basis In determining taxes, it is that value from which gains, losses, and depreciation are computed.

Basis point One-hundredth of one percent.

Bay The unfinished area or space between a row of columns and the bearing wall. This area is usually the smallest area into which a building floor can be partitioned.

Bay depth The distance from the corridor wall to the real window or wall.

Before-tax cash flow (BTCF) The cash flow available prior to paying income taxes.

Before-tax cash flow multiplier A payback method equal to the equity divided by the before-tax cash flow.

Before-tax equity reversion (BTER) The remaining value of the expected sales price less any selling expenses less the unpaid mortgage principal at the time of the sale.

Beneficiary An individual who receives or is to receive the benefits resulting from certain acts.

Benefit cost ratio An alternative financial technique that measures the ratio of the benefit per dollar of costs, typically on a discounted cash flow basis.

Best efforts The effort made by an underwriter of a limited partnership in raising the equity for a transaction.

Bid The amount an individual offers to pay.

Bilateral contract A contract in which each party must perform.

Bill of sale A written instrument used to pass title of personal property from a seller to a buyer.

Binder The earnest money deposit made to secure a piece of property at agreed upon terms.

Blanket mortgage A mortgage which covers more than one piece of real property.

Blended rate mortgage An interest rate which applies to a refinanced loan where the new interest rate is the average of the old and the new rates.

Blind pool An investment by a partnership in which the property is not designated in advance, but is acquired after the funds are raised.

Blue sky laws State laws which protect the public against securities fraud.

BOMA Building Owners and Managers Association.

BOMA standard method A standard method of measuring office space developed by BOMA.

Book value The owner's original cost plus the cost of any improvements less the depreciation taken for tax purposes. This is the value which is carried on the owner's accounting records.

Boot In a property exchange, the unlike property which is included to balance the value in the transaction.

Breach of contract A violation of the terms of a contract that causes a default.

Break-even cash flow ratio The percentage of the total operating expenses plus the debt service to the effective gross income.

Break-even point The income required to cover all operating expenses and the debt service.

Bridge loan A mortgage loan used between the termination of one loan and the beginning of another loan.

Broker An individual who acts as an intermediary between two parties. This individual receives a commission for the services rendered.

Broker-dealer One who is licensed by the Commissioner of Corporations to sell securities.

Budget A prediction of the income and expenses for a property over a specified time period.

Building codes Standards established by local governmental agencies to enforce minimum safety requirements.

Building core The central or arterial part of a multi-story building that integrates functions and service needs for established building occupants. Such areas are usually composed of the bathroom facilities, elevator banks, janitorial areas, utility room and mechanical rooms, smoke shafts, and stairwells.

Building module A unit of length and width by which the plan of the building can be standardized and which facilitates the design and layout of the office space. The module places constraints on the size and shape of many of the elements of the physical systems. In contrast, buildings of a nonmodular design may present many problems in the initial design process.

Building permit The approval that must be obtained by the local governmental authority prior to the commencement of construction.

Building shell The skeleton of the building to which the finished exterior skin and interior finishes are applied.

Building skin All the materials that cover the building's shell.

Building standards The specific construction standards that have been established by the building owner and the architect to achieve a uniform element of design throughout the building and to establish a cost basis for fitting up charges and/or allowances.

Build-to-suit An agreement between a developer and a new tenant whereby the developer assumes the obligation of fitting up the demised space to the tenant's specifications within the constraints of the building standards. The tenant takes possession when the space is completed.

Bundle of rights A doctrine that views the interests in real property as a collection of property rights.

Buy-back sales agreement A provision in a sales agreement in which the seller agrees to repurchase the property in the future.

Buydown The payment of additional monies to reduce the rate of interest charged on a loan.

Buyer's market A real estate marketplace in which there are more sellers than buyers, giving the buyer an opportunity to negotiate a better purchase price and terms.

Buy-sell agreement An agreement between parties in which either party can purchase the other party's interest.

Bylaws A set of regulations according to which an organization conducts its business or activities.

C

Call provision A clause in a mortgage document giving the lender the right to accelerate the debt upon the occurrence of a specified event prior to the original maturity date.

Cancellation clause A clause in a contract giving the right to terminate the agreement upon a specified event.

Capital expenditure A property improvement which will last longer than a repair. This item is added to the basis of the property rather than being expensed.

Capital gains The gains or profit realized from the sale of property and taxed at a rate lower than earned income.

Capitalization The conversion of an income stream into a property valuation.

Capitalization rate The current rate of return derived by dividing the net operating income by the estimated value or resale price.

Capital loss A loss from the sale of a capital asset.

Carrying costs Those costs associated with holding a property.

Cash basis An accounting method that recognizes revenue when cash is received and recognizes expenses when cash is paid out.

Cash on cash return The rate of return of an investment. Calculated by dividing the cash flow by the down payment.

Cash flow The positive difference between the revenue generated from the property and the expenses paid out. This cash flow is the owner's net spendable income.

Caveat emptor (Latin) "Let the buyer beware." The purchaser must examine the property prior to closing and is buying at his own risk.

Central business district (CBD) The center of the downtown in a city, the main commercial area.

Certificate of insurance A document issued by an insurance company verifying the property insurance coverage.

Certificate of occupancy A document issued by a local government permitting occupancy of a property.

Certificate of payment A certificate that is issued by the architect to a contractor for such amount as the architect decides is properly due.

Certificate of title A opinion given by an attorney of the status of the title to a property.

Chain A measurement of land used in surveying equal to 66 feet in length. Each chain contains 100 links.

Chain of title A history of ownership of a piece of property from date the original patent was granted until the present.

Change order An order issued any time when there is a change in the specifications, price, or time set forth in the building contract as authorized in writing by the owner or architect.

Chattel Personal property that can be moved.

Chattel mortgage A mortgage secured by personal property.

Circulation allowance The space that is required to have sufficient access to, from, and around work spaces.

Clear span The amount of floor area that is clear of interference from columns.

Clear title A title that is not encumbered by or burdened with any defects.

Client An individual who engages another individual to perform a service.

Closed-end fund An offering by a partnership which, after the sale of a maximum number of units, is closed unless there is an amendment to the partnership.

Closing The consummation of the real estate transaction in which the ownership rights are transferred to the buyer in exchange for consideration paid to the seller.

Closing costs The expenses associated with the closing.

Closing date A date on which a transaction is closed.

Closing statement A document used to account all of the funds from a real estate sale, listing all of the buyer's and seller's costs.

Cloud on title An outstanding claim or encumbrance against a property that impairs the title to property.

Coinsurance A clause in an insurance policy stating the minimum percentage of value that is insured in order to collect the full amount of a loss.

Collateral Marketable real or personal property that a borrower pledges as security for a loan.

Commercial property Real property that is intended to be used for commerce, such as offices, motels, hotels, and retail outlets.

Comingle The act of mixing funds, as in mixing personal and business funds together in one checking account.

Commission The fee paid to the real estate broker or mortgage broker for services rendered, usually based on a percentage of the purchase price.

Commitment The act of promising to complete an obligation.

Commitment fee The fee paid to a lender for a loan.

Common area The space not used or occupied by tenants, for example, hallways, lobbies, restrooms, or stairways.

Common area maintenance charge (CAM) A provision in a shopping center lease requiring the tenant to pay a share of the common area operating expenses.

Community shopping center A medium-sized shopping center with a small department store or supermarket as the anchor tenant and another 50 smaller retail stores. The typical size is 150,000 square feet.

Co-mortgagor An individual who cosigns a mortgage.

Comparables Properties with similar economic characteristics.

Comparative market approach An appraisal method basing its value estimate on the recent sale prices of comparable properties.

Comparison year During the term of a lease with an escalator clause, any year that is compared with the base year for the purpose of establishing a rise or fall in operating costs.

Completion bond A legal document guaranteeing completion of the construction of a property.

Compound interest Interest paid on the original principal and also on the unpaid accumulated interest.

Concessions Discounts in a lease or sales contract used to induce a party to sign an agreement.

Concurrence estates Estates in land with more than one owner.

Condemnation A government act of taking property for public use with compensation to the owner of the property.

Conditions Certain provisions in an agreement on which the fulfillment of the agreement depend.

Condominium A type of ownership in which each individual has fee-simple title to a specific unit in a multi-tenant building. Each unit owner has an individual mortgage and contributes a share of the common area maintenance and operating expenses of the property.

Condominium association The nonprofit governing body of a condominium property. Each condominium owner automatically belongs to the association upon purchasing a unit.

Condominium conversion The subdivision of an existing rental property into condominium ownership, either in a residential or commercial property.

Consideration The cash or services given in exchange for property.

Constant payment loan A loan in which the payments made are equal during the term of the repayment.

Construction allowance A landlord's contribution to the cost of construction and/or alteration that is necessary to prepare a space for a tenant's occupancy. This allowance may be an established amount, or it may vary from one kind of transaction to another.

Construction cost The total expense, plus normal overhead and profit, that must be paid for the project.

Construction cost estimate A figure that is submitted prior to the start of construction, that estimates the total cost of the construction project.

Construction draw Periodic advances on a construction loan.

Construction loan A loan that is made for the purpose of constructing a property, usually for a term of under three years. They are usually based on prime rate and paid interest only with a balloon payment due at maturity of the loan.

Constructive eviction Any disturbance by the landlord of the tenant's possession of the leased premises, whereby they are rendered unsuitable for occupancy. In such a case, the tenant is not liable for further payment of the rent.

Constructive notice The legal presumption that all individuals have knowledge of a fact when that fact is a matter of public record.

Consumer price index (CPI) An index that is published monthly by the U.S. Department of Labor, Bureau of Labor Statistics, showing the cost of a cross-section of consumer goods and services.

Contingency fund A fund set aside for the use of unforeseen expenses.

Contingent liability The liability assumed by a third party. If the original obligor defaults, the third party will be responsible for the obligation.

Contiguous Adjacent and touching properties.

Contract An agreement between two or more parties that creates or modifies a legal relationship, generally based upon an offer and acceptance.

Contract for deed An agreement in which the seller will deliver title to the purchaser after all payments have been made.

Contractor An individual who contracts to supply goods or services.

Contractor's affidavit A written statement by a contractor, that is made under oath before a notary public, stating the facts regarding the contract, subcontracts, material suppliers, and labor. This affidavit sets forth the amounts paid and unpaid and the balance of payments that are due.

Contract price The price at which a property is contracted for.

Conventional mortgage loan A loan made by a source other than by a federal agency.

Conveyance An instrument by which title to property is transferred.

Coop An arrangement between two individuals to split a real estate commission.

Cooperative ownership A corporate ownership in which each individual owns shares of stock. Each shareholder then gets a proprietary lease to occupy a unit.

Core space The space in a building that includes the square footage used for the public corridors, elevators, restrooms, stairways, electrical and telephone rooms, and the janitorial closet.

Corporation A legal entity registered by the secretary of state, limiting the individual liability of the individuals comprising it.

Cost approach An appraisal method that estimates the value of the property based on the cost to reconstruct the property plus the land cost.

Cost basis The original price of an asset used in determining a capital gain, usually the purchase price.

Counteroffer An offer, instead of an acceptance, made in response to an offer.

Covenant Promise written into a deed or other instrument by which a party agrees to perform or not to perform certain acts.

Covenant not to compete A contract restricting one party from competing with another party.

Creative financing Any financing arrangement other than a conventional level-paid amortizing loan.

Credit The capacity to obtain financing.

Creditor An individual to whom money is owed.

Curable depreciation Deterioration of a property that can be corrected.

Curb appeal The aesthetic image and appearance projected by a property on a first impression.

Current yield Current income divided by the investment cost.

D

Dealer An individual who buys and sells property.

Debt An obligation to be repaid by a borrower to a lender.

Debt coverage ratio A ratio used by a lender which expresses the loan amount in relationship to the net operating income, usually between 1.05 and 1.30.

Debt service The monthly cost of repaying a mortgage loan, including interest on the outstanding balance and, in many cases, a reduction in the loan principal.

Declining balance depreciation A method of depreciation in which a rate is applied to the remaining balance to derive the depreciation deduction.

Dedication The gift of property by its owner for public use.

Deed A written document signed by the seller transferring title in a piece of real estate.

Deed in lieu of foreclosure A deed that is given by an owner to the lender in lieu of foreclosure.

Deed of trust A mortgage that conveys real property to a third party by holding in trust the deed until the loan is repaid.

Deed restrictions A clause in a deed that limits the use of the conveyed property.

Default The failure to perform on an obligation as agreed in a contract.

Defeasance clause A clause giving the mortgagor the right to redeem the property on payment of his obligation to the mortgagee.

Defect in title Any recorded instrument that prevents the seller from giving clear title to a property.

Deferred maintenance The ordinary maintenance that is not performed and will negatively affect the property's use and value.

Deferred payment The taking of a promissory note for payment of a debt to be repaid over time.

Deficiency judgment court order stating that the debtor still owes money on a debt that is in default.

Degree of operating leve re (DOL) A measure that, at any occupancy level is the percentage change in net operating income from a change in occupancy level.

Delinquency The failure to make a payment on an obligation when due.

Delivery The transfer of a property from one party to another.

Demised premises Premises, or parts of the real estate, in which an interest or estate have been transferred temporarily, such as an interest in real estate conveyed in a lease.

Demising clause A clause in a lease whereby the landlord leases and the tenant takes the property.

Demographics Statistical information on the population of an area.

Demolition clause A clause written into a lease denoting the fact that if or when the ground lease expires, the building will be demolished per such clause. The landlord must notify the tenant within a predetermined time period prior to exercising this clause.

Density The average number of individuals or units in a given space.

Deposit Money taken in good faith to assure performance of a contract.

Depreciable life For tax purposes, the number of years in which to depreciate an asset.

Depreciation An expense reflecting the loss in value of the improvements to real estate.

Depreciation recapture The excess of the sales proceeds on a property over the initial cost, limited to the amount of accumulated depreciation taken on the property up until the resale period.

Description A formal depiction of the dimensions and location of a property.

Descent The act of acquiring property when an heir is deceased and leaves no will.

Design development The process by which, upon approval of the schematic design, the architect proceeds with the development of the plans and specifications of the building.

Deteriorating neighborhood An area in which the properties have been neglected and are in disrepair.

Developer An individual who transforms raw land into improved property.

Developing neighborhood An area that is growing with recently constructed property.

Development contract An agreement between a developer and a purchaser in which the developer will construct a particular type of property and the purchaser will buy the property within a specified time period.

Development loan A loan to construct improvements on real property.

Devise A gift of property by will.

Devisee An individual who inherits property through a will.

Direct participation program (DPP) A program that lets investors participate directly in the cash flow and tax benefits of an investment.

Disclosure The release of all important information, both positive and negative, needed to make an investment decision.

Discounted cash flow The present value of an expected future cash flow, reduced by an estimated discount rate reflecting the difference in the value of the money now and the value of the money received at a later time period.

Discount points The amount of money a borrower must pay a lender to obtain a mortgage with a stated interest rate.

Discount rate A percentage rate used to compute the present value of a future cash flow.

Distraint The legal right of a landlord to seize a tenant's personal property to satisfy payment of back rent.

Distressed property Property that is about to be foreclosed on or has been foreclosed on due to insufficient cash flow.

Diversification Investing in different areas so that the average results will not threaten the success of the overall investment program.

Donee The recipient of a gift.

Donor The giver of a gift.

Double-declining-balance depreciation method A method of accelerated depreciation in which twice the annual straight line depreciation is taken.

Dower rights A legal life estate of a wife's interest in her husband's property.

Downpayment The initial equity paid on a piece of property at closing.

Down zoning The act of rezoning a property for a less intensive use.

Dragnet clause A mortgage clause that pledges several properties as collateral, whereby a default on one property constitutes a default on the other properties.

Dry mortgage A nonrecourse mortgage.

Dual contract The illegal practice of providing two contracts for the same transaction.

Due diligence The investigation of all the important facts regarding a potential investment.

Due-on-sale clause A mortgage clause requiring the mortgage to be paid in full at the time of resale. This type of loan cannot be assumed by a new purchaser.

Duplex Two dwelling units under one roof.

Dwelling A place of residence.

E

Early repayment The making of additional debt service payments prior to the required time.

Earnest money The deposit that is made by the purchaser when a purchase contract is made, evidencing the purchaser's serious intent.

Easement A right, privilege, or interest that entitles the holder to a specific limited use.

Economic base The industry within a geographic market area that provides employment opportunities needed to support a community.

Economic benefits The total benefits of an investment exclusive of the tax benefits, such as the equity buildup, cash flow, and the resale profits.

Economic depreciation The loss of value of a property due to outside forces.

Economic feasibility study An in-depth analysis of the potential real estate investment detailing the economic and financial factors.

Economic life The period of time over which a building can be used to produce a service or asset.

Effective age The age of a property based on wear and tear, not its chronological age.

Effective cost of borrowing The true cost of borrowing funds.

Effective gross income The scheduled gross income, plus any miscellaneous income, minus the vacancy rate.

Effective rate The true rate of return taking into consideration all of the costs and discounts.

Egress Access from a property to an exit or public road.

Electrified floor A floor in a commercial building that contains the house telephone and power lines, which emerge from the floor at frequent intervals for easy installation of the telephones and power equipment.

Eminent domain The right of the government or a public utility to acquire property needed for public use.

Encroachment A building or part of a building that physically intrudes upon the property of another.

Encumbrance A lien or liability that affects the fee-simple title to property.

End loan A permanent mortgage.

Equalization board A governmental agency that determines the fairness of any taxes levied against a property.

Equitable title The interest held by a party who has agreed to purchase a property but has not closed on the transaction.

Equity The ownership interest in a property after all debt is subtracted.

Equity buildup The amount of net worth that results from paying down the mortgage debt.

Equity dividend rate A simple rate of return measure equal to the before-tax cash flow dividend by the equity.

Equity kicker The participation in the cash flow or resale proceeds that a lender can receive for making a loan.

Equity REIT A real estate investment trust that invests in the ownership of income-producing property.

Escalation clause A contract clause requiring an upward adjustment in price.

Escalation payments The payments that are made under an escalation clause.

Escheat The reversion of a property to the state in the event the owner dies without a will or any heirs.

Escrow Property or other consideration held by a third party in accordance with an agreement.

Escrow agent An individual who holds an escrow payment.

Established neighborhood A sound, stable, healthy area in which all the land has been developed.

Estate The degree of interest an individual has in real property.

Estate at sufferance The wrongful occupancy by a tenant when his lease has expired.

Estate at will The occupation of a property by a tenant for an indefinite period. It can be terminated by either party.

Estate for life An interest in property that terminates upon the death of a specified individual.

Estate for years An interest in land that allows possession for a specified and limited time period.

Estate in reversion An estate left by a grantor that begins after the termination of estate granted by that individual.

Estate tax The tax based on the value of a property left by a decedent.

Estoppel A doctrine of law prohibiting a party from denying facts which that person once acknowledged were true and others accepted in good faith.

Estoppel certificate A document signed by tenants or underlying lender stating any and all claims they may have against the property owner. These certificates protect the buyer from any claims made at a later date by any of these parties.

Et al (Latin) "and others."

Eviction, actual The removal of a party from a property either by force or by process of law.

Eviction, constructive The termination of a lease by lessor when the property is unfit for the purposes it was leased for.

Eviction notice A notice given to a tenant when a tenant is in default of the rental obligations.

Evidence of title A document demonstrating ownership of property.

Exchange A tax-free exchange of like properties under Section 1031 of the Internal Revenue Code.

Exclusive agency listing An agreement between a seller and a broker in which the broker has the exclusive right to sell a property during a specified time period. This agreement also gives the seller the right to sell the property himself without paying the broker a commission.

Exclusive right-to-sell listing An agreement between a seller and a broker giving the broker the exclusive right to sell a property during a specified time period. The broker can collect a commission no matter who sells the property.

Exculpatory clause A mortgage provision stating that borrower shall not be personally liable in case of default.

Execute To sign a contract.

Executed contract A contract whose terms have been satisfied.

Executory contract A contract in which one or more parties have not yet performed.

Expected cash flow The most likely cash flow under all possible states of the world.

Expenses The costs incurred in the process of operating, acquiring, or organizing an investment entity.

Expense ratio The relationship between the total expenses, exclusive of the debt service, and the gross income.

Expenses of the syndicator The expenses incurred by the syndicator which he intends to pay himself without reimbursement.

Expense stop A ceiling or limit on the dollar amount that the landlord will pay for an expense category. This ceiling is determined by adding a percentage or dollar amount to the base year costs.

Extension An agreement between two parties extending the term of a contract.

F

Facade The exterior front of a building.

Face interest rate The rate of interest that appears on a mortgage document.

Face value The dollar amount shown on a document.

Factory outlet A shopping center comprising of manufacturers' retail outlet facilities where the goods are sold directly to the public in stores that are owned and operated by the manufacturer.

Fact sheet The data presented on a property for sale.

Fair market rent If available, the amount of rent a property could demand at a given time.

Fair market value The value of a property at a given time.

Fannie Mae The nickname for the Federal National Mortgage Association (FNMA).

Farmers Home Administration (FmHA) A governmental agency, under the U.S. Department of Agriculture, that administrates assistance to buyers of homes and farms in rural areas.

Fashion-oriented center A shopping center that consists of a concentration of apparel shops, boutiques, and handcraft shops that carry selected merchandise that is usually of a high quality and a high price. It may include a small specialty department store. Usually located in a high income area.

Feasibility study A report that takes into consideration many factors that relate to an investment and gives an opinion as to the probability of success of the same.

Federal Deposit Insurance Corporation (FDIC) A public corporation that was established in 1933. It insures up to $100,000 for each depositor in most commercial banks.

Federal Home Loan Mortgage Corporation (FHLMC) An organization that buys mortgage loans.

Federal Housing Administration (FHA) An agency of the U.S. Department of Housing and Urban Development (HUD) that administers many loan programs, loan guarantee programs, and loan insurance programs. It is designed to create more housing.

Federal National Mortgage Association (FNMA) A corporation that specializes in purchasing mortgage loans.

Federal Savings and Loan Insurance Corporation (FSLIC) An agency of the government that insures deposits of savings and loan associations against loss of principal.

Fee simple A term denoting title to property without any encumbrances.

Fenestration The design and placement of windows in a building.

Fidelity bond A bond on an employee insuring against theft of funds or valuables.

Fiduciary A person, company, or association holding assets in trust for a beneficiary and charged with investing the money wisely for the beneficiary's benefit.

Financial leverage The increase in the rate of return to the equity investor due to borrowing the funds.

Financial management rate of return (FMRR) A variation of the internal rate of return measurement in which two after-tax reinvestment rates are used.

Financial risk The risk due to the use of borrowed money and the difficulty that will result if the investor is unable to meet the necessary debt service.

Financial statement A statement showing income and expenses for an accounting period or assets, liabilities, and equity as of a certain date.

Financing The borrowing money to acquire property.

Finder's fee A fee to someone other than a broker who performs a service.

First mortgage A first lien against a property.

First right of refusal The right of one party to have the first right to purchase or lease a property.

Fiscal year A 12-month time period used for financial reporting that may or may not coincide with the calendar year.

Fit-up The construction necessary within the enclosing walls (leased space). It includes the partitioning, doors, telephone and electrical outlets, finished wall surfaces, painting or wallcoverings, flooring, and lighting fixtures.

Fixed expenses The operating expenses that tend to be fixed in amount each income period. They tend not to vary with occupancy.

Fixtures Improvements or personal property attached to the land that becomes part of the real estate.

Flood insurance Insurance that covers property damage due to natural flooding.

Floodplain An area of land that is subject to periodic flooding, usually designated by a local government.

Floor area ratio (FAR) Total floor area of a building (gross or net) divided by the total square footage of the land.

Floor loan The minimum loan amount a lender is willing to lend.

Floor plan The arrangement of the rooms in a building.

Foot candle A measurement of light level. It is equivalent to the light intensity made by one candle at a distance of one foot.

Footprint The shape and configuration of a building.

Force majeure clause A clause in a construction contract that allows additional construction time to complete a building due to an unavoidable cause of delay, such as weather, labor disputes, or accidents.

Foreclosure A legal process whereby the rights of the owner who is in default on a loan payment are lost.

Forfeiture The loss of money or other valuables due to a failure to perform under a contract.

Freddie Mac The nickname for the Federal Home Loan Mortgage Corporation (FHLMC).

Free and clear rate of return Another name for the overall capitalization rate.

Free and clear title Real property against which there are no liens.

Freehold An interest in a property for an unspecified time period.

Frontage A linear distance a property has along a road, lake, river, or ocean.

Frontend load The total compensation that is received by the syndicator on the sale of property to a partnership, including commissions on the sale of the units, loans or acquisition fees, or a resale markup of the property to be sold to the partnership.

Front foot A measurement of land based on its frontage.

Front money The sum of money used to initiate a transaction prior to its closing.

Full disclosure The requirement to disclose any and all material relevant to a financial transaction.

Functional depreciation A loss of value of a property determined from within the property and not due to physical deterioration. Examples: poor floor plan or outdated plumbing fixtures.

Functional obsolescence The same as functional depreciation.

Future interest A property right or interest available in the future.

Future return The estimated worth of an asset at some future period.

G

Gain An increase in money or value of property.

Gap loan A mortgage that fills a spread in mortgage financing.

Garden apartment A low-rise apartment property, usually in a suburban area.

General contractor An individual or firm who constructs a building for another party for a fee.

General lien A lien on a debtor of all property, both real and personal.

General partner An individual or corporation acting as the managing partner in a limited partnership and is responsible for the debts of the partnership.

General partnership An entity in which all partners are jointly and severally liable for the debts and obligations of the partnership.

General warranty deed A deed in which a seller agrees to protect the purchaser against any claims to the title of the property.

Gift deed A deed for which the consideration is not money but love and affection.

Ginnie Mae The nickname for the Government National Mortgage Association (GNMA).

Good faith An act which is done honestly between two parties.

Government National Mortgage Association (GNMA) A government agency which assists in financing housing.

Grace period A period of time allowed to a party before being considered in default.

Graduated lease payment A lease payment that increases by a specific dollar amount over the term.

Graduated payment mortgage (GPM) A mortgage featuring lower payments in the early years and increasing payments over a specified time period.

Grandfather clause A clause allowing activities which were legal under an old law to continue under a superseding law.

Grantee A person who acquires an interest in a property by deed or grant.

Grantor A person who transfers an interest in a property to a grantee by deed or grant.

Gross floor area The total floor area including all common areas.

Gross income The total rental income received from an income property.

Gross lease A lease under which the landlord pays all the expenses normally associated with the ownership of the property.

Gross leasable area (GLA) The total floor area designed for tenant occupancy and exclusive use, and on which rent is paid, including any basement, mezzanines, or upper floors, measured in square feet from the centerline of joining partitions and from outside wall faces.

Gross potential income (GPI) The amount of rental income that would result from 100 percent occupancy.

Gross rent multiplier (GRM) The ratio of the sales price of a property to the gross rents collected.

Gross profit ratio (GPR) In an installment sale, the gross profit divided by the contract price.

Ground lease An agreement in which for a fee a lessor can lease a piece of land for a specified term.

Growing equity mortgage (GEM) A mortgage in which the payment is increased by a predetermined amount each year. The additional payments are used to pay off the principal balance. Due to this repayment of principal, the mortgage will be paid off over a shorter time period.

Guaranty A pledge by a borrower to repay a debt or creditor.

H

Hard construction cost The costs of constructing a building shell plus most of the covering materials.

Hard dollars Money given in exchange for an improved equity or ownership position in a transaction, for example the down payment.

Hazard insurance Insurance that protects against fires or certain weather conditions.

Hectare A measurement of land equal to 2.471 acres or about 107,637 square feet.

Heir An individual who inherits property.

Highest and best use The use that is most likely to produce the greatest return at a specific time on a piece of land or a piece of property.

High-rise A building that is over six stories.

Historic structure A building that is officially recognized by a governmental agency for its historic significance, usually receiving special tax treatment to encourage rehabilitation.

Holdback Funds retained until certain events occur.

Holder in due course An individual who acquires a bearer instrument in good faith and is eligible to keep it even though it may have been stolen.

Hold harmless clause A contract clause in which one party agrees to indemnify another party against any claims.

Holding area A receiving area, usually in the freight-docking area where the deliveries to a tenant may be held.

Holding costs Carrying costs.

Holding period That time period during one owns a property.

Holdover tenant A tenant who remains in possession of leased property after the lease has expired.

Homeowner's association An association that is formed by a subdivision or condominium property to enforce deed restrictions and manage common elements.

Homestead exemption In certain jurisdictions, a reduction in assessed property value allowed on one's principal residence.

Horizontal property laws A statute that enables condominium ownership of property.

Housing and Urban Development (HUD) A government department set up in 1965 to assist in stimulating housing development in the United States.

Housing codes Codes set up by local governments setting certain minimum safety and sanitation standards for housing.

Housing starts The number of housing permits issued in an area during a certain time period.

HVAC An abbreviation for heating, ventilation, and air conditioning.

Hybrid REIT A real estate investment trust that invests in both property and mortgages.

I

Illiquid Not easily converted into cash.

Implied contract A contract created by actions but not necessarily written or spoken.

Implied warranty A warranty that is not written but exists under the law.

Impound account An escrow account.

Improved land Land on which there are improvements.

Improvements Additions to raw land that tend to increase its value, such as buildings, streets, and utilities.

Improvements to land Usually publicly owned structures such as curbs, sidewalks, streets, streetlights, and sewers that are constructed to enable the development of privately owned land.

Income The revenue that is generated by an investment property.

Income approach An appraisal method used to calculate value based on the income generated, when the income is capitalized at the current market rate for the particular type of property.

Income property Real estate capable of producing an income stream.

Income stream The regular flow of money generated by an investment.

Incorporeal interest A nonpossessory right in real estate.

Incurable depreciation A defect that cannot be corrected or is not financially practical to correct.

Indemnify To protect another individual against damage or loss.

Independent contractor A contractor who is self-employed.

Index A benchmark indicating a current economic or financial condition.

Indexed lease A lease in which the lease rate can increase or decrease at specified times based on a specified index.

Indexed loan A loan in which the interest rate can increase or decrease at specified times based on a specified index.

Individual metering utility system A metering system in which each tenant has its own utility meter.

Industrial development bond (IDB) A bond that is issued by a local or state government to help finance an industrial plant or facility to be leased to a private business.

Industrial park An area that is zoned for industrial use.

Industrial property Real property that is intended to be used for industry, such as manufacturing or warehousing.

Inducement Negotiable points in a lease or sales contract document resolved in the tenant's/buyer's favor that are used in an effort to induce them to sign the contract.

Industrial district or park A controlled parklike development that is designed to accommodate specific types of industry. It provides all public utilities, streets, railroad sidings, etc.

Inflation A general increase in prices, resulting in a decrease in purchasing power.

Inflation risk The likelihood of losses in real estate due to the changes in nominal prices.

Inner city An older area in a city adjacent to the central business district.

Inspection A review of documents or of the physical aspects of a property.

Inspection period A time period during which a purchaser reviews the property and the documents relating to a transaction.

Installments The periodic payments on a debt.

Installment contract A land contract.

Installment sale A sale in which the proceeds are paid in installments over a fixed period of time, allowing the capital gains to take place over a number of years.

Instrument A written legal document that creates the rights and obligations of the parties to it.

Insurable title A title that can be insured by a title company.

Insurance An agreement in which one party agrees to pay a sum of money to another if the latter suffers a particular loss in exchange for a premium paid by the insured.

Insurance coverage The amount of money and type of insurance that a property carries.

Interest A payment for the use of money.

Interest expense Payments that are made for the use of the borrowed capital.

Interest-only loan A loan in which only interest is paid during the term of the loan.

Interest rate A percentage of a sum of money charged for its use.

Interior partitions All types of interior nonload-bearing partitions that enclose or subdivide tenant space.

Internal rate of return (IRR) The discounted rate that produces a zero value for the net present value. The internal rate of return can be interpreted as the rate of return on the investment.

Internal rate of return on equity A discounted cash flow technique that finds the rate to equate the present value of each after-tax cash flow plus the after-tax equity reversion with the cost of equity.

Internal rate of return on total investment A discounted cash flow technique that finds the rate to equate the present value of the net operating income plus the expected net selling price with the total cost of an investment.

Internal Revenue Code The law specifying how and what income is taxed and what expenses can be deducted.

Internal Revenue Service (IRS) The governmental agency that administers the collection of Federal income taxes.

Interim financing A loan made prior to permanent financing.

Interstate offering An offering to residents of one or more states.

Intestate A person who dies having no valid will.

Intrastate offering An offering in which all the investors reside in the state that the property is located in.

Inventory Property held for sale or use.

Investment life cycle The time span of property ownership.

Investment property Property that is acquired for its current income and capital appreciation.

Investment tax credit A reduction in income tax based on the cost and life of certain assets purchased.

Investment value of equity A discounted cash flow technique that values after-tax cash flow and after-tax equity reversion.

Investor An individual or company that invests in a financial transaction.

Investor note financing The financing of investor promissory notes.

Involuntary lien A lien placed on property without the consent of the owner.

J

Joint and several liability When two or more parties guarantee repayment of debt, all or any one of the parties are obligated to pay the debt.

Joint tenancy Joint property ownership, in which two or more persons take title jointly for life. Upon death, the survivors acquire the decedent's interest in the property.

Joint venture An agreement by two or more parties to work on a project together.

Judgment A decree by a court evidencing the amount of and the parties to an indebtedness.

Judgment lien A claim upon a property of a debtor that results in a judgment.

Judgment foreclosure The sale of a defaulted debtor's property according to court approved terms.

Junior mortgage A mortgage that is subordinate to a first mortgage lien.

K

Kicker Additional payment of interest or rent required in a contract.

L

Land The surface of the earth that is not water.

Land banking The purchase of land to hold for future need.

Land contract A sale of property wherein the seller retains the title of the property; the purchaser is given possession and obtains title upon a predetermined loan paydown.

Land lease Ground lease.

Landlocked A condition of a property having no access to a public street.

Landlord The entity that owns a property which is leased to a tenant.

Land packaging The assembly of several tracts of land into a larger tract for a specific use.

Land sale leaseback The sale of land and the simultaneous leasing back of the land by the seller, who becomes the tenant of the landowner.

Land trust An ownership form that permits limited liability, ordinary tax treatment, and private ownership of real property.

Latent defects Defects that are hidden but will appear in the future.

Lease A contract for the use of rental property.

Leasehold An interest or estate on which a tenant has a lease.

Leasehold mortgage A lien on the tenant's interest in property.

Lease with option to purchase A lease giving the lessee the right to purchase property at an agreed-upon price and terms at a specific date.

Leasing agent A person responsible for the leasing of space in a building.

Legal description A description of a piece of property that enables it to be located on government surveys or recorded maps.

Legal name The name used for official purposes.

Legal notice A notification of other parties using the method required by law.

Legatee An individual who receives property by will.

Lender An individual or firm who lends money to a borrower for a fee with the expectation of being repaid in the future.

Lessee The tenant under a lease.

Lessor The owner who gives the lease to a lessee.

Letter of intent A nonbinding expression of intent conditioned upon the approval and further documentation of a second party.

Level payment mortgage A mortgage having the same payment due each month during its amortization period.

Leverage The use of borrowed capital to make an investment.

Levy To impose or access a tax on a person or property.

Liability A general term encompassing all types of debt and obligations.

Liability insurance Insurance protection for a property that covers any claims from injuries or damage to another's property.

License Permission.

License laws The laws of a state governing the activities of real estate salespersons.

Lien A claim against a property for a debt.

Life estate A freehold interest in property that will expire upon the death of the owner or some other specified person.

Life tenant An individual who is allowed use of property for life or the lifetime of another specified person.

Like-kind property In an exchange, property that has the same nature.

Limited liability Liability limited to the amount invested.

Limited partners Passive investors in a limited partnership who have no personal liability beyond their investment.

Limited partnership A partnership in which some partners' contributions and liabilities are limited.

Liquidated damages An agreed-upon amount that one party will reimburse the other party in the event of a breach of contract.

Liquidity Assets that are readily converted to cash.

Lis pendens (Latin) "suit pending."

List To obtain a listing.

Listing A contract authorizing an agent to sell property for an owner.

Loan A granting of the use of money for a specified time.

Loan application A written application giving all information required by a lender prior to issuing a loan commitment.

Loan commitment A written document drafted by a lender outlining the terms and conditions of a mortgage loan.

Loan constant A factor or multiplier used to compute the monthly mortgage payments that amortize a loan.

Loan-to-value ratio (LVR) The percentage that a lender will lend a borrower against the appraised value of the property.

Location A reference to the comparative advantages of one site in consideration of factors such as convenience, transportation, and social benefits.

Lock-in period A specified period of time during which a loan may not be prepaid.

Long-term capital gains For income tax purposes, the gain on a capital asset that is held for a specified time period.

Lot and block A method of identification of a parcel of land.

Low-rise A building of from one to three stories, typically without an elevator.

M

Maintenance Activities required to correct normal wear and tear on a property.

Maintenance fee A fee that is charged by an owner's association to cover the costs of operating the property.

Mall An enclosed public area connecting individual retail stores in a shopping center.

Management contract The contract between an owner of property and a management company, stipulating the duties, term, and fees to be paid to the management company.

Managing partner In a limited partnership, that partner who makes the decisions and bears the largest part of the risk.

Marginal property Property that is barely profitable to use.

Marginal tax rate The income tax rate charged on the last dollar of income.

Market analysis The study of the economic forces of supply and demand and their impact on real estate returns, risks, and values.

Market approach An appraisal method that values property based on the market value of similar buildings sold in a recent time period in a comparable market area.

Marketable title A title free of any defects.

Market research The research done to review market conditions in a specified area.

Market risk The likelihood of failing to meet expectations in the net operating income due to changes in the economic conditions in the marketplace.

Market value The price a qualified buyer is willing to pay for a property.

Master lease A controlling lease.

Maturity The date on which a loan is due.

Mechanic's lien A lien filed for nonpayment of a labor or material debt.

Meeting of the minds An agreement of all parties to a contract.

Merchant's Association An association set up by the merchants in a shopping center to promote the tenants' businesses.

Metes and bounds A land description giving the boundary lines of a parcel of land, together with their terminal points and angles.

Millage A rate used by local taxing authorities, equal to one-tenth of a cent.

Mini-warehouse A warehouse providing small storage areas for commercial and residential users.

Mixed-use project A planned development in which there are at least two different types of real estate projects involved.

Mobile home A factory manufactured dwelling without a permanent foundation, located on a fixed lot and connected to local utilities.

Mobile home park A subdivision of land used for mobile homes.

Model unit A representative unit in a property used to demonstrate the future appearance of the space.

Month-to-month tenancy A lease agreement cancelable each month.

Mortgage A legal instrument used to secure the payment of a debt or an obligation.

Mortgage banker An individual who originates, sells, and services mortgage loans.

Mortgage broker An individual who specializes in bringing a borrower and a lender together for a commission.

Mortgage commitment An agreement between a borrower and a lender, whereby the lender agrees to lend the borrower money at a future date, subject to the conditions of the commitment.

Mortgage correspondent An individual who will originate and service a loan for a fee.

Mortgagee One who holds a lien on a property as security for a loan.

Mortgage insurance Insurance that is used to protect a lender against any financial loss resulting from a mortgagor defaulting on a loan.

Mortgage lien An encumbrance on a property that is used to secure a mortgage loan.

Mortgage note A description of the debt and the promise by the mortgagor to repay.

Mortgage REIT A real estate investment trust that lends money on property.

Mortgage release A disclaimer of any further liability on the mortgage note issued by the mortgagee.

Mortgagor One who pledges property as security for a loan.

Mullion Metal strips that are placed at regular intervals along a window line. They are designed to receive a wall partition in a manner ensuring a smooth, soundproof connection.

Multi-family housing A residential structure with more than one dwelling unit in the same building.

N

Negative amortization A loan in which the loan balance increases rather than decreases overtime.

Negative cash flow When expenses exceed income.

Negative leverage Reverse leverage.

Negotiation The dealings between two or more parties to reach an agreement on terms and conditions of a transaction.

Neighborhood An area in which there are common characteristics of population and land use.

Neighborhood shopping center A small shopping center with a supermarket or drugstore as the anchor tenant and another 20 retail stores. The typical size is 50,000 square feet.

Net leasable area (NLA) The floor space that is leased to a tenant.

Net listing A listing in which the real estate commission is not added in.

Net net lease A lease agreement which the tenant pays the agreed-upon rent plus the utilities, real estate taxes, insurance, and maintenance.

Net net net lease An agreement in which the tenant pays all maintenance and operating expenses, plus the property taxes and insurance. Also called a triple net lease.

Net operating income (NOI) The income available after all expenses are paid out of the income received.

Net operating income multiplier The ratio of the sales or selling price to the net operating income of the property. The reciprocal is the overall capitalization rate.

Net present value (NPV) The present value of the cash inflow from an investment less the present value of the cash outflow.

Net (single) lease A lease agreement which the tenant pays the agreed-upon rent plus the utilities and real estate taxes.

Nondisturbance clause A mortgage clause providing for a continuation of any leases in the event of a loan foreclosure.

Non recourse No personal liability.

Normal wear and tear The physical depreciation that arises through ordinary use of a property.

Note A written promise to repay a specified amount to an entity on a specified date.

Notice of default A letter sent to a defaulting party as a reminder of the default.

Notice to quit A notice by a tenant to vacate the rental property.

Notorious possession Generally acknowledged possession of real property.

Null and void A contract that is not enforceable.

O

Obligee An individual in whose favor an obligation is entered into.

Obligor An individual who makes an obligation to another party.

Obsolescence A loss in property value brought about by changes in design, technology, taste, or demand.

Occupancy level A percentage of space that is currently rented.

Offer to purchase A buyer's purchase offer, which if accepted becomes a binding document.

Off-price shopping center A shopping center that consists of retail stores offering brand name merchandise usually found in specialty shops and department stores for 20 percent to 70 percent below the manufacturer's suggested price.

One-hundred percent location A location where a retail establishment will achieve the highest sales volume compared to other locations in a market area.

Open-ended mortgage A mortgage written to secure the advancement of additional funds over and above the original amount disbursed.

Open listing A listing contract under which the broker's commission is contingent upon the broker producing a buyer before the property is sold by the owner or another broker.

Open mortgage A mortgage that has matured or is overdue and is therefore subject to foreclosure at any time.

Operating expense ratio The ratio of the total operating expenses to the effective gross income.

Operating expenses The expenses essential to operating a property.

Operating lease A lease between the lessee and a sublessee who actually occupies and uses the property.

Operating leverage A financial technique where a small increase in the gross income results in a large increase in the net operating income.

Operating statement The financial statement that lists the income and expenses for an income property.

Opinion letter A written opinion of an attorney relating to the tax and legal consequences of certain aspects of a syndication.

Opinion of title A certificate, usually by an attorney, confirming the validity of the title to property being sold.

Option The right to purchase or lease property at an agreed-upon price within a specified time period.

Option fee The consideration paid by the optionee to obtain an option.

Option price The negotiated price the optionee is willing to pay to obtain the option.

Oral contract A verbal agreement.

Ordinary income As defined by the Internal Revenue Service, any income that is taxed at regular tax rates, such as fees, commissions, and interest.

Ordinary loss For tax purposes, loss that is deductible against ordinary income.

Organizational fee A fee that a general partner receives for his services in organizing a syndicate.

Origination fee A fee charged by a mortgage loan company for services rendered in connection with processing a loan application.

Other income The income that is derived from an income property, but not from the rental of the tenant space.

Other people's money (OPM) The use of borrowed funds for investment purposes.

Outstanding loan balance The amount currently outstanding on a loan.

Overage lease Additional rental charged in some retail leases based on a percentage of sales over a predetermined sales base.

Overall capitalization rate An investment rule of thumb equal to the net operating income divided by the total costs or sales price.

Overall rate of return (ORR) The percentage of net operating income divided by the purchase price of a property, the capitalization rate.

Overimprovement A land or building use that is considered too intense.

P

Parcel A piece of property that is under one ownership.

Partial release The removal of a general mortgage lien from a specific portion of the property pledged.

Partial taking In a condemnation, the taking of only a part of the property or property rights.

Participation loan A loan whereby the lender will participate in the future cash flow and resale profits of a property.

Partition The division of property between those who own the property with undivided interest.

Partnership An association of two or more individuals as co-owners for the purpose of carrying on a business for profit.

Partnership agreement An agreement between partners describing the duties and rights of each party.

Passive income Income derived from rents, royalties, dividends, interest, and gains from the sale of securities.

Passive investor An individual who invests money in an investment but does not take an active part in management.

Pass-through Expenses or a portion of expenses associated with tenancy that are "passed through" from the landlord and paid by the tenant.

Payback method Rules of thumb that result in multipliers for real estate investment criteria.

Payback period Rules of thumb that result in years, for the benefits of an investment, usually income or cash flow, to repay the total cost or equity costs of the investment.

Penalty A fee charged for breaking the law or violating the terms of a contract.

Percentage lease A lease in which the rental is based on a percentage of the gross business conducted by the lessee.

Percolation test A test designed to measure the drainage characteristics of soil.

Performance bond A bond issued by an insurance company to guarantee completion of a construction contract.

Perimeter space A prescribed area at the outer periphery of a building.

Permanent financing A long-term mortgage on a piece of real property.

Personal guarantee A guarantee given by an individual to endorse a note or obligation.

Personal income tax rates The federal tax rates that are applied to personal income to measure the tax liability due the government.

Personal property A possession or item that is not real property, personalty.

Personalty All the assets that are not permanently attached to the land.

Phantom income Income that is taxed but that might not have been received.

Physical depreciation The loss in value of property from all causes of age and action of the elements.

Physical life The length of time that a building is a sound structure, dependent on the quality of maintenance.

Piggyback loan A combination construction and permanent loan.

Planned unit development (PUD) A zoning classification that allows flexibility in the design of a subdivision.

Plat A plan or map of a specific land area.

Plat book A public record that contains the maps of land and the division of streets.

Pledged account mortgage (PAM) A mortgage in which the mortgagor must pledge a sum of money at loan closing to be set aside to be used to supplement periodic mortgage payments.

Plot plan A diagram showing the proposed or existing use of a specific parcel of land.

Plumbing walls The walls that are provided along areas, as in the kitchen and bathrooms, where there are no provisions for pipe shafts.

Points A charge made by a lender equal to one percentage point of the principal loan amount.

Possessions The right of an owner to occupy property. When property is occupied by a tenant, the owner has constructive possession by right of title.

Power of attorney An instrument granting another person the right to act as an agent of the grantor.

Power of sale A mortgage clause giving the lender the right to sell the property upon default.

Preclosing A rehearsal of the closing.

Prelease To obtain a lease commitment prior to the certificate of occupancy.

Preliminary cost estimates The first cost estimates, which are usually considered "ballpark" figures. These figures are arrived at prior to more detailed analysis.

Premium The cost of an insurance policy.

Prepaid expenses Expenses paid prior to the period that they cover.

Prepayment clause A mortgage clause defining the terms of early payment of the mortgage loan.

Prepayment penalty A penalty charged by a lender for early retirement of a loan.

Presale The sale of a property prior to its completion.

Prescription The acquisition of rights to property through adverse possession.

Present value A sum of money, which if invested today at a specified interest rate, would be equivalent to a specified amount of money in the future.

Present value of future selling price The amount of the expected future selling price times the present value of $1.00 factor.

Preventive maintenance A program designed to regularly inspect the various physical aspects of a property.

Primary lease A lease between the owner and a tenant whose interest, all or part, has been sublet.

Prime rate The rate of interest charged by a lender to its most credit-worthy borrowers.

Prime tenant An anchor tenant in a commercial property.

Principal The major party in a transaction.

Principal amount The amount of the mortgage loan.

Principal and interest payment (P & I) The periodic loan payment, usually paid monthly, of both the principal reduction and the interest due.

Private limited partnership A limited partnership in which the shares are not offered to the general public and having a relatively small number of investors.

Private mortgage insurance (PMI) Insurance coverage on a mortgage that pays off in case of a default.

Procuring cause A broker will be regarded as the procuring cause of a transaction, so as to be entitled to the real estate commission, if his efforts are the foundation on which the negotiations resulted in a closing.

Profit and loss statement A statement showing the operating results of a property.

Proforma A projection of future income and expenses.

Project A proposed development plan for a property.

Projection The estimate of the future performance of a property.

Promoter A syndicator.

Property The rights that an individual has in lands or goods to the exclusion of all others.

Property line The recorded boundary of a parcel of land.

Property management The operation of property as a business.

Property management fee A fee that is received by a management company for services rendered, usually based on a percentage of the income collected.

Property residual technique In appraisal, a method for estimating the value of a property based on the estimated future income and the reversionary value of the improvements and land.

Property rights The legal rights and responsibilities associated with ownership, typically called the "bundle of rights."

Property taxes A tax levied by a local government on the assessed value of a piece of property.

Proprietary lease A document giving a shareholder in a cooperative the right to occupy a unit under certain terms and conditions.

Prorations The prepaid or accrued expenses that are due at the time of sale and are split between the buyer and seller.

Prospectus A document that describes the details of an investment offering.

Public limited partnership A limited partnership in which the shares are offered to the general public, thus having a large number of investors.

Public sale An auction sale of a property with notice to the general public.

Punch list A list of items that need to be finished or corrected prior to a sale.

Purchase contract A formal agreement in which the seller agrees to sell and the buyer agrees to buy a property.

Purchase money mortgage A mortgage that the purchaser gives the seller simultaneously with the purchase of real estate to secure the unpaid balance of the purchase price.

Q

Quadraplex Four dwelling units that are connected or under one roof.

Quiet enjoyment A covenant, usually inserted into a lease that conveys on the part of the landlord a promise that the tenant shall enjoy possession of the premises in peace and without disturbances.

Quiet title suit A suit to remove a defect, cloud, or questionable claim against the title to the property.

Quitclaim deed A deed in which the grantor conveys whatever interest he may have in the property without even implying that any interest exists.

R

Rate of return The percentage return on an investment.

Raw land Unimproved land.

Ready, willing, and able An individual capable of either buying or selling a piece of property.

Real estate Land and the attached improvements, including any minerals and resources inherent to the land.

Real estate broker Any person or entity, who is licensed by a state authority, to sell or lease property on behalf of others.

Real estate commission A fee paid to a real estate broker or agent when a transaction is consummated.

Real estate cycle A period of time during which real property goes through predevelopment to maturity to decline, and then renovation or demolition.

Real estate investment strategy An overall investment plan in which the real estate investor makes a set of decisions that helps to achieve their goals.

Real estate investment trust (REIT) A trust that invests in real estate. By law, 95 percent of the profits must be distributed to the investors.

Real estate security A form of personal property that is secured by real property and which is evidence of real estate ownership or indebtedness.

Realized gain In an exchange, a gain that has occurred financially, but is not necessarily taxed.

Realtors© A registered trademark term reserved for the sole use of active members of local boards of REALTORS© affiliated with the National Association of REALTORS©.

Realty Real estate.

Recapture The amount of gain charged by the IRS on the sale of depreciable property taken by the excess depreciation taken over the straight line depreciation.

Recapture clause A contract clause permitting the party who grants an interest or right to take it back under certain conditions.

Recognized gain In an exchange, the portion of gain that is taxable.

Recording Filing a legal document in the public records of a county.

Recourse loan A loan in which the borrower is personally liable for the debt in the event of a default.

Recreational property Homesites with recreational amenities, including campgrounds and recreational vehicle parks, or properties that offer fishing, boating, skiing, hunting, or other such activities.

Recycling The process of reclaiming an old building for an adaptive re-use.

Redemption period A period in which a former owner can reclaim foreclosed property.

Red herring A proposed prospectus that has not been approved by the Securities and Exchange Commission (SEC) or the state securities commission.

Refinancing The process of paying off an old loan with a new loan.

Regional shopping center The largest type of shopping center with two to five major department stores as anchors and from 100 to 150 smaller retail stores. Usually the centers are called "malls" and are enclosed. These centers range from 400,000 to more than 1,000,000 square feet.

Regulation D A regulation of the Securities and Exchange Commission (SEC) that sets forth the conditions necessary for a private placement exemption.

Rehabilitation Renovating property for use or for resale.

Rehabilitation tax credit A tax credit for expenditures to rehabilitate nonresidential buildings placed in service prior to 1939. The rehabilitated property must be depreciated by using the straight-line method in order to qualify for this tax credit.

Release clause A mortgage clause allowing the release of the pledged property after full payment of the debt.

Relocation clause A clause in a lease that gives the landlord the right to relocate a tenant.

Renegotiate To legally revise the terms of a contract.

Renegotiated rate mortgage (RRM) A mortgage in which the mortgage interest rate is adjusted over the term of the loan.

Renewal option An option to renew a lease at a specified term and rent.

Rent The consideration received from a lessee for the use of the occupied space.

Rentable area Net rentable area. The following three methods can be used.

1. International Association of Building Owners and Managers (BOMA). From the inside of the outside wall (or in new buildings from the glass line) to the outside of the inside wall (or hall wall), and center to center on the division walls. Columns are included.
2. General Services Administration (GSA). Same as above except all columns, division walls, service closets, etc., are included. Net usable space only. In making leases to the federal government, this method must be used.
3. New York Method. Space is measured right across the floor from the glass line, subtracting only the elevator shafts and stairwells. In the case of multiple occupancy on one floor, the common space—usable and nonusable—is apportioned among the tenants according to the size of their respective areas.

Rental concessions Concessions given by the lessor to the lessee to induce the lessee to sign a lease.

Rent control Regulation by a local governing board restricting the amount of rent a lessee can charge to tenants.

Rent roll A balance sheet for the account of each tenant, listing the name, unit number, lease term, and rent.

Rent schedule A listing of the rent levels for the various types of units in a property.

Rent-up period The period of time it takes for a property to become fully rented up following the completion of construction.

Repairs Work performed to return property to a former condition without exceeding its useful life.

Replacement cost approach An appraisal method in which the value is based on the estimated cost to replace the improvements less any depreciation plus the appraised value of the land.

Replacement reserve A cash reserve for the future replacement of fixed assets.

Reproduction cost The cost to duplicate a property as of a certain date.

Resale proceeds The profit an individual receives after selling a property and deducting all sales expenses.

Rescind To withdraw a contract.

Rescission A cancellation of a contract.

Reserve fund An account set aside for funding upcoming capital expenditures or negative cash flow.

Residential property Real estate that is intended for the owner's living quarters.

Resident manager An individual who supervises the care of an apartment property while residing in one of the apartment units.

Restriction A limitation that is placed on the use of a property.

Resyndication A partnership that has been resold to new investors.

Retainage An amount of money that is held back in a construction contract until the contractor has completed contractual obligations.

Retire a mortgage To pay off a mortgage.

Return of capital The return of the original investor's capital contribution, not directly taxable.

Return on equity The amount that is returned to the investor on his original contribution, expressed as a percentage.

Revenue sharing The profit and tax benefit split between the general partners and the limited partners.

Reverse annuity mortgage A mortgage that is designed for the elderly with substantial equity, in which the lender periodically pays an amount to the borrower, creating negative amortization.

Reverse leverage A situation in which the financial benefits from ownership accrue at a lower rate than the mortgage interest rate.

Reversion The right of a landlord to possess leased property upon the termination of a lease.

Revisions Changes in the work that require the architect to provide substitute drawings or revise the original working drawings.

Rider An attachment to a contract.

Right of redemption The right to recover property that has been transferred by a mortgage or lien by paying off the debt prior to or after a foreclosure.

Right of survivorship A right that entitles one owner of a property that is held jointly to take title to it when the other owner dies.

Right-of-way The right or privilege to pass across the lands of another, an easement.

Riparian rights A legal theory of water rights. It maintains that the use of the water belongs to the natural users, especially those adjacent to it.

Risk The possibility that the financial return of an investment will not be as expected.

Risk return relationship The financial principle that recognizes that in order to obtain a chance at a high rate of return, the investor will have to take a high risk.

Rod A linear unit of measurement equal to 16½ feet.

Rollover mortgage A mortgage loan amortized over a long-term with the interest rate adjusted periodically.

Rollover option An option agreement in which the potential buyer has the right to renew the option one or more times upon the payment of a specified amount.

Rules of thumb Shorthand benchmarks used to calculate investment decisions. Common examples are the gross rent multipliers and the overall capitalization rate.

S

Sale The transfer from one entity to another entity, for a consideration, of the possession and right of use of some particular article of value to both parties.

Sale leaseback A commercial financing technique where the owner of the property sells to an investor, who then leases the property back to the original property owner.

Sales contract An agreement by which a buyer and seller agree to the terms of a sale.

Salvage value The amount realized at the final sale of an asset at the end of its useful life.

Sandwich lease A lease that is held by a lessee who becomes a lessor when he sublets his space.

Save harmless To indemnify another, to secure another against loss or damage or claims to a third party.

Savings and Loan Association (S & L) A financial institution established to accept members' deposits and to make real estate loans.

Scheduled gross income The rental rate of a property multiplied by the total rental space.

Schematic design A design concerning the building program resulting from inspection of the site and conferences with the architect's client. The client's needs and requirements are carefully analyzed together with the local zoning regulations, and proposed construction budget.

Seasoned loan A mortgage loan in which many payments have been collected.

Secondary financing A loan secured by a second mortgage on real property.

Section of land One square mile.

Securities and Exchange Commission (SEC) The Federal agency created by the Securities Exchange Act of 1934 that administers said act. The act outlaws misrepresentations in any securities offerings.

Securities Instruments that signify an ownership position in a corporation or a limited partnership.

Security deposit The amount of money required to be paid by a tenant at the start of the lease term to cover any damage to the property over and above normal wear and tear.

Security interest An interest in property in which the real estate serves as collateral.

Seed money Monies that are needed to begin a real estate transaction.

Self-amortizing mortgage A mortgage loan that will retire itself through periodic payments of principal and interest.

Selling expenses Those expenses incurred by the seller on a particular piece of property during the money raising or resale period.

Selling group The group of dealers appointed by the syndicate manager to underwrite the offering.

Seller's market In a real estate marketplace, when there are more buyers than sellers, enabling the seller to obtain a higher sales price.

Sensitivity analysis The multiple analyses of future cash flow, resale, and rates of return on an investment using different assumptions each time.

Settlement The process at the closing of a sale of real estate, whereby the broker usually accounts to the principal for the earnest money and deducts his real estate commission by use of a form of closing or settlement statement.

Shared appreciation mortgage (SAM) A mortgage in which the lender reduces the interest rate below market rate and then shares in the future appreciation of the property.

Shared equity mortgage (SEM) A mortgage in which an outside investor puts up all or part of the equity requirements and shares in the future benefits of the property.

Shop drawings Construction drawings that are made by various construction trades that reflect items on the contract documents. Shop drawings speak both the language of the trade and the shop in which the work is to be completed.

Shopping center A collection of retail stores with a common parking area.

Short-term capital gains A gain on the sale of a capital asset that was held under the prescribed time period to achieve a long term capital gain.

Sign restriction clause A lease restriction prohibiting the use of a particular type of signage.

Single-family housing A type of residential dwelling designed to house one family.

Sinking fund A fund set aside, which when compounded will equal a specified sum after a specified time period.

Site A plot of land.

Slab The reinforced concrete floor between the beams, supporting columns, and the walls.

Slum An area of a city in which the properties are deteriorating.

Social obsolescence A loss in value brought about by the social conditions of an area.

Soft construction costs The costs of constructing and leasing a building other than the costs of building the actual physical structure.

Soft dollars Money that does not improve the equity position of the payor, such as prepaid interest or fees paid to the seller.

Sole proprietorship A form of ownership in which there is only one individual owner.

Sources and applications of funds The funding analysis of where the funds come from and how they are applied.

Space analysis An analysis of an existing office situation to locate problem areas and to provide a basis for judgment in evaluating major changes. It can also be the form of a planning tool that will be used by the client in developing a planning situation.

Space planning The process and act of laying out and designing space for the tenant's needs.

Special assessment A charge against the real estate made by a unit of the government to cover the proportionate cost of an improvement, such as a street or sewer.

Special lien A lien that affects or is attached to only a certain specific parcel of land or a piece of property.

Special purpose building A structure that is designed for the particular needs of its occupant, such as a restaurant or a bowling alley.

Special warranty deed A deed in which the grantor limits the title warranty given to the grantee to anyone claiming by, from, through, or under him, the grantor, the grantor does not warrant against any title defects.

Specifications A list of instructions provided with working drawings detailing the material and how the property will be constructed.

Specific performance An action that forces the performance of an agreement.

Specified fund A fund in which the properties to be purchased are already selected.

Speculation The acquisition of a property not for use but for resale at a high profit, often after only a short holding period.

Speculative building A building where construction is undertaken without the prior commitment from a prime tenant or tenants.

Square footage The area measured in square feet.

Staging area A place to store and work with materials and equipment prior to their movement into the space where they will finally be used.

Standby fee A fee paid by a borrower to a lender to provide a standby loan.

Standby loan A loan made available to a borrower at a specified interest rate for a specified time period in the future.

Standard tenant improvement allowance An allowance for the building of tenant improvements at no extra cost to the tenant.

Statue of frauds A state law that requires certain classes of contracts, engagements, and/or transfers of interest in real estate to be made in writing in order to be enforceable in a court of law.

Stepped-up basis An accounting term used to describe a change in the adjusted tax basis of property, allowed for certain transactions.

Stick-built A method of construction that uses wood frame construction.

Stipulations The terms and conditions outlined within a written contract.

Stop clause A lease clause stipulating an amount of operating expenses above which the tenant must bear.

Straight-line depreciation method The depreciation method allowed by the Internal Revenue Service (IRS), calculated by dividing the depreciable basis by its useful life as determined by the Internal Revenue Code.

Straw man An individual who purchases property for another individual who wishes to conceal his identity.

Strip center A retail shopping center that is a straight line of stores, usually narrow in proportion to its length.

Structure Any constructed improvements to a site.

Subchapter S corporation A corporation with a limited number of stockholders that elects not to be taxed as a regular corporation. The tax benefits can be passed through to the individual stockholders. Corporate limited liability is still available.

Subdivision A tract of land that is surveyed and divided into smaller lots for the purpose of resale or development.

Subject to To acquire property with an existing mortgage, but not becoming personally liable for the debt.

Sublease A lease given to another by a tenant for a part of the leased premises or for a specified term.

Subordinated ground lease A ground lease in which the owner places his right in relation to the structure behind that of others, such as the holder of the construction or permanent mortgage loan.

Subordination In mortgage terms, being secondary, a mortgagee or lien holder is willing to accept payment after another creditor.

Subordination clause A mortgage clause prohibiting a mortgage to be recorded at a later date which mortgage would have priority over an existing mortgage.

Subrogation The act of replacing one person with another in regard to a legal right, interest, or obligation. Substituting, such as an insured transferring the claim rights to the insurance carrier in return for direct payment of the loss.

Subscription The signing of a binding contract to purchase an interest in a syndicated security.

Substitution clause That portion of the work letter that specifies what materials may be substituted for the standard construction materials ordinarily supplied by the landlord.

Sum of the years' digits depreciation method A depreciation method that results in a higher depreciation than that of straight line depreciation, by allowing depreciation based on the inverted scale of the total of digits for the years of the useful life.

Super-regional center A shopping center that provides an extensive variety of general merchandise. It is usually built around three or more department stores with at least 100,000 square feet each. The total center consists of a minimum of 750,000 square feet.

Supply and demand The principle stating that prices will increase as the supply of the product is decreased, or will decrease when there is an oversupply of the product.

Surety One who guarantees the performance of another.

Survey The measurement and description of a piece of land by a surveyor.

Surveyor An individual who prepares a survey.

Survivorship The right of a joint tenant or tenants to maintain ownership following the death of another joint tenant.

Sweat equity The equity the investor creates by labor performed.

Syndicate Any general or limited partnership, joint venture, or other type organization that is formed for the sole purpose of investing in a property for a profit.

Syndication The action taken by the syndicate to acquire a property.

Syndicator An individual whose business it is to sell investments in real estate partnerships.

T

Take-out mortgage loan A mortgage loan that takes out a construction loan at a specified time.

Tax A government levy usually made on a regular basis and based on the relative value of the object being levied.

Taxable income The portion of income after all allowable deductions are taken that is subject to tax.

Tax deductible An expense that may reduce the taxable income.

Tax deferred income The cash flow that is received in a given year, but in which no taxes are currently due because of tax shelter.

Tax-free exchange An exchange of property for other property of like kind, resulting in no immediate tax effect, because the taxes are deferred.

Tax map A map showing the location and dimensions of parcels of property that are subject to property taxes.

Tax preference items Certain types of income or deductions that are added to the adjusted gross income to calculate the alternative minimum tax.

Tax rate The ratio of tax assessed to the amount being taxed.

Tax sale A sale of property held for the nonpayment of taxes.

Tax sheltered Income that is not subject to a tax.

Tenant One who pays rent to occupy real estate.

Tenancy at sufferance A tenancy that is established when a lease has expired and the tenant remains on the property.

Tenancy at will A license to use or occupy property at the will of the owner.

Tenancy by the entirety An estate that exists only between a husband and wife with equal rights of possession and enjoyment during their joint lives and with the right of survivorship.

Tenancy for years A lease for a fixed period of time.

Tenancy in common Ownership by two or more individuals who have undivided interests in a particular piece of property without the right of survivorship. The undivided interests do not have to be equal.

Tenancy in severalty The ownership of property by one person or one legal entity.

Tender To make an offer.

Term The time period within which a loan must be repaid.

Terminal value The economic worth of an investment at the time of the sale.

Terms The conditions and arrangements specified in a contract.

Testament A will.

Testate Having made a valid will.

Testator A person who makes a will.

Theme/specialty center A shopping center that is diverse in format, size, and market orientation. These centers usually have a common architectural design throughout the center. These centers are usually anchored by restaurants and entertainment facilities that appeal to tourists and the local market. The tenants usually offer unusual merchandise.

Time is of the essence A phrase used in a contract that requires that all references to specific dates and times of day noted in the contract be interpreted exactly.

Time sharing A type of ownership in which a property is held by a number of individuals for a specified time period.

Time value of money The concept that the value of money is related to when the money is received.

Title The legal evidence of an individual's right to ownership of real property.

Title company A company that examines the title to property and then issues title insurance.

Title defect Any legal right held by others to claim property or to make demands upon the owner.

Title insurance Insurance issued against the loss or damage from defects or failure of title to a particular piece of property.

Title report A document that indicates the current state of the title.

Title search An examination of the public records, laws and court decisions to discover the current facts regarding the ownership of property.

Title theory The theory of mortgage law that views the existence of a mortgage as a conveyance to title from the borrower to the lender.

Topography The features of the land's surface, such as hills, valleys, etc.

Townhouse A type of single family housing built as an attached or semi-detached row house.

Township A six-square-mile parcel of land.

Tract In some states a unit of subdivided land that is numbered and recorded with the county recorder's office.

Trades A classification of worker skills: carpenters, plumbers, etc.

Trade fixtures Articles that are installed by a tenant under terms of a lease and removed by the tenant prior to the lease expiration.

Traffic flow study A study made by a traffic consultant to review the vehicular traffic patterns. A study completed by an interior space planner regarding the interactions among different departments and operations to create better function and communications.

Traffic report A record of the prospects who inquired about renting a property.

Transaction costs The costs associated with the buying and selling of property.

Transfer tax A tax that is charged on the transfer of an asset or mortgage.

Triple A tenant A tenant that has a triple A credit rating, considered a prime tenant.

Triple net lease A lease in which the lessor receives a net amount, and the lessee pays the taxes, insurance, and all the maintenance expenses.

Triplex Three dwelling units that are connected under one roof.

Trust An arrangement whereby a property is transferred to or held by a third party or trustee.

Trust deed A conveyance of property to a third party to be held for the benefit of another.

Trustee A person holding property in trust.

Trustees deed A deed executed by a trustee that conveys land held in a trust.

Trustor A grantor of property to a trustee.

Turnaround property A property that with creative planning and hard work can be made to return a positive cash flow.

Turnkey project A development in which a developer completes an entire project and then turns the property over to a buyer.

U

Underwriter An individual or corporation that coordinates the process of raising the investor money.

Undivided interest An ownership right to use and possess a property with others.

Unencumbered property Property with free and clear title.

Unilateral contract An obligation given by one party that is contingent on the performance of another party, but without obligation of the second party to perform.

Unimproved property Land that has no improvements.

Unit A pro-rated share of ownership in a limited partnership. A single dwelling.

Unleveraged Purchased for cash.

Unleveraged program A limited partnership that invests in a property with 50 percent or less of the property mortgaged.

Unpaid mortgage principal The outstanding balance on the loan.

Unrealized gain The excess of the current market value over the cost for the asset that is unsold.

Usable area Any area in a given floor that could be used by a tenant. This area includes a point from the perimeter glass line to the demising walls; it also includes the column areas within such a space.

Useful life In appraisal for the purpose of sale, the true economic value of a structure in terms of years of use to the owner.

Use clause A lease provision indicating the purpose for which the leased space will be used.

Usury Excessive interest charged by a lender as determined by state law.

Utilities Essential services, usually including electric, gas, water, sewer, and telephone.

Utility easement An easement for the use of laying the utilities.

V

Vacancy factor A property's anticipated percentage of vacancy.

Vacant land Land that is unimproved.

Vacate To move out.

Value The worth or usefulness of a good or service, expressed in terms of a specific sum of money.

Variable expenses The operating expenses, paid by the owner, that tend to vary with the occupancy of the property.

Variable rate mortgage (VRM) A mortgage with interest that varies with a specified index rate, an adjustable rate mortgage.

Vendee A purchaser of real property.

Vendor A seller of real property.

Veterans Administration (VA) A governmental agency that provides home loans for eligible veterans.

Void Having no legal force.

Volume per square feet This method of estimating probable total construction cost by multiplying the adjusted gross building volume in square feet by a predetermined cost per unit of volume.

Voluntary lien A lien placed on property with the full consent of its owner.

W

Warehousing a loan The packaging of a number of mortgages with the intent to sell them in the secondary mortgage market.

Warranty A promise contained in a contract.

Warranty deed An instrument of conveyance containing an agreement by the grantee to defend the premises against the lawful claims of a third party and an assurance that he is the property owner and will defend the title given.

Wet columns Columns where provisions are made to have a plumbing fixture for drinking, sinks, and so on; the pipes are taken through the small enclosure (chase) against the column.

Wholesaler A middleman who coordinates the raising of equity.

Will The disposition of one's property that takes place after one's death.

Without recourse A mortgage that secures a note without recourse, which allows the lender to look only to the property in the event of a default.

Working capital The difference between the current assets and current liabilities.

Working drawings Detailed floor-space plans that diagram all the improvements to be made. They are designed as instructions to the various contractors involved.

Work letter That part of the lease that states in detail all the work to be completed for the tenant by the landlord.

Workout loan A loan in which the lender has agreed to reduce the debt service payment to avoid foreclosure of the property.

Wraparound mortgage A mortgage that secures a debt and also includes the balance due under the existing debt plus any new funds advanced.

Write-off The excess deductions from an investment which may be used to offset income taxes on income from other sources.

Y

Yield A rate of return as calculated by the profit earned on the investment over a specified time period.

Z

Zoning The act of a governing authority that specifies the uses for which property may be used or developed in a specific area.

Index

A

Absorption cycle (AC), 10
AC. *See* Absorption cycle (AC)
Accelerated amortization mortgage, 387
Accountant, 160
Accounting/draw requests/payment of billings, 187
Accounting system, 570
  accounting chart of accounts, 571, *illus.* 572
  accrual method of accounting, 570
  cash method of accounting, 570
  management of accounting, 571
  monthly accounting report, 571, *illus.* 573–77, 577–78
  use of computer, 578
Accrual mortgage, 385
Adjustable rate mortgage, 386
Advertising, 511, 529
Advertising agencies, 159, 186, 496
Aerials photography, 60, *illus.* 69, 70, 71
After-tax cash flow, 304, *illus.* 305, 306
After-tax cash flow multiplier, 327
After-tax equity reversion, 325
After-tax rate (ATR), 327
Agreements, 187
Air pollution regulations, 134, 142
Air traffic, 130–32
Agricultural zoning, 123
All-adult rental housing, marketing, 26
All-inclusive trust deed, 411
Amenity package, 193
Anchor tenant:
  office space user, 29
  retail center, 28
  space planning, 271–72
Annual loan constant (ALC), 402
Application and certification for payment form, *illus.* 484
Appraisal, 94, *illus.* 316
Appraisal process, 396
  outline, 397–401

Appraised value to total cost ratio, 329
Appraiser, 158
Archeological sites, 78
Architect/engineer:
  cost estimations, 151–52
  design team, 154
  inspection reports, 212
  master planning design, 182–83
  selecting, 163
Architect selection form, *illus.* 228
Architect's inspection report form, *illus.* 230
Asbestos, 142
Asset manager, 159
Athletic/sporting club single purpose building, 32
Attorney, 160, 200
Auction companies, 65
Average rate of return, 328

B

Backdoor approach to financial feasibility, 312, *illus.* 313
Before-tax cash flow, 304, 566
Before-tax cash flow multiplier, 327
Bidding documents, 248
Bidding/negotiations, 254
Blanket mortgage, 388
Blue sky law, 430
BOMA. *See* Building Owners and Managers Association (BOMA)
Bonds:
  bid/proposal, 456
  labor/material payment, 457
  maintenance, 457
  performance, 457
  release of lien, 457
  special indemnity, 457
  surety, 456
Boundary/topographical surveys, 75, 179, *illus.* 180, 181

Bowling alley single purpose building, 32
Break-even cash flow ratio, 326
Bridge loan, 361
Brokerage commission, 93
Brokers/leasing agents, 159, 528
Budget, managing, 164–68
    during construction seed money/equity
        advances, 166–68
    preconstruction/preclosing seed money, 166
    predevelopment seed money, 165
    site selection seed money, 165
Budget, predevelopment, 164, *illus.* 168,
    illus. 170
    management, 166–69, *illus.* 168, *illus.* 170,
        illus. 172
    and strategic planning, 186
Budget forecast form, *illus.* 581
Building codes, 138–39
Building description, 147–48
Building/development fees, 125
Building Owners and Managers Association
    (BOMA), 559
Bulk-distribution industrial property, 30
Business directories, 527
Business lodging property users, 31
Business parks office buildings, 30
Buy down mortgage, 388
Buying/holding land for future development, 3
Buy-sell agreement, 361

C

CACI, 73
Capital expenditures, 566
Car care center retail property, 28
Cash downpayment, 92
Cash flow, 435
    development reward, 15
Cash flow/operating proforma, 301
Chamber of commerce, 71
Change order request form, *illus.* 486
Chattle mortgage, 388
Chemicals for clearing/landscaping, 142
City/county zoning boards, 129
Civil engineer, 155
Closing cost, 92–93
Closing date, 92
Closing extension, 93
Closing prorations, 93
Closing sale, 531–32
Cluster housing, 24

CMO. *See* Collateralized mortgage obligations
    (CMO)
Code synopsis, 153
    form, *illus.* 225
Cold calling, 528
Collateralized mortgage obligations (CMO), 383
Commercial banks, 358
Commercial data form, *illus.* 540
Commercial interior design, 261–64
Commercial lease summary form, *illus.* 542
Commercial measurements, 257, *illus.* 258
Commercial property:
    industrial, 30–31
    lodging, 31
    mixed-use developments, 31–32
    office, 29–30
    other types, 32
    retail, 27–29
Commercial tenant, mini warehouse property,
    31
Commercial Times, 65
Commercial zoning, 124
Commitment dates form, *illus.* 476
Community center retail property, 27–28
    acreage size of, 29
Community politics/issues, 76–78
Compaction tests, 181
Compromise, 7
Computers, 331–32, 578
    Software Directory, 332
Condemnation proceedings, 93
Condominium, 24
    commercial property, 32
Construction administration, 183, 185,
    254–55
Construction cost, controlling, 447
    bid award contracts, 447–48
    cost-plus contract, 448–49
    fast track/guaranteed maximum/negotiated
        contract, 448
    fixed price incentive contract, 449
    fixed price prospective price
        redetermination, 449
    lump-sum contract, 449
    lump-sum with escalation contract, 449
    unit pricing contract, 449
Construction cost analysis form, *illus.* 226
Construction cost estimates, 185
Construction costs form, 480
Construction costs/schedules control, 6,
    195–96

Construction documents, 233–34
    bidding documents, 248
    bidding/negotiations, 254
    construction administration, 254–55
    construction documentation, 248, *illus.* 253
    contract documents, 248, 252, 254
    design development phase, 245–48, *illus.*
        250–51
    design process, *illus.* 235
    master planning phase, 237–43
    master site plan, *illus.* 238
    site plan, *illus.* 239
    research/planning design phase, 234,
        236–37
    schematic design phase, 243, *illus.* 244,
        illus. 249
Construction expenses, preclosing seed
    money, 166
Construction loan, 359
    bridge loan, 361
    buy-sell agreement, 361
    commitment, 363–81
    forward commitment, 360–61
    gap loan, 361
    issues, 362–63
    loan participation, 361
    open-ended mortgage, 360
    piggyback mortgage, 360
    standby/take-out loan, 60
Construction management fee, 15
Construction manager, 154
    general contractor, 157
    job superintendent, 157
    materials supplier, 157
    quality/assurance/quality control, 157
    subcontractor, 157
    tenant construction contractor, 157
    testing service, 157
Construction preparations, 232–33
    creating documents, 233–55
    design forms, 288–89
    design team members, 255–56
    miscellaneous design criteria, 256–71
    plans/specifications reviewing checklist,
        276–88
    tenant development design, 271–76
Construction process, 437–38
    change order requests, 471
    construction draws, 471
    construction management progress reports,
        471–72

contractor/developer agreements, 450–53
    controlling costs, 447
    cost monitoring, 460–63
    development/building permits, 471
    final as-built survey, 472
    final inspection, 472
    insurance/risk containment, 453–57
    management process, 457
        contractor's team/responsibilities, 460,
            illus. 461
        preconstruction meeting, 457–60
    mobilization, 471
    owner's operation/material manual,
        472–74
    punching out building, 472
    quality assurance/control, 466, 468
        proposals, 468–70
    role of general contractor, 438–40
    schedule summary form, 474, *illus.* 475
    scheduling, 463–466, *illus.* 467
    selecting general contractor, 440–56
    strategies, 445–47
        construction methods, *illus.* 446
        design-build, 445
        few primes, 445
        force account, 447
        general contractor, 445
        joint venture, 447
        multiple primes, 445
    warranties callback period, 472
Construction reports, 211–13
Construction scheduling, 463, *illus.* 464–65,
    465, *illus.* 467
Consultants, selection of, 163
    meeting schedule/monthly reports, 212
    team player checklist form, *illus.* 224
Consumer marketing study, 38
Contract documents, 248, 252, 254
    from proposals to, 268–71
Contractor/developer:
    agreements, 450–53
    cost monitoring, 460, 462–63
Contractor organizational chart, *illus.* 461
Contractor selection, 185
    form, *illus.* 229
Contractor's insurance, 455
Contracts, predevelopment, 164
Convenience center (strip center) retail
    property, 27
Convention lodging property users, 31
Conversions, for-sale housing, 25

Convertible mortgage, 387
Conveyance, 93
Cooperative, 24
Corporate suites rental housing, marketing, 26
Corporation, 54
Cost control report form, *illus.* 231
Cost monitoring, contractor/developer, 460,
    462–63
Cost/pricing estimation, 150
    architectural/engineering, 152
    contractor, 152
    graphics designer, 152
    interior design, 152
    landscape architecture, 152
County planning/zoning, 67, 71
County plat books, 68
County tax books, 68
Credential, 16
Credit companies, 381
Criss-cross directories, 527
Crittenden Newsletter, 354
Customer mentality, 8

D

Day care/education single purpose building, 32
DC. *See* Down cycle (DC)
DCR. *See* Debt coverage ratio (DCR)
Deal contingencies, 94–95
Debt coverage ratio (DCR), 402
Debt/equity financing, 157–58, 187
Debt service coverage ratio (DSCR), 325
Delay claims analysis phase, 196–97
Demographic information companies, 72–73
Demographic site studies, 58
Demographic study, components of, *illus.* 59
Department of Transportation (DOT), 72
Depreciation, 320
    tables, *illus.* 321–22
Deregulation of savings and loan industry,
    600–601
Design/construction scheduling, 178, 195
Design costs form, 479
Design development phase, 245–46, *illus.*
    250–51
    exterior design/use of materials, 257, 259
    interior design specialty issues, 259–64
    landscape architectural design, 264, *illus.*
        265–66, 267
    space measurement, 256–57, *illus.* 258
Design fees/expenses, 165, 166

Design forms, 288, *illus.* 289
Design process, *illus.* 235
Design research/planning, 234, 236–37
    schematic design, 243, *illus.* 244, *illus.* 249
Design study, 38, 121
Design team, predevelopment:
    architect, 154
    graphics designer, 155
    interior designer, 154
    land architect, 154
    land planner, 154
    schedule 173, *illus.* 176
    space planner, 154
Design team members, 255
    relationships/composition, 255–56
Detailed construction schedule, 463, *illus.*
    465
Detailed foundation and superstructure
    schedule, 463, *illus.* 464
Developers:
    decision to pass on venture, 200
    "go" "no go" decision, 197–98
    setting up development files, 201–11
    types of, 18
Development, successful real estate, 4–8
    art of compromising, 7
    components of, *illus.* 5
    construction costs/schedules control, 6
    financial staying power, 6
    healthy economy, 7
    location, 4–5
    management control, 7
    market timing, 6
    planning, 5–6
    properly marketed/targeted, 6–7
    quality/service, 7
    well-conceived financing package, 7
    See also Real estate development; Real
        estate development rewards; Real estate
        development target
Development activities, diversification, 13
Development challenges, 36–37
    financial objectives, 37
    social objectives, 37
Development criteria:
    construction type, 36
    feasibility study, 38–39
    potential tenants, 36
    quality of, 36
    size, 36
Development fee, 15

Development management, governmental
    regulations affect:
  design/construction, 121
  finance/accounting, 121
  leasing/marketing/brokerage, 121
  property management/operations, 121
Development proforma:
  contingency category, 301
  form, *illus.* 351
  hard/direct costs, 293–96
  proceeds applications, 293
  proceeds/incomes, 291–92
  soft/indirect costs, 296–301
Development scheduling, 178
Development team:
  construction manager, 154
  developers, 153
  land brokers, 154
  project/development manager, 154
  schedule consultant, 154
  tenant development coordinator, 154
Development to sell/hold, 52
Direct mail, 529
Directory of Major Malls, 57
Donnelly Marketing, 72
DOT. *See* Department of Transportation
  (DOT)
Down cycle (DC), 9–10
Draw request letter form, *illus.* 485
DSCR. *See* Debt service coverage ratio (DSCR)
Due-on-sale clause, 98
Duplex homes, 24

E

Earnest money, 92
Easy money, 602
Economic area growth potential, 33
Economy, healthy, 7
Economy/budget lodging property users, 31
Effective gross income (EGI), 302
Effective gross income multiplier (EGIM), 327
EGI. *See* Effective gross income (EGI)
EGIM. *See* Effective gross income multiplier
  (EGIM)
EIS. *See* Environment impact study (EIS)
Electrical engineer, 155
Employee safety:
  automobile insurance, 142
  OSHA, 142
  Worker's Compensation Insurance, 142

Energy use, 149
Engineering, predevelopment, 155
  specialist, 178–87
Entry level for-sale housing, 26
Environmental assessment studies, 75–76
Environmental/conservation groups, 76–77
Environmental engineer, 156
Environmental issues:
  air quality, 142
  asbestos, 142
  chemicals for clearing/landscaping, 142
  ozone layers, 142
  underground tanks, 142
Environmental Protection Agency (EPA),
  136
Environmental testing, 181
Environment impact study (EIS), 38
EPA. *See* Environmental Protection Agency
  (EPA)
Equifax Marketing Decision Systems, 73
Equity, 187, 413–14
  definition, 413
  developer's fees, 433–35
  finding, 415
  limited partnership, checklist, 428–32
  money raiser, 158
  partnership, 427–20
  profit/tax losses, 435–36
  preparing investor package, 416
    outline, 416–24
  professional raising of, 424
  references, 425–26
  required, development, 51, 414–15
    working capital reserves, 415
  responsibilities of partners, 432–33
  selecting potential investors, 424–25
  sources, 414
  structuring transaction, 426
    establishing joint venture, 426–27
  terminating partnership, 432
Equity dividend rate (EDR), 327
Equity REIT, 55
Equity to total cost ratio, 329
Equity to value ratio, 330
Erosion/sediment control 133
Escrow account, 431–32
Escrow clause, 98
Estate sales, 66
Executive suite tenant, office space user, 29
Exposure items form, *illus.* 481
Extended stay lodging property user, 31

Exterior building, cost reducing, 192–92
Exterior design/use of materials, 257, 259

F

Factory outlet center retail property, 28
Family rental housing, marketing, 26
Fashion oriented center retail property, 28
FDIC. *See* Federal Deposit Insurance
    Corporation (FDIC)
Feasibility study, 38–39
    outline, 39–51
Federal Deposit Insurance Corporation
    (FDIC), 603
Federal Home Loan Mortgage Corporation
    (FHLMC), 384–85
Federal housing administration (FHA), 65, 384
Federal National Mortgage Association
    (FNAM), 383, 384
Federal Saving and Loan Insurance
    Corporation (FSLIC), 603
Fee developers, 19
Fees, generating up-front, 15
FHA. *See* Federal housing administration
FHLMC. *See* Federal Home Loan Mortgage
    Corporation (FHLMC)
Finance/accounting, project regulations, 121,
    139–40
    reports, 213
Financial consultant (investment banker), 158
Financial criteria, 51
    development to sell/hold, 52
    equity required, 51
    payback period, 52
    rates of returns, 53
    return required, 52
Financial feasibility, 290
    approaches to, 308, 310–12
        frontdoor, *illus.* 310, 311–12
    backdoor approach to, 312, *illus.* 313
    cash flow, 301, *illus.* 305
    development proforma, preparing,
        291–301
    development value judgment, 332–50
    financial forms, 350
        development proforma form, 350, *illus.* 351
        operating proforma form, *illus.* 352
    financial rules of thumb, 326–31
    five-to-ten year operating forecasts, 306–7
    lender financial ratios/other measurement
        tools, 325–26

    operating proforma, preparing, 301–4,
        306
    projecting taxable income, 319–25
    refinement process, 308, *illus.* 309
    sensitivity analysis, 312–15
    using computers, 331–32
    value/real estate development, 315–19
Financial guarantees, 405
    additional collateral, 406
    credit enhancements, 406–7
    credit tenants, 407
    jointly/severally, 406
    letters of credit, 406
    recourse versus nonrecourse guarantees, 406
Financial Institutions Reform, Recovery and
    Enforcement Act of 1989 (FIRREA), 602
Financial management rate of return (FMRR),
    329
Financial returns, 355–56
    borrowing to reduce equity, 357
    nonleverage for risk aversion, 357
    use of leverage, 356–57
Financial return type required, 52
Financial risk, 10–11
Financial rules:
    average rates of return, 328
    development ratios, 329–29
    financial management rate of return
        (FMRR), 329
    net present value (NPV), 329
    payback period, 326–27
    property measurements, 330–31
    rates of return, 327
    time-value methods of return, 328–29
Financial staying power, 6
Financial study, 39
Financing, 94, 187
    closing preparations, 200
    concessions, 509
    sources, 381, *illus.* 382, 383–84
Financing expenses, predevelopment seed
    money, 166
Financing forms, 411, *illus.* 412
Financing package, 7
Fire protection engineer, 155
FIRREA. *See* Financial Institutions Reform,
    Recovery and Enforcement Act of 1989
    (FIRREA)
Five-to-ten year operating forecasts, 306–7
    capital expenditure items, 307
    commercial forecasting, 306–7

inflation increases, 306
space absorption, 306
Fixed payment mortgage, 385
Fixed payment rate with accrual, 385
Fleet's Guide, 354
Flipping the land, 3–4
Flood plains, 133
FMRR. *See* Financial management rate of
    return (FMRR)
FNMA. *See* National Mortgage Association
    (FNMA)
Foreclosure reports, 65
For-sale housing types, 24–25
    marketing levels, 26–27
Forward commitment, loan, 360–61
Frontdoor approach, financial feasibility, 310
FSLIC. *See* Federal Saving and Loan
    Insurance Corporation (FSLIC)

G

Gap loan, 361
GEM. *See* Growing equity mortgage (GEM)
General contracting fee, 15
General contractor, 438, 445
    building/lease-up, 439
    deal making/financing/risk containment, 439
    predevelopment, 438–39
    selecting, 440
        data checklist, 444–45
        evaluation considerations, 442–43
        numerical evaluation system, 443–44
        representative/relevant project data, 440
    substantial completion/certificate of
        occupancy, 439–40
General contractor measurements, 257
General partners, 54, 427
Geodetic maps/surveys, 72
Geo-technical engineer, 156
Geo-technical studies:
    compaction tests, 181
    perk tests, 181
    seismic tests, 181
    soil borings, 181
GNMA. *See* Government National Mortgage
    Association (GNMA)
Governmental agencies, 116, *illus.* 117–120
Governmental regulations, 115
    affect on development management, 121
    environmental concerns, 116
    government officials, working with, 143–44

permits, 134–39
project finance/accounting, 139–40
safety/protection of building occupants,
    141–43
sale/leasing of real estate, 140
site acquisition, considerations, 122–34
Governmental regulatory policies, 8
Government National Mortgage Association
    (GNMA), 383, 385
GPI. *See* Gross potential income (GPI)
GPM. *See* Graduated payment mortgage
    (GPM)
Graduated payment mortgage (GPM), 487
Graphics designer, 155, 185
"Greater fool theory," 82
GRM. *See* Gross rent multiplier (GRM)
Gross potential income (GPI), 301
Gross rent multiplier (GRM), 326
Ground cover, landscaping, 182
Ground lease, 99–100
Ground lease with purchase option, 100
Growing equity mortgage (GEM), 387

H

Hazardous waste, 132
Health/family/ego risk, 12
Historic building/sites, 132
Historic preservation groups, 78
Historic renovation, 27
Hotel, lodging property, 31
*How to Work the Competition into the Ground
    and Have Fun Doing It* (John T. Molly),
    632
Hyper-center retail property, 28

I

Impact fees, 125
Incubator space, mini warehouse property, 31
Industrial buildings, 30–31
Industrial development agencies, 67
Industrial zoning, 124
Inflationary risk, 11
In-house management, 546
Inspection architect, 158
Inspection period, 92
    ongoing, 143
Institute of Real Estate Management
    (IREM), 559
Institutional zoning, 124

Insurance:
  contractor's, 455
  fire/explosion legal liability, 456
  liability, 455
  multi-peril crime, 456
  property, 455–56
  water legal liability, 456
Insurance agent, 158
Insurance carrier, 158
Insurance companies, 359
Insurance coverage, 568, 569–70
  pricing, 569
  proper amount of deductible, 569
  types of, 568–70
  workman's compensation, 569
Insurance/risk containment, 453
  contractor's insurance, 455
  damage containment, 454–55
  design, 454
  letter of credit, 457
  liability insurance, 455
  property insurance, 455–56
  miscellaneous insurance, 456
  risks/exposure identification, 454, *illus.* 482
  types of bonds, 456–57
Interest only mortgage, 387
Interest rate, 98
Interior building, cost reducing, 193
Interior design, 149, 185, 259
  commercial, 261–64
  residential, 260–61
Interior designer, 154
Internal rate of return (IRR), 328–29
Inventory/supplies, 578–79
Investment banker, 158
Investment strategy, creating, 4
Investors, 415
  information package outline, 416–24
  reference checklist, 425–26
  selecting potential, 424–25
Invoicing instructions, predevelopment,
  illus. 172
IREM. *See* Institute of Real Estate
  Management (IREM)
IRR. *See* Internal rate of return (IRR)

J

Joint tenancy, right of survivorship, 53
Joint venture, 55, 89, 99, 187, 447
  establishing, 426–27

K

Kiosk tenant, retail centers, 28

L

Land, finding available, 64–67
  architects/engineers, 66
  attorneys/accountants, 65
  auction companies, 65
  county planning, 67
  developers, 66
  estate sales, 65
  foreclosure reports, 65
  local banking community, 65
  local federal housing administration
    (FHA), 65
  local industrial development agencies, 67
  local/national newspapers, 64
  property management companies, 66
  property owners/real estate brokers, 66
  real estate property tax services, 66
  title companies, 65
  trade magazines, 64–65
  visual inspection, 66
  zoning department, 67
Land acquisition:
  contracting/financing, 89–114
  finance structuring, 98
  site selection seed money, 165
Land acquisition forms:
  land checklist form, 82, *illus.*
    83–86, 87
  land rating form, 87, *illus.* 88
Land banking, 81–82
Land broker, 64, 154
Land checklist form, 82, *illus.* 83–86, 87
Land contract, 100
Land cost adjustments, 80
Land cost evaluation:
  adjustments, 80
  as percentage of total development costs,
    80
  price per acre, 78–79
  price per building footage, 79
  price per front foot, 79–80
  price per square foot of land, 79
  price per unit, 79
Land developers, 18
Land development:
  selection criteria, 58, 60–64
  See also Site; Site selection

Land development trends, 67, *illus.* 68
  dormant phase, 67
  growth phase, 67
  maturity phase, 67
Land location, 60
  surrounding uses, 61
Land offer, determining, 95–98
  backdoor approach to land value, 97–98
  comparable properties land appraisal, 95–96
Land planner, 154
Land price, 61
Land purchase:
  agreement, 177
  legal documents, 100 114
  risk management, 13
  sales agreement, 103–14
Land purchase techniques, 90–92, 99
  alternate plans, 91
  ground lease, 99
  ground lease with purchase option, 100
  joint venture, 99
  land contract, 100
  options, 99
  patience, 91–92
  research/knowledge of use, 91
  research seller, 91
  verify facts, 92
Land rating form, 87, *illus.* 88
Land restrictions/covenants, 75
Landscape architect, 154
  cost reducing, 192
Landscape architectural design, 264,
  illus. 265–66, 267
Land spin-off, 94
Land subdividing, 82
Land survey, 94
Land use plans, 124
Lease checklist form, *illus.* 541
Leasehold mortgage, 388
Leases:
  predevelopment existing, 178
  service contracts, current, 94
  tenant, sales contracts, 186
Leasing agreement, 532
  commencement date, 535
  commitment deposit, 537
  deal concessions, 535–36
  design fee allowance, 537
  expansion options, 535
  first right of refusal, 535
  lease term, 535

  renewal options, 535
  security deposit, 537
  tenant improvement (TI) allowance, 537–38
  tenants percentage of total building area, 534
  termination fee, 537
  terms/conditions, 534
  types of, 532–33
  types of operating leases, 538
  use of premise, 537
Leasing commissions, 434, 566–67
Leasing/marketing/brokerage, 121, 159
Leasing/sales, 503
  case study, 504
  closing the sale, 531–32
  fee structure for outside brokers, 504–5
  market share/absorption, 503
  pricing schedule, 503
  reporting procedures, 511
Leasing status report form, *illus.* 543
Legal agreements:
  bylaws, 505
  condominium documents, 505
  leasing agreements, 505
  reservation agreement, 505
  sales agreement, 505
  warranty agreements, 505
  workletters, 506–7
Legal costs, 93
Legal matters, predevelopment, 177–78
Legal study, 38
Lender financial ratio, 325
  break even cash flow ratio, 326
  debit service coverage ratio (DSCR), 325
  loan-to-value ratio (LVR), 325
  operating expense ratio, 326
Lender ratio, *illus.* 403
Lenders, list of sources, 354
Letter of intent, 100–103
Letters of credit, 457
Level payment mortgage, 385
Liabilities/warranties, 93
Liability insurance, 455
Licensing, 136
Lien release:
  bonds, 457
  form, *illus.* 488
Limited partnership, 54, 427
  checklist for establishing, 428–30
    blue sky law compliance, 430
    escrow account, 431–32
    investor subscription package, 431

Limited partnership *(cont.)*
  offering brochure, 430
    securities marketing, 431
    selling agreement evaluation, 430
  master, 428
  organizational chart, *illus.* 433
  private placement, 428
  public, 428
Limiting financial liability, 13
Linear responsibility matrix, 160,
    illus. 161–62
  selecting architect/contractor, 163
  selecting team members, 160
Liquidity risk, 11–12
Loan:
  closing, 408
  negotiating terms/conditions, 401
    financial guarantees, 405–7
    lender's decision-making process, 401–4
    points to remember, 407
    pricing loan, 404–5
  participation, 361
  permanent, 381–92
  prepare package, 392–96
Loans, sources of, 358
  commercial banks, 358
  insurance companies, 359
  local development/housing authorities,
    358
  mortgage real estate investment trusts
    (REIT), 359
  pension funds, 359
  small business administration (SBA), 358
  savings and loans, 358
Loans, types of:
  construction, 359–61
  land acquisition, 359
Loan-to-construction cost ratio, 402
Loan-to-value ratio (LVR), 325, 404
Local building department, 184
Local department of transportation, 184
Local development/housing authorities, 358
Local fire department, 184
Local planning department, 183–85
Local tenant:
  for retail center, 28
  office space users, 29
Local utility departments, 184
Local zoning/land use policies, 122–23
  impact fees, 125
  local moratoriums, 124–25
  plans, 124
  zoning, 123–24
Location, successful development, 4–5
Lodging property, 31
  users of, 31
Low income rental housing, marketing, 25
Luxury level for-sale housing, 27
LVR. *See* Loan-to-value ratio (LVR)

M

Mail list companies, 528
Management company responsibilities,
    551–52
  analysis of property, 552–55
Management control, 7
Management systems reports, 213
Manufacturing facilities industrial property,
    30
Market analyst, 158–59
Market constraints:
  customer mentality, 8
  governmental regulatory policies, 8
  market versus investor demand, 8–9
  mortgage rates, 8
Market cycles, *illus.* 9
Marketing, 2, 200–201
  agreements, 186
  definition, 3
  forms, 538–43
  residential property, 25–27
Marketing budget, 522–23
  preparing, 523–26
  scheduling/marketing budgets, 523
Marketing business plan, 498
  outline, 498–502
  proper name for development, 502–3
  theme/image of product, 502
Marketing campaigns, 526
Marketing centers/visual aids, 186
Marketing expenses, predevelopment seed
    money, 165
Marketing feasibility, 186
Marketing files, 507–8
  prospecting, 508
Marketing/leasing fee, 15
Marketing manager, 159
Marketing process, 489
  budget preparation, 522–26
  business plan, 498
  campaigns, 526

closing the sale—leasing/sale agreement, 531–32
  postclosing follow-up, 532
description packages, 520–22
files, 507–8
financing/concessions, 509
finding users, 526–29
leasing agreement, 532–38
leasing/sales, 503
legal agreements, 505–7
marketing forms, 538–43
media placement, 509–11
model suite, 520
preparing market study, 490–94
preselling market, 529–30
presentation/sale, 530–31
professionals, 494–98
reporting procedures, 511
sales/leasing offices, 518–20
visual aids/collateral materials, 511–18
Marketing program/target, 6–7
Marketing reports, 213
Marketing team, 494–95
  advertising agencies, 496
  brokers/leasing/sales agents, 496
  marketing agents, 496–97
  marketing consultants, 496
  negotiating agreements, 497–98
  public relations agencies, 496
Market research, 2, 12, 149–50
  errors to avoid, 2–3
  identifying the need, 20–23
Market saturation cycle (MSC), 10
Market study, 38, 94
  preparing, 490
    analyze data, graphing, 494
    competition comparative analysis, 493
    information to include, 491–92
    obtaining unit mix/square footage/
      property's age information, 493
    reviewing demographics/area
      trends/occupancy rates, 494
    verifying occupancy/rental rates, 492–93
  research firms, 57
Market study summary, *illus.* 495
Market timing, 6
  absorption cycle (AC), 10
  down cycle (DC), 9–10
  market cycles, *illus.* 9
  market saturation cycle (MSC), 10
  new construction cycle (NCC), 10

Market versus investor demand, 8–9
Master limited partnership, 54
Master plan:
  creating development, 4
  planning phase, 237, *illus.* 238–39,
    239–43
  predevelopment program, 147, 183
    architectural/engineering design, 182–83
Material defects, warranties, 93
Maturity period, 98
Mechanical engineer, 155
Media placement, 509
  billboards, 510
  local magazines, 510
  newspapers, 509
  radio, 510
  signage, 510
  specialty advertising, 511
  television, 510
  trade journals, 509
  yellow pages, 510
Medical office space user, 30
Meetings, predevelopment coordination of,
  188–89
Merchant builders, 18–19
Military rental housing, marketing, 26
Mines, site evaluation, 75
Mini-permanent (bullet or balloon) mortgage,
  388
Mini warehouse industrial properties, 30
Mixed-use developments, 31–32
MJJTM Publications, 57
Mobile homes, 24
Mobile lot rentals, 24
Model suite, 520
Moderate income rental housing, marketing, 25
Mortgage amortization period, 98
Mortgage amount, 98
Mortgage-backed securities, 383
Mortgage broker/banker, 157, 355
Mortgage lender, 158
Mortgage limited partnerships, 381–82
Mortgage payment, 98
Mortgage rates, 8
Mortgage recourse, 98
Mortgage registration tax, 92
Mortgage servicing fee, 434–35
Motel, lodging property, 31
Move-down level for-sale housing, 27
Move-up level for-sale housing, 26–27
MSC. *See* Market saturation cycle (MSC), 10

Multi-family apartments:
    garden style, 24
    high-rise, 24
    mid-rise, 24
    townhouse, 24
Multi-Housing News, 65

N

National Mall Monitor, 65
National Planning Data Corporation, 73
National Real Estate Investor, 64
National Research Bureau, 58
National Roster of Realtors Directory, 528
National soil/water conservation, 77
National tenant:
    for retail center, 28
    office space user, 29
NCC. *See* New construction cycle (NCC)
Near-term schedule, 463, 466, *illus.* 467
Negative/accelerated amortization mortgage,
    387
Neighborhood center retail property, 27
    acreage size of, 29
Neighborhood opposition, 77
Net income multiplier (NIM), 327
Net operating income (NOI), 301, 304,
    566
Net present value (NPV), 329
Net spendable cash flow prior to taxes, 567
New construction cycle (NCC), 10
NIM. *See* Net income multiplier (NIM)
NOI. *See* Net operating income (NOI)
Novick's Financial Newsletter, 354
Nursing facilities, for sale, 25

O

Occupational Health and Safety
    Administration (OSHA), 136–38, 142
Offer site selection negotiations, 92–95
Office buildings, 29
    business parks, 30
    types of, 29–30
Office of Thrift Supervision (OTS), 602
Office space users, 29
    Class A, B, C type, 29
    leases, 29
    square feet space required, 29
Office-warehouse industrial property, 30
    space requirements, 30

Off-price center retail property, 28
Open-ended mortgage, 360
Operating budgets, 557
    before-tax cash flow, 566
    capital expenditures, 566
    debt service, 566
    leasing commissions, 566–67
    net operating income (NOI), 566
    net spendable cash flow prior to taxes, 567
    operating expenses, 559
    revenue calculations, 557–59
    tenant improvement (TI), 566
Operating expense ratio, 326
Operating forecasts, five-to-ten year. *See*
    Five-to-ten year operating forecasts
Operating proforma/cash flows:
    after-tax cash flow, 304, *illus.* 305, 306
    before-tax cash flow, 304
    below bottom line expenses, 304
    effective gross income (EGI), 302
    net operating income (NOI), 304
    operating expenses, 302–4
    revenues, 301–2
Operating proforma form, *illus.* 352
Opportunity risk, 11
OSHA. *See* Occupational Health and Safety
    Administration (OSHA)
OTS. *See* Office of Thrift Supervision (OTS)
Overall capitalization rate (OR), 327
Owner's association, 580
Ownership investment vehicle, 13
    choosing appropriate, 53–55
Ozone layer, 142

P

PAM. *See* Pledged account mortgage (PAM)
Parcel size, 60
Parking consultant, 156
Participating mortgages, 387
Partnerships, 427–28
    management fee, 434
Partners/joint ventures, 187
Payback period, 52
PDP. *See* Project development plan (PDP)
Pension funds, 359
Perk tests, 181
Permanent loan, 381
    commitment, 390
        clauses, 390–92
        financing sources, 381, *illus.* 382, 383–84

funding, 381–84
   private mortgage insurance (PMI), 388–89
   questions/issues, 389–90
   secondary mortgage markets, 384–85
   sources of, 381 types of, 385–86
   variable rate mortgages, 386–88
Permits:
   building, 135
   building codes, 139
   certificate of occupancy/occupancy permit,
      135
   compliance with codes during construction,
      138
   construction safety, 136–38
   land disturbance, 134–35
   process, 135
   programming using code synopsis review,
      135–36
Personal care housing, for sale, 25
Piggyback mortgage, 360
Physical destruction risk, 11
PLA. *See* Potential loan amount (PLA)
Planned unit development (PUD), 25
Planning, successful development, 5–6
Plans/specifications review checklist, 276–88
Pledged account mortgage (PAM), 386
Plumbing engineer, 155
Poor soil conditions, site evaluation, 74
Postclosing report, 213
   development memorandum outline, 214–22
Potential loan amount (PLA), 403–4
Power to sell, 93
Preconstruction/preclosing seed money, 166
Predevelopment budget, 164
   form, *illus.* 168
   management, 166–67
   scheduling, 173
Predevelopment process, 145
   coordination of meetings, 188–89
   creating a program, 146–53
   developer's "go" "no go" decision, 197–200
   linear responsibility matrix, 160–63
   managing, 173, 177
   managing budget, "seed money," 164–67,
      illus. 168, 169, *illus.* 170–72
   managing process, 173, 177
   monitoring systems, 201–13
   postclosing report, 213–22
   preparing to close financing, 200–201
   project management phases, 194–97
   requesting proposals/budgeting, 163–64

   responsibility of, 177–87
   scheduling work tasks, 169, 172–73, *illus.*
      174–76
   selecting a team, 153–60
   selecting consultants, 163
   team selection forms, 222–23, *illus.* 224
   value engineering, 189–94
Predevelopment program, 146, 194–95
   area calculations, 150
   building description, 147–48
   code synopsis, 153, *illus.* 161
   energy use optimization, 149
   existing data, 149
   interior design, 149
   marketing, 149–50
   master planning, 147
   objectives, 147
   philosophy, 149
   presentations, 150
   pricing/cost estimates, 150, 151
   scheduling, 150
   team/team relationships, 130, *illus.* 151
   technical data, 153
   tenant allowances, 152
   traffic, 148
   zoning, 148
Predevelopment schedule, *illus.* 170
Predevelopment seed money, 165
Predevelopment work order system, 167–68
Prepayment clause, 98
Preselling the market, 529–30
   promotions, 530
Presentation, 530–31
Price per acre formula, 78–79
Price per building footage formula, 79
Price per front foot formula, 79–80
Price per square foot of land formula, 79
Price per unit formula, 79
Pricing, predevelopment. *See* Cost/pricing
   estimates
Prison facility single purpose building, 32
Private mortgage insurance (PMI), 388–89
Proceeds and incomes, 291–92
Process of refinement, 308, *illus.* 309
Product types, project economics for, 645
   corporate summit, 668–84
   industrial building, 658–67
   residential subdivision, 685–91
   retail, 646–57
Professional Builder, 65
Profit/tax losses, structuring, 435–36

Project cost report form, *illus.* 487
Project/development manager, 154
Project development plan (PDP), 198–99
Project economics/capital costs/cash flow:
  hard costs, 186
  soft costs, 186
Project feasibility, 94
Projecting taxable income on sale, 323–24
  adjusted cost basis, 324
    excess depreciation, 324
  capital gain, 324
  taxes due on resale, 324
Project management phases:
  construction, 195–96
  delay claims analysis, 196–97
  design, 195
  predevelopment, 194–95
Project studies, 165
Project status reporting, 178
Property insurance, 455–56
Property management, 545
  accounting system, 570–78
  agreement, 549–51
  company responsibilities, 551–52
    analysis of property, 552–55
  companies, 66
  fee, 15, 433
  forms, 580, *illus.* 581–82
  in-house, 546
  insurance coverage, 568–70
  inventory/supplies, 578–79
  maintenance, 159
  manager, 159, 187
  maximizing returns, 544–45
  operating budget, 557–67
  operations, 121, 159, 187
  owner's association, 580
  policies/procedures, 555–56
  real estate taxes, 567
  service contracts, 556–57
  service vendors, 159
  staffing, 546, *illus.* 547, 548–49
  tenant leases, 579–80
  third-party companies, 546
 Property management agreement, 549
  assignment of contract, 551
  authorization to sign service documents, 550
  collection of monies, 550
  compliance with legal requirements, 551
  employees, 550
  fee structure, 549–50

  insufficient income, 551
  major repairs, 550
  management firm expenses, 550
  management firm responsibilities, 550
  operating/capital expenditure budget, 551
  reporting systems, 551
  termination clause/penalty, 551
  terms of agreement, 550
Property management forms, 580, *illus.* 581
Property management policies/procedures, 555
  employee schedules/benefits, 556
  maintenance service, 555–56
  rental rates/collections, 555
  tenant record keeping, 556
Property management staffing, 546, *illus.* 547,
    548–49
Property uses, 182
Proposals, requesting predevelopment, 163–64
  contracts, 164
Public infrastructure group, 18
Public relations agencies, 159, 186, 529
PUD. *See* Planned unit development (PUD)
Purchase price, 92

Q

Quadraplex homes, 24
Quality assurance/quality control engineers
    report, 212, 466, 468
  proposals, 468–70

R

RAM. *See* Reverse annuity mortgage (RAM)
Real estate brokers/agents, 528
Real estate decline in 1980s, 600–603
Real estate development:
  choosing a target, 3
  creating investment strategy, 4
  definition, 1–2
  managing risks, 12–13
  market constraints, 8
  marketing, 2
  marketing research, 2–3
  market timing, 9–10
  public/private interface, 16–18
  rewards, 13–16
  setting a goal, 3
  successful developments, 4–8
  types of developers, 18
  weighing risks, 10–12

Real estate development financing, 353–55
  appraisal process, 396–401
  closing the loan, 408
  development phase financing, 357–81
  financial returns, 355–57
  financing forms, 411, *illus.* 412
  funding permanent loan, 381–92
  maximizing financial returns, 355–57
  mortgage brokers/bankers, 355
  negotiating loan terms/conditions, 401–8
  permanent lender's closing checklist, 408–11
  preparing loan package, 392–96
Real estate development public/private
  interface:
  public infrastructure group, 18
  space consumer group, 16
  space producer group, 16, 18
Real estate development relationships, *illus.* 17
Real estate development rewards, 13–16
  cash flows, 15
  credential, 16
  residual, creating net worth, 16
  tax shelter, using available, 15
  up-front fees, 15
  versus risks, *illus.* 14
Real estate development target, 3–4
  buying/holding for future, 3
  creating master plan, 4
  flipping land, 3–4
  selecting a target, 23–32
  successful development components, *illus.* 5
Real estate industry, changing cycles, 598–600
  causes of decline in 1980s, 600–603
  developer's awareness of 1990s/economic
    factors, 642–44
  development business prescriptions:
    inability to make it happen, 631–32
    inability to obtain financing, 621–22
    inability to retain staff, 626–28
    inability to use predevelopment seed
      money effectively, 622
    in lack of business growth, 632–38
    in loss of operating capital, 628–31
    in potential losses of business due to legal
      action, 638
    in preparing winning proposals, 622–26
  diagnosis of potential problem areas, 603–6
  prescriptions for personal life:
    protecting your family, 640–41
    protecting your personal resources, 641–42
    protecting yourself, 639–40

  project development prescriptions:
    construction failure, 613–15
    debt service payments failure, 615–16
    design failures, 611–13
    legal action by development team
      member/joint venture partner/lender,
      621
    monthly debt service payment
      modification, 616–21
    shortfalls in cash flow projections,
      606–10
  solutions for problem areas, 606
Real estate investment trusts (REIT), 55, 359
Real Estate Mortgage Investment Conduit
  (REMIC), 303
Real estate owned (REO), 65
Real estate property tax service, 66
Real estate research companies, 528
Real estate sales/leasing, 141
Real estate taxes, 94, 567
Recording costs, 92
Recycling commercial properties, 32
Referrals, 528
Refinancing fee, 434
Refinancing proceeds, 435
Refinancing property, 411
  second mortgages, 411
    wraparound mortgage, 411
Refinement process, 308, *illus.* 309
Regional center retail property, 28
  acreage size of, 29
Regional tenant:
  for retail center, 28
  office space users, 29
Rehabilitation, for-sale housing, 25
REIS Report, address, 57
REIT. *See* Real estate investment trust (REIT)
Release clause, 98
REMIC. *See* Real Estate Mortgage Investment
  Conduit (REMIC)
Renegotiated rate mortgage, 386
Renovate/convert developer, 19
Rental properties housing types, 24
  marketing of, 25–26
Rental risk, shift, 13
Rental/sales history, 33
REO. *See* Real Estate Owned (REO)
Residential data form, 538, *illus.* 539
Residential interior design, 260–61
Residential lease summary form, 582
Residential measurements, 256

Residential properties, 23
  types of, 24–25
Residential tenant, mini warehouse property, 30
Residential zoning, 123
Residual, creating net worth, 16
Resolution Trust Corporation (RTC), 603
Resort, for sale, 25
Restaurant/fast-food convenience outlet single
  purpose building, 32
Retail property, 27
  building area square feet, 28
  center-type acreage, 29
  parking area square feet, 28
  types of, 27–29
Retail user directories, 527
Retirement housing, for sale, 25
Returns, rates of, 53
Reverse annuity mortgage (RAM), 387
Rewards, real estate development. *See* Real
  estate development rewards
Rezoning process, *illus.* 131
Rezoning signs, 127
Right-of-assignment clause, 95
Right-of-transfer clause, 98
Risk-identification-damage containment
  form, *illus.* 482–83
Risks:
  financial, 10–11
  health/family/ego, 12
  inflationary, 11
  liquidity, 11–12
  opportunity, 11
  physical destruction, 11
Risks, managing:
  diversifying development activities, 13
  land purchase contingencies, 13
  limiting financial liability, 13
  market research, 12
  ownership investment vehicle/legal liability,
    13
  risk-yield curve, *illus.* 12
  shifting rental risk, 13
Risk-yield curve, *illus.* 12
Road widening, 94
Rock, site evaluation, 74
RTC. *See* Resolution Trust Corporation (RTC)

S

Safety/protection, building occupants, 141–43
Sale brokerage fee, 434

Sale of development, 583
  profitable sale, ten steps, 589–96
  reasons, 583–84
  sale packages, 587
    outline, 587–88
  sale price, terms/conditions, 584
  sale prospect form, *illus.* 597
  sale transactions, 585–87
Sales/leasing, 518–19
  furnishing office, 519
  office design
  office location, 519
  staffing office, 519
  use of office, 519–20
  See also Real estate sales/leasing
Sale pricing, terms/conditions, 584
Sale proceeds, 436
Sale transactions, 585
  cash sale, 585
  deed-in-lieu of foreclosure, 586–87
  donations, 586
  foreclosures, 586
  incorporation of interests, 586
  installment sales, 585
  presale with earn-out, 585
  sale leaseback, 587
  sale of partnership interest, 586
  tax-free exchange, 585
SAM. *See* Shared appreciation mortgage (SAM)
Savings and loans, 358
SBA. *See* Small Business Administration (SBA)
Schedule consultant, 154
Schedule summary form, 474, *illus.* 475
Scheduling, 150
  design/construction scheduling, 178
  development, 178
  project status reporting, 178
  work tasks, 169, 172–73
Schematic design phase, 243, *illus.* 244,
  illus. 249
Secondary mortgage markets, 384–85
Second mortgage, 411
Securities marketing, 431
Seed money, 164–68
Seismic tests, 181
Self-amortizing mortgage, 385
Seller financing terms, 92, 98
Seller warranties, 93–94
Senior citizen:
  for-sale housing, 25
  rental housing, marketing, 26

Sensitivity analysis, 312–13, *illus.* 314, 315
Service contracts, 556–57
  types of, 557
Service/quality, real estate development, 7
Shared appreciation mortgage (SAM), 387
Shopping Center Directory, 58
Shopping Center World, 64
Single-family homes:
  for sale, 24
  rental, 24
Single purpose building commercial property,
  32
Site:
  absorption trends, 33
  analysis process, site for use, *illus.* 34
  analysis process, use for site, *illus.* 35
  best land parcel for product type, 33–36
  characteristics of, 62
  correct product type, 32–33
  demographic criteria, 58
  economic growth potential, 33
  land price, 61
  location, 60
  market studies overview, 57–58
  parcel size, 60
  price of land, 61
  rental/sales history, 33
  selecting, 56–57
  shape of property, 62
  support services availability, 63
  surrounding land uses, 61
  target market, 33
  traffic pattern, 62
  use/use for site, 33–36
  uses, current/past, 60
  utilities, 63
  visibility/access to consumer, 62
  visits, 73–74
    flying, 74
    sighting, 73
    walking, 73
  zoning classification, 60
Site acquisitions, considerations:
  air pollution regulations, 134
  air traffic, 130–32
  erosion/sediment control, 133
  flood plains, 133
  hazardous waste, 132
  historic buildings/sites, 132
  local zoning/land use policies, 122–25
  storm water management, 134

stream banks protection, 134
  waterways, 134
  wetlands, 133
  zoning, 125–30, *illus.* 131
Site analysis, 56
Site development costs, 94
Site evaluation:
  boundary/topographical surveys, 75
  environmental assessment studies, 75–76
  land restrictions/covenants, 75
  mines, 75
  poor soil condition, 74
  rock, 74
  surface water, 75
  underground water, 74–75
Site location 56, 60, 61
Site purchase, 56
  do's and don'ts, 80–81
  land banking, 81–82
  land subdividing, 82
Site research, 68–73
  aerials photography, 68, *illus.* 69–70, 71
  chamber of commerce, 71
  county planning/zoning departments, 71
  county plat books, 68
  county tax books, 68
  demographic information companies, 72–73
  department of transportation (DOT), 72
  geodetic maps/surveys, 72
  local chamber of commerce, 71
  local newspapers, 72
  local real estate guide, 71
  utility companies, 71
  yellow pages, 71
Site selection, 56–88
  offer negotiation, 92–95
  seed money 165
Site visibility/access to consumer, 62
Site work, reducing costs, 192
Small Business Administration (SBA), 358
Soil borings, 181
Soil conditions, 93
Soil/environmental tests, 94
Sole ownership, 53
Sound control, 181
Southeast Real Estate News, 64
Southwest Real Estate News, 64
Space consumer group, 16
Space planner, 154
Space producer group, 16, 18
Specialty consultant, 156–57

Speculative developers, 18
Spinoff effect, 602–3
Square footage calculation form, *illus.* 289
SRO. *See* Weekly rental apartments—single room occupancies (SRO)
Standby loan, 360
Storm water management, 134, 182
Strategy planning, 20
   conducting a feasibility study, 38–39
   developing a strategy, *illus.* 22
   evolution of real estate market information, *illus.* 23
   feasibility study, 39–51
   flexibility, 55
   identifying development criteria, 36
   identifying financial criteria, 51–53
   identifying unique challenges, 36–37
   market research, 20–21
   ownership vehicle, appropriate, 53–55
   proper site, 32–36
   target selecting, 23–32
      commercial, 27–32
      residential, 23–27
Strategy review, development, 38
Stream banks protection, 134
Structural engineer, 155
Student rental housing, marketing, 26
Subchapter S corporation, 54
Subcontractor selection, 185
Suites, lodging property, 31
Summary costs form, *illus.* 478
Summary schedule 173, *illus.* 174
   design/construction, 173, *illus.* 175
Super regional center acreage, 29
Support services availability, site, 63–64
Surface water, site evaluation, 75
Survey, predevelopment, 178
Survey costs, 93
Surveyor, 155
Syndication fees, 433

T

Take-out loan, 360
Target. *See* Marketing program/target; Real estate development, choosing a target
Target choosing, 3
Target market, 33
Target selecting, 23–24
Tax. *See* Real estate tax

Taxable income, projecting, 319–20
   after-tax equity reversion, 325
   capital expenditures/tenant improvement depreciation, 323
   closing costs amortization, 323
   depreciation tables, *illus.* 321–22
   leasing commissions amortization, 323
   loss schedule, 320
   points on permanent mortgage amortization, 323
   profit, 325
   projecting taxable income on sale, 323–24
Tax benefits, 435
Tax consultant, 158, 187
Tax Reform Act of 1986, 601
Tax shelter, development reward, 15
Team, 150
   accountant, 160
   asset manager, 159
   appraiser, 158
   attorney, 160
   construction, 157
   debt/equity financing, 157–58
   design team, 154–55
   development, 153–54
   engineering, 155–57
   insurance, 158
   marketing, 158–59
   property management, 159
   selecting members, 160
   tax consultant, 158
Team member's checklist form, 222–23 *illus.* 224
Team relationships diagram, 150, *illus.* 151
Telemarketing, 529
Tenant:
   development construction, 143
   development design, 271
      anchor space planning, 271–72, *illus.* 273
      systems, 272, 274–76
   leases/sales contracts, 186
   potential, for development, 36
   for retail centers, 28
Tenant allowances form, *illus.* 227
Tenant development coordinator, 154
Tenant improvements (TI), 537–38, 566
   depreciation, 323
Tenant leases, 579–80
Tenants in common, 53

Ten steps of profitable sale, 589
  broker's services, 589
  counteroffer negotiations, 591
  deal closing, 595
  development agreement prior to
      construction completion, 593–94
  distribution of profits, 595, *illus.* 596
  making the deal, 592
  potential purchasers, 590–91
  purchase agreement preparation, 592–93
  reviewing offers, 591
  soliciting partner response, 594–95
Terminating contracts, 94–95
Theater single purpose building, 32
Theme center retail property, 28
  types of, 28
Third-party companies, 546
Time share, for sale, 25
Time-value methods of return, 328–29
Title companies, 65
Title insurance, 92
Title search, 177
Topographical/boundary surveys, 75, 179,
    illus. 180, 181
Townhouse:
  for sale, 24
  rental, 24
Trade magazines, 64–65
Traffic engineer, 156
Traffic patterns, site, 62, 148, 181
  curb/median cuts, 63
  ingress/egress from site, 62
  side of street, 63
  speed of, 63
  traffic courts, 63
Transfer costs, 98
Transfer tax, 92
Triplex homes, 24

U

ULI. *See* Urban Land Institute (ULI)
Underground tanks, 142
Underground water, site evaluation, 74–75
Unresolved issues form, *illus.* 477
Up-front fees, 15
Upscale rental housing, marketing, 25–26
Urban Land Institute (ULI), 559
Utilities, 94
  warranties, 93

Utilities availability, site, 63
Utility/building moratoriums, 77, 94
Utility companies, 71
Utility services, 181

V

Vacation/resort lodging property users, 31
Value engineering, 189–94,
Value/real estate development, 315, *illus.* 316
  appraisal approaches summary, 319
  cost approach, 317
  cost versus market value, 319
  income/capitalization, income approach,
      317–19
  sales/market comparison approach, 315, 317
Variable rate mortgages, 386
Visual aids/collateral materials, 511–12
  architectural models, 518
  audio-visual presentations, 518
  brochures, 512
  business cards, 512
  fliers, 512
  presentation drawings, 512, *illus.* 513–17, 518
  stationary, 512

W

Wall Street brokerage firms, 383
Waterlands, 133
Waterways, 134
Weekly rental apartments—single room
    occupancies (SRO), 24
Weekly/short-term rental housing, marketing,
    26
*What They Don't Teach You in Harvard
    Business School* (Mark H. McCormack),
    632
Workers Compensation Insurance, 136, 142,
    455
Workman's Compensation, 569
Work order system procedure, *illus.* 167–68,
    169
  request, *illus.* 171
World economy, 601–2
Wraparound mortgage, 411

Y

Yellow pages, 71, 510, 528

Z

Zero lot line, 24
Zoning, 122–24, 148, 177
    administrative approval, 127
    appeal process, 130
    application, preparing, 125
    attorney, 125
    building density allowances revisions, 127
    city/county zoning boards, 129
    density, 127
    hearings, 129

local planning/development agencies, 128
local politics, 130
neighborhood planning areas, 128–29
negotiating with city officials, 128
notice to neighbors, 127
questions asked developer, 126
rezoning signs, 127
variances, 94, 126–27
Zoning attorney, role of, 125
Zoning classification, 60